THE GREATEST BATTLES IN HISTORY

THE GREATEST BATTLES IN HISTORY

AN ENCYCLOPEDIA OF CLASSIC WARFARE FROM MEGIDDO TO WATERLOO

GENERAL EDITOR: JACK WATKINS

amber
BOOKS

Reprinted in 2019

This edition first published in 2017

Published by
Amber Books Ltd
United House
North Road
London N7 9DP
United Kingdom
www.amberbooks.co.uk
Instagram: amberbooksltd
Facebook: www.facebook.com/amberbooks
Twitter: @amberbooks

Previously published as *The Encyclopedia of Classic Warfare*

Project Editor: Helen Vick
Design: Joe Conneally

ISBN: 978-1-78274-641-6

Printed in China

4 6 8 10 9 7 5 3

Contributors: Simon Anglim, Matthew Bennett, Jim Bradbury, Robert B. Bruce, Kelly DeVries, Iain Dickie, Martin J. Dougherty, Michael E. Haskew, Phyllis G. Jestice, Christer Jörgensen, Kevin Kiley, Chris McNab, Eric Niderost, Michael F. Pavkovic, Stuart Reid, Rob S. Rice, Scott M. Rusch, Frederick C. Schneid, Chris L. Scott, John Serrati, Jack Watkins

Parts of this book have been previously published by Amber Books Ltd in the following titles: *Battles That Changed Warfare, Battles of the Ancient World, Battles of the Bible, Battles of the Crusades, Battles of the Medieval World, Fighting Techniques of the Ancient World, Fighting Techniques of Naval Warfare, Fighting Techniques of the Medieval World, Fighting Techniques of the Oriental World, Fighting Techniques of the Early Modern World, Fighting Techniques of the Colonial Era, Fighting Techniques of the Napoleonic Age.*

Contents

INTRODUCTION

A book on 'classic' warfare raises the question, Why end it at the Battle of Waterloo in 1815? It's true that a soldier fighting in that battle would have felt just as familiar with the weaponry in use half a century later, for it was really in the quarter of a century before World War I that weapons and armour changed most rapidly. Belt-fed machine guns, steam-powered gunships, tanks deployed en masse – these were among the features of late nineteenth century and early twentieth century warfare that would have rendered it so different to combatants in the Napoleonic age.

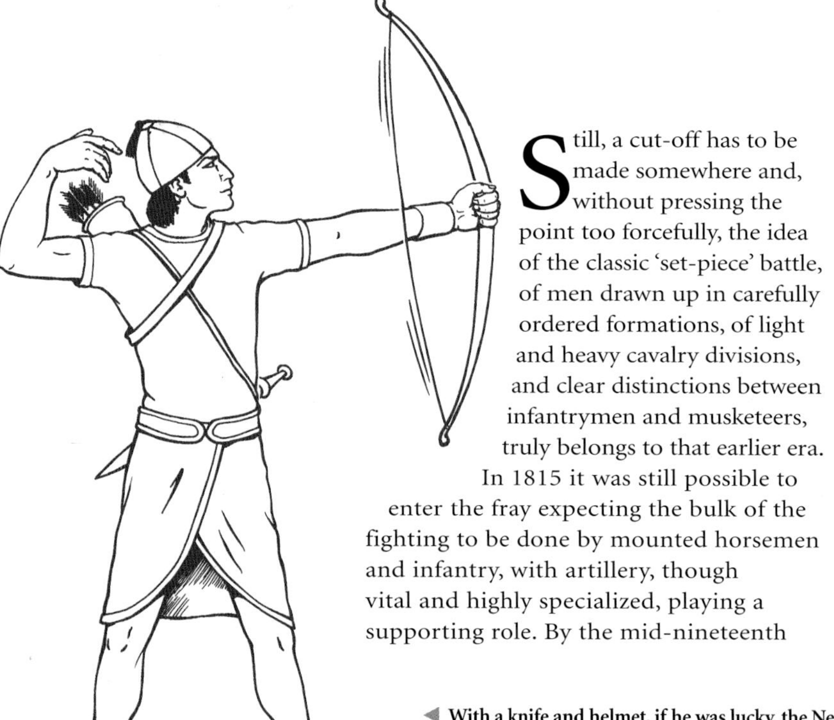

Still, a cut-off has to be made somewhere and, without pressing the point too forcefully, the idea of the classic 'set-piece' battle, of men drawn up in carefully ordered formations, of light and heavy cavalry divisions, and clear distinctions between infantrymen and musketeers, truly belongs to that earlier era. In 1815 it was still possible to enter the fray expecting the bulk of the fighting to be done by mounted horsemen and infantry, with artillery, though vital and highly specialized, playing a supporting role. By the mid-nineteenth century, the rifle had replaced the musket, firearms were issued to the entire infantry, and open order formations were common. Warfare was increasingly technological, even if – contrary to popular perception – the mounted horsemen of the Light Brigade did still achieve their objectives at Balaclava in 1854, despite riding into the teeth of withering gunfire.

FROM MEGIDDO TO WATERLOO

This book begins with Megiddo, one of the first battles to be properly recorded, with its thundering chariots, used by archers as mobile firing platforms. At Marathon, it was the spear-bearing hoplites who held sway. These massed ranks of disciplined

◀ With a knife and helmet, if he was lucky, the Neo-Hittite archer (fifteenth century BC) would depend on his bow and speed to protect him during a battle or a siege. The quality of his bowmanship would depend on his familiarity with his weapon, and skill was the product of years of use and practice.

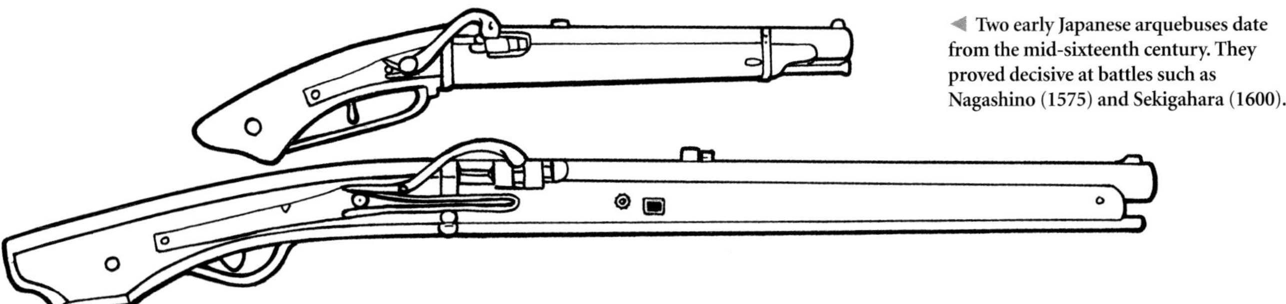

◀ Two early Japanese arquebuses date from the mid-sixteenth century. They proved decisive at battles such as Nagashino (1575) and Sekigahara (1600).

footsoldiers formed the bedrock of the armies of the Greek city states for years.

The age of the great cavalry charge belonged to later times. It was the lightly armoured horsemen from the east, notably the Huns, who taught many bitter lessons to Western soldiers – astride quick, agile horses, they also had the advantage of stirrups. Subsequently, the social cachet of the heavily armoured galloping knight would remain a glamorous figure in the West long after having been proven ponderously ineffective on many occasions during the Crusades.

The book also features some of the great sea battles, from Salamis to Gravelines to Trafalgar, and some of the curiosities too – the early cannon lugged around the boggy fields of northern France by the English and used – to no great effect – at Crécy (1346); the 'turtle' ship, with its smoking dragon's head, deployed by the Koreans at Sacheon (1592); the elephants of countless armies, including those of Darius and Hannibal deployed at Gaugamela (331BC) and Trebia (218BC) respectively; the Zungharian camel wall at Ulan Butung (1690); and the remarkable Venetian hybrid ships, the galleases, of Lepanto (1571).

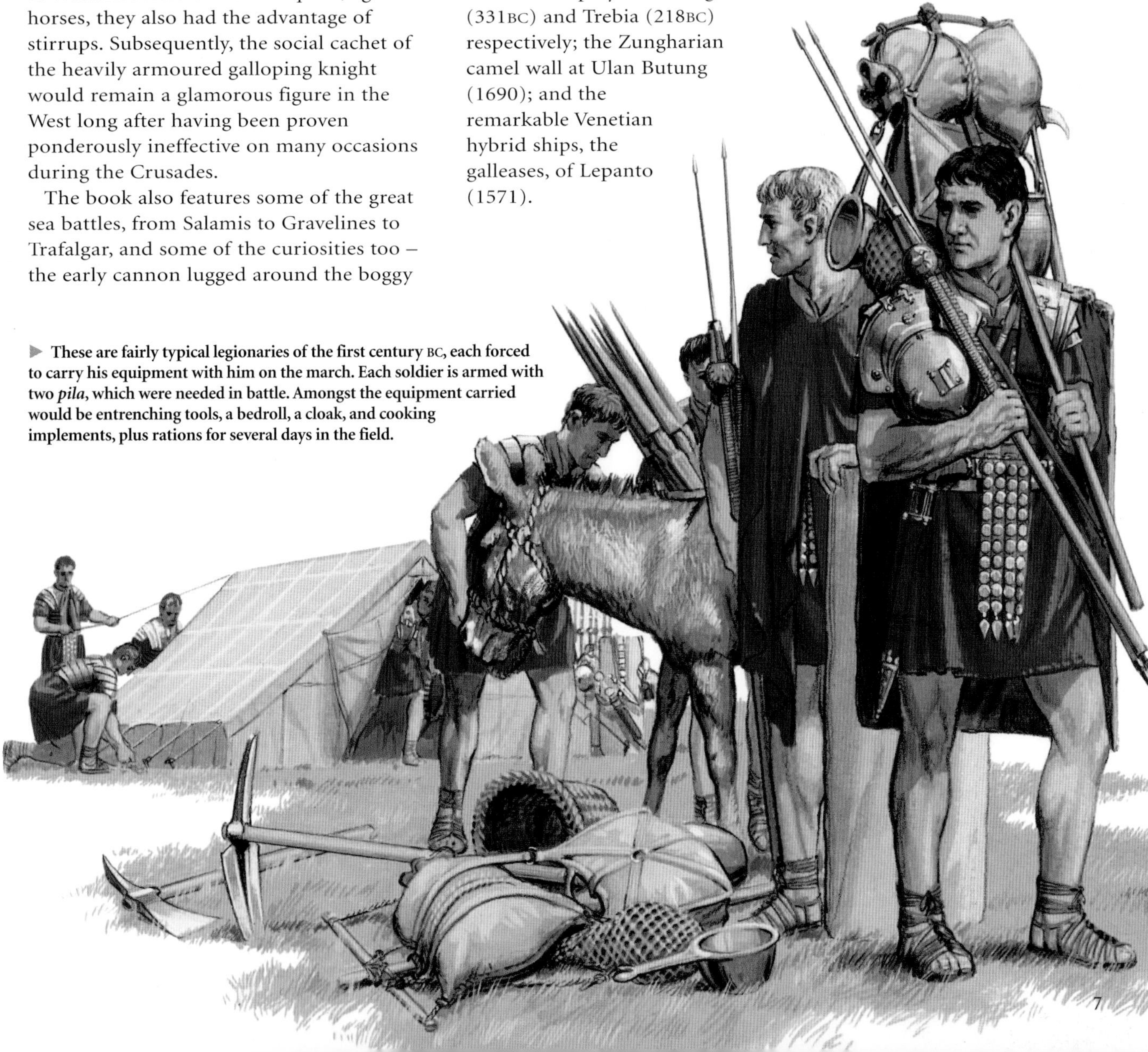

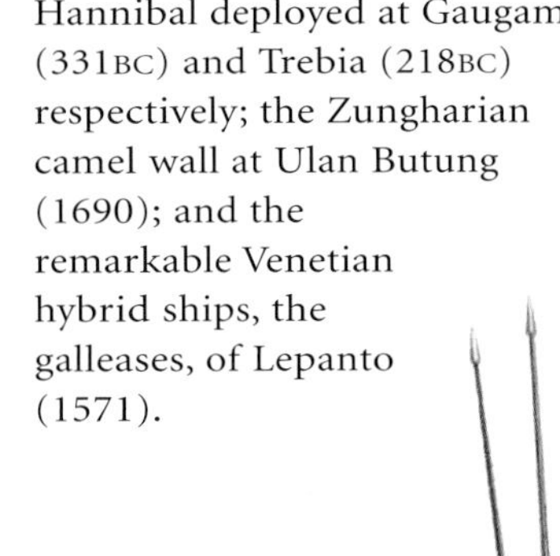

▶ **These are fairly typical legionaries of the first century BC, each forced to carry his equipment with him on the march. Each soldier is armed with two *pila*, which were needed in battle. Amongst the equipment carried would be entrenching tools, a bedroll, a cloak, and cooking implements, plus rations for several days in the field.**

CHAPTER 1

The Ancient World

The determining characteristic in most battles of the ancient world was the heavy reliance on infantry, from the Greek hoplites and Macedonian phalangists to the Roman legions.

Greek infantrymen fought with a spear, the Romans with a javelin (*pilum*) and sword, which made them, ultimately, the more formidable adversary once the formations broke up into close knit, hand-to-hand fighting. Yet warfare took other forms. The Canaanites were the early masters of chariot technology, but the Egyptians used them to better effect at Megiddo (1457BC). Others were masters of siegecraft. The Assyrians seem to have deployed siege towers and rams at Damascus and Lachish in the eighth century BC long before anyone else. What of the cavalry?

In fact, a steadfast, well-trained group of infantrymen, in the pre-stirrup age, could hold their own against a cavalry charge, although the elite Companion Cavalry were vital to Alexander the Great's victories over the Persians at Granicus River (334BC) and Issus (333BC). Psychological warfare had a role too, such as the elephants deployed by, among others, Darius at Gaugamela (331BC) and Hannibal at Trebia (218BC).

◀ **Early warfare was largely a matter of foot soldiers, fortified citadels and siege warfare carried out by the most primitive means. Armour was generally minimal, and casualties inevitably high.**

Megiddo 1457BC

KEY FACTS

WHO An Egyptian army under the command of Pharaoh Thutmose III (d. 1425BC) versus a Canaanite army under Durusha, king of Kadesh.

WHAT The Egyptians took a risky and unexpected route to the battlefield and achieved surprise.

WHERE Near the ancient city of Megiddo, Canaan; now in Israel.

WHEN 1457BC (some sources suggest other dates)

WHY The Canaanites had rebelled against their Egyptian overlords.

OUTCOME After being defeated in the field, the rebels fled into the city and were besieged.

Megiddo is the first battle to have been recorded in a methodical manner. It is noteworthy for the extreme risks taken by the Egyptian commander in making his approach march. The gamble paid off and resulted in a complete victory for the Egyptian army and its disciplined chariot force.

EGYPTIAN/CANAANITE WARS

EGYPTIAN VICTORY

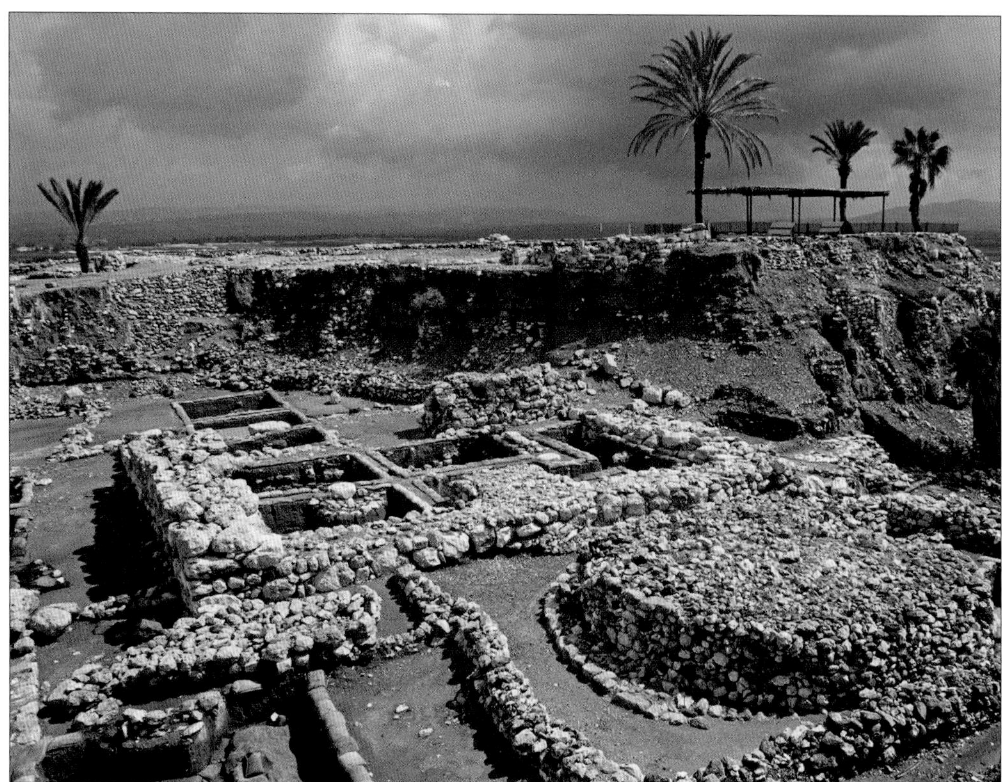

The ruins of Megiddo. The city stood in a strong, high place and was protected by good fortifications. These almost proved the undoing of the defeated Canaanites, who could not get into the city.

LOCATION

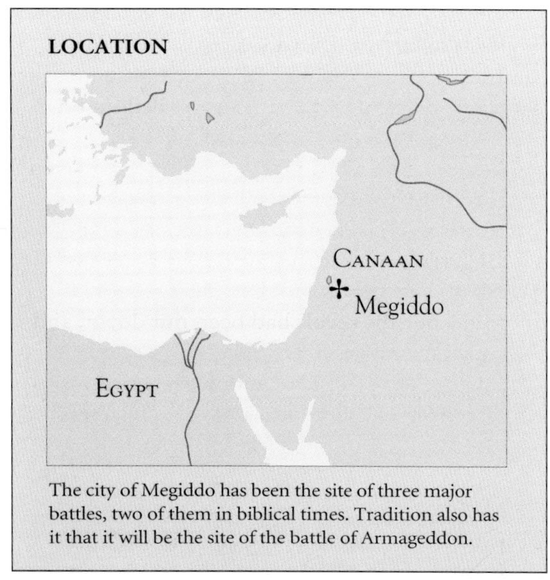
CANAAN
Megiddo
EGYPT

The city of Megiddo has been the site of three major battles, two of them in biblical times. Tradition also has it that it will be the site of the battle of Armageddon.

Thutmose III (d.1425BC) was one of the great Egyptian pharaohs, learned, wise and a great general. But the first 22 years of his reign were spent in the shadows of his powerful stepmother and aunt Hatshepsut, who ruled as co-regent. When she died in 1457, a confederate of Canaanite princes under the leadership of Durusha, king of Kadesh, chose the moment to revolt, forcing Thutmose to quickly mobilize his army and set out across the Sinai Desert in the direction of Canaan with about 20,000 men.

In approaching Megiddo, Thutmose faced a tough choice: he had to pass through the steep Carmel Ridge if he was to reach the battlefield plain. There were three passes through the ridge, of which two – the northerly and southerly passes – offered slow but relatively safe approaches. The central route, the Aruna Pass, was more direct, but it was so narrow, in parts, that men would have to go in single file, with chariots manhandled over obstacles. Even if they weren't ambushed, the army would be strung out, meaning that lead elements could be attacked before the rear had cleared the pass.

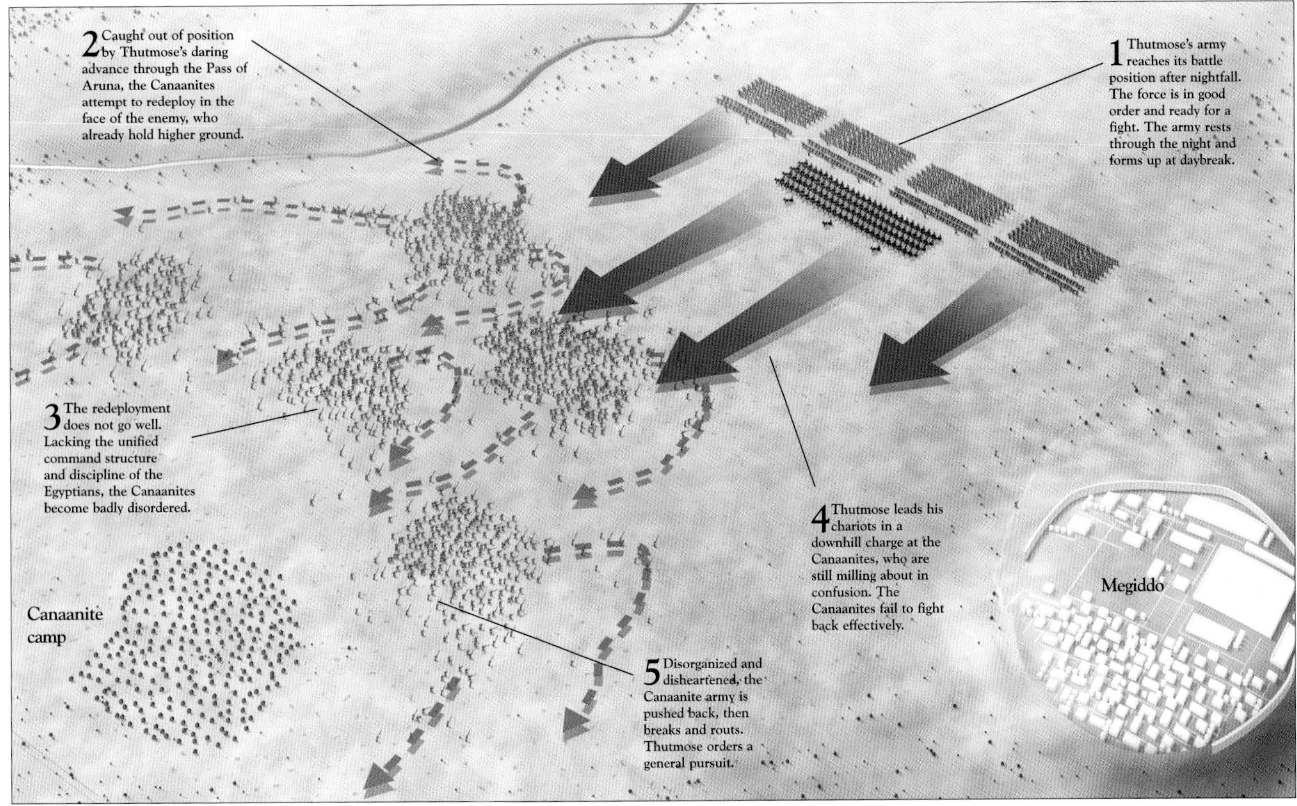
2 Caught out of position by Thutmose's daring advance through the Pass of Aruna, the Canaanites attempt to redeploy in the face of the enemy, who already hold higher ground.
1 Thutmose's army reaches its battle position after nightfall. The force is in good order and ready for a fight. The army rests through the night and forms up at daybreak.
3 The redeployment does not go well. Lacking the unified command structure and discipline of the Egyptians, the Canaanites become badly disordered.
4 Thutmose leads his chariots in a downhill charge at the Canaanites, who are still milling about in confusion. The Canaanites fail to fight back effectively.
Megiddo
Canaanite camp
5 Disorganized and disheartened, the Canaanite army is pushed back, then breaks and routs. Thutmose orders a general pursuit.

Egyptian accounts of the battle suggest the Canaanite forces under Duresha's leadership were huge, and included 350 princes. More likely, it was little larger than the Egyptian army. What was decisive was its lack of cohesion compared to the well-organized Egyptian formations and the latter's mastery of the chariot.

Ignoring the counsel of his subordinate officers, Thutmose chose the Aruna Pass. It was a gamble but it paid off. It took 12 hours to move the whole army through, but Durusha of Kadesh had predicted that Thutmose would take the southerly route, and when the Egyptians unexpectedly emerged on the plain on their flank, there was alarm in the Canaanite camp.

Added to the fact that the Egyptians were able to occupy the higher ground, the Canaanite army was not as well organized as their opponents, whose massed ranks of infantry and archers formed combined divisions. The main strength of the Egyptian army, though, was its chariot corps – long before the invention of the stirrup, which would make the cavalry a battle-winning weapon. Whereas the chariot had been invented in Canaan, it was the Egyptians who most skilfully employed them at Megiddo, as vehicles for fast-firing mobile archers to spread terror among the enemy ranks.

When the pharaoh, in a command chariot decorated in gold and gleaming in the sunlight, gave the advance signal, the chariots hurtled downhill, their arrows raining down on the Canaanites while the infantry crashed their weapons against their shields and trumpets blared. It was an alarming sight, and disorder turned to demoralization, and then quickly to rout.

Seeing the Canaanite army breaking up and men fleeing, Thutmose's chariots and infantry pursued them, but a large segment of Durusha's army reached the city of Megiddo. While the high walls made access difficult, and many men were massacred beneath the fortifications, others did get inside, including Durusha, hauled up on ropes made of clothing.

The Egyptians now laid siege to the city, and after seven months Thutmose finally took its surrender. Mercifully, he spared it the custom of putting the defenders of a city to the sword when it fell, and was rewarded with oaths of loyalty from the former rebels. Durusha of Kadesh did manage to escape, but the revolt had been put down, and Egyptian governors installed in the region.

Thutmose could return to Egypt and take up the reins of power that had been denied him by his stepmother for so long.

Kadesh 1258BC

In a conflict of cultures – Egyptian and Hittite – disinformation and personal leadership drove thousands into an epic battle. Pharaoh Ramses II's use of divisional chains of command proved to be vulnerable in the heat of the fight, and he failed to re-take the city of Kadesh.

SECOND SYRIAN CAMPAIGN OF RAMSES II

NO CLEAR VICTORY

KEY FACTS

WHO The rich and powerful kingdom of Egypt under Pharaoh Ramses II (d. 1213BC) clashed in northern Syria with the militarily innovative Hittite Empire under their king Muwatallis.

WHAT Egyptian chariots and light-armed infantry played a sanguinary game of hide-and-seek around the walls of a fortified city until finally an all-out clash resulted.

WHERE Kadesh was a rich and powerful fortified city that offered an excellent outpost to defend an empire, or to expand one from.

WHEN 1285BC

WHY Kadesh was a Hittite obstacle to Ramses' efforts to make Egypt's claims of world supremacy more than empty boasting.

OUTCOME Hittite cunning and technology were almost too much for Egyptian numbers and organization. A tactical victory for the Egyptians, a strategic one for the Hittites – and in the end a draw.

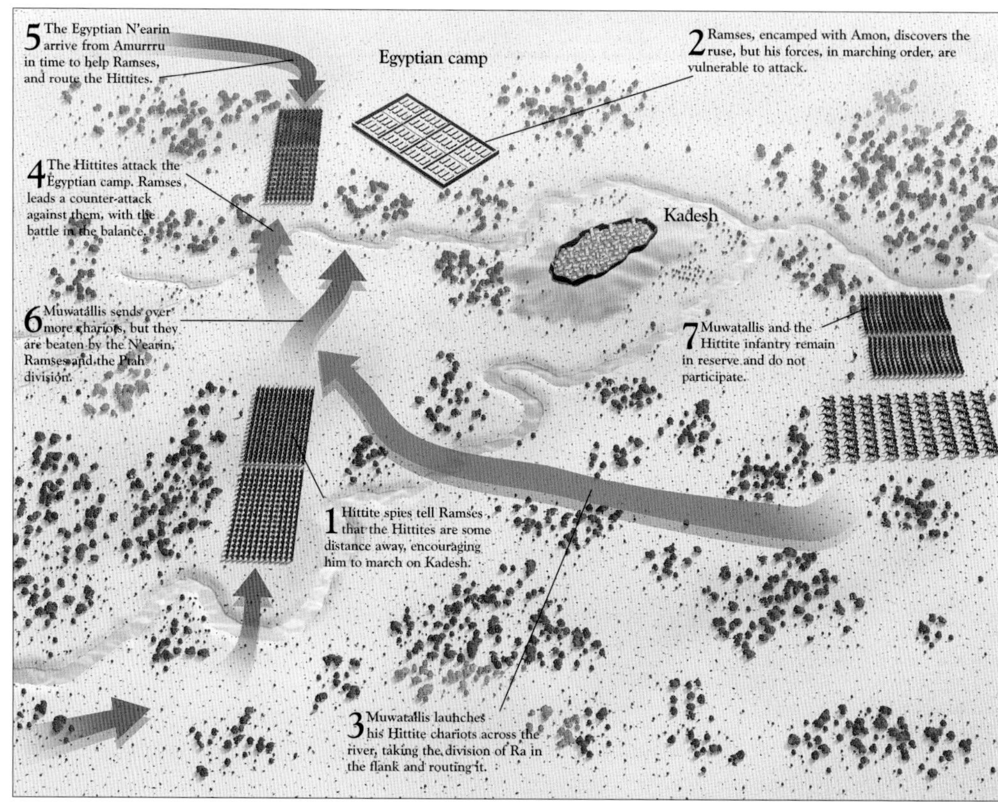
5 The Egyptian N'earin arrive from Amurrru in time to help Ramses, and route the Hittites.
Egyptian camp
2 Ramses, encamped with Amon, discovers the ruse, but his forces, in marching order, are vulnerable to attack.
4 The Hittites attack the Egyptian camp. Ramses leads a counter-attack against them, with the battle in the balance.
Kadesh
6 Muwatallis sends over more chariots, but they are beaten by the N'earin, Ramses and the Ptah division.
7 Muwatallis and the Hittite infantry remain in reserve and do not participate.
1 Hittite spies tell Ramses that the Hittites are some distance away, encouraging him to march on Kadesh.
3 Muwatallis lauhches his Hittite chariots across the river, taking the division of Ra in the flank and routing it.

Moving vast armies over long distances was an operational nightmare. Ramses tried to solve the problem by breaking his up into divisions. But detached chains of command made the divisions vulnerable to misinformation from a wily opponent.

LOCATION

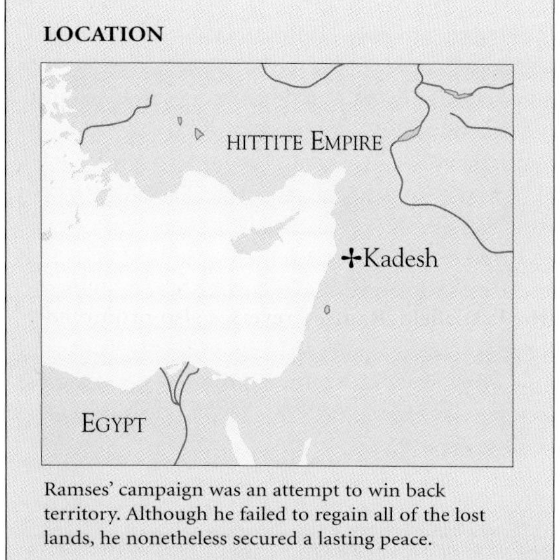
HITTITE EMPIRE
Kadesh
EGYPT

Ramses' campaign was an attempt to win back territory. Although he failed to regain all of the lost lands, he nonetheless secured a lasting peace.

Pharaoh Ramses II's great battle of 1285BC resulted from his desire to surpass the achievements of his illustrious ancestor Thutmose III, and to quell the Hittite Empire's expansion southwards from Asia Minor. Two competing imperial tides clashed around the walls of a fortified city.

Ramses' army was huge – around 20,000 – but controlling such a force on the march and in battle was difficult in terms of command structure. The restricted ability of a single man to control an army required compensatory measures. Ramses' solution was to divide it into four divisions of equal size under trusted subordinates.

During the march towards Kadesh, these four divisions moved at some distance apart. The speed of the march risked causing problems such as sudden attack from the Hittites, with the army's component parts encountering the enemy while still separate, but the tactical advantage was great in terms of surprise and preparation.

However, Muwatallis, the Hittite king, was no supine foe and had managed to produce a matching army of his own by the time the Egyptian forces approached Kadesh.

A relief from Abu Simbel showing Ramses II slaying a foe. Such carvings would have impressed foreign visitors and native Egyptians with the terror and power of Egypt.

He also cannily fed some 'disinformation' by planting two spies in the path of his enemy's army. The captured pair informed Ramses that the Hittite army was still some distance off, prompting Ramses to make another tactical gamble and try to seize Kadesh before their arrival.

The Hittite army thus had the advantage that Ramses was unaware of their actual position. As two of Ramses' divisions approached from the south and west of the city, the Hittites moved to the east, poised to move across the Egyptian line of march.

The Hittites struck the second of Ramses' divisions as it approached their new positions and hit it in the flank. The Egyptians were surprised, panicked and fled for safety towards the following division, similarly throwing that formation into disorder and confusion, just as the Hittites attacked again from the south directly across the Egyptians' escape route. Disaster loomed.

The panic and disorder of fully half of his forces left Ramses physically unable to transmit orders. But Muwatallis also found his command disintegrating when his men stopped to plunder the Egyptians' camp as the disorganized Egyptian forces gave ground.

In desperation, Ramses now led his own bodyguard into a headlong counter-attack, inspiring a general movement against them, which allowed one division to strike the Hittites in the rear just as another pitched into them from the flank.

Muwatallis withdrew into Kadesh, sheltered against any further Egyptian surprises, but forfeiting the advantage of holding the battlefield. Ramses' reverses also prompted him to withdraw his remaining forces from the vicinity of Kadesh, and negotiate peace. It had been a tactical win for the Egyptians, a strategic victory for the Hittites, and, in the light of the treaty, an international 'draw'.

Ramses v Sea Peoples 1190BC

KEY FACTS

WHO The army and navy of Egyptian pharaoh Ramses III against those of the confederation of Sea Peoples.

WHAT Ramses was able to trap the Sea Peoples ships in the slow waters of the Nile, while out-mobilizing them on land, where their armies were slowed by travelling in company with their families.

WHERE Nile delta, Egypt.

WHEN During the reign of Ramses III, 1186–1155BC

WHY The Sea Peoples were a band of migratory tribes who, in looking for somewhere to settle, had been launching small attacks on Egyptian soil for years.

OUTCOME Ramses III was slowly able to overcome the threat posed to his kingdom by the Sea Peoples, a number of whom finally settled in Canaan.

Invasions by migratory bands of peoples presented a different kind of military problem to those of massed armies. Finally, in the twilight years of the Egyptian empire, Ramses III found a way to deal with the persistent nuisance of the Sea Peoples.

SEA PEOPLES' CAMPAIGN

EGYPTIAN VICTORY

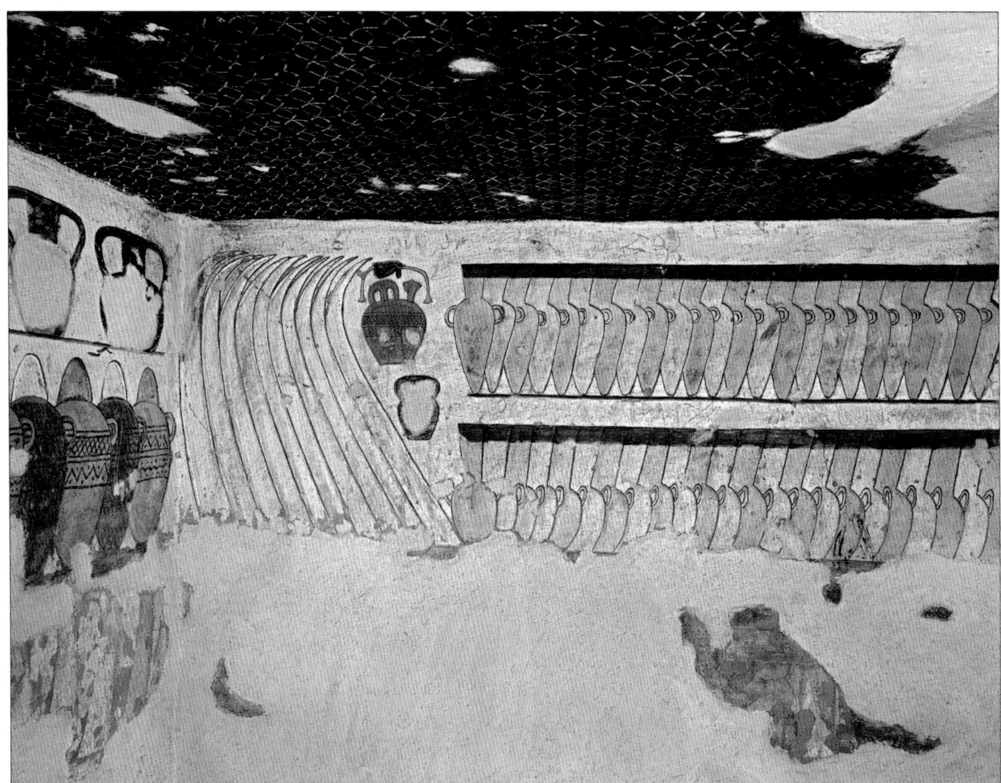

Little is known about the Sea Peoples, other than depictions shown on Egyptian wall paintings. They were essentially a collection of seafaring tribes seeking new land to settle, rather than to make conquests.

LOCATION

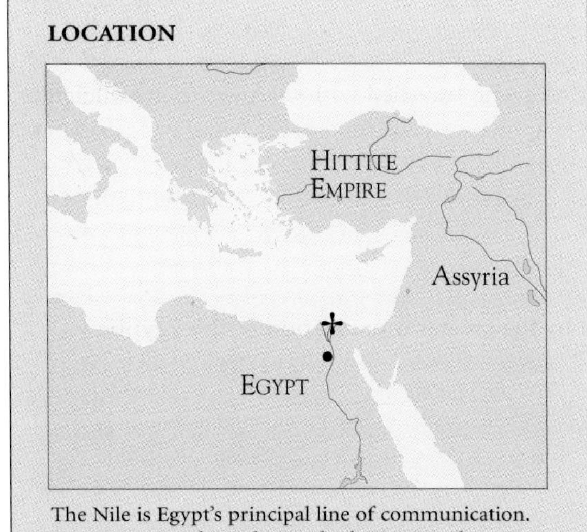
HITTITE
EMPIRE
Assyria
EGYPT

The Nile is Egypt's principal line of communication. Trying to enter from the north, the Sea Peoples were trapped in the labyrinthine channels of the delta.

By the reign of Ramses III, the Egyptian New Kingdom had entered a period of slow decline. New enemies were emerging and Egyptian records painted a picture of uproar in the Aegean Sea. They recounted tales of the islands in these waters pouring out hordes of tribes so that 'no land stood before them.' However, the Egyptians remained a force to be reckoned with, and Ramses would ensure that they at least remained so for the duration of his long reign.

The so-called Sea Peoples were effectively groupings of migratory tribes active in the waters of the eastern Mediterranean throughout the second millenium BC. There had been reports of their activities during the heyday of Ramses II, and some of them were even recorded as having fought against his army at Kadesh, as allies of the Hittites, in 1285BC. While these attacks were beaten off, Ramses III, the last of the great Egyptian pharoahs, was forced to deal with a second wave of their invasions. These seem not to have been based around a quest for military glory, but rather to have been

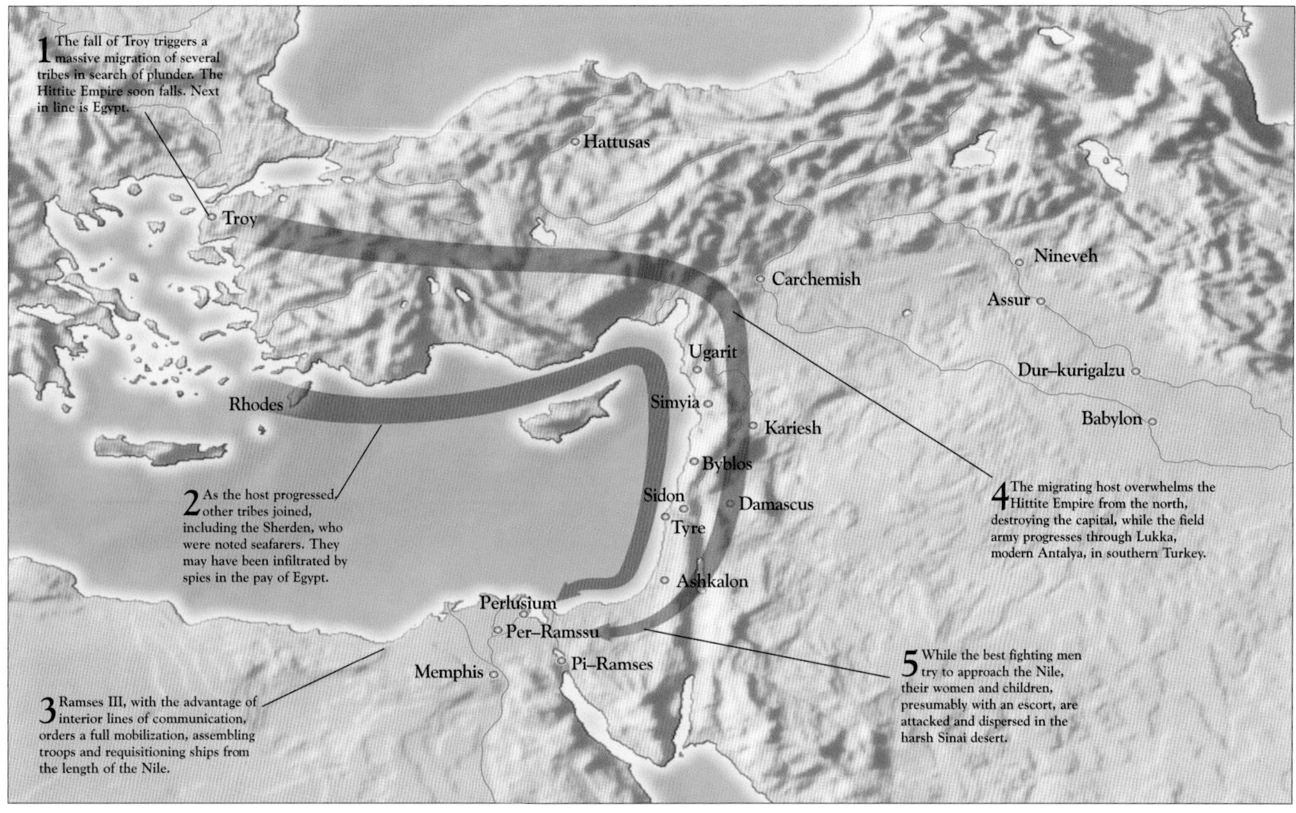
1 The fall of Troy triggers a massive migration of several tribes in search of plunder. The Hittite Empire soon falls. Next in line is Egypt.
Hattusas
Troy
Carchemish
Nineveh
Assur
Ugarit
Dur-kurigalzu
Rhodes
Simyia
Kariesh
Babylon
Byblos
2 As the host progressed, other tribes joined, including the Sherden, who were noted seafarers. They may have been infiltrated by spies in the pay of Egypt.
Sidon
Damascus
Tyre
4 The migrating host overwhelms the Hittite Empire from the north, destroying the capital, while the field army progresses through Lukka, modern Antalya, in southern Turkey.
Ashkalon
Perlusium
Per-Ramssu
Memphis
Pi-Ramses
5 While the best fighting men try to approach the Nile, their women and children, presumably with an escort, are attacked and dispersed in the harsh Sinai desert.
3 Ramses III, with the advantage of interior lines of communication, orders a full mobilization, assembling troops and requisitioning ships from the length of the Nile.

To begin with, the Sea Peoples could use the element of surprise in their ventures into Egypt from the ocean. Egypt was not a major seapower, but Rameses II was eventually able to set a trap for them as they broached further along the Nile.

comprised of large groups of migrants looking for new land on which to settle.

The Sea Peoples appear to have made at least one invasion earlier in Ramses III's reign, but by dividing themselves into two parties for concurrent invasions by land and sea they diluted their strength, and seem to have been confidently repelled. When they returned in Year 8 of his reign, Ramses was even waiting for them at the mouth of the Nile with a specially prepared fleet of ships.

The Egyptians were not a great seafaring nation, whereas their opponents were doubtless hardened seamen, but around the calmer waters of the Nile the Sea Peoples' primitive crafts were easier to ambush, and the greater numbers and discipline of the Egyptians would have overwhelmed them. Rather than being able to launch shock raids in the style deployed by later maritime warrior peoples such as the Vikings, they instead found themselves surprised by Egyptian ships lurking unseen amongst the tall papyrus reeds of the Nile delta. The Egyptians also employed superior tactics, with their ships ramming and then withdrawing to ram again – and again. Volleys of arrows were fired from the cover of the reed beds, and grappling hooks used to drag the ships in close, after which the Egyptians poured on board to overwhelm them in hand-to-hand fighting with their superior weaponry. The Sea Peoples' leaders were dragged ashore and executed.

DEMISE OF THE SEA PEOPLES

Meanwhile, the invasion by land fared little better. The Sea Peoples' deeply flawed plan of dividing their army into sea and land forces once again left their women and children, who travelled with them, with insufficient protection in open country – making them easy prey for the marauding Egyptian chariotry, backed by their tribal allies. The invaders' strike force also used outdated technology and failed to achieve surprise or numerical superiority.

The end of the great conspiracy of the Sea Peoples was achieved by the greater organization of the Egyptian empire. The survivors from the Sea Peoples' army were captured and used as slaves. Very few escaped, bringing an end to the culture of the Sea Peoples and the threat they posed in the Eastern Mediterranean.

TIMELINE

1500–1000BC	1000–500BC	500BC–0AD	0–500AD	500–1000AD	1000–1500AD	1500–2000AD

Siege of Jerusalem 1000BC

WARS OF THE ISRAELITES

ISRAELITE VICTORY

The capture of Jerusalem was a pivotal moment in world history. After defeating its Canaanite defenders with a surprise attack, King David spared them vicious reprisals but brought the Ark of the Covenant there, and made it his capital and the founding block of a more united Israeli nation.

KEY FACTS

WHO The primitively armed force of David, king of Israel c. 1003–970BC, against the Canaanite defenders of the great city of Jebus.

WHAT Israelites launch missiles at the fortifications, creating time for the foot soldiers to scale the walls.

WHERE The ancient city of Jebus, renamed Jerusalem by David.

WHEN 1000BC

WHY David needed a new capital to unify the northern and southern Israeli tribes.

OUTCOME In spite of being ill-equipped to launch a siege, David's sudden attack is enough to secure a rapid surrender.

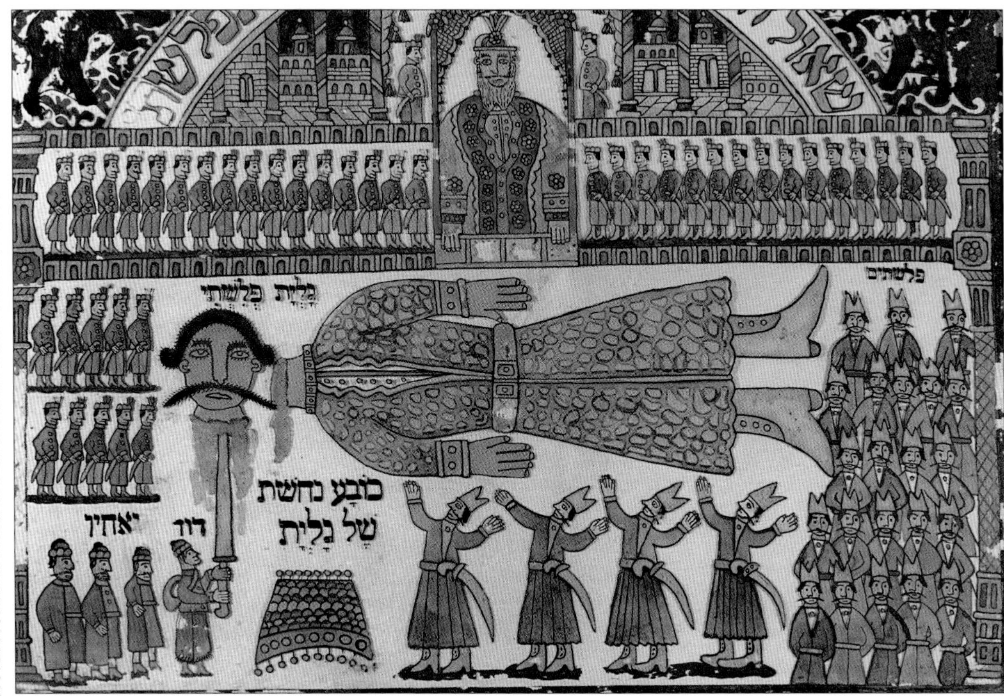
גלית פלשתי
פלשתים
דוד
אחיו
של גלית

King David was, according to the Bible, the founder of Jerusalem and uniter of the Israeli tribes. But first, he had to fight a bitter war against the Canaanites and take the mighty fort of Jebus.

LOCATION

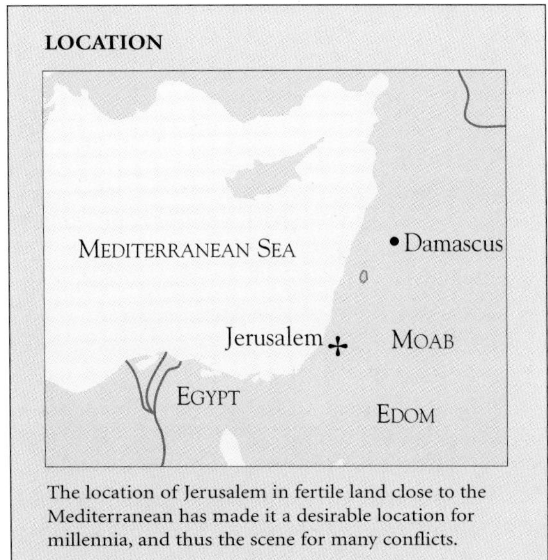
MEDITERRANEAN SEA
• Damascus
Jerusalem
MOAB
EGYPT
EDOM

The location of Jerusalem in fertile land close to the Mediterranean has made it a desirable location for millennia, and thus the scene for many conflicts.

King David, ruler of disparate Israelite tribes, decided that Jebus – modern Jerusalem – was ideally situated to unite the north and south portions of his realm. But the fortress city, located on a rock escarpment, was impressively fortified. Its Canaanite defenders bragged that a handful of blind and lame men could defend it.

David's force was effective in guerrilla mountain combat, but vulnerable to missiles launched by the defenders. Many men wore no armour at all, simply carrying a spear and shield. But a sudden attack, with archers and slingers providing covering fire with a hail of missiles, caught the defenders by surprise, forcing their heads down long enough for the Israelites to scale the walls.

After some hard fighting, the defence collapsed. The surrendering Jebusites were treated magnanimously by David, who spared the life of their king. David brought the Ark of the Covenant to Jebus, which he renamed Jerusalem and made his capital, passing on a mainly united Israelite nation to his son Solomon (d. 922BC).

TIMELINE

1500–1000BC	1000–500BC	500BC–0AD	0–500AD	500–1000AD	1000–1500AD	1500–2000AD

Siege of Samaria 890BC

WARS OF THE ISRAELITES

ISRAELITE VICTORY

KEY FACTS

WHO Benhadad II, king of Syria, against Ahab, king of Samaria.

WHAT Benhadad led a huge army, supported by 32 other tribal leaders, and laid siege to the outnumbered Samarians in their city.

WHERE Samaria, the wealthy capital of the northern half of the Israelite kingdom after its division on the death of Solomon.

WHEN c. 890BC

WHY Benhadad believed Samaria's flourishing economy and ambitions to be a threat to his own kingdom.

OUTCOME Benhadad, taking victory for granted, set impossible conditions of surrender. While indulging in drunken revelry, a bold sortie of young Samarian officers took him by surprise.

When King Solomon died in 922BC, the united Jewish kingdom was divided in two. In the following century, King Benhadad II of Syria launched an attack on Ahab, ruler of the northern half in his capital of Samaria. His siege of the city, however, was undone by complacency.

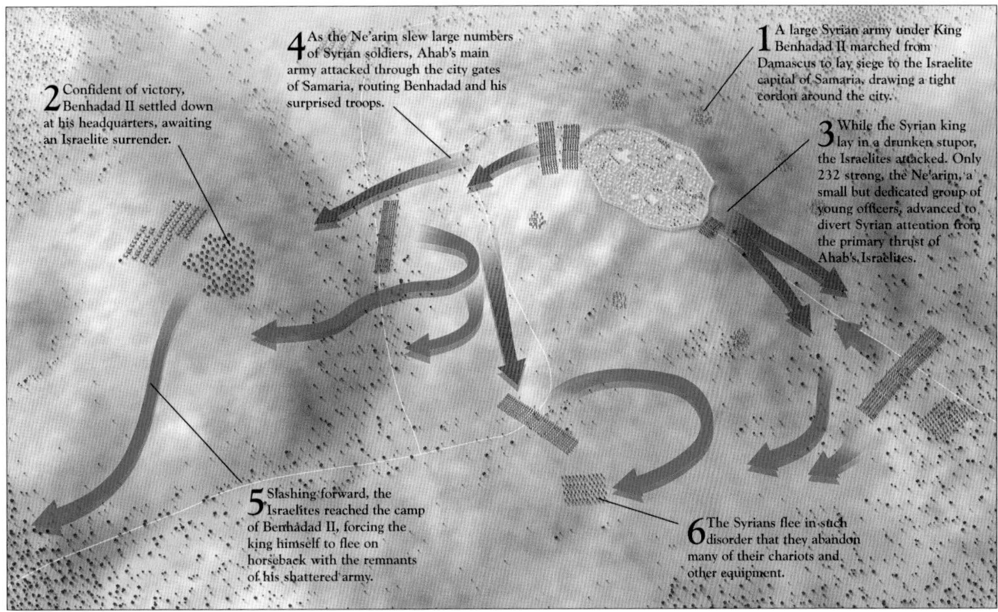

1 A large Syrian army under King Benhadad II marched from Damascus to lay siege to the Israelite capital of Samaria, drawing a tight cordon around the city.
2 Confident of victory, Benhadad II settled down at his headquarters, awaiting an Israelite surrender.
3 While the Syrian king lay in a drunken stupor, the Israelites attacked. Only 232 strong, the Ne'arim, a small but dedicated group of young officers, advanced to divert Syrian attention from the primary thrust of Ahab's Israelites.
4 As the Ne'arim slew large numbers of Syrian soldiers, Ahab's main army attacked through the city gates of Samaria, routing Benhadad and his surprised troops.
5 Slashing forward, the Israelites reached the camp of Benhadad II, forcing the king himself to flee on horseback with the remnants of his shattered army.
6 The Syrians flee in such disorder that they abandon many of their chariots and other equipment.

The siege of Samaria is an example of what happens when a complacent superior opponent meets a determined smaller fighting force. As Benhadad's men sat back beyond the city and partied, the Samarians launched a surprise attack.

Under King Ahab (c. 890–850BC) the flourishing Israelite city of Samaria was a threat to neighbouring Aram (modern Syria), whose king Benhadad II decided to besiege it. Benhadad considered the city's fall to be a foregone conclusion. But delivering a stiff ultimatum to Ahab succeeded only in galvanizing the Samarians to make a stand.

While Benhadad II and his lieutenants drank to excess in their tents, a cadre of 232 young officers, known as the Ne'arim, marched out in full view of the Syrians. In his drunken stupour, the cavalier Benhadad II was captivated by the opportunity to annihilate these brave but foolish Israelites. But the Ne'arim proved an unexpectedly formidable foe, paving the way for Ahab and the main Israelite force to advance through the gates and fall upon the confused Syrians.

So great was the rout that Benhadad II, caught completely by surprise, realized that his only option was to flee the field. Ahab's soldiers inflicted heavy losses on the Syrians, but they were far from completely defeated. Dark days lay ahead for both sides, with further conflicts lying in wait in the years that followed.

LOCATION

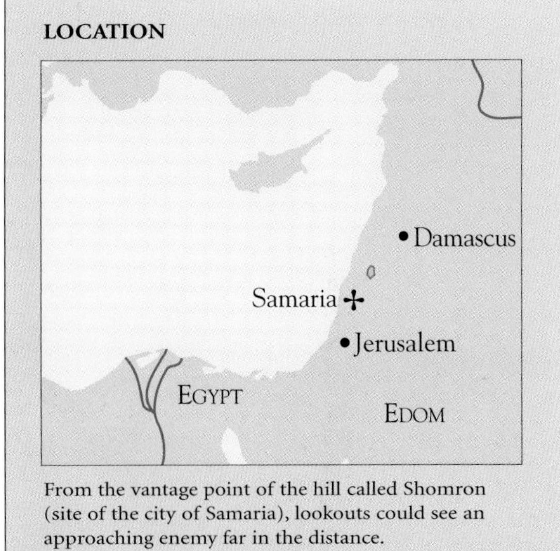

Damascus
Samaria
Jerusalem
EGYPT
EDOM

From the vantage point of the hill called Shomron (site of the city of Samaria), lookouts could see an approaching enemy far in the distance.

TIMELINE

1500–1000BC	1000–500BC	500BC–0AD	0–500AD	500–1000AD	1000–1500AD	1500–2000AD

Samaria

SAMARIA

The battle of Samaria took on a form that seems characteristic of many of the battles and wars that were waged in the biblical period – that of a weaker tribe offering stout resistance in a heavily fortified town, and their stronger opponent settling in for a long siege. Samaria was a classic, thick-walled desert stronghold, ideally located for its command of all surrounding approach routes. It was partly this that enabled its garrison to mount a successful stand against King Benhadad's better equipped Syrians. Essentially, however, the eventual outcome – defeat for Benhadad – rested on the unprofessional attitude of the Syrians, who literally allowed their guard to slip as they caroused outside the walls, awaiting what they believed was certain victory.

Golan Heights 874BC

KEY FACTS

WHO	The Israelite army of King Ahab (889–850 BC) against the Syrian army of King Benhadad II.
WHAT	Ahab undertook a campaign to defend against a second invasion by the reconstituted army of Benhadad II, defeating the Syrians.
WHERE	The Golan Heights, northwest of the Israelite capital of Samaria.
WHEN	874BC
WHY	Following his defeat at Samaria, Syrian King Benhadad II intended to invade the kingdom of Israel a second time. Ahab, the Israelite king, was determined to prevent another invasion.
OUTCOME	The Syrian army was routed a second time and, after begging for his life, Benhadad was spared by Ahab.

Defeat at Samaria did not deter the Syrian King Benhadad II from his aggressive intentions towards its ruler Ahab. When Ahab launched a march into the disputed Golan Heights, Benhadad determined to resume hostilities. The result was carnage – and another Syrian defeat.

WARS OF THE ISRAELITES

ISRAELITE VICTORY

Ben-Hadad was a Syrian king with a powerful his reputation as a military leader, but few battles are won sitting drinking in a tent, and his love of hedonistic pleasures undermined his achievements as a war leader.

LOCATION

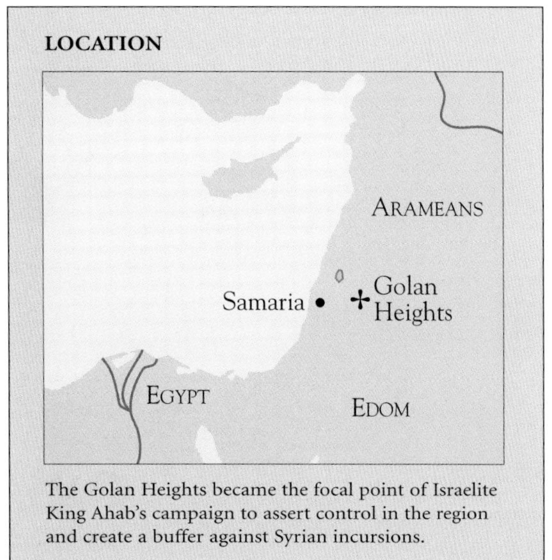
ARAMEANS
Samaria
Golan Heights
EGYPT
EDOM

The Golan Heights became the focal point of Israelite King Ahab's campaign to assert control in the region and create a buffer against Syrian incursions.

The rejoining of battle was inevitable after Benhadad II's humiliation at Samaria. Prophets warned the latter's ruler, Ahab, to expect another invasion by the Syrians. Instead, though, Ahab launched an offensive of his own to prevent the Syrian host from invading his homeland and bringing war once again to the heart of the kingdom. So he led his army into the long disputed territory of Golan Heights.

Benhadad was convinced he'd defeat Ahab if the fighting took place in a narrow valley called Aphek, but this proved a massive tactical error. Fighting in these narrow confines limited the mobility of his larger army, and sheer weight of numbers probably became a hindrance rather than an advantage. The Israelites were said to have inflicted a hundred thousand casualties on the foot soldiers in a day – a biblical exaggeration clearly, but indicative of a massive defeat. Ahab spared the life of his long-time foe, however, in exchange for the return of lands lost in previous generations. In future, the two men would even fight together against the Assyrians.

TIMELINE

1500–1000BC	1000–500BC	500BC–0AD	0–500AD	500–1000AD	1000–1500AD	1500–2000AD

Revolt of Mesha 850BC

WARS OF THE ISRAELITES

STALEMATE

KEY FACTS

WHO Moab king Mesha, against his Israelite overlords, who were in alliance with Edom.

WHAT Jeroham, king of Israel, decides to extinguish a revolt by storming into Moab territory.

WHERE The walled citadel of Kir-Haraseth, thought to be modern day Kerak, in Jordan.

WHEN c. 850BC

WHY On the death of King Ahab, the Israelites were wracked by internal divisions, and Moab king Mesha, believed he could exploit the situation by revolting.

OUTCOME Jeroham inflicted heavy casualties on the Moabs, but the Kir-Haraseth was able to hold out, and force the Israelites to withdraw.

When Mesha, Moabite vassal of Israel, learnt of the death of old king Ahab, he seized the moment to rebel. Despite eventually being forced to retreat to the great citadel of Kir-Haraseth, Mesha managed to stave off the Israelites and their Edomite allies, and retain his newly won independence.

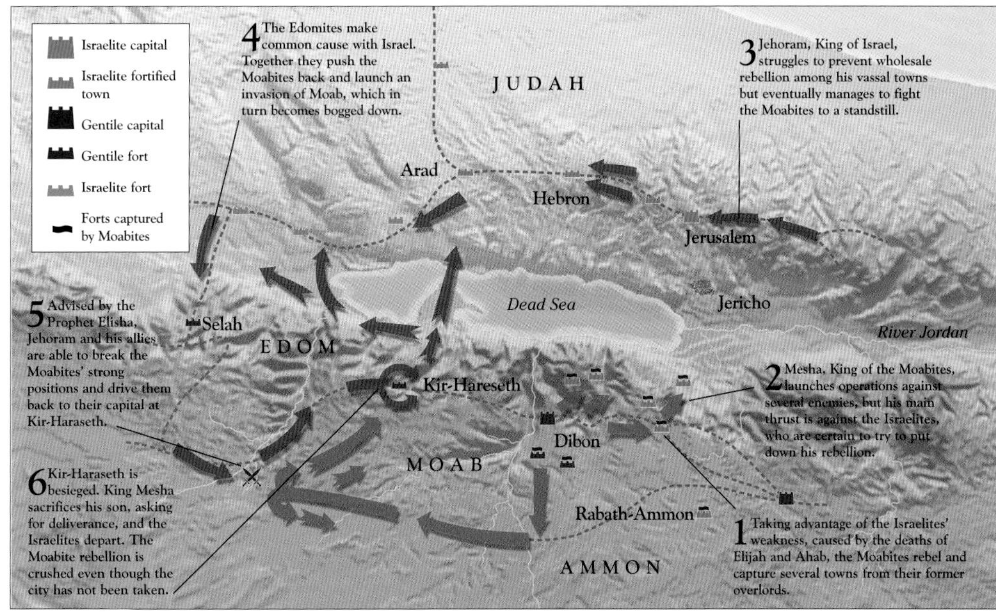
Israelite capital
Israelite fortified town
Gentile capital
Gentile fort
Israelite fort
Forts captured by Moabites
4 The Edomites make common cause with Israel. Together they push the Moabites back and launch an invasion of Moab, which in turn becomes bogged down.
JUDAH
3 Jehoram, King of Israel, struggles to prevent wholesale rebellion among his vassal towns but eventually manages to fight the Moabites to a standstill.
Arad
Hebron
Jerusalem
Dead Sea
Jericho
River Jordan
5 Advised by the Prophet Elisha, Jehoram and his allies are able to break the Moabites' strong positions and drive them back to their capital at Kir-Haraseth.
Selah
EDOM
Kir-Hareseth
2 Mesha, King of the Moabites, launches operations against several enemies, but his main thrust is against the Israelites, who are certain to try to put down his rebellion.
Dibon
MOAB
6 Kir-Haraseth is besieged. King Mesha sacrifices his son, asking for deliverance, and the Israelites depart. The Moabite rebellion is crushed even though the city has not been taken.
Rabath-Ammon
AMMON
1 Taking advantage of the Israelites' weakness, caused by the deaths of Elijah and Ahab, the Moabites rebel and capture several towns from their former overlords.

Kir-Haraseth was a formidable fortress on the Dead Sea. When the Moabs were forced to retreat behind its walls after their rebellion had lost its impetus, the Israelites faced an uphill struggle to take it.

Mesha, King of Moab, revolted against his vassals, the Israelites. He enjoyed early success, recapturing much lost territory, but Jehoram, king of Israel, soon fought back. In alliance with another vassal state, Edom, he invaded Moab, forcing Mesha to retreat into the formidably fortified city of Kir-Haraseth.

Assault of such an intimidating fortification was impossible. Instead the allies laid siege to the city, throwing a ring of troops around it and posting slingers on high ground, harassing any defenders who showed themselves. With no chance of a relief force arriving, the allies merely had to wait for the defenders to starve.

COUNTER-ATTACK

Mesha, making a bold stroke to reverse his fortunes, gathered some 700 swordsmen and came out fighting. Predictably, his force was driven back into the city in total defeat. Yet, in a perverse way, he got what he wanted. For unexplained reasons and despite inflicting heavy casualties on Mesha and his army, the allies disengaged and retired from Kir-Haraseth, withdrawing from the land of Moab, which was left unreconquered.

LOCATION

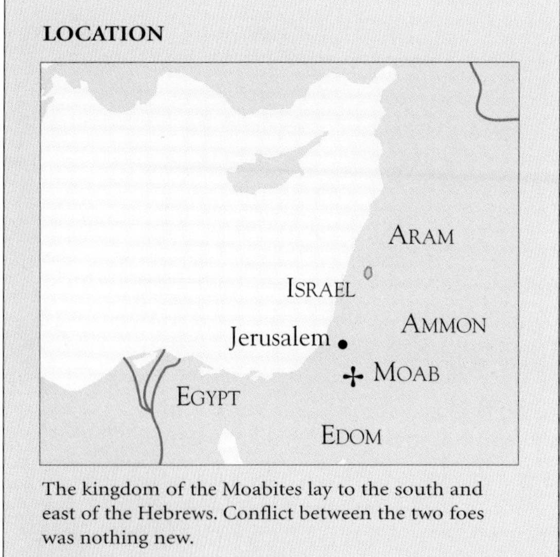
ARAM
ISRAEL
AMMON
Jerusalem
MOAB
EGYPT
EDOM

The kingdom of the Moabites lay to the south and east of the Hebrews. Conflict between the two foes was nothing new.

TIMELINE

1500–1000BC	1000–500BC	500BC–0AD	0–500AD	500–1000AD	1000–1500AD	1500–2000AD

Campaign against Edom 785BC

JUDEAN CAMPAIGN

JUDEAN VICTORY

Edom, southeast of Judah, on important trade routes to the Dead Sea, was often the target of the expansionist Judean kings. But their chariot forces proved ineffective on rocky desert terrain. Only when cavalrymen were deployed by King Amaziah was conquest achieved.

KEY FACTS

WHO King Azamiah of Judah leads the cavalry into the important strategic territory of Edom.

WHAT Azamiah is able to deploy cavalrymen for the first time in his kingdom's history to try to seize a valuable prize.

WHERE According to the Bible, in the Valley of Salt, near the Dead Sea.

WHEN c. 785BC

WHY The Judeans had long coveted neighbouring Edom for its access to sea trade routes.

OUTCOME A massive victory for Judah, as its well-equipped soldiers inflict heavy casualties on the nomadic Edomites.

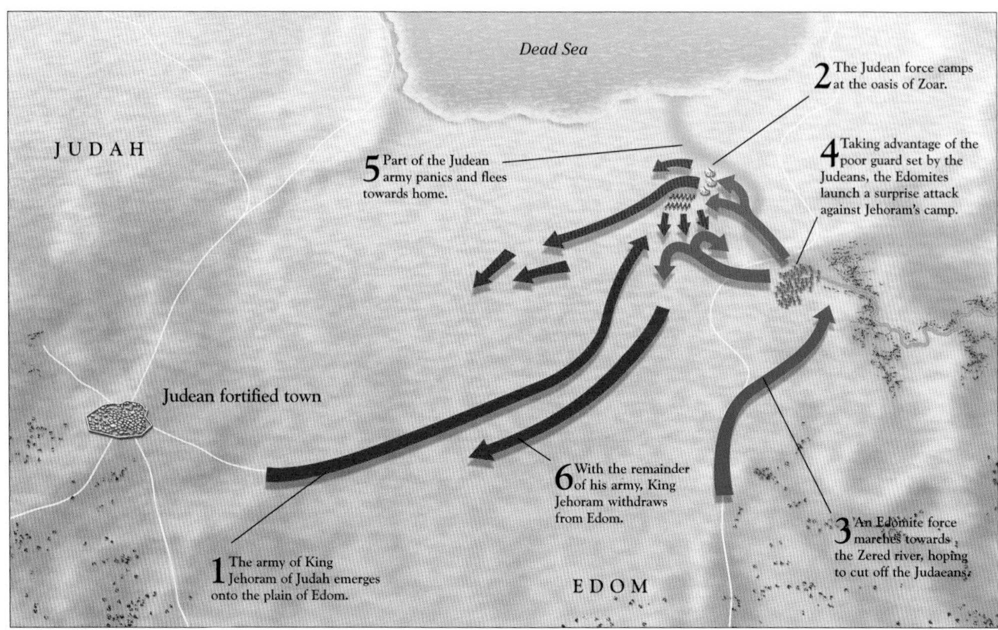
Dead Sea
JUDAH
EDOM
Judean fortified town
1 The army of King Jehoram of Judah emerges onto the plain of Edom.
2 The Judean force camps at the oasis of Zoar.
3 An Edomite force marches towards the Zered river, hoping to cut off the Judaeans.
4 Taking advantage of the poor guard set by the Judeans, the Edomites launch a surprise attack against Jehoram's camp.
5 Part of the Judean army panics and flees towards home.
6 With the remainder of his army, King Jehoram withdraws from Edom.

The desert kingdom Edom had many times thwarted the Judean chariot army whose wheels had difficulty moving through its cracked, rocky plains. Mobile cavalry were ideal, however, and were the key to Amaziah's success.

Edom was an arid, sparsely populated, desert land, but strategically important for its control of Dead Sea trade routes. Neighbouring Judah's past attempts to take it had been thwarted, as its chariot forces were unsuited to campaigning on the cracks and crevices of the terrain.

But when King Amaziah began a new campaign c. 785BC, he probably left the chariots behind, taking instead a cavalry corps, with more manoeuvrable mounted bowman. He also had archers, slingers and infantry equipped with spears, daggers and shields. Elite troops were clad in body armour. The Edomite force, by contrast, were better equipped for raiding and guerrilla fighting. Few of their soldiers possessed body armour although, given their largely pastoral lifestyles, it is likely that they could muster at least some cavalry.

The two armies met in battle south of the Dead Sea, at a location the Bible calls the Valley of Salt, and the superiority of the Judean army was clearly apparent. The result was a major Judean victory with 10,000 Edomites killed in fighting, and another 10,000 captured and then thrown off a cliff. Amaziah was thereafter quickly able to establish Judean overlordship over all of northern Edom.

LOCATION

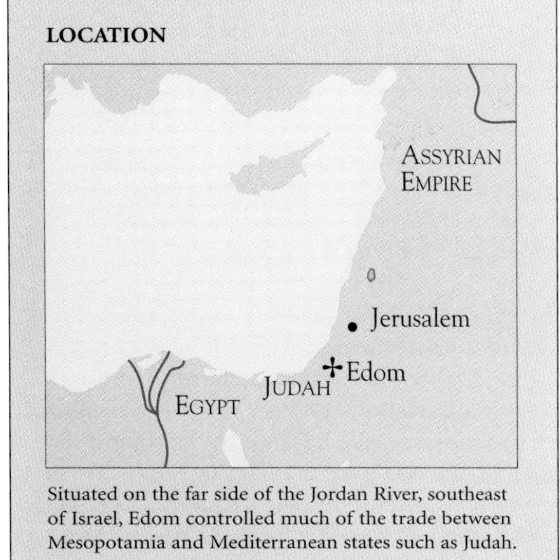
ASSYRIAN EMPIRE
Jerusalem
Edom
JUDAH
EGYPT

Situated on the far side of the Jordan River, southeast of Israel, Edom controlled much of the trade between Mesopotamia and Mediterranean states such as Judah.

TIMELINE

1500–1000BC	1000–500BC	500BC–0AD	0–500AD	500–1000AD	1000–1500AD	1500–2000AD

Palestine and Syria 734BC

KEY FACTS

Who The formidable Assyrians under Tiglath-Pileser III against the coalition of Israel and Damascus.

What While carrying out a siege of Damascus, Tiglath-Pileser's troops also marauded through the adjoining terrain, reducing the Israelites to submission.

Where Damascus, Tyre and the surrounding countryside and city ports along the Mediterranean coast.

When 733–734BC

Why Assyria was a mighty force on the Middle Eastern stage but, being landlocked, it had its eyes on the Mediterranean conquests.

Outcome A decisive Assyrian victory and an emphatic statement of its military prowess.

Israel and Damascus knew that only by combining forces could they hope to resist the mighty army of Assyria, under Tiglath-Pileser III. But when he invaded Palestine and Syria in 734–32BC, in an effort to take control of Mediterranean trade routes, they were substantially beaten.

ASSYRIAN WARS

ASSYRIAN VICTORY

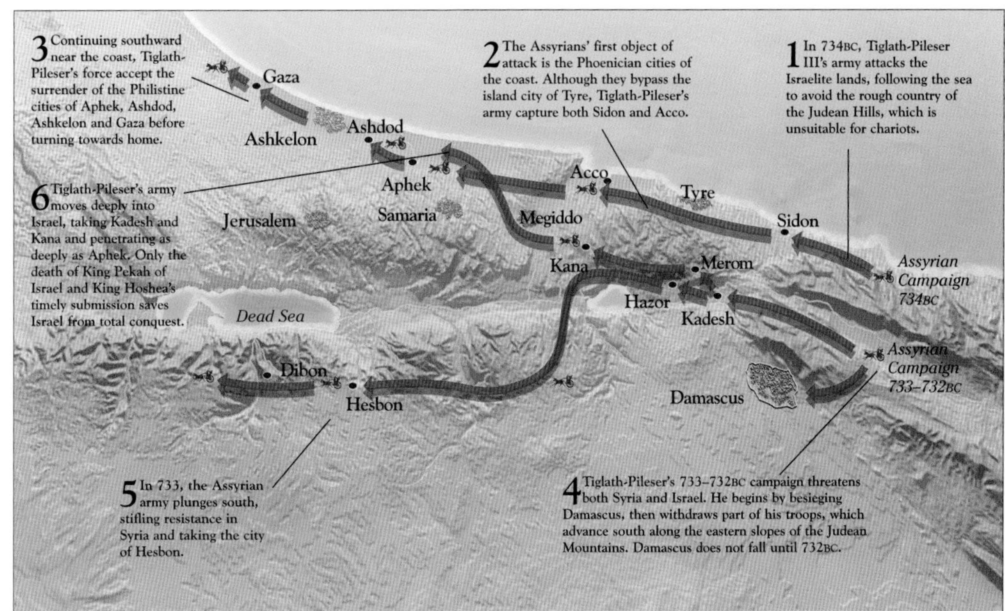
3 Continuing southward near the coast, Tiglath-Pileser's force accept the surrender of the Philistine cities of Aphek, Ashdod, Ashkelon and Gaza before turning towards home.
2 The Assyrians' first object of attack is the Phoenician cities of the coast. Although they bypass the island city of Tyre, Tiglath-Pileser's army capture both Sidon and Acco.
1 In 734BC, Tiglath-Pileser III's army attacks the Israelite lands, following the sea to avoid the rough country of the Judean Hills, which is unsuitable for chariots.
6 Tiglath-Pileser's army moves deeply into Israel, taking Kadesh and Kana and penetrating as deeply as Aphek. Only the death of King Pekah of Israel and King Hoshea's timely submission saves Israel from total conquest.
5 In 733, the Assyrian army plunges south, stifling resistance in Syria and taking the city of Hesbon.
4 Tiglath-Pileser's 733–732BC campaign threatens both Syria and Israel. He begins by besieging Damascus, then withdraws part of his troops, which advance south along the eastern slopes of the Judean Mountains. Damascus does not fall until 732BC.
Gaza
Ashkelon
Ashdod
Aphek
Samaria
Jerusalem
Acco
Tyre
Sidon
Megiddo
Kana
Merom
Hazor
Kadesh
Dead Sea
Dibon
Hesbon
Damascus
Assyrian Campaign 734BC
Assyrian Campaign 733–732BC

The Assyrian Tiglath-Pileser III's awesome professional army moved along the coastline, picking off the Phoenician cities one by one before turning its attention on Damascus. This was more challenging, but it went the same way.

Tiglath-Pileser III, king of Assyria from 744–727BC, had a standing army that set new standards of training and professionalism. It was a fully integrated force, complete with infantry, cavalry, a small force of chariots – declining in significance in warfare since the ninth century BC and eventually totally replaced by cavalry – and a corps of engineers.

Only Israel and Damascus offered much regional opposition, but they were powerless to stop Tiglath-Pileser subjecting independent Phoenician city-states along the Mediterranean, probably by applying the Assyrians' usual terror tactics of flaying and impaling citizens – tactics designed to intimidate future opponents into surrendering without a fight. When Tyre submitted and paid tribute, others followed suit.

Damascus held out for two years after a siege began in 733BC, while Tiglath-Pileser set about subduing the rest of the region, and punishing King Pekah of Israel for his opposition. But the campaign proved conclusively that the army of Israel was too small and amateurish to face the Assyrian military machine, which at that period was more than a match for any rival force in the region.

LOCATION

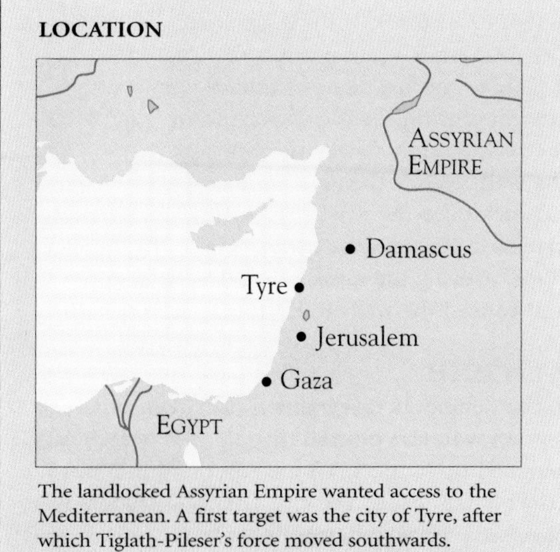
Assyrian Empire
Damascus
Tyre
Jerusalem
Gaza
Egypt

The landlocked Assyrian Empire wanted access to the Mediterranean. A first target was the city of Tyre, after which Tiglath-Pileser's force moved southwards.

TIMELINE

1500–1000BC	1000–500BC	500BC–0AD	0–500AD	500–1000AD	1000–1500AD	1500–2000AD

Siege of Lachish 700BC

KEY FACTS

WHO Sennacherib, king of the Assyrians (704-681BC), invades Judah to stamp out a rebellion.

WHAT Lachish was a well-fortified town en route to Jerusalem. Sennacherib used it for a terrifyingly efficient demonstration of how to conduct siege warfare.

WHERE Historical city of Lachish, south of Jerusalem.

WHEN 700BC

WHY Hezekiah of Judah 9726–697BC) had planned for a long-term defensive campaign of resistance against his Assyrian overlords.

OUTCOME A decisive Assyrian victory, after which Sennacherib marched on Jerusalem. Although the latter did not fall, a sufficiently intimidating point had been made and rebellion quelled.

ASSYRIAN WARS

ASSYRIAN VICTORY

King Sennacherib of Assyria marched against Judah to suppress its rebellious king, Hezekiah. The first major obstacle in his path was Lachish, a powerful Judean fortress that protected the southwest approach to Jerusalem. Sennacherib responded with a classic Assyrian siege.

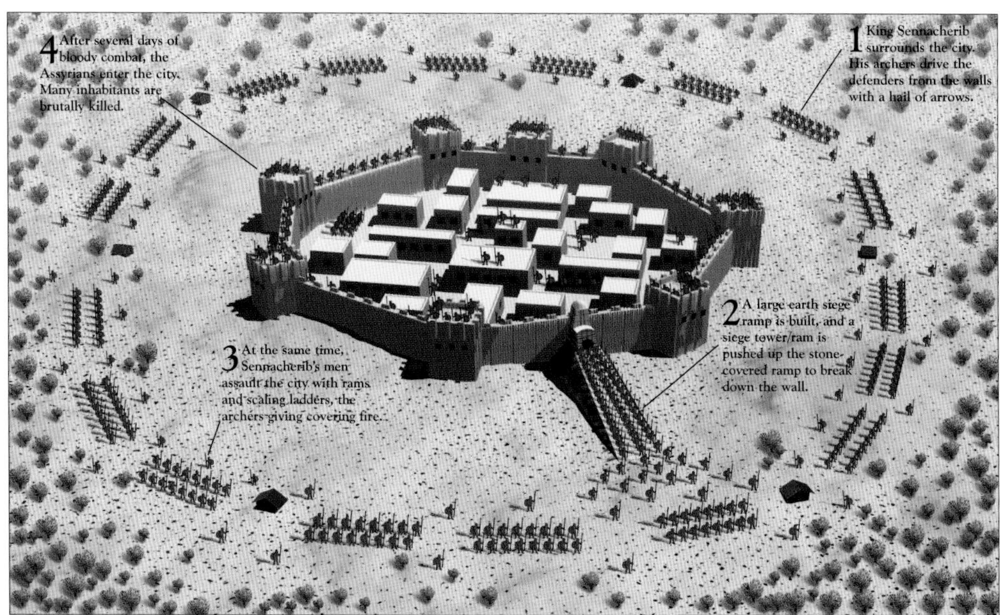

4 After several days of bloody combat, the Assyrians enter the city. Many inhabitants are brutally killed.
1 King Sennacherib surrounds the city. His archers drive the defenders from the walls with a hail of arrows.
3 At the same time, Sennacherib's men assault the city with rams and scaling ladders, the archers giving covering fire.
2 A large earth siege ramp is built, and a siege tower/ram is pushed up the stone-covered ramp to break down the wall.

When it came to siegecraft, the Assyrians were the absolute masters, deploying technology sometimes centuries ahead of other warring states. The full panoply would be brought into play at Lachish.

By 700BC, Assyria was one of the most militaristic states in the world, with a huge professional army. When King Hezekiah of Judah revolted, King Sennacherib launched an immediate attack. Hezekiah hoped his many strong fortresses would wear down the Assyrians until they gave up – but the Assyrians were masters of siege warfare.

Setting siege to the key city of Lachish, engineers constructed siege ramps, wide enough to operate sharp-pointed battering rams, swinging from suspended ropes, against the walls. While the defenders showered arrows, spears and rock onto the workers, Assyrian archers sniped back in retaliation from siege towers level with the crenellations. Aiming the rams at joints gradually eroded mortar and caused the walls to crumble.

FALL OF LACHISH

Although the defenders threw down fire down onto the rams, Assyrian warriors poured through the breach, while others swarmed up ladders. Women and children were killed as the victors looted the city. Lachish's leaders were horridly impaled. Hezekiah, trembling in Jerusalem, sent an immediate surrender.

LOCATION

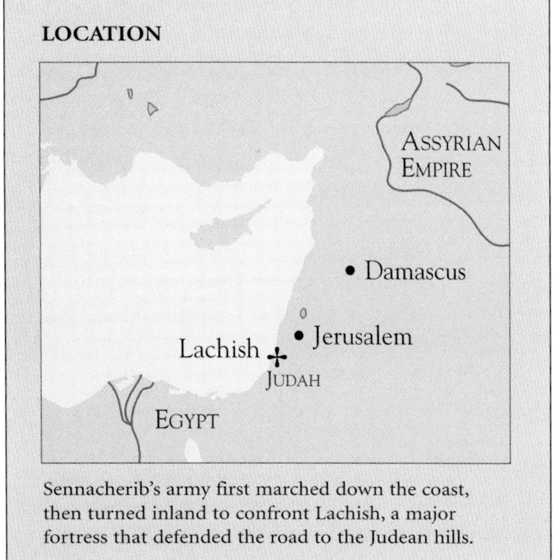

ASSYRIAN EMPIRE
Damascus
Jerusalem
Lachish
JUDAH
EGYPT

Sennacherib's army first marched down the coast, then turned inland to confront Lachish, a major fortress that defended the road to the Judean hills.

TIMELINE

1500–1000BC	1000–500BC	500BC–0AD	0–500AD	500–1000AD	1000–1500AD	1500–2000AD

Fall of Judah 586BC

BABYLONIAN CAMPAIGN

BABYLONIAN VICTORY

Nebuchadnezzar II, ruler of the neo-Baylonian empire, ran out of patience with the rebellious King Zedekiah of Judah. After capturing a series of Judean towns, his campaign culminated in an 18-month siege of Jerusalem, ending with thousands of Jews being led into the 'Babylonian captivity'.

KEY FACTS

WHO King Nebuchadnezzar II of Babylon (c. 605–562BC), decides to teach the rebellious Zedekiah of Judah (c. 597–586BC) a lesson.

WHAT Zedekiah banked on Jerusalem's 'impregnability', but the Babylonians proved as ruthless masters of the siege as the Assyrians.

WHERE Jerusalem

WHEN 586BC

WHY Judah, squeezed between the feuding empires of Egypt and Babylon, sought to exploit the situation, provoking the wrath of Babylon.

OUTCOME Nebuchadnezzar II broke the defences of Jerusalem, put Zedekiah in chains and hauled thousands of Judeans into captivity, temporarily extinguishing the Judean state.

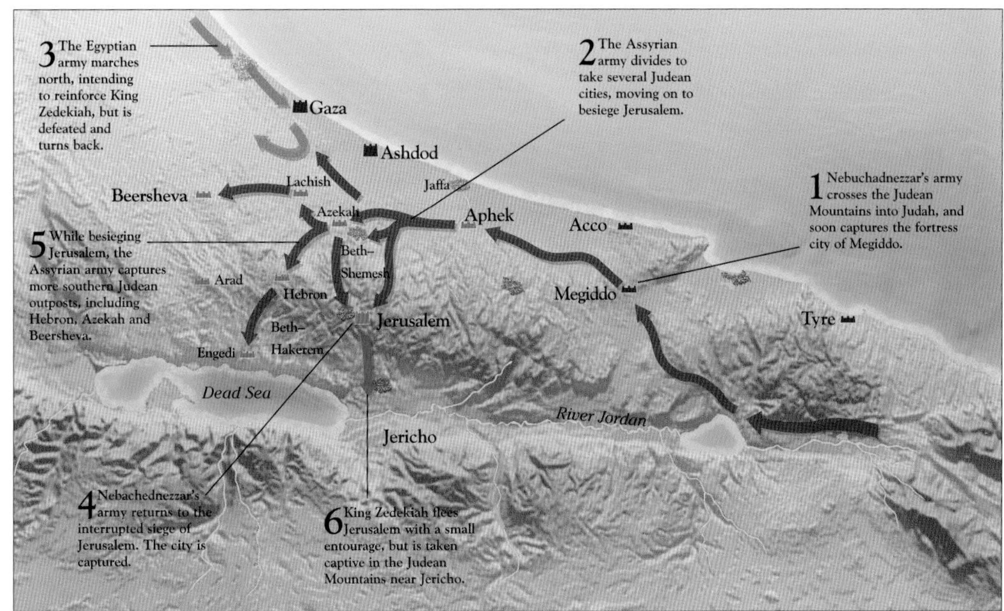

3 The Egyptian army marches north, intending to reinforce King Zedekiah, but is defeated and turns back.
2 The Assyrian army divides to take several Judean cities, moving on to besiege Jerusalem.
1 Nebuchadnezzar's army crosses the Judean Mountains into Judah, and soon captures the fortress city of Megiddo.
5 While besieging Jerusalem, the Assyrian army captures more southern Judean outposts, including Hebron, Azekah and Beersheva.
4 Nebachednezzar's army returns to the interrupted siege of Jerusalem. The city is captured.
6 King Zedekiah flees Jerusalem with a small entourage, but is taken captive in the Judean Mountains near Jericho.
Gaza
Ashdod
Lachish
Jaffa
Beersheva
Azekah
Aphek
Acco
Beth-Shemesh
Arad
Hebron
Megiddo
Jerusalem
Beth-Hakerem
Engedi
Tyre
Dead Sea
River Jordan
Jericho

If the Hebrew kingdoms thought there would be a let-up after the decline of the Assyrian Empire, they were in for a shock. The Babylonians were just as terrifying, as Zedekiah of Judah discovered when he tried to take on Nebuchadnezzar.

LOCATION

BABYLONIAN EMPIRE

Israel

Jerusalem

JUDAH

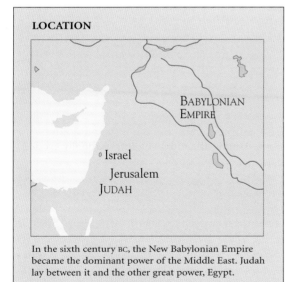

In the sixth century BC, the New Babylonian Empire became the dominant power of the Middle East. Judah lay between it and the other great power, Egypt.

When the mighty Assyrian Empire collapsed in 612BC, Babylon soon took over as the new regional superpower, but vassal state Judah wanted independence. Jerusalem, its capital, was the greatest cosmopolitan centre of the region, and formidably defended. King Zedekiah determined on resistance to Babylonian King Nebuchadnezzar II, expecting to hold out against a siege until the arrival of help from Egypt.

The siege began on 10 January 587BC, pausing only for Nebuchadnezzar to beat off an Egyptian army. It lasted 18 months, before famine and disease spread through the city. Starving mothers reportedly boiled and ate their own children. King Zedekiah fled but was recaptured, and Nebuchadnezzar exacted gruesome revenge on the man he regarded as a disloyal, oath-breaking vassal. First, he had Zedekiah's sons slaughtered before their father's eyes. Then, Zedekiah himself had his eyes bored out, after which he was loaded with chains and sent into captivity. Nebuchadnezzar also took steps to dissolve the Judean state, with Jews deported to Babylonia – the start of the 'Babylonian captivity', which was to be seen as one of the pivotal events in Jewish history.

TIMELINE

1500–1000BC	1000–500BC	500BC–0AD	0–500AD	500–1000AD	1000–1500AD	1500–2000AD

Marathon 490BC

GRECO-PERSIAN WARS

GREEK VICTORY

The Marathon is the only Olympic event named after a battle. It is a race of 42km (26 miles) to retrace the distance run by the Greek messenger Philippides from Marathon to Athens to announce the victory of the Athenian and Platean forces over a substantially larger Persian invasion force.

KEY FACTS

WHO An Athenian army under Miltiades attacked a Persian invasion force commanded by King Darius' general Datis.

WHAT The Greek hoplites charged the Persian line, broke the light infantry on the flanks and turned in on the heavy infantry in the centre. The Persians were pursued to their ships and great numbers were killed.

WHERE Marathon, 42km (26 miles) from Athens, in Greece.

WHEN 490BC

WHY Darius invaded Greece to punish Athens for its support of a rebellion of the Ionian Greek cities in Asia Minor.

OUTCOME The Persian army was all but wiped out, and the Greek peninsula was saved from Persian conquest.

The primary weapon of the hoplite was the spear. They wore helmets topped with horsehair plumes and chest armour. A disciplined hoplite phalanx on the charge was an overwhelming sight.

Early in the fifth century BC, the Persian Empire was the largest state in the Eastern Mediterranean region. Military encounters with the Greeks, however, were rare until the revolt of Ionia. The Persian emperor Darius crushed the Ionian revolt and was so determined to exact revenge on Greece that he insisted a slave whisper 'Remember Athens!' to him while serving him his evening meals.

His campaign against mainland Greece began in 491BC, but while several of the Greek *polis* (city state) submitted, Athens and Sparta were prepared to fight. When Datis, the Persian commander, moved on Eretria, quickly destroying it and enslaving the population, the Athenians sent the legendary Philippides, their swiftest messenger, to enlist military assistance. But while the Spartans were prepared to come to their aid, they would not do so until religious celebrations were completed. A militaristic society, the Spartans were nevertheless highly religious, and not even war was allowed to interrupt their festivities and rituals.

The Persian fleet disembarked its army near the battlefield of Marathon, but it was the Athenians who

LOCATION

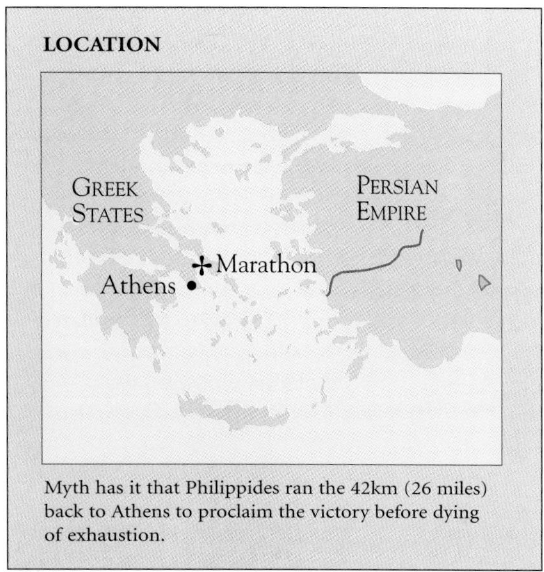
GREEK STATES
PERSIAN EMPIRE
Marathon
Athens

Myth has it that Philippides ran the 42km (26 miles) back to Athens to proclaim the victory before dying of exhaustion.

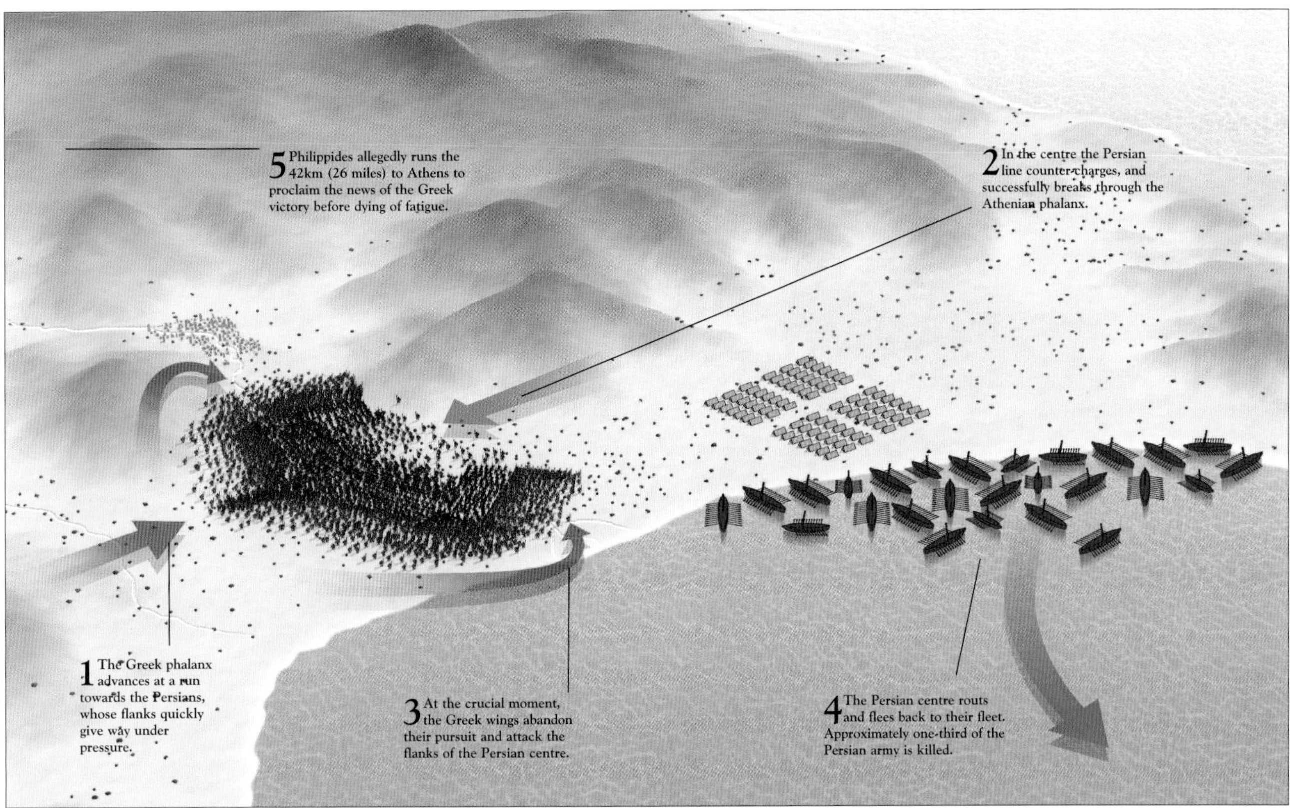
5 Philippides allegedly runs the 42km (26 miles) to Athens to proclaim the news of the Greek victory before dying of fatigue.
2 In the centre the Persian line counter-charges, and successfully breaks through the Athenian phalanx.
1 The Greek phalanx advances at a run towards the Persians, whose flanks quickly give way under pressure.
3 At the crucial moment, the Greek wings abandon their pursuit and attack the flanks of the Persian centre.
4 The Persian centre routs and flees back to their fleet. Approximately one-third of the Persian army is killed.

The Greek phalanx made a remarkable running advance at their adversaries' deeper lines. But while the Persian centre launched a successful counter-charge, its wings folded. Suddenly under fire from all directions, the Persians fled for their boats. Philippides then made his heroic run to Athens to break the good news.

chose to fight there, rather than to try and shelter behind their city walls as the Eretrians had attempted to do. However, when the Athenians saw the immense size of the Persian force – possibly 25,000 men, including cavalry, compared to their own roughly 10,000 combined Athenian and Plataean infantry – several of them wavered until the general Miltiades spoke up in favour of fighting.

Miltiades was placed in overall command of the Greek forces and, choosing to go into battle without waiting for the arrival of the Spartans, he formed his Athenian and Plataean troops into their battle formation. With the force stretched thinly in the middle – 'only a few ranks deep', according to the Greek historian Herodotus – to approximate the length of the deeper Persian line that faced them, the two wings were actually stronger than the centre.

According to Herodotus, the Greek hoplites – armed with spears or javelins, swords and shields – now charged the invaders, which the Persians regarded as madness, since they were unsupported by cavalry or archers. The clash of the two forces must have been loud and violent. Quickly the two wings of the Persian army began to fail, but the centre – which included the Immortals, a select group of Persian heavy infantry whose bravery, experience and fraternity made them feared throughout the Ancient World – held and soon began to gain the upper hand against the Greeks who faced them.

However, by this time, it seems, the soldiers on the Persian wings had begun to flee to the beach. Instead of pursuing them, though, the Greek wings folded in on the Persian centre – 'the two wings combined into a single fighting unit', wrote Herodotus. Whatever early advantage the Persians had gained on their opponents soon dissolved, as they began to be attacked on all sides. They, too, eventually fled towards the beached Persian ships.

The Greeks had won the battle, and although all but seven Persian ships were able to escape, Philippides made his run to Athens, 42km (26 miles) away, to tell its elated citizens the good news. The Spartans arrived the following day on the battlefield and congratulated their fellow Greeks on victory. They had kept the peninsula free from Persian conquest.

TIMELINE

1500–1000BC	1000–500BC	500BC–0AD	0–500AD	500–1000AD	1000–1500AD	1500–2000AD

Salamis 480BC

GRECO-PERSIAN WARS

GREEK VICTORY

Both the previous land and naval battles between the Greeks and Persians had been fought on lines of communication, but this was not. If King Xerxes could establish command of the seas, he could bypass the wall being built near Corinth across the isthmus connecting the Peloponnese to the Greek mainland.

KEY FACTS

WHO A Persian fleet of at least 700 triremes, under the command of the Phoenician admiral Ariabignes, but with King Xerxes (d. 465 BC) in command of the nearby land army, was opposed by a fleet of about 310 ships contributed by member states of the Greek League.

WHAT The marine exchanges of arrows and javelins were succeeded by ramming and boarding of enemy vessels.

WHERE In the Salamis Strait, between the island of Salamis and the mainland of Attica.

WHEN 20 September 480BC

WHY Xerxes had launched a massive invasion in revenge for Greek interference in a Persian rebellion and the Athenian victory over a Persian force at Marathon in 490BC.

OUTCOME The Greeks won a resounding victory. The Persians lost over 200 ships sunk and many more captured and disabled.

Salamis was fought in the confines of a harbour. The end result was a ramming and grappling match, with the Greeks eventually able to board the Persian ships and assert their superiority in hand-to-hand combat.

LOCATION

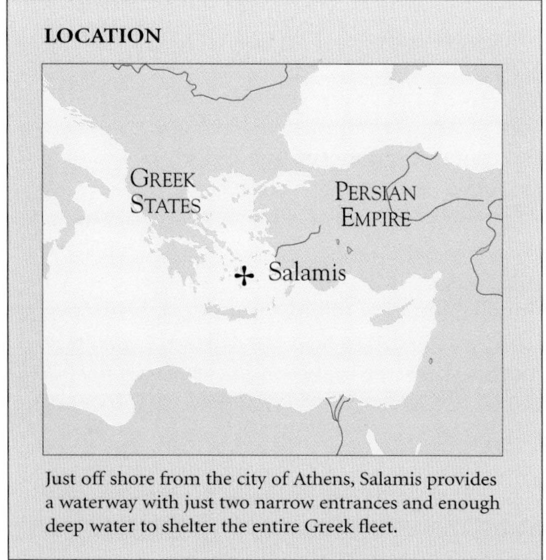
GREEK STATES
PERSIAN EMPIRE
Salamis

Just off shore from the city of Athens, Salamis provides a waterway with just two narrow entrances and enough deep water to shelter the entire Greek fleet.

King Xerxes was eager to restore the Persian Empire after its defeat by the Athenians at Marathon, and launched a massive invasion of the Greek peninsula by land and sea. The united Greek fleet met the larger one of the Persians at Artemisium. Thanks to storms that wreaked havoc among the Persian ships, it was able to hold its own, but when news came that a Persian land force had defeated the Spartans at Thermopylae, it retreated to the strait off the island of Salamis, to defend Athens.

The Greek ships at Salamis numbered between 300–400, whereas the Persian fleet had twice that amount. But the Salamis strait was an ideally chosen location for the Greeks to engage the Persians, as well as to protect Athenian refugees gathered on the island. The passage between the mainland and the isle, at just 1.6km (1 mile) wide and little over 4.8km (3 miles) long, would neutralize their enemies' overwhelming numerical superiority, whereas in the open sea Xerxes would have been able to surround the Greeks ships and destroy them.

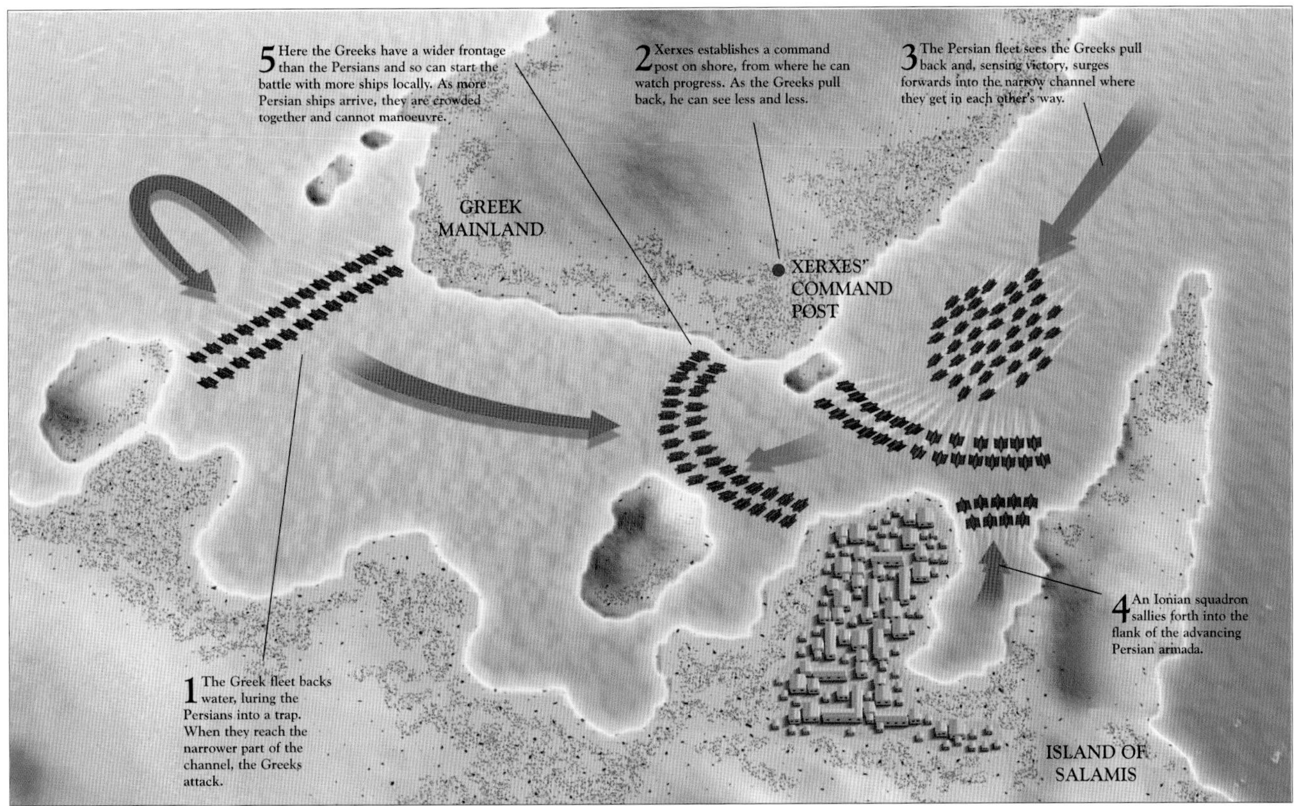
5 Here the Greeks have a wider frontage than the Persians and so can start the battle with more ships locally. As more Persian ships arrive, they are crowded together and cannot manoeuvre.
2 Xerxes establishes a command post on shore, from where he can watch progress. As the Greeks pull back, he can see less and less.
3 The Persian fleet sees the Greeks pull back and, sensing victory, surges forwards into the narrow channel where they get in each other's way.
GREEK MAINLAND
XERXES' COMMAND POST
4 An Ionian squadron sallies forth into the flank of the advancing Persian armada.
1 The Greek fleet backs water, luring the Persians into a trap. When they reach the narrower part of the channel, the Greeks attack.
ISLAND OF SALAMIS

The Greek tactics at Salamis involved drawing the Persian fleet into the narrow strait, where their numerical advantage was reduced. Once they got close enough to the ships to board them, the age-old superiority of the hoplite soldier in close conflict situations was telling.

The Greeks, as ever an uneasy alliance of rival states, were hampered by disagreements within the high command, and news of this trickled back to Xerxes. When Themistocles, admiral of the Athenian fleet, tricked him with a note telling him of his plans to defect and that Greeks ships were planning to escape in the night, he readily believed him. The Persians deployed their fleet that night to block both exits from the Salamis basin, preventing the Greek contingents from escaping.

SUPERIOR STRATEGY

All night, the Persians stayed at sea. Their crews, unable to rest other than on their rowing benches, would have been exhausted by the time battle finally began.

The following morning, the main Greek fleet did deploy as if to break out, but then started to back water into the narrowest part of the strait. This position suited the Greeks since their ships were on the outside of the curve and could enjoy local numeric superiority and the advantages of a flank attack. The Persians took the bait and pursued the Greeks into the narrow waters.

As they crowded into the strait, the Persian ships became so bunched up that they could not row without interfering with the neighbouring vessels, never mind manoeuvre to ram or counter-ram. The Greeks, being better able to manoeuvre, were more successful, but when the water was so choked with waterlogged ships, they had to resort to boarding where they could and fighting hand to hand on blood-soaked decks.

PERSIAN CASUALTIES

During this, the superiority of the Greek hoplite's equipment, training and motivation quickly began to tell and the Persian king's men fell in droves. As Xerxes watched from his throne on the hillside overlooking the strait, the unengaged ships from the head of the Persian column turned to try and escape back out to sea, some unintentionally ramming others from their own side. Many of the Persian sailors who were thrown into the water drowned because they were unable to swim. Among the thousands of Persian casualties during the battle was Xerxes' own brother.

TIMELINE

1500–1000BC	1000–500BC	500BC–0AD	0–500AD	500–1000AD	1000–1500AD	1500–2000AD

Salamis

SALAMIS

In land battles, it was an ancient tactic characteristic of a wily commander of a small force to mount a feigned withdrawal or retreat to lure an inherently stronger opponent onto less favourable terrain. Such a move was harder to achieve at sea, but it could be done if battles were fought near land, as many of those involving the Greek states were. At Salamis, the numerically superior Persian fleet ceded their advantage by allowing themselves to be drawn into restricted waters by the seemingly retreating Greeks, who then turned on them to inflict a heavy defeat.

Plataea 479BC

GRECO–PERSIAN WARS

GREEK VICTORY

KEY FACTS

Who The Persian army under the command of Mardonius, against a Greek coalition of Athens and Sparta.

What Mardonius is killed in a land battle in which the Greeks, boasting the largest number of hoplites ever sent onto a battlefield (38,000), end Persian ambitions to take control of Greece.

Where About 8km (5 miles) east of the ancient town of Plataea.

When 479BC

Why Although the Persian fleet at Salamis had been destroyed, its army remained undefeated. Sparta formed a fragile alliance with Athens to administer the coup de grâce.

Outcome The well-armoured hoplites prove better suited to the conditions in which this encounter was fought. Mardonius was killed, and the Persians withdrew from Greece.

Despite its comprehensive defeat at Salamis, Persia retained a massive fighting capability on Greek soil, with the potential to inflict serious damage on Athens. Sparta, recognizing its own vulnerability should Athens fall, decided it had no option but to form an uneasy alliance with its old rival.

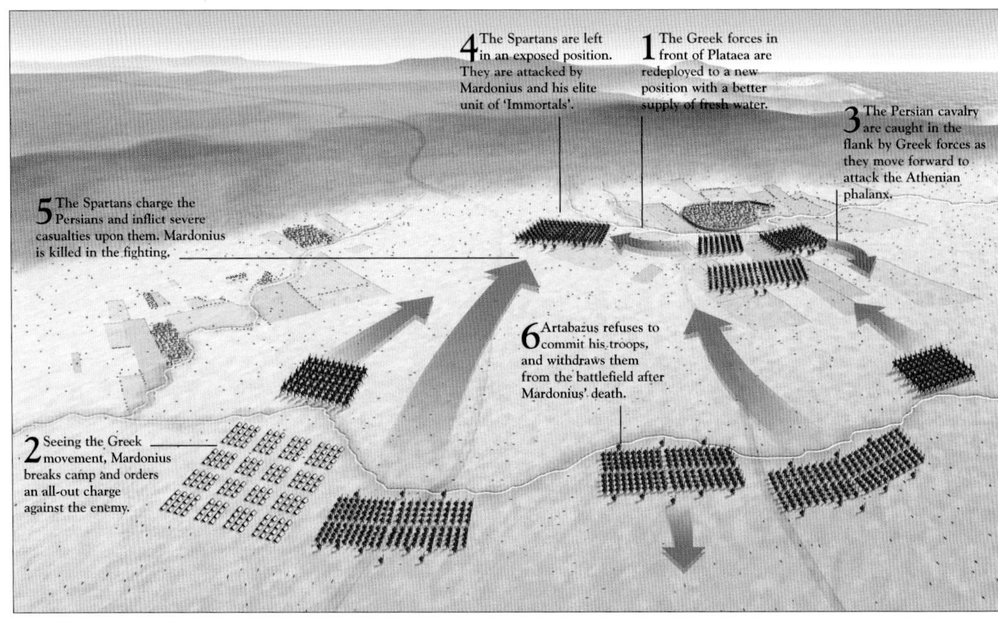
4 The Spartans are left in an exposed position. They are attacked by Mardonius and his elite unit of 'Immortals'.
1 The Greek forces in front of Plataea are redeployed to a new position with a better supply of fresh water.
3 The Persian cavalry are caught in the flank by Greek forces as they move forward to attack the Athenian phalanx.
5 The Spartans charge the Persians and inflict severe casualties upon them. Mardonius is killed in the fighting.
6 Artabazus refuses to commit his troops, and withdraws them from the battlefield after Mardonius' death.
2 Seeing the Greek movement, Mardonius breaks camp and orders an all-out charge against the enemy.

Loss of the commander in battle often swung the result. Although the Greeks were in seeming disarray at Plataea, when the Persian general Mardonius was killed, the remaining divisions hurriedly withdrew from the field.

LOCATION

Greek States
Persian Empire
Plataea

The battle at Plataea saw the ultimate defeat of the invading Persian army and their Greek allies after the loss of the Persian fleet at Salamis the previous year.

The Greeks had assembled a 38,000-strong hoplite force, but found themselves attacked by Persian mounted archers near the River Asopos. A retreat from the Asopos towards Plataea began at night, but the Spartan Amompharetus refused to withdraw his own small command in the face of the enemy. Pausanias, the Greek commander, was forced to countermarch in mid-redeployment.

Mardonius, the Persian commander, noticed the disorder in the Greek line and launched an all-out attack. A slower Athenian withdrawal allowed those forces to take the charging Persians partly in the flank. The élite Persian unit of 1000 picked troops, 'The Immortals', surrounding Mardonius in the centre, were attacked by Spartan heavy infantry. Mardonius was killed in the savage hand-to-hand fighting, for which the better armoured Greek hoplites were more suited.

This prompted a crisis in Persian command, with Mardonius' subordinate Artabazus holding his own forces out of a battle he considered lost. With the battle clearly now in the Greeks' favour, Artabazus assumed command of the entire Persian army and retreated swiftly.

TIMELINE

1500–1000BC	1000–500BC	500BC–0AD	0–500AD	500–1000AD	1000–1500AD	1500–2000AD

Syracuse 415BC

KEY FACTS

WHO An Athenian expedition attacked the Corinthian colony of Syracuse.

WHAT An Athenian feint to the north of the city allowed their main force to land unopposed in the harbour and bottle up the surprised garrison in the inner city.

WHERE Syracuse in Sicily.

WHEN 415BC

WHY To restrict the flow of grain to the Peloponnesian League and complete Athens' domination.

OUTCOME Although the Athenians had limited initial success, further land and naval reinforcements were sucked in and destroyed by the Syracusans, reversing Athens' earlier successes in the war.

Athens' attempt to conquer the Corinthian colony of Syracuse during the Peloponnesian War was a disaster. The drain on manpower and resources as the campaign escalated into a prolonged siege crippled the city. The final defeat ended Athenian hopes of dominating the Greek world.

PELOPONNESIAN WAR

SYRACUSAN VICTORY

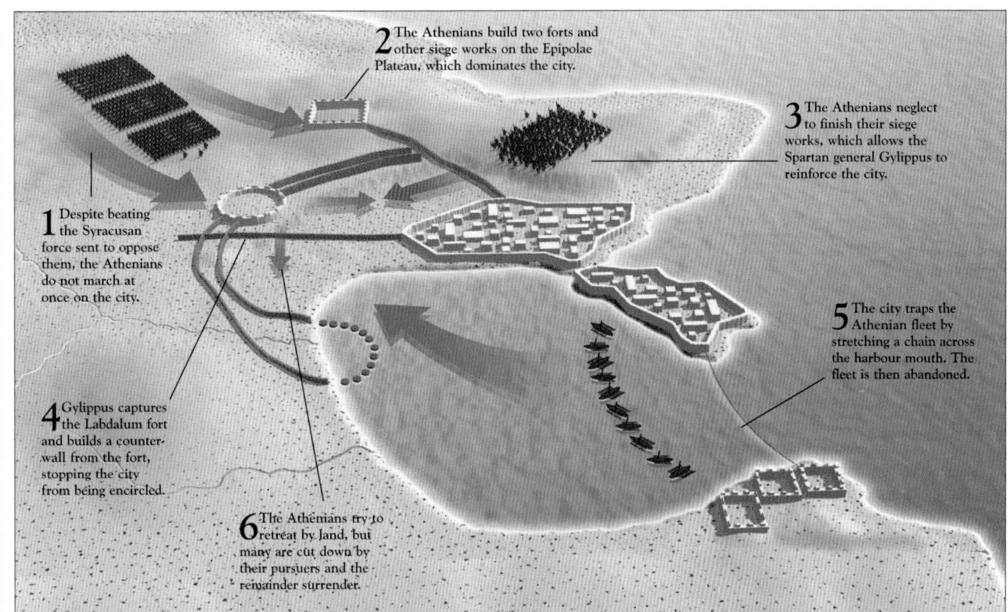

1 Despite beating the Syracusan force sent to oppose them, the Athenians do not march at once on the city.
2 The Athenians build two forts and other siege works on the Epipolae Plateau, which dominates the city.
3 The Athenians neglect to finish their siege works, which allows the Spartan general Gylippus to reinforce the city.
4 Gylippus captures the Labdalum fort and builds a counter-wall from the fort, stopping the city from being encircled.
5 The city traps the Athenian fleet by stretching a chain across the harbour mouth. The fleet is then abandoned.
6 The Athenians try to retreat by land, but many are cut down by their pursuers and the remainder surrender.

Many battles between the Greek states involved intense fighting in confined areas around the cities and their harbours. At Syracuse, the locals actually managed to run a chain across the harbour mouth, turning the tables on the besiegers.

LOCATION

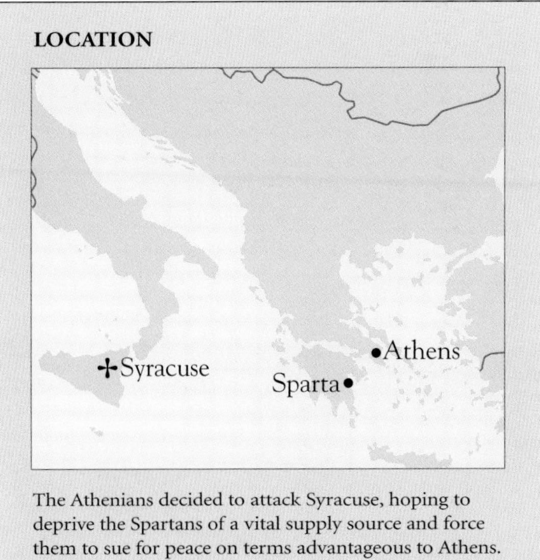

Syracuse
Athens
Sparta

The Athenians decided to attack Syracuse, hoping to deprive the Spartans of a vital supply source and force them to sue for peace on terms advantageous to Athens.

In 415BC the Athenians invaded Syracuse, a colony of its rival city state, Corinth, which fought alongside Sparta against Athens in the Peloponnesian War, 431–404BC. They were initially successful, but when the Syracusans received aid from Corinth and Sparta, they faced a long campaign.

Gradually the Syracusans gained the upper hand, blocking harbour routes and harrying foraging parties, so that the Athenian besiegers became the besieged. A naval battle to gain the harbour failed, a damaging blow to the morale of Athens, the greatest of Greek seafaring cities. Reinforcement ships, bringing 500 hoplites and other troops, brought hopes of renewing the struggle. A further naval battle around the harbour and shoreline saw 100 Athenians ships deployed against 76 of the Syracusans – rarely can a naval battle have involved so many ships in so confined an area. During it, the Syracusans deployed a fire ship – perhaps the first use of this weapon. It inflicted little damage, but they still carried the day.

This disastrous campaign crippled Athens and destroyed her ability to dominate Greece.

TIMELINE

1500–1000BC	1000–500BC	500BC–0AD	0–500AD	500–1000AD	1000–1500AD	1500–2000AD

Leuctra 371 BC

GREEK WARS

THEBAN VICTORY

KEY FACTS

WHO Theban forces numbering 7000–9000 under Epaminondas (d. 362 BC) versus around 12,000 Spartans under King Cleombrotus (d. 371BC).

WHAT A Spartan cavalry attack was repulsed, then Epaminondas used unusual tactics to break the Spartan right flank, killing their king and forcing a retreat.

WHERE 16km (10 miles) west of Thebes, in Greece.

WHEN July 371 BC

WHY The Spartans invaded Theban territory in response to a request from several Boeotian cities for assistance in overthrowing their Theban overlords.

OUTCOME Up until this point, the Spartans were thought to be invincible. Their defeat at the hands of an inferior force caused irreparable damage to Spartan prestige.

The Battle of Leuctra was notable for two things – the defeat of the supposedly invincible Spartans, and the method of that defeat. The Theban army used innovative tactics, including a 'refused' flank, to break the conventionally deployed Spartan force.

In the fifth century BC, other Greek states recoiled before the Spartans' military prowess, and King Cleombrotrus. But in the Theban Epaminondas they met their match.

LOCATION

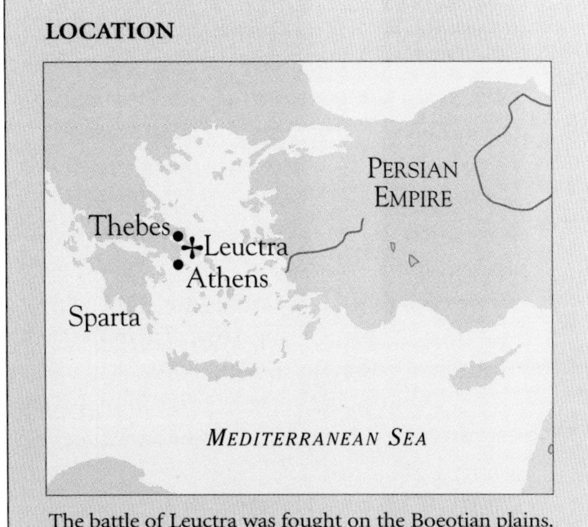
Persian Empire
Thebes
Leuctra
Athens
Sparta
Mediterranean Sea

The battle of Leuctra was fought on the Boeotian plains. It was ideal country for hoplite tactics, and proved that the previously invincible Spartans could be beaten.

Ever since her defeat of Athens in 404BC, Sparta was the ascendant Greek city state. She owed her position mainly to her impressive military prowess, with martial skills imbued in the male citizenry from childhood. (Spartan boys began a harsh form of military training from the age of seven, at which point they were effectively removed from the care of their mothers.)

Sparta's great mass of spear-armed citizen-soldiers creating a hoplite phalanx that was better than anyone else's. Conventionally the weakest side in battle formations was the left – owing to the tendency of foot soldiers in a phalanx to edge right when in combat towards the protection of the shield carried by the man on their right flank – but even the Spartan left was a match for the right-flank units of most foes. So powerful was the Spartan army that it won battles on reputation alone.

Thebes, however, was also a rising power, and when it captured Spartan-controlled cities in Boeotia, the stage was set for conflict. A Spartan army under King Cleombrotus marched on Thebes, taking an unexpected route and in the process capturing a Theban fortress. Epaminondas of Thebes placed himself at the head of his army and advanced to meet the Spartans.

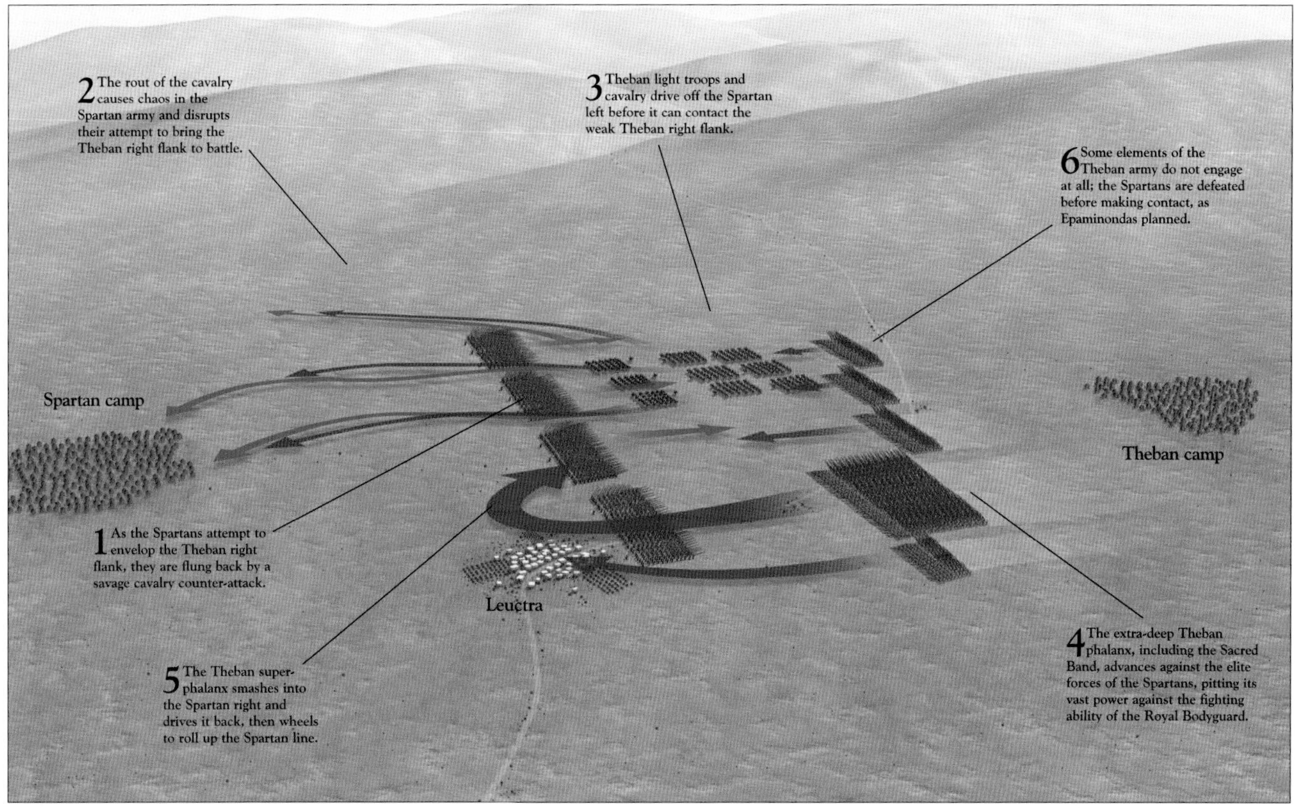
2 The rout of the cavalry causes chaos in the Spartan army and disrupts their attempt to bring the Theban right flank to battle.
3 Theban light troops and cavalry drive off the Spartan left before it can contact the weak Theban right flank.
6 Some elements of the Theban army do not engage at all; the Spartans are defeated before making contact, as Epaminondas planned.
Spartan camp
Theban camp
1 As the Spartans attempt to envelop the Theban right flank, they are flung back by a savage cavalry counter-attack.
Leuctra
4 The extra-deep Theban phalanx, including the Sacred Band, advances against the elite forces of the Spartans, pitting its vast power against the fighting ability of the Royal Bodyguard.
5 The Theban super-phalanx smashes into the Spartan right and drives it back, then wheels to roll up the Spartan line.

Leuctra brought to an end a long period of Spartan military supremacy, owing greatly to the Thebans unusual formations, with massed phalanxes on the left – contrary to battle convention of the time.

Epaminondas cannot have had any great confidence of success, not least because the mighty Spartans heavily outnumbered his forces. But he had no choice other than to fight, so he offered battle near Leuctra.

Contrary to the conventions of the time, Epaminondas deployed his army with his strongest troops on the left of his line, and created a massive hammer in the form of a 50-deep phalanx there. In order to find the troops for this formation he had to thin the rest of his line to a dangerous extent. Instead of deploying the usual 12-man-deep formation, Epaminondas placed most of his troops in very thin lines facing the Spartans' more conventional formation. There was no chance that these weak units could withstand the impact of a deeper phalanx, but Epaminondas had planned for this. He drew up his army in echelon from left to right, with each unit positioned slightly further back than the one to its left. This created a 'refused' flank that was well back from the enemies facing it. With this tactic, Epaminondas was hoping to achieve a local superiority and use it to decisive advantage before his refused flank and centre could be broken.

The Spartan force tried to perform an encirclement, but the Theban cavalry launched a vigorous attack on the Spartan horse and routed it, sending a shattered mob of horsemen reeling into the Spartan lines. Then under cover of the chaos caused by the cavalry fight, Epaminondas sent the powerful left-flank phalanx at the Spartan lines. The Spartan force was deployed traditionally, 12 men deep, which meant that for every man in the Spartan phalanx there were four on the Theban side. Faced with such enormous pushing power, the Spartans were shoved bodily back and suffered many casualties in the press.

In the ensuing mêlée, fallen men were trampled to death or despatched with spear butts. Among the dead was King Cleombrotus. Never before had a Spartan king fallen in battle against fellow Greeks. The shock rippled though the Spartan force, which began to fall apart. The right wing, traditionally the strongest part of the army, was in disarray.

Realizing that they were losing, the Spartans began a retreat. Epaminondas sent his cavalry in pursuit. A truce was eventually agreed, Boeotia remaining under Theban control and the myth of Spartan invincibility dispelled.

Granicus River 334BC

MACEDONIAN CONQUESTS

MACEDONIAN VICTORY

Alexander the Great was only 20 when he succeeded his father Philip II as king of Macedon in 336 BC. But he quickly realised that smashing the might of the Persian Empire was vital if he was to line up Greek support for his rule. Granicus River was his first great victory, but nearly cost him his life.

KEY FACTS

WHO Alexander the Great (356-323 BC) led the Macedonians and their Greek allies in the first of his great battles with the Persians

WHAT The Persians' positional advantage on the banks of the Granicus proved ineffective against the valour of Alexander and his cavalry

WHERE At a crossing point of the Granicus (now Biga) River, Asia Minor, near what is now Ergili, Turkey

WHEN May 334 BC

WHY Alexander wanted to put into action his father's unfulfilled dream of breaking the Persian Empire

OUTCOME Alexander's success established a bridgehead in Asia Minor and enabled him to press deeper into Persian territory

Alexander the Great (foreground), here seen riding at the head of his army on his famous horse Bucephalus, had a character moulded by the martial traditions and great victories of his father, Philip of Macedon.

LOCATION

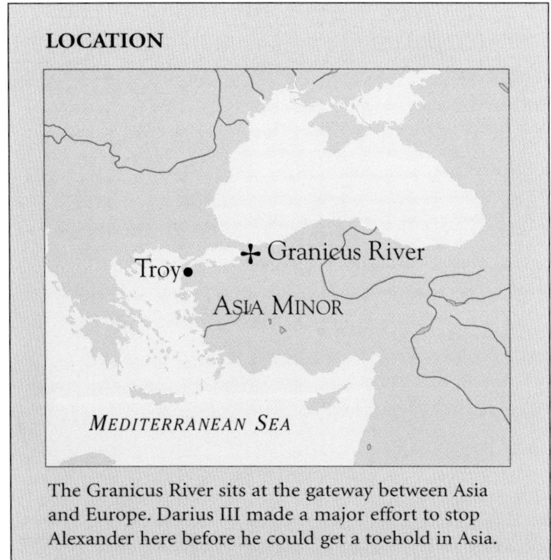
Granicus River
Troy
ASIA MINOR
MEDITERRANEAN SEA

The Granicus River sits at the gateway between Asia and Europe. Darius III made a major effort to stop Alexander here before he could get a toehold in Asia.

Alexander II, known as the Great, succeeded his father, the assassinated Philip II, as king of Macedon in 336 BC at the youthful age of 20. Almost immediately he faced the challenge of Greek cities chafing to regain a measure of independence at the end of his father's firm rule. Alexander realized that a way of binding them more fully behind his leadership was to launch a war on the detested Persians.

Alexander launched his campaign in the spring of 334, crossing the Hellespont (now Dardenelles) onto the Asia Minor mainland with a 40,000-strong army, made up of Macedonians, Balkans and Greeks, along with mercenaries. As he marched north–east, the Persian satraps (provincial governors) held a special council of war. Deciding against a scorched earth policy of burning crops and laying waste to farms and villages to force Alexander to abort his campaign due to lack of supplies, the Persians assembled their army in a defensive position on the Granicus River.

The Persians were famed for the strength and skill of their cavalry which, numbering around 10,000 men, was double the size of the one Alexander could call upon. Their battle

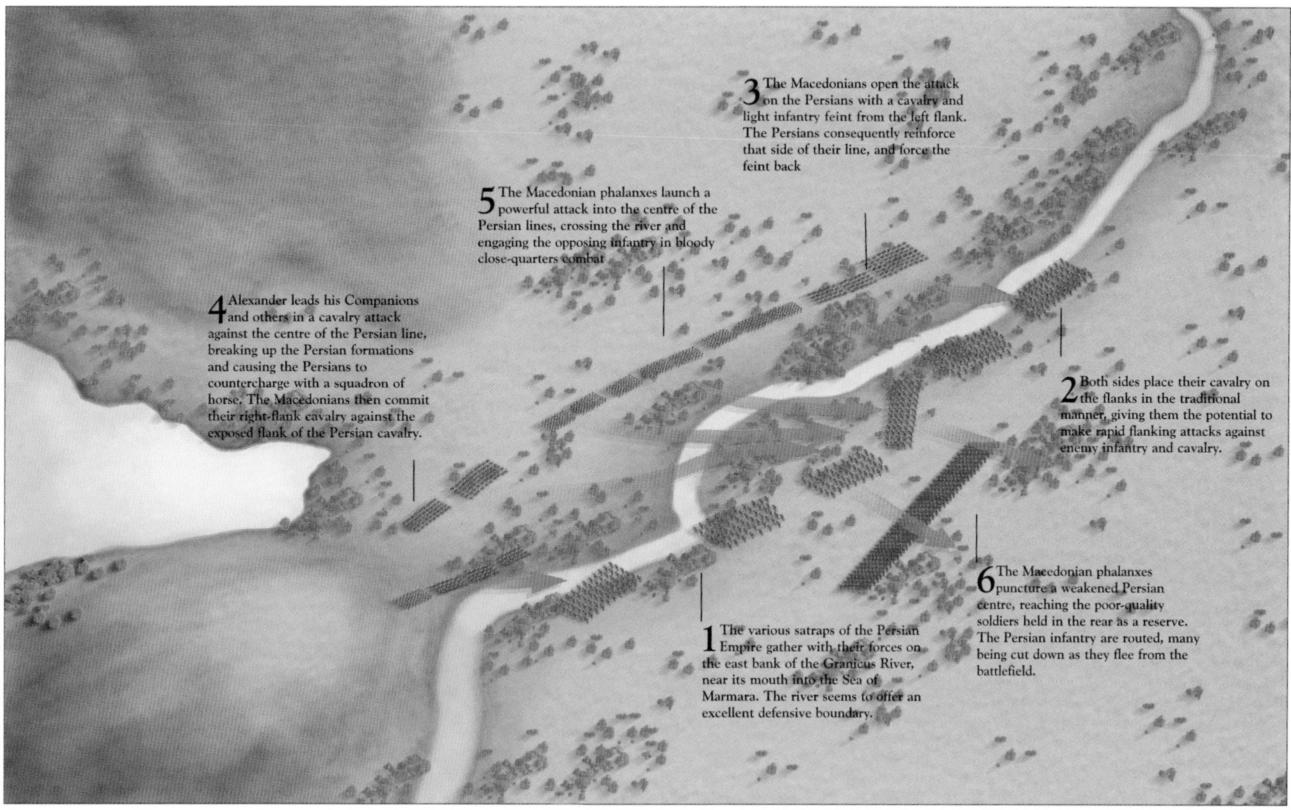
3 The Macedonians open the attack on the Persians with a cavalry and light infantry feint from the left flank. The Persians consequently reinforce that side of their line, and force the feint back
5 The Macedonian phalanxes launch a powerful attack into the centre of the Persian lines, crossing the river and engaging the opposing infantry in bloody close-quarters combat
4 Alexander leads his Companions and others in a cavalry attack against the centre of the Persian line, breaking up the Persian formations and causing the Persians to countercharge with a squadron of horse. The Macedonians then commit their right-flank cavalry against the exposed flank of the Persian cavalry.
2 Both sides place their cavalry on the flanks in the traditional manner, giving them the potential to make rapid flanking attacks against enemy infantry and cavalry.
6 The Macedonian phalanxes puncture a weakened Persian centre, reaching the poor-quality soldiers held in the rear as a reserve. The Persian infantry are routed, many being cut down as they flee from the battlefield.
1 The various satraps of the Persian Empire gather with their forces on the east bank of the Granicus River, near its mouth into the Sea of Marmara. The river seems to offer an excellent defensive boundary.

The battle of Granicus illustrates perfectly Alexander's talents as a military tactician. In the above diagram, we see how Alexander unbalances his opponent, weakening the centre of the defence and choosing the right moment to launch his main infantry thrust.

array sought to capitalize on this by placing the cavalry at the head of the infantry, forming a wide front over a mile on the east bank of the river. Alexander had little choice but to advance to meet them even though the requirement to cross the river, and the massing of his enemies on the high bank beyond put him at a considerable positional disadvantage.

It seems that Parmenio, Alexander's trusted second in command, had advised resting after a day's marching when they approached the Granicus, crossing the river further upstream, and attacking the Persians the following day after a refreshing night's sleep. However, Alexander ordered an immediate cavalry charge, backed by light infantry. While this was predictably met with showers of Persian javelins, and sustained heavy casualties, it did succeed in breaking the left flank of the Persian cavalry formation. Now Alexander led the elite of his own Cavalry – the Companions - across the river and, with trumpets blaring, a frantic battle ensued. Alexander himself was in the thick of the combat, but when his sarissa (cavalry lance) was splintered, it was some time before he received a replacement. He sustained injuries when an enemy scimitar sliced off a portion of his helmet, but he killed several high-ranking Persians in the onslaught.

After a time, the Persian line was steadily driven back beyond the riverbank and, as a gap was prized open in their centre, the Macedonian infantry were able to pour through, engaging with, and inflicting heavy casualties upon, the Persian infantry stranded in the rear. With this achieved, panic now began to break out amongst the Persian cavalry, who turned and fled from the battlefield, leaving it to Alexander's men to slaughter or enslave those of the infantry behind.

Alexander's victory at Granicus seemed to owe much to his personal courage in the heat of the battle and his ability to see that, while his opponent literally occupied the high ground, the defensive formation adopted negated the mobility of the much-vaunted Persian cavalry, enabling him to seize the initiative while other more experienced voices counselled caution. Victory not only liberated the Greek cities of Asia Minor, but paved the way for further triumphs for Alexander ahead.

TIMELINE

1500–1000BC	1000–500BC	500BC–0AD	0–500AD	500–1000AD	1000–1500AD	1500–2000AD

Granicus River

GRANICUS RIVER

There is no more exciting image in the history of battles than that of the cavalry charge, and Alexander the Great was clearly an early exponent, even in the days before the stirrup. Granicus River was the first of his great victories over the Persians. There, despite an initially unfavourable position, he hurled his Macedonian army into a headlong attack over the river and up the opposing banks into the opposition lines. Alexander nearly lost his life in the fighting, but greater valour won the day, and his reputation as a great warrior and leader was confirmed.

Issus 333BC

MACEDONIAN CONQUESTS

MACEDONIAN VICTORY

After victory at Granicus River, the reputation of Alexander the Great was beginning to spread far and wide. At Issus, it seemed he had been outwitted by the Persian king Darius, whom he was meeting in battle for the first time, but once again the brilliant Macedonian would prevail.

KEY FACTS

WHO Alexander the Great (356–323BC) against the Persians led by King Darius III (reigned 336–330BC).

WHAT Alexander seemed at first to have been outthought by his opponent, but once again the courage, tenacity and quick thinking of Alexander and his men would prove critical in the heat of the battle.

WHERE On the banks of the stream or river Pinarus, near the town founded by Alexander as Alexandria (now Iskenderun).

WHEN 3 November 333BC

WHY Alexander the Great's launching of a campaign in Asia Minor, and his success at Granicus River, had stirred the attention of the Persian ruler Darius III.

OUTCOME Darius III fled the battlefield, leaving the west part of Asia Minor decisively in Alexander's hands.

At Issus, Alexander the Great finally encountered the Persian king Darius himself in battle. Darius was a considerable figure in his own right, but on the battlefield even he would prove no match for the valorous young Macedonian.

LOCATION

Issus
SYRIA
CYPRUS
MEDITERRANEAN SEA
EGYPT

Issus was fought on the edge of the Mediterranean. Retaining a foothold here was critical for Alexander if his army were to maintain supply lines.

After his success at the Battle of Granicus River, Alexander the Great swiftly moved to assert his control over Asia Minor. But his military exploits had roused the attention of the Persian King Darius II, based at Babylon, who now began mobilizing a vast army and heading in Alexander's direction.

Memnon, a Greek who had fought bravely at Granicus River in the service of the Persians and who was now in command of the Persian forces based in Asia Minor, began menacing Greek towns along the Mediterranean coast. While he was doing so, Darius advanced westwards, aware that if he could reach the coast he could cut the Macedonian invader's supply lines. Alexander had fallen ill with a fever in the city of Tarsus and sent ahead the loyal, long-serving Parmenio – who had been in the service of his father Philip II and had been his own second-in-command at Granicus River – to capture the harbour town of Issus and at the same time to keep watch for signs of the approach of Darius's army.

PERSIAN RUTHLESSNESS

When Alexander finally arrived in Issus, he left sick and wounded in the town and moved south, anticipating that he could catch Darius's army in a disorganized state as it

In the run-up to the battle, much ground had to be covered by both armies, with Alexander having roved across much of Asia Minor, and Darius advancing from the East from Babylon.

emerged through the narrow mountain Pass of Jonah. In fact, Darius had received word of Alexander's location and taken a more northerly route, meaning he was now at Alexander's rear. He took Issus and brutally cut the hands off the sick soldiers and paraded them through his camp before turning them loose to spread the word about the horror's awaiting those who rose against the Persians.

BATTLE ON THE BANKS OF THE PINARUS

By now Alexander was advancing north again, covering a remarkable 112km (70 miles) in two days, aware that Darius had managed to cut his supply lines, and finding that he had taken up a defensive position on the opposite side of the Pinarus river, in a long line from the sea to the west to the mountains foothills to the east.

Parmenio was put in charge of leading the advance on the left wing, with strict instructions to keep close to the Mediterranean shore, so that the Persians could not turn them on that flank. Alexander, meanwhile, astride his legendary horse Bucelphalus, led the distinguished Companion Cavalry on the right.

As the Macedonian army advanced, it became clear that the Persians had placed sharpened stakes on the banks of the Pinarus at the point where it was at its lowest to impede their enemy's crossing. These slowed the advance of the Macedonian phalanx, at the same time as Alexander launched a furious cavalry charge that crashed into the Persian right. Even though the latter folded at this attack, a gap had appeared in the Macedonian line and the Persians moved to exploit it.

MACEDONIAN TRIUMPH

However, Alexander's cavalry, spotting the danger, swiftly wheeled leftwards to cut them down, before Alexander turned back to advance on the splendidly ornamented chariot of Darius himself. Darius, fearing for his life, abandoned this hefty vehicle for a much faster one, and fled the field. Once he was gone, any sense of order or purpose within the Persian ranks disintegrated.

Victory was soon Alexander's and the whole of the Levant was now his for the taking. The masterly Macedonian had once again prevailed.

TIMELINE

1500–1000BC	1000–500BC	500BC–0AD	0–500AD	500–1000AD	1000–1500AD	1500–2000AD

Siege of Tyre 332BC

KEY FACTS

WHO Alexander the Great's (356–323BC) Macedonian and Greek army aided by several Phoenician cities and Cyprus, versus Tyre, a major Phoenician city subject to Persia.

WHAT Macedonian siege of Tyre, which resisted Alexander in his effort to control the eastern seaboard of the Mediterranean.

WHERE Tyre (modern Sur, southern Lebanon), approximately 0.8km (0.5 miles) off the Phoenician coast.

WHEN January–August 332BC

WHY Alexander did not have a sufficient naval force to meet the Persian fleet, so he eliminated the threat by taking the Persian-held seaports of the eastern Mediterranean coast, including Tyre.

OUTCOME After seven months of resistance, Alexander took Tyre, killing most of the male population and enslaving the women and children.

The Phoenician city of Tyre was one of the best fortified cities of all time, but subduing it was vital to Alexander the Great's conquest of the Persian Empire. It took seven months for his siege to achieve a breakthough, but the resolve shown displayed the great military skills of Macedonia.

MACEDONIAN CONQUESTS

MACEDONIAN VICTORY

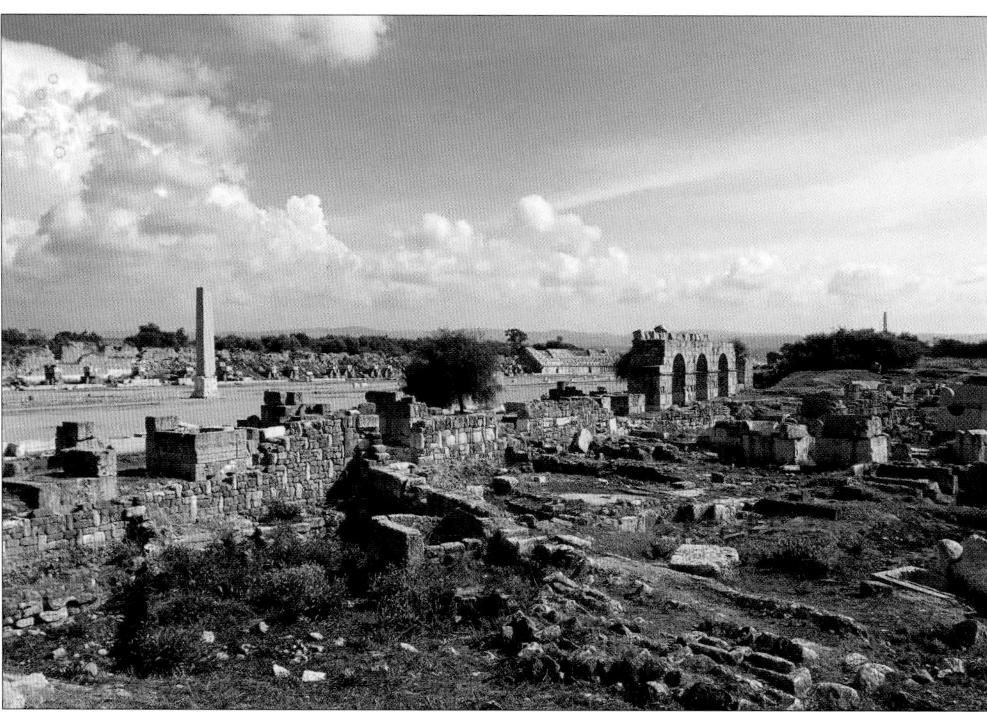

Tyre was one of the most impressive Phoenician cities, protected by walls rising sheer from the sea, and 46m (150ft) high on the landward side. Its citizens confidently believed they could withstand even the attentions of Alexander the Great.

LOCATION

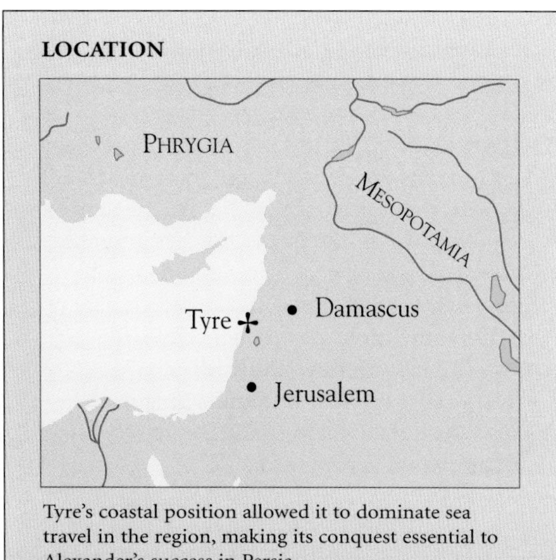
PHRYGIA
MESOPOTAMIA
Tyre
Damascus
Jerusalem

Tyre's coastal position allowed it to dominate sea travel in the region, making its conquest essential to Alexander's success in Persia.

Capturing the Phoenician naval bases along the Mediterranean coast was vital to Alexander the Great if his plans to break the Persian Empire were to succeed. However, he did not have sufficient sea power to challenge the Persian-controlled Phoenician fleet. His only option, therefore, was to take control of the city ports along the Mediterranean coast of Anatolia and Phoenicia.

Most of the Phoenician cities, never happy as Persian subjects, opened their gates to the Macedonian conqueror, but Tyre was at bitter enmity with its fellow Phoenician city Sidon. When Sidon went over to Alexander, the Tyrians decided to resist.

The Tyrians had every right to be confident in their ability to withstand Alexander. The city had held off sieges by the greatest military powers of earlier ages, the Assyrians and the Babylonians. Situated on an island 800m (2625ft) off the mainland, Tyre was strongly fortified all around, and its walls on the landward side were 46m (150ft) in height, rising from the edge of the sea so that no attacker could gain a foothold from which to stage an assault. Catapults were mounted all around the walls. A strong Tyrian fleet of about 80 ships, mostly triremes, seemed sufficient to keep the waterways open.

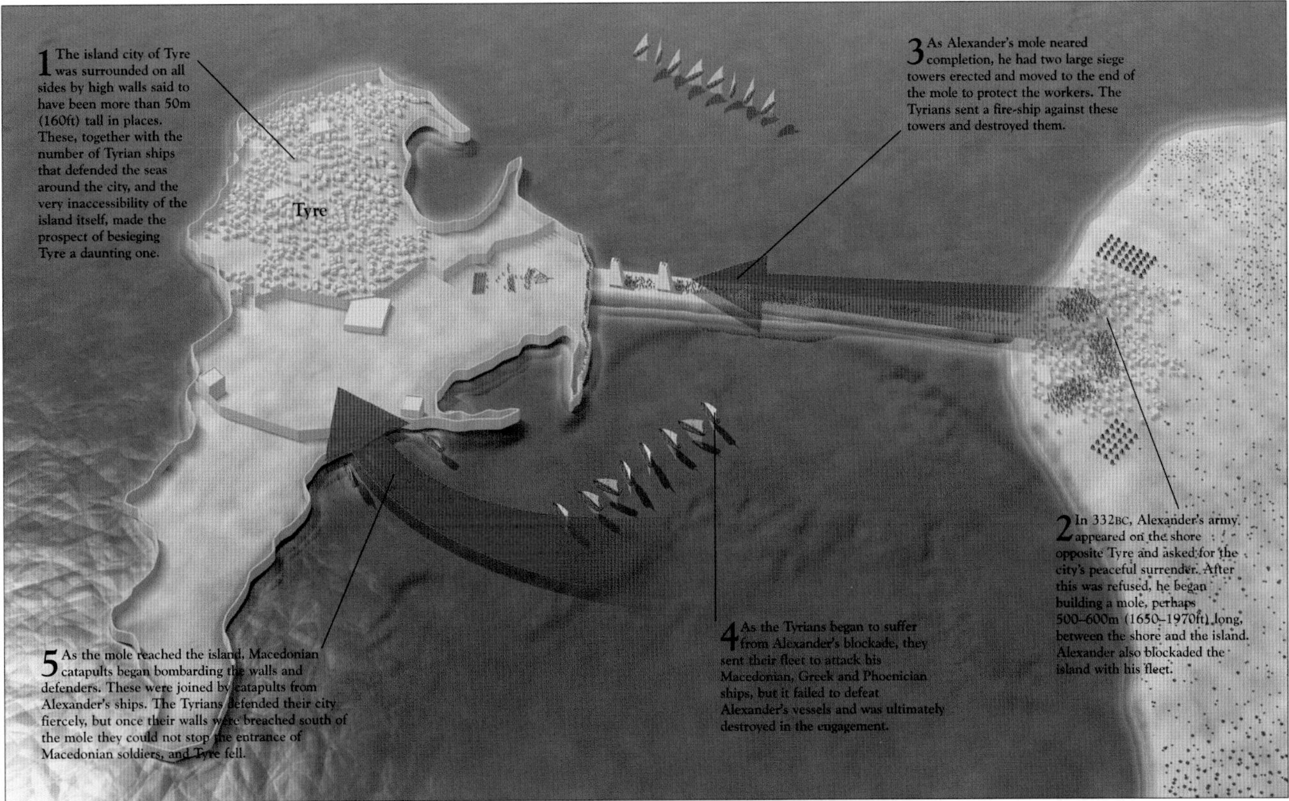
1 The island city of Tyre was surrounded on all sides by high walls said to have been more than 50m (160ft) tall in places. These, together with the number of Tyrian ships that defended the seas around the city, and the very inaccessibility of the island itself, made the prospect of besieging Tyre a daunting one.
Tyre
3 As Alexander's mole neared completion, he had two large siege towers erected and moved to the end of the mole to protect the workers. The Tyrians sent a fire-ship against these towers and destroyed them.
2 In 332BC, Alexander's army appeared on the shore opposite Tyre and asked for the city's peaceful surrender. After this was refused, he began building a mole, perhaps 500–600m (1650–1970ft) long, between the shore and the island. Alexander also blockaded the island with his fleet.
4 As the Tyrians began to suffer from Alexander's blockade, they sent their fleet to attack his Macedonian, Greek and Phoenician ships, but it failed to defeat Alexander's vessels and was ultimately destroyed in the engagement.
5 As the mole reached the island, Macedonian catapults began bombarding the walls and defenders. These were joined by catapults from Alexander's ships. The Tyrians defended their city fiercely, but once their walls were breached south of the mole they could not stop the entrance of Macedonian soldiers, and Tyre fell.

Alexander's plan to take Tyre involved the building of a mole, perhaps 500–600m (1650–1970ft) long, from the Phoenician mainland to the island on which the city stood. Siege towers were also built, and floating battering rams were used to breach the walls of a hitherto impregnable city.

Alexander's siege began in January 332BC with the construction of a mole, a causeway from the mainland that gradually inched towards the island city. Tyrian soldiers attacked the workers, employing torsion catapults mounted on the city walls, while also drawing close to the mole with their ships to pelt them with arrows and missiles.

Alexander responded to the threat of ship harassment by erecting a palisade to shelter his work gangs. He also constructed two siege towers at the end of the mole. They stood 46m (150ft) high, perhaps the tallest siege towers ever built. But the Tyrians floated out a cavalry transport ship filled with combustibles, which succeeded in igniting both Macedonian towers. As they burned, Tyrian soldiers in small boats tore down the palisade that Alexander had erected and set much of Alexander's smaller siege machinery alight. Soon afterwards, high seas submerged most of the mole.

However, the arrival of 80 Phoenician triremes augmented the fleet at Alexander's command, enabling him to defeated the Tyrians in a naval battle, and blockade both Tyrian harbours. Another mole was constructed, with new siege towers, guarded by patrol ships that made another naval attack impossible. Alexander also began to probe Tyre's sea walls with floating battering rams: he had ships tied together so that they could provide stable platforms for rams, the ship platforms moored close against a segment of wall with anchors all around.

Early in August, the battering rams discovered a weak spot on the south side of the city walls, and a breach was made. Alexander brought in ships with siege machinery to widen it, and launched a massive assault on all fronts. He himself led the attack on the breach, at the same time as ship attacks took place all around Tyre. The Tyrians did not have enough defenders to fight off so many challenges at once. Alexander's force beat its way through, the fleets broke into both harbours and started fighting street to street, and the main Macedonian force was then able to enter the city along the mole.

Tyre was burned, and the assault is known to have cost the lives of about 8000 Tyrians. Alexander had won control of the eastern Mediterranean, thereby gaining a foothold in Phoenicia and Palestine.

Gaugamela 331BC

Elite forces faced exotic tactics and weaponry in the battle that decided the fate of the known world in the Near East. Could the military genius of Alexander the Great overcome the collected resources of the world's largest empire?

MACEDONIAN CONQUESTS

MACEDONIAN VICTORY

KEY FACTS

WHO Alexander the Great (356–323BC) and his battered Macedonian army faced the final stand of the Persian Great King Darius (reigned 336–330BC).

WHAT War elephants from India stood ready to smash the legendary Macedonian phalanx – while scythed chariots and special troops awaited their own part in the final struggle for control of the Persian Empire.

WHERE Gaugamela near the city of Arbela.

WHEN 1 October 331BC

WHY To Alexander, the Persian Empire stood as the very definition of world power. That taken, Alexander and his army would neither face nor fear a rival.

OUTCOME In a staggering display of tactical adaptability and superb military training, Alexander's army resisted and destroyed every Persian weapon and tactic. However, one subordinate's error resulted in a crisis of Macedonian command.

Darius was murdered by one of his own men after his defeat, but Alexander's propagandists claimed he'd lived long enough to indicate that he wished Alexander to inherit his Persian domains.

LOCATION

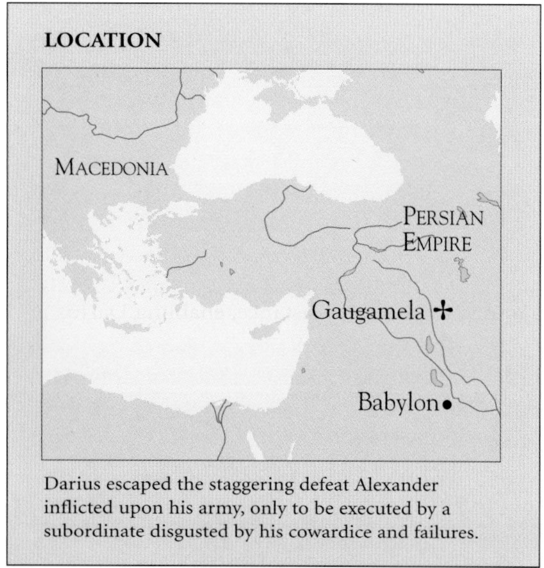
MACEDONIA
PERSIAN EMPIRE
Gaugamela
Babylon

Darius escaped the staggering defeat Alexander inflicted upon his army, only to be executed by a subordinate disgusted by his cowardice and failures.

Alexander had been blessed in his principal opponent, Darius III, during his campaigns against Persia from 336 to 331BC. For five years the boy-king of Macedon had laboured brilliantly to complete his father's dream of conquering the latter's empire and territories in the East. The Persian Great King Darius was a good leader but a below-par general, whose ability to bring huge numbers of Persia's military assets into the field did not live up to his skill in using them.

However, at Gaugamela, Darius felt more confident going into battle, thanks to the procurement of two new 'secret' weapons. From his Indian subjects, Darius had secured a number of war elephants, transported from the easternmost frontiers of Persian suzerainty. Untrained horses could endure neither the sight nor appearance of the strange monsters, who bore archers and javelin throwers upon their backs, and whose strength, Darius thought, might crack the Macedonian phalanx.

Besides the elephants, Darius also had in his arsenal 200 of the most terrifying weapons from the traditions of

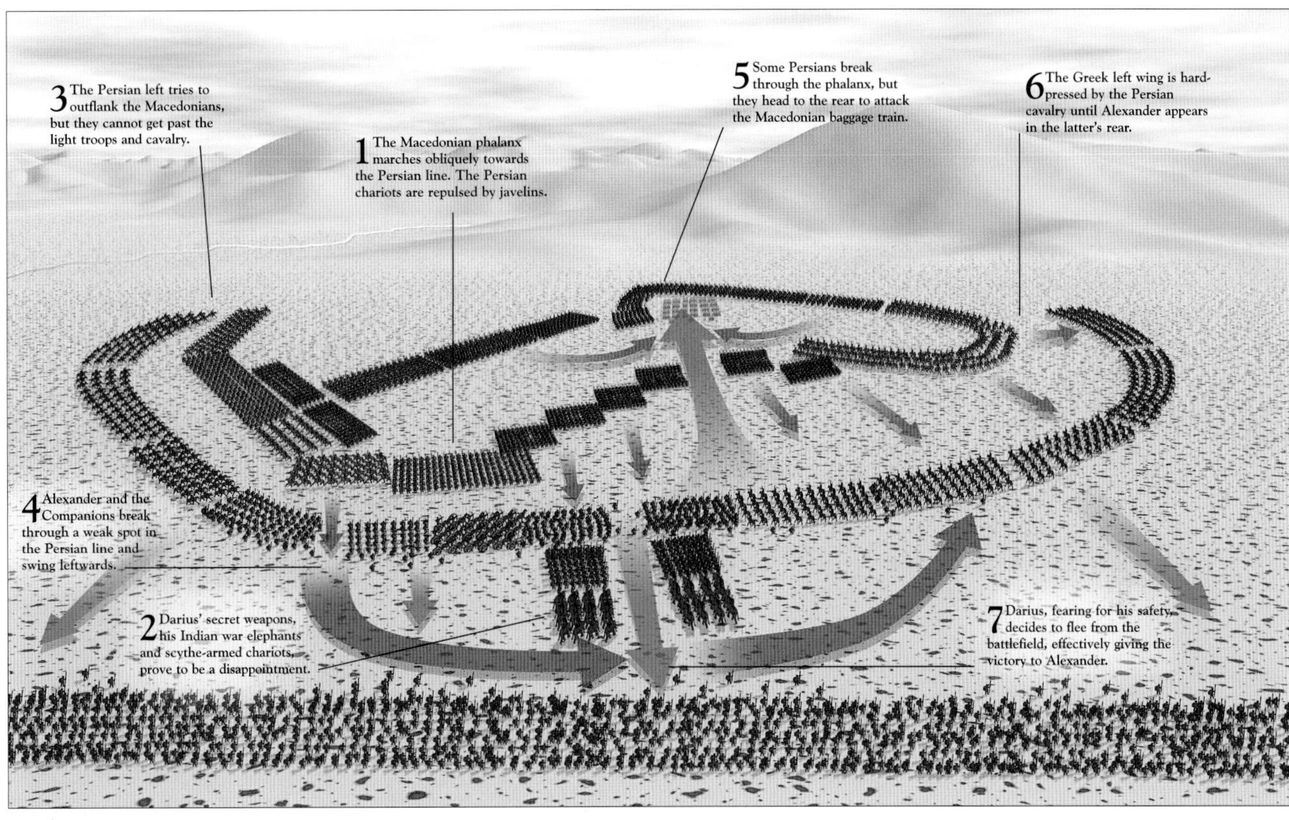
3 The Persian left tries to outflank the Macedonians, but they cannot get past the light troops and cavalry.
1 The Macedonian phalanx marches obliquely towards the Persian line. The Persian chariots are repulsed by javelins.
5 Some Persians break through the phalanx, but they head to the rear to attack the Macedonian baggage train.
6 The Greek left wing is hard-pressed by the Persian cavalry until Alexander appears in the latter's rear.
4 Alexander and the Companions break through a weak spot in the Persian line and swing leftwards.
2 Darius' secret weapons, his Indian war elephants and scythe-armed chariots, prove to be a disappointment.
7 Darius, fearing for his safety, decides to flee from the battlefield, effectively giving the victory to Alexander.

Gaugamela was remarkable for the Persian deployment of scythe-chariots and Indian war elephants, but both proved ineffective against a Macedonian phalanx that advanced in an oblique line which drew their opponents out of position.

Eastern warfare: chariots equipped with scythe blades upon their wheels and traces, weapons designed to inflict dire casualties upon Alexander's infantry.

He had also managed to assemble his forces to meet Alexander on ground of their own choice, a flat plain naturally suiting the deployment of the elephants and chariots. But to counter the threat, Alexander devised a clever plan of his own. Both Alexander's elite cavalry and the awe-inspiring Macedonian phalanx would move at an oblique angle into the much longer Persian line, impact, as usual, being set directly for Darius' visible position in the centre of his line. Layer after layer of the dreaded Macedonian pike, the *sarissa,* would menace the Persians and hold their attention. The Macedonian line would move at an angle as it advanced, and create a gap in the ranks of the apprehensive enemy.

While his attack was being launched, Alexander knew that Darius' forces would attempt to flank him and get behind his army. He would counter with his own selected special forces – a unit new in Western warfare, crack light infantry called *hypaspists.* Experienced veterans, these men could move rapidly to oppose an attack with support from Alexander's allied Thessalian cavalry positioned at either end of his line. Both the *hypaspists* and the Thessalians fought in small units capable of dispersing in the face of a threat, then re-forming at need. In the course of the battle, these sub-formations would move aside in the face of elephants and chariots, showering javelins on those and the cavalry as they would inevitably be driven back by the Persian thrusts at Alexander's flanks.

For the most part, the tactics worked. Alexander's archers and javelin throwers killed the charioteers. Meanwhile the elephants proved uncontrollable. But Parmenio, Alexander's long-serving general, leading the left wing, panicked under fierce assault from the Persians, and sent frantically to the front to Alexander for assistance. Just as he was pursuing Darius, Alexander was forced to return to provide assistance, enabling Darius to escape the battlefield once more.

It was, however, Darius's most humiliating defeat. A few weeks later he was murdered by his entourage, leaving Alexander virtual master of the Greek and Persian worlds.

Hydaspes 326BC

MACEDONIAN CONQUESTS

MACEDONIAN VICTORY

KEY FACTS

WHO The army of Alexander the Great (356–323BC) against the army of the Indian king Porus.

WHAT Porus' army stood blocking Alexander's crossing of the River Hydaspes, but was outmanoeuvred and outfought by the tactically brilliant Alexander.

WHERE The banks of the Hydaspes river, now the Jhelum river on the northwest frontier of what is now Pakistan.

WHEN 326BC

WHY Alexander sought to carry his conquests on into India, to subjugate the known world to his rule.

OUTCOME Alexander accepted Porus' submission and appointed him a client king, but his plans for further conquest were later thwarted when his men finally refused to go any further.

Alexander the Great's last major victory saw his mastery of battlefield tactics once more outmanoeuvre and outfight a superior enemy army, this time against massed war elephants that could have panicked the cavalry – who provided the main element of his striking force.

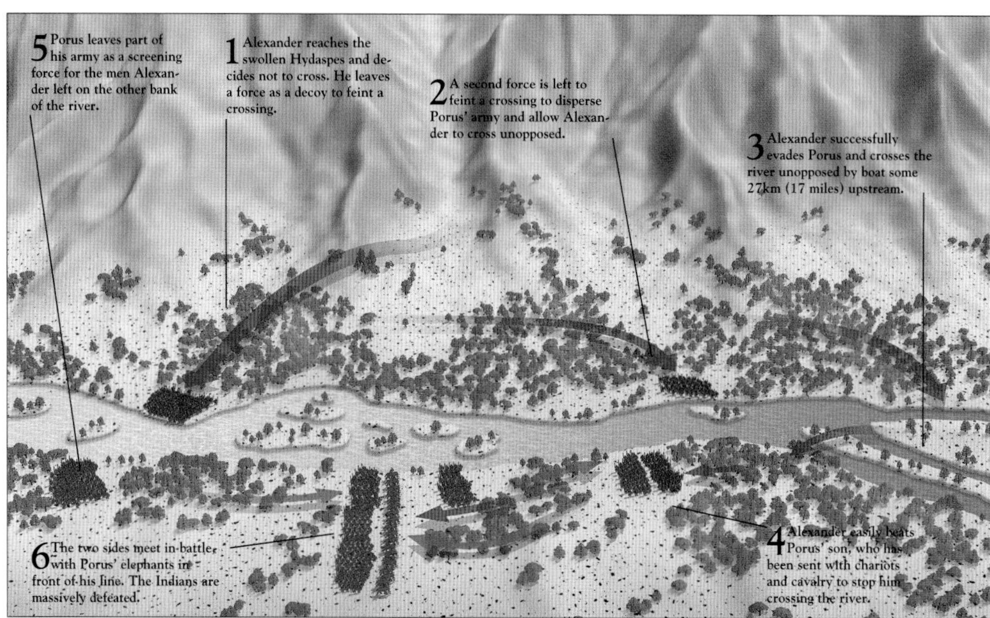

5 Porus leaves part of his army as a screening force for the men Alexander left on the other bank of the river.
1 Alexander reaches the swollen Hydaspes and decides not to cross. He leaves a force as a decoy to feint a crossing.
2 A second force is left to feint a crossing to disperse Porus' army and allow Alexander to cross unopposed.
3 Alexander successfully evades Porus and crosses the river unopposed by boat some 27km (17 miles) upstream.
6 The two sides meet in battle with Porus' elephants in front of his line. The Indians are massively defeated.
4 Alexander easily beats Porus' son, who has been sent with chariots and cavalry to stop him crossing the river.

Elephants were a weapon of early warfare, used for their intimidation factor. Needless to say, they didn't frighten Alexander, who just charged round them with his Companion Cavalry.

LOCATION

Hydaspes

• Persepolis

INDIA

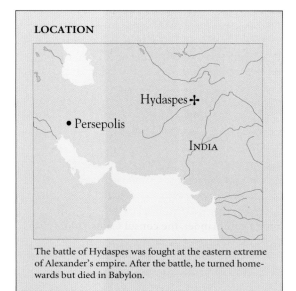

The battle of Hydaspes was fought at the eastern extreme of Alexander's empire. After the battle, he turned homewards but died in Babylon.

Alexander faced an Indian army led by King Porus, containing a large number of war elephants. Capable of trampling its enemy, clubbing him with its trunk, and goring him with its tusks, the elephant was a weapon of psychological terror. But Alexander responded to the challenge by charging his Companion Cavalry around them, quickly outflanking them, while a second cavalry unit of Companions, moving across the rear of the Indian army, attacked the Indian cavalry on Porus' right flank.

Porus drove his elephants at the approaching infantry, but the well-disciplined Macedonian soldiers did not break from their phalanxes. By contrast, Porus' elephants panicked and could not be controlled by their drivers. They charged into their own men, mowing them down, flinging their riders to the ground and trampling on them. More terrified than menacing, the beasts were driven like cattle from the battlefield.

Indians who could not flee, surrendered. One of these was Porus himself, who had stayed on the field, fighting until his elephant was killed under him. Only then did he surrender. Alexander, suitably impressed, preserved Porus' life and even returned him to power, as a client king.

TIMELINE

1500–1000BC	1000–500BC	500BC–0AD	0–500AD	500–1000AD	1000–1500AD	1500–2000AD

Mylae 260BC

FIRST PUNIC WAR

ROMAN VICTORY

KEY FACTS

WHO The fleets of Rome and Carthage meet in the first real naval battle of the First Punic War (264–241 BC).

WHAT The Romans deploy *corvi* for the first time in a sea battle to seize the initiative in the contest for control of the Mediterranean.

WHERE Mylae (modern-day Milazzo) off the Sicilian coast.

WHEN 260BC

WHY Rome at this period was still a largely land-based power. It needed control of the seas if its colonial ambitions were to be pursued.

OUTCOME A surprise victory for the Romans, given the Carthaginians' superior maritime experience, paving the way for further sea victories ahead.

In 260BC Carthage was the major force in the Mediterranean world, but it was facing a challenge from an emergent Rome, impatient to flex its growing military might beyond the Italian peninsula. Sicily occupied a key strategic position, over which conflict between these two powers was inevitable.

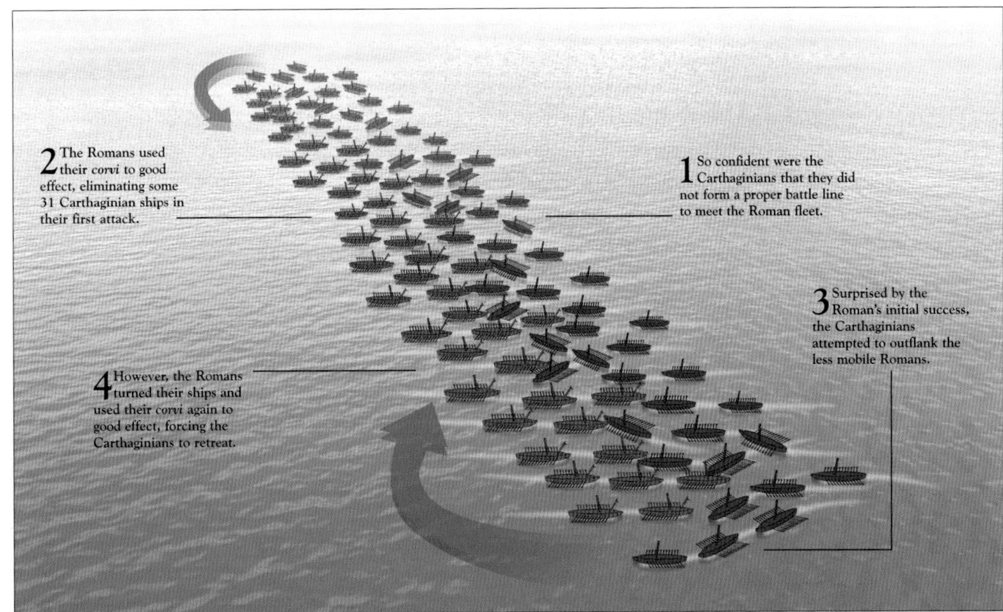
1 So confident were the Carthaginians that they did not form a proper battle line to meet the Roman fleet.
2 The Romans used their *corvi* to good effect, eliminating some 31 Carthaginian ships in their first attack.
3 Surprised by the Roman's initial success, the Carthaginians attempted to outflank the less mobile Romans.
4 However, the Romans turned their ships and used their *corvi* again to good effect, forcing the Carthaginians to retreat.

Early sea battles, in the absence of gunpowder, were about ramming, grappling and boarding. Mylae was a classic example, but the supposed maritime maestros, the Carthaginians, nevertheless were beaten by the up-and-coming Romans.

Mylae was the first significant sea battle of the war between Rome and Carthage. The Carthaginian and Roman fleets were well-matched, but the Carthaginians were so confident of victory that they did not form proper battle lines. Some Roman ships were rammed, but the Carthaginians then found themselves grappling with the *corvi* – planks used for holding and then boarding enemy ships – and Roman marines swarming to board them in superior numbers. In the first attack, the Romans took 31 ships, including the Carthaginian flagship. The Carthaginians attempted to encircle the Romans, but despite their more unwieldy ships and lack of training, the Roman crews were able to turn their vessels around, dropping the *corvi* in their bows again to grappling the enemy. Finally the Carthaginians, caught completely by surprise by the *corvi,* disengaged and retreated, at a cost of 31 vessels captured and 13–14 destroyed.

The Roman commander, the consul Caius Duilius, was granted Rome's first naval triumph, decorating the speaker's platform in the forum with the prows (*rostrata*) of the Carthaginians' captured ships, thus giving the 'rostrum' its name.

LOCATION

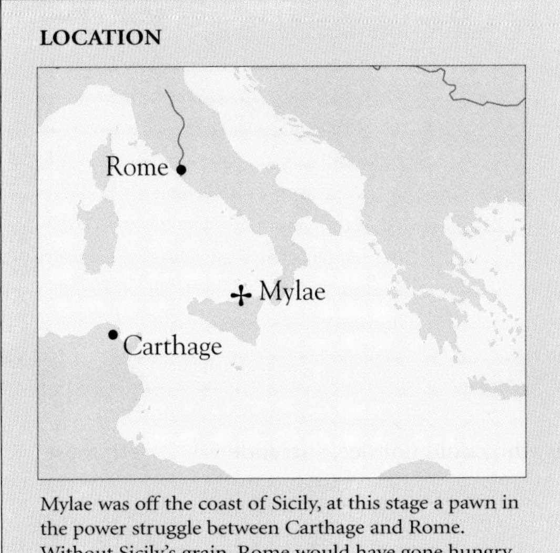
Rome
Mylae
Carthage

Mylae was off the coast of Sicily, at this stage a pawn in the power struggle between Carthage and Rome. Without Sicily's grain, Rome would have gone hungry.

TIMELINE

1500–1000BC	1000–500BC	500BC–0AD	0–500AD	500–1000AD	1000–1500AD	1500–2000AD

Mylae

MYLAE

Early sea battles were pretty crude affairs, with much deployment of ramming tactics, and great expenditure of energy for often little gain. However, at Mylae, for the first time the *corvus* grappling plank was deployed by the Romans. It was to be used for gripping hold of the enemy ship and boarding it. Once that happened at Mylae, it became a matter of hand-to-hand conflict as the Romans swarmed on board the Carthaginian vessels and overwhelmed them. This was a surprise defeat for the Carthaginians, at that time considered a major military sea power.

Trebia 218BC

SECOND PUNIC WAR

CARTHAGINIAN VICTORY

KEY FACTS

WHO Four Roman legions and their allies under Publius Scipio and Tiberius Sempronius Longus faced a collected band of barbarians, mercenaries, elephants, and an elite officer corps under the direct command of Carthaginian general Hannibal Barca (247–183 or 182BC).

WHAT The Carthaginians would require overwhelming brilliance and guile to overcome the morale and experience of the Roman army fighting upon its native soil.

WHERE The banks of the river Trebia, near what is now Piacenza in northern Italy.

WHEN December 218BC

WHY The first Punic War had set the hatred of Carthage for Rome in stone. Hannibal had to be stopped from entering Italy, if he was to be stopped at all.

OUTCOME Rome's greatest military disaster in the field would soon be followed by others.

At the threshold of world empire, the Roman military machine gloried in an unbroken record of success, proven tactics and the finest soldiers in the world. In response, the hated city of Carthage thrust forth mercenaries, elephants – and an avenger in the form of Hannibal.

The Alps presented a formidable obstacle for armies to cross for centuries. For Hannibal to have marched an army, including elephants, across them in the middle of winter was an almost unbelievable feat.

LOCATION

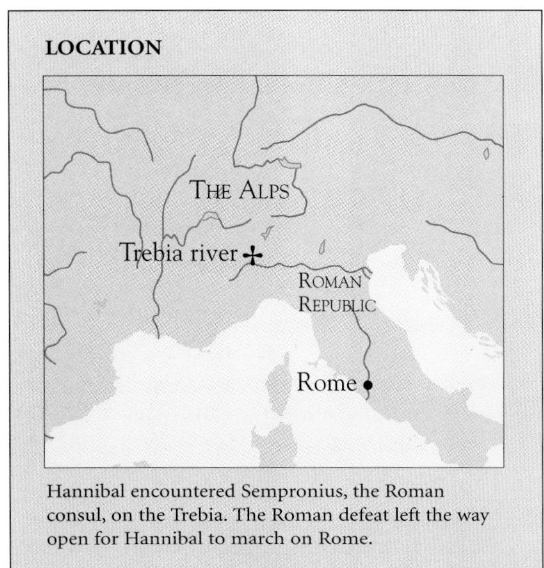
THE ALPS
Trebia river
ROMAN REPUBLIC
Rome

Hannibal encountered Sempronius, the Roman consul, on the Trebia. The Roman defeat left the way open for Hannibal to march on Rome.

Rome had defeated Carthage in the First Punic War of 264–241BC, instilling a hatred and lust for revenge in Hannibal, Carthage's greatest general. The Romans had attempted to thwart his successful military operations in Spain, prompting Hannibal to move his mostly mercenary army from Spain to Italy through the Alpine passes in the dead of winter. Hannibal's deft handling of his army, on top of the incredible feat of transporting elephants over wide rivers and tall mountains in winter, made him by far the fiercest opponent Rome ever had or would encounter.

Publius Scipio, appointed consul to meet the threat, was injured in an encounter with Hannibal's superbly trained and skilfully handled cavalry and light infantry at the crossings of the Ticinus river, and forced to retreat into the fortified city of Placentia (modern Piacenza). So the Roman Senate quickly despatched reinforcements, and a second consular army under Scipio's co-consul, Sempronius Longus, soon arrived at Placentia.

A minor success in a skirmish with the Carthaginian advance guard convinced Sempronius that a decisive

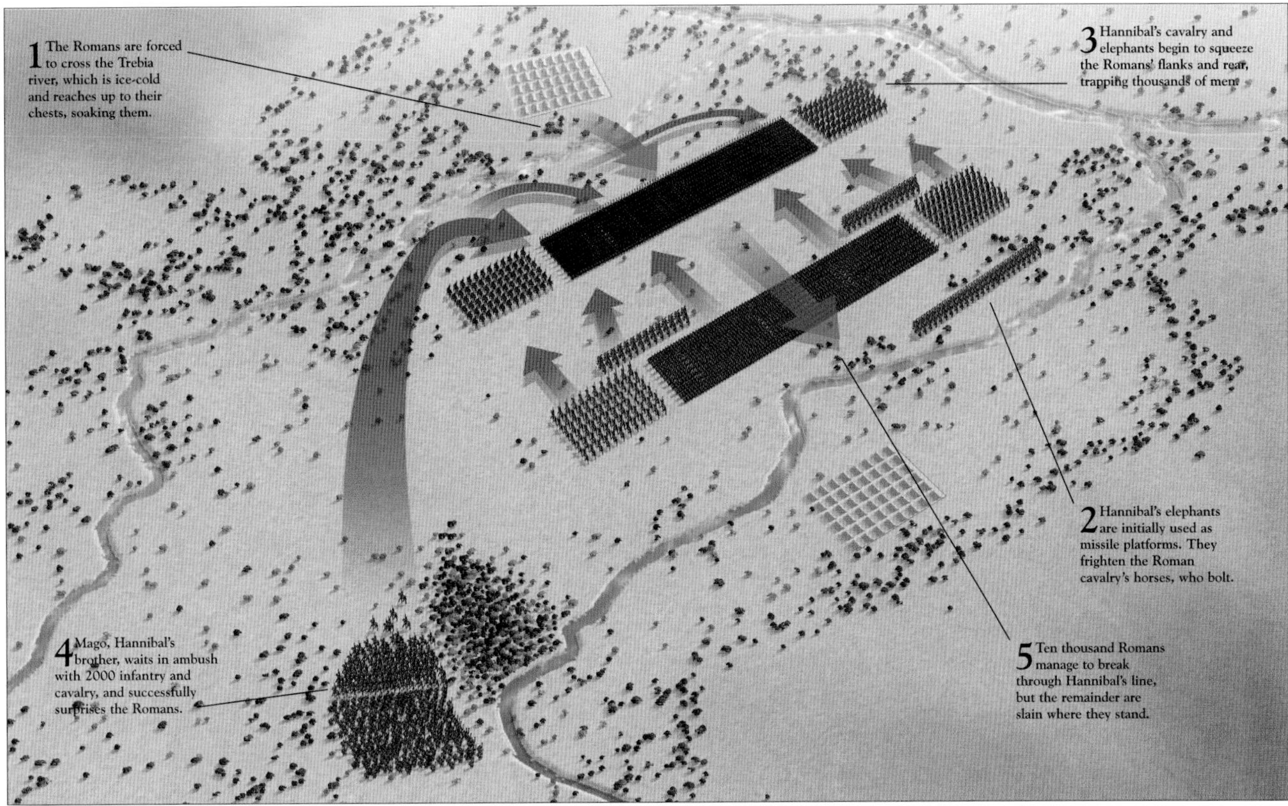
1 The Romans are forced to cross the Trebia river, which is ice-cold and reaches up to their chests, soaking them.
2 Hannibal's elephants are initially used as missile platforms. They frighten the Roman cavalry's horses, who bolt.
3 Hannibal's cavalry and elephants begin to squeeze the Romans' flanks and rear, trapping thousands of men.
4 Mago, Hannibal's brother, waits in ambush with 2000 infantry and cavalry, and successfully surprises the Romans.
5 Ten thousand Romans manage to break through Hannibal's line, but the remainder are slain where they stand.

Hannibal's formation included keeping the elephants back from the front line so that they could be used as missile platforms. When the Roman cavalry charged through, they halted on sight of these strange beasts.

victory and political success were his for the taking from an enemy that could not have been anything but weakened by its winter crossing of the Alps. With Scipio still suffering from his wound, Sempronius took sole command and moved to the Trebia river with the combined consular armies of some 40,000 men.

At dawn, Hannibal's Numidian cavalry appeared in front of Sempronius' fortified camp and invited the Romans to battle with a shower of javelins and other missiles.

Sempronius at once sent his own cavalry and light infantry to exhaust their bodies and missile weapons in a vain response, despite a worsening winter storm and his men's lack of food or fire. The Trebia river was bitterly cold, and came up to the chests of the Roman infantry as they advanced toward the Carthaginian camp, where Hannibal's well-fed and well-warmed troops awaited them.

Hannibal's plan of battle was to set light infantry in front of his line containing the heavier infantry. These skilled soldiers retreated in good order as the enemy advanced, and showered the lumbering Romans with javelins at a safe distance.

Hannibal kept his elephants behind his line of battle, where they could serve as missile platforms in some safety, while his light infantry made a well-organized withdrawal behind the long line of Hannibal's 20,000 Spanish infantry.

Sempronius's legionaries made a strong response to Hannibal's bombardment, throwing javelins as the legions drew near to the very centre of the Carthaginian line. However, the Italian horses could not abide the sight and smell of the huge elephants and bolted, and Hannibal's superior cavalry began to drive in the Roman flanks.

Sempronius responded to a worsening tactical situation by continuing his central advance. Hannibal turned his elephants against the Roman light infantry (*velites*) who, while fighting them off in worsening weather conditions, lost all contact with the centre. Sempronius thought he had the victory when a quarter of his army burst through the Carthaginian centre, but those 10,000 men proved to be the sole survivors of a disastrous defeat. While Sempronius and the survivors escaped to Placentia in small groups, Hannibal's forces methodically set about slaughtering the remaining three-quarters of the Roman army.

Raphia 217BC

KEY FACTS

WHO The army of the Seleucid king Antiochus III against that of Ptolemy IV of Egypt.

WHAT While the Seleucid's Indian elephants were more dependable in battle, the vast size and better training of the Ptolemaic phalanx of pikemen men proved decisive.

WHERE Modern Rafah, near Gaza.

WHEN 22 June 217BC

WHY Coele-Syria was a much disputed borderland between the Ptolemaic Egyptians and the Seleucid empire, and long fought over.

OUTCOME Ptolemy's success would secure the borders of Coele-Syria for a time, but after his death in 204BC, Antiochus III would later capture it from his son, Ptolemy V.

Many early armies made considerable use of elephants as 'fighting machines'. In reality, they were highly unpredictable, and it was unwise to set too much faith in them. They could have cost Ptolemy IV the battle at Raphia, but fortunately his infantry proved rather more reliable.

HELLENISTIC WARS

PTOLEMAIC VICTORY

Despite a taste for culture, which extended to temple building, Ptolemy IV was a not one of the great Egyptian pharaohs. Success at Raphia, however, was a high point in his reign.

LOCATION

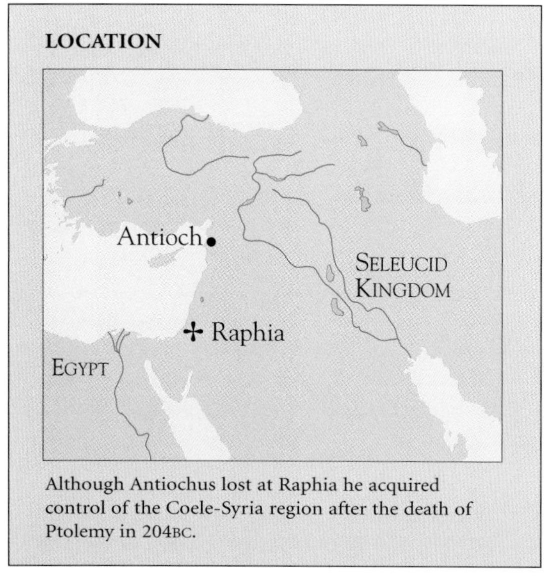
Antioch
SELEUCID KINGDOM
Raphia
EGYPT

Although Antiochus lost at Raphia he acquired control of the Coele-Syria region after the death of Ptolemy in 204BC.

Antiochus III would in time earn the epithet 'The Great' for his distinguished rule and unification of the Seleucid Empire. However, he faced much opposition in his early years and it was only some time after his succession in 222BC that he was fully able to turn his attention to the province of Coele-Syria – essentially what is now Lebanon, Palestine/Israel, Jordan and southern Syria – a long disputed borderland between his Syrian kingdom and that of his Ptolemaic Egyptian neighbours to the south. Ptolemy IV of Egypt, by contrast, was not to prove, in the long run, a great ruler, and he spent much of his reign under the thumb of stronger advisors and other members of his family. But these advisors at least sensed the growing threat that Antiochus III represented, and major preparations had been undertaken to retrain and expand the size of the Ptolemaic army.

The two sides met near the town of Raphia on the eastern edge of the Sinai peninsula, where Antiochus based his army not far away from that of his enemy. Several days of skirmishing followed, and on one occasion

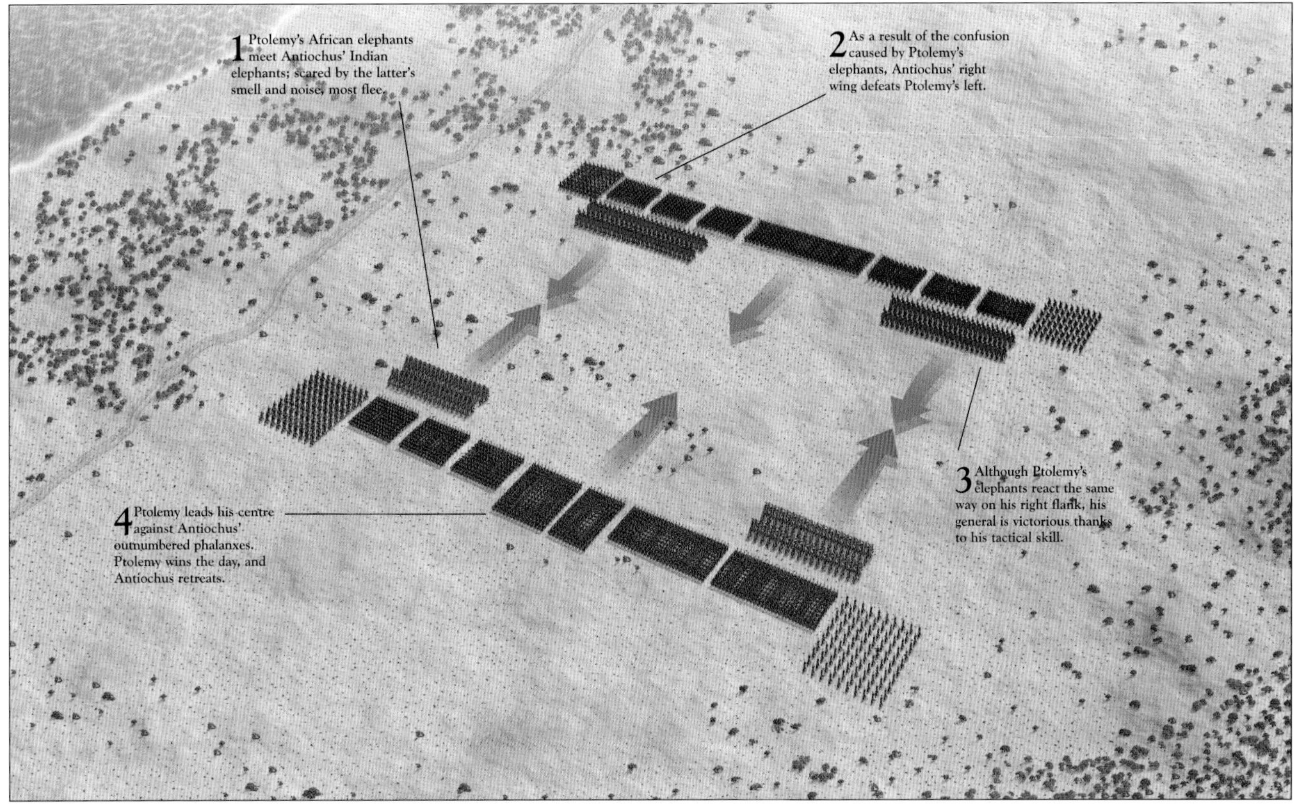
1 Ptolemy's African elephants meet Antiochus' Indian elephants; scared by the latter's smell and noise, most flee.
2 As a result of the confusion caused by Ptolemy's elephants, Antiochus' right wing defeats Ptolemy's left.
3 Although Ptolemy's elephants react the same way on his right flank, his general is victorious thanks to his tactical skill.
4 Ptolemy leads his centre against Antiochus' outnumbered phalanxes. Ptolemy wins the day, and Antiochus retreats.

Fought on a broad desert plain, the massed armies at Raphia must have made for terrific spectacle, not least the lines of war elephants which, although this was not always the case, seemed to have been used to good effect.

an officer who had switched sides to join Antiochus's men managed to gain access to the opposing camp and steal into Ptolemy's tent. Only the latter's absence thwarted this assassination attempt.

The battleground of Raphia was a desert plain some 40km (25 miles) southwest of Gaza. Both armies were immense: Antiochus could draw upon 62,000 infantry, 6000 cavalry and 102 Indian elephants. Ptolemy had 70,000 infantry, 5000 cavalry and 73 African Forest elephants. The centres of both armies were formed of heavy infantry phalanxes armed with the Macedonian *sarissa,* or long spear, and there was lighter infantry on both flanks and cavalry on the wings. In front of the cavalry and some of the infantry on each wing, the kings deployed their elephants.

ELEPHANTS ENGAGE

The battle began with a clash of the elephants, urged on by the men in the 'towers' on their back, who struck at their opponent with their *sarissas* at close quarters, while the elephants met forehead to forehead, tusks firmly interlocked, shoving against each other until one gave ground. Once one elephant began to give ground and it turned away, its flank would be exposed, and the 'winning' elephant would gore it with its tusks. In this fight, it was the Seleucid elephants who came off best. African elephants were unable to stand the smell and trumpeting of Indian elephants, and were probably intimidated by their greater size and strength. Gradually, they began to turn and take flight, and this caused disarray in Ptolemy's infantry, lined up behind them.

However, while this meant that Antiochus' right wing triumphed over its Ptolemaic opponents, and the elephants on his left wing enjoyed a similar outcome, clever manoeuvring by Ptolemy's general on the right ensured the overall defeat of Antiochus' left flank. Meanwhile, in the centre, Ptolemy's phalanx enjoyed the numerical advantage, and Antiochus' infantry lines collapsed, just as he returned from having led a successful cavalry charge. In defeat, Antiochus retreated, though he would gain his revenge a decade later against Ptolemy's son.

Cannae 216BC

KEY FACTS

WHO A Roman army under the consul Varro moved to attack the Carthaginians under Hannibal Barca (247–183 or 182BC).

WHAT The Roman cavalry were driven from the field by their enemy. The Roman and allied infantry pushed the Carthaginians back until their own flanks were exposed to the longer Carthaginian line, which squeezed their formation even more. The returning Carthaginian cavalry attacked the rear of the Roman infantry, severely restricting the ability of individuals to respond.

WHERE Apulia, Italy

WHEN 216BC

WHY Hannibal was attempting to wrest Rome's recently acquired Italian allies from her and so weaken her ability to continue the war.

OUTCOME More than half the Roman force was cut down. But Rome raised another army and continued the war to ultimate victory.

After the battles of Trebia (218BC) and Trasimene (217BC), Hannibal won his third and greatest victory over the armies of Rome in Italy, at Cannae. A tactical masterpiece, the battle has provided a model for generals for over 2000 years. Yet Rome survived this catastrophe to defeat the Carthaginians.

SECOND PUNIC WAR

CARTHAGINIAN VICTORY

The death of the Roman general Paullus at Cannae, at which battle over half the Roman army was cut down in one of its most catastrophic defeats.

LOCATION

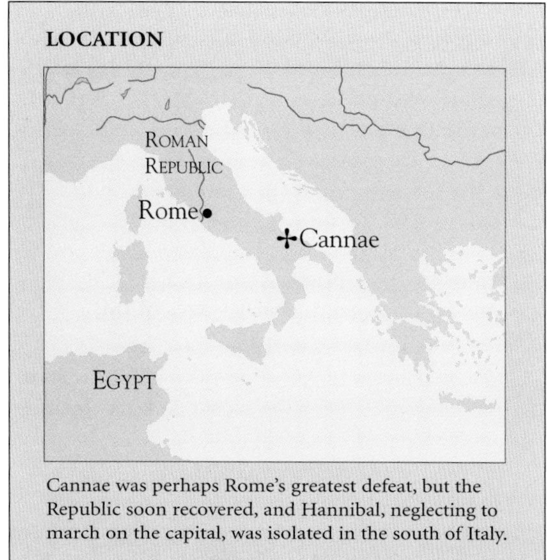
ROMAN
REPUBLIC
Rome
Cannae
EGYPT

Cannae was perhaps Rome's greatest defeat, but the Republic soon recovered, and Hannibal, neglecting to march on the capital, was isolated in the south of Italy.

Most of the Second Punic War (218–202BC) between Carthage and Rome was fought in Spain, but by taking the fight to the Roman power base in Italy, the Carthaginian general Hannibal Barca hoped to reduce Rome's power in the field. Roman strategy had been, initially, to immediately confront the invader in the field, but Hannibal had outthought his opponents on every occasion and slaughtered Roman soldiers in their tens of thousands. By winter, however, he was experiencing problems in obtaining food for his army – which during its long campaign was forced to live off the countryside – and so he relocated into Apulia, in southern Italy.

His movements were tracked by Roman scouts, and soon their army, under the joint consulship of Paullus and Varro, caught up with him near the village of Cannae. But Hannibal had been shrewd in his choice of a location, which provided him with several advantages. Firstly, his army was deployed on hills, giving them a height advantage. Secondly, they had their backs to the prevailing wind, which was prone to kick up dust squalls and impair

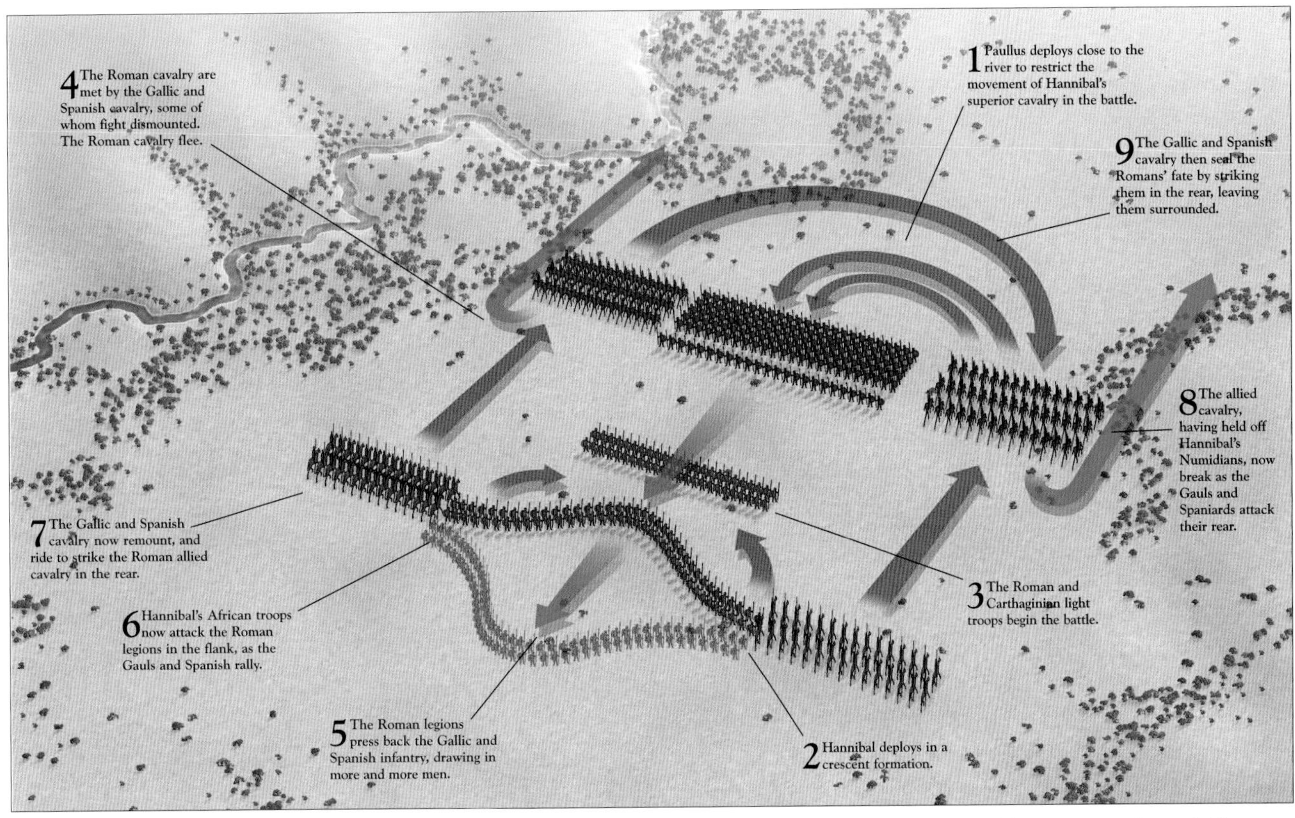

1 Paullus deploys close to the river to restrict the movement of Hannibal's superior cavalry in the battle.
2 Hannibal deploys in a crescent formation.
3 The Roman and Carthaginian light troops begin the battle.
4 The Roman cavalry are met by the Gallic and Spanish cavalry, some of whom fight dismounted. The Roman cavalry flee.
5 The Roman legions press back the Gallic and Spanish infantry, drawing in more and more men.
6 Hannibal's African troops now attack the Roman legions in the flank, as the Gauls and Spanish rally.
7 The Gallic and Spanish cavalry now remount, and ride to strike the Roman allied cavalry in the rear.
8 The allied cavalry, having held off Hannibal's Numidians, now break as the Gauls and Spaniards attack their rear.
9 The Gallic and Spanish cavalry then seal the Romans' fate by striking them in the rear, leaving them surrounded.

While Hannibal's army was outnumbered at Cannae, he cleverly chose his position to nullify this by forcing the Romans to fight on a narrow front, which restricted their advantage.

the vision of anyone advancing into it. Thirdly, but perhaps most importantly of all, the frontage was restricted. Hannibal knew the Roman army outnumbered him almost two to one. The ground he chose forced them to deploy with a river on their right and steep hills to their left. It restricted the Romans' frontage, and forced their infantry into a much denser formation than normal, with only their front rank able to fight. Hannibal had negated the principal Roman advantage at a stroke.

LET BATTLE COMMENCE

When the battle began, the Roman cavalry were the first to give ground. Hemmed in by the river on one side and the massed infantry on the other, and outclassed by the veteran Gallic and Spanish cavalry led by Hannibal's brother Hasdrubal, they turned and fled. Now skirmishers on both sides exchanged missiles, buoyed up by the war horns and shouts of their own men. The lines collided in mêlée, shield clashing against shield. Slowly but surely the Roman infantry pushed back the centre of the Gallic/Spanish line. This, though, was Hannibal's trap. As the Romans pushed forward the line flattened and then went concave, crowding the already cramped Roman infantry, restricting the space they needed to wield their weapons.

The Gauls and Spaniards feigned a retreat, which left the two tips of African troops on the wings of the infantry to launch themselves at their flanks. As the African steamroller hit, the confused Romans were thrown closer together, unable to fight back. Historical sources speak of butchery rather than fighting. A slingshot had injured Paullus, commanding the right wing of the army. Unable to stay mounted, he ordered his bodyguard to dismount to continue the fight. When Hannibal heard of this, he is reported to have said: 'They might as well be delivered up to me in chains.'

As casualties mounted and men started to leave the field, Hasdrubal launched Numidian cavalry – a formidable band of fighting horsemen so skilled they did not need bridles to control their mounts – into a bloody slaughter of the fugitives. In the early stages of this pursuit, they cut down the consul Paullus, who was still trying to make a fight of it.

The Roman dead numbered 48,000, and they had suffered their heaviest ever battlefield defeat.

Gaixia 202BC

KEY FACTS

WHO Han Xin and Liu Bang and the Han forces, against those of Xiang Yu of the Chu.

WHAT Xiang Yu, in attempting to free his wife when she was taken prisoner by the Han, marched into an ambush in a canyon near Gaixia with tragic consequences.

WHERE Gaixia, modern day Suzhou.

WHEN 202BC

WHY China had become divided between the rival rulers of the Han in western China, and the Chu in the east.

OUTCOME After his victory, Liu Bang was effectively able to unite China, and he declared himself emperor of the newly established Han dynasty.

The Han dynasty were to rule China for two hundred years, leaving behind them enduring cultural traditions. In 202BC, however, they were involved in a desperate scrap for power in the wake of the fall of the Qin dynasty. Victory at Gaixia paved the way for the first Han emperor.

CHU–HAN WARS

HAN VICTORY

羽
塗山の澤中に

Artists of a later generation would find the warring Han and Chu clans a source for highly imaginative woodblock art, as this image of a ferocious warrior in battle illustrates.

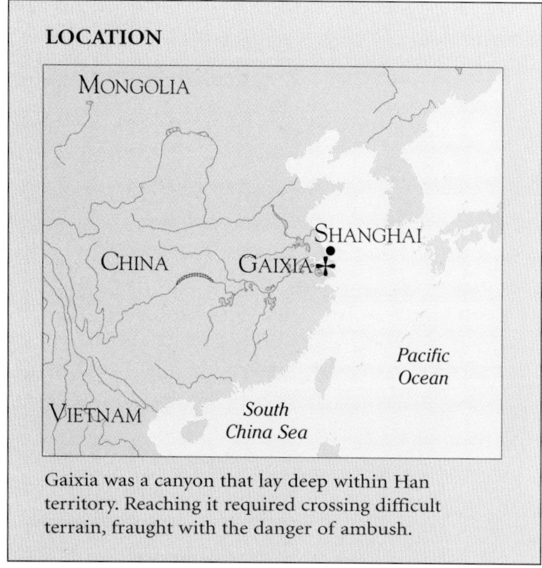
LOCATION
MONGOLIA
CHINA
GAIXIA
SHANGHAI
Pacific Ocean
VIETNAM
South China Sea

Gaixia was a canyon that lay deep within Han territory. Reaching it required crossing difficult terrain, fraught with the danger of ambush.

After a lengthy era of Chinese disunity known as the age of the Warring States, the Qin emerged from the west of the country, and after a series of conquests over its rivals brought a period of stability and prosperity. However, the Qin dynasty had been displaced through rebellion by 206BC and the country was pitched into further bitter warfare between various warring states.

Among the most formidable figures who emerged during the turmoil was Xiang Yu, who had set himself up as king of the Western Chu, having shown himself to be a skilled commander on the battlefield, achieving several victories over the Qin. Xiang Yu awarded Liu Bang the title King of the Han after the latter had inflicted the final defeat on the Qin, after which Xiang Yu had split China up into 18 kingdoms.

However, in doing so, he had also allocated land that rightfully should have gone to Liu Bang. What followed was a power struggle known as the Chu-Han contention, eventually to be resolved in Liu Bang's favour at the battle of Gaixia.

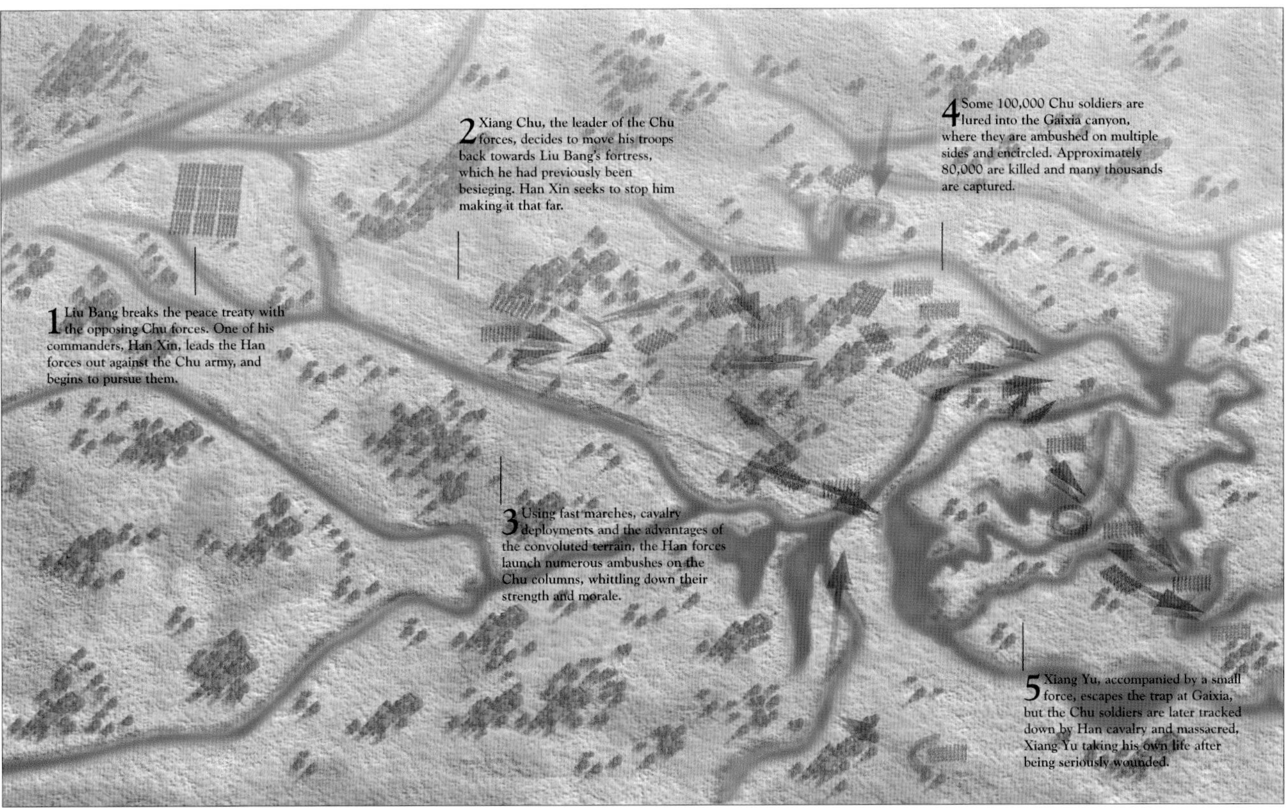
1 Liu Bang breaks the peace treaty with the opposing Chu forces. One of his commanders, Han Xin, leads the Han forces out against the Chu army, and begins to pursue them.
2 Xiang Chu, the leader of the Chu forces, decides to move his troops back towards Liu Bang's fortress, which he had previously been besieging. Han Xin seeks to stop him making it that far.
3 Using fast marches, cavalry deployments and the advantages of the convoluted terrain, the Han forces launch numerous ambushes on the Chu columns, whittling down their strength and morale.
4 Some 100,000 Chu soldiers are lured into the Gaixia canyon, where they are ambushed on multiple sides and encircled. Approximately 80,000 are killed and many thousands are captured.
5 Xiang Yu, accompanied by a small force, escapes the trap at Gaixia, but the Chu soldiers are later tracked down by Han cavalry and massacred, Xiang Yu taking his own life after being seriously wounded.

This bird's eye view of the terrain around Gaixia illustrates its suitability for a Han campaign based on ambush and encirclement, with rivers, valleys, canyons and numerous areas of woodland helping channel the Chu forces into confined killing grounds.

After a series of battles, it seemed by 203BC that the Han had gained the upper hand. So Xiang Yu managed to negotiate an armistice, known as the Treaty of Hong Canal, which agreed to the division of China under the rule of the Chu in the east and the Han in the west. However, Liu Bang had no intention of keeping to the pact. Within a short time he had launched an attack on the Western Chu, with support from the forces of Han Xin, the king of Qi and Peng Yue, later to be made king of Liang.

RETREAT TO PENGCHENG

Xiang Yu, forced to retreat with his army though he had been leading the siege of a Han fortress, now found himself under attack from three directions, and attempted to move his forces back to his capital city, Pengcheng. He was harassed all the way, however, by ambushes set by Han Xin and Liu Bang, and in one of these, the Chu ruler's wife, Yuji, who had been travelling with the army, was captured near a canyon at Gaixia. Xiang Yu was determined to rescue her from his detested enemies, and while he sent most of his troops on toward Pengcheng, he gathered together a smaller force of around 100,000 men and headed towards the canyon.

RAID ON THE CANYON

Han Xin had made sure Yuji was held captive deep within the area of the canyon. As Xiang moved in to reach her, he marched straight into the trap set for him by Han Xin and faced 'ambush from ten sides.' The Chu sustained heavy casualties, and many of them began to flee from the canyon. Distraught that she had been the cause of the disaster, Yuji committed suicide, which did little to raise the already plummeting morale of Xiang Yu. Still, with now less than 1000 loyal men at his side, Xiang Yu was able to break out of the canyon, reaching the Wu River before the Han soldiers caught up with him. Xiang Yu refused to surrender, however. He was wounded in a desperate last-ditch battle to avoid capture, and chose to commit suicide by slitting his throat. With this defeat, the era of the great Han Dynasty was about to begin, with Liu Bang, as its first emperor.

TIMELINE

1500–1000BC	1000–500BC	500BC–0AD	0–500AD	500–1000AD	1000–1500AD	1500–2000AD

Chios 201 BC

KEY FACTS

WHO The fleet of Philip V, King of Macedon (reigned 221 BC–179 BC) against the combined ships of Rhodes, Pergamon, Byzantium and Cyzicus.

WHAT Philip was able to call upon a sparkling new fleet for his campaign against Rhodes and its allies, but the lack of experience of its crews would prove critical in a fight with a canny old maritime power.

WHERE Off the island of Chios, Aegean Sea.

WHEN 201 BC

WHY The Macedonians under Philip V were determined to crush the maritime power of Rhodes.

OUTCOME After this embarrassing defeat, the Macedonian fleet would play little further part in the battles against its Greek enemies.

Alexander the Great cast long shadows over his Macedonian successors. The able Philip V dreamt of reviving his Empire, but found himself thwarted at Chios by an alliance of two wily Greek opponents.

CRETAN WAR

GREEK VICTORY

ΒΑΣΙΛΕΩΣ
ΦΙΛΙΠΠΟΥ

Philip V cast himself in the heroic mold of his illustrious Macedonian predecessor, Alexander the Great. Even the latter had never truly trusted the Greeks, however, and they won the day at Chios.

Philip V of Macedon dreamt of matching the achievements of Alexander the Great. Among the regional powers standing in his way were the island democracy of Rhodes, with the most superlative navy in the ancient world, and the fortress-city of Pergamon under King Attalus I. When the two joined in an alliance, Philip in turn responded by building up his navy, including some of the heaviest, most dangerous warships known to exist at that time, as well as lighter vessels carrying rams.

LAYING SIEGE

Philip sought to divide the forces of Rhodes and Pergamon with a siege of the island of Chios, from which he would be well situated to prevent Attalus and the Rhodians from aiding each other. Attalus had quite correctly realized that Philip intended an eventual strike against him and was feverishly steeling his fortress-city for the onslaught. The shrewd Rhodian admiral Theophiliscus, however, equally correctly understood that Pergamon could resist any attack Philip could mount. He convinced Attalus to abandon his preparations and join his fleet with Rhodes' while he was still able to do so.

Philip had been digging away beneath the Chians' walls when the news came of the allied fleet's arrival. From the first moment, Theophiliscus had seized the

LOCATION

MACEDONIA
Pergamon
Athens
Chios
Rhodes

Philip knew that if he could capture Chios he would be able to defeat the allies in turn. His strategic loss at Chios gave the allies breathing space.

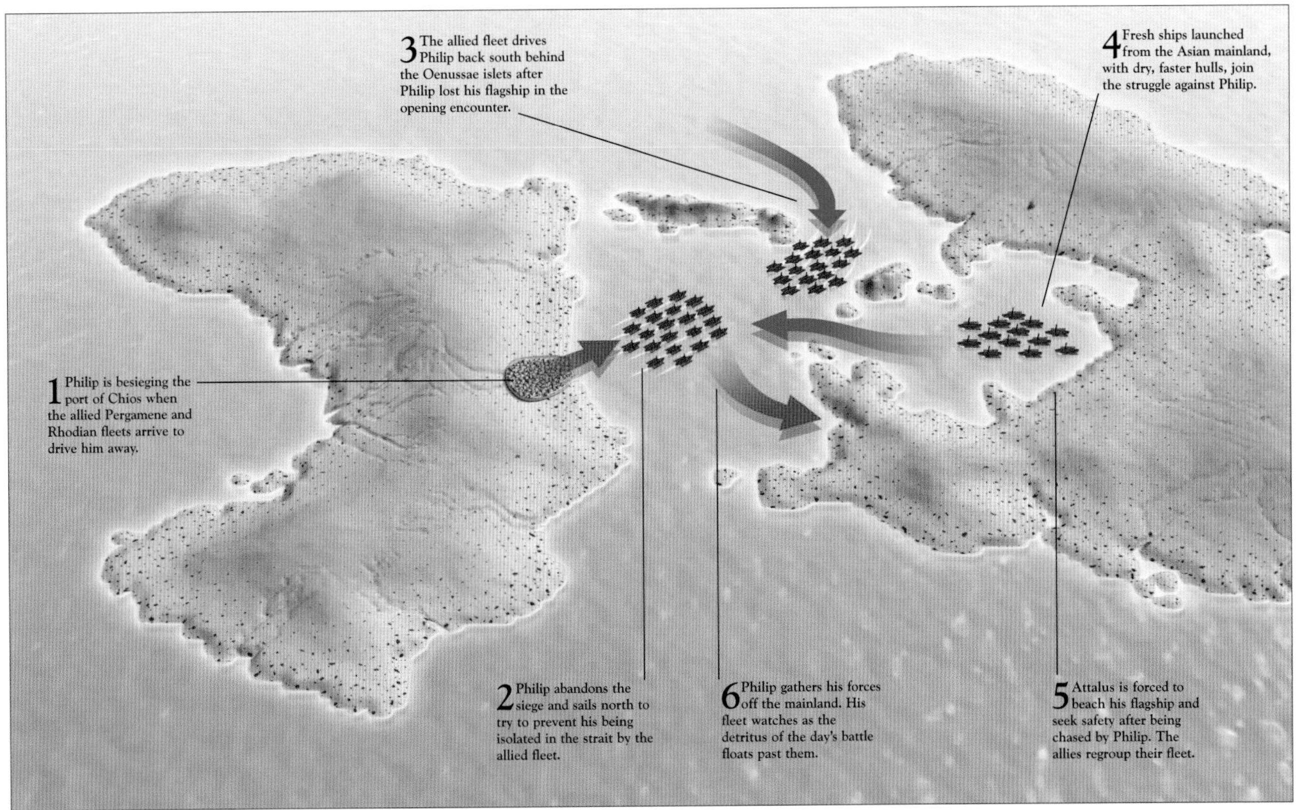
3 The allied fleet drives Philip back south behind the Oenussae islets after Philip lost his flagship in the opening encounter.
4 Fresh ships launched from the Asian mainland, with dry, faster hulls, join the struggle against Philip.
1 Philip is besieging the port of Chios when the allied Pergamene and Rhodian fleets arrive to drive him away.
2 Philip abandons the siege and sails north to try to prevent his being isolated in the strait by the allied fleet.
6 Philip gathers his forces off the mainland. His fleet watches as the detritus of the day's battle floats past them.
5 Attalus is forced to beach his flagship and seek safety after being chased by Philip. The allies regroup their fleet.

Philip V went into battle with some of the heaviest fighting vessels known to have been put to sea at that time, but the Greeks were simply more experienced in the art of sea fighting.

initiative from the Macedonian king, who suddenly found himself trapped on an island with a hostile fleet across his supply lines.

Philip moved slowly to deploy his fleet, which enabled the allies to convert their own picket formation into a line of battle, and the engagement took place in the strait between Chios and the Erythraean promontory of the Asian coast. Attalus took his own lavishly appointed flagship directly into the line, while Philip preferred to wait in the vanguard with his own squadron of lighter ships. The Pergamene fleet crossed the strait at speed to prevent Philip's escape around the northern end of Chios.

FLAGSHIP ATTACK

In the confusion of the prow-to-prow rush of the Pergamene and Macedonian squadrons that followed, one of Philip's lighter vessels accidentally turned her broadside into the Macedonian flagship. As the flagship's bow was trapped under the overhang of the lighter vessel's topmost oarbenches, two of Attalus' vessels moved sharply in to ram and sink the ship, with its admiral and full complement of crewmen still on board.

Philip's ships tried to withdraw around the island inlets, but they lost their line abreast formation and were rammed in their unprotected sterns, while others had their oarbanks shattered by the beaks and well-trained crews of the Rhodian galleys.

DECEPTION

However, as Attalus chased the faster enemy fleeing toward the Asian shore, he passed the islands where Philip and his personal flotilla were waiting. The Macedonian king moved to intercept him and while Attalus was able to beach his ships, enabling him to flee to the shore, Philip captured his flagship and, taking it in tow, was able to convince the Pergamenes that the king was dead. As the enemy ships discreetly decided the moment had come to withdrew, Philip himself was only too happy to disengage from a battle in which his own fleet, though seemingly larger and better equipped, had come off worst.

Cynoscephalae 197BC

KEY FACTS

WHO A Roman army of about 26,000 men under the command of Consul Titus Quinctius Flaminius (c. 228–174BC), opposed by an approximately equal number of Macedonians under Philip V (238–179BC).

WHAT Manoeuvres by both sides led to an encounter battle that pitted the frontal power of the phalanx against the flexibility of the legion.

WHERE Southeast Thessaly, Greece.

WHEN 197BC

WHY Rome was concerned at the expansionist intent displayed by Philip V, and moved to counter his ambitions.

OUTCOME A crushing defeat for the Macedonians despite some local successes.

The Battle of Cynoscephalae matched the tactical flexibility of the Roman legion against the fighting power of the Macedonian phalanx. While nothing could stand against the head-on attack of the phalanx, good tactics were capable of defeating it.

SECOND MACEDONIAN WAR

ROMAN VICTORY

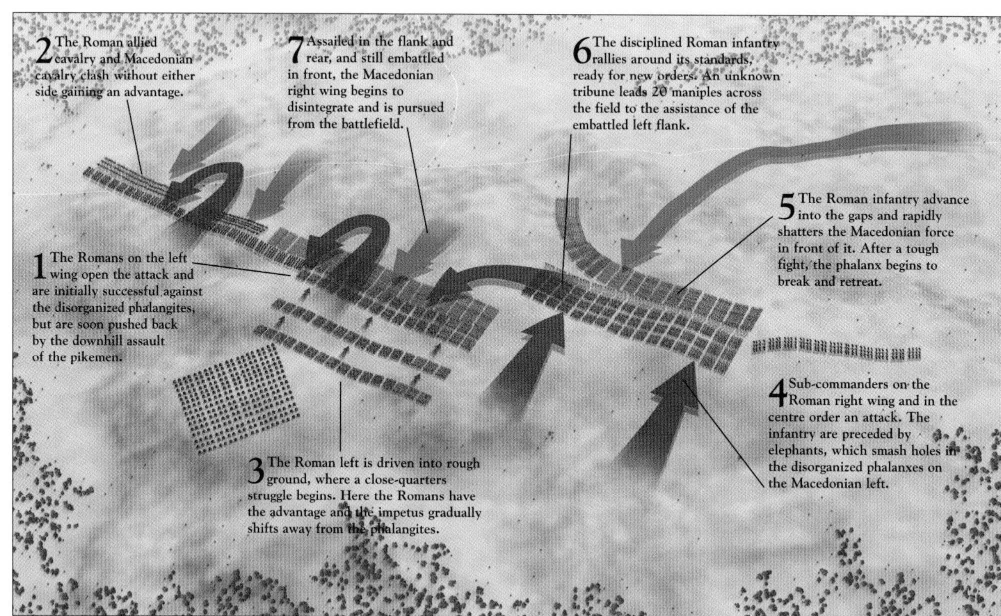

2 The Roman allied cavalry and Macedonian cavalry clash without either side gaining an advantage.
7 Assailed in the flank and rear, and still embattled in front, the Macedonian right wing begins to disintegrate and is pursued from the battlefield.
6 The disciplined Roman infantry rallies around its standards, ready for new orders. An unknown tribune leads 20 maniples across the field to the assistance of the embattled left flank.
5 The Roman infantry advance into the gaps and rapidly shatters the Macedonian force in front of it. After a tough fight, the phalanx begins to break and retreat.
1 The Romans on the left wing open the attack and are initially successful against the disorganized phalangites, but are soon pushed back by the downhill assault of the pikemen.
4 Sub-commanders on the Roman right wing and in the centre order an attack. The infantry are preceded by elephants, which smash holes in the disorganized phalanxes on the Macedonian left.
3 The Roman left is driven into rough ground, where a close-quarters struggle begins. Here the Romans have the advantage and the impetus gradually shifts away from the phalangites.

The massed phalanx of spearmen had held sway for centuries, but the Romans, splitting their legions into smaller combat groups, suddenly made it look slow to adapt to the often rapidly changing directions of attack on the battlefield.

LOCATION

THRACE
ROME
MACEDONIA
CYNOSCEPHALAE

Cynoscephalae was an 'encounter battle', in which the goal was the destruction of the enemy force rather than a terrain objective.

Philip V of Macedon fought the Romans under the command of consul Titus Quinctius Flaminius near a ridge known as Cynoscephalae. At first, the Macedonian phalangites had a significant advantage in a head-on combat, but Flaminius' tactical retreat drew them into rough ground, where Philip's traditionally arrayed spear-carrying infantrymen were at a disadvantage. As the massed ranks broke up and the advance lost momentum, the phalangites dropped their pikes and resorted to swords and long daggers. In this sort of close-quarter fight, individuals and small combat teams counted for more than large formations and, together with their more flexible command structure of officers in charge of smaller units, the Romans soon gained the upper hand.

Faced with hard-fighting enemies in front and assailed in the rear, and with its flank supports rapidly disappearing over the ridgeline, the Macedonian right collapsed into rout. Huge numbers of casualties were inflicted as the phalangites tried to fight their way free. The collapse of the Macedonian army at Cynoscephalae effectively marked the end of the Second Macedonian War. The day of the phalanx was over and the legion was in the ascendant.

TIMELINE

1500–1000BC	1000–500BC	500BC–0AD	0–500AD	500–1000AD	1000–1500AD	1500–2000AD

Pydna 168BC

THIRD MACEDONIAN WAR

ROMAN VICTORY

KEY FACTS

WHO Roman legions and supporting forces under Lucius Aemilius Paullus (c. 229–160 BC) versus Macedonian forces under Perseus, king of Macedon (c. 212–165BC).

WHAT A clash between troops gathering water developed into a full-blown battle, which was won by the Roman legions after initial reverses. The Macedonian left was shattered by elephants and the central phalanx massacred.

WHERE Near the city of Pydna, Macedon.

WHEN 22 June 168BC

WHY Roman dissatisfaction with the indecisive Third Macedonian War, which had begun in 172BC, resulted in a new campaign to subdue the increasingly anti-Roman Macedonians.

OUTCOME The Macedonians were decisively defeated in battle and Macedon became a Roman province.

The Battle of Pydna was the pivotal moment of the Third Macedonian War. It was a classic phalanx versus legion clash, with the legions emerging victorious. The battle also marked a major shift in power, with Roman military might firmly establishing the new order in the Mediterranean.

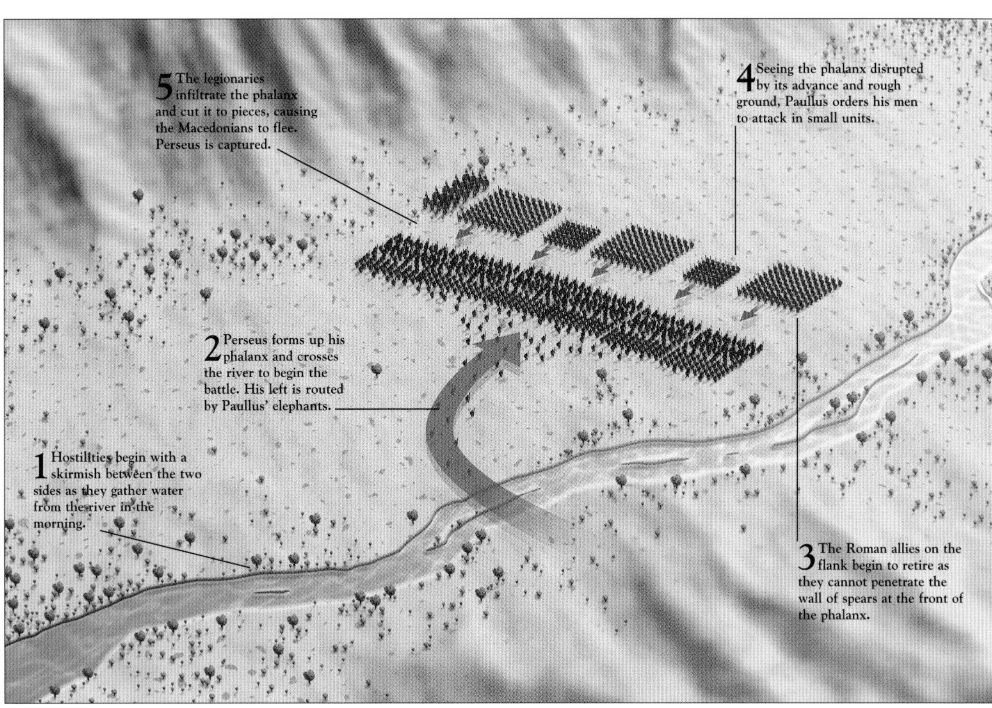
5 The legionaries infiltrate the phalanx and cut it to pieces, causing the Macedonians to flee. Perseus is captured.
4 Seeing the phalanx disrupted by its advance and rough ground, Paullus orders his men to attack in small units.
2 Perseus forms up his phalanx and crosses the river to begin the battle. His left is routed by Paullus' elephants.
1 Hostilities begin with a skirmish between the two sides as they gather water from the river in the morning.
3 The Roman allies on the flank begin to retire as they cannot penetrate the wall of spears at the front of the phalanx.

Pydna marked a confirmation that the old order was changing. Perseus dreamt of reviving the old Macedonian empire. It was another legion versus phalanx battle and Roman versatility prevailed in the end.

LOCATION

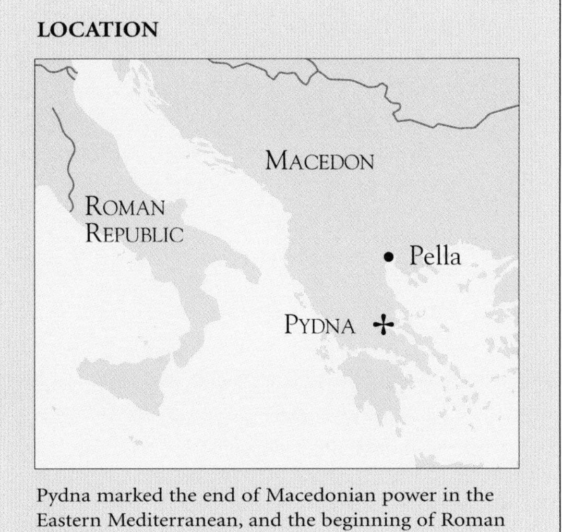
MACEDON
ROMAN REPUBLIC
Pella
PYDNA

Pydna marked the end of Macedonian power in the Eastern Mediterranean, and the beginning of Roman hegemony. Macedon came under Roman protection.

Although Macedonia's days of greatness were over, it remained a thorn in the Roman side. In 168BC, legions under the consul Lucius Aemilius Paullus marched on its king, Perseus, to teach him a lesson. At the Battle of Pydna, the mighty Macedonian phalanx – a huge wall of long spears – pressed forward in the traditional manner, crushing its foes like a giant spiked steamroller. But it inevitably lost some of its cohesion as it advanced uphill, and the battle dissolved into a desperate infantry struggle, with the smaller, nimbler maniple groups of the Roman legion more adept at the hand-to-hand fighting that ensued.

Although equipped with small shields and swords or daggers, the Macedonians had received minimal training. When the great phalanx was shattered, massacre followed, with around 25,000 Macedonians killed or taken prisoner, while Roman casualties amounted to around 100 men. Perseus was among those of the Macedonian cavalry who fled the field back to his capital at Pella, his dreams of reviving the glories of Alexander the Great in tatters.

TIMELINE

1500–1000BC	1000–500BC	500BC–0AD	0–500AD	500–1000AD	1000–1500AD	1500–2000AD

Emmaus 165BC

MACCABEAN REVOLT

JUDEAN VICTORY

KEY FACTS

WHO The Jewish rebel army of Judas Maccabeus against the Seleucid army of Ptolemy, Gorgias and Nicanor.

WHAT The punitive expedition of the Seleucid government was defeated and put to flight as Judas Maccabeus adapted his original battle plan to exploit his enemy's vulnerability.

WHERE Emmaus, near the foothills of Judea.

WHEN 165BC

WHY The Seleucid government sought to put down the troublesome revolt of the Jews led by Judas Maccabeus.

OUTCOME The Jewish rebels continued a string of victories against the numerically and technologically superior Seleucids, defeating them again at Beth-Zur a year later, entering Jerusalem and rededicating their Temple.

For over a century, the inhabitants of Judea had lived with a great degree of religious freedom, as subjects of the Egyptians and then of the Seleucid government after the province had been taken by force in 198BC. Attempts to force them to change their religious practices, however, incited revolt.

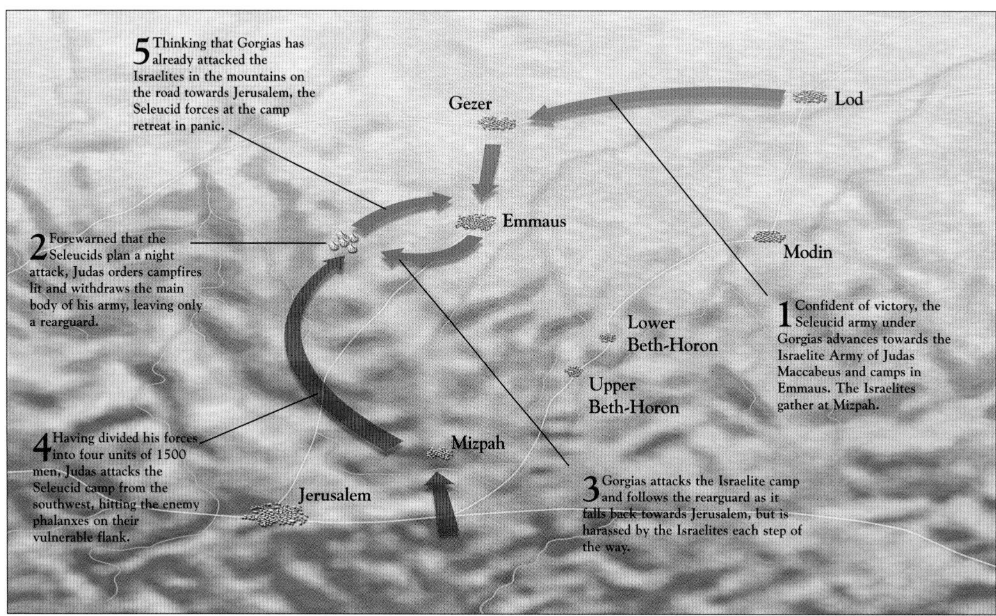
5 Thinking that Gorgias has already attacked the Israelites in the mountains on the road towards Jerusalem, the Seleucid forces at the camp retreat in panic.
Gezer
Lod
Emmaus
Modin
2 Forewarned that the Seleucids plan a night attack, Judas orders campfires lit and withdraws the main body of his army, leaving only a rearguard.
Lower Beth-Horon
Upper Beth-Horon
1 Confident of victory, the Seleucid army under Gorgias advances towards the Israelite Army of Judas Maccabeus and camps in Emmaus. The Israelites gather at Mizpah.
4 Having divided his forces into four units of 1500 men, Judas attacks the Seleucid camp from the southwest, hitting the enemy phalanxes on their vulnerable flank.
Mizpah
Jerusalem
3 Gorgias attacks the Israelite camp and follows the rearguard as it falls back towards Jerusalem, but is harassed by the Israelites each step of the way.

Judas Maccebeus could never beat the Seleucids in a set-piece battle, so his tactics were geared to splitting up his army into units and harassing the larger massed forces of the enemy at opportune moments.

Judas Maccabeus of Judea revolted against attempts by the Seleucids to 'Hellenize' Judea, forcing them to follow the gods and mores of Greek tradition. Judas commanded a ragtag band of patriots against overwhelming numbers of professional soldiers and knew he could not win a direct confrontation against the Seleucids' up-to-date Greek army, settling for guerrilla tactics. When three commanders – Ptolemy, Nicanor and Gorgias – marched on Judea to put down the Jewish rebellion, Judas responded accordingly.

Ordering his troops to leave their campfires burning, plainly visible to the Seleucids, he slipped away with his entire force, except for a small rearguard of 200 men. Gorgias attacked the vacated Jewish camp and took the bait, believing that the rearguard, withdrawing up the valley towards Jerusalem, was the entire army of Judea. As they pursued the rearguard, the Seleucids were set upon by small bands of rebels, who harassed them relentlessly in the darkness. Further attacks led to the disintegration of the Seleucid phalanx. As they fled to the plains, Judas maintained tight control of his forces, urging them to complete the rout of the Seleucids before halting to plunder. It had been a stunning victory against the odds.

LOCATION

SELEUCID EMPIRE

Emmaus

Jerusalem

EGYPT

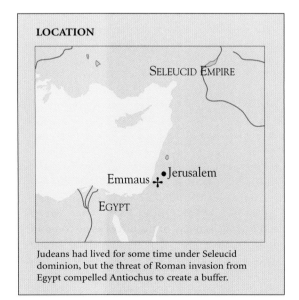

Judeans had lived for some time under Seleucid dominion, but the threat of Roman invasion from Egypt compelled Antiochus to create a buffer.

TIMELINE

1500–1000BC	1000–500BC	500BC–0AD	0–500AD	500–1000AD	1000–1500AD	1500–2000AD

Beth–Zechariah 162BC

KEY FACTS

WHO Judas Maccabeus and his rebels had defeated the Seleucid general Lysias two years previously, but Lysias was more than ready for a second encounter.

WHAT To succeed in his ultimate goal of restoring Israel as an independent power, Judas Maccabeus knew that he would have to defeat Lysias in a pitched battle.

WHERE The citadel at Beth-Zechariah, Jerusalem's last external defence.

WHEN 162BC

WHY Either Israel would defend its capital or it would fail as a nation – Judas Maccabeus had sufficient faith in his own skills and his army to risk a fight to the finish.

OUTCOME One of the most feared weapons in the Hellenistic arsenal – elephants – broke the Jewish army and almost completely destroyed a resurgent Israel.

Only a single fortress remained to the Seleucid overlords of Judea, but the latter's resourceful, brave leader Judas Maccabeus found that his hopes of prolonging his state's defiance would be crushed under the feet of an intimidating elephant core.

MACCABEAN REVOLT

SELEUCIDIAN VICTORY

The Seleucids would put on a crushing show of force in reducing the Judeans, but Lysias later showed unusual restraint in allowing them to continue with their religious practices.

LOCATION

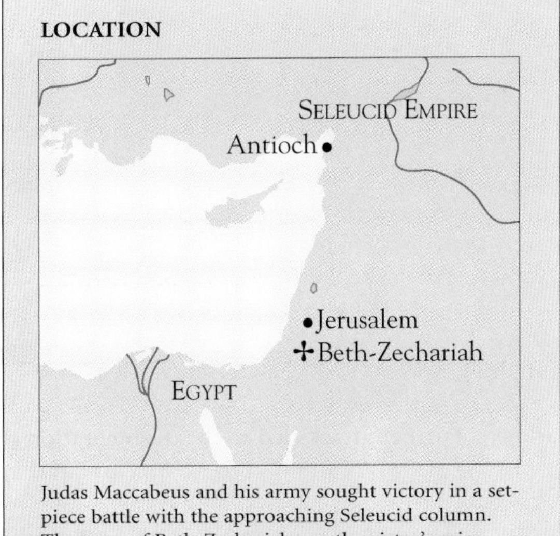
SELEUCID EMPIRE
Antioch
Jerusalem
Beth-Zechariah
EGYPT

Judas Maccabeus and his army sought victory in a set-piece battle with the approaching Seleucid column. The town of Beth-Zechariah was the victor's prize.

On five occasions, Judas Maccabeus had fought and beaten the armies of the Seleucid Empire, reducing its presence in Jerusalem to an isolated garrison, but now General Lysias, a viceroy of the Seleucid Empire, determined to meet him in a massive set-piece battle.

Lysias' force included a terrifying elephant core, and as his huge column of some 50,000 men moved up towards Beth-Zur, Maccabeus moved back to narrower terrain, where he hoped there would not be room for the weight of the elephants and their support forces to bear down upon his army. But as the Seleucid elephant column ground onwards, a collapse of his line was inevitable.

Judas Maccabeus had no choice but to retreat into the fortification of Beth-Zechariah, leading his army through the city, and leaving as many of his forces as he could in the fortifications. He was clearly not yet ready to submit, but Lysias, by a display of military strength, and by then permitting the Jews to continue with their religious rites and sacrifices, had dampened the flame of rebellion.

TIMELINE

1500–1000BC	1000–500BC	500BC–0AD	0–500AD	500–1000AD	1000–1500AD	1500–2000AD

Beth–Zechariah

BETH-ZECHARIAH

For years, Judea had cheekily resisted the might of the Seleucid Empire, its small army's guerilla tactics proving quite fruitful. However, meeting a full-strength army in a set-piece battle was never likely to work in their favour, and they were forced to beat a retreat towards the hilltop fortress of Beth-Zechariah. The Seleucid army was no less than 50,000 strong, but if that was not daunting enough, it could also call upon an elephant core. Judea's rebellion would literally be crushed beneath their feet, though the Seleucids would be merciful in victory.

Aquae Sextae 102BC

KEY FACTS

WHO A Roman consular army under Gaius Marius (157–86BC), consisting of two legions and two *alae* of cavalry, plus supporting units for a total of around 30,000–35,000 Roman troops, versus the Germanic Teutones tribe.

WHAT Migration by the Germanic tribes threatened the security of Rome. Marius brought the enemy to decisive battle.

WHERE Aquae Sextae (now Aix-en-Provence) in southern France.

WHEN 102BC

WHY Friction between Rome and the Germanic tribes was constant, and the migratory nature of some tribes inevitably brought them into conflict with Rome.

OUTCOME The Germanic barbarians tried to charge uphill against formed and waiting legionary troops, and were crushingly defeated.

Aqua Sextae proved the superiority of the professional, well-equipped Roman legion to the physically brave, but poorly armed German warrior. Its decisive victory also led to the eternal glory of Gaius Marius himself, named as the third founder of Rome.

ROME V GERMANIC TRIBES

ROME WIN

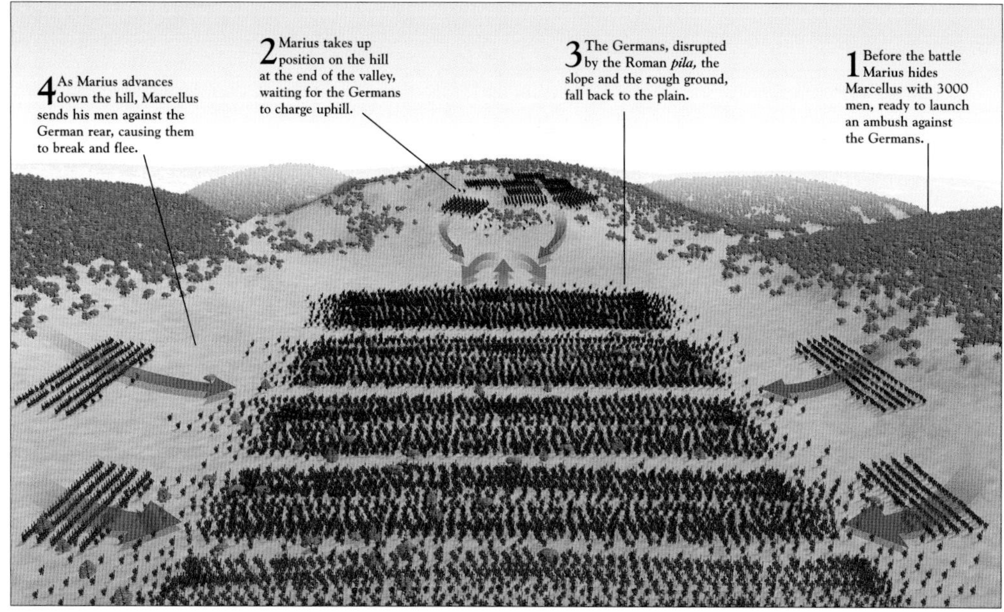

4 As Marius advances down the hill, Marcellus sends his men against the German rear, causing them to break and flee.
2 Marius takes up position on the hill at the end of the valley, waiting for the Germans to charge uphill.
3 The Germans, disrupted by the Roman *pila*, the slope and the rough ground, fall back to the plain.
1 Before the battle Marius hides Marcellus with 3000 men, ready to launch an ambush against the Germans.

The Germanic warriors were noted for their tenacity, but, confronted by the disciplined legions of Rome at Aqua Sextae, they had no answers to the short *gladius* swords of the legionaries.

When a Germanic invasion of Rome threatened in 102 BC, Gaius Marius, a leading figure in the development of the Roman Army, led a consular army north to intercept the enemy near Aquae Sextae. The barbarians' soldiers were experienced, disciplined warriors, but their weapons were poor, and they had little armour. Their dense formation made an easy target for missile weapons such as the massed pila (javelins) of the Roman legions.

The battle took place in a heavy forested valley surrounded by steep sides, and as the Germans advanced uphill to attack, they received a shower of pila. As the two forces came into contact, Romans stabbed confidently at their tired opponents, the legionaries' gladius, a short sword, ideally suited to such combat.

The Teutones were pushed back downhill where they rallied and began to form a shield wall, but a rear attack smashed their resistance. The barbarians' camp was stormed, sacked and burned and several German chieftains taken back to Rome for public execution by strangulation. Marius was hailed as a great hero and revered as a third founder of Rome, serving as consul no less than seven times.

LOCATION

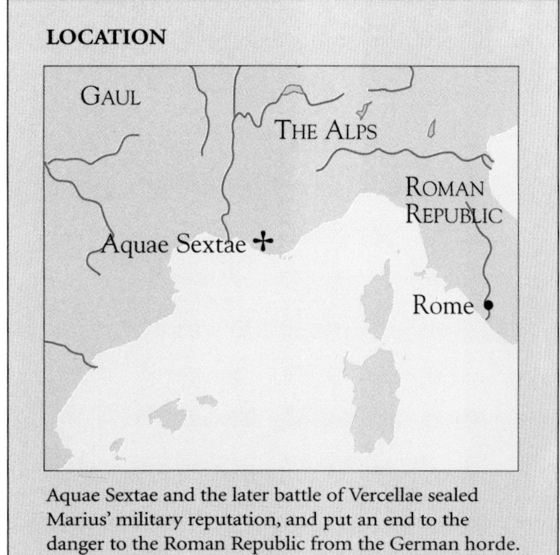

GAUL
THE ALPS
ROMAN REPUBLIC
Aquae Sextae
Rome

Aquae Sextae and the later battle of Vercellae sealed Marius' military reputation, and put an end to the danger to the Roman Republic from the German horde.

TIMELINE

1500–1000BC	1000–500BC	500BC–0AD	0–500AD	500–1000AD	1000–1500AD	1500–2000AD

Pompey's Sea Campaign 67BC

Piracy was rife on the Mediterranean in the first century BC, not merely preying on ships, but even raiding Italian ports. Pompey, the Roman consul, was put in command of a naval fleet to deal with the problem.

ROME v PIRATES

ROMAN VICTORY

KEY FACTS

WHO Gnaeus Pompeius Magnus (Pompey) (106–48BC) at the head of a 50-strong fleet of ships, against a mixed band of Mediterranean pirates.

WHAT In a rapid 45-day campaign, Pompey swept across the seas to rid them of the scourge of piracy.

WHERE The Mediterranean waters off Italy, Sicily, North Africa, Sardinia and Spain.

WHEN 67BC

WHY Piracy had been rife for over a century, after the decline of Greek Rhodes, which had acted as police force. Increasingly bold pirates had been carrying their raids inland. Grain cargo routes were affected.

OUTCOME Pompey achieved rapid results, though his campaign of re-exacting tribute and resettling the pirates did not go down well with all Romans, and piracy would remain an issue.

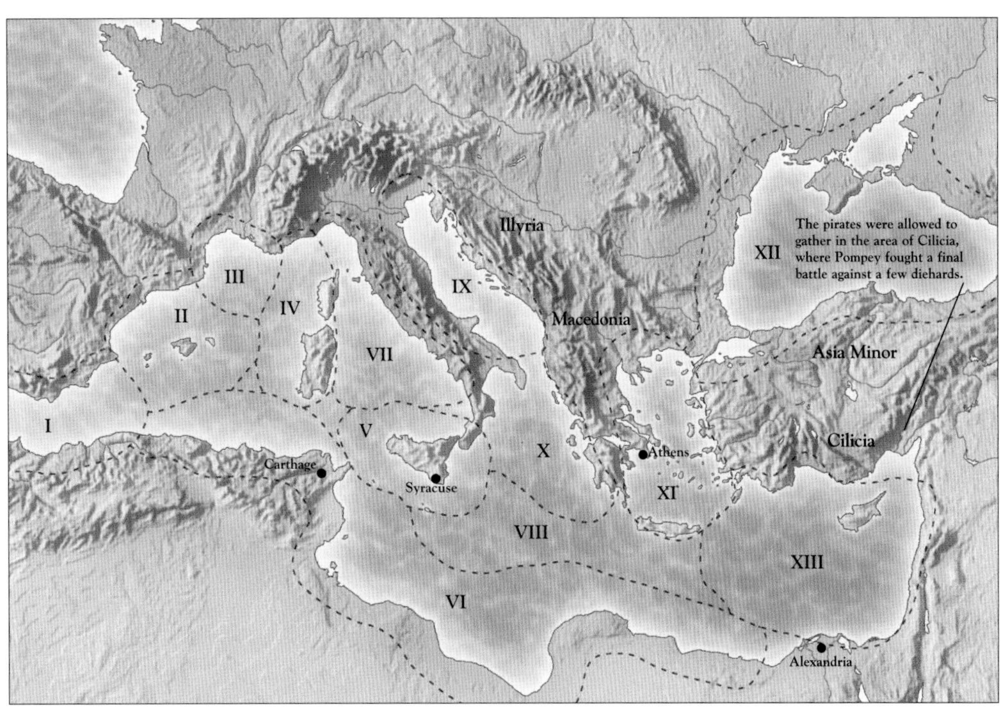
Illyria
III
II
IV
IX
XII
The pirates were allowed to gather in the area of Cilicia, where Pompey fought a final battle against a few diehards.
Macedonia
VII
Asia Minor
I
V
X
Athens
Cilicia
Carthage
Syracuse
XI
VIII
XIII
VI
Alexandria

Pompey's ships took on the pirates in a series of Mediterranean sea battles, before bottling the residue up for one last clash at Cilicia. Pompey divided into the Mediterranean into 13 units leaving Cilicia (deliberately) unguarded.

LOCATION

THE MEDITERRANEAN

The success of Pompey's campaign against the pirates ensured that no challenge to Rome's navy would emerge again.

In the first century BC, pirates were freely plundering the coasts of Italy, Greece and Asia Minor. Rome was concerned because it threatened critical grain supplies. Pompey, who had built up such an impressive military reputation that at the age of 35 he had been elected consul, was put in a charge of a naval fleet. He was given autonomous command to clear the entire Mediterranean and Black Seas, as well as land within 80km (50 miles) of the sea, from the scourge of pirates. His resources were formidable, as he took charge of 500 ships, 120,000 soldiers and 5000 cavalry.

Within three months, the seas were entirely swept clean of pirates. Pompey drove them from Sicily and the coasts of North Africa, before sweeping across the Mediterranean from Spain to the east. A pirate rabble duly gathered in Cilicia for a last stand, and there was a final sea battle in the bay of Coracesium. Although most pirates surrendered easily, Pompey's clemency proved controversial, and piracy remained an issue a decade later.

TIMELINE

1500–1000BC	1000–500BC	500BC–0AD	0–500AD	500–1000AD	1000–1500AD	1500–2000AD

Siege of Jerusalem 63BC

KEY FACTS

WHO A Roman army under Gnaeus Pompeius Magnus (Pompey) (106–48BC) versus Jewish forces loyal to Aristobulus (104–103 BC).

WHAT Pompey's forces gradually wore down the defences around the Temple and then launched a successful assault.

WHERE The city of Jerusalem in Judea.

WHEN 63BC

WHY Pompey had wide-ranging powers to end a threat to Rome, and decided that there were sufficient grounds for intervention in Jerusalem.

OUTCOME Pompey's forces were successful and captured the Temple. He then installed a High Priest of his own choosing.

Disputes among Jewish factions were common. In 63BC, the Jewish princes Aristobulus and Hyrcanus were in conflict, and this led to disaster when the Romans under Pompey decided to become involved.

ROMAN CAMPAIGN

ROMAN VICTORY

The defilement of their temple by Roman troops caused many Jews to commit suicide rather than face the indignity of seeing their oppressors impose their own High Priest.

Pompey, the Roman general, was involved in a Jewish power struggle between two Judean princes, Aristobulus and Hyrcanus. While Pompey sided with Hyrcanus, Aristobulus' supporters remained in control of Jerusalem's Temple and its environs. Pompey laid siege for three months before ordering an attack. Covered by intense shooting by their artillery and auxiliary missile troops, the assault columns made their way forwards. The gates were attacked with battering rams, while infantrymen charged up a specially built ramp and onto the wall. Attacking at multiple points split the defenders and made it difficult to reinforce a threatened area.

The assault was bloody and one-sided. When defeat was obvious, many Jews committed suicide rather than see their Temple defiled by the Romans. Judea became a Roman possession and Hyrcanus was named 'Ethnarch' (National Leader) of Judea, while Aristobulus and his children were taken as prisoners to Rome, where they were forced to take part in Pompey's triumphal entry to the city.

LOCATION

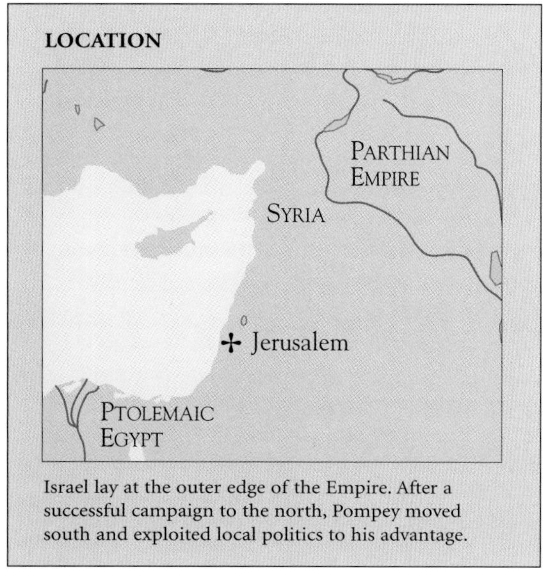

PARTHIAN EMPIRE
SYRIA
Jerusalem
PTOLEMAIC EGYPT

Israel lay at the outer edge of the Empire. After a successful campaign to the north, Pompey moved south and exploited local politics to his advantage.

TIMELINE

1500–1000BC	1000–500BC	500BC–0AD	0–500AD	500–1000AD	1000–1500AD	1500–2000AD

Carrhae 53BC

WARS OF THE FIRST TRIUMVIRATE

PARTHIAN VICTORY

Crassus' Parthian Campaign of 53BC was one of the great military disasters of Roman history. A Roman infantry force of 42,000 was harried to defeat by horse archers, whose tactic of the 'Parthian shot' has entered modern language.

KEY FACTS

WHO The Romans under Marcus Licinius Crassus (115–53BC) made an unprovoked invasion of Parthian territory.

WHAT The Romans formed a hollow square, but 5500 were lured out in pursuit of the horse archers and massacred by the cataphracts. The rest were steadily shot down. An overnight halt at the unprovisioned town of Carrhae failed to halt the killing.

WHERE Carrhae, 48km (30 miles) south of Edessa in Syria.

WHEN 53BC

WHY Crassus needed a military success to further his political rivalry with the other Triumvirs, Pompey and Julius Caesar.

OUTCOME Only 5000 of the Roman army escaped, 10,000 surrendered, and the rest, including Crassus, were slaughtered.

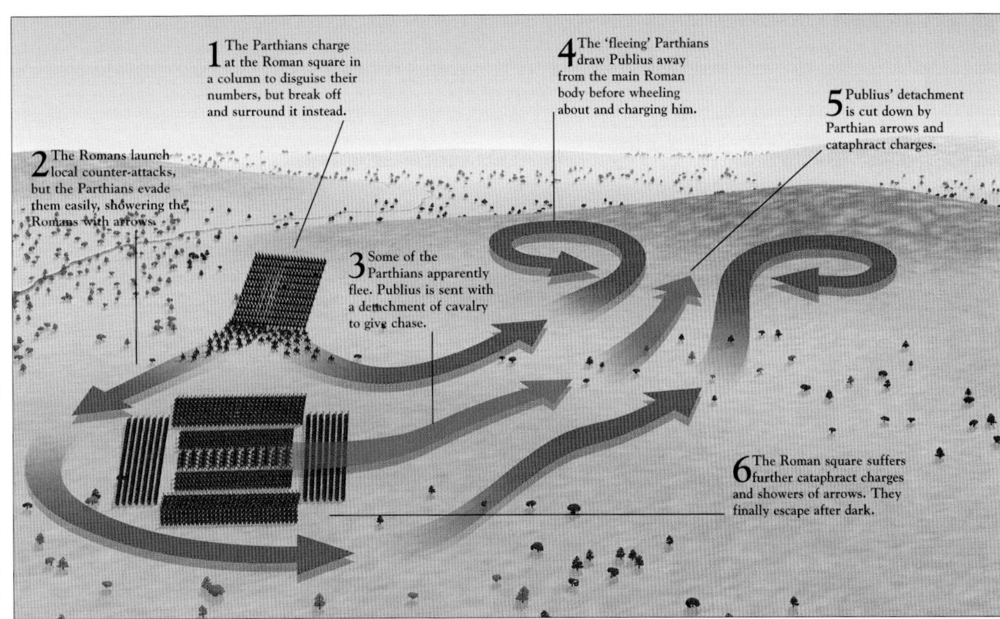
1 The Parthians charge at the Roman square in a column to disguise their numbers, but break off and surround it instead.
2 The Romans launch local counter-attacks, but the Parthians evade them easily, showering the Romans with arrows.
3 Some of the Parthians apparently flee. Publius is sent with a detachment of cavalry to give chase.
4 The 'fleeing' Parthians draw Publius away from the main Roman body before wheeling about and charging him.
5 Publius' detachment is cut down by Parthian arrows and cataphract charges.
6 The Roman square suffers further cataphract charges and showers of arrows. They finally escape after dark.

Experienced Roman campaigners probably thought there were few tricks anyone could teach them, but caught in the vast empty terrain of the Syrian desert, they were helpless against these lightly armoured, swift-moving mounted archers.

Marcus Licinius Crassus needed military success to equal his rivals Pompey and Julius Caesar, and invaded Parthia. But at Carrhae, he faced a Parthian army based around a new troop type, the cataphract – a fully armoured, lance-carrying horseman – supported by rapid-firing mounted archers, against whom the Romans had little overall combat experience.

In the vast emptiness of the Syrian Desert, Crassus' huge, hollow square formation was attacked by the horse archers whose nimble ponies kept them out of reach while they displayed their mastery of the 'Parthian shot' – a tactic involving riding directly away from the enemy at speed, and then skewing anti-clockwise round in the saddle and shooting the bow directly over the horse's rump.

When Crassus ordered his son Publius to lead a desperate foray out to attack the horse archers, the result was slaughter. Meanwhile the cataphracts made a series of controlled charges, murderously effective in a small area, but quickly pulled back if they seemed threatened. When Crassus fled, the Parthians pursued him and he was eventually slaughtered along with, perhaps, as many as 20,000 Romans.

LOCATION

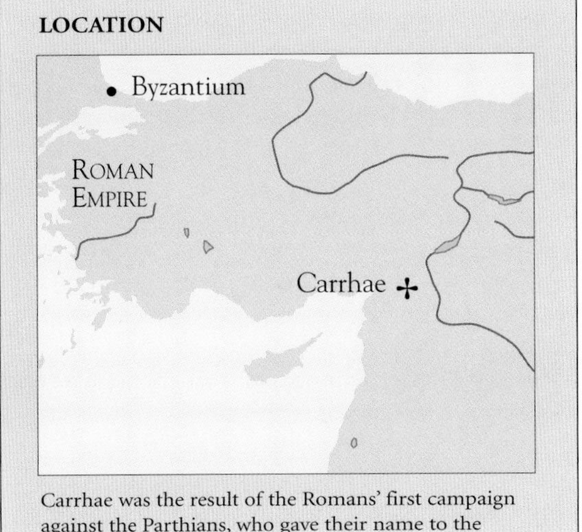
Byzantium
ROMAN EMPIRE
Carrhae

Carrhae was the result of the Romans' first campaign against the Parthians, who gave their name to the 'Parthian shot', an arrow delivered as the bowman fled.

TIMELINE

1500–1000BC	1000–500BC	500BC–0AD	0–500AD	500–1000AD	1000–1500AD	1500–2000AD

Alesia 52BC

KEY FACTS

WHO Roughly 70,000 Roman troops under Gaius Julius Caesar (100–44BC), versus around 80,000 infantry and 15,000 cavalry under the Gallic chieftain Vercingetorix (d. 46 BC) besieged inside the fortress.

WHAT The Roman forces built extensive field fortifications to pen the Gauls within their fortress and to prevent relief. Gallic reinforcements and relief efforts were beaten off and the siege was maintained.

WHERE Mount Auxois, near what is now Dijon.

WHEN 52BC

WHY Julius Caesar embarked on a campaign to pacify Gaul and bring the Gallic tribes within the empire. The Gauls resisted fiercely.

OUTCOME Break-out and relief attempts were contained, and the starving Gauls were forced to surrender.

The fall of Alesia was the death knell for Gallic independence. Defeated by the Roman armies under Gaius Julius Caesar, the Gauls fell under the sway of the expanding Republican empire. Operations continued into the following year, but it was at Alesia that the Gauls were broken.

GALLIC WAR

ROMAN VICTORY

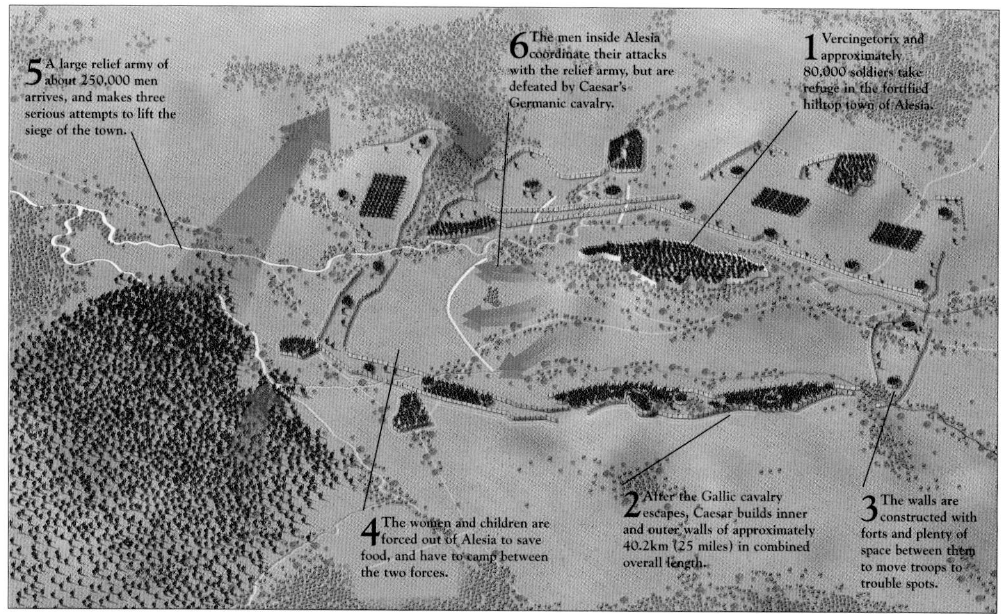

5 A large relief army of about 250,000 men arrives, and makes three serious attempts to lift the siege of the town.
6 The men inside Alesia coordinate their attacks with the relief army, but are defeated by Caesar's Germanic cavalry.
1 Vercingetorix and approximately 80,000 soldiers take refuge in the fortified hilltop town of Alesia.
4 The women and children are forced out of Alesia to save food, and have to camp between the two forces.
2 After the Gallic cavalry escapes, Caesar builds inner and outer walls of approximately 40.2km (25 miles) in combined overall length.
3 The walls are constructed with forts and plenty of space between them to move troops to trouble spots.

The Gauls fought a strong rearguard action at Alesia, forcing the Romans to erect a series of field fortifications, and to face attack on two fronts. In the end, however, proud Vercingetorix, in full battle armour, had to ride out to surrender.

LOCATION

GERMANIA

GAUL

Alesia

The town of Alesia is now called Alise-Ste.-Reine, on Mount Auxois. It was in Central Gaul, a province that Caesar himself had added to Rome's empire.

Under chieftain Vercingetorix, the Gauls put up ferocious resistance to Julius Caesar's campaign of conquest, but when he forced them to retreat into the hilltop town of Alesia, they became trapped, as the Romans erected a series of field fortifications, including wide ditches and earth and timber walls. Cut off from supplies, Vercingetorix held out for the relief army. When it arrived, Caesar was forced to defend his positions from attack from outside, while Vercingetorix was leading an attack from within.

A confused and bloody battle erupted with Roman troops defending their positions using javelins and light siege engines called scorpions, and hurling stones that had been readied for just such an occasion. Eventually, Vercingetorix's assault faltered and with it any hope of linking up with the relief army. Disheartened, the latter melted away, leaving the siege unbroken.

The following day, the starving defenders of Alesia agreed to Caesar's demand for unconditional surrender. Vercingetorix, dressed in his most impressive armour and riding a fine horse, laid down his weapons before Caesar and was taken away as a prisoner.

TIMELINE

1500–1000BC	1000–500BC	500BC–0AD	0–500AD	500–1000AD	1000–1500AD	1500–2000AD

Actium 31BC

WARS OF THE SECOND TRIUMVIRATE

OCTAVIAN VICTORY

KEY FACTS

WHO Octavian, the Roman Princeps (first citizen), against the combined forces of Mark Antony and Cleopatra in a Roman civil war.

WHAT Mark Antony's ships got trapped at Actium where the more mobile fleet of Octavian was able to out-flank him.

WHERE Off the promontory of Actium in the Ionian Sea.

WHEN 31BC

WHY The Second Triumvirate of Octavian, Mark Antony and Lepidus had broken down and there were fears Mark Antony threatened a break-up of the Empire through his alliance with Cleopatra.

OUTCOME Mark Antony's fleet was destroyed and Octavian, eventually to become Augustus, was left in complete control.

Mark Antony's affair with the Egyptian Queen Cleopatra seemed to threaten the unity of Rome. When Octavian declared war on Cleopatra, he had effectively also declared war on his fellow Roman who, while his position in Italy was weak, still posed a considerable threat at sea.

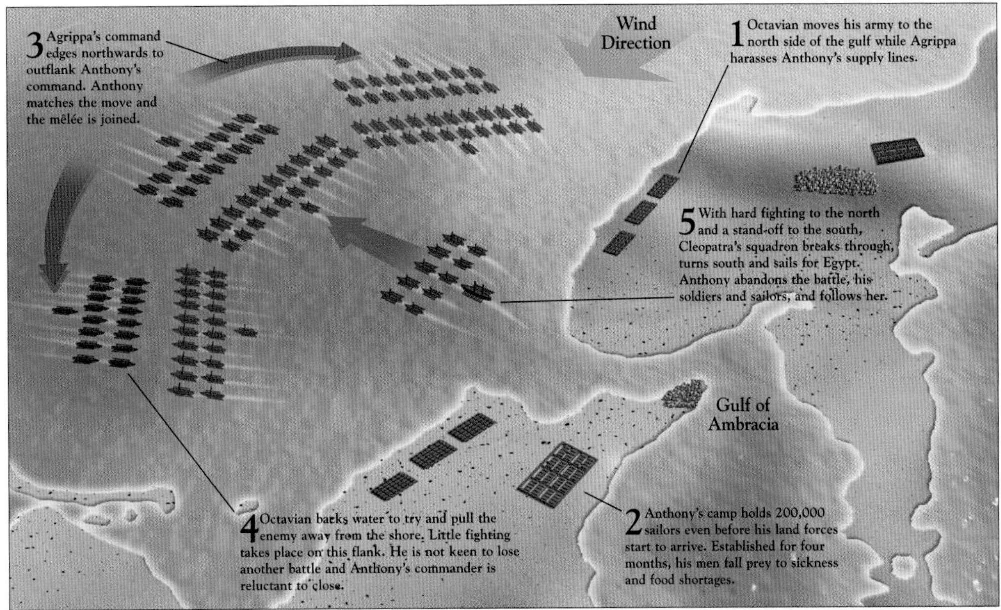
Wind Direction
1 Octavian moves his army to the north side of the gulf while Agrippa harasses Anthony's supply lines.
2 Anthony's camp holds 200,000 sailors even before his land forces start to arrive. Established for four months, his men fall prey to sickness and food shortages.
3 Agrippa's command edges northwards to outflank Anthony's command. Anthony matches the move and the mêlée is joined.
4 Octavian backs water to try and pull the enemy away from the shore. Little fighting takes place on this flank. He is not keen to lose another battle and Anthony's commander is reluctant to close.
5 With hard fighting to the north and a stand-off to the south, Cleopatra's squadron breaks through, turns south and sails for Egypt. Anthony abandons the battle, his soldiers and sailors, and follows her.
Gulf of Ambracia

Agrippa was able to wage a war of attrition when Mark Antony locked up his fleet at Actium, and when a sea battle finally began, the smaller, more mobile ships of Octavian had the advantage.

Anthony knew his best hope of success over Octavian was at sea where, although his opponent had more ships, they were smaller and less well-equipped. He also knew that an invasion on mainland Italy using his Egyptian soldiers would be regarded as a foreign attack on the homeland, not civil war.

But by planting his fleet and army at Actium, he gave the initiative to Octavian's general, Agrippa, who took full advantage, interrupting food supplies and waging a war of attrition that left Antony's men seriously under strength.

OUTMANOEUVRED

Mark Antony's warships were mostly gigantic quinqueremes, huge galleys with massive rams, whereas Agrippa had smaller, more mobile ships and better-trained crews who were fresh and healthy. When battle began, they proved more adept at outmanoeuvring Mark Antony's larger ships in the Gulf, firing their volleys of arrows and catapulted stones and then quickly retreating out of shot. While Mark Antony and Cleopatra were able to escape to Egypt, the majority of their ships surrendered or were set on fire.

LOCATION

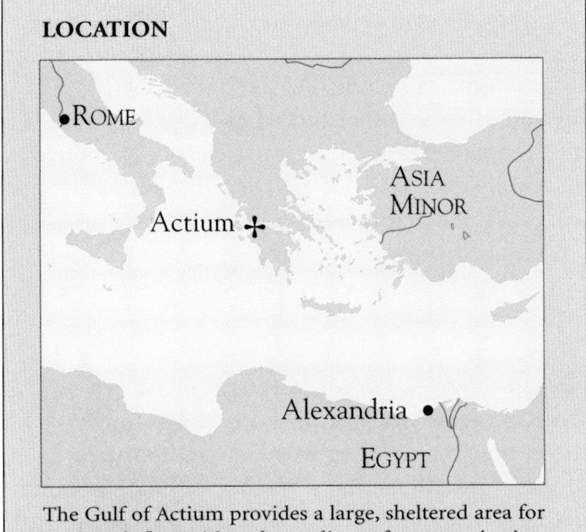
ROME
ASIA MINOR
Actium
Alexandria
EGYPT

The Gulf of Actium provides a large, sheltered area for Anthony's fleet with seaborne lines of communication and supply back to Egypt.

TIMELINE

1500–1000BC	1000–500BC	500BC–0AD	0–500AD	500–1000AD	1000–1500AD	1500–2000AD

Teutoberger Wald AD9

KEY FACTS

WHO Three Roman legions under Publius Quinctilius Varus (d. AD9), with supporting cavalry, versus Germanic troops of the Cherusci tribe under their chief Arminius (18BC–AD19).

WHAT The Roman forces were betrayed, ambushed and massacred by the Cherusci in the Teutoberger Wald.

WHERE Along the line of march towards winter quarters in the deep forest, near Osnabrück in northwest Germany.

WHEN September–October AD9

WHY Tiring of Roman policies, the Cherusci turned on their allies and used guerrilla tactics to destroy them in the forests, where standard legionary formations were ineffective.

OUTCOME Three Roman legions and supporting troops were annihilated. The Roman Empire never regained control of the Germanic frontier.

Teutoberger Wald was a shocking defeat for the Roman Empire, and one that ensured that the Germanic frontier was never fully pacified. The battle had consequences that changed the course of European history.

ROME'S GERMANIC WARS

GERMANIC VICTORY

Varius, the Roman general, prepares to commit suicide as his legions are slaughtered around him in the massacre at Teutoberger Wald.

LOCATION

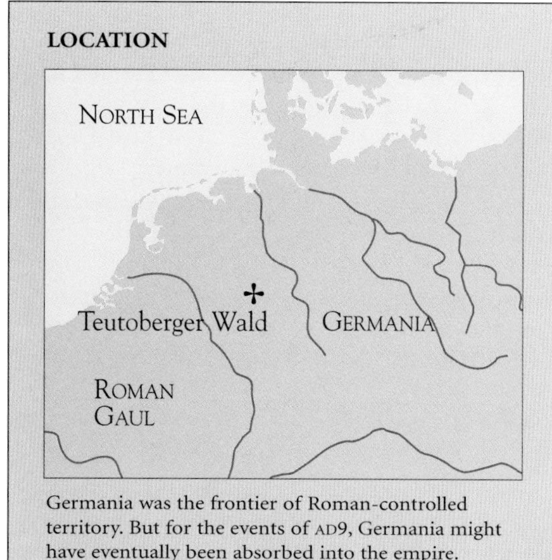

NORTH SEA
Teutoberger Wald
GERMANIA
ROMAN GAUL

Germania was the frontier of Roman-controlled territory. But for the events of AD9, Germania might have eventually been absorbed into the empire.

The Romans had been involved in a lengthy campaign to secure the Germanic frontier. But when Varus became governor of the province of Germania in AD6, his policies alienated several tribal leaders and their people. Arminius of the Cherusci tribe determined to remove the Roman presence from the frontier and when, after a successful campaign putting down various rebellions, Varus retired towards his winter quarters, Arminius' men tracked him through the wilds.

The route chosen by Varus was through the densely forested Teutoberger Wald. The thick forest was tough going, made worse by appalling weather conditions. As such, the well-drilled formations that were their strength became disorganized and fragmented. Troops became lost and straggled off into the forests. Shortly after, the attacks began.

The annihilation of the legions began with hit-and-run attacks by Germanic tribesmen at various points on the fragmented column. The slow-moving baggage and camp-followers meant that the legionaries could only plod on through the forest between attacks.

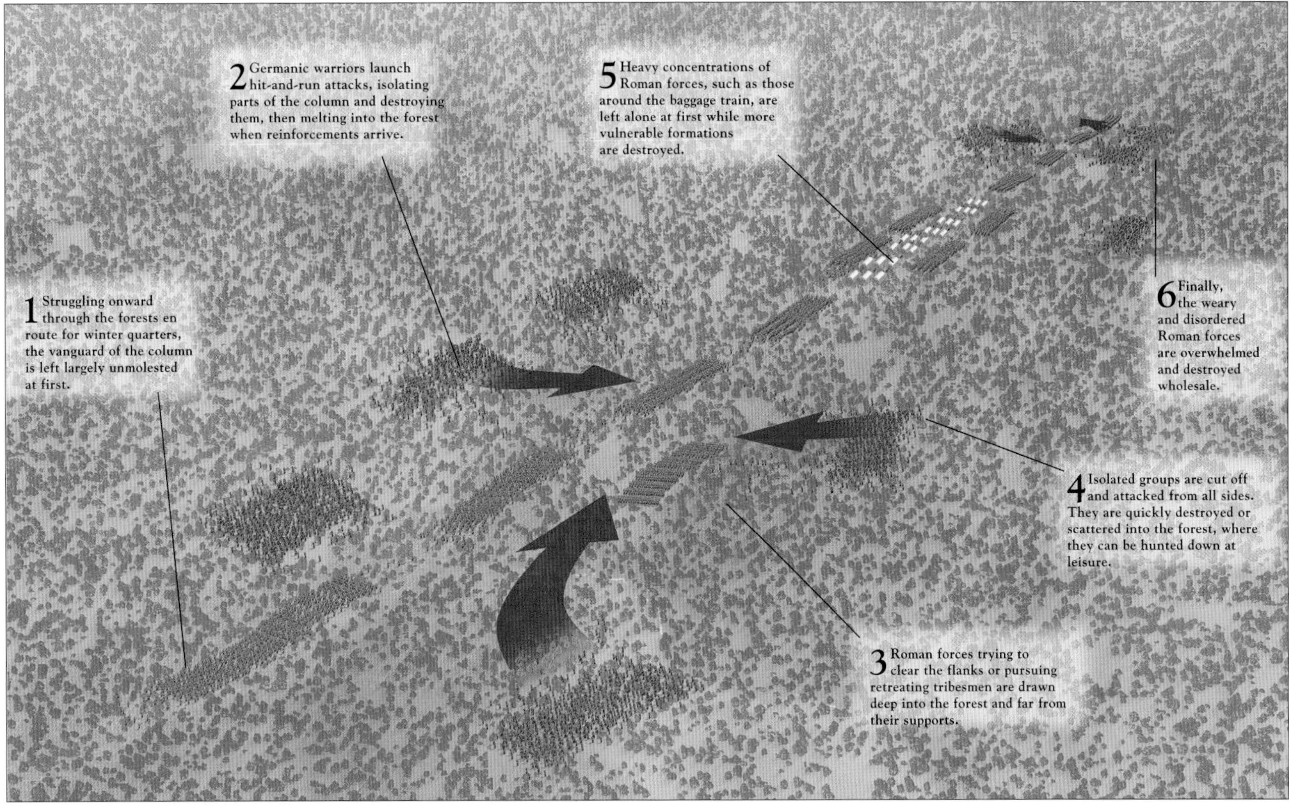
2 Germanic warriors launch hit-and-run attacks, isolating parts of the column and destroying them, then melting into the forest when reinforcements arrive.
5 Heavy concentrations of Roman forces, such as those around the baggage train, are left alone at first while more vulnerable formations are destroyed.
1 Struggling onward through the forests en route for winter quarters, the vanguard of the column is left largely unmolested at first.
6 Finally, the weary and disordered Roman forces are overwhelmed and destroyed wholesale.
4 Isolated groups are cut off and attacked from all sides. They are quickly destroyed or scattered into the forest, where they can be hunted down at leisure.
3 Roman forces trying to clear the flanks or pursuing retreating tribesmen are drawn deep into the forest and far from their supports.

Teutoberger Wald was grim terrain for the Roman army to fight a battle. Surrounded by thick forest and preyed upon by Germanic guerrilla warriors, it turned into a rain-soaked nightmare of ambush and sudden death.

The Romans fought back hard, their long training and excellent combat skills giving small groups of legionaries a fighting chance even against enemies who sprang out from ambush with no warning. But gradually the Roman force was worn down despite its best efforts.

Varus ordered his section of the column to halt and to prepare a fortified camp. Despite the attentions of Germanic warriors, Varus' legionaries fortified themselves with earthworks and cut logs, creating formidable defences. The baggage and camp-followers were placed within, defended by legionaries who were fighting for their very lives.

The camp held out for several days, during which additional groups straggled in. All were sadly depleted. They described a rain-soaked nightmare of ambush and sudden death; the forest filled with vast numbers of tribesmen. Gradually the Roman force was whittled down until only those holding out in their fort were left alive. Now the field fortification had become a prison around which the tribesmen gathered their strength. When they were ready, the final attack went in.

The Roman infantry on the walls of the camp put up a good fight. For a while it seemed that superior equipment and discipline might prevail over the raw courage of the tribal warriors, but there were simply too many of them. More and more barbarians poured into the camp, overwhelming what reserves there were and forcing the defenders away from their fortifications, back into the camp. It was all over but for the massacre.

The Roman cavalry, which had numbered about 1800 at the beginning of the action, made an attempt to break out and escape but it was dragged to a halt and cut down. Seeing that all was lost, Varus fell upon his own sword, thereby avoiding capture. Many tribunes and centurions also evaded the disgrace of capture by suicide or, more often, by being cut down as they fought on.

The head of Varus was sent to the Emperor Augustus in Rome, and the captured survivors were used as human sacrifices to the Germanic gods. The image of Rome as the invincible conqueror had been shattered at Teutoberger Wald, and helped ensure that Germany would never be fully absorbed into Roman Mediterranean culture.

TIMELINE

1500–1000BC	1000–500BC	500BC–0AD	0–500AD	500–1000AD	1000–1500AD	1500–2000AD

Siege of Jerusalem 70

KEY FACTS

WHO	A Roman army numbering around 35,000 under Titus Flavius Vespasianus – opposed by at least 24,000 rebel Jews led by Simon bar Giora.
WHAT	Jerusalem was besieged for much of the war and finally taken by storm.
WHERE	The city of Jerusalem in Judea.
WHEN	70
WHY	Outraged by practices allowed by the Romans, the Jews rebelled against their conquerors.
OUTCOME	The Jews were utterly defeated.

Although it started well for the rebels, the Jewish revolt that began in 66 ended in catastrophic defeat at the hands of Titus Flavius. The Jews suffered massive casualties, and Roman reprisals were savage.

ROMAN–JEWISH WARS

ROMAN VICTORY

Sickened by the disrespect shown by Romans to their religion, the Judeans had risen in revolt, but were pitilessly put down by the Romans who, not for the first time, stormed the walls of Jerusalem and the Temple.

LOCATION

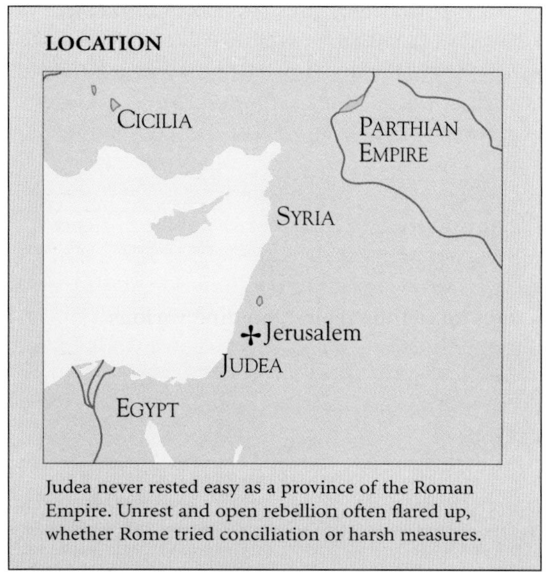
CILICIA
PARTHIAN EMPIRE
SYRIA
Jerusalem
JUDEA
EGYPT

Judea never rested easy as a province of the Roman Empire. Unrest and open rebellion often flared up, whether Rome tried conciliation or harsh measures.

Judea had been a Roman province for many years when the Jews broke out in rebellion in 66. The Roman general Titus Flavius Vespasianus made some progress in stamping out the insurrection, but when he was forced to return to Rome during a civil war (68–69) – from which he emerged as the Emperor Vespasian – the rebels continued their offensive. In 70, Vespasian appointed his son, also called Titus Flavius Vespasianus, to lead a new campaign to put down the revolt.

Titus's efforts centred around taking Jerusalem, strongly held and well fortified. Built on high ground, with two hills forming natural strong points, the Temple itself, surrounded by good, strong walls, was a formidable fortress and the Jews were prepared to defend their city fanatically. The leader of the Jewish revolt, Simon bar Giora, and his followers provided the main Jewish fighting forces. They were well equipped, experienced and also highly motivated.

Titus's army approached its objective cautiously, and set about establishing itself in position for a siege and

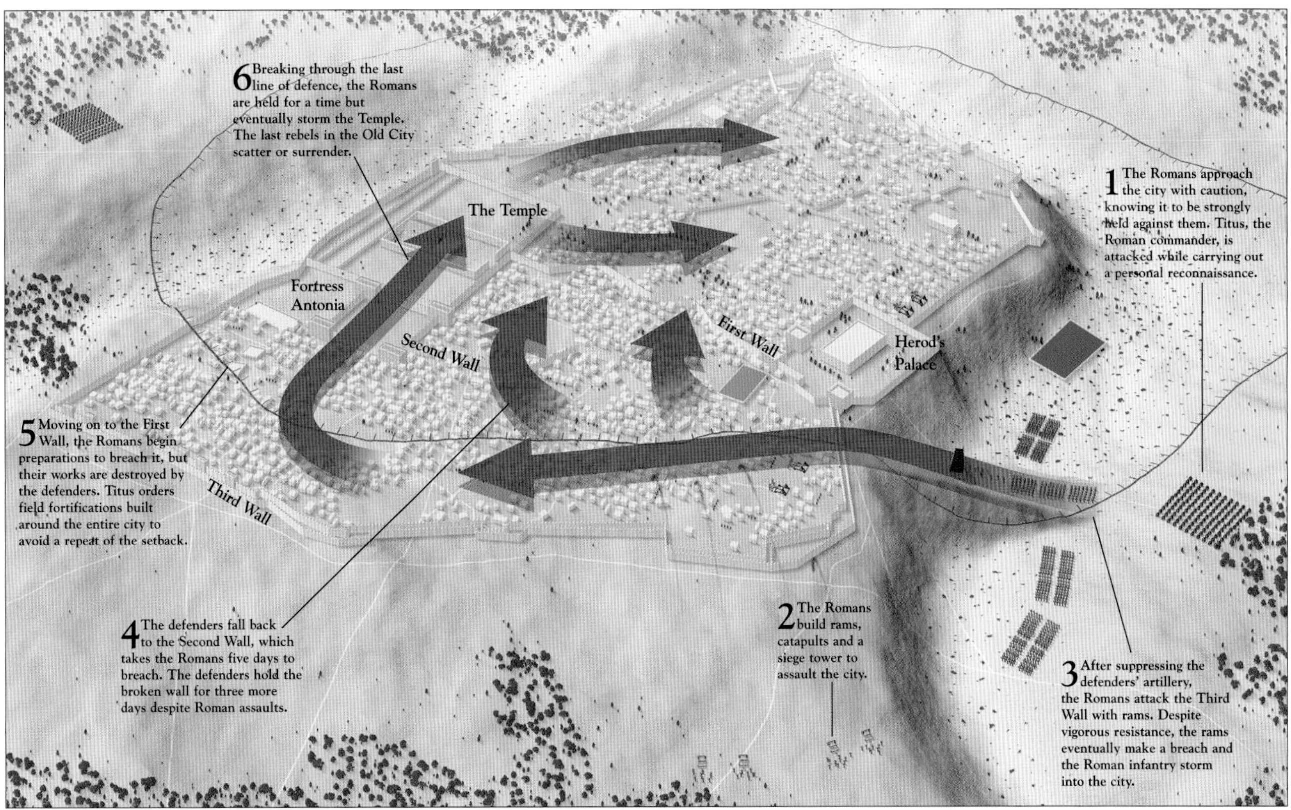
6 Breaking through the last line of defence, the Romans are held for a time but eventually storm the Temple. The last rebels in the Old City scatter or surrender.
The Temple
Fortress Antonia
Second Wall
First Wall
Herod's Palace
Third Wall
1 The Romans approach the city with caution, knowing it to be strongly held against them. Titus, the Roman commander, is attacked while carrying out a personal reconnaissance.
5 Moving on to the First Wall, the Romans begin preparations to breach it, but their works are destroyed by the defenders. Titus orders field fortifications built around the entire city to avoid a repeat of the setback.
4 The defenders fall back to the Second Wall, which takes the Romans five days to breach. The defenders hold the broken wall for three more days despite Roman assaults.
2 The Romans build rams, catapults and a siege tower to assault the city.
3 After suppressing the defenders' artillery, the Romans attack the Third Wall with rams. Despite vigorous resistance, the rams eventually make a breach and the Roman infantry storm into the city.

If the Romans were to suppress the Jewish revolt, it inevitably meant Jerusalem would eventually have to be taken. But this was a formidably located and fortified city, and it would take all the Roman's know-how to lower it.

eventual assault. However, while the legions were thus engaged, a large force sallied out of the east side of the city and attacked them. Some units fell back in disorder and others openly fled. Further attacks followed and Titus led a series of counter-attacks, in which he personally fought like a common trooper. Finally, the attack was beaten off.

Even though the siege was re-established, the defenders had no intention of being defeated easily. They tried various stratagems, including successfully luring a group of Roman soldiers close to the walls by offering to surrender. Many of the Romans were cut down in a hail of missiles.

Gradually, ramps were created which enabled battering rams to be deployed against the walls. Protected by the fire of artillery and archers, the rams began their work. The defenders did what they could, but after 15 days a breach was created, and the Romans were able to establish themselves in the city.

Further challenges lay ahead, not least the breaching of the inner 'First Wall', a strong fortification, determinedly held. Storming it was a hard task, and when more siege ramps were built against one of its towers, mines deliberately dug by the Jews underneath collapsed, bringing the ramps with them. Gradually, the siege work resumed, and eventually, they reached the Great Temple. Titus was keen this should not be damaged, understanding its huge symbolic meaning to the Jews, but at some point in the close-quarters fighting, it caught fire. Some efforts were made to douse it, but as the rebels were driven out, the victors were more interested in plunder than civil defence.

Now, the only part of the city still in Jewish hands was the Old City, which the Romans had access to via the wrecked Temple. Titus ordered an assault and began building ramps once again. By the time they were ready, the defenders were starving and demoralized. In the final assault most of the defenders scattered before the Romans could reach them and the rebellion more or less ended.

Titus paraded his troops and showered them with honours, then toured the region, holding various ceremonies and putting the seal on the re-conquest of Judea. Finally, he returned to Italy, in triumph, the high point of a special celebratory event being the formal execution, by strangulation, of Simon bar Giora.

Masada 73

KEY FACTS

Who In the mopping-up operations following the suppression of the Jewish revolt, the Romans commanded by Lucius Flavius Silva besieged a small Jewish force lead by Eleazar ben Yair in their hilltop fortress at Masada.

What The Romans built an encircling wall and eight camps to command the various approaches, followed by a huge ramp and a siege tower to assault the position.

Where Masada, overlooking the Dead Sea in modern Israel.

When 72 – May 73

Why After a prolonged period of terrorist atrocities, the Romans were determined to end the disruption to civil life and tax-collecting.

Outcome The Jews slew each other, rather than face the Roman swords.

In the aftermath of the Jewish revolt of 66, a Roman legion besieged a small garrison of religious zealots in the seemingly impregnable fortress of Masada. But Roman siege techniques were triumphant, and the zealots took their own lives to escape capture.

ROMAN–JEWISH WARS

ROMAN VICTORY

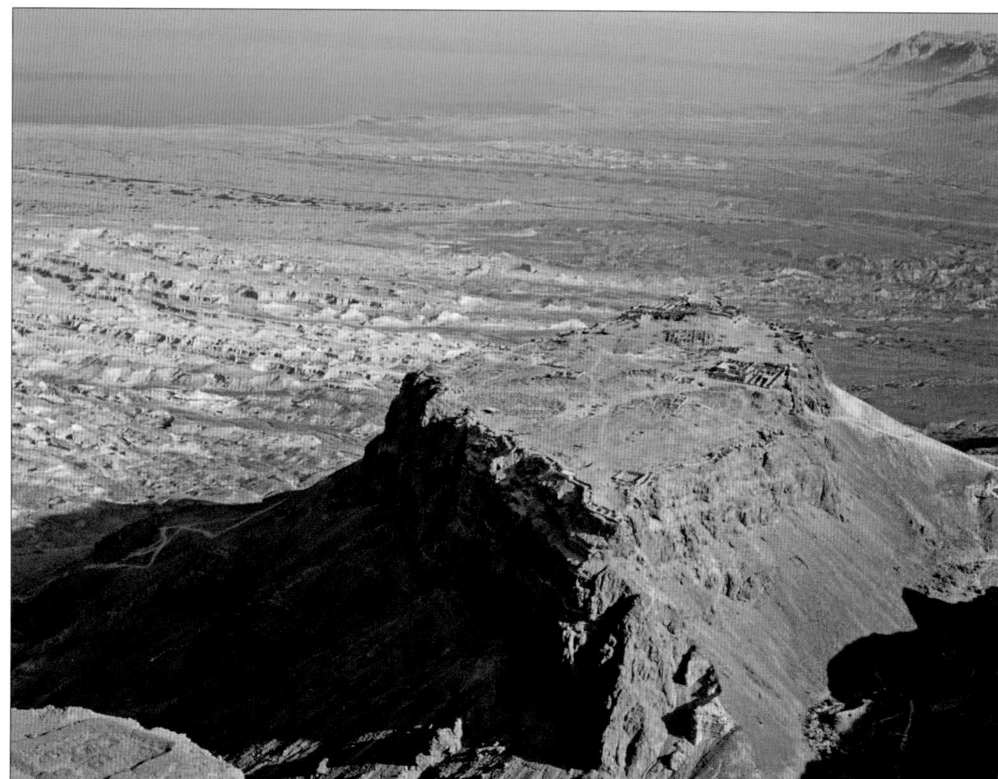

Of all the fortifications near the Dead Sea, Masada was among the most impregnable, situated atop an almost sheer-sided mountain. However, it also made breaking out impossible for the defenders if it was besieged by an adversary.

LOCATION

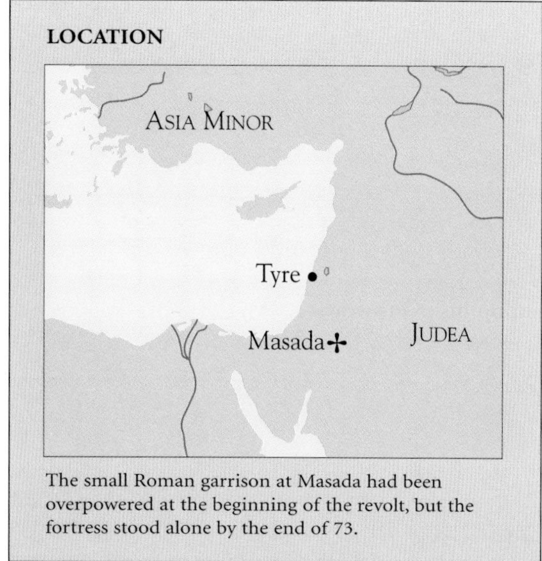
Asia Minor
Tyre
Masada
Judea

The small Roman garrison at Masada had been overpowered at the beginning of the revolt, but the fortress stood alone by the end of 73.

After Titus Flavius had suppressed the Jewish revolt with the storming of Jerusalem in 70, several garrisoned fortresses still held out, of which the most intractable was Masada. Lucius Flavius Silva was the Roman commander charged with recapturing the fort, which overlooked the Dead Sea, perching on top of sheer cliffs with just two approach paths.

The hardest route, on the side of the Dead Sea, was over 3km (1.8 miles) long, and twisted and turned interminably. To the west was an easier route, guarded at its narrowest point by its own tower, 500m (546 yd) from the summit. The 1.5km (0.9 mile) perimeter was surrounded by a wall 5m (16ft) high and 3.5m (11.5ft) thick. This was strengthened by 37 towers, each more than 20m (65ft) high. Inside the walls the ground was cultivated so the garrison would always have access to some food. Water was available from cisterns cut into the rock.

Led by Eleazar ben Yair, the Sicarii who held the fort watched from their seemingly impregnable vantage

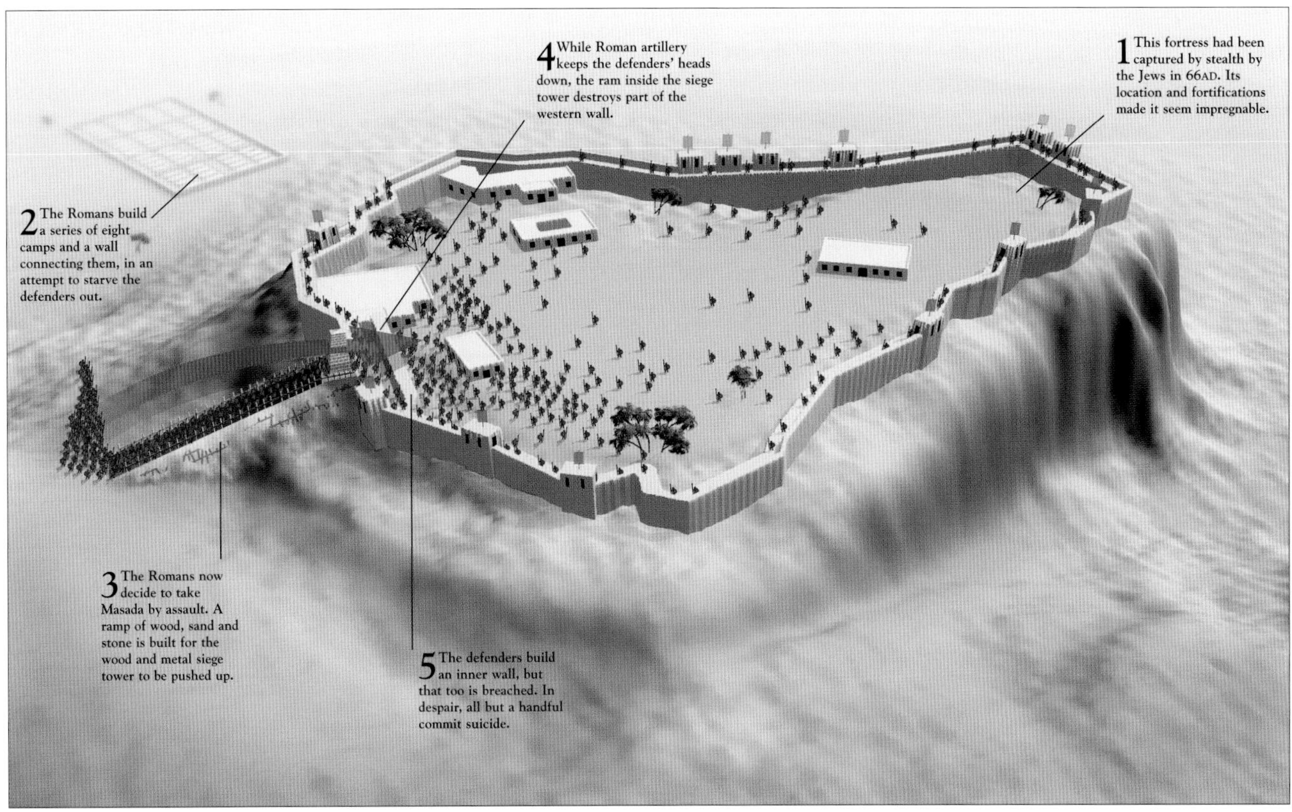
1 This fortress had been captured by stealth by the Jews in 66AD. Its location and fortifications made it seem impregnable.
2 The Romans build a series of eight camps and a wall connecting them, in an attempt to starve the defenders out.
3 The Romans now decide to take Masada by assault. A ramp of wood, sand and stone is built for the wood and metal siege tower to be pushed up.
4 While Roman artillery keeps the defenders' heads down, the ram inside the siege tower destroys part of the western wall.
5 The defenders build an inner wall, but that too is breached. In despair, all but a handful commit suicide.

At first the Romans chose to starve the defenders out, before realizing that their only option was to climb the approaches and assemble ramps, rams and siege towers. Masada fell soon after.

point 370m (1214ft) above, as the column of steadily trudging infantry crept ever closer on the desert floor below. Silva followed standard procedure. The legionaries built eight fortified camps at the likely points of egress from the fortress while the cavalry swept the immediate area in search of forage and to check for surprise attack. The next phase was the construction of a wall, 3.3km (2 miles) long, complete with towers every 80m (87 yards), close enough for mutual archery and sling support. This sealed the fortress off from any outside help or communication.

ASSAULT ON THE GARRISON

The next step was the construction of a ramp. This was built on a cliff projecting from the main rock 140m (459ft) below the fortress. At the foot of this ramp a wooden shell took shape. The shell was built higher and higher and the garrison must have realized this was going to be higher than their wall. The shell was clad in timber and metal plates so there was no chance to set fire to this monster. As the tower grew, so spirits in the fortress fell.

This tower was even larger than the three towers Titus had completed for the siege of Jerusalem, and when complete it was fitted out with stone- and arrow-throwing engines. With a range of 400m (437 yards), these could shoot anyone whose head appeared above the ramparts and allowed a more sinister machine to operate below: a ram. This was suspended from ropes tied to overhead beams in the tower and swung back and forth against the wall. Eventually the wall collapsed, and the end of the siege was a matter of time.

To escape was impossible, to fight was hopeless. Eleazar knew they would all be butchered by the Romans. He decided not to wait and give the Romans satisfaction for all their efforts. The warriors killed their own families and set fire to their possessions, then one in ten killed his fellows, then one man took the life of the other nine and then fell upon his own sword.

Mission accomplished, Silva departed. Later, the lands of Jewish families who had revolted were confiscated and given to retiring legionaries, thus setting up a kind of colony and military reserve in the province.

TIMELINE

1500–1000BC	1000–500BC	500BC–0AD	0–500AD	500–1000AD	1000–1500AD	1500–2000AD

Red Cliffs 208

WARS OF THE THREE KINGDOMS

LUI & SUN VICTORY

Leading an 800,000-strong army against the southern kingdoms, the northern Chinese warlord Cao Cao suggested that they might consider surrendering or face inevitable defeat. When his fatigued, diseased soldiers limped onto Red Cliffs several weeks later, it was in defeat.

KEY FACTS

WHO Cao Cao's Wei army and fleet against the forces of Liu Bei of the Shu and Sun Quan of the Wu.

WHAT While he had a vastly larger army, Cao Cao had reckoned without the difficulties of moving huge numbers of men across difficult terrain, and they proved easy prey for their southern enemies.

WHERE On the south bank of the Yangtze river, southwest of modern Wuhan, China.

WHEN Winter of 208/209

WHY Cao Cao, the northern Chinese warlord, wanted to add land south of the Yangtze river to the territories under his control.

OUTCOME Cao Cao's defeat ensured the two halves of China remained separate and paved the way for future bitter confrontations.

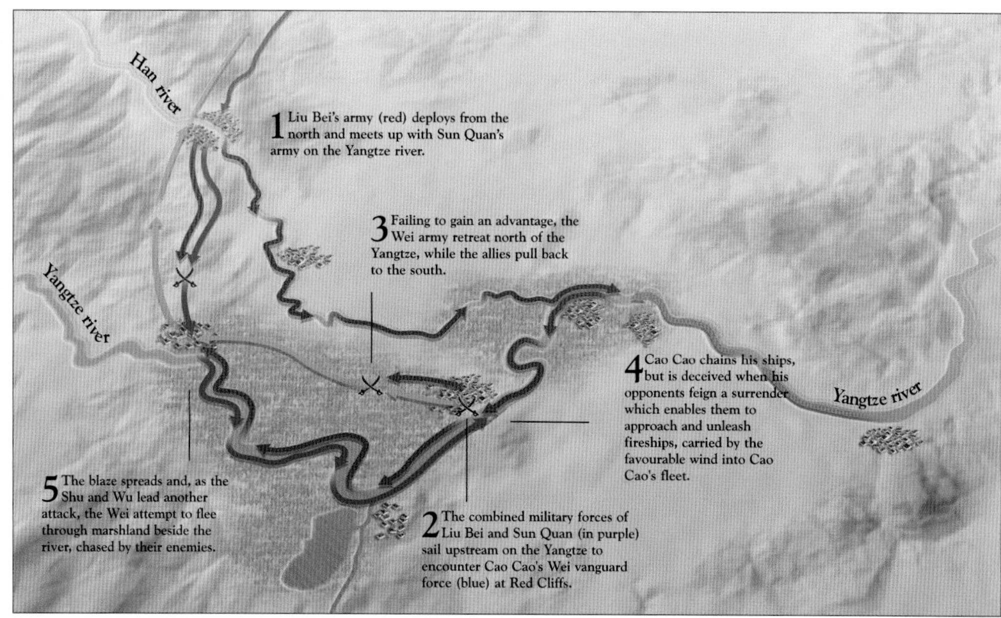
Han river
Yangtze river
Yangtze river
1 Liu Bei's army (red) deploys from the north and meets up with Sun Quan's army on the Yangtze river.
2 The combined military forces of Liu Bei and Sun Quan (in purple) sail upstream on the Yangtze to encounter Cao Cao's Wei vanguard force (blue) at Red Cliffs.
3 Failing to gain an advantage, the Wei army retreat north of the Yangtze, while the allies pull back to the south.
4 Cao Cao chains his ships, but is deceived when his opponents feign a surrender which enables them to approach and unleash fireships, carried by the favourable wind into Cao Cao's fleet.
5 The blaze spreads and, as the Shu and Wu lead another attack, the Wei attempt to flee through marshland beside the river, chased by their enemies.

The battle of Red Cliffs was as much about deception as it was about open tactics. Warfare in the ancient Far East put a high value on being able to confuse or deceive the enemy – ethics often came second to victory.

Cao Cao made his reputation as a great warlord by uniting the Chinese northern kingdoms, but the lands beyond the Yangtze remained independent. Putting himself at the head of an 800,000-strong army, he headed south, but while confident of success, he found that the Shu and Wu southern kingdoms had allied against him, calculating that moving an army of that size, many of them conscripts, over land and water would be a logistical nightmare.

ARMY IN DISARRAY

They were right. By the time the sides met at Red Cliffs, Cao Cao's men were wracked by disease, fatigue and low morale. After a short battle the Wei retreated, while Cao Cao tied his fleet with iron chains to achieve a kind of defensive fortification. The Wu general Zhou Yu pretended to surrender, but it was merely a trick to get close enough to unleash a series of fire ships. The fire spread through the fleet and onto the banks, decimating the Wei army and forcing the remainder to flee as their opponents gave chase alongside the river. Cao Cao's dreams had literally gone up in smoke.

LOCATION

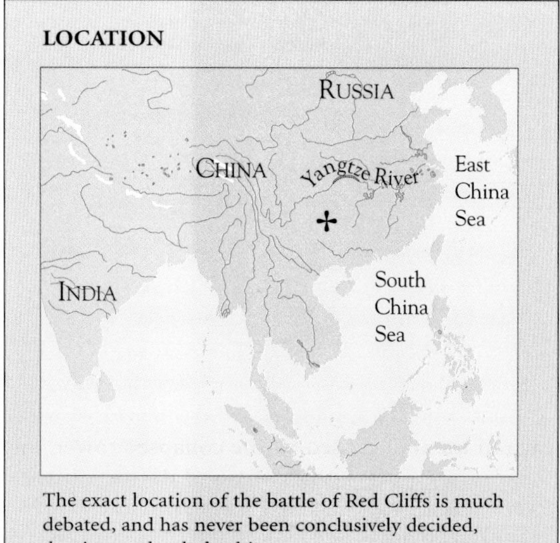
RUSSIA
CHINA
Yangtze River
East China Sea
INDIA
South China Sea

The exact location of the battle of Red Cliffs is much debated, and has never been conclusively decided, despite much scholarship.

TIMELINE

1500–1000BC	1000–500BC	500BC–0AD	0–500AD	500–1000AD	1000–1500AD	1500–2000AD

Dura Europos 256–257

KEY FACTS

WHO The Sassanid Persians under Shapur I against a Roman garrison.

WHAT The Sassanids, masters of seigecraft, set to undermine the walls of this old castle on an east-west trade route.

WHERE Dura Europos, near Salhiye, in modern Syria.

WHEN 256–257

WHY The Sassanids were trying to revive the glories of the ancient Persian empire, and posed a major threat to the Roman territories in the East.

OUTCOME The siege proved successful, and after the Sassanids pillaged it, the fortress was abandoned, never to be rebuilt.

The Sassanid Persians laid siege to the Roman outpost at Dura Europos, and constructed three different mines in a bid to cause a breach in the walls. These tactics, supplemented by a siege ramp, resulted in the collapse of the tower and the garrison was sacked.

SASSANID–ROMAN WARS

SASSANID PERSIAN VICTORY

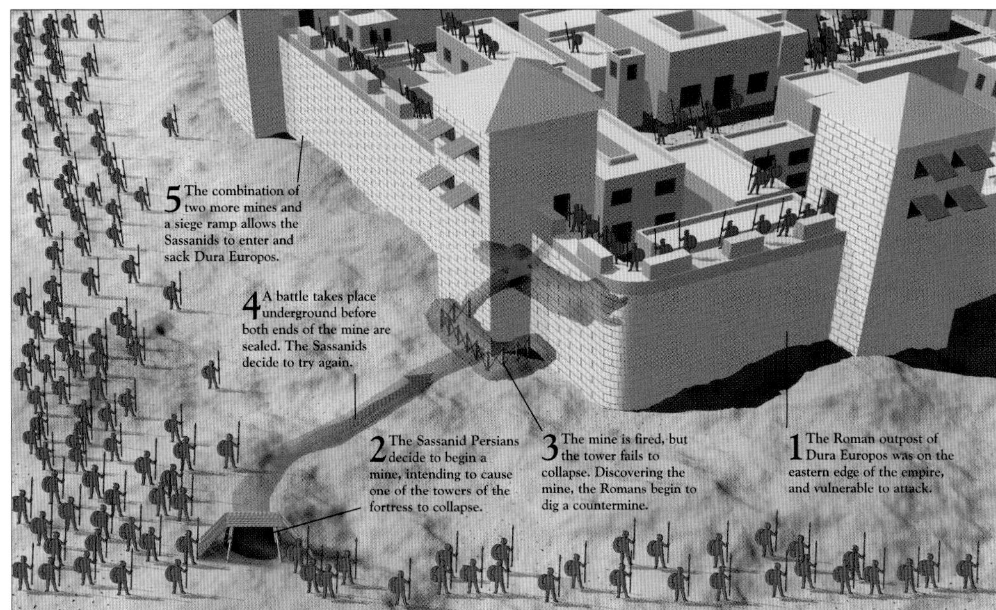
5 The combination of two more mines and a siege ramp allows the Sassanids to enter and sack Dura Europos.
4 A battle takes place underground before both ends of the mine are sealed. The Sassanids decide to try again.
2 The Sassanid Persians decide to begin a mine, intending to cause one of the towers of the fortress to collapse.
3 The mine is fired, but the tower fails to collapse. Discovering the mine, the Romans begin to dig a countermine.
1 The Roman outpost of Dura Europos was on the eastern edge of the empire, and vulnerable to attack.

The Sassanid campaign to take the fort involved mining beneath its walls, and even encompassed a skirmish between the two opposing forces underground in one of the tunnels.

Dura Europos was located on an ancient east-west trade route. It was founded in c. 300BC by a Successor king, Seleukos I. The Romans had captured the fort in AD165, but as the Sassanids tried to build a new Persian bulwark against their expansion eastwards, this outpost on the edge of two civilizations seemed an obvious target to attempt to take.

First the Sassanids constructed a mine to make a breach in the walls, but this was unsuccessful, as the structure only sagged. The mine was then intercepted by a Roman countermine, and it appears that a battle took place underground. At some point, the mine caved in, trapping those inside, who were left to die. The Sassanids then began construction of two new mines: one was successfully fired and brought down a significant portion of a tower, while another went under the city walls and allowed the attackers access to the city. The combination of the breach in the wall caused by the collapsed tower, the assault from the mine under the walls, and the assault via the siege ramp appears to have been successful.

Having gained access, Dura Europos was sacked by the Sassanids, and any survivors hauled off as slaves.

LOCATION

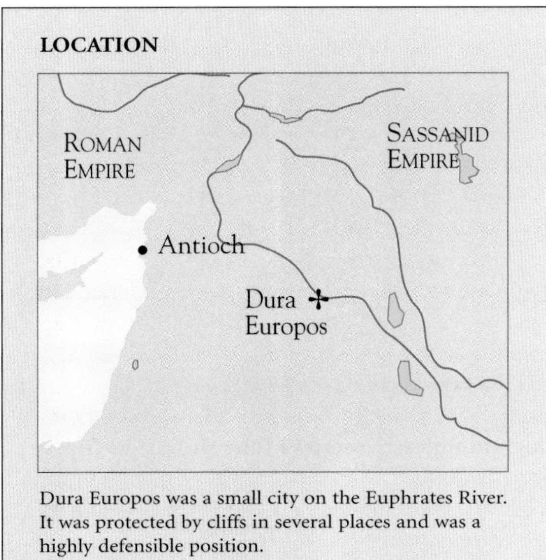
Roman Empire
Sassanid Empire
Antioch
Dura Europos

Dura Europos was a small city on the Euphrates River. It was protected by cliffs in several places and was a highly defensible position.

TIMELINE

1500–1000BC	1000–500BC	500BC–0AD	0–500AD	500–1000AD	1000–1500AD	1500–2000AD

Milvian Bridge 312

An empire hung in the balance as two men – Constantine and the man he was to succeed, Maxentius – made vital decisions on the sides of a famous river across a ruined bridge. It was to be the last of Rome's disastrous civil wars.

ROMAN CIVIL WAR

CONSTANTINE VICTORY

KEY FACTS

WHO The army of Constantine (d. 337) clashed with that of the Emperor Maxentius (d. 312).

WHAT Maxentius decided to face Constantine, who had invaded Italy from Gaul, in the open field on the far side of the Tiber. His army was routed, the bridge they fled over collapsed, and Maxentius was drowned.

WHERE At the Pons Milvius, the last bridge before Rome on the Appian Way.

WHEN 28 October 312

WHY Constantine sought to overthrow Maxentius and seize sole control of the Roman Empire.

OUTCOME Constantine takes a great victory, ascribing it to divine intervention, and enters the capital.

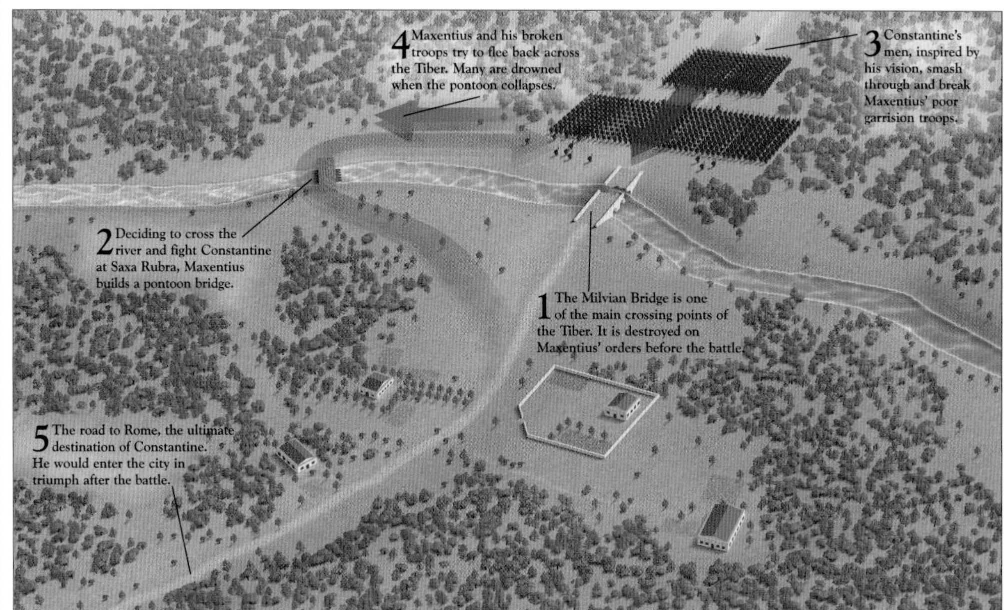
4 Maxentius and his broken troops try to flee back across the Tiber. Many are drowned when the pontoon collapses.
3 Constantine's men, inspired by his vision, smash through and break Maxentius' poor garrision troops.
2 Deciding to cross the river and fight Constantine at Saxa Rubra, Maxentius builds a pontoon bridge.
1 The Milvian Bridge is one of the main crossing points of the Tiber. It is destroyed on Maxentius' orders before the battle.
5 The road to Rome, the ultimate destination of Constantine. He would enter the city in triumph after the battle.

This was a battle decided by bridges – first, the major stone bridge over the Tiber, which Maxentius smashed to cut Constantine off; and then a smaller pontoon bridge, which he had to hastily assemble after deciding to engage his enemy.

Constantine, after military successes in Gaul, challenged the position of Emperor Maxentius by invading Italy. He moved swiftly towards the capital, so Maxentius had a wide stone bridge over the Tiber, the Pons Milvius, cut in order to delay his progress, and to hinder his supply lines during an expected siege of Rome. Quixotically, however, Maxentius then decided to offer battle on the far side of the Tiber at a place called Saxa Rubra, forcing his engineers to hastily construct a wooden pontoon bridge to move his forces across the river.

Constantine, personally leading his cavalry in a headlong attack, seized the initiative and soon had his counterparts in headlong retreat towards the wooden bridge, leaving the flanks of Maxentius' infantry fatally exposed. With the complete collapse of his army's discipline came the complete collapse of both the remnants of the Pons Milvius, and the wooden bridge, and among those thrown into the waters of the Tiber was the Emperor himself.

Maxentius drowned in his armour, but just to make sure of the fact, the victorious Constantine had the river dredged the next day.

LOCATION

GAUL

Rome

Milvian Bridge

A roadblock on the Appian Way: the Pons Milvius was Maxentius' last chance to halt Constantine's advance on Rome.

TIMELINE

1500–1000BC	1000–500BC	500BC–0AD	0–500AD	500–1000AD	1000–1500AD	1500–2000AD

Strasbourg 357

KEY FACTS

Who The Alamanni tribal confederation led by King Chnodomar took on a Late Roman army under the command of Julianus.

What Although the Roman forces under Julianus were relatively small, greater discipline and their ability to hold positions in a drill unit proved decisive.

Where Near Strasbourg, Alsace, France.

When 357

Why In the fourth century, the German barbarian tribes had become increasingly bold in their attacks across the frontiers of Gaul, and threatened the Roman hold on the province.

Outcome Julianus was successfully able to evict the barbarians and restore the security of Roman defensive forts along the Rhine.

The youthful Julianus was thought to face a difficult task when he was placed at the head of an army charged with reasserting Roman control in one of its most important provinces in northern Europe. But he proved an unexpectedly adept commander.

ROMAN–ALAMANNI WAR

ROMAN VICTORY

Roman cavalry lock swords with Alamanni warriors on the banks of the Rhine. Although this artwork focuses on mounted troops, the battle of Strasbourg was really decided by the Roman infantry.

LOCATION

GERMANIA
Strasbourg
GAUL
Rome

The battle of Strasbourg is unusual, for most actions fought against Germanic migrants were on a much smaller scale.

Roman civil wars had weakened defences in Gaul along the Rhine frontier, encouraging increasingly confident attacks from the Germanic Alamanni tribes. Julianus, despatched to confront them with a modest-sized army, decided to meet the Alamanni in battle near Strasbourg.

When he ordered a general advance, the Germans countercharged, but they were driven back by the Roman legions. As the Roman cavalry was less effective, the battle revolved around infantrymen: the Romans rained arrows onto the barbarians, who, lacking the training of their opponents, began to lose their discipline.

Next, the Romans formed a shield wall, and the Alamanni tried to push them back. Some broke through the Roman line, but as casualties mounted, they fled. The Romans broke formation and chased them to the Rhine, where many Germans drowned attempting to swim across under heavy missile fire. While the Alamanni lost 6000 men, and King Chnodomar was captured and sent to Rome, the Roman losses were negligible.

TIMELINE

1500–1000BC	1000–500BC	500BC–0AD	0–500AD	500–1000AD	1000–1500AD	1500–2000AD

Adrianople 378

ROMAN–GOTHIC WARS

GOTHIC VICTORY

The Battle of Adrianople was the only great victory in a battle of the Germans who overran the Western Roman Empire. The Gothic victory demonstrated Roman weaknesses and exposed the empire to further attack, beginning a domino effect that ended imperial rule in the West.

KEY FACTS

WHO The field army of the Eastern Roman Empire, commanded by the Emperor Flavius Valens (328–378), met a mixed Gothic army.

WHAT The battle took place between the rebellious Goths and a Roman army that had been called together to suppress the rebellion.

WHERE About 13km (8 miles) from Adrianople, modern Edirne in European Turkey.

WHEN 9 August 378

WHY Having made a treaty with the Romans in 376, which allowed them to settle within the empire, the Goths rebelled against the ill-treatment they received. Valens intended to end this Gothic threat but attacked based on a mistaken report of Gothic strength, without waiting for the Western Roman army to arrive.

OUTCOME The Roman army was defeated. Two-thirds of the Roman forces, perhaps 10,000 men, were killed, including Valens.

SPQR

Emperor Valens concludes a treaty with the Goths in 376, just two years before the massacre at Adrianople.

LOCATION

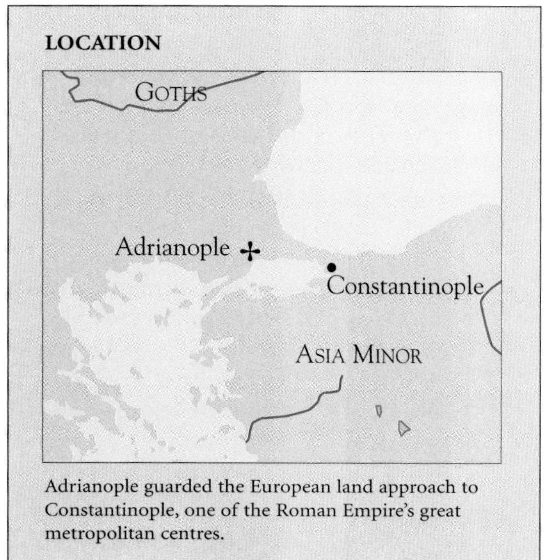
GOTHS
Adrianople
Constantinople
ASIA MINOR

Adrianople guarded the European land approach to Constantinople, one of the Roman Empire's great metropolitan centres.

By 378, rampaging Gothic tribes were proving to be a major embarrassment to the Eastern Roman emperor, Valens. He was an unpopular ruler, but an experienced and successful commander who had spent much of his reign in the field. About 50 years old at the time of the battle of Adrianople, he had won several noteworthy battles against Goths in the 360s. Arranging for the Western Roman emperor, his nephew Gratian, to join him in a joint attack against the Goths, Valens assembled his men outside Constantinople, but then news came that Gratian's arrival would be delayed. Valens, seeking glory for himself, moved the short distance towards the approaching Goths to join battle near Adrianople.

On the morning of 9 August 378, the Roman army marched about 13km (8 miles) from its camp outside Adrianople to where the Gothic Tervingi under the command of Fritigern had been sighted north of the city. Most of Fritigern's force was lined up along a ridge, from which they could charge the Roman army at full speed. On arrival, the Romans deployed in a traditional

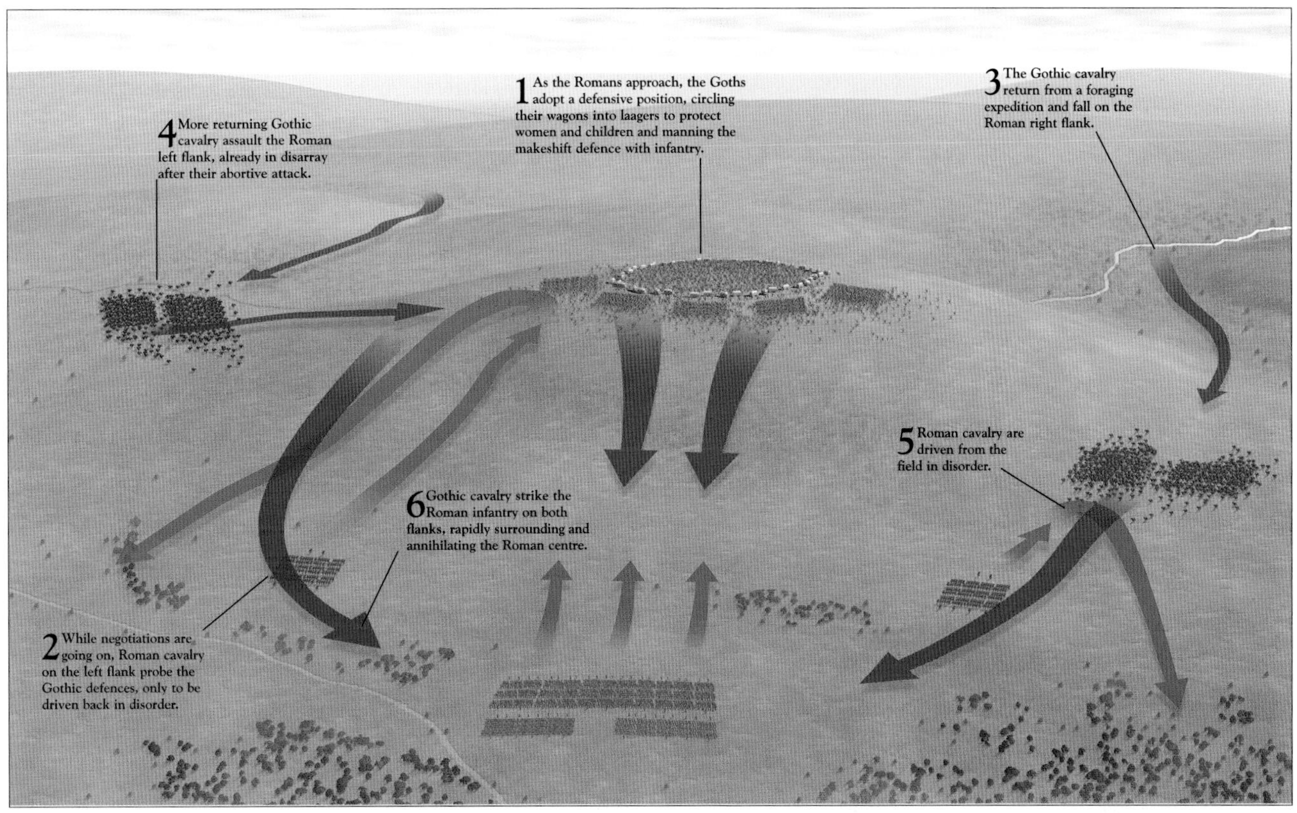
1 As the Romans approach, the Goths adopt a defensive position, circling their wagons into laagers to protect women and children and manning the makeshift defence with infantry.
2 While negotiations are going on, Roman cavalry on the left flank probe the Gothic defences, only to be driven back in disorder.
3 The Gothic cavalry return from a foraging expedition and fall on the Roman right flank.
4 More returning Gothic cavalry assault the Roman left flank, already in disarray after their abortive attack.
5 Roman cavalry are driven from the field in disorder.
6 Gothic cavalry strike the Roman infantry on both flanks, rapidly surrounding and annihilating the Roman centre.

By the fourth century, the Romans were losing their reputation for invincibility. The armies increasingly made use of mercenaries, and cavalry took their place alongside foot soldiers without being fully integrated. The Goths exploited the disorganization at Adrianople.

formation: two lines of heavy infantry forming the centre, with a screen of skirmishers thrown out before them, and cavalry on both flanks. It is almost certain that the cavalry included both regular heavy cavalry – an increasingly sizeable force in the Roman army as the fourth century progressed – and horse archers. Most of the heavy infantry would have been equipped with chain mail, round or oval shields, and the longer swords favoured by the late Roman military, and there were also archers.

Unfortunately for Valens, cavalry had never been fully integrated into Roman warfare and tended to be unpredictable. A pre-emptive attack by the cavalry on the right wing was easily driven back. While an attack by those on the left wing at first made more progress, catastrophe struck the Roman cause with the sudden arrival of another large Gothic force – mainly mounted army of the Greuthungi, which also included Huns and Alans. Overlooked by Roman scouts, they appeared on the battlefield just as the Roman left wing's cavalry attack stalled, and fell on this Roman force, shattering it while the rest of the Roman left wing was still forming up to support them. The surviving Romans of the left wing fled for their lives, abandoning the battlefield.

Now the Tervingi, who until then had held their position on the ridge, deployed all along the increasingly exhausted Roman infantry line, which was left fully exposed by the flight of the cavalry. They soon found themselves surrounded, Gothic archers adding to the confusion and panic by shooting deep into the Roman ranks.

Most of the Roman soldiers soon broke and fled, to be cut down by Gothic cavalrymen as they tried to escape. Only two elite legions held firm in a desperate last stand, Emperor Valens apparently with them. Some stories told of how he was killed by an arrow, and his body never found in the carnage. Another reported he was wounded, then taken to a nearby farmhouse by his bodyguard. A group of Goths attacked and, meeting resistance, burned the place down without realizing that such a valuable potential captive was inside.

In all, two-thirds of the Roman army was left dead on the battlefield. The Goths had proven that they could meet and defeat a Roman emperor in the field.

The Huns' Campaign vs Eastern Rome 441–443

HUNNIC–ROMAN WARS

HUNNIC VICTORY

In the fourth century, riding off the Central Asian Steppes came an army of nomadic warriors, the Huns. Famous for the speed and breadth of their conquests, infamous for their ruthlessness, the Huns were diverse people who were united by charismatic leaders, the most famous of whom was Attila.

KEY FACTS

WHO A large Hunnic army led by the famous Attila (406–453) and his brother, Bleda (c. 390–445), campaigned throughout the Eastern Roman Empire.

WHAT The Huns marched through Southeastern Europe virtually to Constantinople.

WHERE The Eastern Roman Empire from the Danube River throughout the Balkans and into Anatolia.

WHEN From 441 to 443

WHY Breaking a peace treaty with the Huns, Emperor Theodosius provoked a campaign that devastated much of his empire.

OUTCOME The numerous victories of the Huns forced the Romans to negotiate the Treaty of Anatolius, which, among other things, markedly increased their tribute payments.

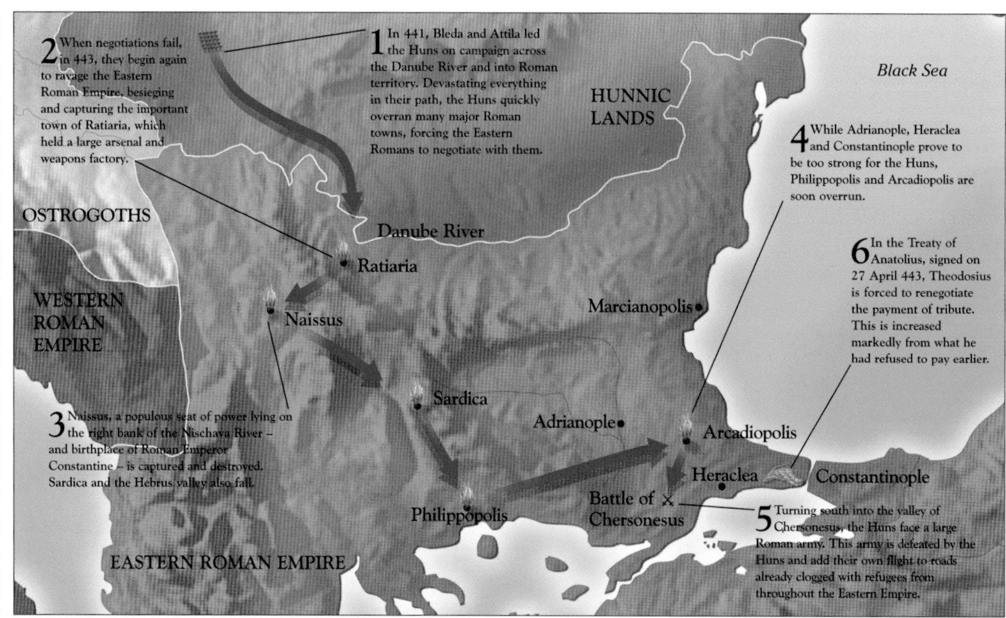
1 In 441, Bleda and Attila led the Huns on campaign across the Danube River and into Roman territory. Devastating everything in their path, the Huns quickly overran many major Roman towns, forcing the Eastern Romans to negotiate with them.
2 When negotiations fail, in 443, they begin again to ravage the Eastern Roman Empire, besieging and capturing the important town of Ratiaria, which held a large arsenal and weapons factory.
3 Naissus, a populous seat of power lying on the right bank of the Nischava River – and birthplace of Roman Emperor Constantine – is captured and destroyed. Sardica and the Hebrus valley also fall.
4 While Adrianople, Heraclea and Constantinople prove to be too strong for the Huns, Philippopolis and Arcadiopolis are soon overrun.
5 Turning south into the valley of Chersonesus, the Huns face a large Roman army. This army is defeated by the Huns and add their own flight to roads already clogged with refugees from throughout the Eastern Empire.
6 In the Treaty of Anatolius, signed on 27 April 443, Theodosius is forced to renegotiate the payment of tribute. This is increased markedly from what he had refused to pay earlier.
HUNNIC LANDS
Black Sea
OSTROGOTHS
Danube River
Ratiaria
WESTERN ROMAN EMPIRE
Naissus
Marcianopolis
Sardica
Adrianople
Arcadiopolis
Heraclea
Constantinople
Battle of Chersonesus
Philippopolis
EASTERN ROMAN EMPIRE

The Hunnic armies were built around brilliant horsemen who were able to sweep through southeastern Europe and menace Constantinople, forcing the Eastern Empire to pay them expensive tributes that only fuelled further attacks.

The Huns, primarily fighting as cavalry and mounted archers deploying the recurved composite bow, used a speed and agility against Roman forces not seen for centuries. When the Eastern Emperor Theodosius broke a treaty by witholding tribute, their attacks, led by Attila and his brother Bleda, grew in intensity. The brutality of an assault on the Romans near the Danube in 441 – made at market-time when many civilians were present – shocked Constantinople.

By 443, no population, fortification or city seemed safe. When a Roman army was at last despatched to do battle, it was defeated several times. Using the speed, agility and lethality of their cavalry, the Huns then forced their opponents – led by Germanic generals Aspar, Areobindus and Arnegisclus – into the Chersonesus valley, cutting off their retreat to Constantinople, and inflicting defeat.

Theodosius was forced into begging for terms before Bleda and Attila turned their forces against Constantinople. Tensions remained high between the Eastern Romans and the Huns for several years following the Treaty of Anatolius. Surprisingly, though, they never again developed into further large-scale warfare.

LOCATION

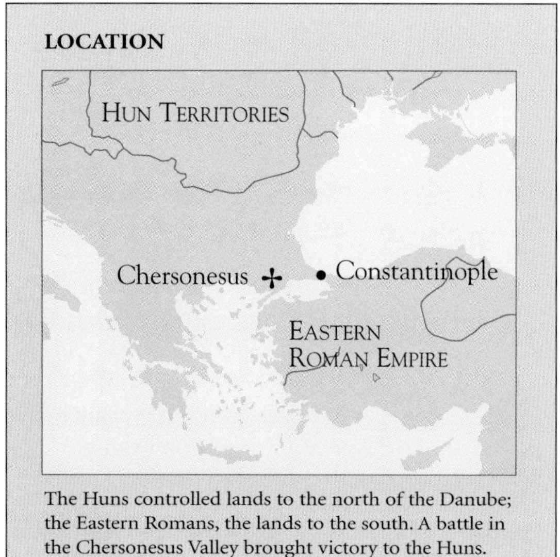
HUN TERRITORIES
Chersonesus
Constantinople
EASTERN ROMAN EMPIRE

The Huns controlled lands to the north of the Danube; the Eastern Romans, the lands to the south. A battle in the Chersonesus Valley brought victory to the Huns.

TIMELINE

1500–1000BC	1000–500BC	500BC–0AD	0–500AD	500–1000AD	1000–1500AD	1500–2000AD

Catalaunian Fields 451

KEY FACTS

WHO The army of the Huns under Attila (d. 453) was checked by an army of Romans, Visigoths and Alans commanded by Flavius Aetius (d. 454).

WHAT Aetius' army occupied the high ground at the start of the battle, from which the Huns were unable to drive them despite hard fighting. After a few days' stalemate, the Huns withdrew but the Romans did not pursue them.

WHERE The Catalaunian Fields, between Troyes and Châlons-sur-Marne in what is now the Champagne region of France.

WHEN June 451

WHY Aetius sought to halt the Huns' invasion of Gaul.

OUTCOME Attila withdrew with his army and loot intact, but his reputation was damaged and the conquest of Gaul was prevented.

In 451, the Roman general Aetius met the hitherto invincible Hunnic hordes, led by the 'scourge of God' himself, Attila. This time the Huns were driven off, and for the time being at least, the Western Roman Empire would stagger on intact.

HUNNIC–ROMAN WARS

ROMAN VICTORY

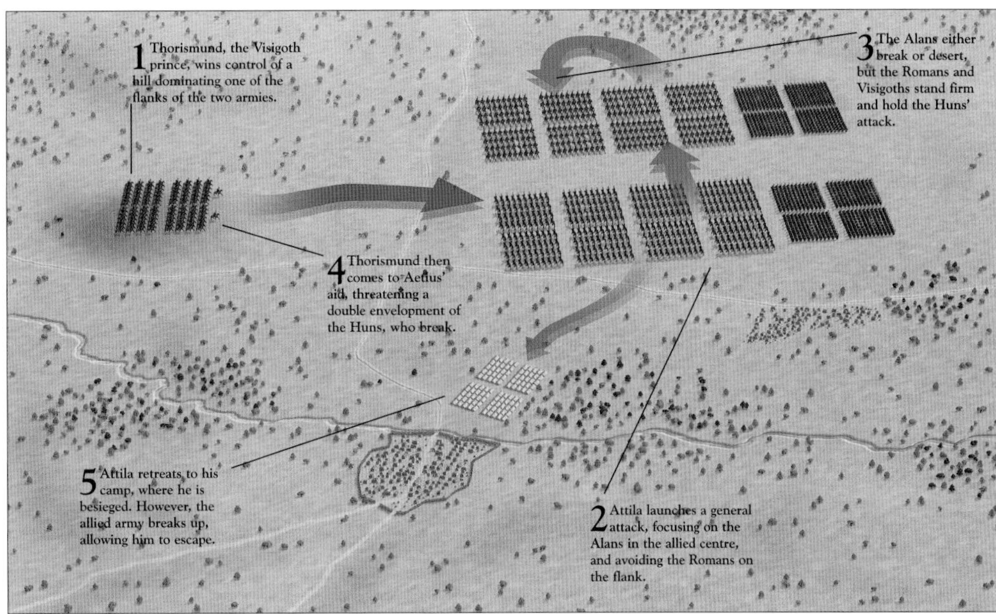
1 Thorismund, the Visigoth prince, wins control of a hill dominating one of the flanks of the two armies.
2 Attila launches a general attack, focusing on the Alans in the allied centre, and avoiding the Romans on the flank.
3 The Alans either break or desert, but the Romans and Visigoths stand firm and hold the Huns' attack.
4 Thorismund then comes to Aetius' aid, threatening a double envelopment of the Huns, who break.
5 Attila retreats to his camp, where he is besieged. However, the allied army breaks up, allowing him to escape.

The Huns, even under Attila, were not invincible, and the able Roman general Flavius Aetius was able to exact revenge for years of terror campaigns near Champagne, in Gaul. The myth of the unbeatable Hun had been smashed.

LOCATION

GERMANIA
Catalaunian Fields
GAUL
Rome

The location of the Catalaunian Fields has never been determined, although sources agree that the battle took place in June or July not far from the town of Châlons.

In the spring of 451, Attila the Hun was back on the warpath, this time against the Western Roman Empire, possibly even reaching as far as Paris. A Roman army commanded by the experienced Flavius Aetius finally caught up with him on the Catalaunian Fields. By this time, the Roman forces comprised a large number of Germanic soldiers, including the Visigoths, within its ranks. The Romans, occupying the high ground, quickly succeeded in pushing the Huns back in confusion, and Attila had to harangue them to return to the fight. During fierce hand-to-hand fighting, King Theodoric of the Visigoths was killed. But rather than discouraging the Visigoths, their king's death enraged them and they fought with such spirit that the Huns were driven back to their camp as night fell.

For several days the Huns did not move from their encampment, but their archers succeeded in keeping the Romans at bay. The desertion of the frustrated Visigoths allowed Attila to withdraw his army from the battlefield, and with his wagons of booty intact. The Romans did not pursue him, but his aura of invincibility had been shattered.

TIMELINE

1500–1000BC	1000–500BC	500BC–0AD	0–500AD	500–1000AD	1000–1500AD	1500–2000AD

Catalaunian Fields

CATALAUNIAN FIELDS
The galloping Huns struck fear into everyone in the fifth century AD. They symbolized frontier breakdown and the long painful decline of the Roman Empire. Yet it wasn't all one-way traffic, and Rome could still strike out for moments of glory. Its army by now was making use of 'barbarian' soldiers within its own ranks, and they would play their part at the Catalaunian Fields, with King Theodoric of the Visigoths fighting at the side of the Roman general Flavius Aetius. Even when the former was slain, it only encouraged his men to fight with even more bitter resolve, to secure Roman victory.

Ad Decimum 533

KEY FACTS

WHO An Eastern Roman army numbering about 15,000 under the command of Flavius Belisarius (505–565), opposed by about 11,000 Vandal troops under King Gelimer (480–553).

WHAT The Romans, advancing on the Vandal capital, Carthage, were intercepted by Vandal forces, resulting in a hard-fought battle.

WHERE 16km (10 miles) south of Carthage, North Africa.

WHEN 13 September, 533

WHY Belisarius and his army had been sent against the Vandals as part of the planned reconquest of the Western Roman Empire.

OUTCOME After almost being defeated, Belisarius' force emerged victorious.

The battle of Ad Decimum was one of many victories won by the extremely talented Belisarius. The Vandals' defeat by his expedition marked the end of their ascendancy and a renewal of Roman glory, with the use of heavily armoured cavalrymen, called cataphracts, proving decisive.

VANDALIC WAR

ROMAN (BYZANTINE) VICTORY

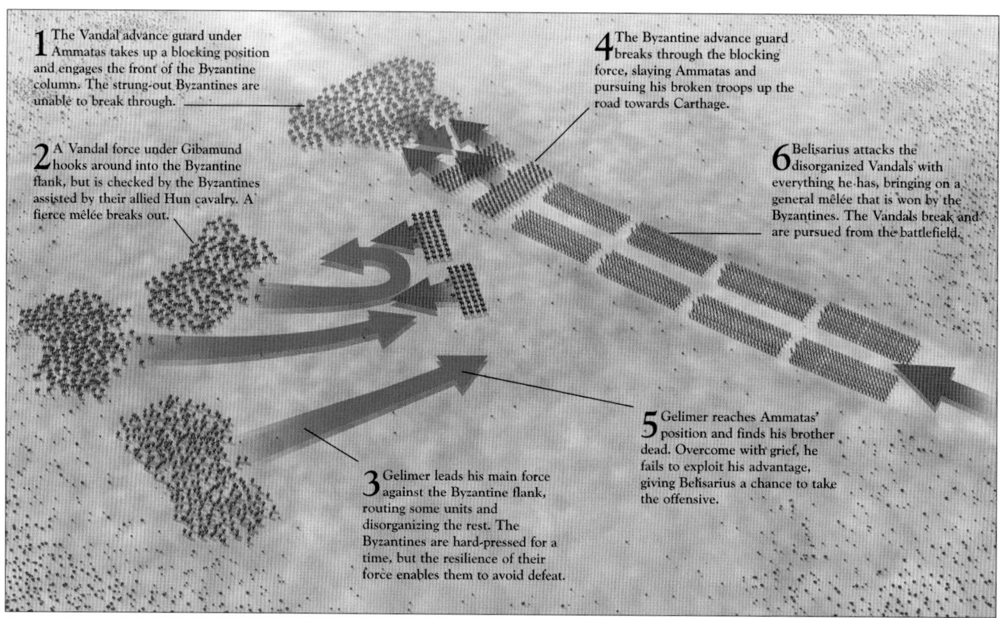
1 The Vandal advance guard under Ammatas takes up a blocking position and engages the front of the Byzantine column. The strung-out Byzantines are unable to break through.
2 A Vandal force under Gibamund hooks around into the Byzantine flank, but is checked by the Byzantines assisted by their allied Hun cavalry. A fierce mêlée breaks out.
3 Gelimer leads his main force against the Byzantine flank, routing some units and disorganizing the rest. The Byzantines are hard-pressed for a time, but the resilience of their force enables them to avoid defeat.
4 The Byzantine advance guard breaks through the blocking force, slaying Ammatas and pursuing his broken troops up the road towards Carthage.
5 Gelimer reaches Ammatas' position and finds his brother dead. Overcome with grief, he fails to exploit his advantage, giving Belisarius a chance to take the offensive.
6 Belisarius attacks the disorganized Vandals with everything he has, bringing on a general mêlée that is won by the Byzantines. The Vandals break and are pursued from the battlefield.

Belisarius was one of the greatest generals of the Dark Ages. But at Ad Decimum he owed something to luck, the Vandal leader Gelimer allowing himself to be distracted in the heat of battle by personal grief at the loss of his brother.

The Eastern Roman Emperor Justinian (483–565) wanted to reconquer the West and restore the entire Roman Empire. His main military architect was his capable general Belisarius, who led a campaign against the Germanic Vandals in North Africa headed by the hostile Gelimer. An advance guard under the command of Gelimer's brother, Ammatas, met the advancing Romans outside the Vandal's capital Carthage. But they reached Ad Decimum as a disorganized mob, and Ammatas' force was overwhelmed and their commander was killed.

Gelimer, meanwhile, led his 7000 men straight into the Roman force and met with considerable success. Some imperial units were routed and much of Belisarius' army was thrown into disorder. But when Gelimer found his brother dead, he was overcome with grief, insisting on stopping to bury him on the battlefield. Crucial momentum was lost, a seemingly beaten Belisarius was now able to regroup his forces, and counter-attack.

Total victory was secured when the Vandals broke and fled the field. Gelimer was forced to abandon Carthage which welcomed Belisarius as a liberator. From the Vandal king's own throne, he declared it restored to the empire.

LOCATION

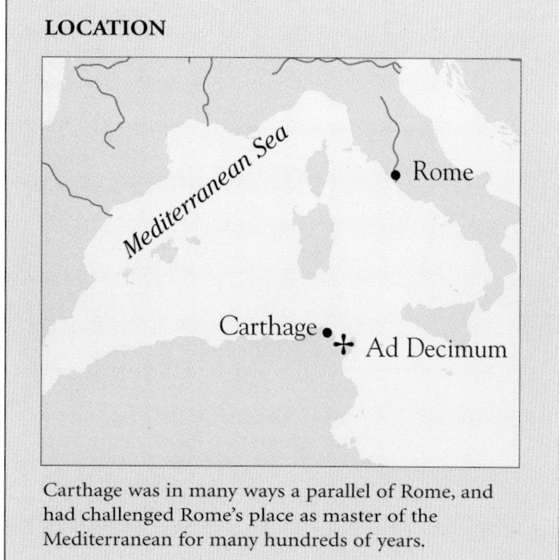
Mediterranean Sea
Rome
Carthage
Ad Decimum

Carthage was in many ways a parallel of Rome, and had challenged Rome's place as master of the Mediterranean for many hundreds of years.

TIMELINE

1500–1000BC	1000–500BC	500BC–0AD	0–500AD	500–1000AD	1000–1500AD	1500–2000AD

Battle of Casilinium 554

BYZANTINE WARS

BYZANTINE VICTORY

In the sixth century, the Byzantine emperor Justinian I had ambitions to restore the former Roman Empire in its western parts. Narses' victory over Gothic tribes at Casilinium was emphatic enough to make it seem, for a time at least, more than just a pipe dream.

KEY FACTS

WHO An army of the Eastern Roman (Byzantine) Empire, led by Narses, against the combined forces of the Gothic Alamanni and Franks.

WHAT Narses marched on Butilin's largely infantry-based army with a better balanced unit, including heavy cavalry and mounted archers as well as foot soldiers.

WHERE Volturno River, Italy.

WHEN 554

WHY The Alamanni chieftain Butilin had ambitions to take control of Italy, at a time when the Byzantine emperor Justinian I was attempting to reunite the two halves of the former Roman Empire.

OUTCOME Narses was triumphant, and the entire opposing army, including Butilin, was massacred.

The Italian peninsula in the sixth century was a battleground in the aftermath of the fall of the Western Empire between the Germanic tribes and the Eastern Roman Empire, which strove to reclaim it.

LOCATION

WESTERN ROMAN EMPIRE

Rome

Casilinium

The Battle of Casilinium was fought beside the River Volturno. The Germans, returning to their base, found Narses' Byzantine army astride their path.

The Goth Butilin had set up a fortified camp near the Volturno River when some of his soldiers fell ill with dysentry. When the Byzantine general Narses learnt of their location, he moved in for the kill, deploying his troops carefully, with the infantry in the centre and cavalry on both flanks largely hidden by surrounding woodland.

Butilin's infantry, in its deep formation, charged against the enemy centre, intending to split it and force a retreat. Initially this seemed to have worked, as the centre of the Byzantine infantry buckled under the sheer depth and ferocity of the Germanic charge. But the Byzantine troop of Herul mercenaries, which had held in reserve, now came into the line just in time to restore the situation.

Meanwhile, Narses, having drawn the Goths into his trap, closed the door on any retreat by manoeuvring his cavalry into outflanking positions. Butilin's men were surrounded and massacred, bringing an end to their rampaging campaign through Italy.

TIMELINE

1500–1000BC	1000–500BC	500BC–0AD	0–500AD	500–1000AD	1000–1500AD	1500–2000AD

CHAPTER 2

The Medieval Period

Many academics furiously reject the term 'Dark Ages' being applied to the early medieval period from the fall of the Roman Empire to the eleventh century. Yet a telling indication of the paucity of our knowledge of the time is that only three set-piece battles between the sixth century and Hastings (1066) feature here, of which the greatest was Lech (955).

The medieval period saw the early use of artillery in some Asian battles as at Bun'ei (1274). Another curiosity was the huge early cannon used by the English at Crécy (1346). Earlier, the resourceful Scottish pikeman had put on a show of which hoplites of an earlier age would have been proud, at Bannockburn (1314).

The Crusades witnessed a fascinating contrast between the heavily armoured, lance-bearing Western knight, charging into headlong attack on a powerful horse, against the Saracens on nimbler steeds favouring the bow and arrow. The Western knight was a figure of great glamour, however. The Black Prince, who led the English to victory at Poitiers (1356), is still one of the most emblematic names of the Age of Chivalry.

◀ A graphic rendering of the battle of Sarmada in 1119, when the Muslim forces of Ilghazi of Mardin destroyed a Crusader army in Syria. The Arab warriors were often more nimble on horseback than their armour-clad opponents.

Poitiers 732

KEY FACTS

Who Charles Martel (688–741) leads a Frankish army against the Muslim Arabs under the leadership of the governor of Al-Andalus (Spain) Abd al-Rahman al-Ghafiqi.

What Charles Martel summoned up an army after a request for aid from the embattled Eudes, prince of Aquitaine. Just north of Poitiers, he was able to kill Abd al-Rahman al-Ghafiqi and stem the Muslim tide.

Where Near Poitiers, France.

When 25 October 732

Why The 'Saracen' army had conquered Spain and had been carrying out raids across the Pyrenees, making increasing advances northwards through Aquitaine.

Outcome Although the Arabs probably never intended to settle in Aquitaine, defeat at Poitiers was a massive blow to their expansionist policies, and was widely proclaimed as the beginning of the Western Christian fightback.

They called Charles Martel 'the Hammer' for his efficient ways of dispatching his enemies on the battlefield. His victory over the Islamic invaders of the Frankish kingdom at Poitiers was celebrated as a symbol of Christian resistance for centuries afterwards.

MUSLIM CONQUESTS

FRANKISH VICTORY

Charles Martel was the founder of the great Carolingian dynasty and grandfather of the later Holy Roman Emperor Charlemagne. Victory over the Muslims at Poitiers burnished his reputation as 'the Hammer'.

LOCATION

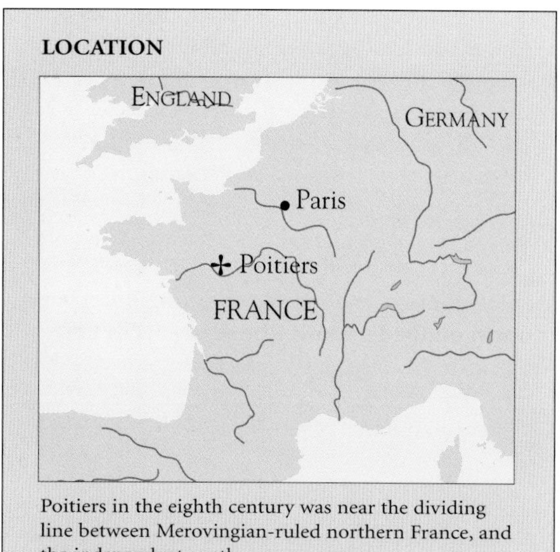
England
Germany
Paris
Poitiers
FRANCE

Poitiers in the eighth century was near the dividing line between Merovingian-ruled northern France, and the independent south.

Charles Martel wasn't officially the Frankish king. He was simply the Mayor of the Palace to the Merovingians – the leading official – but this was an ailing dynasty of ineffective kings, and the mayors had increasingly assumed charge. Charles ruled the Merovingian domains, in effect, and he efficiently defended the borders, leading successful campaigns against the neighbouring Frisians and Saxons in the north, and against the Basques in the south. Still, Aquitaine, retaining a culture more romanized than the Germanic Franks, had maintained a large measure of independence from Merovingian control.

The southern borders of Aquitaine met the western Pyrenees, beyond which was Al-Andalus, the kingdom of Muslim-conquered Spain, under the rule of the Arab Umayyad dynasty. Abd al-Rahman al-Ghafiqi, the Umayyad governor of Al-Andalus, planned an invasion across the Pyrenees – though with a relatively small army. It is possible he was not intending to settle but rather to soften up the area with a series of raids. There were several 'Saracen' booty-gathering missions into areas nominally

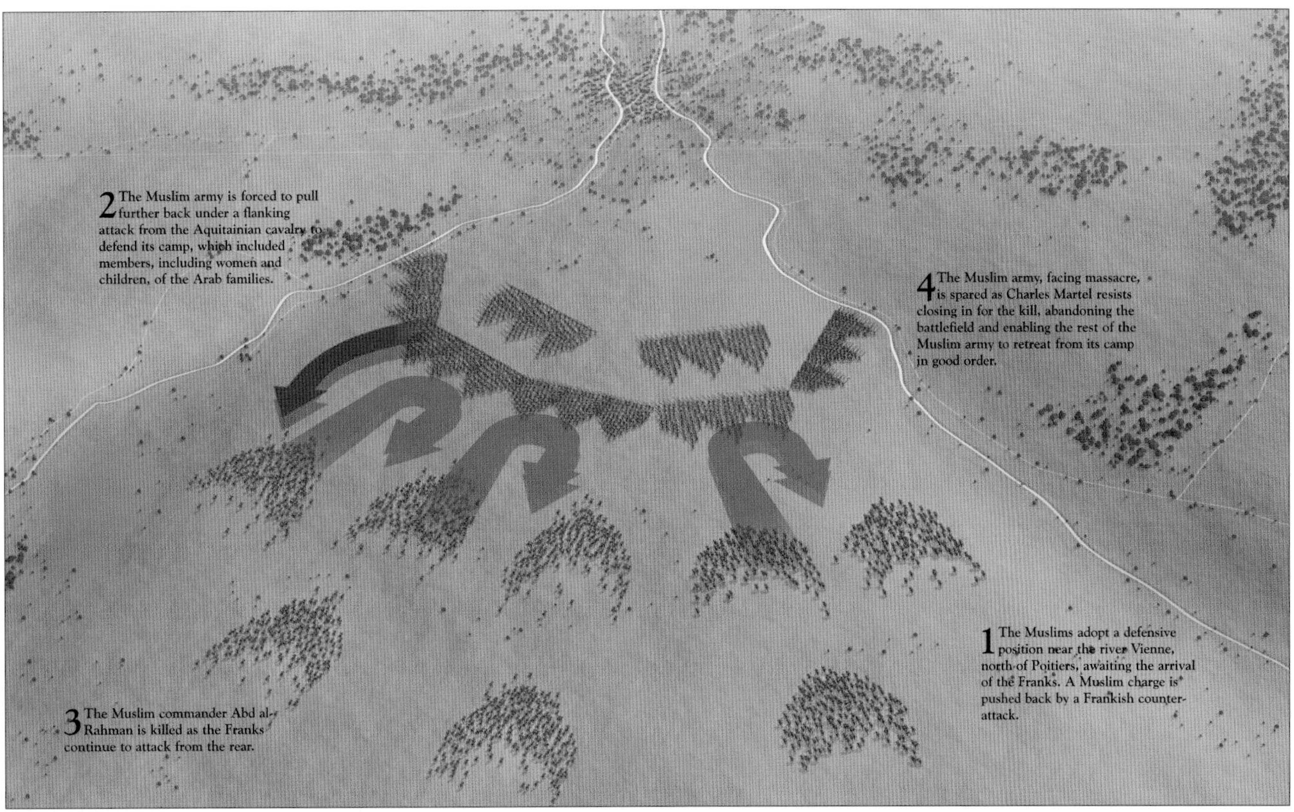
2 The Muslim army is forced to pull further back under a flanking attack from the Aquitainian cavalry to defend its camp, which included members, including women and children, of the Arab families.
4 The Muslim army, facing massacre, is spared as Charles Martel resists closing in for the kill, abandoning the battlefield and enabling the rest of the Muslim army to retreat from its camp in good order.
1 The Muslims adopt a defensive position near the river Vienne, north of Poitiers, awaiting the arrival of the Franks. A Muslim charge is pushed back by a Frankish counter-attack.
3 The Muslim commander Abd al-Rahman is killed as the Franks continue to attack from the rear.

The Arab army arrived at Poitiers having already raided several towns north of the Pyrenees. It had forced the proudly independent Aquitainians to seek the help of Charles Martel's Frankish army.

under the Franks in 731, attacking Arles, in Provence, and up through Burgundy, as far north as Sens. But the invasion of 732 was a far more serious event.

Once across the western mountains, several towns were ransacked and abbeys burned. When the city of Bordeaux was stormed, its governor executed and civilians put to the sword, Prince Eudes of Aquitaine retreated to Reims and, probably with deep reluctance, requested the help of Charles Martel. Charles reacted with typical decisiveness, mustering as large an army as he could and marching south to the border city of Tours, on the River Loire. It was not far south of here that some initial clashes of advanced forces of Franks and Arabs took place, but Abd al-Rahman had positioned his main army in a defensive position beyond the river Vienne, just north of Poitiers, waiting for the arrival of Charles's troops.

Certifiable details of the battle are few, but it appears fighting began with a Muslim charge, which was met by a Frankish counter-attack. The Muslim army's great strength at this time lay in its mounted infantry, carrying spears and swords, many of them of Berber origin, as well as some Turks and Persians. The horsemanship of the professional cavalry element within their ranks was aided by the adoption of the stirrup. This was in contrast to the Frankish horsemen of the time who, although donning helmet and chain mail, still went into battle stirrup-less. As was common amongst Western cavalry of the time, they bore javelins.

THE HAMMER IS VICTORIOUS

While Charles Martel attacked the main Muslim line, Prince Eudes and his Aquitainian cavalry went for the Muslim rear, forcing them to retreat to their fortified camp. During this stand, Abd al-Rahman was killed by a javelin. While this seemed to hand victory to the Franks, the Arab army was able to withdraw from the field in good order. Charles, with pressing concerns still to attend to further north on the Frankish Rhone, seems to have chosen not to pursue them. While there would be further Muslim raids north of the Pyrenees, however, they would never attack Aquitaine again. Charles 'The Hammer' had, as ever, been thoroughly effective.

TIMELINE

1500–1000BC	1000–500BC	500BC–0AD	0–500AD	500–1000AD	1000–1500AD	1500–2000AD

Viking Seine Campaign 841–911

KEY FACTS

Who Viking raiders against West Francia, under rule of the Carolingian king Charles the Bald (reigned 840–877).

What When the Vikings began launching amphibious raids on the settlements along the waterways of northern France, Charles the Bald adopted a dual policy of paying them off while gradually building up fortified bridges to bar their way.

Where Northern France.

When 841–911

Why Viking raids had become increasingly frequent across Northern Europe during the ninth century in the 'First Viking Age'.

Outcome Charles the Bald's policy slowed the Viking advances, but did not prevent Paris from being threatened in 885.

To the Christian Franks, the Vikings seemed the epitome of godlessness in their relentless targeting of Church properties and their valuable furnishings. Paying them protection money was one way of dealing with them, but the improvement of fortification was a better long-term policy.

VIKING SEINE CAMPAIGN

VIKING VICTORY

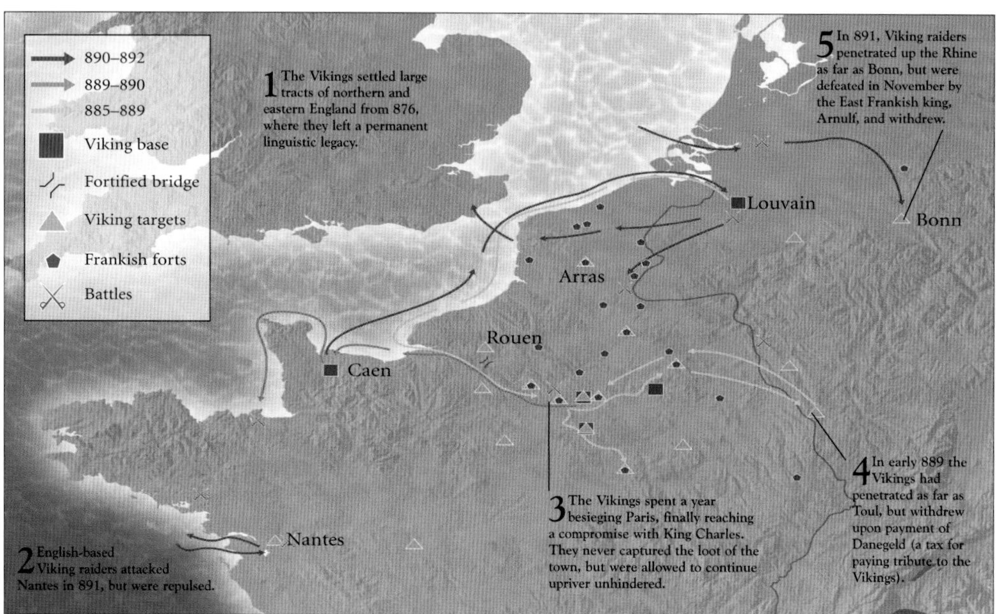
890–892
889–890
885–889
Viking base
Fortified bridge
Viking targets
Frankish forts
Battles
1 The Vikings settled large tracts of northern and eastern England from 876, where they left a permanent linguistic legacy.
5 In 891, Viking raiders penetrated up the Rhine as far as Bonn, but were defeated in November by the East Frankish king, Arnulf, and withdrew.
Louvain
Bonn
Arras
Rouen
Caen
Nantes
2 English-based Viking raiders attacked Nantes in 891, but were repulsed.
3 The Vikings spent a year besieging Paris, finally reaching a compromise with King Charles. They never captured the loot of the town, but were allowed to continue upriver unhindered.
4 In early 889 the Vikings had penetrated as far as Toul, but withdrew upon payment of Danegeld (a tax for paying tribute to the Vikings).

The Viking raids on northern France concentrated on the use of the riverways to move inland, with the Seine providing especially lucrative territory with its rich monasteries.

The lightning amphibious attacks of Viking raiding parties struck terror into local populations, not only because of the bloodshed, enslavement, burning and pillaging that ensued, but because, as pagans, they had no compunction about targeting churches and monasteries, whose furnishings, books and monuments provided valuable loot.

BLOCKADING WATERWAYS

The raids grew increasingly frequent from 841. Not only did they use their boats to terrorize settlements along the Seine, Loire and Garonne, but they began setting up winter camps at the river mouths. In the 850s, Paris was sacked twice. King Charles the Bald's policy was to pay them off with 'protection money', but it only kept bringing them back for more. Gradually, though, he was able to limit their mobility by constructing forts and fortified bridges on the main rivers. By blocking points upriver, it forced the Vikings to give up the advantage of their ships and maraud across land. It slowed the attacks for a time, although the Vikings would be back in 885.

LOCATION

SCANDINAVIA
IRELAND
BRITAIN
FRANCIA
MAGYARS
BYZANTINE EMPIRE

Vikings also raided southern France and Spain, even penetrating into the Mediterranean Sea as far as the southern coast of Italy.

TIMELINE

1500–1000BC	1000–500BC	500BC–0AD	0–500AD	500–1000AD	1000–1500AD	1500–2000AD

Siege of Paris 885–886

VIKING SEINE CAMPAIGN

STALEMATE

The Vikings were a persistent threat to the inhabitants of northern France in the ninth century. Much of their success owed itself to the surprise element inherent in rapid movements of their raiding parties along rivers, or over land. But in 885, they found Paris was prepared for them.

KEY FACTS

WHO The Viking hordes against the inhabitants of Paris, led by their Count Odo.

WHAT The Vikings sailed up the Seine to extract their usual protection money, but found their way thwarted by newly fortified barrage bridges across the river.

WHERE Paris, France.

WHEN 885–886

WHY The Vikings had carried out periodic attacks on Paris in the ninth century, and were usually paid off. But stronger fortifications now encouraged the Parisians to trust in the effectiveness of barrage bridges to thwart further attacks.

OUTCOME The Vikings were frustrated by the Parisians' resistance and after negotiations they were eventually persuaded to raise their siege, though their maraudings continued elsewhere.

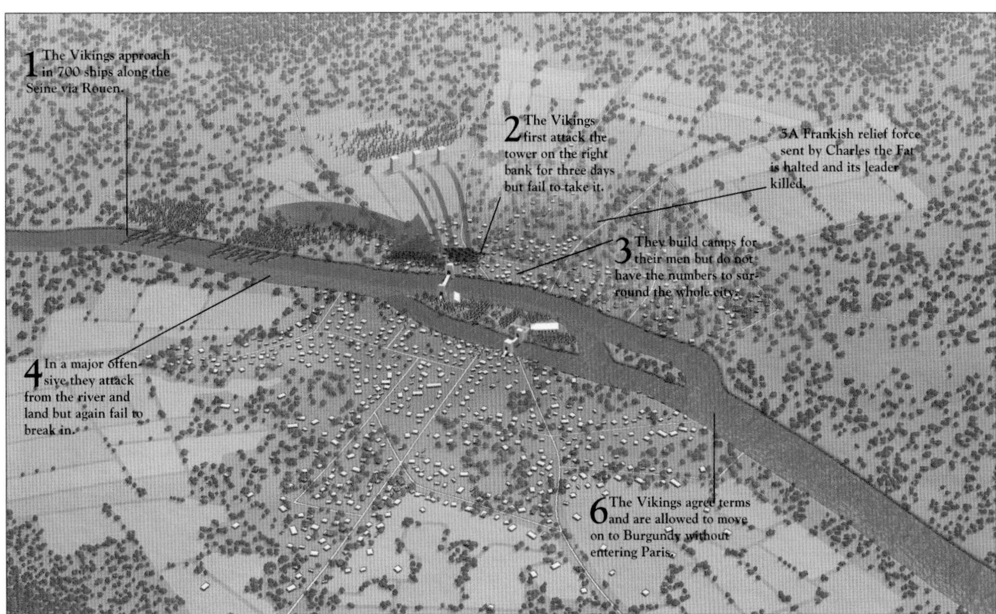
1 The Vikings approach in 700 ships along the Seine via Rouen.
2 The Vikings first attack the tower on the right bank for three days but fail to take it.
3 They build camps for their men but do not have the numbers to surround the whole city.
4 In a major offensive they attack from the river and land but again fail to break in.
5 A Frankish relief force sent by Charles the Fat is halted and its leader killed.
6 The Vikings agree terms and are allowed to move on to Burgundy without entering Paris.

The Vikings had been sailing down the Seine for years to raid Paris, but by 885 the citizens had better defences. These didn't solve the problem entirely, but it gave more hope of holding out and taking the fight to the Vikings inland.

The marauding Vikings approached Paris by sailing up the River Seine with 700 ships, sacking the town of Rouen on the way. However, Count Odo of Paris refused to let them through. The main city was centred on an island – the Isle de France – with fortified bridges to the left and right banks, built by the Carolingian rulers. The Vikings began by attacking a tower defending the bridge on the right bank, using engines and belfries, fire and mines, but they failed to break in. Next, they built a camp with the intention of starving the city into submission. But they lacked the manpower to surround and close off all routes into the city, and consequently the defenders' supply lines remained open.

The Vikings made one major attempt by storm, attacking from both land directions and from the river at the same time, but this was no more successful, and the city held out, despite being hit by an outbreak of plague. A relief force sent by the king of West Francia, Charles the Fat, was repelled and lost its leader, but the Vikings were persuaded to leave. They were allowed to go on to continue their campaign in Burgundy, but Paris was never entered.

LOCATION

ENGLAND

FRANCIA

Paris

Paris was the key city defending the Seine from Viking approach into Francia. Its bridges were aimed at preventing the Vikings from going on up the river.

TIMELINE

1500–1000BC	1000–500BC	500BC–0AD	0–500AD	500–1000AD	1000–1500AD	1500–2000AD

Siege of Paris

SIEGE OF PARIS

Imagine being an inhabitant of one of the towns along the Seine in the ninth century as the longboats of the Vikings suddenly rowed into view. The Parisians had lived with this terrifying experience for decades, and were heartily sick of it. The Vikings had even began overwintering at the mouth of the Seine. However, the citizens gradually built up the fortifications of Paris, increasingly assuming preeminence among the towns of northern France, so that when a raid came again in 885 the Vikings met greater resistance than previously. It didn't solve the problem completely, but it meant the beleagured local population had a better chance of sleeping at nights.

Lechfeld 955

KEY FACTS

WHO Otto I leads the dukes of Germany and their armies against the Magyars lead by their chieftain Bulcsu.

WHAT The Magyars had exploited a recent revolt against Otto, but at last he was able to draw upon a unified German force to confront them in a set-piece battle.

WHERE On the floodplains of Lechfeld, south of Augsburg, Swabia, on the banks of the Lech river.

WHEN 10 August 955

WHY Magyars from the Hungarian region had launched plundering attacks on the Western European frontier, exploiting disunity amongst the German lord principalities.

OUTCOME Otto's success was a major step towards creating a more united Germany. It not only ended the Magyar threat but also led to them settling down and establishing the kingdom of Hungary.

The Magyars had menaced the borders of Germany for over half a century, but King Otto I's resounding victory over them at Lech ended their threat for ever. Victory meant Otto emerged as the clear leader of Germany, and a few years later he would be crowned Holy Roman Emperor in Rome.

WARS OF THE GERMAN STATES

GERMAN VICTORY

The defeat of the Hungarian army at the battle of Lechfeld by the Holy Roman Emperor Otto I was one of the most celebrated events in German military history, a key moment in engendering a sense of unity and nationhood.

LOCATION

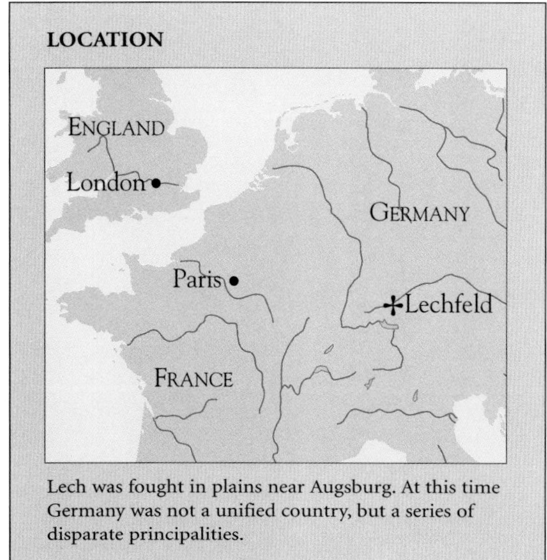
ENGLAND
London
GERMANY
Paris
Lechfeld
FRANCE

Lech was fought in plains near Augsburg. At this time Germany was not a unified country, but a series of disparate principalities.

In the early tenth century, what is now modern Germany was essentially a group of duchies, each with their own local political structures, whose boundaries were readily breached by northern and eastern raiders, including Danes, Slavs, and the semi-nomadic Magyars, or Huns. Gradually, the dukes of Saxony achieved a measure of control over the other princes, thanks to prestigious victories on the battlefield. In 936, Otto of Saxony was crowned as king of Germany in Aachen. This was symbolically important because Aachen was the palace of the former Carolingian emperor Charlemagne, the first of the Holy Roman Emperors, who was crowned in Rome by the Pope in 800 and in whose footsteps Otto would eventually follow after the events at Lech.

GERMAN RESISTANCE

The Magyar continued to attack with success until 955, when they finally found the Germans had at last closed ranks behind their king. After failing to take the city of Augsburg under the leadership of chieftain Bulcsu, they

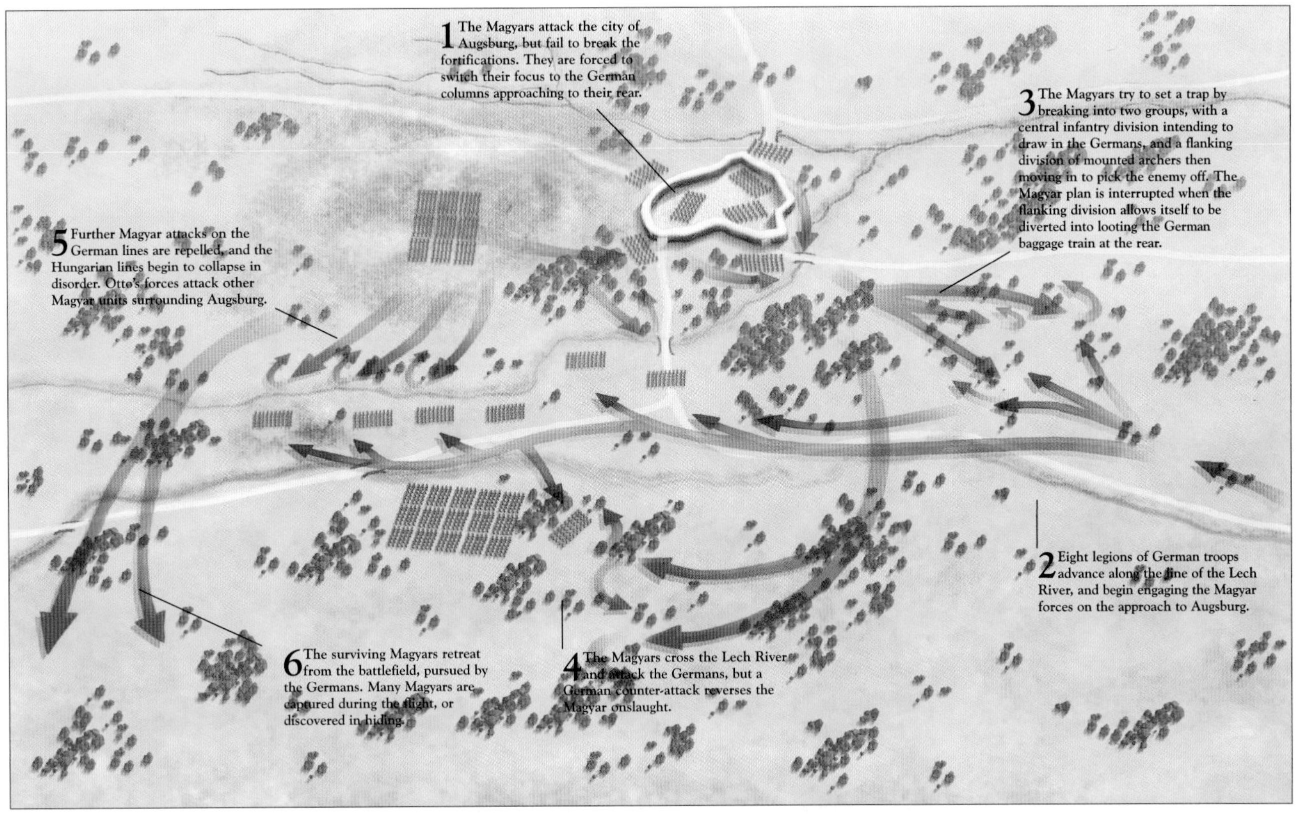
1 The Magyars attack the city of Augsburg, but fail to break the fortifications. They are forced to switch their focus to the German columns approaching to their rear.
3 The Magyars try to set a trap by breaking into two groups, with a central infantry division intending to draw in the Germans, and a flanking division of mounted archers then moving in to pick the enemy off. The Magyar plan is interrupted when the flanking division allows itself to be diverted into looting the German baggage train at the rear.
5 Further Magyar attacks on the German lines are repelled, and the Hungarian lines begin to collapse in disorder. Otto's forces attack other Magyar units surrounding Augsburg.
2 Eight legions of German troops advance along the line of the Lech River, and begin engaging the Magyar forces on the approach to Augsburg.
6 The surviving Magyars retreat from the battlefield, pursued by the Germans. Many Magyars are captured during the flight, or discovered in hiding.
4 The Magyars cross the Lech River and attack the Germans, but a German counter-attack reverses the Magyar onslaught.

The battle of Lechfeld unfolded on a flood plain beside the River Lech. Many of the retreating Hungarians drowned when a feigned withdrawal merely led to their plunging into the river to escape the pursuing Germans.

managed a strategic retreat beyond the Lech river, where they met Otto's Saxon army, buoyed by the arrival of the troops of Henry, Duke of Bavaria, and Otto's son-in-law Charles of Lorraine, and further swelled by divisions from Swabia, Franconia and Bohemia.

The Magyars tried to set a trap. By breaking into two groups, a central infantry division was intended to draw in the Germans, after which mounted archers on the flanks would move to pick them off. Indiscipline, however, proved their undoing when this flanking division stopped off to loot the German baggage train. The mistake was spotted by Otto, who quickly sent a detachment to attack the distracted pillagers. This caused a significant arm of the Magyar army to flee.

ON THE OFFENSIVE

Having secured his rear by seeing off this threat, Otto was now able to concentrate on attacking the main Magyar columns. At this moment he is recorded to have proclaimed, in the inspirational style of many great leaders in the field: 'They surpass us in number, I know, but neither in weapons nor courage. We also know they are quite without the help of God, which is of the greatest of comfort to us.'

Now the two armies faced up to each for a decisive head-to-head clash. Arrows rained down upon the German infantry as it advanced, but its greater discipline held firm, and the Magyars began to retreat in the face of it. Bulcsu, though, had one last card to play – the classic feint, so effectively deployed by Eastern cavalry over the centuries. Hot-headed armies would often be lured to their deaths when charging in headlong pursuit of what they mistakenly thought was a retreating enemy, believing victory was within their grasp, only to find their opponents turning upon them suddenly to renew the attack.

FAILED RETREAT

But it did not work at Lech, where retreat only meant running into the river itself, and many Magyars were drowned. Others fled to nearby villagers or hid out in the countryside. They were ruthlessly rounded up by Otto's men and killed, or sent home, minus their ears and noses.

Battle of Hastings 1066

KEY FACTS

Who A Norman army under William the Conqueror (1028–87) invaded England and fought a battle against an Anglo-Saxon force led by King Harold II Godwinson (c. 1022–1066).

What The battle was fought largely by Norman cavalry who charged several times up a hill into a shield wall formed by Anglo-Saxon infantry.

Where At Senlac Hill, 11km (7 miles) north of Hastings, now called Battle.

When 1066

Why William the Conqueror fought the battle in an effort to press his claim to the throne of England.

Outcome In a lengthy battle, after numerous Norman cavalry charges up Senlac Hill against the Anglo-Saxon shield wall, and two feigned retreats, many of the Anglo-Saxon infantry broke from their formation and ran down the hill into defeat.

Medieval warfare had very few decisive military engagements, but one certainly was the Battle of Hastings, fought between Duke William the Conqueror's invading Norman troops and King Harold II Godwinson's Anglo-Saxon army. The battle would lead to a new era in English history.

NORMAN INVASION OF ENGLAND

NORMAN VICTORY

EDWARD
REX:

Edward the Confessor had brought Normans favourites to England during his reign, and Duke William claimed he had designated him his heir. Then on his deathbed, Edward nominated the Saxon Harold Godwinson as his successor.

LOCATION

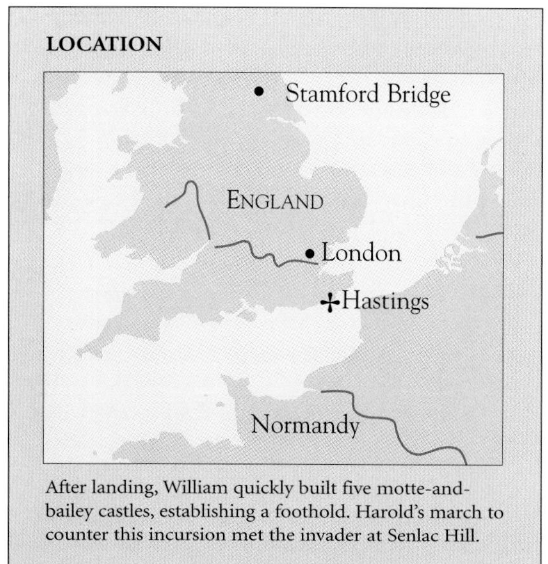
Stamford Bridge
England
London
Hastings
Normandy

After landing, William quickly built five motte-and-bailey castles, establishing a foothold. Harold's march to counter this incursion met the invader at Senlac Hill.

On his deathbed, on 5 January 1066, Edward the Confessor had recognized Harold Godwinson as the new King of England, but his coronation was disputed by Duke William of Normandy and King Harald Hardrada of Norway, who made their separate plans to invade England. Possibly because he thought that William was the greater of the two threats, Harold Godwinson prepared his army for William's invasion along the southern coast of England. But poor weather in the English Channel delayed the Normans, by which time Harald Hardrada had landed further north, and scored several early victories, forcing Harold to march swiftly north to meet him – and defeat him – at Stamford Bridge.

Harold then had to shift his troops south again because, by now, the weather had relented and enabled William's ships to cross the Channel. Finding terrain he believed suitable at Senlac Hill, and correctly guessing that William wanted to fight a battle, he lined up his troops using a well-known tactic, the shield wall. His infantry and dismounted cavalry stood in a tightly packed formation,

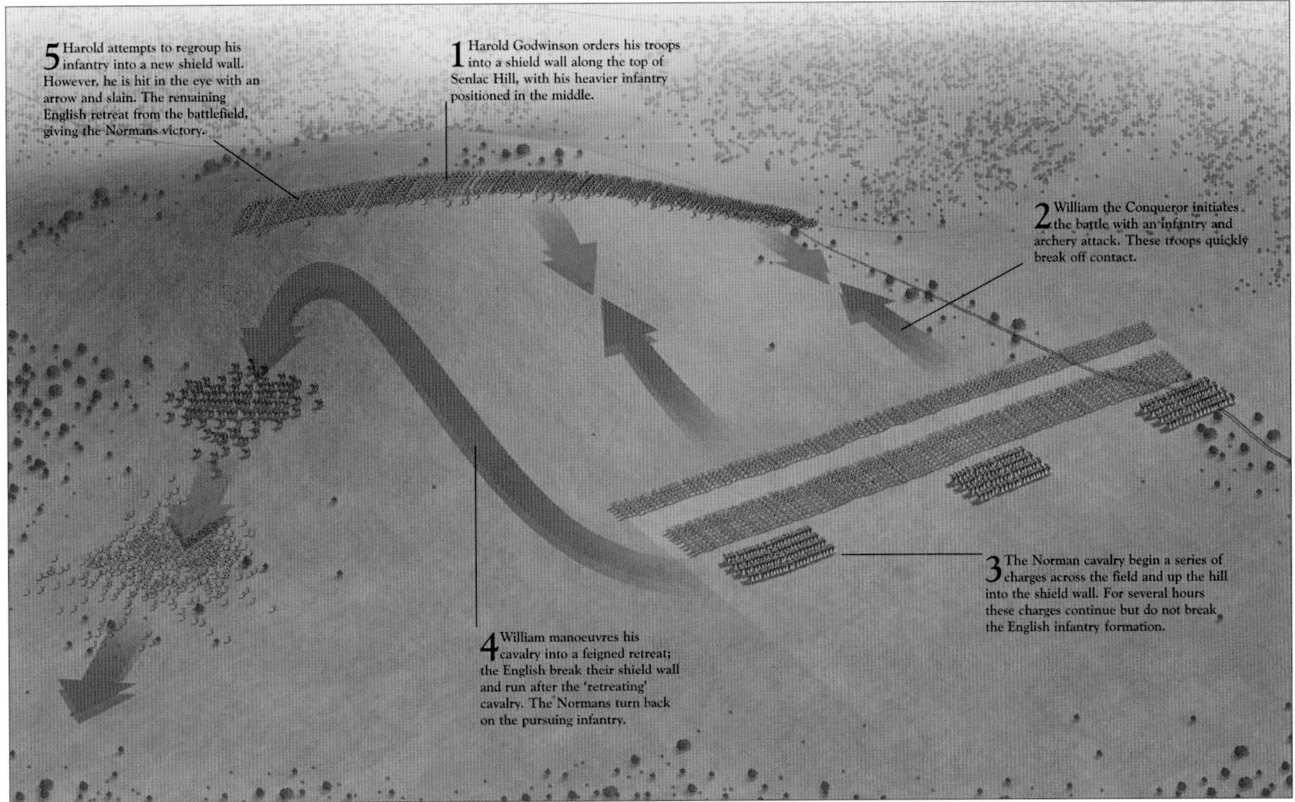
5 Harold attempts to regroup his infantry into a new shield wall. However, he is hit in the eye with an arrow and slain. The remaining English retreat from the battlefield, giving the Normans victory.
1 Harold Godwinson orders his troops into a shield wall along the top of Senlac Hill, with his heavier infantry positioned in the middle.
2 William the Conqueror initiates the battle with an infantry and archery attack. These troops quickly break off contact.
3 The Norman cavalry begin a series of charges across the field and up the hill into the shield wall. For several hours these charges continue but do not break the English infantry formation.
4 William manoeuvres his cavalry into a feigned retreat; the English break their shield wall and run after the 'retreating' cavalry. The Normans turn back on the pursuing infantry.

The Anglo-Saxon army occupied the high ground on Senlac Hill. Their shield wall was like a human fortification, and for a while seemed unbreakable. But it required discipline to hold the line, and the Anglo-Saxons failed in this critical aspect.

their shields overlapping one another in what was in effect a field fortification. If they could hold their position, it was almost impossible to break through.

In the centre of the shield wall fought the royal *huscarls,* Harold's most trusted and skilled troops, armoured in lengthy mail coats and feared for their use of the two-handed battle-axe. On the wings of the shield wall were the *fyrd,* a well-trained and skilled militia, adept with the spear and sword. A small number of archers also fought with the English forces.

Cavalry was the primary arm of William's force at Hastings. They were experienced warriors and horsemen, and formed the best cavalry force seen in centuries. William's tactic was basically for his cavalry to charge up the hill against the Anglo-Saxon shield wall. If stopped, they were to retreat, regroup, and charge again and again.

William began the battle using dismounted Norman archers and infantry, but soon the cavalry charges started, though for some time the shield wall repelled them. Then a rumour passed through the Norman ranks that William had fallen, which he rapidly quashed by lifting his helmet and showing his face. Then his forces regrouped for another charge.

That William was still fighting with them seemed to re-energize the Norman cavalry, enough at least to pull off one of the most widely used but difficult cavalry tactics: the feigned retreat. Some Anglo-Saxon troops were able to remain in their lines, but many others broke and pursued the 'retreating' Normans, only to realize too late that the cavalry had turned around and returned to the attack. Very few of the English troops who had run down the hill after the Normans could escape the re-charging horsemen, and they were ridden down and slain.

The battle had changed so quickly that Harold could do little more than try to regroup those soldiers who had not fallen for the Normans' trick. He attempted to form them again into a shield wall, but they proved to be too fatigued and disorganized to resist the Normans for long. They remained with their king until he was killed, apparently by an arrow that struck him in the eye. With this victory, William, Duke of Normandy and Count of Maine, had become William the Conqueror, King of England, as well.

Manzikert 1071

KEY FACTS

WHO Alp Arslan, Sultan of the Seljuk Turks, against the Byzantine army of Emperor Romanus IV.

WHAT Emperor Romanus assembled a large army to take the fight to the Seljuks, but found himself undone by the Turks deploying classically elusive tactics of advance and retreat on the battlefield.

WHERE Manzikert, modern Malazgirt, Turkey.

WHEN 26 August 1071

WHY Alp Arslan had invaded the Byzantine Empire, and Romanus IV had begun a retaliatory campaign in Anatolia.

OUTCOME Defeat was quickly followed by a coup d'état in Constantinople against the Emperor Romanus, and the further disunity this caused in the empire meant Alp Arslan was soon back on the attack.

Defeat at Manzikert by the Turks has often been painted as the moment the Byzantine Empire went into marked decline. In fact, decline owed much to the Empire's internal political disunity. Still, the defeat was a humiliation and made the papal crusades to rescue Asia Minor more likely.

BYZANTINE CAMPAIGN

TURKISH VICTORY

Alp Arslan's Turks were a much feared fighting force in the 11th century. Although they were implacable adversaries in close combat, they were also skilled bowmen – a decisive combination at Manzikert.

LOCATION

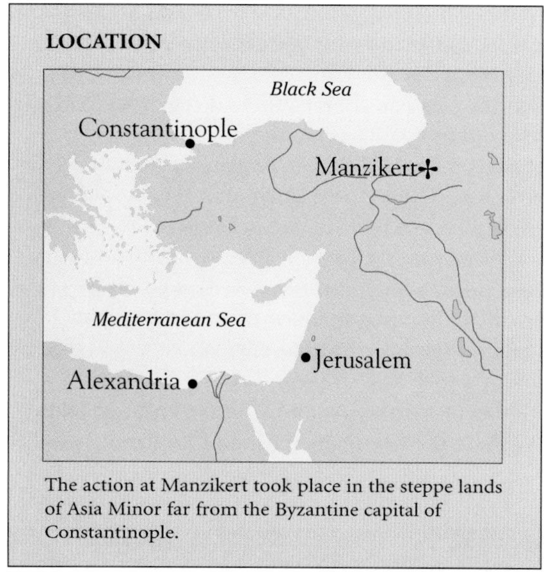
Black Sea
Constantinople
Manzikert
Mediterranean Sea
Jerusalem
Alexandria

The action at Manzikert took place in the steppe lands of Asia Minor far from the Byzantine capital of Constantinople.

Alp Arslan had been a thorn in the side of the Byzantine Empire since he first launched an attack upon it in 1064. Tearing up a truce that had been signed by his predecessor, he had conquered Ani, the capital of Armenia, and followed that up by swallowing up Armenia itself and, a couple of years later, Caesarea. Constantine X had been the ineffective Byzantine emperor in this period, but his successor Romanus IV, coming to power in 1068, determined to take a more aggressive stance, recognizing the threat to the entire empire posed by the Turkish upstart.

Romanus was a courageous general, but the Byzantine army he'd inherited was ill-equipped and deeply dependent on unreliable mercenaries. Meanwhile, there were many people in faction-ridden Constantinople who despised him, and a coup was always on the horizon. Still, he managed to effect some improvements to it before crossing the Bosphorus and marching across Anatolia against the Turks early in 1071. His action was actually in breach of a truce agreed with Alp Arslan the previous year, but when the sultan heard of Romanus's actions, he was

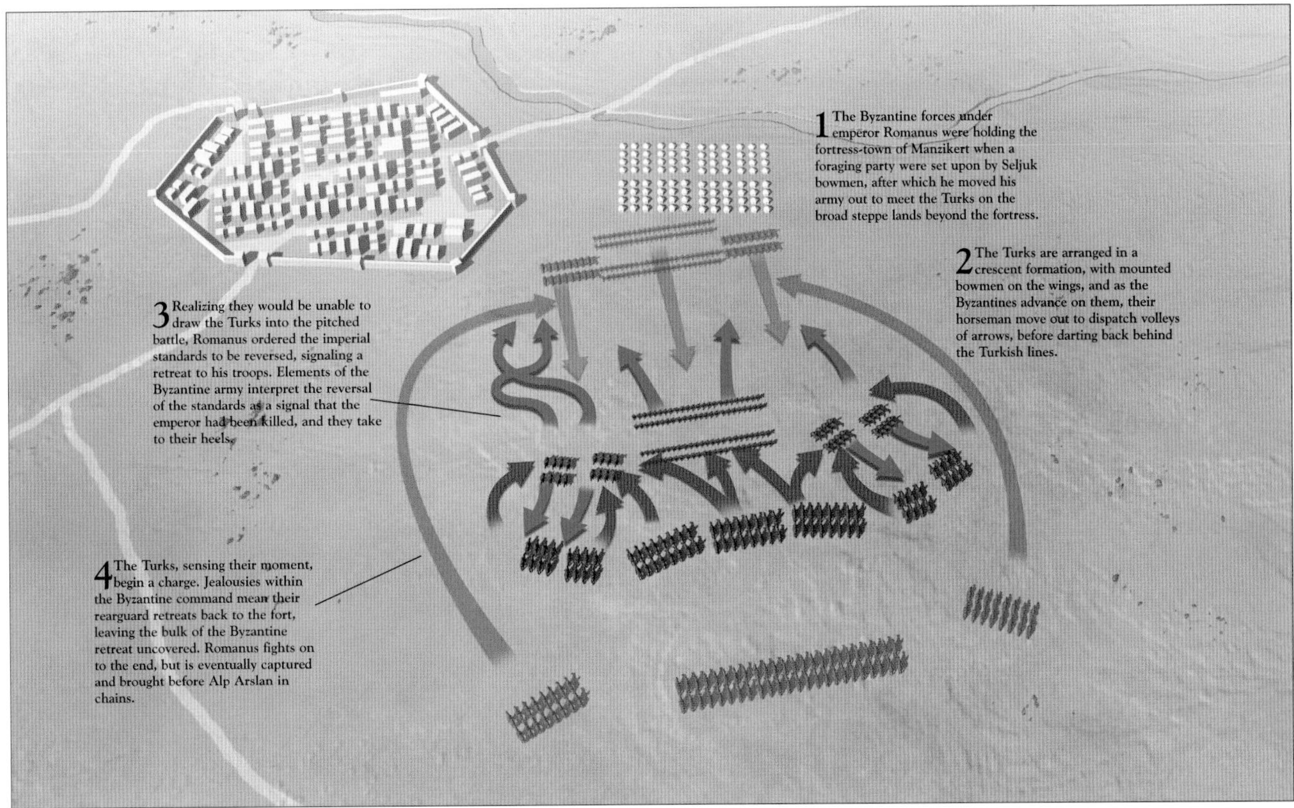
1 The Byzantine forces under emperor Romanus were holding the fortress-town of Manzikert when a foraging party were set upon by Seljuk bowmen, after which he moved his army out to meet the Turks on the broad steppe lands beyond the fortress.
2 The Turks are arranged in a crescent formation, with mounted bowmen on the wings, and as the Byzantines advance on them, their horseman move out to dispatch volleys of arrows, before darting back behind the Turkish lines.
3 Realizing they would be unable to draw the Turks into the pitched battle, Romanus ordered the imperial standards to be reversed, signaling a retreat to his troops. Elements of the Byzantine army interpret the reversal of the standards as a signal that the emperor had been killed, and they take to their heels.
4 The Turks, sensing their moment, begin a charge. Jealousies within the Byzantine command mean their rearguard retreats back to the fort, leaving the bulk of the Byzantine retreat uncovered. Romanus fights on to the end, but is eventually captured and brought before Alp Arslan in chains.

The Byzantine Emperor Romanus assembled a mighty army to confront Alp Arslan at Manzikert, knowing that, given his domestic political fragility, this was a one-off chance to confront the Turkish menace.

forced to break off from a campaign against the Fatimids and make ready to meet him.

Romanus took the fortress-town of Manzikert and the first awareness he had of the imminent arrival of the full Turkish army came soon after its capture, when a foraging party was set upon by Seljuk bowmen. In fact, Alp sent a peace delegation to the Emperor. This, though, was rejected by Romanus, who perhaps realized, given the precarious political situation back in Constantinople, that he could hardly risk spending so much time away again, and that the large army he had managed to assemble represented his best chance of crushing the Turks.

BYZANTINE ADVANCE

The battle, which took place on steppe land beyond the fortress, began with a Byzantine advance against the Turks, who were arranged in a crescent formation, with mounted bowmen on the wings. These would quickly essay out to dispatch volleys of arrows at the Byzantines and then dart back just as quickly before an effective response was possible. As the day wore on, realizing he was unable to draw the Turks into the pitched battle that might have run to his advantage, Romanus ordered the imperial standards to be reversed – the signal for his troops to move back.

RETREAT AND CONFUSION

But this was interpreted in some parts of the Byzantine army as meaning that the emperor had been killed and that the battle was lost. As they took to their heels, Alp Arslan sensed his moment had come and unleashed his men to fall upon the retreating enemy. Now the deep fissures and jealousies within the Byzantine leadership emerged, as Andronikas Doukas, in command of the rear, who should have covered the retreat, deliberately ignored Romanus's signal and retreated all the way back to the fort at Manikert. Romanus himself was captured, fighting defiantly to the end and was taken prisoner. Brought before Alp Arslan in chains, he was honourably treated by his enemy, which was more than could have been said of the commander who had betrayed him so desperately in his moment of need.

TIMELINE

1500–1000BC	1000–500BC	500BC–0AD	0–500AD	500–1000AD	1000–1500AD	1500–2000AD

Dorylaeum 1097

KEY FACTS

WHO Some 50,000 Crusaders, including 7000 knights and a small Byzantine allied contingent under Tatikios, faced a force of 10,000 Seljuk Turks and their Danishmund Turk allies under Kilij Arslan.

WHAT The Turks ambushed the Crusaders as they entered the Anatolian Plateau, while the latter were divided on the march from Nicaea.

WHERE Along the Byzantine military road, in a valley northwest of Dorylaeum.

WHEN 1 July 1097

WHY The Crusaders had taken the capital Nicaea and were marching through central Anatolia. Kilij Arslan now sought to defeat the Crusaders on the march.

OUTCOME The Turks had some initial success against the Crusaders' vanguard, but ultimately the Crusader army inflicted heavy losses on the Turks, opening the way for a conquest of Anatolia.

In November 1095, Pope Urban II (1042–1099) addressed many of the nobility and clergy of France at Clermont. He called for an expedition to aid the Christians of the east, notably the Byzantines, against the Turks, and to liberate Jerusalem and the holy places.

FIRST CRUSADE

CRUSADER VICTORY

The Crusaders looked to be on the back foot for a time at Dorylaeum, but when the contest turned to hand-to-hand fighting, their superior armour and close combat skills with the sword gave them the upper hand.

LOCATION

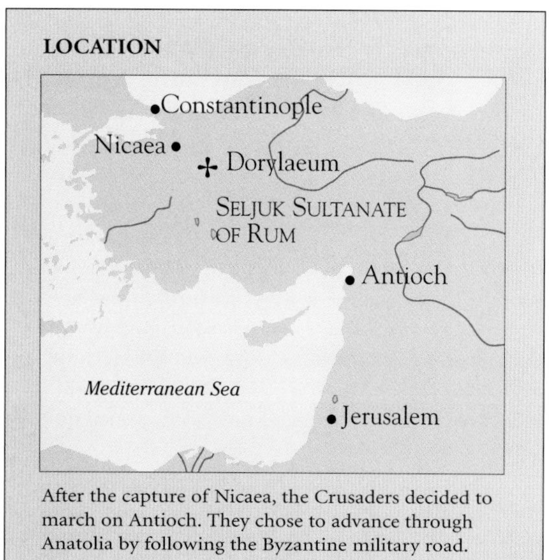
Constantinople
Nicaea
Dorylaeum
SELJUK SULTANATE OF RUM
Antioch
Mediterranean Sea
Jerusalem

After the capture of Nicaea, the Crusaders decided to march on Antioch. They chose to advance through Anatolia by following the Byzantine military road.

The First Crusade got off to a good start with a successful siege of the city of Nicaea, capital of the Turkish Sultan of Rum, Kilij Arslan. From here, the Crusaders planned to continue towards their ultimate objective, Jerusalem, by following the Byzantine military road to the southwest to Dorylaeum and then across the Anatolian Plateau and Syria.

Given the size of the army, and the lack of a truly unified command structure, the Crusader army was divided into two groups. The first was a vanguard, numbering fewer than 20,000 men, with Bohemond, Tancred, Stephen de Blois and Robert of Normandy, and including a small Byzantine force under the leadership of Tatikios. The main body consisted of more than 30,000 men and was accompanied by Robert, Count of Flanders, Godfrey de Bouillon, Raymond of Toulouse and Hugh of Vermandois.

Meanwhile, Kilij Arslan had regrouped his forces and was joined by an army of Danishmund Turks with whom he had forged an alliance, for a total of 10,000 cavalrymen. His plan was to ambush the Crusaders while their forces were divided.

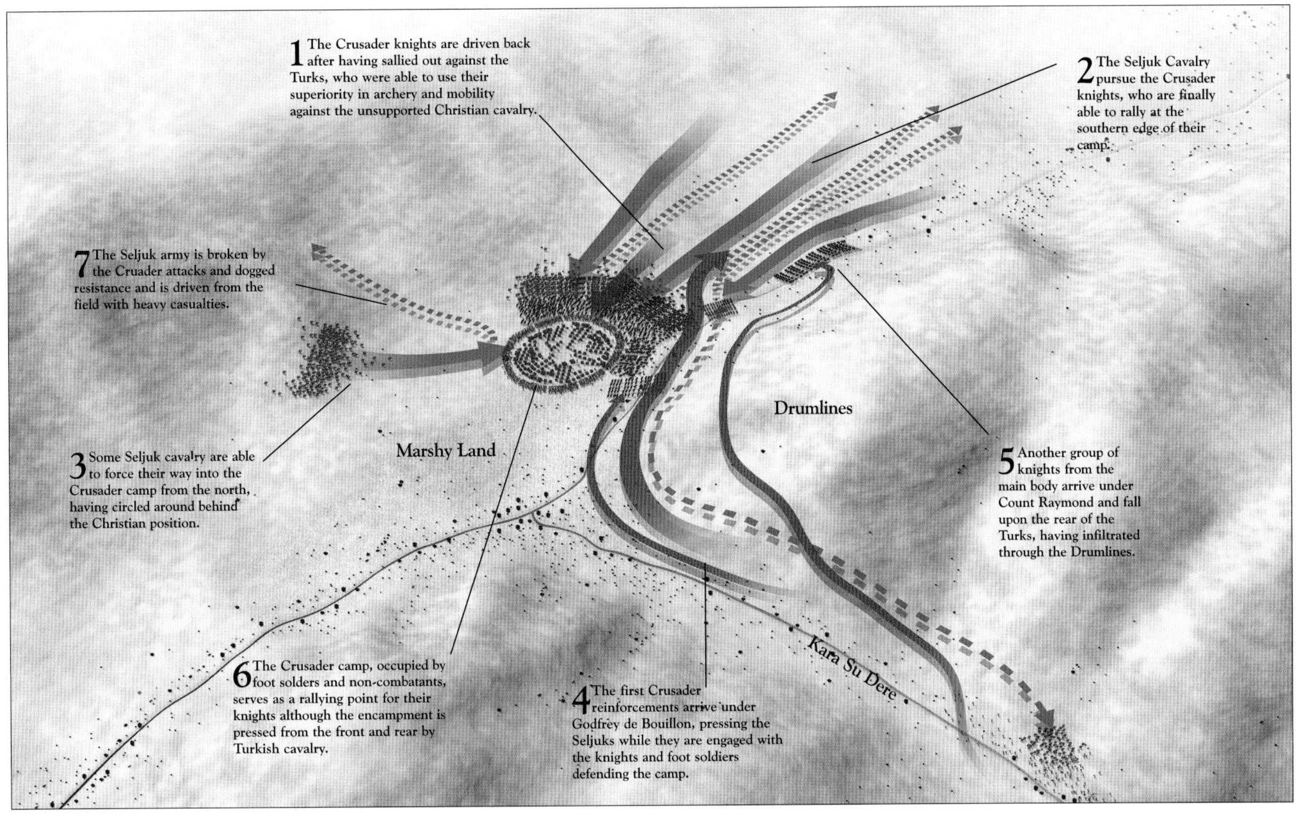
1 The Crusader knights are driven back after having sallied out against the Turks, who were able to use their superiority in archery and mobility against the unsupported Christian cavalry.
2 The Seljuk Cavalry pursue the Crusader knights, who are finally able to rally at the southern edge of their camp.
7 The Seljuk army is broken by the Cruader attacks and dogged resistance and is driven from the field with heavy casualties.
Drumlines
Marshy Land
3 Some Seljuk cavalry are able to force their way into the Crusader camp from the north, having circled around behind the Christian position.
5 Another group of knights from the main body arrive under Count Raymond and fall upon the rear of the Turks, having infiltrated through the Drumlines.
Kara Su Dere
6 The Crusader camp, occupied by foot soldiers and non-combatants, serves as a rallying point for their knights although the encampment is pressed from the front and rear by Turkish cavalry.
4 The first Crusader reinforcements arrive under Godfrey de Bouillon, pressing the Seljuks while they are engaged with the knights and foot soldiers defending the camp.

The Crusaders were pushed back on their heels for much of the battle, and reinforcements in the shape of Count Raymond's army arrived just in time to help swing their fortune.

His chosen spot was at the juncture of two valleys, which then opened into a larger plain. The space would allow him to draw out the Crusader knights and then surround them as they moved out of range of their infantry support. It would also give him local superiority of numbers at a key point on the battlefield and allow his mounted archers room to manoeuvre.

When the Crusaders discovered the presence of the Turks, they pitched camp to provide themselves with a defendable base. Bohemond deployed his mounted knights in front of the camp to intercept the main body of Turkish horsemen advancing from the south. The main body of the Christian force was advancing from the west and was a mere 5–6km (3–4 miles) behind the vanguard.

Soon the battle began in earnest, Bohemond advancing against the Turks with his main body of mounted knights. In doing so, he played to the strength of the enemy. As the knights moved forwards, they found themselves assailed by volleys of arrows from the mounted archers. Separated from the support of their foot soldiers defending the camp, the knights were shot at without being able to come to grips with the nomadic horse archers. At the same time, some of the Turkish cavalry, literally riding circles around the knights, attacked the Christian camp and apparently forced their way into it in the course of fierce hand-to-hand fighting.

The Christian knights were ultimately driven back to the southern edge of their camp, where the Turkish cavalry were no longer able to manoeuvre as freely, and got the worst of an ensuing close-quarters combat. At this point, the larger horses and heavier armour of the Crusaders seemed to give them a distinct advantage over the Turks.

Now reinforcements arrived from the Crusaders' main body, and as they attacked out of the valley from the west, the lightly armoured Seljuk cavalry found themselves caught between two forces of heavily armoured Crusader knights. Additional reinforcements from the Crusader main body under Count Raymond fell upon the rear of the Turkish army and, having suffered heavy casualties, they broke off the combat and retreated to the south. The battle ended with the Crusaders pursuing the Turks off the field. Both sides had suffered major losses, with the Crusaders losing perhaps 4000 men and the Turks about 3000.

Antioch 1098

FIRST CRUSADE

CRUSADER VICTORY

Hailed as miraculous by contemporaries, the Christian victory at Antioch came at a time when the Crusaders were starving and heavily outnumbered by their enemies. The Battle of Antioch was a great tactical triumph that saved the First Crusaders from annihilation.

KEY FACTS

WHO The army of the First Crusade fought a much larger mixed force of Turkish cavalry and Syrian infantry, led by Kerbogah, Atabeg of Mosul.

WHAT The Crusaders exited the recently captured city of Antioch to engage the Turkish besieging forces on the plain outside the city.

WHERE Along the west bank of the Orontes River, just outside the walls of Antioch (modern Antakya, Turkey).

WHEN 28 June 1098

WHY The Turkish force wanted to drive out the invading Crusaders; the Crusaders had to engage with the Turks or face starvation.

OUTCOME The Crusader force won a major tactical victory. Although the majority of Kerbogah's force never engaged the enemy, it withdrew, leaving the Crusaders in control of the region.

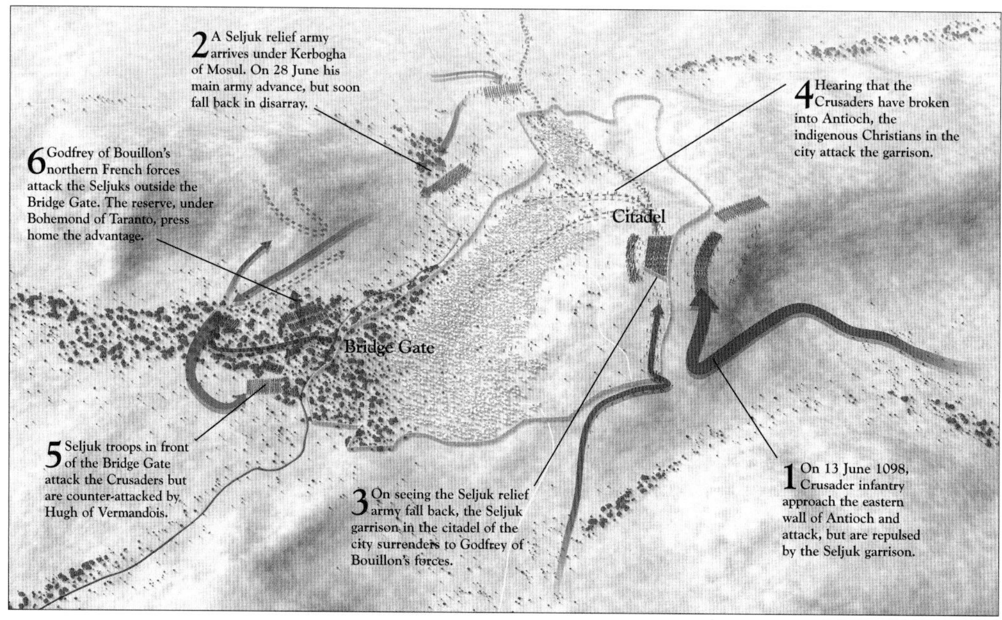

2 A Seljuk relief army arrives under Kerbogha of Mosul. On 28 June his main army advance, but soon fall back in disarray.
4 Hearing that the Crusaders have broken into Antioch, the indigenous Christians in the city attack the garrison.
6 Godfrey of Bouillon's northern French forces attack the Seljuks outside the Bridge Gate. The reserve, under Bohemond of Taranto, press home the advantage.
Citadel
Bridge Gate
5 Seljuk troops in front of the Bridge Gate attack the Crusaders but are counter-attacked by Hugh of Vermandois.
3 On seeing the Seljuk relief army fall back, the Seljuk garrison in the citadel of the city surrenders to Godfrey of Bouillon's forces.
1 On 13 June 1098, Crusader infantry approach the eastern wall of Antioch and attack, but are repulsed by the Seljuk garrison.

The city of Antioch was the key to Syria and ultimately on the road to Jerusalem for the Crusaders. Having taken it from the Muslims, they found themselves under siege and their escape was a narrow-run affair.

Having taken Antioch, the key to Syria, the Crusaders found themselves besieged by a large, mixed Turkish and Syrian relief force, led by Kerbogah, the governor of Mosul.

The Crusaders had to break out or starve, but their escape was aided by the fact that, while small Turkish divisions had been posted on the gates, the main army was some way off to the north. The Crusaders left the city unopposed, save for the brief fire of a few mounted bowmen, driven back by retorting Crusader archers.

Except for Bishop Adhemar's Provencal force, each Crusader contingent turned right after crossing the bridge outside of the city, marching along the bank of the Orontes River, which protected their right flank. This meant that the Turkish cavalry units that made it to the battlefield wasted their attacks on the smaller Crusader force, instead of supporting their infantry along the river. Kerbogah lost faith in his Syrian allies' will to fight, so the main Turkish force never even reached the Crusaders. The force that withdrew at Kerbogah's command massively outnumbered them, but the Crusaders had control of the region.

LOCATION

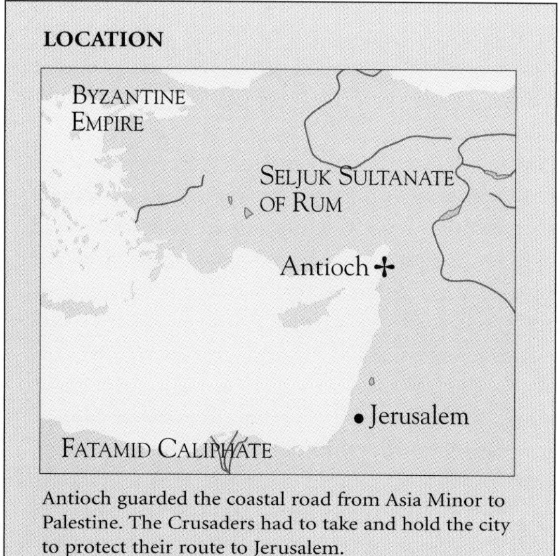

BYZANTINE EMPIRE
SELJUK SULTANATE OF RUM
Antioch
Jerusalem
FATAMID CALIPHATE

Antioch guarded the coastal road from Asia Minor to Palestine. The Crusaders had to take and hold the city to protect their route to Jerusalem.

TIMELINE

1500–1000BC	1000–500BC	500BC–0AD	0–500AD	500–1000AD	1000–1500AD	1500–2000AD

Ascalon 1099

KEY FACTS

Who A Crusader army of 9000 foot and 1200 knights, led by Raymond of Toulouse, Godfrey de Bouillon and Tancred, faced Fatimid Egypt's and Vizier al-Afdal's force of 20,000 men.

What The Crusaders left Jerusalem and moved to attack the Fatimid forces in their camp outside of Ascalon.

Where Just north of the port town of Ascalon, some 80km (50 miles) west of Jerusalem.

When 12 August 1099

Why The Crusaders had captured Jerusalem from the Fatimids after a five-week siege. The Fatimids sent an army to drive the Crusaders from the city, prompting the Crusaders to surprise the Egyptians at Ascalon.

Outcome The Egyptians were poorly coordinated. The Crusaders routed the enemy field army, but were unable to capture Ascalon itself.

With the Crusaders having taken Jerusalem, they had achieved their ultimate goal. Yet their situation remained perilous. When they learnt that an Egyptian army had taken control of the port of Ascalon, they knew immediate action was required, but leadership divisions undermined their response.

FIRST CRUSADE

NO CLEAR VICTORY

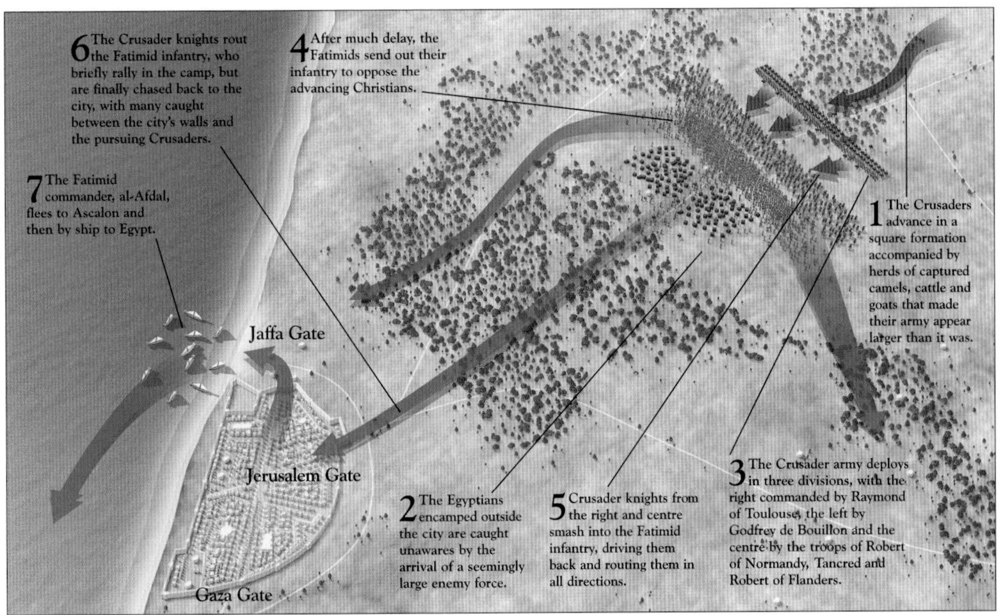
6 The Crusader knights rout the Fatimid infantry, who briefly rally in the camp, but are finally chased back to the city, with many caught between the city's walls and the pursuing Crusaders.
4 After much delay, the Fatimids send out their infantry to oppose the advancing Christians.
7 The Fatimid commander, al-Afdal, flees to Ascalon and then by ship to Egypt.
1 The Crusaders advance in a square formation accompanied by herds of captured camels, cattle and goats that made their army appear larger than it was.
Jaffa Gate
Jerusalem Gate
Gaza Gate
2 The Egyptians encamped outside the city are caught unawares by the arrival of a seemingly large enemy force.
5 Crusader knights from the right and centre smash into the Fatimid infantry, driving them back and routing them in all directions.
3 The Crusader army deploys in three divisions, with the right commanded by Raymond of Toulouse, the left by Godfrey de Bouillon and the centre by the troops of Robert of Normandy, Tancred and Robert of Flanders.

Ascalon's position near the sea made it a key strategic town, but the Crusader leadership were prone to squabbles and, despite a lengthy effort to take the city, this undermined their success.

An Egyptian Fatimid force had established themselves in the port city of Ascalon, some 80km (50 miles) to the west of Jerusalem. Realizing that it represented a potential threat to supply lines, a Crusader army set out to confront them, and their approach caught the Fatimids off guard. As their cavalry were largely unprepared, unarmed and unarmoured, foot soldiers were sent out to engage, but a hotly contested battle ensued with heavy casualties inflicted on both sides. Particularly fearsome were the Fatimid Azoparts with their heavy flails, which smashed through shields and armour. An attack of Christian knights from the right wing and centre finally scattered the Egyptian infantry and a general rout ensued, with many of the Fatimids trapped between the Crusaders and the city walls.

Although the Fatimid army outside the city had been routed, the garrison still held Ascalon itself. Squabbles within the Crusader leadership persuaded the town's commander to hold out and broke off negotiations. The end result was that Ascalon would remain in Muslim hands for another 54 years.

LOCATION

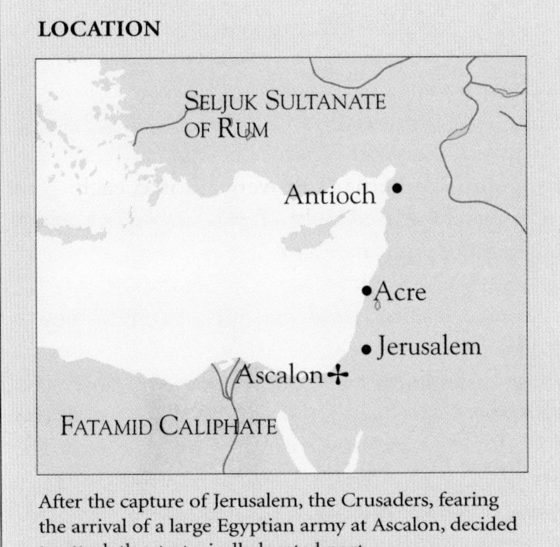
Seljuk Sultanate of Rum
Antioch
Acre
Jerusalem
Ascalon
Fatamid Caliphate

After the capture of Jerusalem, the Crusaders, fearing the arrival of a large Egyptian army at Ascalon, decided to attack the strategically located port.

TIMELINE

1500–1000BC	1000–500BC	500BC–0AD	0–500AD	500–1000AD	1000–1500AD	1500–2000AD

Siege of Jerusalem 1099

FIRST CRUSADE

CRUSADER VICTORY

On 15 July 1099, the First Crusade reached its ultimate goal – the Church of the Holy Sepulchre – but only after a bloody assault that showed yet again the versatility, military skill and perseverance of the Crusader forces.

KEY FACTS

WHO The remnants of the Christian armies of the First Crusade fought the Fatimid Egyptian garrison of Jerusalem, under the command of the governor Iftikhar-ad-Daulah.

WHAT In an extended and hard-fought assault, the Crusaders broke into Jerusalem and claimed it as Christian territory.

WHERE Jerusalem

WHEN 13–15 July 1099

WHY By 1099 the whole focus of the First Crusade had been the conquest of the city of Jerusalem, to regain the city of Christ's death and resurrection as the natural and God-given possession of Christendom.

OUTCOME The Crusaders took the city and established a Christian state with Jerusalem as its capital, electing Duke Godfrey of Lorraine as 'advocate' of the Holy Sepulchre.

Conducting a siege while on Crusade: in truth, it required more than sword and a rickety ladder to reduce some of the mighty fortifications that the Western armies encountered en route to Jerusalem.

LOCATION

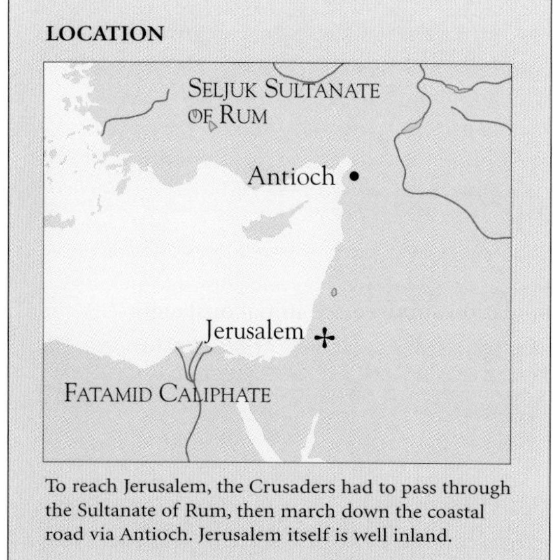
SELJUK SULTANATE
OF RUM
Antioch
Jerusalem
FATAMID CALIPHATE

To reach Jerusalem, the Crusaders had to pass through the Sultanate of Rum, then march down the coastal road via Antioch. Jerusalem itself is well inland.

The Crusader army reached Jerusalem, by now in the control of the Egyptian Fatimid Caliphate, by 7 June 1099, walking barefoot as penitents and overcome with joy at the sight of the Holy City for the final yards. Almost immediately, the council of Crusade leaders planned an assault. When a fleet of six Italian ships arrived at Jaffa, carrying supplies and vital timber, the Crusaders rapidly started building two siege towers and a large ram (suspended in a framework that was moved on rollers), assault ladders, mangonels and other stone and bolt-throwing devices.

ASSAULT ON THE HOLY CITY

The assault proper commenced a month later at the north of the city. A ram was brought up to the wall, with the defenders trying to stop it with a barrage of missiles. By aiming their mangonels at the troops on the walls, the Crusaders inflicted serious damage on the Muslims. As the Crusaders positioned the ram at the foot of the wall, the enemy worked desperately to burn it, with flaming

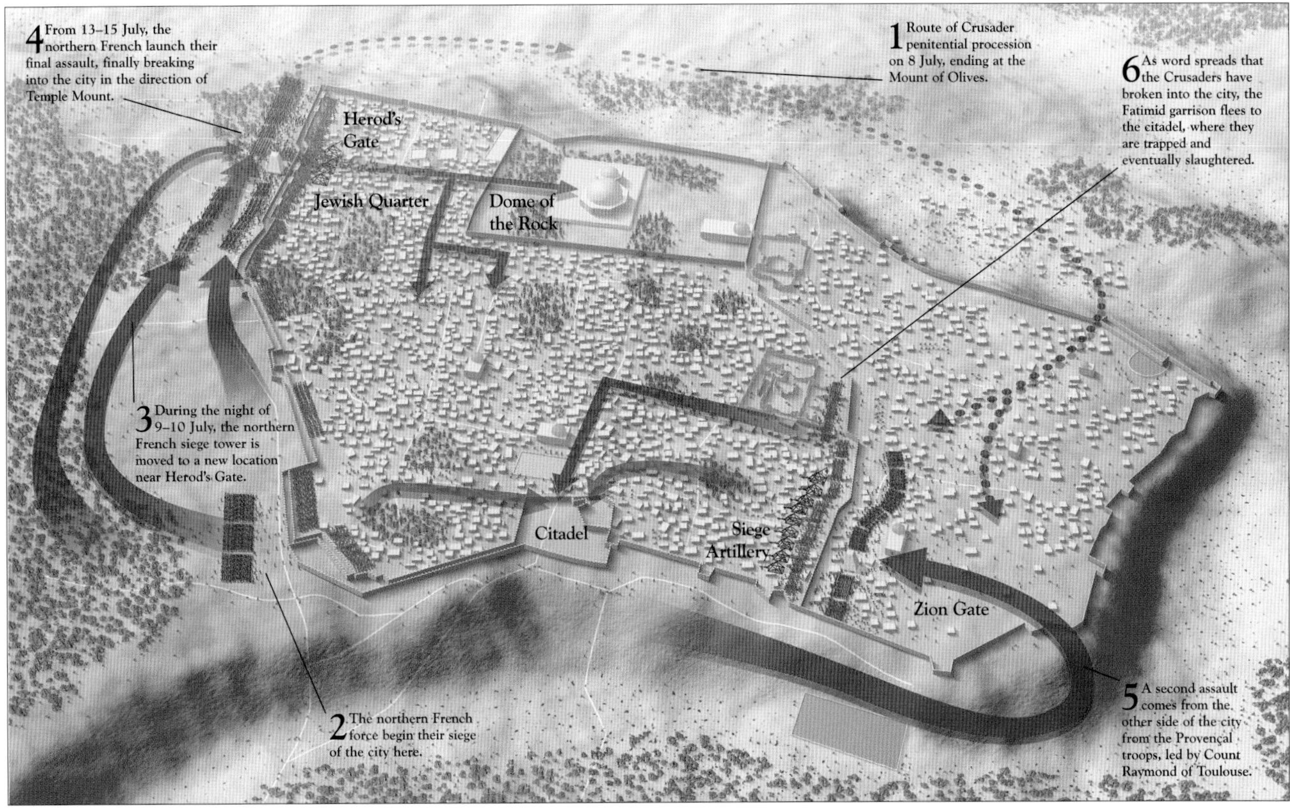
4 From 13–15 July, the northern French launch their final assault, finally breaking into the city in the direction of Temple Mount.
Herod's Gate
Jewish Quarter
Dome of the Rock
1 Route of Crusader penitential procession on 8 July, ending at the Mount of Olives.
6 As word spreads that the Crusaders have broken into the city, the Fatimid garrison flees to the citadel, where they are trapped and eventually slaughtered.
3 During the night of 9–10 July, the northern French siege tower is moved to a new location near Herod's Gate.
Citadel
Siege Artillery
Zion Gate
2 The northern French force begin their siege of the city here.
5 A second assault comes from the other side of the city from the Provençal troops, led by Count Raymond of Toulouse.

They were miles from home, but to take Jerusalem the Crusaders were able to bring into play some heavy-duty siege weaponry, including a siege tower 15–17m (49–56ft) high. They were helped greatly by supply ships that had arrived in the port of Jaffa.

arrows and fire pots. Despite the defenders' efforts, the men operating the ram succeeded in bringing down a portion of the outer wall.

The inner wall was apparently too strong for the ram, and the space was very narrow, causing the ram itself to block the progress of the siege tower. So the Christians now set the ram alight themselves, while the defenders desperately tried to put out the flames. When the ram was finally destroyed, the Crusaders were able to move their siege tower close to the inner wall. The tower was a massive structure, standing about 15–17m (49–56ft) high and looming above the wall. Its purpose was to act as a platform for firing down on the wall's defenders, thus making it possible for other attackers to raise siege ladders and climb the walls in relative safety.

As the tower reached the wall, the defenders tried to tip it over, swinging against it a heavy beamthat they had suspended with ropes between two of the wall's towers. But the Crusaders succeeded in cutting the ropes that supported the beam, using blades attached to long poles for the purpose.

Unlike their north wall counterparts, the resilient defenders of the south wall managed to damage the siege tower deployed there so badly that it could not be brought up to the wall for the assault. But when word arrived that the northern assault was actually succeeding, the Crusader attackers launched a mad scramble for the wall with ladders and ropes.

They too succeeded in forcing their way into the city. The surviving members of the garrison retreated before the Crusaders into the citadel, but surrendered almost immediately when Count Raymond of Toulouse promised to protect them.

BLOODY MASSACRE

The following orgy of killing and looting was typical when an army took a city by assault, but much of the native population survived the initial onslaught – though three days later, the Crusader leaders ordered the massacre of all prisoners. Soon the Latin kingdom of Jerusalem was established, the focal point of Muslim–Christian struggle for the next two centuries.

Harran 1104

CRUSADES

TURKISH VICTORY

KEY FACTS

WHO Prince Bohemond I of Antioch (1098–1111), supported by Prince Tancred of Gallilee (1072–1112) and Lord Joscelin of Turbessel (1098–1131) against the Seljuk Atabeg Jekermish of Mosul and the Artukid Prince of Mardin, Sokman.

WHAT Harran ended the Crusaders' reputation for 'invincibility'.

WHERE Either the River Balikh or near the town of ar-Raqqah.

WHEN 7 May 1104

WHY Bohemond of Antioch and Count Baldwin I of Edessa wished to expand their territories, secure them against Muslim attacks and split the Seljuk states of Syria, Iraq and Anatolia – all to be achieved by taking Harran.

OUTCOME Muslim victory ensured that Edessa remained an isolated outpost surrounded by enemy-held territory.

The First Crusade left the French in control of Edessa, Antioch and Jerusalem. The Crusaders created the Principality of Antioch, ruled by Bohemond, while the Kingdom of Jerusalem and the County of Edessa were ruled by King Baldwin I. Bohemond and Baldwin lead their armies to defeat at Harran.

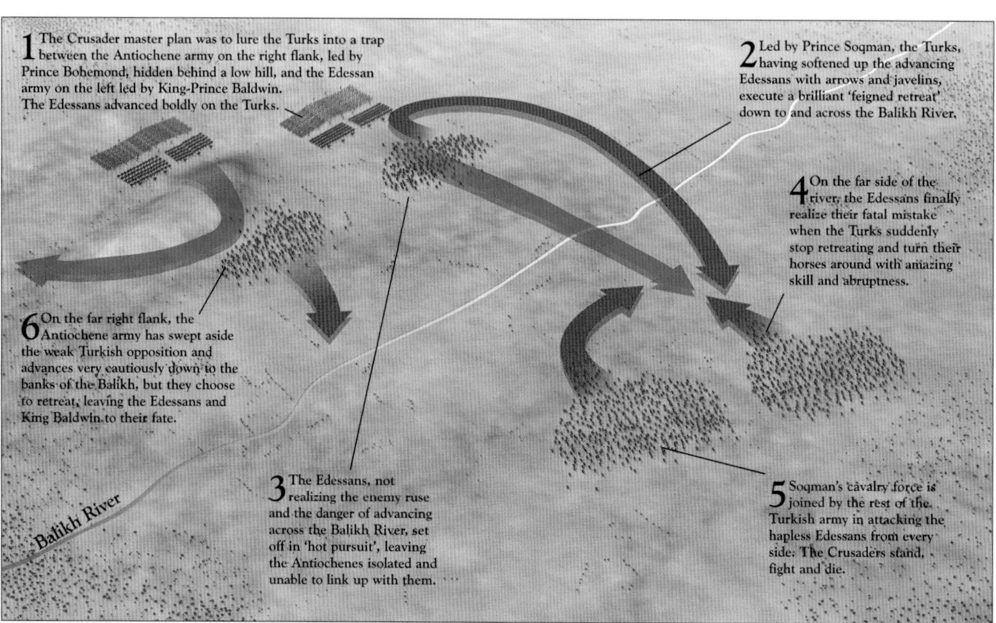
1 The Crusader master plan was to lure the Turks into a trap between the Antiochene army on the right flank, led by Prince Bohemond, hidden behind a low hill, and the Edessan army on the left led by King-Prince Baldwin. The Edessans advanced boldly on the Turks.
2 Led by Prince Soqman, the Turks, having softened up the advancing Edessans with arrows and javelins, execute a brilliant 'feigned retreat' down to and across the Balikh River.
3 The Edessans, not realizing the enemy ruse and the danger of advancing across the Balikh River, set off in 'hot pursuit', leaving the Antiochenes isolated and unable to link up with them.
4 On the far side of the river, the Edessans finally realize their fatal mistake when the Turks suddenly stop retreating and turn their horses around with amazing skill and abruptness.
5 Soqman's cavalry force is joined by the rest of the Turkish army in attacking the hapless Edessans from every side. The Crusaders stand, fight and die.
6 On the far right flank, the Antiochene army has swept aside the weak Turkish opposition and advances very cautiously down to the banks of the Balikh, but they choose to retreat, leaving the Edessans and King Baldwin to their fate.
Balikh River

The feigned retreat was something for which cavalrymen who learnt their craft on the wide, arid plains of the East were especially noted. At Harran, the Turks were able to bring this tactic decisively into play.

Prince Bohemond of Antioch and Count Baldwin I of Edessa (also King of Jerusalem) set out to capture the fortified city of Harran. But fighting took place on the plains beyond the fortress, where the Turks' cavalry and mounted archers' greater mobility, speed and agility was an advantage against the more formidable armour and weaponry of the slower-moving Crusaders.

The plan was for Bohemond's army to enter the fight only at a late stage to administer the knockout blow, but the Turks feigned a flight from the battlefield, luring Baldwin's men into a deadly trap that saw them showered with arrows and javelins from the flanks. As the Turks 'fled' across the Balikh River, Baldwin's men set off in hot-headed pursuit, only to find the rest of the Turkish army arrayed before them.

The Turks mounted a full-scale cavalry attack upon the outnumbered Edessans, who were cut down where they stood. Few prisoners were taken, as the Edessan army was completely destroyed and Baldwin captured. Bohemond, seeing the carnage, kept his men out of the fray, but Harran had done serious damage to the prestige of the crusading armies.

LOCATION

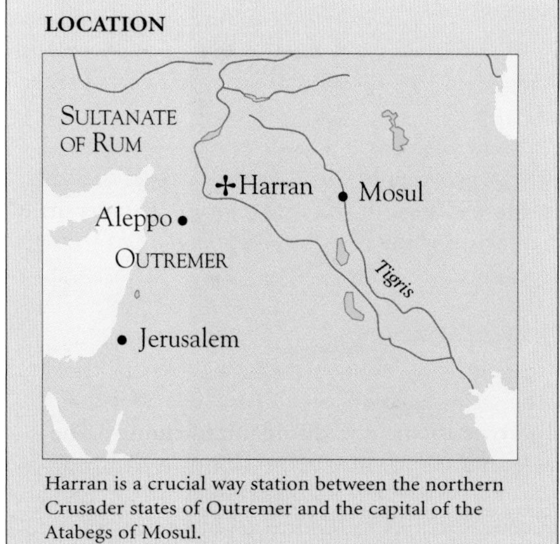
Sultanate of Rum
Harran
Mosul
Aleppo
Outremer
Tigris
Jerusalem

Harran is a crucial way station between the northern Crusader states of Outremer and the capital of the Atabegs of Mosul.

TIMELINE

1500–1000BC	1000–500BC	500BC–0AD	0–500AD	500–1000AD	1000–1500AD	1500–2000AD

Sarmada 1119

CRUSADES

TURKISH VICTORY

KEY FACTS

WHO Crusader forces from the Principality of Antioch under Roger of Salerno (d. 1119), numbering about 3700. They were opposed by a larger force of Turks under Ilghazi (d. 1122).

WHAT The Crusader force was surrounded and attacked by a superior enemy.

WHERE Kadesh was a rich and powerful fortified city that offered an excellent outpost to defend an empire, or from which to expand.

WHEN 1119

WHY The Crusaders responded to an invasion of their territory by the Turks, resulting in a meeting engagement.

OUTCOME The Crusader force was massacred, with few survivors.

The Battle of Sarmada, fought between the French Crusaders and the Turks, is also known as the Field of Blood, and for good reason. Less than 200 of the 3700 Crusader soldiers, led by Roger of Salerno, escaped with their lives.

The fully armoured Western knight charging at full pelt, lance at the ready, made for a magnificent spectacle. Against a nimbler Turkish cavalryman, with a lighter, swifter horse, however, he could just look clumsy and slow.

LOCATION

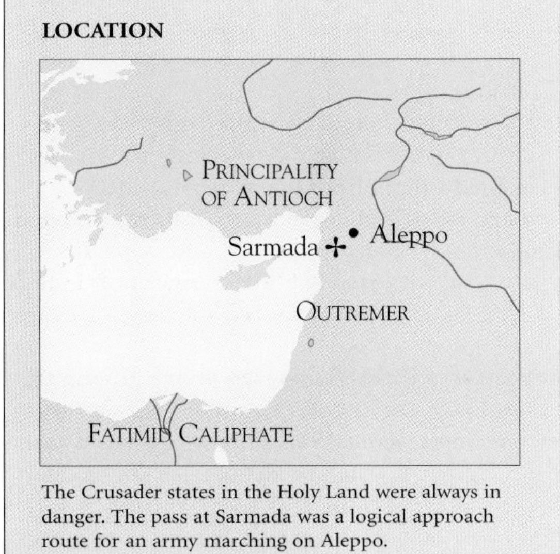
PRINCIPALITY OF ANTIOCH
Sarmada
Aleppo
OUTREMER
FATIMID CALIPHATE

The Crusader states in the Holy Land were always in danger. The pass at Sarmada was a logical approach route for an army marching on Aleppo.

Ilghazi of the Turkish Ortoqid dynasty had invaded the Crusader state of Antioch, and its regent, Roger of Salerno, despite being heavily outnumbered, advanced to meet the Muslim army at the pass of Sarmada. The initial charge of Roger's heavily armoured knights met with success and drove the enemy back, but they and their horses tired fast in the hot desert conditions, and as they became separated from their supports, the Crusader army began to break up, its small fighting groups quickly overwhelmed by their nimbler opponents.

Roger of Salerno tried to rally his men, but it was to no avail. He was struck down by a blow to the face as his army disintegrated.

There was nowhere to run. The Crusaders were now scattered all over the field in disorganized clumps. The Muslims slaughtered the Crusader army until virtually nothing was left of it. Only two of Roger's actual knights survived. In the end, some 3500 of the 3700 Crusaders engaged were killed.

TIMELINE

1500–1000BC	1000–500BC	500BC–0AD	0–500AD	500–1000AD	1000–1500AD	1500–2000AD

Lisbon 1147

KEY FACTS

WHO Northern European Crusaders under a group of minor nobles, along with local Christians, against the inhabitants of Lisbon and their mainly Muslim defenders.

WHAT The Crusaders besieged the fortified city until the eventual surrender of the defenders.

WHERE Lisbon, in Portugal.

WHEN 1 July to 21 October 1147

WHY The European Crusaders were persuaded to divert from their journey to the Holy Land and help Afonso Henriques cement his claim to the throne of Portugal by taking this wealthy port from the Muslims.

OUTCOME The defenders surrendered on terms, although that did not prevent the sacking of the city.

There is little question that the Second Crusade was one of the most disastrous military campaigns ever. Yet at its outset none could have predicted that the taking of Lisbon would be the only significant Christian success of the campaign.

SECOND CRUSADE

CRUSADER VICTORY

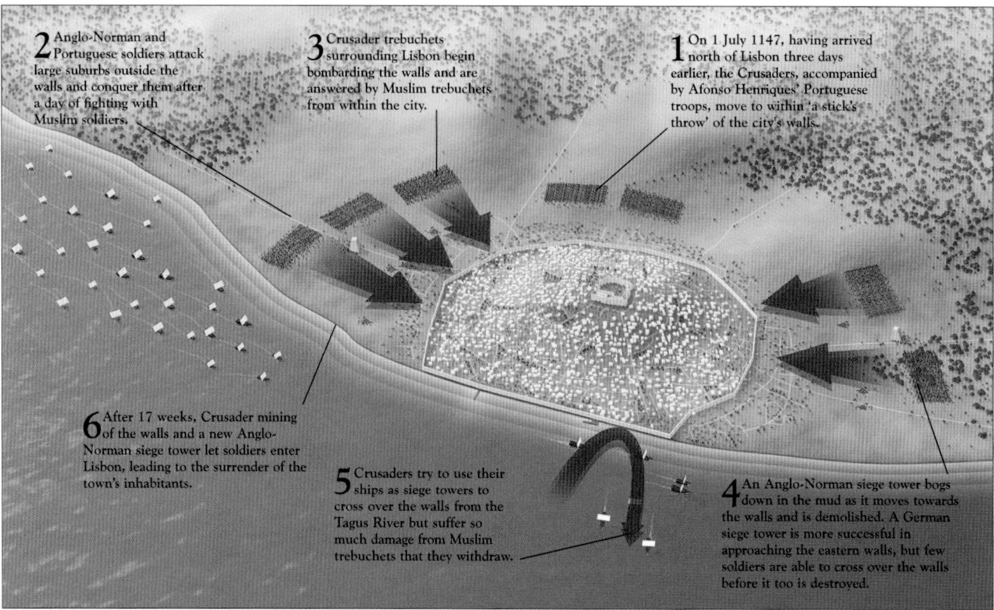
1 On 1 July 1147, having arrived north of Lisbon three days earlier, the Crusaders, accompanied by Afonso Henriques' Portuguese troops, move to within 'a stick's throw' of the city's walls.
2 Anglo-Norman and Portuguese soldiers attack large suburbs outside the walls and conquer them after a day of fighting with Muslim soldiers.
3 Crusader trebuchets surrounding Lisbon begin bombarding the walls and are answered by Muslim trebuchets from within the city.
4 An Anglo-Norman siege tower bogs down in the mud as it moves towards the walls and is demolished. A German siege tower is more successful in approaching the eastern walls, but few soldiers are able to cross over the walls before it too is destroyed.
5 Crusaders try to use their ships as siege towers to cross over the walls from the Tagus River but suffer so much damage from Muslim trebuchets that they withdraw.
6 After 17 weeks, Crusader mining of the walls and a new Anglo-Norman siege tower let soldiers enter Lisbon, leading to the surrender of the town's inhabitants.

The Crusaders moved with efficiency to effect the siege of Lisbon, partly because they were aware it was a major detour from their main purpose to defeat the infidel further east. It was to be their only success of a deeply flawed campaign.

Soldiers on their way to the Holy Land at the start of the Second Crusade made a detour to the wealthy city of Lisbon, to retake it from the Muslims. Lisbon's walls were tall and strong, and the Crusaders resorted to various siege engines, especially trebuchets (mangonels), but the defenders answered with their own smaller stone-throwing versions.

Mining, the oldest of siege techniques, did some damage. An enormous mine, with huge halls and five entrances, was constructed, shored up by wooden supports. Once the attackers were ready, the timber was set on fire, causing the mine to collapse and bring down the stone walls above. But falling timber blocked the breach created, and the assault was halted.

In the end it was dwindling food supplies and the approach of winter that caused the city's surrender. Despite a promise not to ransack the city, agreed by the Crusader leaders anxious to be on their way, their troops rushed through the gates and began pillaging. Before calm could be restored, Lisbon had been ransacked and a number of citizens killed – including the Mozarabic Christian Bishop of the city.

LOCATION

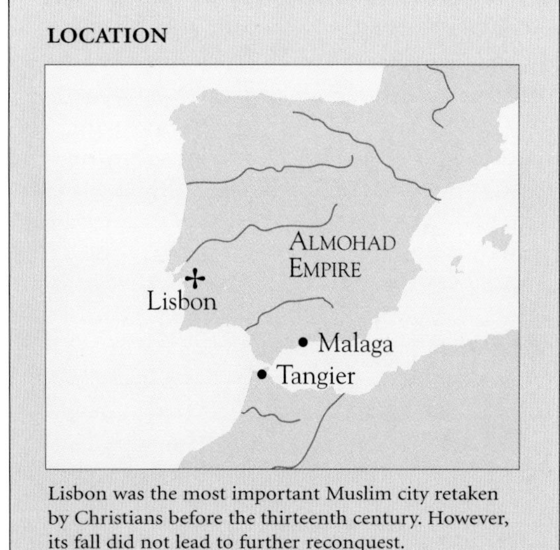
ALMOHAD EMPIRE
Lisbon
Malaga
Tangier

Lisbon was the most important Muslim city retaken by Christians before the thirteenth century. However, its fall did not lead to further reconquest.

TIMELINE

1500–1000BC	1000–500BC	500BC–0AD	0–500AD	500–1000AD	1000–1500AD	1500–2000AD

Siege of Montreuil-Bellay 1149–1152

KEY FACTS

WHO Count Geoffrey of Anjou, against a rebellious vassal, Gerard Berlai.

WHAT Geoffrey lay siege to the castle for three years, eventually taking Gerard as prisoner, only to be released on the mediation of the king of France.

WHERE Montreuil-Bellay, beside the River Thouet, a tributary of the Loire, south of Saumur.

WHEN 1149–1152

WHY Gerard had led a rebellion of local lords against Geoffrey's attempts to assert stronger control over the region of southern Anjou.

OUTCOME Geoffrey used all his Angevin military skills to end Gerard's resistance and further seal his position as the strongest lord in France during his day.

Geoffrey of Anjou was the founder of the Plantagenet dynasty that, beginning with his son Henry II, would rule England for centuries. But as Count of Anjou he faced a continuous battle to extend his authority over his often rebellious vassals; control of the castles in the Loire was the key.

ANGEVIN CAMPAIGN

ANGEVIN VICTORY

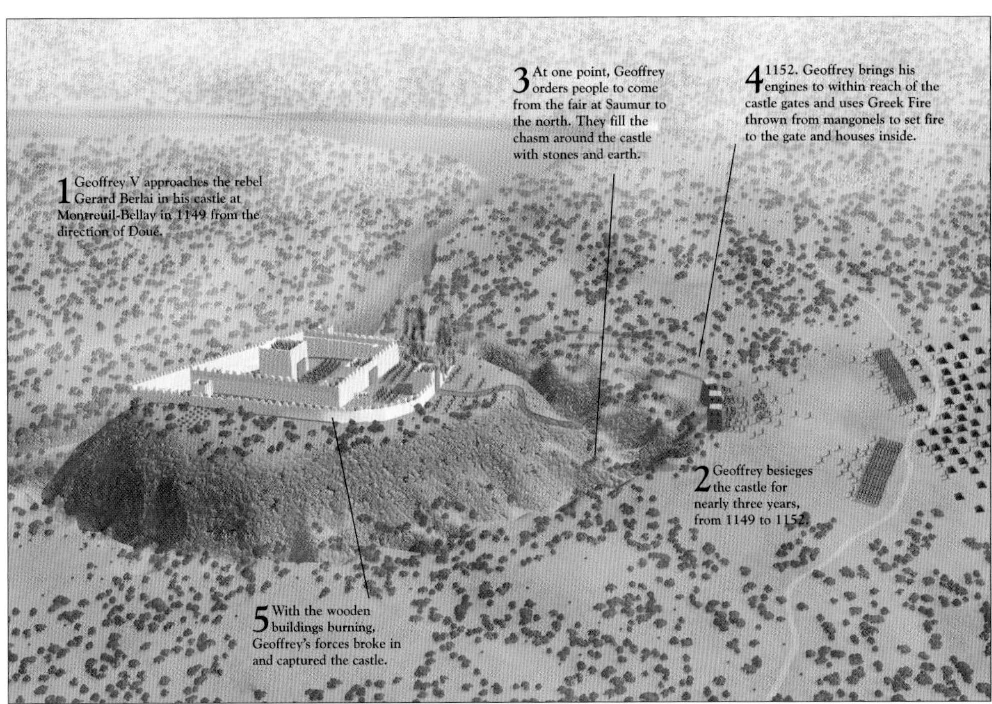
1 Geoffrey V approaches the rebel Gerard Berlai in his castle at Montreuil-Bellay in 1149 from the direction of Doué.
2 Geoffrey besieges the castle for nearly three years, from 1149 to 1152.
3 At one point, Geoffrey orders people to come from the fair at Saumur to the north. They fill the chasm around the castle with stones and earth.
4 1152. Geoffrey brings his engines to within reach of the castle gates and uses Greek Fire thrown from mangonels to set fire to the gate and houses inside.
5 With the wooden buildings burning, Geoffrey's forces broke in and captured the castle.

Gerard Berlai's castle occupied an important location on the river. Geoffrey of Anjou moved to bring his vassal into line, but with the castle's strong defences, this would not be easy.

LOCATION

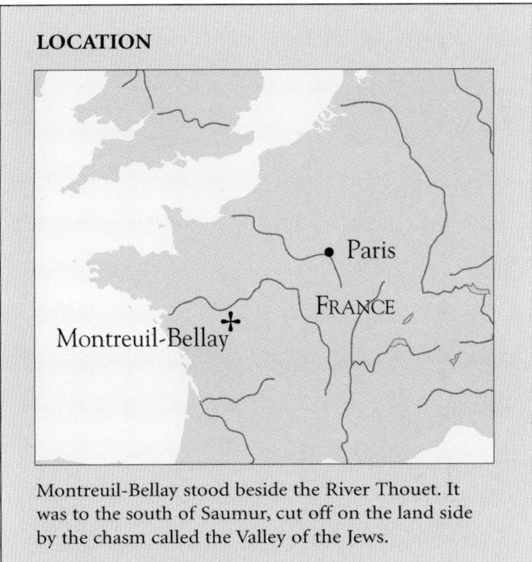
Paris
FRANCE
Montreuil-Bellay

Montreuil-Bellay stood beside the River Thouet. It was to the south of Saumur, cut off on the land side by the chasm called the Valley of the Jews.

Montreuil-Bellay was a castle held by Gerard Berlai who rebelled against his lord, Geoffrey Plantagenet, count of Anjou, in 1149. The castle had a high keep. It was protected on one side by the river, and on the other by a deep natural chasm. Geoffrey, however, was an autocratic ruler, unlikely to accept such a challenge to his position lightly, and he prepared for a long siege.

His first major attempt to break in meant bringing all the people from the nearby fair at Saumur. They were ordered to drop stones and earth in the ditch and fill it. Then Geoffrey could advance his engines and belfries towards the castle. His final effort was to load throwing engines with vases containing Greek Fire (a lethal mix of ingredients that burst into flames when exposed to air). These were hurled at the castle and set fire to the gates and houses inside, causing havoc. Geoffrey broke in and captured the castle, bringing the three-year siege to an end. Gerard was taken prisoner, and only later released through the agency of the French king Louis VII.

TIMELINE

1500–1000BC	1000–500BC	500BC–0AD	0–500AD	500–1000AD	1000–1500AD	1500–2000AD

Siege of Montreuil-Bellay

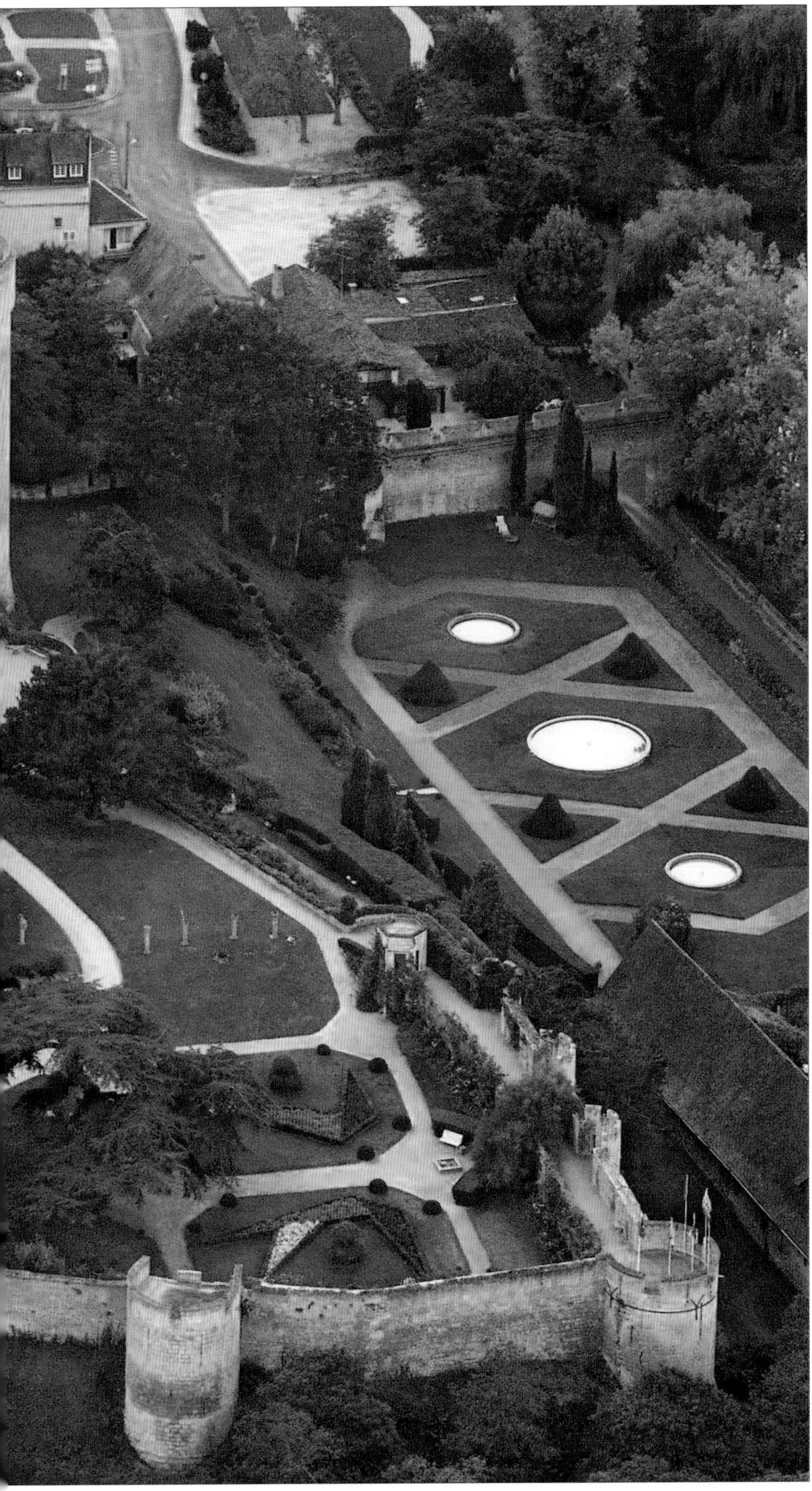

SIEGE OF MONTREUIL-BELLAY

In the twelfth century, he who held the castle held the land, so upstart vassals were not to be tolerated. It was a difficult balance to achieve. Any king or count required the support of local nobles for support in their control of the domain, and a measure of trust was necessary. But an out-of-control lord was a boil that needed lancing and Geoffrey Plantagenet – the man who gave his name to a English dynasty – did not tolerate dissent, spending a lifetime fighting campaigns in Normandy and extending his Angevin estates. Even so, Gerard Berlai's resistance would take three years to stamp out, illustrating the limited military means of even the strongest lords of the time.

Legnano 1176

WARS OF THE LOMBARD LEAGUE

LOMBARD VICTORY

On one of his numerous campaigns through the Alps into Northern Italy, the Holy Roman Emperor Frederick Barbarossa's army was defeated by non-professional soldiers drawn mostly from the town militias. The battle of Legnano was a victory of inexperienced over professional troops.

KEY FACTS

WHO A small German cavalry army, numbering no more than 2500, led by the Holy Roman Emperor Frederick Barbarossa (c. 1123–90), was defeated by an equally small northern Italian army.

WHAT While Frederick Barbarossa's cavalry easily chased off their northern Italian counterparts (the Milanese), Veronese and Brescian infantry stood solidly against the Germans, and defeated them.

WHERE Legnano in northern Italy.

WHEN 29 May 1176

WHY In an effort to stop an alliance between the Lombard League and Pope Alexander III (1159–81), Frederick Barbarossa marched through the Alps to restore his rule.

OUTCOME Having been defeated at Legnano, Frederick Barbarossa was forced to make a truce with the Lombard League.

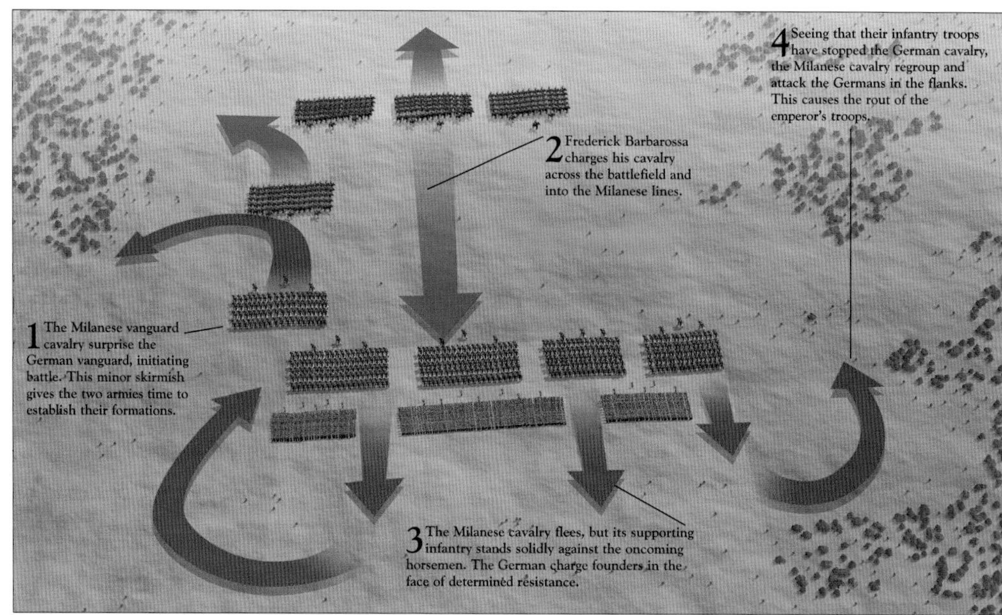
1 The Milanese vanguard cavalry surprise the German vanguard, initiating battle. This minor skirmish gives the two armies time to establish their formations.
2 Frederick Barbarossa charges his cavalry across the battlefield and into the Milanese lines.
3 The Milanese cavalry flees, but its supporting infantry stands solidly against the oncoming horsemen. The German charge founders in the face of determined resistance.
4 Seeing that their infantry troops have stopped the German cavalry, the Milanese cavalry regroup and attack the Germans in the flanks. This causes the rout of the emperor's troops.

The formations of the Italian militia at Legnano are a reminder that determined pikemen organized in tight formations holding steady could still do a job against the cavalry charge.

LOCATION

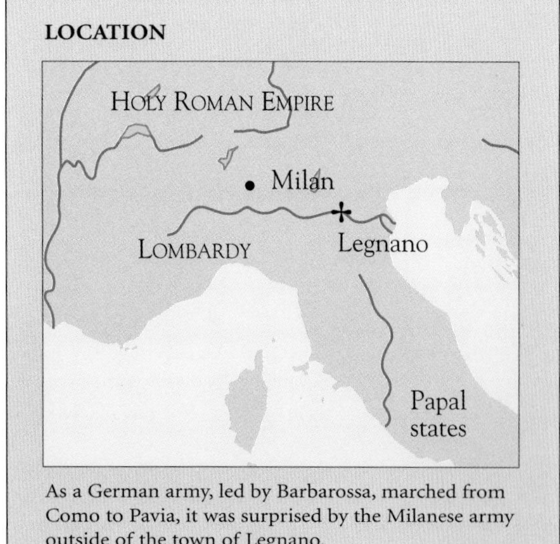
Holy Roman Empire
Milan
Lombardy
Legnano
Papal states

As a German army, led by Barbarossa, marched from Como to Pavia, it was surprised by the Milanese army outside of the town of Legnano.

Frederick Barbarossa wanted to bring the independent-minded Italian cities into closer political and economic union with the rest of his Empire, and launched a military campaign. However, his army had become split, and, at Legano, where he was cut off from his infantry, the Italians were able to catch him by surprise.

Frederick launched a cavalry charge, even though a retreat might have been a wiser strategy. They pushed through the Milanese cavalry quite easily, but they then ran into the Italian infantry, who had held their positions – an important and incredibly courageous stand. The German cavalry charge was halted. The Italian infantry – 'with shields set close and pikes held firm' – caused the German horses to stop, unwilling to run onto their long spears.

LOMBARD ROUT

This allowed the fleeing Milanese cavalry to regroup and return to the battlefield, and a rout followed, during which Frederick's banner was lost to the Milanese, and his horse was killed under him. Frederick was lucky to escape the battlefield with his life.

TIMELINE

1500–1000BC	1000–500BC	500BC–0AD	0–500AD	500–1000AD	1000–1500AD	1500–2000AD

Montgisard 1177

CRUSADES

CRUSADER VICTORY

KEY FACTS

Who A Crusader army containing almost 600 knights and several thousand common soldiers under Baldwin IV, versus approximately 30,000 Muslim troops under Saladin.

What The Crusaders surprised their opponents and, after a brief hesitation, charged headlong at them.

Where Near Montgisard, southwest of Jerusalem.

When 25 November 1177

Why Part of the ongoing war between Crusaders and Muslim states in the Holy Land.

Outcome The Muslim force was routed, suffering further casualties in its subsequent retreat.

Montgisard was a massive defeat for Saladin, from which he only just escaped with his life. In many ways this was the classic Crusader victory, won by a headlong violent charge against superior numbers. Never again, though, would such a small force shatter a huge host in this manner.

Saladin was the most formidable opponent the Western soldiers would encounter in the history of the crusading movement, but he was not unbeatable, and at Montgisard a small but determined force was able to best him.

LOCATION

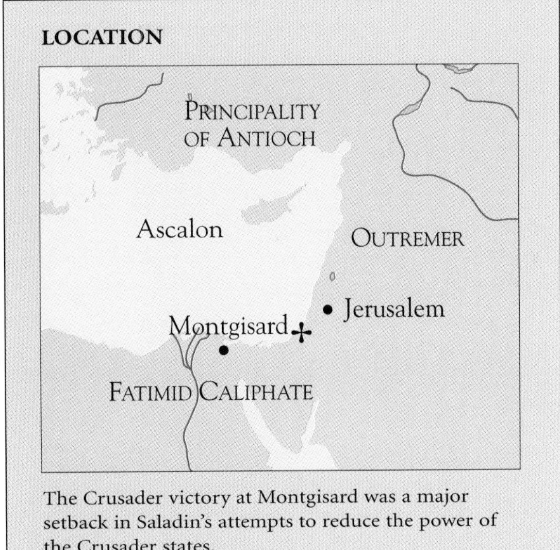
PRINCIPALITY OF ANTIOCH
Ascalon
OUTREMER
Jerusalem
Montgisard
FATIMID CALIPHATE

The Crusader victory at Montgisard was a major setback in Saladin's attempts to reduce the power of the Crusader states.

Saladin had begun a campaign against the Crusader states, but in allowing his forces to launch looting raids, they became overstretched, and he was caught off guard by a relatively small group of Crusaders launching a cavalry charge. Less than 600 lances smashed into the Muslim army, but the line was broken and the infantry followed up their knights' success with a determined advance.

In the Muslim army, it seemed that all was lost. Had the commanders on the spot managed to rally their followers, they might have counter-attacked and overwhelmed the Crusaders. But Saladin's men had started the battle off balance and were facing what looked like a resounding Crusader victory in progress. This swiftly became reality as the Muslim army disintegrated. No quarter was given by the victorious Christians. Wounded men were despatched as the victors advanced. Saladin escaped the carnage on the back of a camel, but not before his elite bodyguard was slaughtered. He gathered what he could of his army and began the long retreat back to Egypt.

TIMELINE

1500–1000BC	1000–500BC	500BC–0AD	0–500AD	500–1000AD	1000–1500AD	1500–2000AD

Hattin 1187

KEY FACTS

WHO A Crusader army of 32,000 men under King Guy of Jerusalem (reigned 1186–92), opposed by 50,000 Seljuk Turks under Saladin (1138–93).

WHAT Thirsty, tired and dispirited Crusaders en route to relieve a castle could not catch the more nimble Turks. Eventually they are too exhausted to fight, at which point the Turks surround and attack the remaining Crusaders.

WHERE The Horns of Hattin, near Tiberias on the Sea of Galilee in modern Israel.

WHEN June 1187

WHY The Turks were responding to the Crusaders who had breached a truce by raiding a Turkish caravan.

OUTCOME Most of the Crusaders were killed or captured. The Turks went on to recapture Jerusalem.

This battle marked the turning point in the Crusades. The more intelligent strategy and flexible tactics of the Islamic army delivered a catastrophic defeat to the army of Jerusalem. The Christians would never again hold as much territory as they had previously.

CRUSADES

TURKISH VICTORY

The Saracens were not as well protected in battle as the Crusaders, but they were masters of the art of the charge and retreat, and their own mounted archers were more than a match for the Crusader infantry at Hattin.

LOCATION

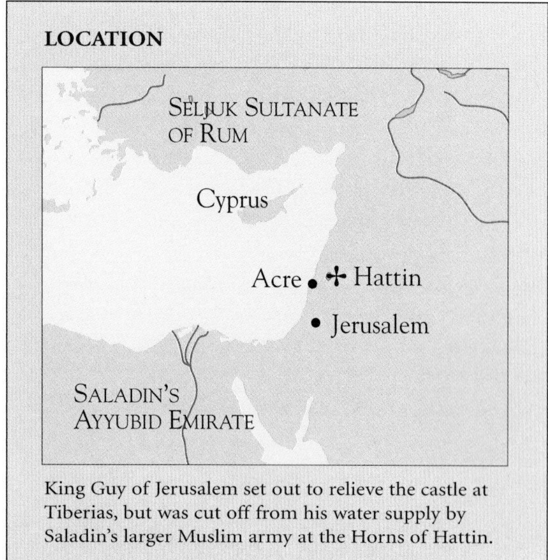
SELJUK SULTANATE OF RUM
Cyprus
Acre
Hattin
Jerusalem
SALADIN'S AYYUBID EMIRATE

King Guy of Jerusalem set out to relieve the castle at Tiberias, but was cut off from his water supply by Saladin's larger Muslim army at the Horns of Hattin.

In the autumn of 1186, when Crusaders raided a Muslim caravan, breaking a long-standing truce, Saladin declared war and summoned his host from a portion of his empire in northern Syria, Aleppo, Damascus and Egypt. Count Raymond of Tripoli and King Guy of Jerusalem resolved to meet him in battle. The mass of their army was made up of 32,000 infantry – some veterans of earlier campaigns, some newly arrived pilgrims. Their weapons included the spear and crossbow, and many wore mail and a helmet for protection. Spearmen also carried a shield.

Saladin's host of perhaps 50,000 included 12,000 regular Egyptian and Syrian cavalry – five times the number of Crusader knights. They were fully equipped, mail-coated cavalry, armed with bow as well as lance and shield. They were as well equipped as their Christian counterparts, but less inclined to charge as ferociously and, more importantly, prepared to skirmish away if the moment was unfavourable.

As the Crusaders advanced via Wadi Hamman, Saladin tried to block them at the Horns of Hattin. The Crusaders

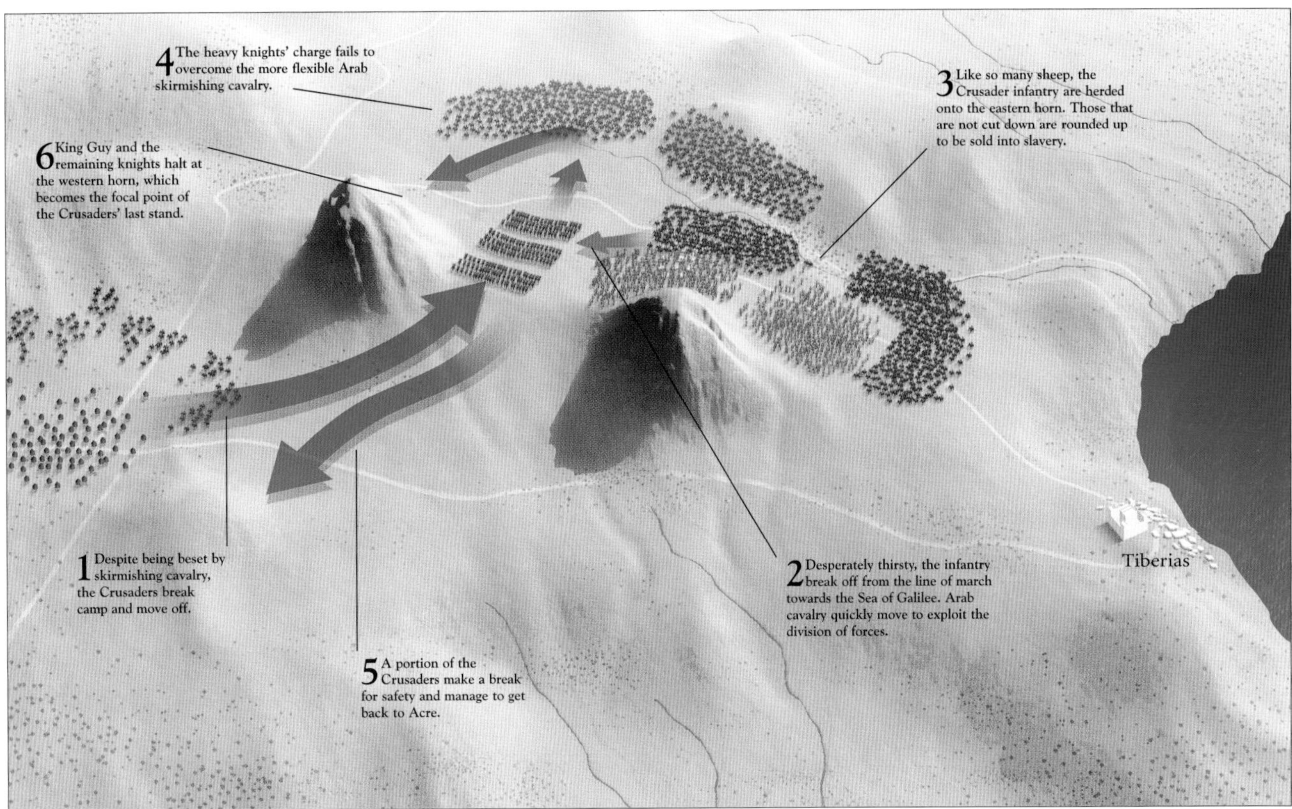
4 The heavy knights' charge fails to overcome the more flexible Arab skirmishing cavalry.
6 King Guy and the remaining knights halt at the western horn, which becomes the focal point of the Crusaders' last stand.
3 Like so many sheep, the Crusader infantry are herded onto the eastern horn. Those that are not cut down are rounded up to be sold into slavery.
1 Despite being beset by skirmishing cavalry, the Crusaders break camp and move off.
2 Desperately thirsty, the infantry break off from the line of march towards the Sea of Galilee. Arab cavalry quickly move to exploit the division of forces.
Tiberias
5 A portion of the Crusaders make a break for safety and manage to get back to Acre.

The settings for so many battles of the Crusades were broad, open landscapes – tailor-made for the skirmishing techniques of the Turkish cavalry, who often left the enemy floundering.

marched on amidst continuous skirmishing from Muslim light cavalry and mounted bowmen, deploying hit-and-run tactics. However, the rearguard was now becoming separated from the main column as casualties mounted, so the whole army was forced to halt in the hot early afternoon and the order was given to make camp even though there was no water available.

Next morning the main Muslim force advanced in a crescent formation, their sweeping arrow fire further reducing the Crusaders' morale. Cavalry charges were simply met by showers of deadly arrows, the Saracens retiring before them, but keeping within bow range and targeting the Crusaders' horses to dismount the heavily armoured knights.

But the tired, disorganized and thirsty Crusader infantry could see blue water ahead, and they surged past the vanguard to push on to the Sea of Galilee, which seemed tantalizingly close. Now they too were met by Muslim arrow fire, and those that weren't cut down were rounded up and later sold into slavery by the Saracens.

King Guy ordered Raymond and the remaining vanguard of about 200 knights to charge. The Muslims opened their ranks and Raymond's charge passed through, receiving more archery casualties on the way, a classic response to the charge of Western knights and a tactic from the steppes with a pedigree of more than a thousand years. Raymond, an experienced crusader thrice wounded in the charge, knew the day was lost and rode from the field into the steep-sided gorge of Wadi Hamman.

THE LAST STAND

The wadi was dry and the Muslims closed behind him. Raymond knew he could not charge back up the slope, so he rode on to the safety of Tyre. He had been expected to follow a suicidal plan by people lacking his experience. The remaining knights made two or three more charges, but were still unable to come to grips with their highly mobile foes. Eventually the survivors were driven back to the hill where King Guy's red tent had been erected. The Muslims circled around the hill, cutting the Crusaders down. Finally, the tent was overrun and about 150 remaining knights surrendered, among them King Guy.

Hattin

HATTIN

Saladin, Sultan of Egypt and Syria, was also the greatest adversary the crusaders would encounter in their campaigns in the Holy Land. Legend made him the beau ideal of Saracenic chivalry, a pagan who yet seemed to act according to knightly customs with which he must have been unfamiliar – such was the intoxicating mystery of his appeal to westerners. At Hattin, fought after the crusaders violated a truce, he captured Guy, the Poitevin adventurer who had become king of Jerusalem. Typically, he spared the life of Guy, who would go on to found a ruling dynasty on Cyprus.

Acre 1191

THIRD CRUSADE

CRUSADER VICTORY

Saladin's victories at Hattin and Jerusalem led to the Third Crusade. Three kings travelled to the Holy Land to regain what had been lost, but although they captured Acre and defeated Saladin at the Battle of Jaffa, they could not recapture the city of Jerusalem.

KEY FACTS

WHO Local Crusaders under King Guy of Jerusalem, (c. 1150–1194) joined by the Third Crusade under Kings Richard I of England (1157–1199) and Philip II of France (1165–1233) against a Muslim army under Saladin (1138–1193).

WHAT Saladin's army failed in repeated attempts to break the Crusader siege, and Christian reinforcements from Europe eventually caused the city to surrender.

WHERE The city of Acre, in the Gulf of Haifa, now northern Israel.

WHEN August 1189 to July 1191

WHY The siege was a Crusader response to Saladin's attempt to retake the Holy Land and consolidate his earlier victories at Hattin and Jerusalem.

OUTCOME The fall of Acre and the later Crusader victory at Arsuf ensured the survival of the Crusader state, although Jerusalem remained in Saladin's hands.

The Crusader army that took Acre was led by two of the medieval period's most fascinating figures, Richard the Lionheart, the handsome epitome of a warrior king, and the more politically gifted, if less soldierly, Philip Augustus.

LOCATION

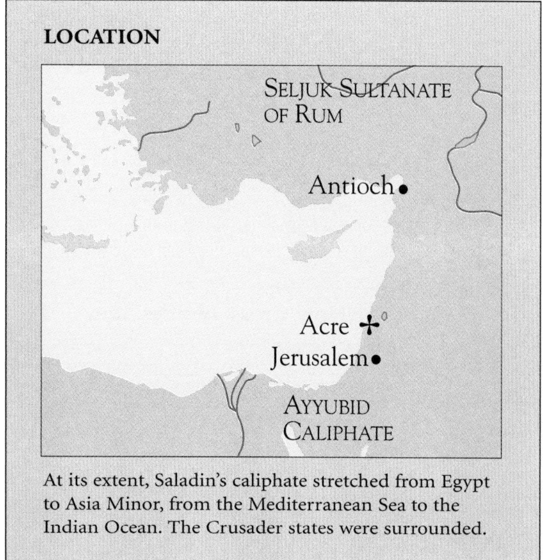
SELJUK SULTANATE OF RUM
Antioch
Acre
Jerusalem
AYYUBID CALIPHATE

At its extent, Saladin's caliphate stretched from Egypt to Asia Minor, from the Mediterranean Sea to the Indian Ocean. The Crusader states were surrounded.

News from the Holy Land of the defeat at Hattin and the loss of Jerusalem to Saladin in 1187 was greeted in Europe by stunned disbelief and fear. Saladin now tried to gnaw away at Crusader-held territory, trying to capture as much of it as possible before the inevitable announcing of another Crusade by the Pope, but those Crusaders still in the East were not idle in the meantime. The siege of Acre had been waged for more than 18 months before Philip Augustus, King of France, and Richard I of England arrived at the port city of Acre. The resident Crusaders, led by Guy, titular king of Jerusalem – who had been freed by Saladin after his capture at the debacle of Hattin four years earlier – had been handling the siege quite skilfully on their own, but once there the status of the two kings quickly surpassed that of local leaders.

During the siege, Acre had been surrounded, blockaded by land and by sea. The naval blockade was especially effective, with Saladin unable to compete against the Crusader ships with his own fleet. On land, the Crusader siege was also strong. As with most medieval sieges,

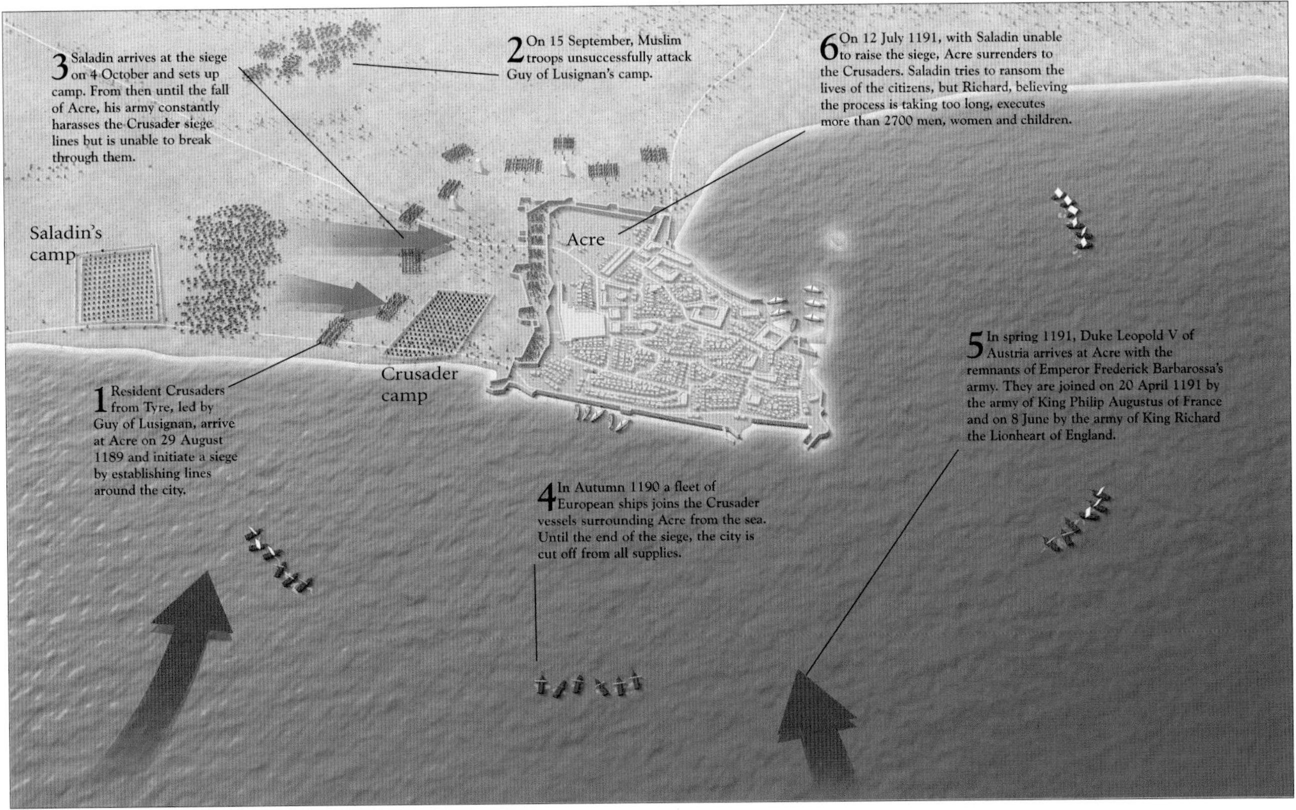
3 Saladin arrives at the siege on 4 October and sets up camp. From then until the fall of Acre, his army constantly harasses the Crusader siege lines but is unable to break through them.
2 On 15 September, Muslim troops unsuccessfully attack Guy of Lusignan's camp.
6 On 12 July 1191, with Saladin unable to raise the siege, Acre surrenders to the Crusaders. Saladin tries to ransom the lives of the citizens, but Richard, believing the process is taking too long, executes more than 2700 men, women and children.
Saladin's camp
Acre
5 In spring 1191, Duke Leopold V of Austria arrives at Acre with the remnants of Emperor Frederick Barbarossa's army. They are joined on 20 April 1191 by the army of King Philip Augustus of France and on 8 June by the army of King Richard the Lionheart of England.
Crusader camp
1 Resident Crusaders from Tyre, led by Guy of Lusignan, arrive at Acre on 29 August 1189 and initiate a siege by establishing lines around the city.
4 In Autumn 1190 a fleet of European ships joins the Crusader vessels surrounding Acre from the sea. Until the end of the siege, the city is cut off from all supplies.

The Crusader blockade of Acre was impressively thorough, though harassment from Saladin's men did enable a few supplies to sneak through. Success was marred by the cruelty of Richard's behaviour once the city surrendered.

however, it seems that the besieged did receive some relief throughout the ordeal, especially as Saladin continually distracted the Crusaders with assaults. Reinforcements for the Muslim garrison even made it into the city and helped convince those in Acre to hang on.

Adding the new soldiers to the Crusaders around Acre, however, increased their number significantly, so much so that it appears any holes in the blockade were closed and the citizens began to suffer heavy bombardment from trebuchets and other siege machines. The walls of the city were also undermined. The Crusaders were now, in fact, so numerous that they set up two siege lines, one that blockaded the city and a second that protected this blockade from Saladin. There was little the Sultan could do. Relief attacks were tried but they failed, and on 12 July 1191, just a little more than a month after the arrival of Richard the Lionheart, Acre surrendered.

Saladin, who had not given his permission for this capitulation but was powerless to do anything about it, was informed by a swimmer who had made his way through the Crusader lines. Surrender negotiations were not only held between the besiegers and the besieged, but also between the Crusader leaders. Philip and Richard shared the captured Muslim ships and also the garrison's leaders – whom Saladin held to ransom. Prisoners were also exchanged.

But these were only Acre's notable and wealthy. The poorer citizens were left in Crusader hands. Perhaps Saladin believed that the Crusaders would respect the lives of the common people, innocent pawns in these wars, and would treat them with the same mercy that he had shown those who could not afford ransom after his capture of Jerusalem in 1187.

Richard, however, did not let them go. Instead, on 20 August, he had them beheaded – men, women and children, some 2700 by his own reckoning. English rationalizers excused the act by claiming that the English king was simply responding to Saladin's unwillingness to return the fragment of the Holy Cross. Besides, they argued, these people had not surrendered immediately after being besieged, a violation of the laws of war. Other chroniclers are not swayed: Richard's actions were heinous – an egregious and cowardly war crime.

Arsuf 1191

KEY FACTS

WHO	A Crusader army under King Richard I of England (1157–99) numbering about 12,000 men was attacked by a Saracen force approximately double in size, commanded by Saladin (1138–93).
WHAT	The Crusaders, attempting to march along the Palestine coast, were attacked by the more mobile Saracens but were able to reach and occupy the town of Arsuf.
WHERE	The town of Arsuf.
WHEN	September 1191
WHY	Having taken Acre, Richard hoped to press on to Jerusalem. Saladin was determined to stop him.
OUTCOME	The Crusaders were able to maintain formation and march under fire to Arsuf. A mounted counter-attack then drove off the Saracen force.

The battle of Arsuf pitted a Crusader army under Richard the Lionheart against a Saracen force under Saladin. It was a severe test of the discipline that Richard hoped to instil in the Crusader armies. Ultimately, the Crusader infantry proved their worth in the face of constant harassment by Muslim cavalry.

THIRD CRUSADE

CRUSADER VICTORY

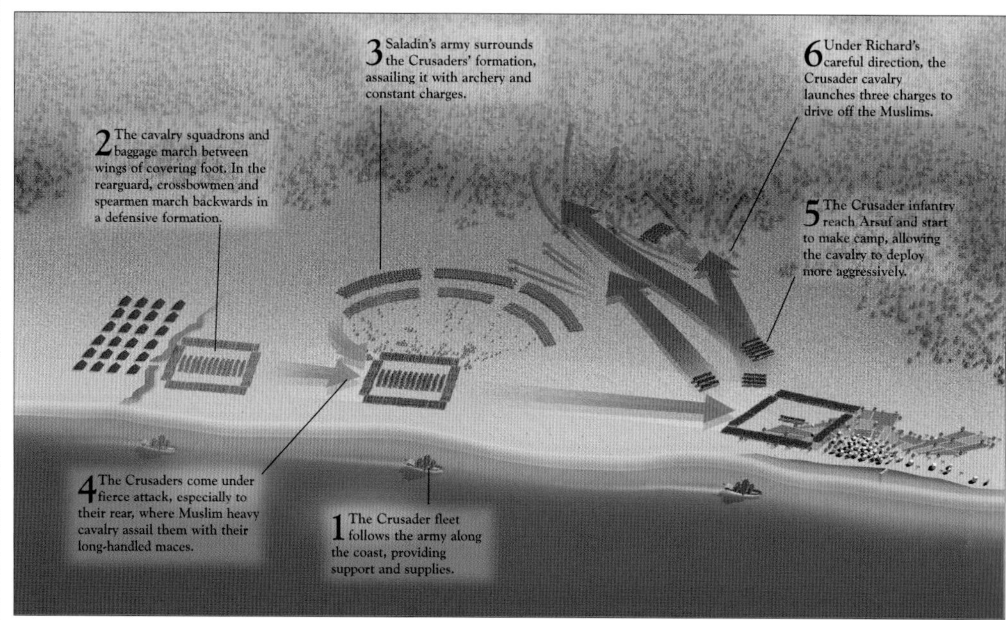

3 Saladin's army surrounds the Crusaders' formation, assailing it with archery and constant charges.
6 Under Richard's careful direction, the Crusader cavalry launches three charges to drive off the Muslims.
2 The cavalry squadrons and baggage march between wings of covering foot. In the rearguard, crossbowmen and spearmen march backwards in a defensive formation.
5 The Crusader infantry reach Arsuf and start to make camp, allowing the cavalry to deploy more aggressively.
4 The Crusaders come under fierce attack, especially to their rear, where Muslim heavy cavalry assail them with their long-handled maces.
1 The Crusader fleet follows the army along the coast, providing support and supplies.

The march on Arsuf showed the discipline of the Crusader forces at their best. Despite the persistent attentions of Saladin's cavalry, they maintained their formations, and clung to the coast, eventually reaching their destination.

Richard the Lionheart, marching his army along the Palestine coast en route to Jerusalem, was attacked by Saladin near the town of Arsuf. The Crusader army was organized in a defensive box around its supply wagons and irreplaceable heavy cavalry. Saladin's men were kept at bay by spearmen protecting the crossbowmen from direct attack, while the heavy bolts of the crossbowmen exacted a steady toll on the enemy.

In reserve, the threat of the heavy armoured cavalry prevented the Muslim army from making an all-out assault. The infantry at the back of the formation marched backwards, keeping their shields and weapons facing the enemy.

Pressure mounted as the Saracen horse archers came in ever closer and more boldly to shoot, but despite extreme provocation the Crusader knights resisted the urge to charge. Then, near Arsuf, Richard unleashed his knights in three sudden bursts forward out of the formation, catching the Saracens by surprise.

Reeling from heavy blows on both flanks, the Saracen army was shattered, and it scrambled into the wooded hills above Arsuf, leaving behind about 7000 casualties.

LOCATION

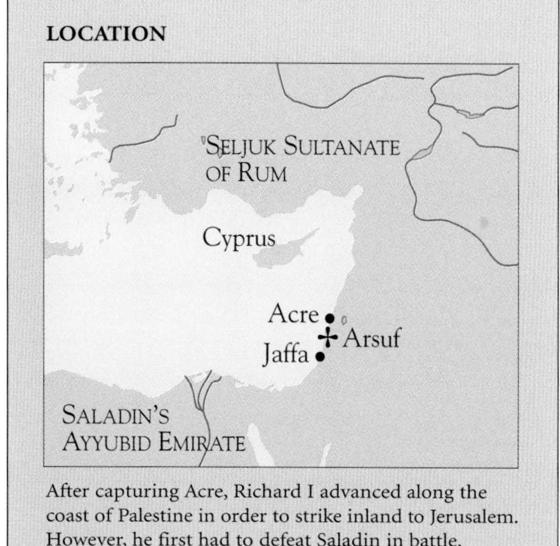

Seljuk Sultanate of Rum
Cyprus
Acre
Jaffa
Arsuf
Saladin's Ayyubid Emirate

After capturing Acre, Richard I advanced along the coast of Palestine in order to strike inland to Jerusalem. However, he first had to defeat Saladin in battle.

TIMELINE

1500–1000BC	1000–500BC	500BC–0AD	0–500AD	500–1000AD	1000–1500AD	1500–2000AD

Château Gaillard 1203–04

KEY FACTS

WHO A French force under King Philip II Augustus of France (1165–1223) besieged an English garrison under Roger de Lacy.

WHAT Determined to take the castle, the French steadily captured the outer and then inner defences.

WHERE Château Gaillard, at the confluence of the Rivers Seine and Gambon in northern France.

WHEN 1203–04

WHY The castle not only guarded an important river crossing but also represented an insulting challenge to the French king, who wanted to regain lands lost to the English.

OUTCOME The French eventually managed to capture enough of the castle's defences to force a surrender.

The siege of Château Gaillard was a lengthy affair in which a determined French force steadily dug and fought its way into a heavily fortified castle held by troops loyal to King John of England. Château Gaillard was a particularly strong fortress, and proved very difficult to capture.

CAMPAIGNS OF PHILIP II

FRENCH VICTORY

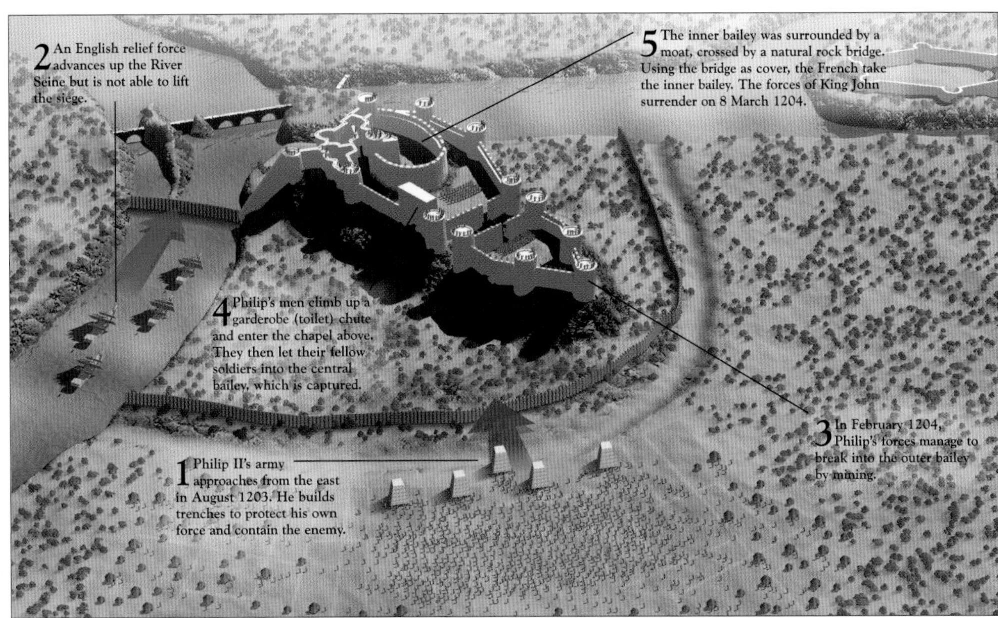

2 An English relief force advances up the River Seine but is not able to lift the siege.
5 The inner bailey was surrounded by a moat, crossed by a natural rock bridge. Using the bridge as cover, the French take the inner bailey. The forces of King John surrender on 8 March 1204.
4 Philip's men climb up a garderobe (toilet) chute and enter the chapel above. They then let their fellow soldiers into the central bailey, which is captured.
3 In February 1204, Philip's forces manage to break into the outer bailey by mining.
1 Philip II's army approaches from the east in August 1203. He builds trenches to protect his own force and contain the enemy.

Château Gaillard was one of the most impressively defended castles of the Middle Ages, in terms of both its geographical location, atop a steep rocky outcrop above the Seine, and its state-of-the-art fortifications.

King Philip wished to remove the English from Normandy. Taking Château Gaillard was key, but was a stiff challenge, for it was a powerful fortress, guarded on two flanks by wide rivers and built on a natural rise.

Access to the outer bailey was gained by use of siege engines and archers, by digging mines to weaken the walls, and by the most basic of castle assault techniques, the escalade – foot soldiers placing ladders against the walls and climbing. But entry to the second bailey was less conventional. Enterprising soldiers found that they could crawl through the chute of a garderobe (a toilet) and from there clamber up into the bailey's chapel.

BRIDGE ASSAULT

Access to the third bailey was only via a rock formation, which bridged the steep gully in front of the walls. Assault across the bridge was suicidal, but perversely, the bridge worked in favour of the attackers, who were able to use it as shelter from the defenders' increasingly desperate rain of missiles, while they mined the bailey walls. By now down to 150 defenders, Château Gaillard was now quick to surrender.

LOCATION

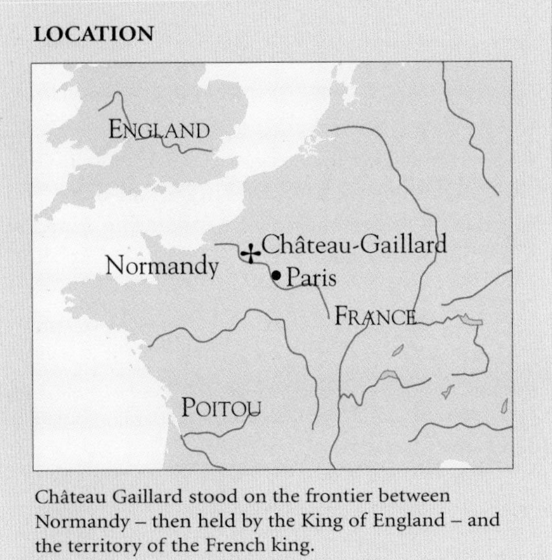

ENGLAND
Normandy
Château-Gaillard
Paris
FRANCE
POITOU

Château Gaillard stood on the frontier between Normandy – then held by the King of England – and the territory of the French king.

TIMELINE

1500–1000BC	1000–500BC	500BC–0AD	0–500AD	500–1000AD	1000–1500AD	1500–2000AD

Constantinople 1203

KEY FACTS

WHO A French Crusader army numbering about 12,000 accompanied by 8000 Venetians led by the Doge Enrico Dandolo (c. 1122–1205), opposed by the larger garrison of Constantinople, commanded by the usurper Emperor Alexius III (d. 1211).

WHAT The Crusader army launched a two-pronged assault against a heavily fortified city.

WHERE Constantinople, modern Istanbul, Turkey.

WHEN July 1203, April 1204

WHY The Crusader army, in debt to Venice, sought to solve its financial woes by restoring the exiled Prince Alexius (d. 1204) to the throne of the Byzantine Empire.

OUTCOME Venetian seaborne forces and French Crusaders attacked the city. Much of it was burned, the usurper fled and the Crusaders installed Prince Alexius as Emperor Alexius IV.

The Venetian and French forces that set out on the Fourth Crusade were 'detoured' and assaulted the city of Constantinople in both 1203 and 1204, marking the largest amphibious attack in the Middle Ages to that date. This battle showed Western military ingenuity at its best.

FOURTH CRUSADE

CRUSADER & VENETIAN VICTORY

The sack of Constantinople would lead to a westerner, Baldwin of Flanders, being elected as a (short-lived) Emperor of Byzantium by the doge of Venice, Enrico Dandolo, and the Crusaders.

LOCATION

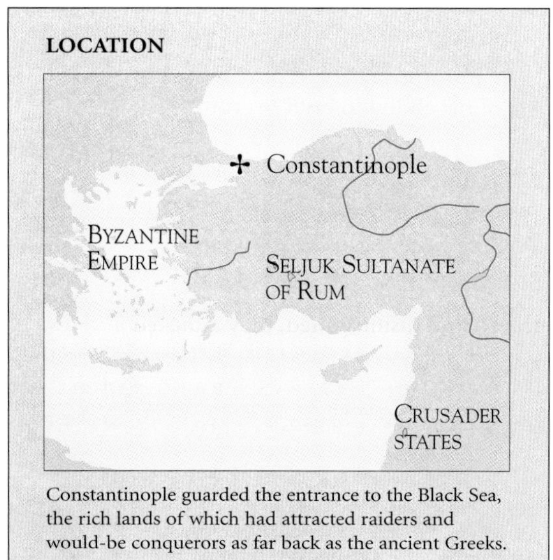
Constantinople
Byzantine Empire
Seljuk Sultanate of Rum
Crusader States

Constantinople guarded the entrance to the Black Sea, the rich lands of which had attracted raiders and would-be conquerors as far back as the ancient Greeks.

French Crusaders on their way to the Holy Land for the Fourth Crusade had made an alliance with the Venetians but found themselves indebted to them, and were unable to raise the funds. When Prince Alexius, whose father the Byzantine Emperor had been deposed, offered to pay their debt if they would attack Constantinople and get rid of the usurper, they agreed. But Constantinople, surrounded by water on three sides, was a hard nut to crack.

The only conceivable weak spot was the Golden Horn, the harbour. On that side of the city, ships were sheltered from the open sea. The Crusaders' first step was to gain control of the Tower of Galata at the harbour mouth, which they did via an amphibious assault – in which the Venetians were skilled – and the use of siege ladders to climb the Tower. Although some warships were present in the Golden Horn and tried to prevent the Venetian vessels from entering, the Byzantine Empire no longer had an effective war fleet. Its ships were decrepit and the forces aboard them inadequate. They were soon beaten and the Crusaders proceeded into the harbour. However, they did

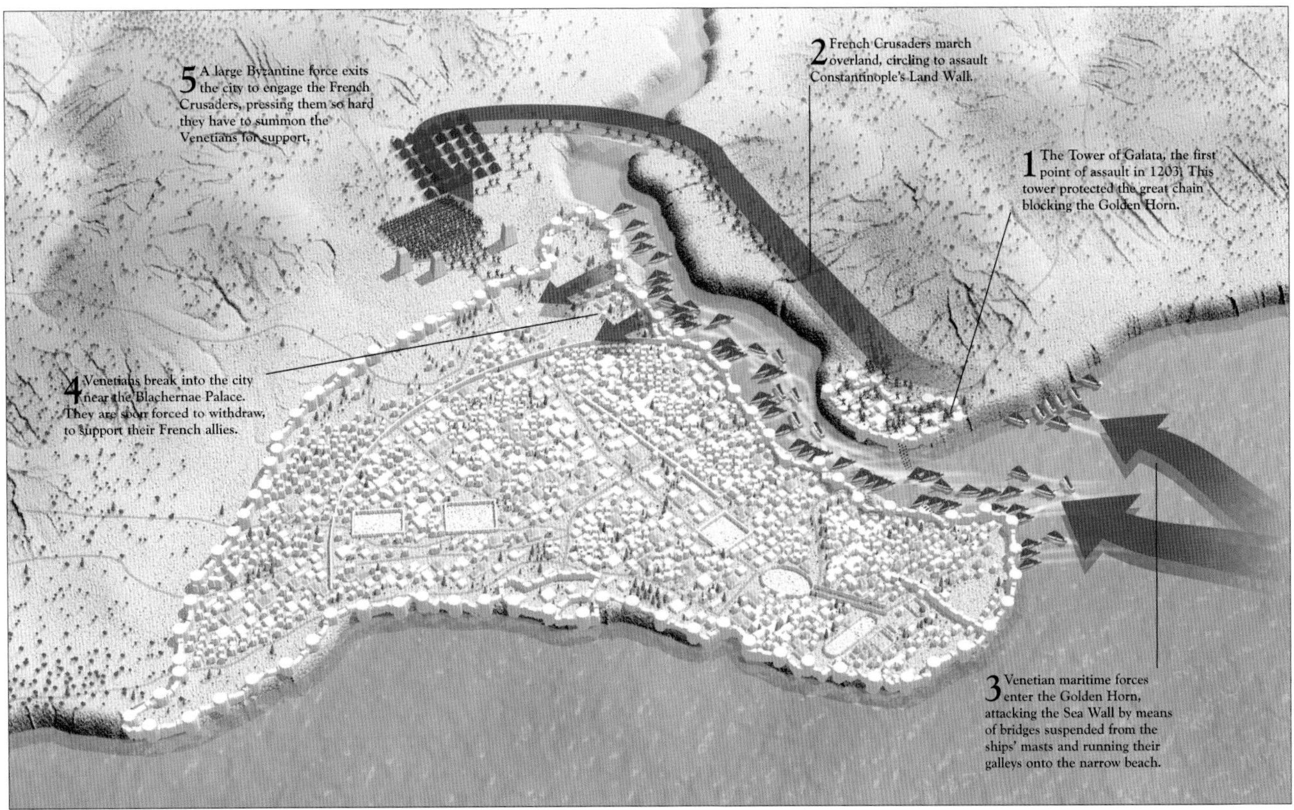
5 A large Byzantine force exits the city to engage the French Crusaders, pressing them so hard they have to summon the Venetians for support.
2 French Crusaders march overland, circling to assault Constantinople's Land Wall.
1 The Tower of Galata, the first point of assault in 1203. This tower protected the great chain blocking the Golden Horn.
4 Venetians break into the city near the Blachernae Palace. They are soon forced to withdraw, to support their French allies.
3 Venetian maritime forces enter the Golden Horn, attacking the Sea Wall by means of bridges suspended from the ships' masts and running their galleys onto the narrow beach.

The key to gaining control of Constantinople was taking charge of the harbour. The Venetians were skilled at marine operations, and faced little serious obstruction from an obsolete Byzantine fleet.

not have the supplies to enter into a lengthy siege, and so the Venetian and French leaders soon settled on a bold plan to assault the city.

The French Crusaders, led by Count Baldwin of Flanders (1172–1205), rode around to the Land Wall, where they could fight using conventional tactics, though they were beaten back by a Greek force that attacked as they tried to raise their siege ladders. Meanwhile, the Venetians launched their own naval assault on the 9m (30ft) high sea walls, defended by archers and engineers working very large catapults.

The Venetians covered their ships with hides, to protect them from Greek Fire, a highly combustible chemical compound, and launched a two-pronged attack. Galleys were to beach before the walls, so their men could disembark and erect siege ladders. The larger roundships were converted into floating siege towers, carrying portable bridges that could be latched to the walls. Several roundships managed to hook their bridges onto towers and send their men pouring up and into Constantinople. They then opened the gates for the galley crews that had landed on the beaches. In this way the Venetians gained a large section of the Sea Wall.

Despite their gains, the Venetians did not enter the actual city. Instead, they were forced to withdraw to lend support to the French Crusaders, who were still in serious difficulties at the Land Wall. While withdrawing, though, the Venetians set fires that spread and consumed a large part of the city.

The battle was won. The usurping Emperor Alexius III, despairing of his ability to hold his throne in face of such determined assault and the growing hatred of his own people, fled that very night. The city gates were soon peaceably opened, and Prince Alexius was admitted to be crowned as co-emperor with his father Isaac. Victory did have an unpleasant aftermath, however. The new emperor, Alexius IV, failed to keep his promises to the Crusaders and, betrayed and disillusioned, they attacked Constantinople again in April 1204, this time taking the city by storm, subjecting it to a vicious sack, and establishing a Westerner, Baldwin of Flanders, as the new Byzantine emperor.

TIMELINE

1500–1000BC	1000–500BC	500BC–0AD	0–500AD	500–1000AD	1000–1500AD	1500–2000AD

Constantinople

CONSTANTINOPLE
In medieval times, the city of Constantinople was of huge symbolic significance. A link to our classical past, it remained the capital city of the Byzantine emperors in the thirteenth century, even if it was in a long, slow decline. However, a schism between the churches of Rome and Constantinople symbolized a deepening ideological divergence between East and West, and the behaviour of pilgrims and crusaders in the Holy Land had gradually strengthened Byzantine suspicions against Westerners. The city's residual wealth remained a lure for these adventurers, and the sack of the city in 1204 was a deeply disturbing event.

Adrianople 1205

KEY FACTS

WHO A Crusader army including 300 knights under Baldwin I, opposed by several thousand Bulgar soldiers under Tsar Kaloyan of Bulgaria.

WHAT The Crusaders were goaded into pursuing lighter troops they could not catch, and once drawn out were attacked from all sides.

WHERE Adrianople, Bulgaria.

WHEN 14 April 1205

WHY The Crusader army had invaded the Balkans with the intention of recapturing Adrianople.

OUTCOME The Crusaders were decisively defeated.

Adrianople was a battle which showed that well-handled lighter troops could defeat an army which included powerful forces of armoured knights. As usual, Crusader impetuosity resulted in a battle on the enemy's terms, and brought the whole enterprise to ruin.

BULGARIAN UPRISING

BULGARIAN VICTORY

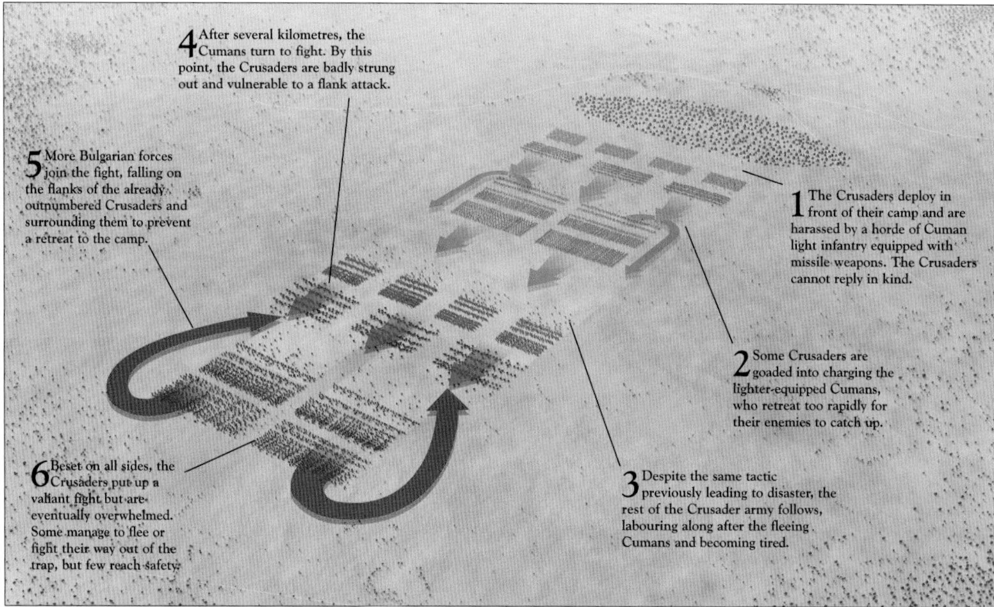
4 After several kilometres, the Cumans turn to fight. By this point, the Crusaders are badly strung out and vulnerable to a flank attack.
5 More Bulgarian forces join the fight, falling on the flanks of the already outnumbered Crusaders and surrounding them to prevent a retreat to the camp.
1 The Crusaders deploy in front of their camp and are harassed by a horde of Cuman light infantry equipped with missile weapons. The Crusaders cannot reply in kind.
2 Some Crusaders are goaded into charging the lighter-equipped Cumans, who retreat too rapidly for their enemies to catch up.
6 Beset on all sides, the Crusaders put up a valiant fight but are eventually overwhelmed. Some manage to flee or fight their way out of the trap, but few reach safety.
3 Despite the same tactic previously leading to disaster, the rest of the Crusader army follows, labouring along after the fleeing Cumans and becoming tired.

At Adrianople, the Crusaders fell for the classic trick beloved of Eastern light cavalry over the centuries – the feigned retreat that culminated in the sudden switchback into the path of an overly belligerent charging enemy.

LOCATION

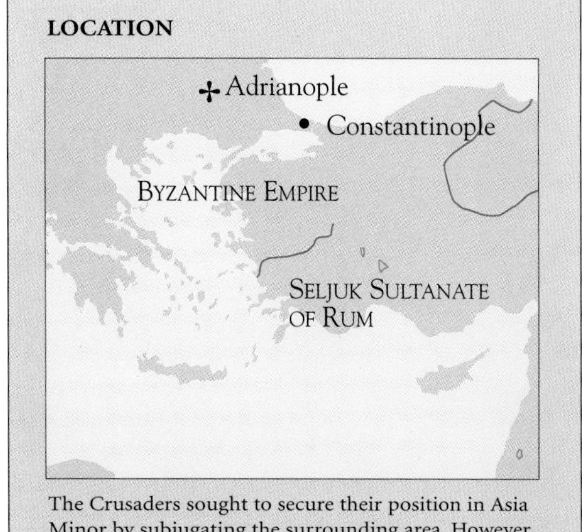
Adrianople
Constantinople
BYZANTINE EMPIRE
SELJUK SULTANATE OF RUM

The Crusaders sought to secure their position in Asia Minor by subjugating the surrounding area. However, the loss at Adrianople severely limited their ambitions.

The fall of Constantinople led to the dividing up of the Byzantine Empire among the leaders of the Fourth Crusade and of Venice, under the rule of Baldwin, formerly Count Baldwin of Flanders. But this 'Latin Empire' found itself under attack from all directions, and in 1205 the Greek populace of Thrace revolted in alliance with Tsar Kaloyan of Bulgaria and ousted the Latin garrison at Adrianople.

Baldwin tried to retake the city, but Kaloyan's forces included the lightly equipped Cuman allies, adept at blunting the potentially devastating charges of the Crusader knights. Kaloyan sent a large force of them to make an attack on the Crusaders, who naturally responded aggressively. The Cumans 'fled' and were pursued for several kilometres. This tired out the more heavily equipped Crusader infantry and especially the knights' horses. As the weary Crusaders broke off their pursuit, the Cumans turned and attacked them, shooting arrows into the Crusaders. They were joined by the rest of Kaloyan's army. Disorganized and exhausted, the Crusaders could not unleash their devastating knightly charge, and were soon beset on all sides. Baldwin was captured, and Kaloyan had him blinded and imprisoned.

TIMELINE

1500–1000BC	1000–500BC	500BC–0AD	0–500AD	500–1000AD	1000–1500AD	1500–2000AD

Beziers 1209

KEY FACTS

WHO The Duke of Burgundy (1166–1218) and the Count of Nevers (d. 1219) aided by the Abbot of Citeaux with about 11,000 soldiers, prepared to besiege Beziers. The opposing leader, Viscount Beziers, Raymond-Roger Trancavel (1185–1209), had already fled to raise a relief force, leaving the town elders to maintain the defence.

WHAT On the first night a scuffle on the bridge outside the city was won by the *ribaud* militia from the Crusaders and they forced their way in.

WHERE Beziers, in the foothills of the Pyrenees.

WHEN 21–22 July 1209

WHY The Pope insisted on crushing the heretical Cathar sect that had evolved in the region.

OUTCOME Everyone in the city was killed. The *ribauds* were robbed of their loot by their own knights and the city was burned.

The Catholic Church continually tried to crush those who promoted a different version of Christianity to that coming from the Vatican. And when the Cathar sect spread over a wide area of the Pyrenees, the Church turned its crusading zeal on the heretics.

ALBIGENSIAN CRUSADE

PAPAL CRUSADER VICTORY

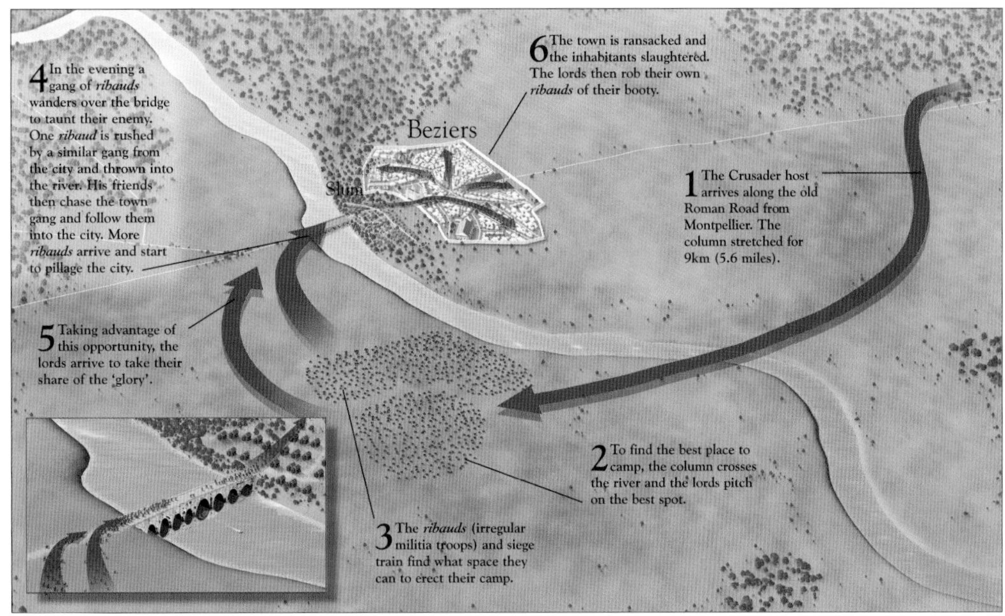
Beziers
Shim
1 The Crusader host arrives along the old Roman Road from Montpellier. The column stretched for 9km (5.6 miles).
2 To find the best place to camp, the column crosses the river and the lords pitch on the best spot.
3 The *ribauds* (irregular militia troops) and siege train find what space they can to erect their camp.
4 In the evening a gang of *ribauds* wanders over the bridge to taunt their enemy. One *ribaud* is rushed by a similar gang from the city and thrown into the river. His friends then chase the town gang and follow them into the city. More *ribauds* arrive and start to pillage the city.
5 Taking advantage of this opportunity, the lords arrive to take their share of the 'glory'.
6 The town is ransacked and the inhabitants slaughtered. The lords then rob their own *ribauds* of their booty.

This was an example of the medieval religious crusade at its most brutally unpleasant. Women and children were helplessly mowed down in the onslaught when the soldiers, sanctioned by the Pope, burst through the city gates.

When the Crusading host arrived at Beziers, the elderly Bishop who had been left in charge following Raymond-Roger Trancavel's absence advised the townsfolk to accept the inevitable. But its citizens refused, trusting to its tall, strong walls and wide river to provide an adequate defence. But a scuffle on the bridge outside the city enabled a few of the Crusaders to force access through the city gates. Women and children ran through the narrow streets screaming as the defenders, caught unawares, were unable to respond. The butchery soon began, and lasted three hours. Even those Catholics who sought sanctuary at the very altars of their own churches were mowed down.

ANNIHILATION

By noon all the Catholics in the city were killed. Abbot Amaury's subsequent missive to the Pope boasted that he had carried out orders to the letter: 'Neither age, nor sex nor status have been spared.' Estimates of the death toll vary between 7000 and 60,000, and widespread looting was carried out that disgusted even some of the Crusader knights who were present. Just to round off this work of annihilation, the wretched city was also set on fire.

LOCATION

Paris
FRANCE
Toulouse
Beziers

The town of Beziers lies at the lowest crossing point of the River Orb – a true bottleneck on the routes from eastern Spain to France and Italy beyond.

TIMELINE

1500–1000BC	1000–500BC	500BC–0AD	0–500AD	500–1000AD	1000–1500AD	1500–2000AD

Las Navas 1212

KEY FACTS

WHO An army of Crusaders from Spain and the rest of Europe under Alfonso VIII of Castile (1155–1214) against a larger Muslim force led by Abu 'Abd Allah al-Nasir (d. 1214)

WHAT Al-Nasir's deployment on open ground allowed Crusader heavy cavalry and infantry to destroy his much larger force.

WHERE Las Navas de Tolosa, southern Spain.

WHEN 16 July 1212

WHY Al-Nasir had launched an attack in 1211 to defend and expand Muslim territory in the Iberian Peninsula. This was countered by a united Spanish and European Crusade in 1212, led by Alfonso VIII of Castile.

OUTCOME The Crusader victory was decisive, with some three-quarters of the Muslim force being killed. It heralded the Reconquista of the Iberian peninsula.

When the squabbling Spanish Christian kings finally united under the banner of a Crusade, they were able to inflict a crushing defeat on the Almohad dynasty that controlled southern Spain and much of north Africa.

RECONQUISTA

SPANISH CHRISTIAN VICTORY

In close combat, heavily armoured Western soldiers, wielding heavy-duty swords, maces and axes tended to be more than a match for the more thinly protected Arabs soldiers, who were better suited to darting skirmishes and ambushes.

LOCATION

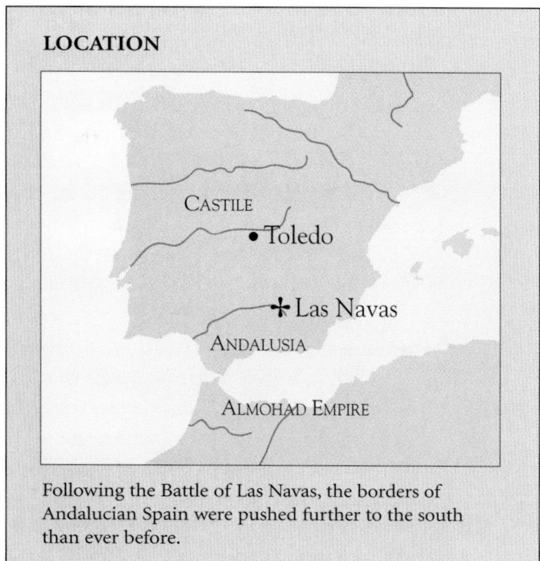
CASTILE
Toledo
Las Navas
ANDALUSIA
ALMOHAD EMPIRE

Following the Battle of Las Navas, the borders of Andalucian Spain were pushed further to the south than ever before.

An alliance of several Spanish Christian kings and Provencal nobles under Alfonso VIII of Castile met Al-Nasir's Muslim Andalusian army in the Sierra Morena Mountains. Al-Nasir's soldiers were mostly infantry and archers, lightly armoured and carrying swords, spears, maces, axes or bows.

The Crusaders, however, typical of Western European armies of the time, were based around heavily armoured cavalry and heavy infantry. It was better suited to the flat, wide terrain of the battlefield and Alfonso VIII took the offensive by charging his intimidating heavy cavalry forward, followed up immediately with the infantry. Within seconds they had slammed into the Andalusian defensive lines, but the Muslims had planned for this, their infantry line folding to allow their cavalry to sweep in from the sides. Alfonso responded by unleashing a smaller unit, which he had held in reserve, just as the Andalusians were becoming fatigued. A short time later, Muslims began fleeing the field, and soon the combat was over.

TIMELINE

1500–1000BC	1000–500BC	500BC–0AD	0–500AD	500–1000AD	1000–1500AD	1500–2000AD

Battle of the Passes 1213

KEY FACTS

Who General Jebe leading a group of soldiers of Genghis Khan's Mongol army against an army of the Chinese Jin Dynasty.

What The Mongols baited the Jin army by appearing to be retreating, but suddenly turned on their pursuers and slaughtered them.

Where Near the village of Huailai, north west of Beijing, northern China.

When 1213

Why Genghis Khan had invaded the Jin Empire to his south and was determined to take their capital, Jin Yenching (Beijing).

Outcome Jebe was able to march on to Beijing, but although the following year the Jin were forced to make a humiliating peace treaty, they managed to retain control of their capital city.

Genghis Khan united the nomadic Mongol tribes and transformed them into one of the most formidable, all-conquering war machines the world has ever known. In 1211 he launched an unsuccessful invasion of the lands of the Chinese Jin Dynasty. But he was victorious two years later.

MONGOL–JIN DYNASTY WAR

MONGOL VICTORY

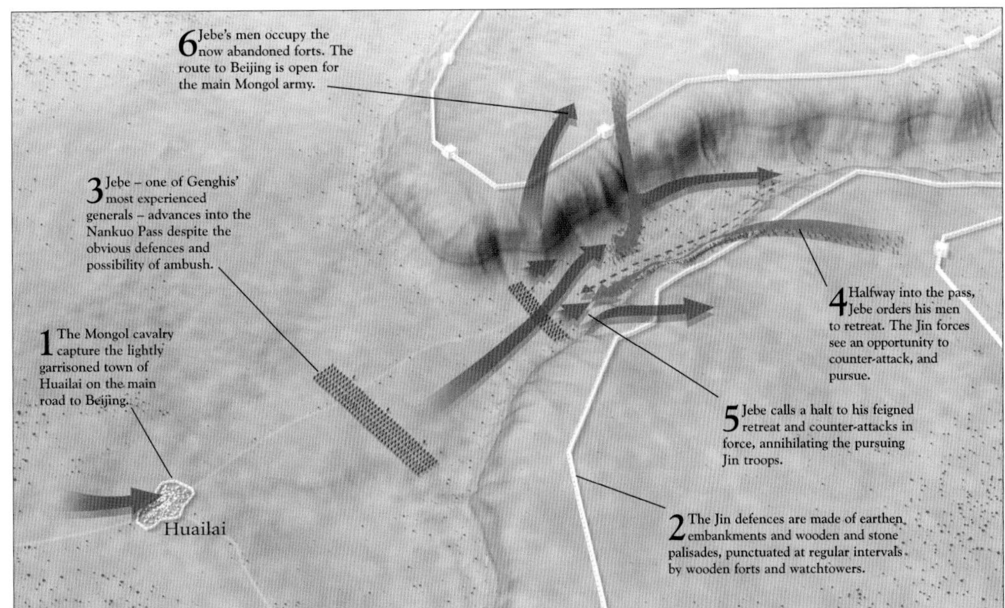
6 Jebe's men occupy the now abandoned forts. The route to Beijing is open for the main Mongol army.
3 Jebe – one of Genghis' most experienced generals – advances into the Nankuo Pass despite the obvious defences and possibility of ambush.
1 The Mongol cavalry capture the lightly garrisoned town of Huailai on the main road to Beijing.
4 Halfway into the pass, Jebe orders his men to retreat. The Jin forces see an opportunity to counter-attack, and pursue.
5 Jebe calls a halt to his feigned retreat and counter-attacks in force, annihilating the pursuing Jin troops.
2 The Jin defences are made of earthen embankments and wooden and stone palisades, punctuated at regular intervals by wooden forts and watchtowers.
Huailai

General Jebe was one of Genghis Khan's ablest generals. At Nankuo Pass, though, the odds of him being successful must have seemed as steep as the walls of the canyon through which he led his army on a feigned reconnaissance mission.

Genghis Khan's efforts to take Jin Yenching (Beijing) had proved unsuccessful in 1211 and 1212, but he was back with a vengeance in 1213. The shortest, but most perilous, route to the Jin capital lay via the Nankuo Pass to the northwest, between the fortified village of Huailai and Nankuo village.

This village lay at the edge of the 'Plateau of Dragon and Tiger', a mere 30km (20 miles) from the walls of the capital. But to reach it the Mongols had to pass through the narrow, deep, gorge-like pass – a distance of 22km (14 miles) from one end to the other, with Jin forts, towers, palisades and troops atop steep hills on either side.

General Jebe was ordered by Genghis Khan to take his cavalry down the Nankuo Pass, tricking the enemy by appearing to be conducting a reconnaissance operation. He advanced halfway down the pass before he ordered his men to retreat. The Jin took the bait, abandoned their fortified posts, gave chase and realized only when the Mongols halted their 'retreat' that they had walked into a deadly trap.

The Jin infantry were slaughtered, their positions occupied and Jebe marched on Beijing.

LOCATION

Mongolia

Nankuo Pass • Jin Yenching

Jin Empire

Song Empire

Less than 30km (20 miles) from Beijing (Jin Yenching), Nankuo Pass protected the shortest and fastest road from the north to the Chinese capital.

TIMELINE

1500–1000BC	1000–500BC	500BC–0AD	0–500AD	500–1000AD	1000–1500AD	1500–2000AD

Battle of Muret 1213

KEY FACTS

WHO Simon de Montfort against Pedro II, the king of Aragon.

WHAT Pedro crossed the Pyrenees, where he was joined by soldiers from Toulouse, and rode to meet de Montfort's much smaller army, encamped at Muret. Despite bravely leading his own men from the front line, he was quickly undone by a cavalry charge.

WHERE Muret, France.

WHEN 12 September 1213

WHY De Montfort led the Albigensian Crusade to rid southern France of the Cathar heretics. Pedro of Aragon was alarmed by his ambitions and territorial conquests in the area, however, and determined to fight him at Muret.

OUTCOME De Montfort's outnumbered cavalry charged the Aragonese, killing Pedro, and the disheartened troops turned and fled.

Simon de Montfort was a warrior baron of much courage, who had taken part in the Fourth Crusade and led another against the heretic Cathars of southern France. In doing so, though, he deposed many local nobles and his acquisitive actions were alarming for King Pedro, in nearby Aragon.

ALBIGENSIAN CRUSADE

SIMON DE MONTFORT'S VICTORY

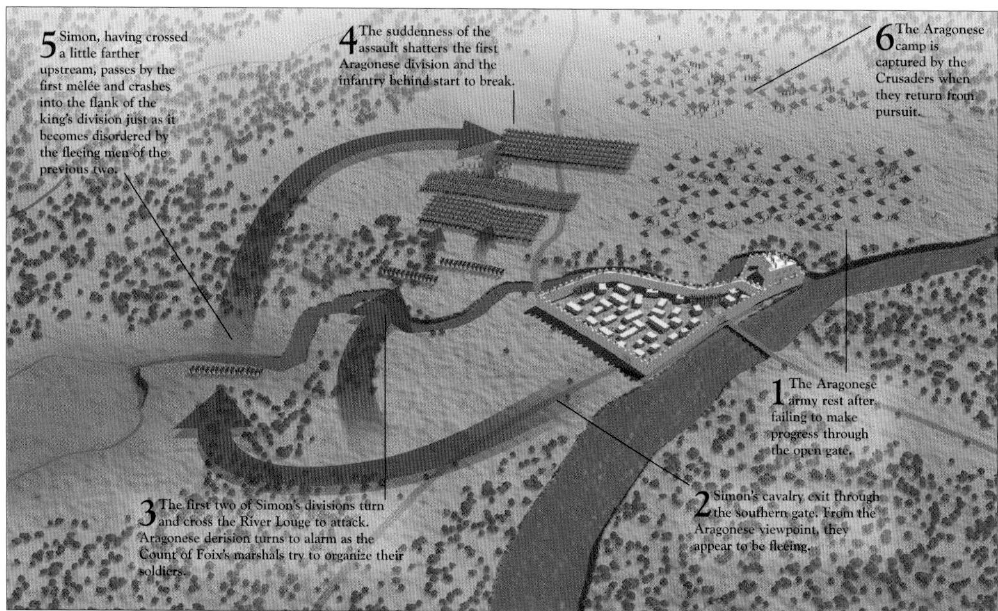

5 Simon, having crossed a little farther upstream, passes by the first mêlée and crashes into the flank of the king's division just as it becomes disordered by the fleeing men of the previous two.
4 The suddenness of the assault shatters the first Aragonese division and the infantry behind start to break.
6 The Aragonese camp is captured by the Crusaders when they return from pursuit.
1 The Aragonese army rest after failing to make progress through the open gate.
2 Simon's cavalry exit through the southern gate. From the Aragonese viewpoint, they appear to be fleeing.
3 The first two of Simon's divisions turn and cross the River Louge to attack. Aragonese derision turns to alarm as the Count of Foix's marshals try to organize their soldiers.

Southern France, particularly Toulouse, remained an anarchic, fractious region in the thirteenth century, just the sort of area for an ambitious noble such as Simon de Montfort to try to carve out his own domain.

King Pedro II's Aragonese army had a clear numerical advantage over that of Simon de Montfort's when it reached the walled city of Muret. However, Pedro's men were still in a state of disorder when they perceived a column of cavalry moving swiftly out from one of the gates. At first, it looked as if the column was fleeing, but suddenly it turned, split into three and became an attacking formation.

THREE-PRONGED ATTACK

Two divisions launched themselves directly into the front of the surprised Aragonese, who overlooked the third division to focus on this immediate threat – a common occurrence in battle at close quarters. Reeling from the frontal hammer blow, they fell back, disrupting the division behind. At just this point, Simon de Montfort's third division of crusader cavalry appeared from their right, shieldless flank, slamming into the king's reserve division. Pedro was unhorsed and, despite his cries, he was slain. This caused his men to panic and they fled the battlefield, decisively beaten by forces amounting to a fraction of their own number.

LOCATION

FRANCE

Toulouse

Muret

SPAIN

Transforming from God-fearing crusader to greedy baron in a few short months, Simon de Montfort tried to carve out his own fiefdom in the Pyrenees.

TIMELINE

1500–1000BC	1000–500BC	500BC–0AD	0–500AD	500–1000AD	1000–1500AD	1500–2000AD

Bouvines 1214

WARS OF PHILIP AUGUSTUS

FRENCH VICTORY

On 27 July 1214, at the bridge of Bouvines, west of Tournai, in the County of Flanders, a battle was fought that involved most of the major principalities of Western Europe. King Philip II Augustus (1165–1223) defeated an allied army led by the Holy Roman Emperor Otto IV of Brunswick (c. 1180–1218).

KEY FACTS

WHO The French led by King Philip II met the allies under Holy Roman Emperor Otto IV.

WHAT The battle was fought in three phases: cavalry vs. cavalry; cavalry/infantry vs. cavalry/infantry; infantry vs. infantry.

WHERE At Bouvines near Tournai in northern France.

WHEN 27 July 1214

WHY Several French princes rebelling against Philip II were joined by King John of England (1167–1216), who had lost lands to Philip, and Otto IV, because Philip was supported by Pope Innocent III (1160–1216).

OUTCOME Philip II Augustus's patient tactics easily defeated the allied princes, who rushed into battle without waiting for the arrival of their entire army and without any united leadership.

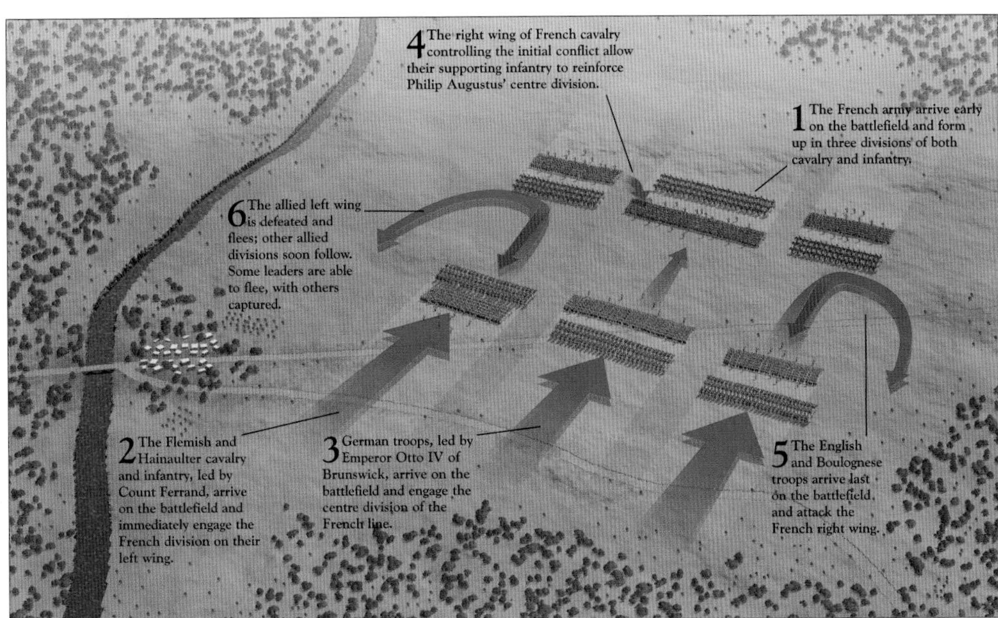
4 The right wing of French cavalry controlling the initial conflict allow their supporting infantry to reinforce Philip Augustus' centre division.
1 The French army arrive early on the battlefield and form up in three divisions of both cavalry and infantry.
6 The allied left wing is defeated and flees; other allied divisions soon follow. Some leaders are able to flee, with others captured.
2 The Flemish and Hainaulter cavalry and infantry, led by Count Ferrand, arrive on the battlefield and immediately engage the French division on their left wing.
3 German troops, led by Emperor Otto IV of Brunswick, arrive on the battlefield and engage the centre division of the French line.
5 The English and Boulognese troops arrive last on the battlefield, and attack the French right wing.

Philip Augustus's victory at Bouvines would establish France as the political powerhouse of thirteenth-century Europe, leaving King John of England and Otto IV of Germany to return to dire situations on their home fronts.

When the leaders of the allied army heard that the French under Philip Augustus had stopped at Bouvines, their vanguard, in an excess of enthusiasm for battle, charged on, without allowing the other elements to catch up and so exploit their numerical superiority. Some soldiers did not reach the field until the fight was over.

FRENCH STRENGTH

The battle began with a simultaneous cavalry charge – horse against horse, lances couched – as if a tournament mêlée was being fought. The French attack was stronger, and penetrated the Flemish echelons, who within the space of an hour took flight. Philip delayed his own attack, but Emperor Otto was unwilling to await the outcome and charged recklessly into the French line. Initially, the Germans pushed the French back, the energy of the charge even knocking Philip from his saddle. But soon the attack petered out. Otto's own horse was wounded and, turning away from the fighting, it fled, taking the emperor with it. By the end only six knights remained standing by the side of the defiant Count of Boulogne. All the other allies had fled or surrendered.

LOCATION

England
Calais
Bouvines
Paris
Normandy
France
Poitou

Philip Augustus and his French army, being pursued by an equally large coalition of forces from the Holy Roman Empire, fought outside Bouvines.

TIMELINE

1500–1000BC	1000–500BC	500BC–0AD	0–500AD	500–1000AD	1000–1500AD	1500–2000AD

Bouvines

BOUVINES

Philip Augustus of France wasn't much of a crusader. A jealous suspicion that he was never going to keep up with the deeds of his ally on the Third Crusade, Richard the Lionheart, may have been one of the reasons why he retuned home early. Once back on home terrain, however, he reigned supreme. At Bouvines, despite the embarrassment of being unhorsed in the conflict, he won a decisive victory over the forces of the Holy Roman Emperor, Otto IV, in alliance with the counts of Boulogne and Flanders. In so doing, he put an end to King John of England's troubled Angevin Empire.

Battle of the River Kalka 1223

KEY FACTS

Who A Mongol force under Subutai Bahadur and Jebei Noyan against several Rus principalities, led by Galich, Kiev and their Cuman allies.

What The Mongols employed a classic strategy of appearing to be beating a retreat, before turning on their pursuers and annihilating them with their rapid arrow fire and lightning cavalry movements.

Where Kalka River, near Donetsk, Ukraine.

When 31 May 1223

Why Mongol raiding parties had been active in the region for years, but when news arrived that they were planning to turn their attention on Russia, the Rus princes gathered together a substantial army and prepared to meet them.

Outcome The resounding Mongol victory opened the door to full-scale invasion and the conquest of vast territories in Eastern Europe.

For years Genghis Khan's Mongols had rampaged through central Asia, but by the 1220s he was ready to turn his attentions further west. Now it was the Russians' turn to receive a taste of Mongol military prowess.

MONGOL INVASION OF EUROPE

MONGOL VICTORY

By the thirteenth century Eastern Europe seemed powerless to resist the advance of Genghis Khan and his Mongol invaders. Kalka River was one of their most resounding victories.

LOCATION

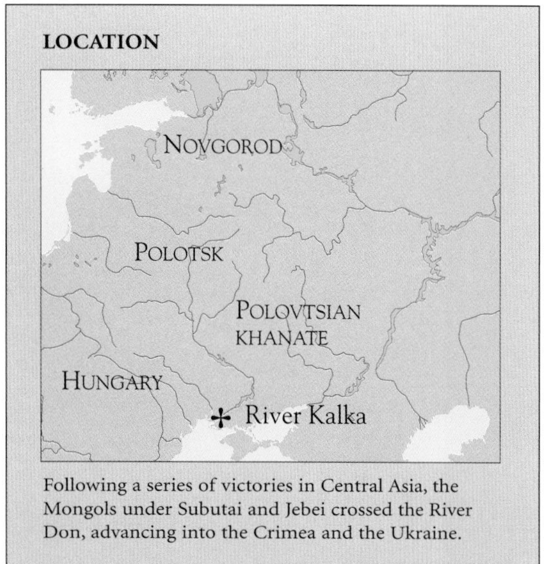
NOVGOROD
POLOTSK
POLOVTSIAN KHANATE
HUNGARY
River Kalka

Following a series of victories in Central Asia, the Mongols under Subutai and Jebei crossed the River Don, advancing into the Crimea and the Ukraine.

Two of Genghis Khan's most trusted generals, Subutai Bahadur and Jebei Noyan, had scored some easy wins in Russia and requested permission to lead a Mongol army on a more ambitious campaign. Passing through the Caucasus, they had administered a heavy defeat on the Cuman army, and its leader had fled to the court of the Rus prince Mstislav the Bold of Galich, who joined with Mstislav of Kiev and others in an alliance to meet the growing Mongol threat.

Numbering at peak strength no more than 40,000, the Mongols under Subutai and Jebei were heavily outnumbered by a Russian army nearly twice their size. The Kievan Rus were, however, prone to internal strife and discord, and disunity of command, with each general advocating his own strategy for the annihilation of the invaders. To compound the problems faced by the Russians, only about a quarter of their troops had received any proper military training. Those who had been trained or had actually experienced combat had faced only Western-style opposition. The tactics of the Mongols

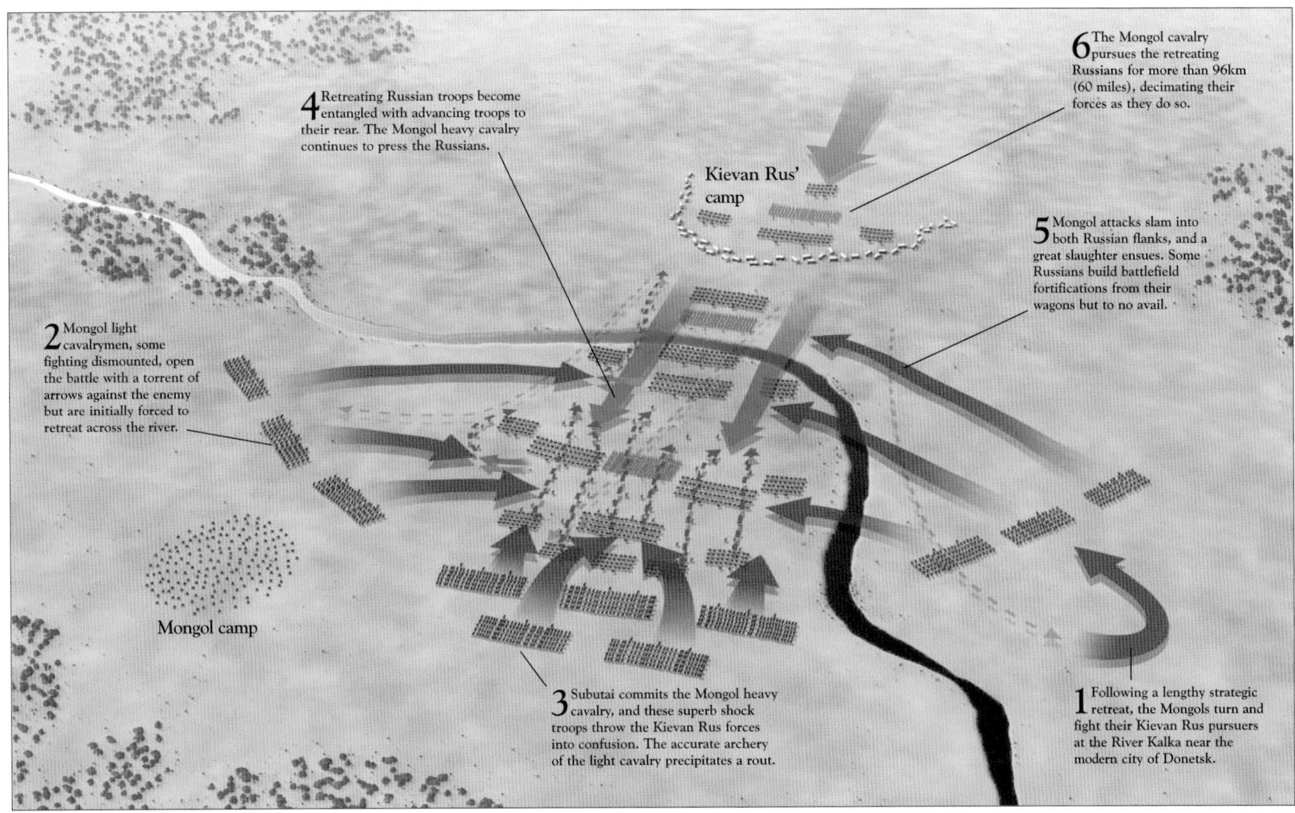
6 The Mongol cavalry pursues the retreating Russians for more than 96km (60 miles), decimating their forces as they do so.
4 Retreating Russian troops become entangled with advancing troops to their rear. The Mongol heavy cavalry continues to press the Russians.
Kievan Rus' camp
5 Mongol attacks slam into both Russian flanks, and a great slaughter ensues. Some Russians build battlefield fortifications from their wagons but to no avail.
2 Mongol light cavalrymen, some fighting dismounted, open the battle with a torrent of arrows against the enemy but are initially forced to retreat across the river.
Mongol camp
3 Subutai commits the Mongol heavy cavalry, and these superb shock troops throw the Kievan Rus forces into confusion. The accurate archery of the light cavalry precipitates a rout.
1 Following a lengthy strategic retreat, the Mongols turn and fight their Kievan Rus pursuers at the River Kalka near the modern city of Donetsk.

An alliance of Rus kingdoms finally thought they had enough manpower to confront and rid themselves of the persistent terror of the Mongols. But they were simply lured into a death trap on the banks of the Kalka.

would prove very different from anything previously encountered.

For nine days, the Mongols, in one of their favoured tactics, 'gave ground.' The divided Russians began to fragment even further in the pursuit, weakening their decided advantage in numbers. Finally, on 31 May 1223, the advance elements of the Russian army, the Volhnyians and Polovtians, drew up along the River Kalka.

With a predetermined signal, the light cavalry of the Mongols assumed the offensive. The initial contact again seemed to be favouring the Russians, and the Mongols executed a coordinated retreat across a bridge spanning the Kalka. The Russians, though, were unable to press their temporary advantage and their pursuit faltered. Subutai sensed that the time was right for a decisive blow and committed the Mongol heavy cavalry to the fray. These more heavily armed and armoured horsemen bowled into the Russians and put their main body to flight, while the light cavalrymen fired withering barrages of arrows as they repeatedly crossed the enemy's route of advance.

Turning in confusion, the Polovtians and Volhynians panicked and attempted to cross the bridge to the western bank of the Kalka. In doing so, they became hopelessly tangled with an allied contingent from Galicia, which had just arrived. Milling about at the crossing point, the Russians were easy targets for the sledgehammer blows of the Mongol heavy cavalry. Soon the Galicians had either been trampled or panicked and had joined the retreat.

With the enemy pressed in the centre, Subutai ordered attacks from the left and right flanks. The Chernigov army and the Kievan contingent had arrived, but came upon the scene too late to alter its outcome. The Chernigov soldiers were cut down in great numbers and fell back, while the Kievans attempted to stem the Mongol tide by building makeshift fortifications with their wagons and equipment. The effort was futile. The swift light cavalry of the Mongols was said to have pursued the fleeing Russians for more than 96km (60 miles), inflicting horrific casualties and showing no mercy. The Kievan soldiers who had made a defensive stand managed to hold out for two days but were forced to surrender.

TIMELINE

1500–1000BC	1000–500BC	500BC–0AD	0–500AD	500–1000AD	1000–1500AD	1500–2000AD

Leignitz 1241

KEY FACTS

WHO A Mongol army comprising 20,000 warriors under Baidar on an 'diversionary raid' was confronted by an army of Silesians, Germans and the Holy Orders of 20–30,000 men under Henry II of Silesia (d. 1241).

WHAT Mongol skirmishers repulsed the initial allied assault, but the Silesian army renewed the attack. The Mongols feigned retreat and then attacked from both front and flank. They then carried away the infantry waiting in reserve.

WHERE Leignitz, now in modern Poland, between Prague and Breslau.

WHEN 9 April 1241

WHY The Mongols attacked all who did not submit to them.

OUTCOME The allied army was utterly destroyed and the Mongols slaughtered everyone in the Oder valley as a lesson to the rest.

They ruled the greatest land empire there has ever been: from Korea in the Far East to the shores of the Baltic, from the Arctic Circle to the tip of India, the Mongols were supreme. Popes, Kings and Emperors had no answer to the scale of their strategy or their discipline on the battlefield.

MONGOL INVASION OF EUROPE

MONGOL VICTORY

Within sight of the steeples of the city of Leignitz, a Mongol army slaughtered something like 150,000 men in less than a week, the Silesians having no answer to the superior tactics of their opponents.

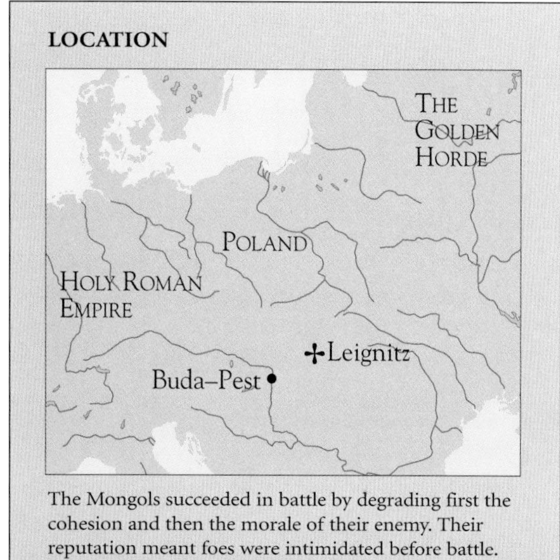
LOCATION
THE GOLDEN HORDE
POLAND
HOLY ROMAN EMPIRE
Leignitz
Buda–Pest

The Mongols succeeded in battle by degrading first the cohesion and then the morale of their enemy. Their reputation meant foes were intimidated before battle.

The Mongols planned an advance west between the Black Sea and the Baltic, with Hungary as the main target. Meanwhile a diversionary raid was planned under two leaders – Baidar and Kadan – which would sweep northwest into Poland and Lithuania before heading south to support the main effort.

Soon Baidar and Kadan had burnt the cities of Lublin and Zawichost (Volodymyr) on the road to Warsaw. Next was Sandomir, taken with barely a fight. But this was not the plan. They were supposed to be drawing forces towards themselves and away from the main action in Hungary. No one seemed to want to come out and fight. They had to try harder. So they split their army in two, cunningly attempting to make each part a more tempting target. It was Baidar who got the desired result. News of the Mongols' terrifying attacks had reached Henry of Silesia, who formed an extensive alliance and was at Leignitz, not from Baidar's army. Also King Wenceslas of Bohemia (1205–53) was on his way with another army 50,000 strong. Baidar sent out messages to

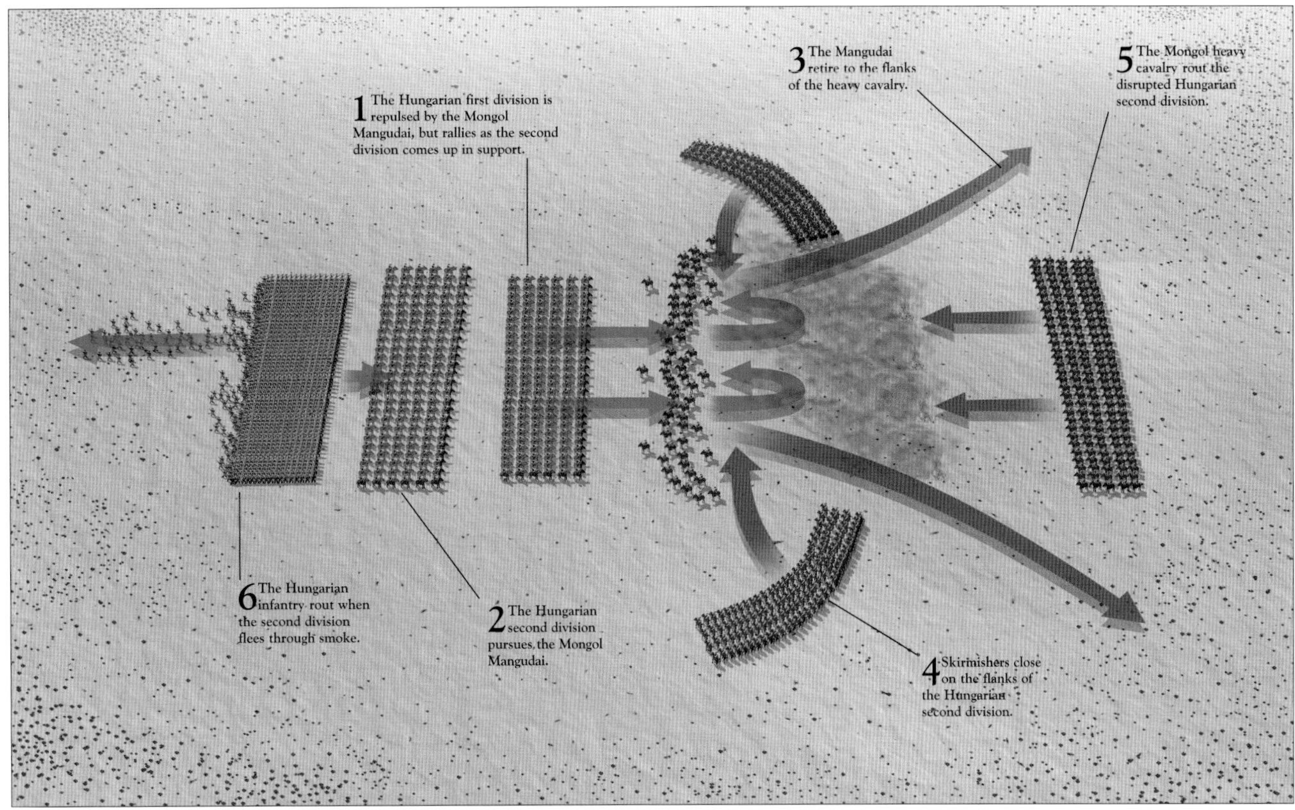
1 The Hungarian first division is repulsed by the Mongol Mangudai, but rallies as the second division comes up in support.
2 The Hungarian second division pursues the Mongol Mangudai.
3 The Mangudai retire to the flanks of the heavy cavalry.
4 Skirmishers close on the flanks of the Hungarian second division.
5 The Mongol heavy cavalry rout the disrupted Hungarian second division.
6 The Hungarian infantry rout when the second division flees through smoke.

Both armies that met at Leignitz were, to some extent, amalgams of different forces and tribes, but somehow the Mongols were able to forge a disciplined unit out of theirs, whereas large parts of the Silesian ranks were a disorganized rabble.

ensure Kadan's forces could get to Leignitz before the two armies could unite.

Henry's army included his own Silesians plus contingents from the Holy Orders of Teutonic Knights, Templars and Hospitalars, few in number but strong in determination. Apart from the Holy Orders, most of those at his disposal were poorly trained feudal levies.

The Mongols also included men from many different tribes and cultures. But all had been subsumed into the higher Mongol organization. Surrounded by veterans with thousands of miles on horseback and numerous raids and battles behind them, they could not fail to fight well.

SUPERIOR MONGOL TACTICS

The Mongols sent forward their Mangudai light cavalry, proficient in feigned flight. They were met by Henry's Silesian cavalry, who were of such bad quality that they ran from the Mangudai. Henry next sent forward the Polish cavalry and Teutonic Knights. These succeeded in slowly forcing back the Mangudai – but too slowly, so he joined in himself with the rest of his cavalry. The Mangudai now withdrew.

Mistaking this for a rout, the knights followed and pursued deep into the deadly embrace of the Mongol army. The cavalry on their flanks closed in, showering the knights with arrows. They even set fire to a smokescreen which they had prepared in the path of the knights after having ridden over it. Thus, for the remaining infantry the knights would have appeared to be swallowed up. And then there was the awful wait before worst fears were realized. The knights reappeared, a few to begin with, but soon followed by the rest – routed.

The best the region had – lords and masters over all they surveyed – had been beaten by heathens thanks to unknown means. The infantry couldn't stand it; they too routed and the Mongols pursued. Relentless pursuit by an enemy mounted on faster horses, as the Mongols were, was an awful thing. There was no escape, no time to hide, no let-up in the killing. This is when armies are utterly destroyed. In half a week, the Mongols had slaughtered three armies totalling 150,000 men.

Peipus 1242

NORTHERN CRUSADES

RUSSIAN VICTORY

KEY FACTS

WHO A Russian force of 5000 under Alexandre Nevskii (1220–63), opposed a Crusader army of perhaps 1000 under Bishop Hermann von Buxhoved of Tartu (d. 1248).

WHAT The power of the knightly charge was dissipated by mounted archery, and the remaining knights overwhelmed by the more numerous enemy.

WHERE Lake Peipus, on the border between modern Estonia and Russia.

WHEN April 1242

WHY The Russians had launched a raid into enemy territory in revenge for one by the Crusaders and were in the process of withdrawing when they were caught by the pursuing Crusaders.

OUTCOME Almost half of the Crusaders were killed, a few were captured and even fewer escaped.

Alexander Nevskii, revered in Soviet propaganda, was caught between Catholic intolerance and Pagan indulgence. However, he knew whom to kneel before and whom he could fight. He accepted the Mongol Yoke and at Lake Peipus defeated the Teutonic Knights and their allies.

Sergei Eisenstein's celebrated film *Alexander Nevsky* (1938) restaged the so-called Battle on the Ice, with dramatic scenes of soldiers plunging through the cracking ice to their deaths. In reality, the lake was quite shallow.

LOCATION

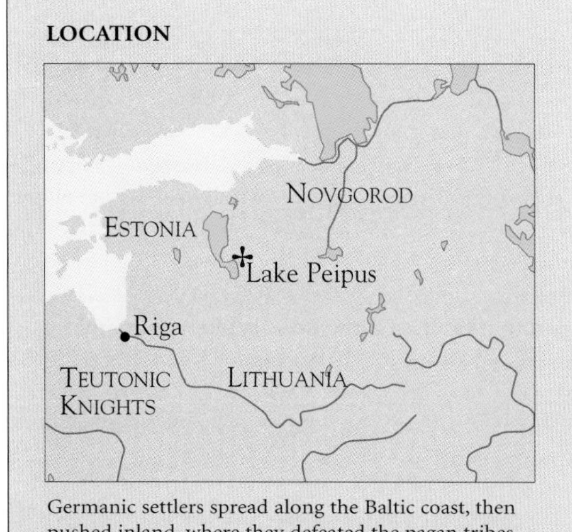

Novgorod
Estonia
Lake Peipus
Riga
Teutonic Knights
Lithuania

Germanic settlers spread along the Baltic coast, then pushed inland, where they defeated the pagan tribes. Here they met the Orthodox Christians of Russia.

The Russian state of Novgorod, which observed Orthodox Christianity, was under pressure from the Pope to accept the Latin creed. It fell to Alexander Nevskii to lead the defence against a Crusader army led by Bishop Hermann von Buxhoved of Tartu.

Alexander had scored a great victory over the Swedish element among the Crusading forces. But when a dispersed group of Russians was virtually wiped out by Bishop Hermann's army at a bridge near the village of Mooste, survivors escaped to warn Alexander, and he turned his army eastwards across the frozen Lake Peipus. Bishop Hermann, perhaps exhilarated by his recent success, and seriously underestimating his opponent's strength, pursued him via a parallel course.

The Russians reached the further shore of the lake first and turned north to await the Crusaders from firm ground on the beach at a place called Raven Rock. The prevailing wind in this area is from the west and this, plus the tendency of ice to thaw and refreeze, forced the ice to build up into wave-like ridges on the eastern

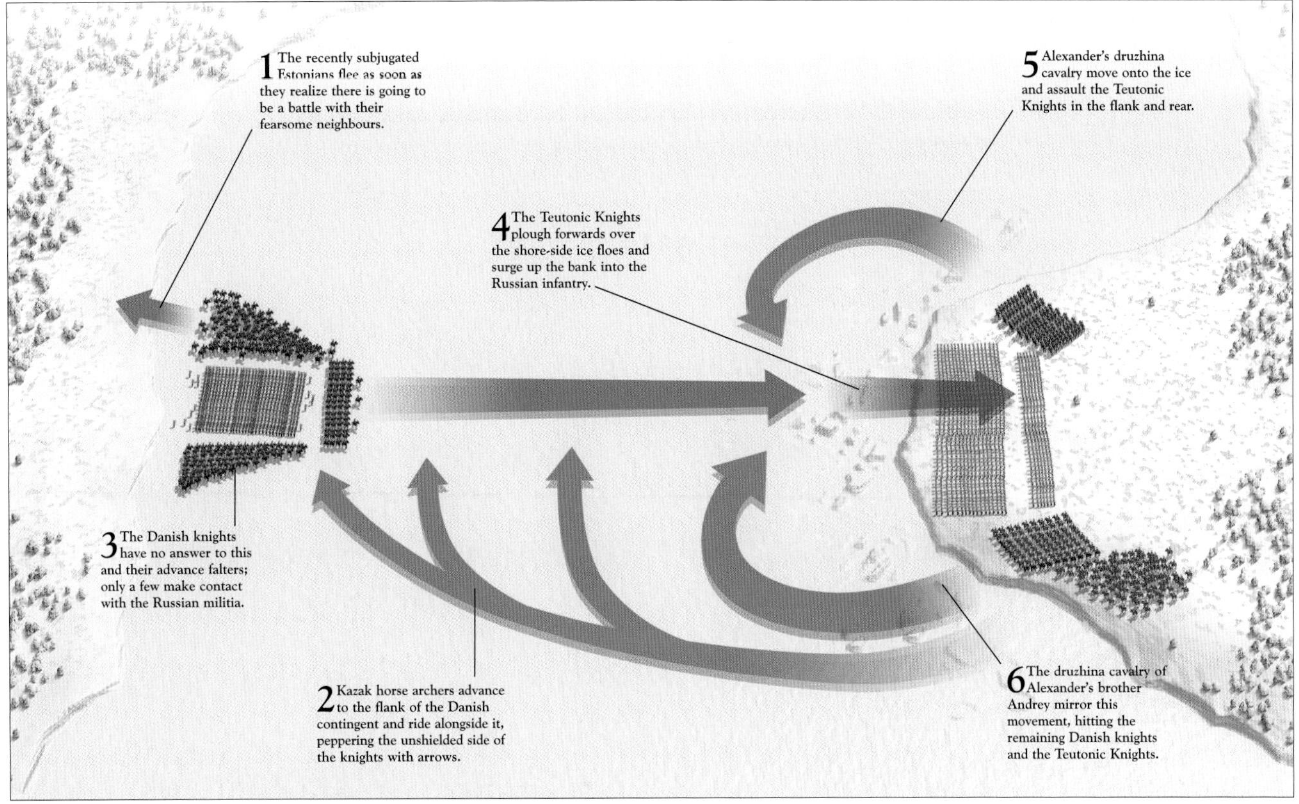
1 The recently subjugated Estonians flee as soon as they realize there is going to be a battle with their fearsome neighbours.
5 Alexander's druzhina cavalry move onto the ice and assault the Teutonic Knights in the flank and rear.
4 The Teutonic Knights plough forwards over the shore-side ice floes and surge up the bank into the Russian infantry.
3 The Danish knights have no answer to this and their advance falters; only a few make contact with the Russian militia.
2 Kazak horse archers advance to the flank of the Danish contingent and ride alongside it, peppering the unshielded side of the knights with arrows.
6 The druzhina cavalry of Alexander's brother Andrey mirror this movement, hitting the remaining Danish knights and the Teutonic Knights.

The Estonians tried to line up in the classic wedged cavalry charge formations known as the Boar's Head. But a gallop on ice must have quickly become a slide and slither into chaos and ultimate defeat.

shore, thus forming an area of broken ground in front of the deployed Russians. Alexander positioned his infantry, armed with a mixture of spears, bows and axes, in the centre. On his flanks he placed his cavalry with horse archers.

BOAR'S SNOUT CHARGE

The Estonian levies, forced to fight by their masters, fled from the field at the sight of the Russian army without making any contribution. The outnumbered Crusaders then did what they knew best. They formed a 'Boar's snout', a blunt wedge formation with the best troops, the Teutonic Knights, at the front, and charged. This cannot have been easy with horses slipping on the ice, so it is doubtful they managed the full momentum of the classic knightly charge. All the same, despite the slippery and uneven ice and the arrows of the enemy, they struck the militia in the centre of the Russian line with great force, driving into their lines and killing many. But in such a mêlée neither the militia nor the Crusader knights could see what was happening on the flanks.

As the knights were cutting down the militia in the centre, the Russian cavalry was falling on their flanks. Suffering serious casualties, many of the Danes began to turn and fall back across the lake. The remaining knights continued to drive into the Russian foot but were undermined by the arrival of more cavalry. With the limited peripheral vision provided by their helmets and their own concentration on the enemy in front, many of them would have been cut down, unaware of this new foe.

Those Crusaders who either could not or would not escape, fought on until they were beaten. Six Teutonic Knights were captured plus 44 other Danish and German men-at-arms. The small Crusader force left 400 bodies on the ice. Those that fled were pursued only to the far shore of the lake.

In spite of the legend of the 'Battle on the Ice', Lake Peipus is remarkably shallow, so it is likely that any knights who did drown in the rout probably did so as the result of falling off their horses. The casualties on both sides were high, but the Crusaders suffered the worst, losing 45 per cent of their force.

TIMELINE

1500–1000BC	1000–500BC	500BC–0AD	0–500AD	500–1000AD	1000–1500AD	1500–2000AD

La Forbie 1244

KEY FACTS

WHO A Crusader army containing about 6000 western soldiers plus 4000 local allies, opposed by 10,000 Khwarezmid Egyptians and 6000 Mamluk Turks.

WHAT After their allied troops were broken by a sudden attack, the Westerners launched their own assault, driving deep into the enemy army.

WHERE Near La Forbie, northwest of Gaza.

WHEN 17–18 October 1244

WHY Jerusalem had fallen to Khwarezmid Egyptians, prompting a campaign to defeat them in the field and restore the situation.

OUTCOME Surrounded in the middle of the enemy army, the Crusaders were defeated with massive casualties.

La Forbie was the worst defeat suffered by the Crusaders and caused a sharp decline in their power in the Holy Land. Casualties among the knightly orders were especially serious. It also marked the beginning of Mamluk dominance in Egypt.

CRUSADES

KHWAREZMID/MAMLUK VICTORY

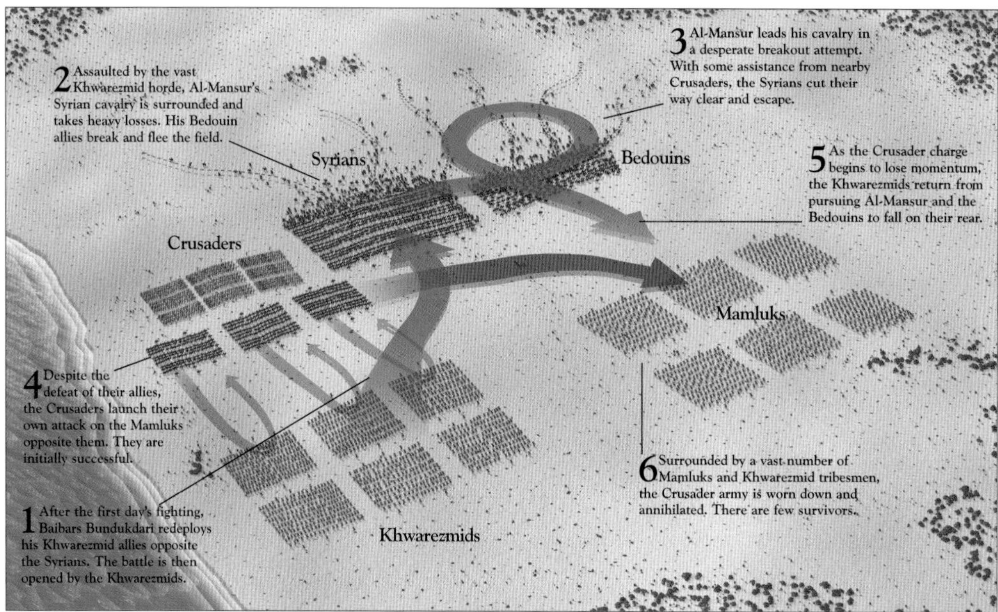
2 Assaulted by the vast Khwarezmid horde, Al-Mansur's Syrian cavalry is surrounded and takes heavy losses. His Bedouin allies break and flee the field.
3 Al-Mansur leads his cavalry in a desperate breakout attempt. With some assistance from nearby Crusaders, the Syrians cut their way clear and escape.
Syrians
Bedouins
5 As the Crusader charge begins to lose momentum, the Khwarezmids return from pursuing Al-Mansur and the Bedouins to fall on their rear.
Crusaders
Mamluks
4 Despite the defeat of their allies, the Crusaders launch their own attack on the Mamluks opposite them. They are initially successful.
6 Surrounded by a vast number of Mamluks and Khwarezmid tribesmen, the Crusader army is worn down and annihilated. There are few survivors.
1 After the first day's fighting, Baibars Bundukdari redeploys his Khwarezmid allies opposite the Syrians. The battle is then opened by the Khwarezmids.
Khwarezmids

At La Forbie, crusaders fought in alliance with Syrians and Bedouins, but these were driven from the field relatively quickly, leaving the crusaders, after a serious of defiant but unavailing cavalry charges, to be picked off in hand-to-hand combat.

In 1244 Jerusalem fell to a large force of Khwarezmids allied to the Sultanate of Egypt, and local Muslim and Christian states allied to launch a retaliatory campaign. At La Forbie they faced the Khwarezmids, who were supported by the Mamluk Turks' elite heavy cavalry.

The allies began to advance, and the Crusaders launched a predictable succession of cavalry charges, largely absorbed by the Khwarezmid tribesmen, whose larger numbers allowed them to soak up casualties. The following day, however, a horde of Khwarezmids launched a wild charge against the Syrians in the centre, badly mauling them. Walter of Brienne, leading the Crusaders, ordered his knights to support their allies, but it was too late. The Syrians fled the field in disorder, and those that that did not were set upon by the victorious Khwarezmids and slaughtered. The Crusaders launched further charges, but the battle degenerated into a static hand-to-hand fight, with the Crusaders surrounded on all sides by large numbers of enemies.

Something like 5000 Christians were killed, and the Crusader army was virtually wiped out.

LOCATION

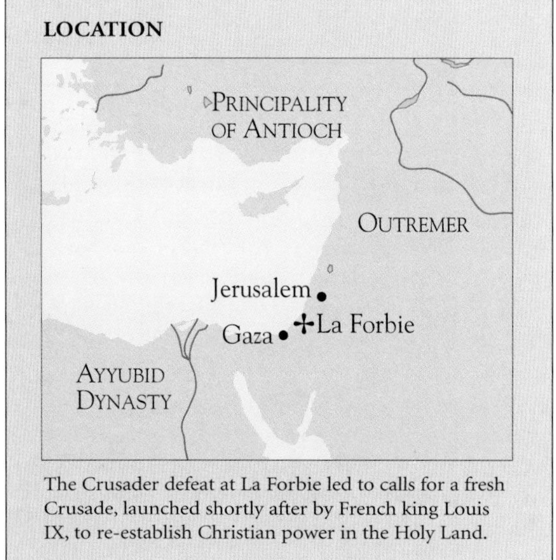
PRINCIPALITY OF ANTIOCH
OUTREMER
Jerusalem
Gaza
La Forbie
AYYUBID DYNASTY

The Crusader defeat at La Forbie led to calls for a fresh Crusade, launched shortly after by French king Louis IX, to re-establish Christian power in the Holy Land.

TIMELINE

1500–1000BC	1000–500BC	500BC–0AD	0–500AD	500–1000AD	1000–1500AD	1500–2000AD

Mansura 1250

KEY FACTS

WHO King Louis IX of France (1226–70) led an army of 25,000 men against the Aybid Sultanate of Egypt.

WHAT Having captured Damietta, he was defeated in an ambush at Mansura.

WHERE The Nile Delta city of Mansura (Mansûrah) in Egypt.

WHEN 10 February 1250

WHY Louis hoped to cripple the Aybid dynasty and wrench back Jerusalem from Muslim control.

OUTCOME It was a massive defeat and brought the Outremer Christians' worst enemy into power.

King Louis of France launched this attempt to take the Nile Delta and Cairo. Yet again, however, an impetuous commander caused the Crusader army to run into a well-planned ambush and crushing defeat.

SEVENTH CRUSADE

EGYPTIAN VICTORY

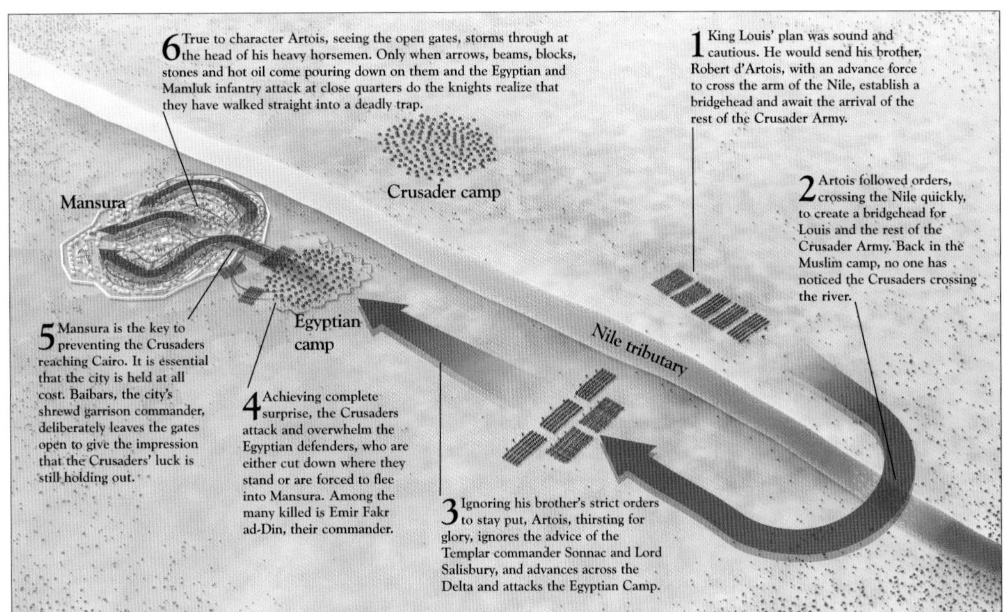
6 True to character Artois, seeing the open gates, storms through at the head of his heavy horsemen. Only when arrows, beams, blocks, stones and hot oil come pouring down on them and the Egyptian and Mamluk infantry attack at close quarters do the knights realize that they have walked straight into a deadly trap.
1 King Louis' plan was sound and cautious. He would send his brother, Robert d'Artois, with an advance force to cross the arm of the Nile, establish a bridgehead and await the arrival of the rest of the Crusader Army.
Crusader camp
Mansura
2 Artois followed orders, crossing the Nile quickly, to create a bridgehead for Louis and the rest of the Crusader Army. Back in the Muslim camp, no one has noticed the Crusaders crossing the river.
Egyptian camp
Nile tributary
5 Mansura is the key to preventing the Crusaders reaching Cairo. It is essential that the city is held at all cost. Baibars, the city's shrewd garrison commander, deliberately leaves the gates open to give the impression that the Crusaders' luck is still holding out.
4 Achieving complete surprise, the Crusaders attack and overwhelm the Egyptian defenders, who are either cut down where they stand or are forced to flee into Mansura. Among the many killed is Emir Fakr ad-Din, their commander.
3 Ignoring his brother's strict orders to stay put, Artois, thirsting for glory, ignores the advice of the Templar commander Sonnac and Lord Salisbury, and advances across the Delta and attacks the Egyptian Camp.

Louis IX of France was one of the outstanding monarchs of his age. He couldn't be everywhere, however, and when his brother Robert of Artois disobeyed orders at Mansura, the result was disaster.

The beleaguered Christian states in the Holy Land thought they had gained a formidable champion when King Louis IX of France took his crusading vows, but a plan to take the city of Mansura on the Nile was undone by a deadly trap set by Baibars Bundukdari, a Mamluk Turk and the garrison commander. Baibars left the city gates deliberately open to lure the 'infidels' into the city's narrow, winding lanes. When Louis's brother Robert of Artois led in a contingent, the men were met with stones, arrows, beams and scalding hot oil poured down on them from the roof tops. Hundreds of knights, including Artois, were slaughtered, and Louis and the remainder of the army found itself trapped.

Louis attempted to retreat towards Damietta, his supply base, but was soon forced to accept the fact that the army would not reach the port in time. There was little choice but to negotiate with the Egyptian Sultan, Turan Shah. At the end of April, an agreement was struck. In return for paying the Sultan some 800,000 gold bezants, the knights, nobles and higher-ranked members of the Crusader army would be spared.

LOCATION

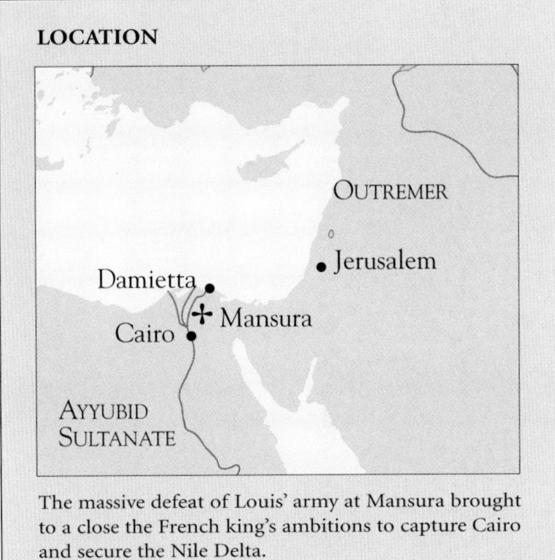
OUTREMER
Jerusalem
Damietta
Mansura
Cairo
AYYUBID SULTANATE

The massive defeat of Louis' army at Mansura brought to a close the French king's ambitions to capture Cairo and secure the Nile Delta.

TIMELINE

1500–1000BC	1000–500BC	500BC–0AD	0–500AD	500–1000AD	1000–1500AD	1500–2000AD

Mansura

AMRO AHMED

MANSURA

The Mamluk Turks were as guileful as they were cruel. At Mansura they played on a repeated failing of many a Western crusader over the centuries – the irresistible desire to be the hero. Robert of Artois was the brother of the French king Louis IX, a man so esteemed he would later be granted sainthood. Robert, however, had little of Louis' wisdom. When he neglected orders to guard a route over the Nile and entered the open gates of Mansura, he found he had been lured into a death trap. His lack of judgement would lead to the aborting of Louis's crusading expedition.

Siege of Xiangyang 1267–1273

KEY FACTS

WHO Lu Wenhuan and Zhang Tianshun under the Song Emperor Duzong (1265–74), under siege led by Chinese general General Shi Shu, in the employ of Kublai Khan's Yuan Mongols.

WHAT The garrison mounted stiff resistance in their near impregnable fortress city, until fearsome counter trebuchets brought the city to submission in a matter of days.

WHERE Xiangyang, near modern day Hubei, China.

WHEN 1267–1273

WHY The River Han was the most important waterway into southern China, so as long as the Song held the fortresses they could effectively block Yuan ambitions of territorial expansion.

OUTCOME The taking of the city cleared the routes through into southern China, and the Song dynasty would fall soon after.

For 30 years the Chinese Song dynasty had beaten back attacks by the Mongols Yuan dynasty. But when the fortified city of Xiangyang finally fell after a protracted six-year siege, the path was clear for the Mongols to push on through southern China.

SONG–YUAN WARS

MONGOL VICTORY

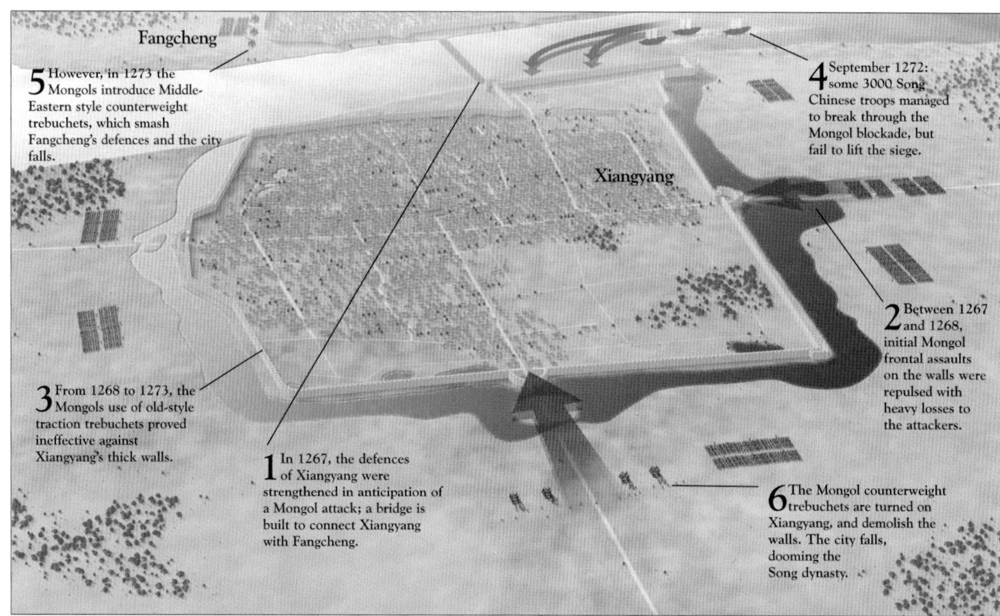

Fangcheng
Xiangyang
5 However, in 1273 the Mongols introduce Middle-Eastern style counterweight trebuchets, which smash Fangcheng's defences and the city falls.
4 September 1272: some 3000 Song Chinese troops managed to break through the Mongol blockade, but fail to lift the siege.
2 Between 1267 and 1268, initial Mongol frontal assaults on the walls were repulsed with heavy losses to the attackers.
3 From 1268 to 1273, the Mongols use of old-style traction trebuchets proved ineffective against Xiangyang's thick walls.
1 In 1267, the defences of Xiangyang were strengthened in anticipation of a Mongol attack; a bridge is built to connect Xiangyang with Fangcheng.
6 The Mongol counterweight trebuchets are turned on Xiangyang, and demolish the walls. The city falls, dooming the Song dynasty.

Xiangyang seemed to be an impenetrable walled city. It had defied the Mongol siegemen for six years. But when a new kind of trebuchet was suddenly hauled into place, walls that had seemed unbreachable crumbled within a matter of days.

For six years Kublai Khan's men besieged the fortress city of Xiangyang which, on the River Han, the watery highway into southern China, was effectively one of the gateways into the Song heartlands to take them. Traction trebuchets proved ineffective because the Song soldiers had widened the moat, meaning the range was too far for the stones to hit the walls consistently. Those that did hit did little damage, thanks to the net 'padding' that festooned the walls.

An increasingly impatient Kublai Khan sent Shi Shu, a northern Chinese general in Mongol service, to Xiangyang to help tighten the siege, but still the city held out. Finally utilizing skilled Persian engineers, Kublai bought in counterweight trebuchets, the first ever seen in China. These machines were capable of hurling heavy projectiles – stones weighing at least 75 kg (165lb) more than 500m (1640ft).

Their impact was immediate. Huge boulders sailed over the walls and crashed into city streets and houses. Then the great walls themselves crumbled into piles of broken brick and shattered mortar. What the Mongol army could not accomplish in almost six years was achieved in a few days.

LOCATION

GREAT KHANATE

Xiangyang

SONG CHINA

Xiangyang stood close to the River Han. As such, it acted as a gateway into southern China. The Song dynasty soon fell to the Mongols.

TIMELINE

1500–1000BC	1000–500BC	500BC–0AD	0–500AD	500–1000AD	1000–1500AD	1500–2000AD

Battle of Bun'ei 1274

Bune'ei was the first encounter of the mighty Mongol army with the feudal Japanese samurai. It proved a fascinating clash of styles, and the result did not quite go as the all-conquering Mongols invaders would have anticipated.

MONGOL INVASIONS OF JAPAN

JAPANESE VICTORY

KEY FACTS

WHO Kublai Khan's army versus the feudal samurai of Japan.

WHAT The Mongols launched an amphibious attack on Japan, and their fighting discipline seemed about to overwhelm the more individualistic Samurai.

WHERE Hakata Bay, Japan.

WHEN 19 November 1274

WHY Kublai Khan sought to extend the Mongol Empire into Japan.

OUTCOME For all their military superiority, the Mongols were actually outnumbered at Bun'ei, and when the Japanese fell back to a defensive position, fearing the arrival of reinforcements, the Mongols departed.

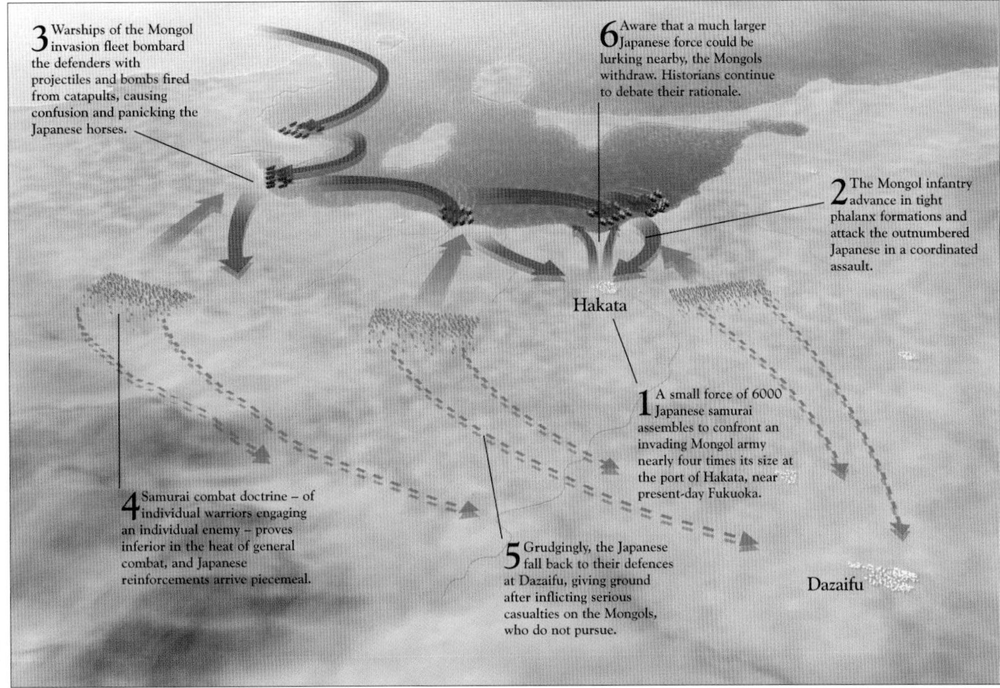

3 Warships of the Mongol invasion fleet bombard the defenders with projectiles and bombs fired from catapults, causing confusion and panicking the Japanese horses.
6 Aware that a much larger Japanese force could be lurking nearby, the Mongols withdraw. Historians continue to debate their rationale.
2 The Mongol infantry advance in tight phalanx formations and attack the outnumbered Japanese in a coordinated assault.
Hakata
1 A small force of 6000 Japanese samurai assembles to confront an invading Mongol army nearly four times its size at the port of Hakata, near present-day Fukuoka.
4 Samurai combat doctrine – of individual warriors engaging an individual enemy – proves inferior in the heat of general combat, and Japanese reinforcements arrive piecemeal.
5 Grudgingly, the Japanese fall back to their defences at Dazaifu, giving ground after inflicting serious casualties on the Mongols, who do not pursue.
Dazaifu

When the Mongols landed at Hakata Bay in 1274, the relatively puny Japanese defending forces must have feared the worst. But the invaders were uncertain of the size of the army that might be lying in wait further inland, and beat an abrupt retreat.

LOCATION

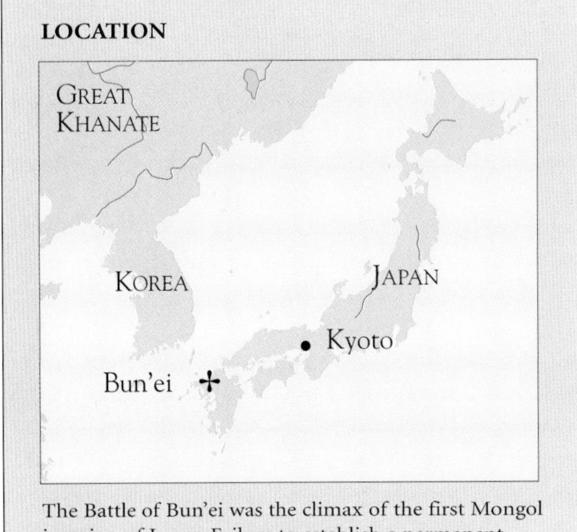

GREAT KHANATE
KOREA
JAPAN
Kyoto
Bun'ei

The Battle of Bun'ei was the climax of the first Mongol invasion of Japan. Failure to establish a permanent bridgehead there ended the Mongols' ambitions.

The battle of Bun'ei began with an amphibious Mongol assault, and as the battle developed, their tactics soon proved superior to those of the Japanese. Fighting in tight infantry formations resembling the phalanxes of ancient Greece, the Mongols also unleashed a storm of arrows from their bows.

Korean sailors aboard the Mongol ships fired rudimentary catapults, sending both hollow bombs and projectiles filled with shrapnel into the Japanese lines. It seems possible that gunpowder was also used.

However, for all the old-fashioned nature of the Japanese samurai approach – adhering to the doctrine that a warrior confront an enemy of similar rank and engage in single combat – they displayed incredible bravery and inflicted severe casualties. Under mounting pressure, however, the Japanese fell back to their defences at Dazaifu, the capital of Kyushu. The Mongols, aware that strong enemy reinforcements might well be just over the next hill, did not pursue them.

TIMELINE

1500–1000BC	1000–500BC	500BC–0AD	0–500AD	500–1000AD	1000–1500AD	1500–2000AD

Vochan 1279

KEY FACTS

WHO The Viceroy of Yunnan, Nazir ud-Din, leads the Mongols against the Burmese army, including war elephants.

WHAT The Burmese proved unexpectedly doughty opponents, thanks greatly to the intimidatory factor of their elephants, but the military know-how of the unflappable Nazir ud-Din ensured the Mongols eventually prevailed.

WHERE Vochan, in the modern day Yunnan province, Burma.

WHEN 1279

WHY The Burmese were a rising military power and posed a threat to the southern Chinese borders of the Mongol Empire.

OUTCOME Although Kublai Khan acquired the elephants captured at Vochan, fighting in the difficult Burmese terrain would continue for many years.

When Kublai Khan unleashed his forces on the troublesome kingdom of Burma, he didn't foresee it posing much of an obstacle for his mighty war machine. As has so often happened in history, however, a smaller, more unconventional army threw up an unexpected challenge.

MONGOL v BURMESE

MONGOL VICTORY

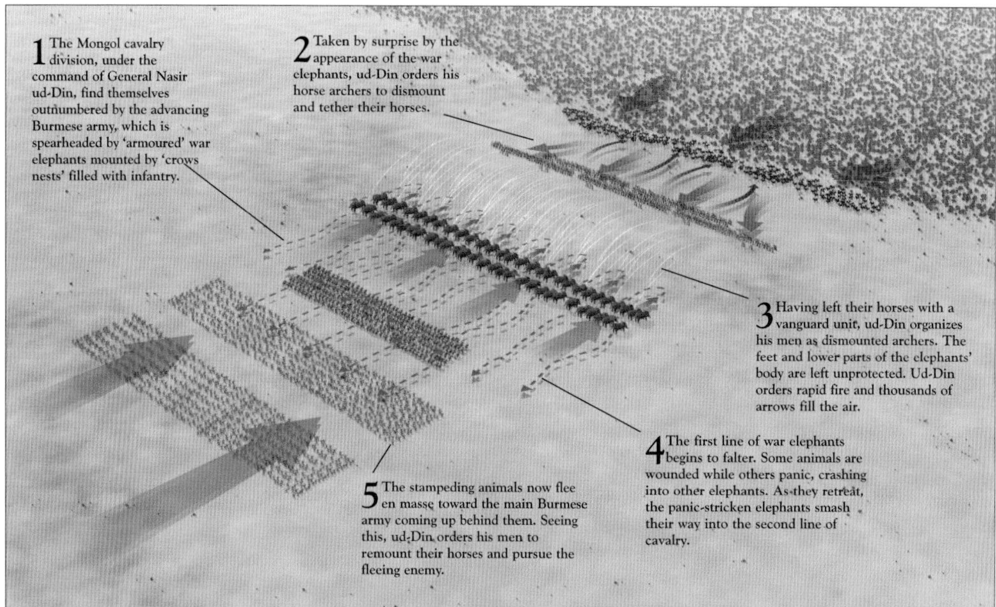
1 The Mongol cavalry division, under the command of General Nasir ud-Din, find themselves outnumbered by the advancing Burmese army, which is spearheaded by 'armoured' war elephants mounted by 'crows nests' filled with infantry.
2 Taken by surprise by the appearance of the war elephants, ud-Din orders his horse archers to dismount and tether their horses.
3 Having left their horses with a vanguard unit, ud-Din organizes his men as dismounted archers. The feet and lower parts of the elephants' body are left unprotected. Ud-Din orders rapid fire and thousands of arrows fill the air.
4 The first line of war elephants begins to falter. Some animals are wounded while others panic, crashing into other elephants. As they retreat, the panic-stricken elephants smash their way into the second line of cavalry.
5 The stampeding animals now flee en masse toward the main Burmese army coming up behind them. Seeing this, ud-Din orders his men to remount their horses and pursue the fleeing enemy.

Throughout history, Burma has thrown up formidable challenges to invaders. At Vochan, the Mongols encountered elephants, but warriors were ultimately undeterred, and the creatures were soon usefully augmenting Kublai Khan's ranks.

Kublai Khan had appointed the Viceroy of Yunnan, Nazir ud-Din, an experienced commander, to deal with the threat posed by the militaristic Burmese to his Chinese borders. But when ud-Din's cavalrymen emerged on the Burmese plains along the River Irrawaddy, they found themselves facing a line of 2000 heavily armed war elephants.

The Mongol riders and their horses were terrified at their appearance. To steady his men in the face of this monstrous apparition, ud-Din ordered them to tether the horses behind the battle line and fight dismounted. Their only chance, as the Burmese war elephants advanced on a broad front, was to open relentless fire upon the beasts.

ELEPHANT ASSAULT

Under this fire, the elephants began to falter, halted and then turned around and fled into the massed ranks of the Burmese troops behind them. Now ud-Din ordered his men to remount and charge the confused enemy. After a tough fight, the Mongols eventually prevailed. Included in the war booty sent back to Beijing were two hundred war elephants that became the nucleus for the Imperial Corps of War.

LOCATION

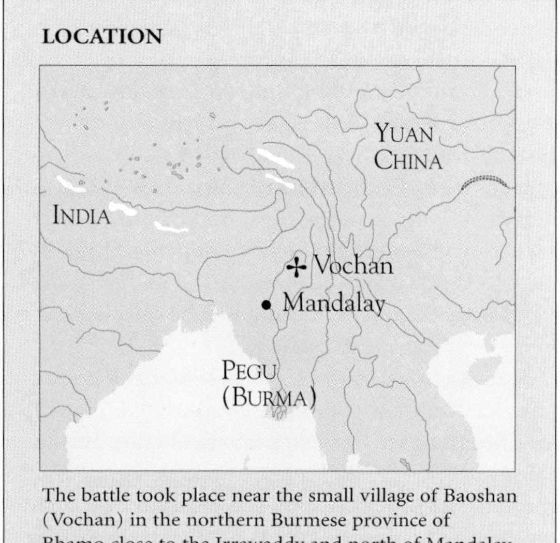
YUAN CHINA
INDIA
Vochan
Mandalay
PEGU (BURMA)

The battle took place near the small village of Baoshan (Vochan) in the northern Burmese province of Bhamo close to the Irrawaddy and north of Mandalay.

TIMELINE

1500–1000BC	1000–500BC	500BC–0AD	0–500AD	500–1000AD	1000–1500AD	1500–2000AD

Kublai Khan: Mongol Invasion of Japan 1281

KEY FACTS

Who A combined army of Mongol soldiers and Korean seamen, against the Japanese samurai and fleet.

What Kublai Khan's men encountered better equipped Japanese defences, and a fleet able to hold its own, but their superior firepower might have finally won the day, had it not been for the intervention of a storm that sunk much of the Mongol fleet.

Where Hakata Bay, Japan.

When June–July 1281

Why Kublai Khan was determined to extend Mongol dominion over Japan, and assembled a force five times the size of his previous army.

Outcome The Mongols lost as many as 100,000 men in the storm, and the invasion was called off. Yet Kublai Khan would still be planning a third invasion attempt at the time of his death ten years later.

In 1281, Kublai Khan launched a second attempt at invading Japan. This time his opponents were better prepared – but they still had the elements to thank for working in their favour at a crucial moment, sinking much of the invading fleet and forcing a Mongol withdrawal.

MONGOL INVASIONS OF JAPAN

NO CLEAR VICTORY

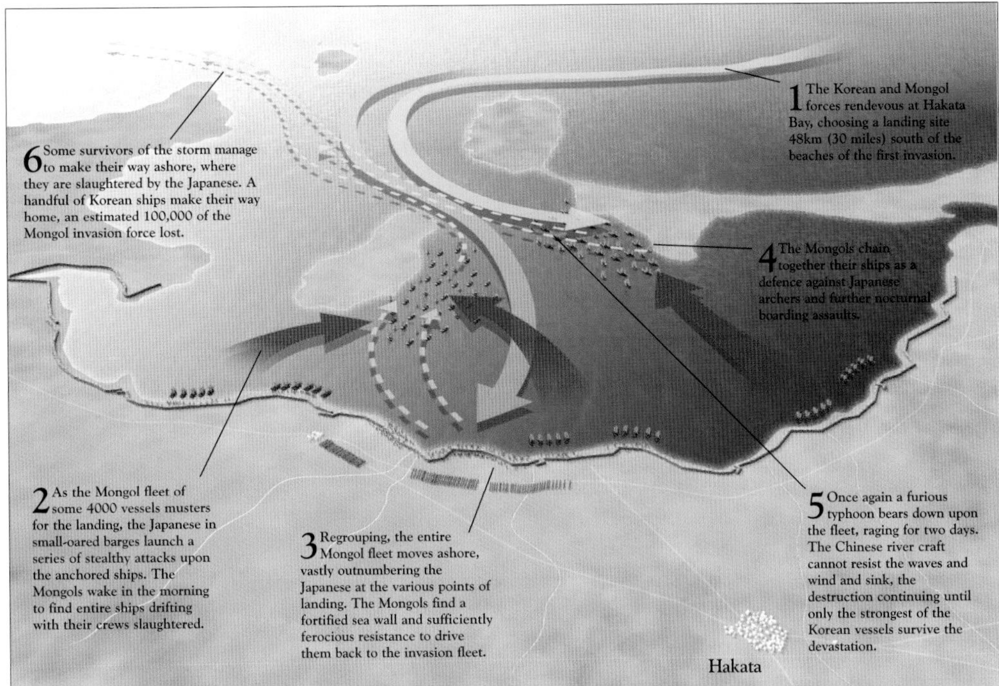
1 The Korean and Mongol forces rendezvous at Hakata Bay, choosing a landing site 48km (30 miles) south of the beaches of the first invasion.
2 As the Mongol fleet of some 4000 vessels musters for the landing, the Japanese in small-oared barges launch a series of stealthy attacks upon the anchored ships. The Mongols wake in the morning to find entire ships drifting with their crews slaughtered.
3 Regrouping, the entire Mongol fleet moves ashore, vastly outnumbering the Japanese at the various points of landing. The Mongols find a fortified sea wall and sufficiently ferocious resistance to drive them back to the invasion fleet.
4 The Mongols chain together their ships as a defence against Japanese archers and further nocturnal boarding assaults.
5 Once again a furious typhoon bears down upon the fleet, raging for two days. The Chinese river craft cannot resist the waves and wind and sink, the destruction continuing until only the strongest of the Korean vessels survive the devastation.
6 Some survivors of the storm manage to make their way ashore, where they are slaughtered by the Japanese. A handful of Korean ships make their way home, an estimated 100,000 of the Mongol invasion force lost.
Hakata

Many factors affect results on the battlefield, but the intervention of nature is easily overlooked. The Japanese were already mounting a doughty defence against the Mongols in 1281, but it was a typhoon that truly came to their rescue.

LOCATION

KOREA

TSUSHIMA

JAPAN

Iki

✢Hakata Bay

The Tsushima Strait ranges from 64km (40 miles) to 97km (60 miles) in width – not an easy voyage for a riverboat, but one conceivable in good weather.

The Mongol force for the second invasion of Japan contained five times as many men as in the previous assault in 1274. But their attack on Hakata Bay on Kyushu found them against an opposition more experienced and more numerous than they had been before.

The Japanese had come up with a way of utilizing their tradition of individual combat against the Mongol hordes. Samurai in small, oared vessels sailed out by day or night to board invasion ships, engaging in an environment where the deadly katana and heavy armour of the individual Japanese could be best applied. Entire crews of the assault fleet fell under the samurai swords.

Still the Mongols countered with a massive floating harbour-fortress of linked ships, from which trebuchets and archers fired upon the smaller Japanese craft. But suddenly a typhoon ripped down the Japanese coast. The samurai retreated inland, but the harbour became a death trap for clustered Mongol fleet. Losing as many as 4000 ships, the invasion was undone by the elements.

TIMELINE

1500–1000BC	1000–500BC	500BC–0AD	0–500AD	500–1000AD	1000–1500AD	1500–2000AD

Malta 1283

KEY FACTS

WHO Charles of Anjou against King Pedro III of Aragon.

WHAT The Angevin fleet tried to engage the Aragonese in a conventional battle of the galleys, but their opponents utilized the unusual design of their own ships to take control of the fighting.

WHERE Malta

WHEN 1283

WHY In the War of the Sicilian Vespers (1282–1302), the princes of Anjou, a junior line of the French royal family, and the royal house of Aragon fought for control of Sicily and southern Italy. The waters around Malta occupied a key position.

OUTCOME Although the Aragonese won the Battle of Malta quite decisively, the Angevins would rebuild their fleet and war would continue for a further 20 years.

The battle of Malta was one of the great sea fights of the thirteenth century. It was the first triumph of a new naval power – Aragon – in battle against a committed enemy. Malta also provides an ideal example of Mediterranean galley warfare in the later Middle Ages.

WAR OF THE SICILIAN VESPERS

ARAGONESE VICTORY

Malta was sought after because it occupied a prime position in the Mediterranean. However, its fortifications made it a formidable obstacle for the invader, and much of the fighting would take place in the surrounding waters.

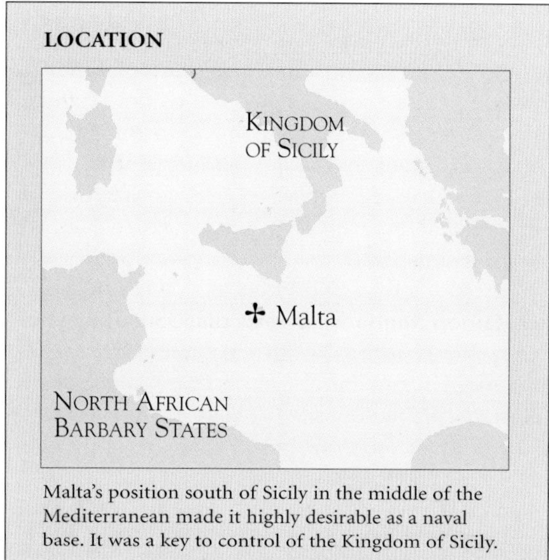
LOCATION
KINGDOM OF SICILY
Malta
NORTH AFRICAN BARBARY STATES

Malta's position south of Sicily in the middle of the Mediterranean made it highly desirable as a naval base. It was a key to control of the Kingdom of Sicily.

Duke Charles of Anjou had claimed the throne of Sicily in 1266, but his system of high taxes alienated the populace. When outright rebellion began in 1282, King Pedro III of Aragon, who also had a claim to Sicily, made common cause with the rebels.

Control of Malta was of central importance, since the island, with its excellent harbour, was ideally located to stage a naval invasion of Sicily. An Angevin garrison retained a precarious hold of the harbour fortifications, but was pinned down by a local insurrection and an Aragonese contingent that had arrived to attack them. In the spring of 1283 an Angevin fleet sailed to relieve Malta, pursued by the galleys of the Aragonese fleet, commanded by Admiral Roger of Lauria, who had never lost a naval battle.

The battle was fought within the harbour. As the fleets closed range, the Angevin fighters launched a barrage of javelins, arrows, stones and even powdered lime to blind their enemies – the traditional opening move of a medieval galley fight, in which, rather than using rams to sink an opponent's boats, the prime aim was to get close enough to

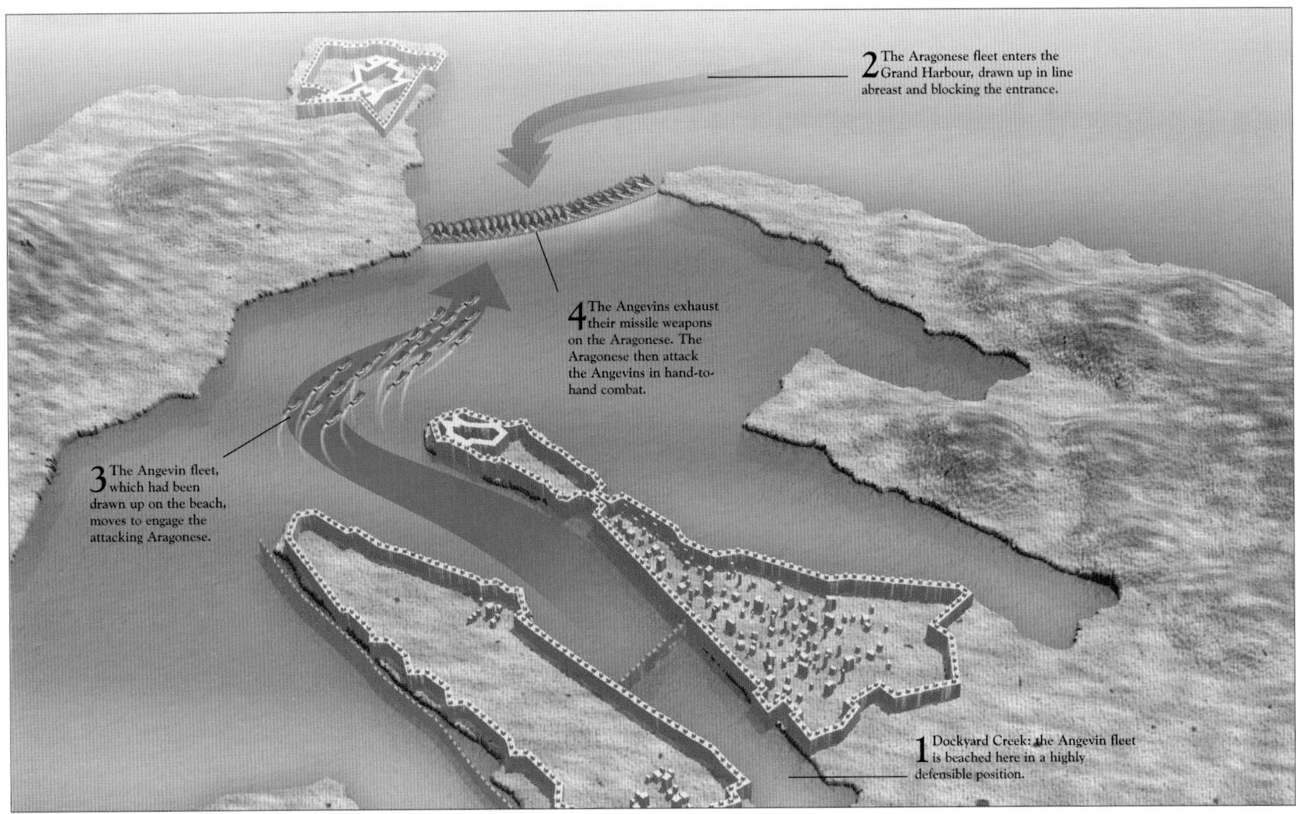
2 The Aragonese fleet enters the Grand Harbour, drawn up in line abreast and blocking the entrance.
4 The Angevins exhaust their missile weapons on the Aragonese. The Aragonese then attack the Angevins in hand-to-hand combat.
3 The Angevin fleet, which had been drawn up on the beach, moves to engage the attacking Aragonese.
1 Dockyard Creek: the Angevin fleet is beached here in a highly defensible position.

The narrow waters around Malta made it ideal for the 'traditional' type of sea battle. The object was to try to get close enough to attach grappling hooks to the enemy boat, and then board it and overcome the crew in close-knit fighting.

board their vessel. Unusually, however, Admiral Roger ordered his men to limit their response. Instead of returning fire with everything at their command, only the crossbowmen were allowed to reply. The rest of the Aragonese fighting men were ordered to shelter from enemy missiles. The Aragonese vessels had high bulwarks for the men to shelter behind, as well as forecastles and sterncastles raised higher and protected more strongly than was normal in the Mediterranean. Although these innovations made the Aragonese ships slower and heavier, they were intended to take advantage of the high-quality Catalan crossbowmen that were available to the fleet.

By about noon the Angevins had run out of ammunition. At that point the Aragonese marines were unleashed. They still apparently had a large supply of crossbow bolts, which were used to good effect by the expert Catalan archers. As the range closed, javelins and stones were added to the barrage.

Unlike the Aragonese, the Angevins did not have effective bulwarks to protect them from missile attack, and the greater height of the Aragonese ships also made their shooting much more effective. The Angevin ships were driven into disarray by the missile attack. Thus, ship by ship, the Aragonese drew near enough that their marines were able to board and continue the fight hand to hand. Lightly armoured and nimble, these Aragonese fighters were more ideally suited to naval warfare than their Angevin counterparts.

Nevertheless, the fighting was fierce; despite the disorder of the Angevins, they still outnumbered the Aragonese in both ships and men. Quarter was not usually given to the losers, whose best hope of survival was to swim for it, so the hand-to-hand battle continued until dusk. At last, Bonvin, the surviving Angevin admiral, broke free of the Aragonese fleet and fled. He took with him perhaps seven damaged galleys, of which two later had to be abandoned because they were no longer seaworthy. The Catalan chronicler Ramon Muntaner reports that 3500 Angevin mariners and marines were killed and nearly 1000 more were captured. By contrast, after the battle, Roger of Lauria recruited some 288 replacements, so his casualties must have been fewer than 10 per cent.

Falkirk 1298

KEY FACTS

WHO An English army commanded by Edward I (1239–1307) defeated the Scots under William Wallace (1270–1305).

WHAT The Battle of Falkirk was a major engagement in the First War of Scottish Independence.

WHERE Falkirk, to the west of Edinburgh.

WHEN 22 July 1298

WHY Edward sought to crush the Scottish uprising and force his authority.

OUTCOME Despite his success, Edward was unable to complete the subjugation of Scotland because his army had been weakened by the scorched-earth tactics used by Wallace prior to the battle.

British history is replete with legends, and those of the longbow and William Wallace have been especially potent. In a moment of great historical resonance, these two legends clashed, at the Battle of Falkirk on 22 July 1298.

FIRST WAR OF SCOTTISH INDEPENDENCE

ENGLISH VICTORY

Two resonant names of British history met at Falkirk – King Edward I, one of the most distinguished of English monarchs, and the Scottish warrior William Wallace. The latter's foot soldiers would be overwhelmed.

LOCATION

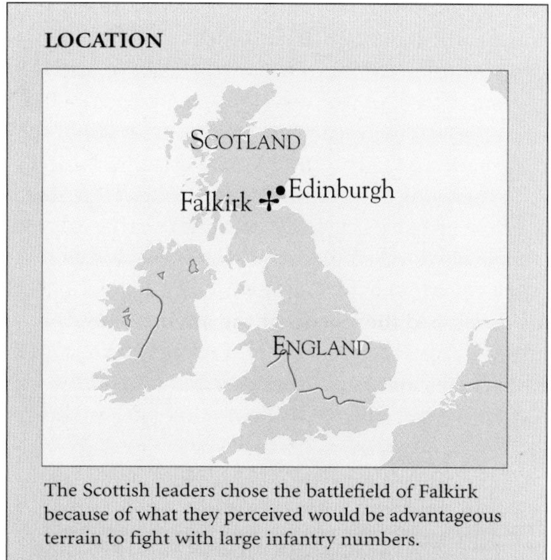
SCOTLAND
Falkirk
Edinburgh
ENGLAND

The Scottish leaders chose the battlefield of Falkirk because of what they perceived would be advantageous terrain to fight with large infantry numbers.

William Wallace had led the Scots to victory over the English at Stirling Bridge in September 1297, and Edward I determined on avenging the defeat the following year. As dawn broke on 22 July 1298, the English army marched from their camp to face Wallace at Falkirk, where his men were already arrayed in their battle formations, mainly based around four 'schiltrons' of spearmen, interspersed by Scottish longbowmen, and the few Scottish cavalry at his disposal held in reserve.

Once on the battlefield, Edward and his generals immediately recognized their advantage in cavalry and decided to charge them into the Scottish schiltrons. Faced by the charge of heavy horsemen, many an enemy would turn on their heels at the fearsome sight, but at Falkirk the Scots stood solidly in formation.

And, at least initially, their faith in their military abilities was confirmed when the charges of the English cavalry were easily turned away, partly owing to the soggy ground at the base of the hill-slope on which the Scots were arrayed, and partly because medieval warhorses, no matter

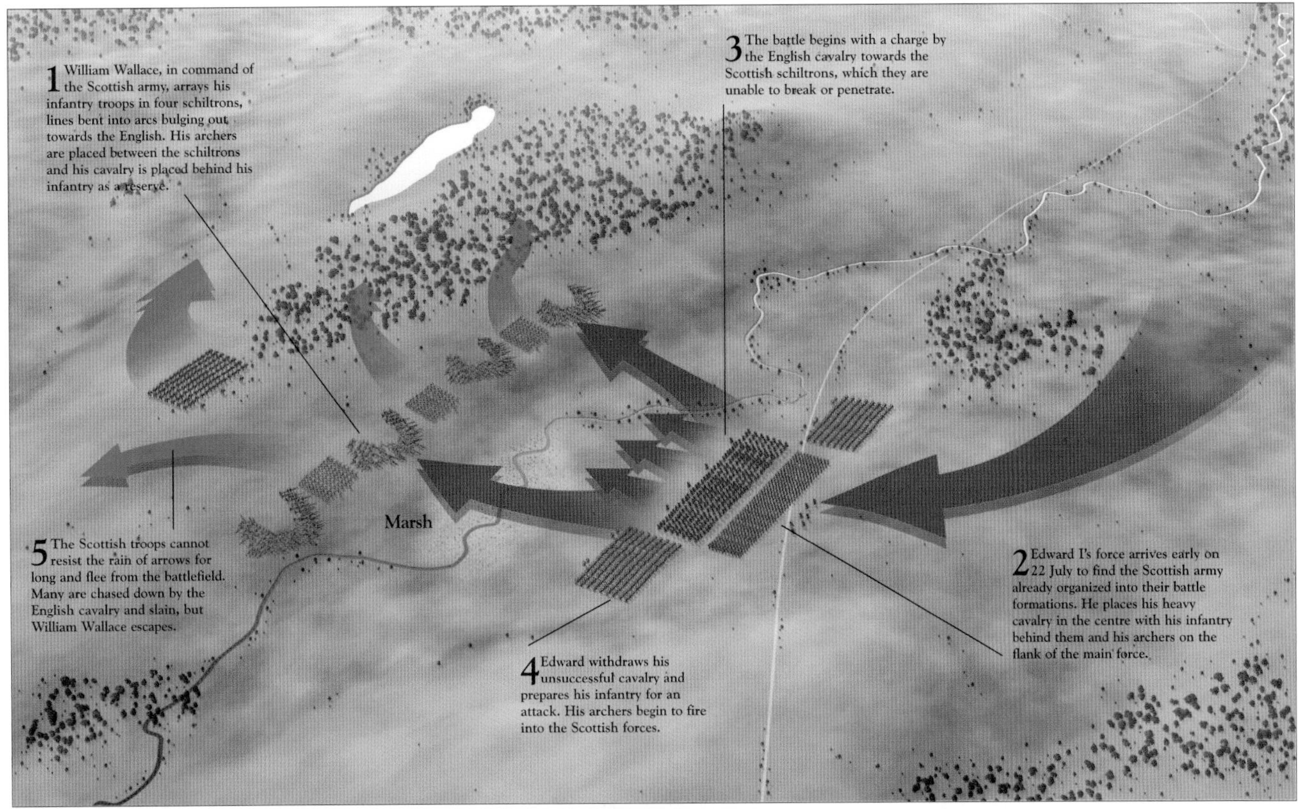
1 William Wallace, in command of the Scottish army, arrays his infantry troops in four schiltrons, lines bent into arcs bulging out towards the English. His archers are placed between the schiltrons and his cavalry is placed behind his infantry as a reserve.
3 The battle begins with a charge by the English cavalry towards the Scottish schiltrons, which they are unable to break or penetrate.
Marsh
5 The Scottish troops cannot resist the rain of arrows for long and flee from the battlefield. Many are chased down by the English cavalry and slain, but William Wallace escapes.
2 Edward I's force arrives early on 22 July to find the Scottish army already organized into their battle formations. He places his heavy cavalry in the centre with his infantry behind them and his archers on the flank of the main force.
4 Edward withdraws his unsuccessful cavalry and prepares his infantry for an attack. His archers begin to fire into the Scottish forces.

The key to victory at Falkirk were the longbowmen that Edward I placed on the flanks. While the Scottish schiltrons resisted cavalry charges, they could not withstand the hail of arrow fire.

how well trained, would usually stop, wheel away or drop to the ground rather than skewer themselves on the spears of determined foot soldiers who held their lines.

However, Edward I, having led armies for more than 30 years, knew not to rely on a single tactic. Recalling the cavalry, he moved his infantry into position. But before they could make their charges, the English longbowmen on the flanks of the other infantry began to fire into the Scottish schiltrons. The English army had arrived at Falkirk with 5000 longbowman in its ranks – the largest force of these troops ever assembled in a single army. Their number greatly dwarfed the 400 crossbowmen.

The chief advantage of the longbow over shorter bows was that its string could be drawn to the ear instead of to the chest, allowing for the discharge of a longer arrow. This increased the range of the arrow to almost twice as far, to perhaps as much as 400m (1312ft), and it also delivered an equally increased ballistic impact. Edward had placed his longbowmen along the wings of the lines of infantry and dismounted cavalry. In such a formation, the archers did not need to kill many men. Their role was simply to harass the enemy to such an extent that they broke into a disordered charge

While their confidence was no doubt increased by their success against the cavalry, few of Wallace's troops were prepared for the rain of arrows that now poured down on them. Most of the Scottish soldiers probably wore little if any armour, with shields and helmets also insufficient in number to provide much relief against such an onslaught. According to one English chronicle, they began to fall, in large numbers, 'like blossoms in an orchard when the fruit has ripened'.

The schiltrons simply dissolved, although some Scottish soldiers, including Wallace, were able to get away. He was not captured until 5 August 1305, when he was found guilty of treason. He was hanged, emasculated, drawn, beheaded and quartered at Smithfield in London 18 days later. Thus developed the legend of the 'invincible' longbow and the 'unbeatable' English longbowmen, a legend still potent today. Wallace's legend also remains vital. However, when these two legends clashed on the battlefield of Falkirk, it was the longbow that triumphed.

Bannockburn 1314

KEY FACTS

WHO An English army numbering 18,000 under King Edward II (1284–1327), opposed by 9500 Scots under King Robert the Bruce (1274–1329).

WHAT The main action took place between blocks of Scottish pikemen and heavily armoured English cavalry.

WHERE 1.6km (1 mile) southeast of Stirling Castle, Scotland.

WHEN June 1314

WHY Marching to relieve Stirling Castle, the English army was intercepted by the Scots.

OUTCOME The English were caught in marshy ground while trying to outflank the Scots, who attacked aggressively and broke the English army.

The battle of Bannockburn pitted an outnumbered force of Scots pikemen against the deadly combination of English archers and men-at-arms. The stakes were high: the ownership of the critical castle at Stirling would be decided by a day of battle.

FIRST WAR OF SCOTTISH INDEPENDENCE

SCOTTISH VICTORY

In the vicious mêlée in the marshes at Bannockburn, the steadfastness of the Scottish pikemen, followed by their assault with swords and axes on the pride of the English cavalry, secured sweet revenge for the defeat at Falkirk.

At Bannockburn, learning lessons from Falkirk, the Scots were drawn up in large blocks of pikemen who had dug pits and strewed caltrops – triangular iron spikes designed to injure horses – at their front, to break up the English cavalry charge.

An early charge of King Edward II's mounted men-at-arms was repulsed by the pikemen, who presented their pikes outwards in a fearsome defensive barrier. The English then changed position, spending the night wearily slogging through boggy ground by the Bannock. As dawn broke, the cavalry were still mired in the marsh as Robert Bruce unleashed his pike columns.

Men were pierced through, or bowled over helpless in the marsh, where they drowned. Horses stampeded, causing further chaos in the rear of the English. The Scots pushed grimly on into the mix of foot and horse, assailing them with lance and spear, sword and axe, until suddenly the English broke and fled. Once the rout had started, it spread swiftly, with men scattering in all directions. With echoes of the Greek hoplites of earlier centuries, it had been a victory for cleverly deployed infantry over mounted knights.

LOCATION

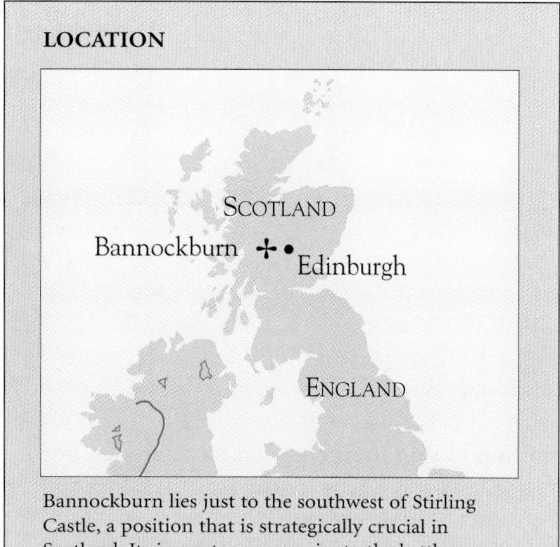
SCOTLAND
Bannockburn
Edinburgh
ENGLAND

Bannockburn lies just to the southwest of Stirling Castle, a position that is strategically crucial in Scotland. Its importance gave rise to the battle.

TIMELINE

1500–1000BC	1000–500BC	500BC–0AD	0–500AD	500–1000AD	1000–1500AD	1500–2000AD

Sluys 1340

Edward III was one of the greatest of English kings, famed for his triumphs over the French at Crécy and Poitiers. But at Sluys he was also able to score a notable naval victory.

HUNDRED YEARS WAR

ENGLISH VICTORY

KEY FACTS

WHO Edward III (1327–77) of England against the combined French, Castilian and Genoese fleets.

WHAT The English caught the French fleet anchored in three defensive lines, and chained together by boarding lines. It meant they were unable to manoeuvre to each other's assistance as the English attacked.

WHERE Sluys harbour on the border between Zeeland and West Flanders.

WHEN 24 June 1340

WHY Edward III had been preparing a fleet to invade France to assert his claim to the throne. To counter the threat, the French had assembled their own ships at Sluys.

OUTCOME Destroying a large proportion of the French fleet made it impossible for the French to invade England.

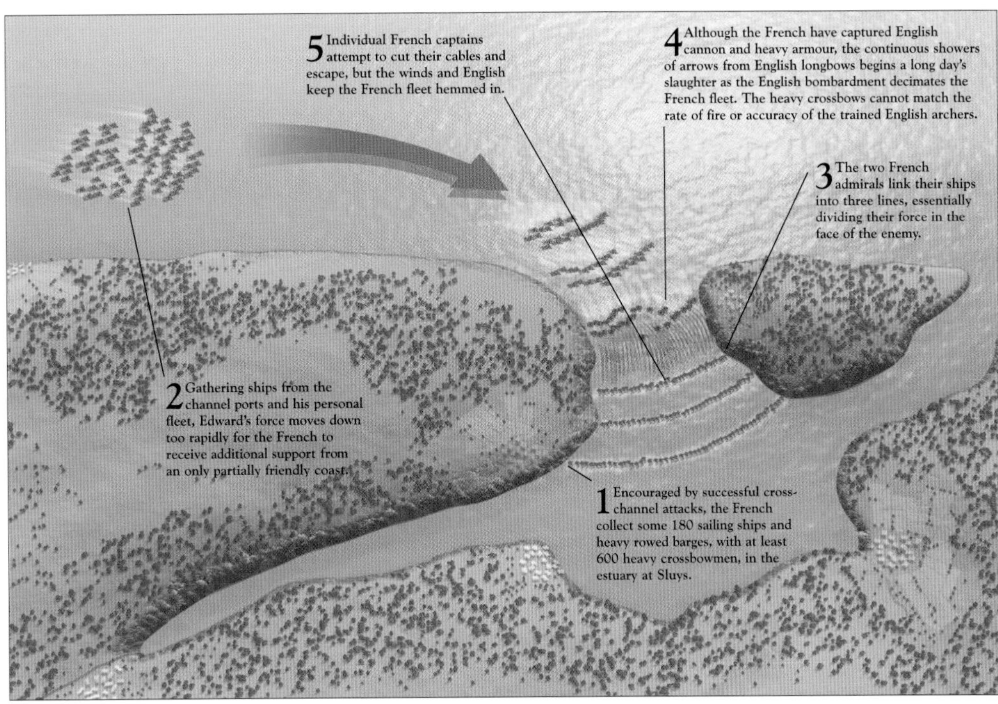
5 Individual French captains attempt to cut their cables and escape, but the winds and English keep the French fleet hemmed in.
4 Although the French have captured English cannon and heavy armour, the continuous showers of arrows from English longbows begins a long day's slaughter as the English bombardment decimates the French fleet. The heavy crossbows cannot match the rate of fire or accuracy of the trained English archers.
3 The two French admirals link their ships into three lines, essentially dividing their force in the face of the enemy.
2 Gathering ships from the channel ports and his personal fleet, Edward's force moves down too rapidly for the French to receive additional support from an only partially friendly coast.
1 Encouraged by successful cross-channel attacks, the French collect some 180 sailing ships and heavy rowed barges, with at least 600 heavy crossbowmen, in the estuary at Sluys.

Chaining ships together while at harbour could make for an intimidating defensive formation. The drawback was a loss of the flexibility to adapt to changing points of attack, as happened at Sluys.

LOCATION

ENGLAND

Sluys

FRANCE

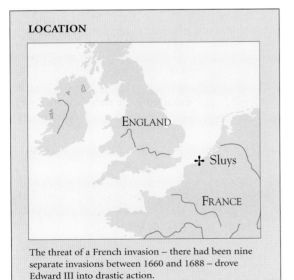

The threat of a French invasion – there had been nine separate invasions between 1660 and 1688 – drove Edward III into drastic action.

The Franco-Scottish alliance had not only stoked up Scottish attacks along the northern border of England, but the French had also attacked several English coastal towns. Caught between the two halves of this alliance, Edward III made the decision to forestall further French raids with a pre-emptive attack.

Edward assembled a large fleet of 120–160 armed cogs and as many as 40 support vessels, and set sail for the Flemish Coast. The French had been amassing their own ships for a full-scale invasion at Sluys. Suddenly cast onto the defensive, the French commanders decided to chain their fleet together with boarding lines in three defensive formations in the shelter of the Sluys estuary, and await battle. The boarding lines were used to enable crewmen to cross from ship to ship to provide aid to comrades, but they also prevented them from moving out of danger. Edward pressed his advantage, his longbowmen and war fleet hammering the French until the local Flemish completed the rout by hitting the French from the rear.

TIMELINE

1500–1000BC	1000–500BC	500BC–0AD	0–500AD	500–1000AD	1000–1500AD	1500–2000AD

Sluys

SLUYS

Rivalry between the kings of France and England dated back centuries, but it fell to Edward III to revive English claims to the French throne. Victory at Sluys in 1340 put him on the front foot, able to dictate the terms of the war. The French navy had been caught at harbour, and their commanders decided to chain the ships together in a defensive formation. This could work effectively, forming a defensive citadel-like structure, but it was at the expense of mobility and left them easy to outflank. This was a big psychological fillip for the English early on in the Hundred Years War.

Crécy 1346

KEY FACTS

Who An English army numbering 9000 under King Edward III (1312–77), opposed by some 30,000 French troops under King Philip VI (1293–1350).

What The main action took place between defensively positioned archers and dismounted men-at-arms, attacked by mounted men-at-arms.

Where The village of Crécy-en-Ponthieu, near Abbeville, France.

When 26 August 1346

Why The English army, marching to link up with Flemish allies, was caught and brought to battle by a vastly superior French force.

Outcome Repeated French charges were slaughtered by intense archery. Over 10,000 casualties were inflicted by the English, for the loss of about 100 men. The French army attacked until after nightfall, then collapsed and scattered.

The battle of Crécy was the beginning of the end for the armoured cavalryman who had dominated warfare for centuries. Pitting a tired and outnumbered English force composed mainly of archers against the flower of French chivalry, Crécy was the shape of things to come.

HUNDRED YEARS WAR

ENGLISH VICTORY

On the battlefield at Crécy, Edward III positioned himself and his army reserve towards the rear, not far from a windmill standing on a ridge.

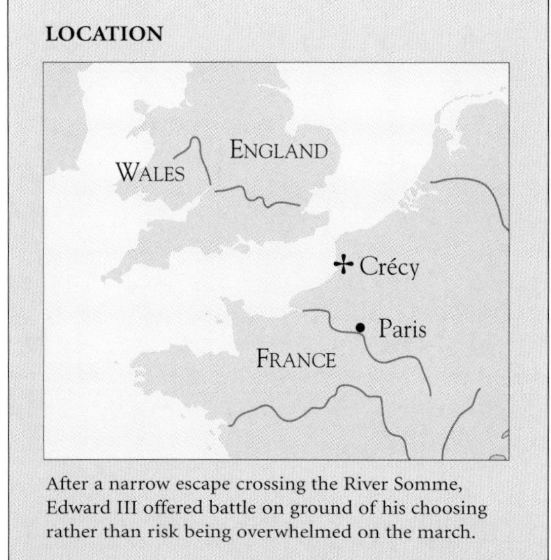
LOCATION
ENGLAND
WALES
Crécy
Paris
FRANCE

After a narrow escape crossing the River Somme, Edward III offered battle on ground of his choosing rather than risk being overwhelmed on the march.

In 1346, the English king, Edward III, was on campaign in France. Moving eastwards to link up with his Flemish allies, the French advance guard was pressing at his heels as he led his men across the wide Somme, and the following day took up a battle position near the village of Crécy-en-Ponthieu. It was an excellent spot, with sloping ground in front of the English – a perfect killing ground for the massed archers with their mighty longbows.

Edward deployed his force defensively, with two main bodies of Welsh spearmen and dismounted men-at-arms under the Earl of Northampton and Prince Edward (the Black Prince). Each of these bodies was flanked by archers in roughly triangular formations that allowed them to sweep their front and flanks with a hail of arrows, bringing intense missile fire to bear at any point on the field. Edward had great faith in his archers, many of whom had received special training in firing rapid volleys – perhaps 20 arrows a minute. Knowing they would soon be attacked by cavalry, the archers dug small pits in the ground in front of their position to impede the charge.

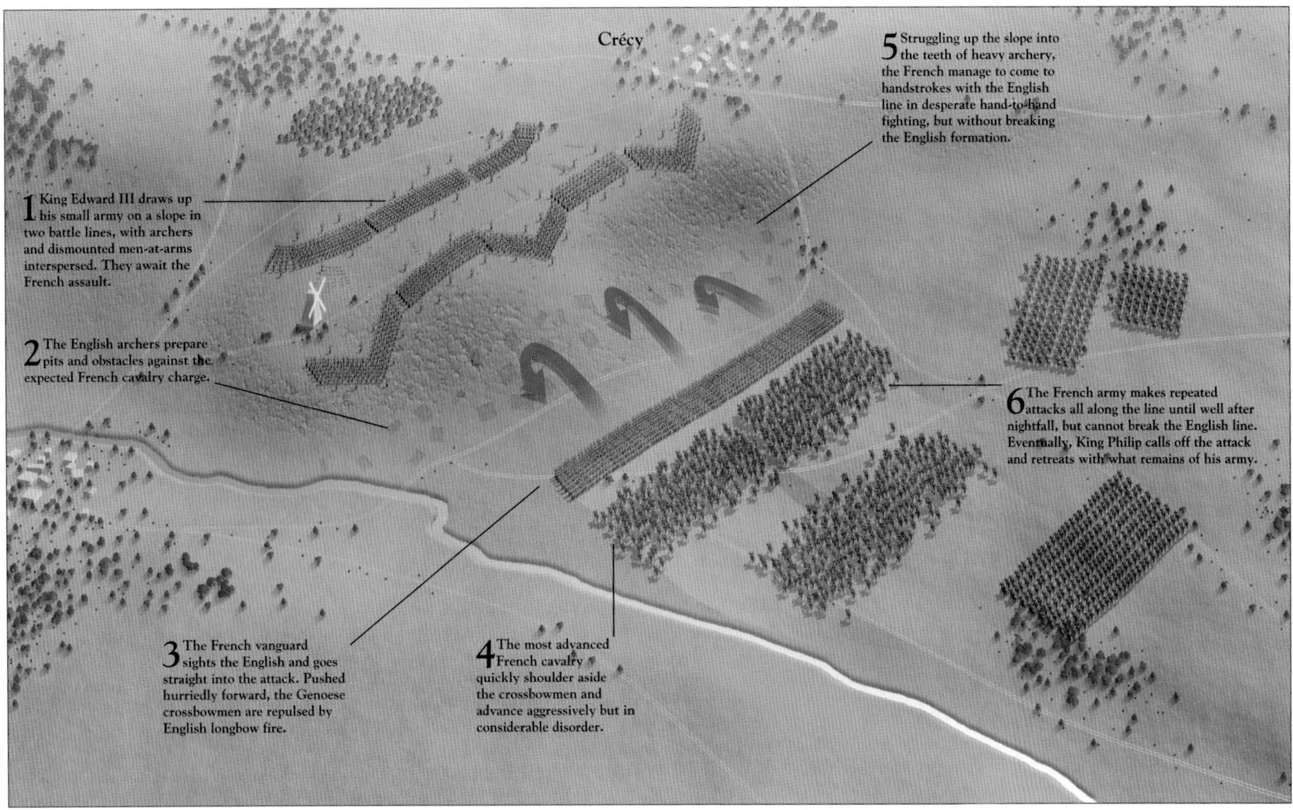
Crécy
5 Struggling up the slope into the teeth of heavy archery, the French manage to come to handstrokes with the English line in desperate hand-to-hand fighting, but without breaking the English formation.
1 King Edward III draws up his small army on a slope in two battle lines, with archers and dismounted men-at-arms interspersed. They await the French assault.
2 The English archers prepare pits and obstacles against the expected French cavalry charge.
6 The French army makes repeated attacks all along the line until well after nightfall, but cannot break the English line. Eventually, King Philip calls off the attack and retreats with what remains of his army.
3 The French vanguard sights the English and goes straight into the attack. Pushed hurriedly forward, the Genoese crossbowmen are repulsed by English longbow fire.
4 The most advanced French cavalry quickly shoulder aside the crossbowmen and advance aggressively but in considerable disorder.

This was a battle that pitted a French army whose tactics were based around the repeated mounted horse charge, against an English army which was largely dismounted. With the advantage, the skills of the English bowmen proved decisive.

The king himself took position with a reserve of men-at-arms and more archers at the top of the slope. His reliance on dismounted soldiers at Crécy was a remarkable tactical innovation that would be much copied.

When the French army arrived, they entered the field in some disorder, with elements of their three divisions intermixed in places and out of contact with their commanders. Even so, the mounted men-at-arms in the vanguard launched an immediate attack.

Impatiently, as they jostled forward, they drove before them 6000 or so Genoese crossbowmen in the advance guard, who were quickly seen off by the English longbowmen and, less effectively, by the fire of a primitive, lumbering cannon, volleying small stones or iron balls massing perhaps 1–2kg (2.2–4.4lb), and possibly being deployed for the first time on a battlefield.

When the French knights advanced, they used the weight of their horses and weapons to force a passage through the longbowmen. But volley after volley of arrow fire smashed into their flanks as they pressed home their ragged charge. Relatively few Frenchmen reached the English line, but those who got there assailed their opponents vigorously.

Now King Philip of France sent the rest of his army hastily forward in a series of uncoordinated charges. The hand-to-hand fighting became increasingly intense, and Godfrey Harcourt, charged with the safety of Prince Edward – the Black Prince – became gravely concerned for the young man's life. King Edward declined to commit his reserve in aid, however, making the – ultimately vindicated – decision to 'let the boy win his spurs'.

Still the French came on. Inspired by the example of their leaders, including blind King John of Bohemia (1296–1346), whose horse was led into battle by two knights, the vainglorious charges continued. Finally, around midnight, King Philip was dissuaded from launching another attack, and drew what remained of the French army off under cover of darkness. There was no pursuit. The weary English slept where they had fought. They had defeated a force three times their size, and without ever being even pushed back from their initial starting positions.

TIMELINE

1500–1000BC	1000–500BC	500BC–0AD	0–500AD	500–1000AD	1000–1500AD	1500–2000AD

Poitiers 1356

KEY FACTS

Who Edward, Prince of Wales, leads an army of English and Gascon soldiers against the French army under King John II and the Dauphin.

What The Black Prince was able to use an enforced adoption of a defensive position behind a hedgerow to reduce the French numerical advantage, and through the sheer tenacity of his soldiers, score an unexpected victory.

Where Near Nouaille-Maupertuis, south of Poitiers, France.

When 19 September 1356

Why Edward, Prince of Wales – known as the Black Prince, and the son of Edward III – had launched a series of raids aimed at destabilizing French operations in the Hundred Years War.

Outcome The capture of their king meant the French people were forced to bear the brunt of the high ransom fee, and many rose in revolt.

The Black Prince had won his spurs at the age of 16 at Crécy, fighting bravely for his father Edward III. At Poitiers, he was to show that he was a thoroughly inspirational leader on the battlefield in his own right.

HUNDRED YEARS WAR

ENGLISH VICTORY

Nothing was more likely to result in the deflation and ultimate defeat of an army in battle than the death or capture of its leader. The taking of John II of France at Poitiers, however, came when the battle was effectively already lost.

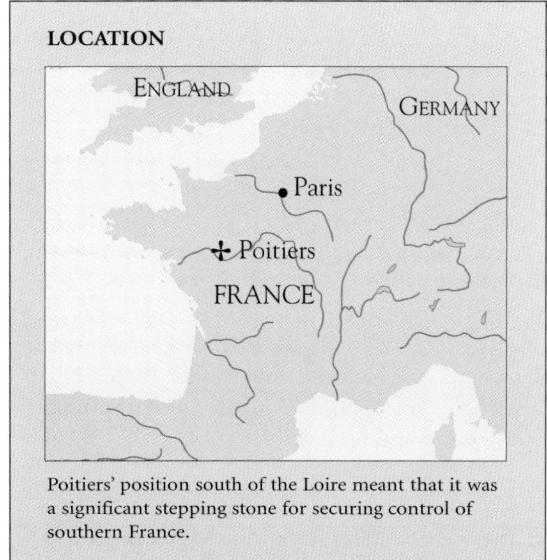
LOCATION
England
Germany
Paris
Poitiers
FRANCE

Poitiers' position south of the Loire meant that it was a significant stepping stone for securing control of southern France.

By 1355, after a halt in hostilities during the ongoing Hundred Years War caused by an outbreak of plague in both countries, Edward III, king of England, was keen to relaunch his campaign to claim the crown of France. His son Edward, the Black Prince, was dispatched on an expedition into southern France, and encountered little opposition as he carried out a series of raids across the countryside, leaving a trail of destruction and attacking such strongholds as Carcassonne, Limoux and Bordeaux.

REINFORCEMENTS

Encouraged by the success of his son, Edward III now sent a force under the command of the Duke of Lancaster to follow suit in the north by invading Normandy, with the eventual aim of the two armies linking up. This left John II, king of France, who had so far avoided entering the fray against the Black Prince, with the dilemma of which army to deal with first. Initially, he moved on the Duke of Lancaster, pushing him back towards the coast, before advancing south to deal with the Black Prince. By now, the

The French army would outnumber that of the Black Prince by two to one at Poitiers, but the English soldiers were experienced men, battle hardened by months of sorties through southern France.

prince was marching northwards, burning and pillaging the countryside as he went, in the mistaken belief that Lancaster's army was somewhere near. Instead, the first forces he would encounter would be that of John's, which had advanced beyond the Loire to reach Poitiers.

An attempt to broker a peace between the two sides was made by the locally based Cardinal Talleyrand, but neither side seems to have taken it very seriously – on the one hand, because John II was leading an army of 14,000 soldiers, thus outnumbering the English by about two to one, and on the other, because the prince had at his disposal an experienced unit, battle-hardened by several fruitful, booty-laden, months on the campaign trail.

During the battle, the English occupied a defensive position at the bottom of the hill held by the French. An initial charge of the French cavalry was met with a flurry of arrows from their crossbowmen, but when the English vanguard attempted to move forward it came under fierce attack and retreated to the cover of a thick hedge.

This gave them a positional advantage, for as the French tried to force their way through a break in the hedge, it reduced their numerical advantage by thinning their front, and making them easier pickings for the waiting English men-at-arms and archers.

This still left the main body of the French forces grouped around King John, which now began a slow march towards the hedge. Deciding to seize the initiative, while rallying his troops for one major advance, the Black Prince also ordered a contingent of soldiers under Sir Jean de Grailly to 'secretly' break off to launch an attack on the French flank by approaching via woods to the side of the battlefield.

SURPRISE ATTACK

As the English burst through the hedgerow, they caught the ponderously advancing French by surprise with their mixture of assault by arrow-fire, mace, spear, sword and axe. In the hard fighting that followed, fighting on two fronts with the arrival of de Grailly's men, the French eventually came off second best, and ultimately John himself was seized and taken prisoner. It was a staggering English win, against the odds, to place bedside Crécy.

TIMELINE

1500–1000BC	1000–500BC	500BC–0AD	0–500AD	500–1000AD	1000–1500AD	1500–2000AD

Poitiers

POITIERS

King John II of France was also known as John the Good, but he wasn't an especially good king. When the English took him captive at Poitiers and shipped him across the English Channel as a prisoner in the Tower London, the treaty he signed to secure his freedom required the paying of such a heavy sum that it caused a revolt by many of his over-taxed subjects. If Poitiers did nothing for his reputation, however, it did much for that of Edward, Prince of Wales. This was truly the Black Prince's finest hour.

Lake Poyang 1363

KEY FACTS

Who Chen Youliang, leading the navy of the Chinese Han dynasty, against that of the Ming dynasty led by Zhu Yuanzhang.

What The Han had laid siege to the Ming capital with monstrous tower ships, but were forced to move out to Lake Poyang to meet the Ming relief force who were advancing down the Yangtze.

Where Lake Poyang, near Nanchang, Jiangxi province, China.

When 1363

Why As Mongol control over China began to disintegrate, ethnic Chinese groups, such as the Han and Wu began to fight among themselves.

Outcome Chen Youliang managed a retreat, but the Ming chased and killed him. The Ming, towing off all his tower ships, went on to become the Ming Dynasty.

When the Chinese Han besieged Nanchang, the capital of their rivals, the Ming, they deployed massive 'tower' ships. These outlandish siege vessels certainly looked like they could lower the walls of a city, but when they were forced to fight in more open waters, their weightiness proved their undoing.

RED TURBAN REBELLION

MING VICTORY

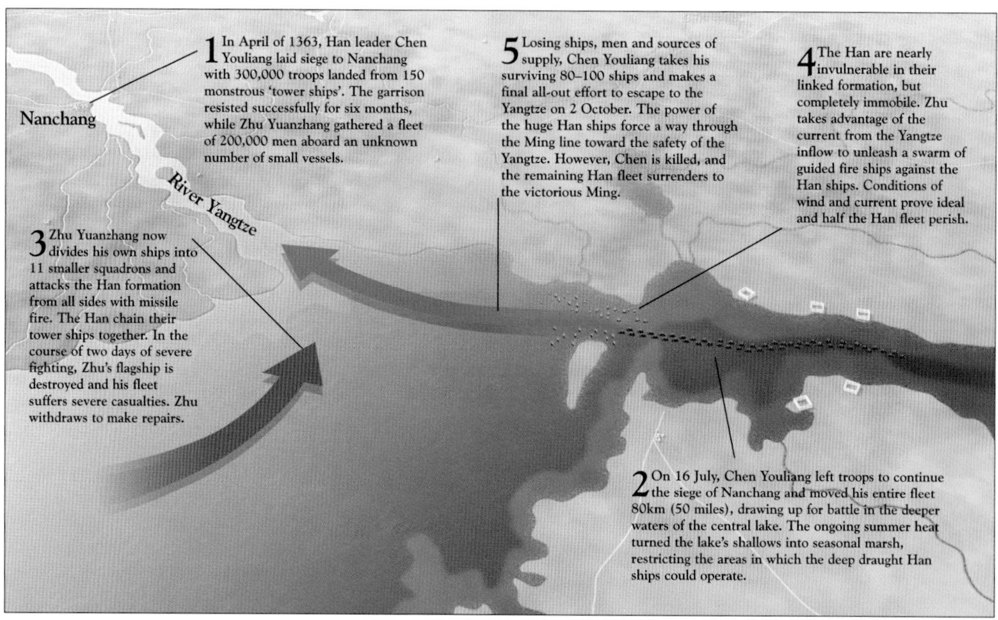

1 In April of 1363, Han leader Chen Youliang laid siege to Nanchang with 300,000 troops landed from 150 monstrous 'tower ships'. The garrison resisted successfully for six months, while Zhu Yuanzhang gathered a fleet of 200,000 men aboard an unknown number of small vessels.
Nanchang
River Yangtze
5 Losing ships, men and sources of supply, Chen Youliang takes his surviving 80–100 ships and makes a final all-out effort to escape to the Yangtze on 2 October. The power of the huge Han ships force a way through the Ming line toward the safety of the Yangtze. However, Chen is killed, and the remaining Han fleet surrenders to the victorious Ming.
4 The Han are nearly invulnerable in their linked formation, but completely immobile. Zhu takes advantage of the current from the Yangtze inflow to unleash a swarm of guided fire ships against the Han ships. Conditions of wind and current prove ideal and half the Han fleet perish.
3 Zhu Yuanzhang now divides his own ships into 11 smaller squadrons and attacks the Han formation from all sides with missile fire. The Han chain their tower ships together. In the course of two days of severe fighting, Zhu's flagship is destroyed and his fleet suffers severe casualties. Zhu withdraws to make repairs.
2 On 16 July, Chen Youliang left troops to continue the siege of Nanchang and moved his entire fleet 80km (50 miles), drawing up for battle in the deeper waters of the central lake. The ongoing summer heat turned the lake's shallows into seasonal marsh, restricting the areas in which the deep draught Han ships could operate.

When the Ming were besieged at Lake Poyang by Han 'tower ships', the situation appeared ominous. But the Han were undone by the oldest of sea battle technologies – the use of fireships.

Han ruler Chen Youliang laid siege to Nancheng using tower ships – three-decked vessels rising pagoda-style above the waterline, pierced with arrow loopholes and crenellated battlements to protect crossbowmen and spearmen. Carrying 2000 men, they seemed well-suited to besieging a city port, or crushing the smaller Ming ships.

But when word came that a relief force was heading down the Yangtze through Lake Poyang under the command of Zhu Yuanzhang, Chen moved to engage him. By chaining the Han ships together, they were transformed into a massive, impenetrable fortress. Zhu countered by deploying fire ships. A strong wind helped them to create a conflagration that destroyed half of the Han fleet.

Next Chen removed the chains, determining on an all-out assault, using the extra weight of their ships to crush their opponents. But Zhu was tipped off about the plan, and took advantage of the Han's newly open formation to move in with grappling hooks and missile fire. As confusion raged among the Han, disintegration set in and Chen was killed in the ensuing fighting. Shortly after, the Ming were able to raise the siege of Nancheng.

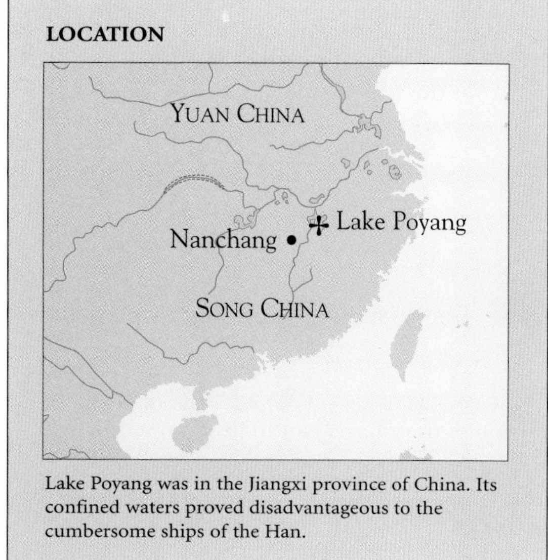

LOCATION
Yuan China
Nanchang
Lake Poyang
Song China

Lake Poyang was in the Jiangxi province of China. Its confined waters proved disadvantageous to the cumbersome ships of the Han.

TIMELINE

1500–1000BC	1000–500BC	500BC–0AD	0–500AD	500–1000AD	1000–1500AD	1500–2000AD

Najera 1367

KEY FACTS

WHO A Spanish army of French mercenaries under King Henry II of Castile (1333–79), opposed an army of mainly English mercenaries under Edward the Black Prince (1330–76).

WHAT Henry's skirmishers distracted the English archers from the advancing French mercenaries and his knights charged the supporting English division, but to little avail. Hand-to-hand fighting ensued between the men-at-arms.

WHERE Najera, northern Spain.

WHEN 3 April 1367

WHY Pedro the Cruel (1334–69) had requested help from the Black Prince in regaining the throne of Castile from Henry of Trastamara.

OUTCOME Although the French vanguard fought well, they were cut down and the Spanish part of the army routed.

Having proved himself on the field of Poitiers in northern France in 1356, Edward the Black Prince further demonstrated his grasp of strategy in the campaign leading to Najera in northern Spain, a battle where the English longbow again showed its superiority.

CASTILIAN CIVIL WAR

CASTILIAN VICTORY

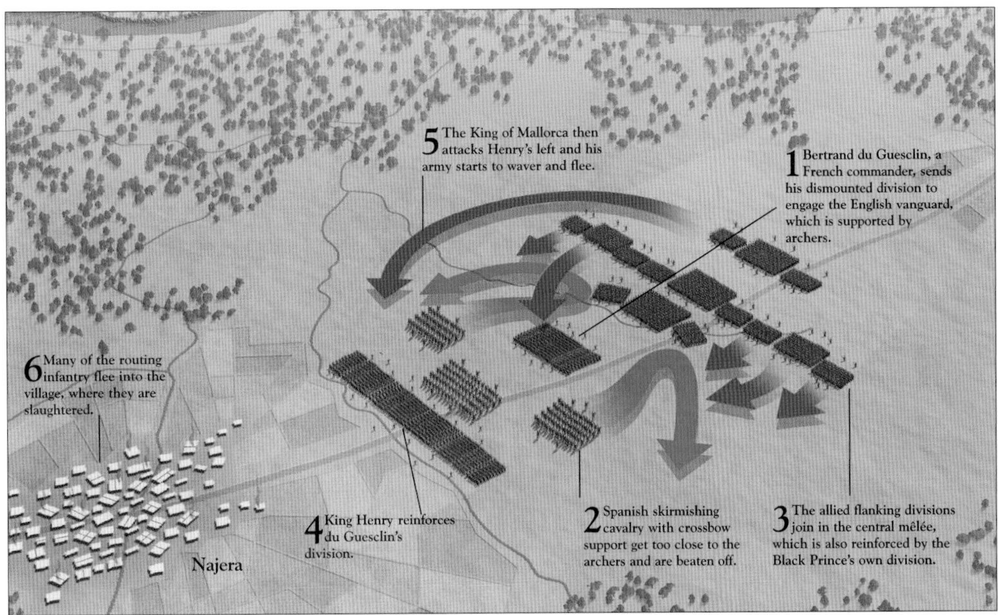
5 The King of Mallorca then attacks Henry's left and his army starts to waver and flee.
1 Bertrand du Guesclin, a French commander, sends his dismounted division to engage the English vanguard, which is supported by archers.
6 Many of the routing infantry flee into the village, where they are slaughtered.
4 King Henry reinforces du Guesclin's division.
2 Spanish skirmishing cavalry with crossbow support get too close to the archers and are beaten off.
3 The allied flanking divisions join in the central mêlée, which is also reinforced by the Black Prince's own division.
Najera

Battles between armies largely comprised of mercenary soldiers were not uncommon in the Middle Ages. But Edward, the Black Prince, was no ordinary military talent, and his forces swung the battle the way of the deposed Pedro of Castile.

King Pedro the Cruel of Castile had lost his throne to his more popular half-brother, Henry of Trastamara, and secured the help of Edward, the Black Prince, to regain his crown. At the head of a band of mercenaries, the pair met Henry's army, likewise deploying many mercenaries – this time from France – just north of the little village of Najera on a broad open plain. Henry's French men-at-arms came forward in a rush, charging three times, but Edward had deployed his men in what was now a classic formation of dismounted men-at-arms and archers and the French were quickly routed from the field.

MASS RETREAT

Heavily outnumbered, the Spanish infantry in the rearguard caught the drift of the moment and they too started to flee. Vast numbers were subsequently caught and killed. Even more drowned in the swollen river running through the village. Not to be left out, the final part of Edward's army came up and joined in the fight. The remaining French, having fought bravely and lost nearly one-third of their number, now surrendered, though Henry escaped to fight another day.

LOCATION

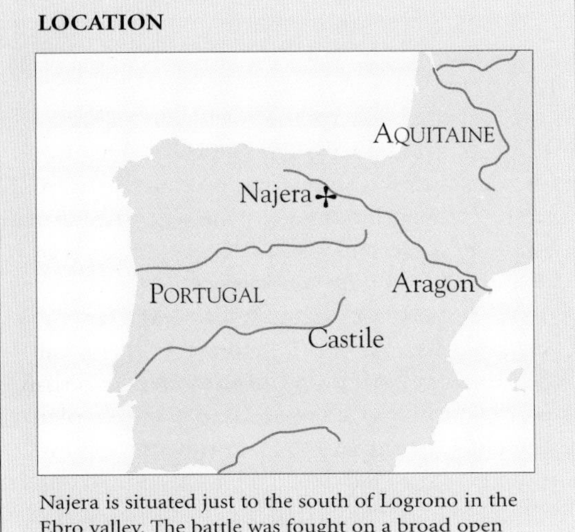
AQUITAINE
Najera
PORTUGAL
Aragon
Castile

Najera is situated just to the south of Logrono in the Ebro valley. The battle was fought on a broad open plain – ideal for the two armies to test their mettle.

TIMELINE

1500–1000BC	1000–500BC	500BC–0AD	0–500AD	500–1000AD	1000–1500AD	1500–2000AD

Nicopolis 1396

OTTOMAN–BALKAN WARS

TURKISH VICTORY

The battle of Nicopolis was the first combined military effort by Western European forces against the Ottoman Turks. Crusaders from numerous western principalities united with more proximate Hungarian, Wallachian and Transylvanian forces to halt the expansion of the Ottoman Empire.

KEY FACTS

WHO A mixed European army of about 12,000, led by John the Fearless of Burgundy (1371–1419), opposed an Ottoman Turkish force under Sultan Báyezîd I (1354–1403), which numbered around 15,000.

WHAT The Crusaders' mounted men-at-arms charged without order into the solid infantry lines of the Turks, were halted and beaten by counter-attacking cavalry.

WHERE On the plains south of the Bulgarian city of Nicopolis.

WHEN 25 September 1396

WHY In the late 1300s the Ottoman Turks began their conquest of southeastern Europe. As Turkish armies began to threaten the kingdom of Hungary, a Crusade was called.

OUTCOME The first encounter of the Crusaders with an Ottoman army led to a devastating defeat. The Turks built on this victory to complete their conquest of southeastern Europe.

Only a few Crusaders survived defeat at the Battle of Nicopolis, managing to beat a hasty retreat towards some boats awaiting on the Danube.

LOCATION

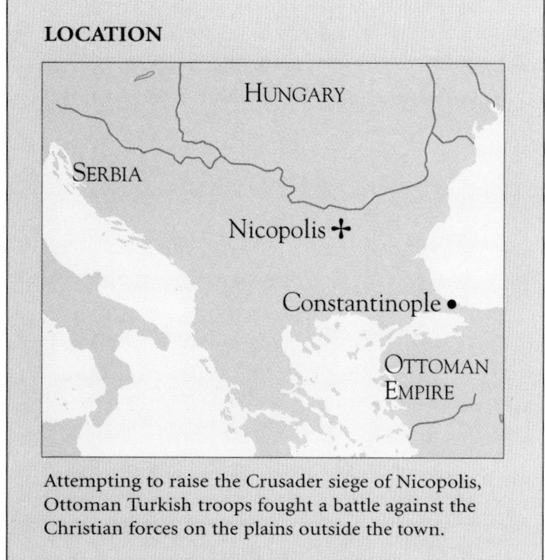
HUNGARY
SERBIA
Nicopolis
Constantinople
OTTOMAN EMPIRE

Attempting to raise the Crusader siege of Nicopolis, Ottoman Turkish troops fought a battle against the Christian forces on the plains outside the town.

By the late fourteenth century, the Ottoman Turks were already in control of a large amount of territory in the eastern Mediterranean, but Western rulers, diverted by wars in their own backyards, were too preoccupied to address the issue, despite attempts by the papacy to launch a new Crusade. So when one was finally announced in 1396, leadership fell to Philip the Good of Burgundy's militarily inexperienced son, John the Fearless, heading a group of English, French and Burgundians soldiers. As they marched through Europe, more Crusaders – including Hungarians, Wallachians, Transylvanians and Germans – swelled the ranks. John's confidence was further buoyed by early successes, when Turkish fortresses at Vidin and Rahova surrendered after strong Crusader attacks. Now they moved on to lay siege to Nicopolis.

But the Crusaders had yet to encounter the full might of the Sultan's army. Báyezîd, at the time attacking the remnants of Byzantium, soon heard of their victories and marched quickly to Serbia to counter them. It was not until the day before the battle of Nicopolis, when the

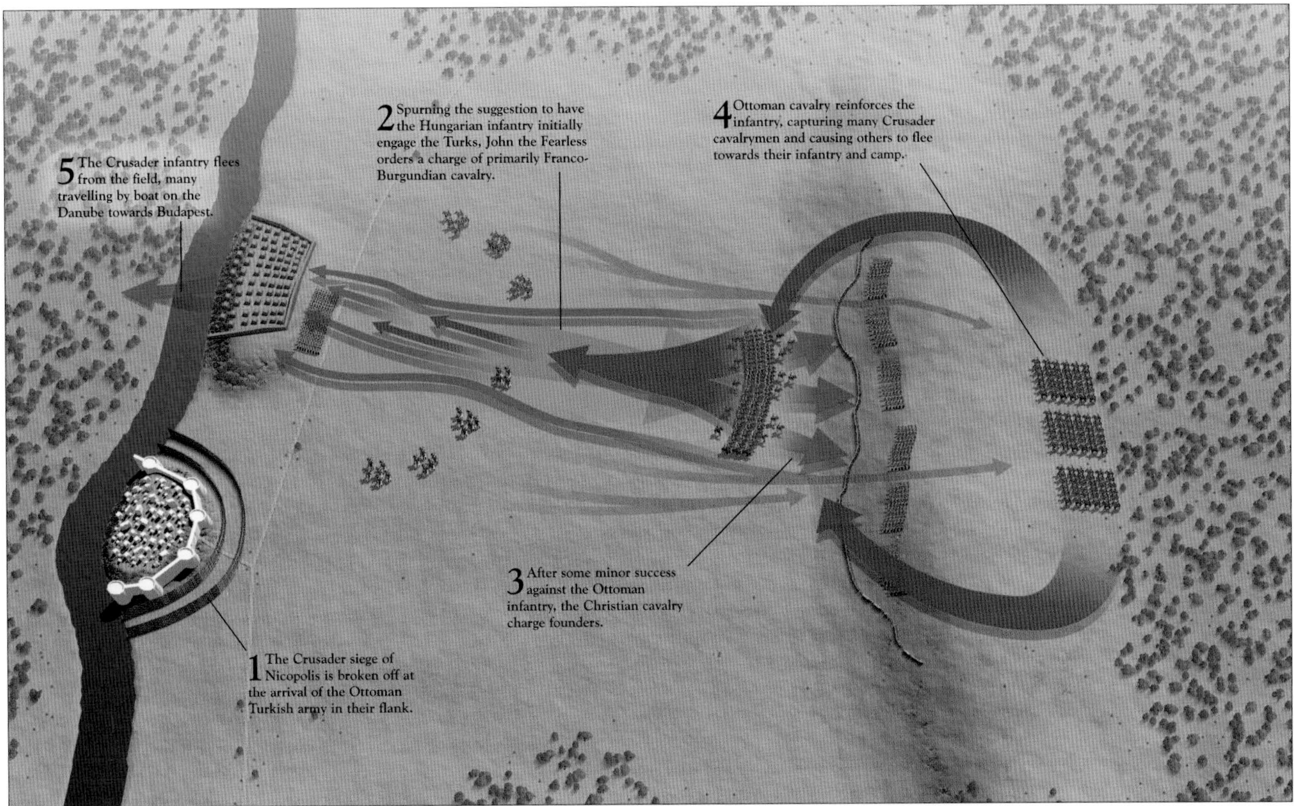
2 Spurning the suggestion to have the Hungarian infantry initially engage the Turks, John the Fearless orders a charge of primarily Franco-Burgundian cavalry.
4 Ottoman cavalry reinforces the infantry, capturing many Crusader cavalrymen and causing others to flee towards their infantry and camp.
5 The Crusader infantry flees from the field, many travelling by boat on the Danube towards Budapest.
3 After some minor success against the Ottoman infantry, the Christian cavalry charge founders.
1 The Crusader siege of Nicopolis is broken off at the arrival of the Ottoman Turkish army in their flank.

A charge of the Burgundian cavalry brought some initial success at Nicopolis, but the lines of Turkish infantry largely held, and the battle was over within an hour. The remaining Crusaders fled to the Danube.

Ottomans were less than 6.4km (4 miles) away, that the Crusader leaders learned that a large enemy army led by the sultan himself was approaching and seeking battle.

The Crusaders broke off their siege of Nicopolis and prepared for a battle, feeling that a great victory was in the offing. John the Fearless called a council of war with all his various generals. King Sigismund of Hungary – who had previous experience of fighting the Ottomans – recommended that the Hungarians and other Central European troops, almost entirely infantry, should be the vanguard. He suggested that they would meet what would be the irregular infantry of the Turks, who were always in front of their own army. He would take a defensive stance to try and provoke the Ottomans into a charge that might be defeated by the contact of the two infantry forces or reinforced by the strong Franco-Burgundian cavalry in the second rank.

But he was overruled by most of the Franco-Burgundian leaders, who believed that a mounted charge of the armoured knights would bring success on the battlefield. They took to their horses and proudly charged headlong into the vanguard of the Turks. This was the very infantry that Sigismund said would be there, safely protected behind a line of stakes. Initially, the shock of this mounted charge brought some success, breaking through the stakes and pushing the Turkish irregular infantry back. However, these Ottoman troops, more disciplined than had been reckoned, did not break, but instead quickly re-formed in the lull before a second cavalry attack could be mounted.

That second Crusader charge also pushed the Ottoman vanguard back, but again they did not flee, and when a counter-attack came from Báyezîd's regular troops – cavalry, infantry and archers – the impetus of the Crusader horsemen had been spent. Although some German and Hungarian infantry rushed to reinforce their cavalry, all were quickly defeated.

The Battle of Nicopolis had lasted only an hour. Among those who managed to get away unscathed were King Sigismund of Hungary and his army, which had never actually taken part in the battle because it had been so short. Only about 300 of the 6000 Crusaders who had actually fought, including John the Fearless, were spared.

Tannenberg 1410

KEY FACTS

Who The Teutonic Knights, led by their Grand Master Ulrich von Jungingen (d. 1410) sought to divide Lithuania from Poland, but were annihilated in a single battle with King Wladislaw II Jagiello's Polish-Lithuanian army.

What Lightly armed but swift-moving Lithuanian cavalry and heavily armed Polish knights outflanked, encircled and destroyed the Teutonic Knights.

Where Between the villages of Tannenberg and Grünwald, in East Prussia.

When 15 July 1410

Why The Teutons took the Polish-Lithuanians by surprise, forcing a reluctant King Jagiello to fight on ground chosen by them.

Outcome Ulrich remained on the defensive, counter-attacking only when the Polish-Lithuanians retreated, but fell into a trap that saw his army destroyed.

The Poles' spectacular victory at Tannenberg, or Grünwald, over the Teutonic Order ensured that the newly created Kingdom of Poland-Lithuania survived and the advance of the German Order was halted.

POLISH–LITHUANIAN–TEUTONIC WAR

POLISH–LITHUANIAN VICTORY

King Wladyslaw II Jagiello would lead the Poles to one of their most significant victories on the battlefield at Tannenberg, handing out an unexpectedly severe drubbing to the order of Teutonic Knights.

LOCATION

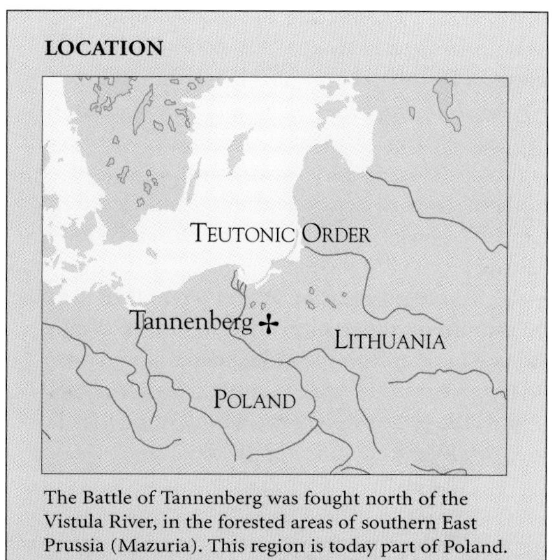
Teutonic Order
Tannenberg
Lithuania
Poland

The Battle of Tannenberg was fought north of the Vistula River, in the forested areas of southern East Prussia (Mazuria). This region is today part of Poland.

The Teutonic Order, originally founded as a Crusader order of knights in Acre, had transferred to the Baltic, fighting Prussian, Latvian, Livonian and Estonian pagans. Gradually they had become a constant presence in the region and, thanks to the backing of a superlative army, made unpleasant neighbours for Polish-Lithuania. An uneasy period of 'peace' came to an end when they clashed over the fate of the province of Samogitia and the Polish-Lithuanians planned a military campaign.

Of the two sides, the Order was militarily the stronger and more experienced. The core of their army consisted of the superbly mounted, armoured and disciplined Teutonic Knights. These were supplemented with German and European mercenary infantry force and specialist troops such as English archers, Genoese crossbowmen and Italian artillery, making for a formidable war machine.

The Polish-Lithuanian army under King Jagiello was, by contrast, composed of two entirely different armies that had almost nothing in common in tactics, strategy, combat experience or equipment. The striking arm of the

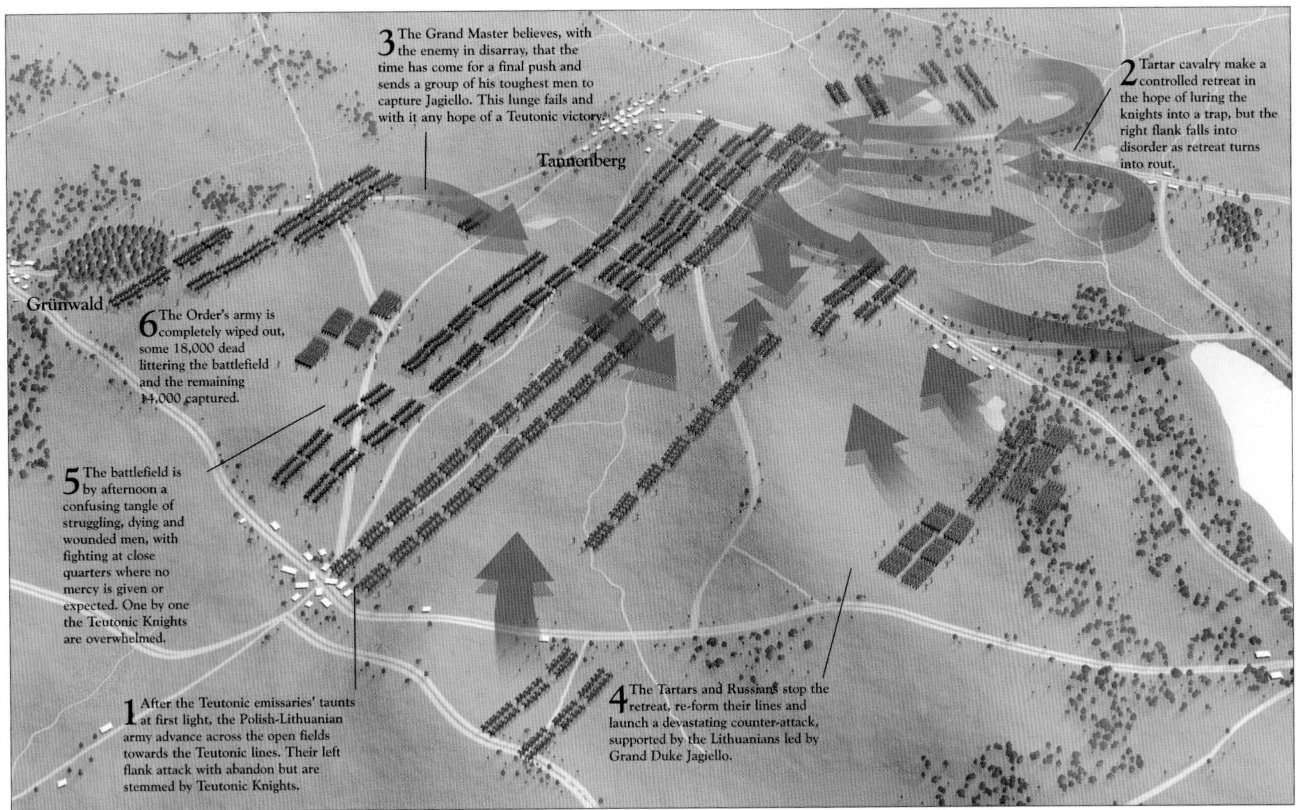
3 The Grand Master believes, with the enemy in disarray, that the time has come for a final push and sends a group of his toughest men to capture Jagiello. This lunge fails and with it any hope of a Teutonic victory.
Tannenberg
2 Tartar cavalry make a controlled retreat in the hope of luring the knights into a trap, but the right flank falls into disorder as retreat turns into rout.
Grünwald
6 The Order's army is completely wiped out, some 18,000 dead littering the battlefield and the remaining 14,000 captured.
5 The battlefield is by afternoon a confusing tangle of struggling, dying and wounded men, with fighting at close quarters where no mercy is given or expected. One by one the Teutonic Knights are overwhelmed.
1 After the Teutonic emissaries' taunts at first light, the Polish-Lithuanian army advance across the open fields towards the Teutonic lines. Their left flank attack with abandon but are stemmed by Teutonic Knights.
4 The Tartars and Russians stop the retreat, re-form their lines and launch a devastating counter-attack, supported by the Lithuanians led by Grand Duke Jagiello.

The Teutonic Order had fought in the Jerusalem Crusades, but had switched its attentions to Northern Europe. It was a mighty fighting unit of experienced soldiers, but the excellence of the Polish cavalry was more than a match at Tannenberg.

Polish army was its cavalry of armoured knights who were more than a match for their Teutonic enemy. But the infantry was poorly equipped and ill-disciplined, and no match for the Teutonic Knights in open battle except in terms of their customary, almost suicidal, Polish bravery.

The Lithuanian army was more Asiatic than European in training, relying upon lightly armed and armoured cavalry that was highly mobile and fought the enemy with lightning raids, skirmishes and ambushes. It also contained a large contingent of 'Tartar' (Mongol) cavalry, armed with bows and lassos and mounted on small, shaggy steppe ponies. Although these Asian warriors and the Lithuanians were superb light cavalry, they were of dubious value in a pitched battle against Teutonic Knights.

The Grand Master of the Teutonic Order, Ulrich von Jungingen, who looked upon the Poles as Slav 'barbarians', thought they would be easy prey when they the two sides met at Tannenberg. He expected them to dash forward in an impetuous rush. In fact, the Poles advanced in good order with lances and spears at the ready. On their right, however, the Lithuanians, with their Russian and Tartar auxiliaries, crashed into the Teutonic lines, sweeping all before them until the Grand Master committed his knights. These heavily armoured troops fought the Lithuanians to a standstill. The Tartars attempted a controlled retreat to lure the Teutonic Knights into a trap but the plan backfired. Their own troops thought the Tartars were fleeing and began to flee themselves. The knights moved forward methodically, coldly butchering the fleeing Tartars, Lithuanians and Russians.

The Poles had in the meantime held more than half of the Order's army at bay and had forced them back in close combat. Re-emboldened Lithuanians streamed back to the fight and the Teutons began to give way when they were surrounded on all sides. But most of the Order, including the Grand Master himself, fought to the death. Others who had been able to disengage from the advancing enemy continued to fight on the road that led to Grünwald. In this village, the Teutonic army made its last stand and fought to the death with the Poles and Lithuanians. By 7.00 p.m. the battle was finally won. The Teutonic Order had ceased to exist as a proper military force.

TIMELINE

1500–1000BC	1000–500BC	500BC–0AD	0–500AD	500–1000AD	1000–1500AD	1500–2000AD

Tannenberg

TANNENBERG

The Teutonic Order were among the orders of fighting Christians who had made their name as crusaders in Acre, in the Holy Land, but by the fifteenth century, they had relocated to northern Europe. Fighting the Muslim infidel was one thing, but to the Baltic states they were a utter nuisance, made more so by their arrogant behaviour and their belief that their new Pole, Lithuanian and Latvian neighbours were as big barbarians as the eastern infidels – and inferior soldiers. They got their come-uppance at Tannenberg, however, particularly as the Polish cavalry showed themselves to be more than a match for a galloping order of ex-crusaders.

Agincourt 1415

KEY FACTS

WHO An English army numbering 5700 under King Henry V (1388–1422), opposed by 25,000 French under Charles d'Albret (1369–1415), Constable of France.

WHAT The main action took place between French men-at-arms (mounted and dismounted) and a combined force of English archers and dismounted men-at-arms.

WHERE East of the village of Agincourt, between Abbeville and Calais.

WHEN 25 October 1415

WHY Marching to winter in Calais, Henry's tired and sick army was brought to battle by a vastly superior French force.

OUTCOME The French initially intended to fight a defensive action, but instead attacked down a narrow frontage between two woods. The result was a shattering defeat for the French.

The Battle of Agincourt pitted a tired and diseased English army against a French host almost five times its size. The French were determined to break the chain of English victories and to prevent King Henry V from reaching Calais with his army.

HUNDRED YEARS WAR

ENGLISH VICTORY

In the heat of fighting at Agincourt, King Henry V made sure he was right in the thick of the action, and distinguished himself by coming to the aid of his fallen noble, the Duke of Gloucester.

LOCATION

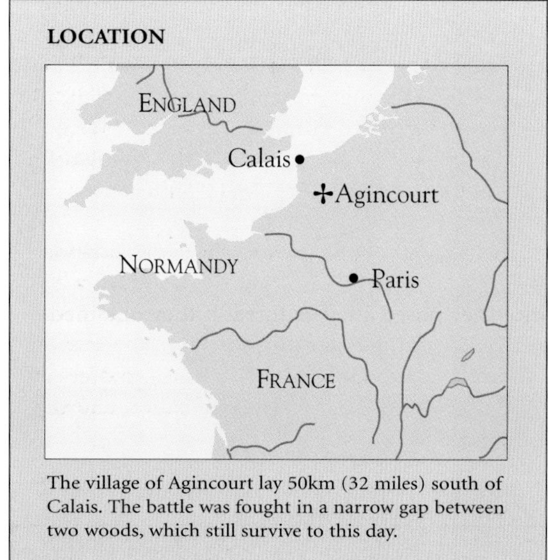
ENGLAND
Calais
Agincourt
NORMANDY
Paris
FRANCE

The village of Agincourt lay 50km (32 miles) south of Calais. The battle was fought in a narrow gap between two woods, which still survive to this day.

The Battle of Agincourt was part of the so-called Hundred Years War (actually 1337–1453) between England and France. The war was not continuous, and at times subsided into an uneasy peace of sorts.

In 1415, Henry V of England had resumed hostilities, but after capturing the fortress of Harfleur, dysentery had hit some of his men, forcing him to retreat with what remained of his army to Calais. The Constable of France, Charles d'Albret, knew the English were sick, weary and short of provisions, and determined to bring them to battle. When Henry's army crossed the Somme at St Quentin, it found d'Albret's powerful host camped across its line of march. With his men starving and soaked by a downpour during the night, Henry had no choice but to fight his way through to safety.

His opponent was determined to force the outnumbered English to come to him. But despite a string of crushing defeats at the hands of the English longbowmen, the French remained wedded to the ideal of the massed charge of lance-armed chivalry. The rivalry between these

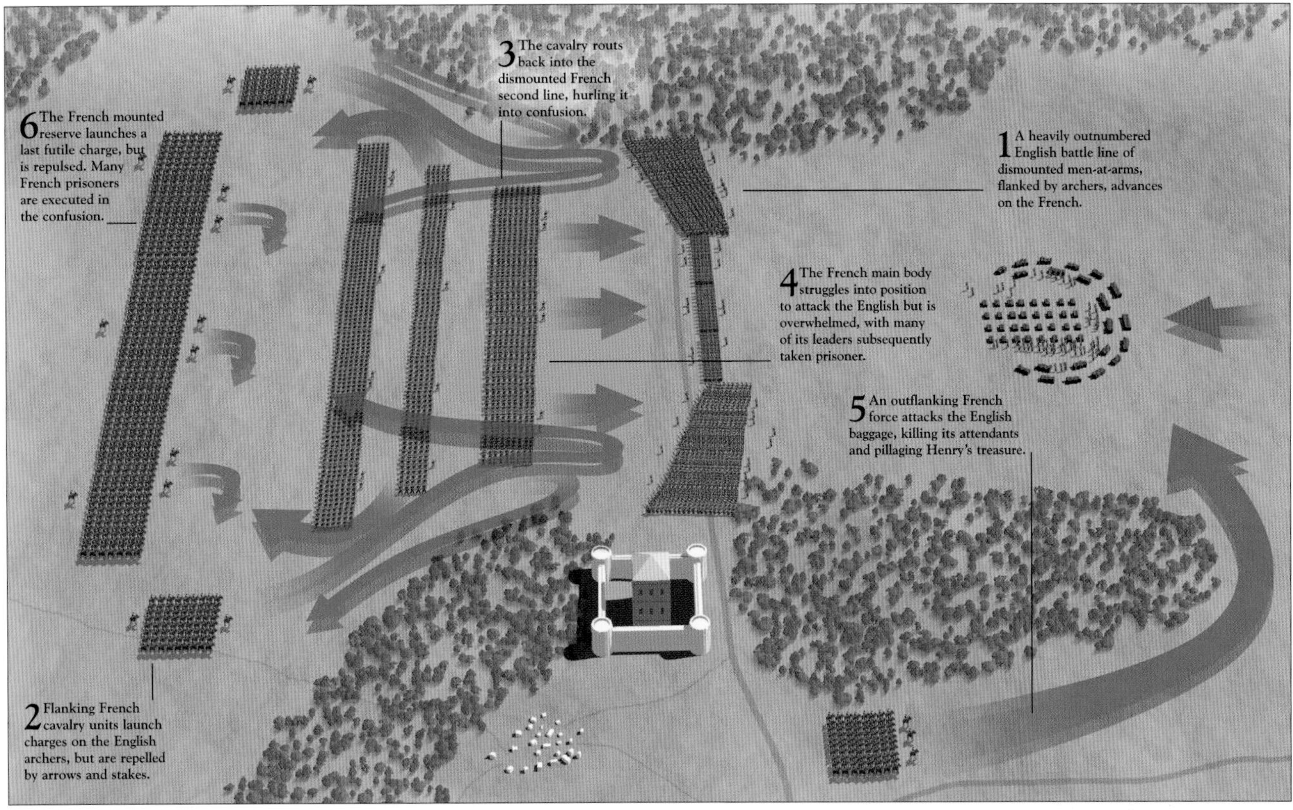
3 The cavalry routs back into the dismounted French second line, hurling it into confusion.
6 The French mounted reserve launches a last futile charge, but is repulsed. Many French prisoners are executed in the confusion.
1 A heavily outnumbered English battle line of dismounted men-at-arms, flanked by archers, advances on the French.
4 The French main body struggles into position to attack the English but is overwhelmed, with many of its leaders subsequently taken prisoner.
5 An outflanking French force attacks the English baggage, killing its attendants and pillaging Henry's treasure.
2 Flanking French cavalry units launch charges on the English archers, but are repelled by arrows and stakes.

By forcing the French to fight on a compressed front funnelled by woods on either side, the English went some way to nullifying their opponents' immense numerical advantage.

noble warriors, whose status in society depended upon what they did on the battlefield, made them impetuous and unreliable. Their charge would be furious, but also uncontrolled. One concession to the dominance of the English archer was to provide many of the knights' horses with barding – horse armour – to give them a measure of protection. Even if barding slowed their mounts down, the French hoped it would enable more of them to reach the enemy line.

The battle took place on rain-sodden ground, and Henry, though heavily outnumbered, had little choice but to attack. The archers advanced to within longbow range, and began firing. The French had no means of reply, since their own crossbowmen were too far to the rear, so they were then forced to take the offensive after all.

Several charges were repulsed by the arrow fire, but the ankle-deep mud was further churned up by the cavalry, weighed down by armour. Headlong charges slowed to advances at a slow walk, offering easy targets for rapid-firing English longbowmen. The French lines were also compressed into smaller formations by woods framing the battlefield, which acted as a funnel so that their numerical advantage was weakened. In fact, so tightly compressed were the French that some men struggled to find room to wield their weapons.

When the lead French soldiers finally came into contact with the English and hand-to-hand fighting began, they were exhausted by their laborious advance and, jammed together, could not fight effectively. The Count d'Alençon and a party of knights, sworn to kill King Henry or die trying, cut their way through to the English monarch, who was fighting heroically in the front rank. Henry covered himself with glory once more, coming to the rescue of the Duke of Gloucester who was in serious trouble at the hands of d'Alençon.

Henry did not have enough men to guard the prisoners taken in battle, and gave orders for them to be put to the sword, since they posed a severe threat if they obtained weapons. The remaining French forces thought better of pressing their attack against the English line and drew off. They left a corpse-strewn field in English hands, and the road to Calais open.

TIMELINE

1500–1000BC	1000–500BC	500BC–0AD	0–500AD	500–1000AD	1000–1500AD	1500–2000AD

Vitkov 1420

HUSSITE WARS

HUSSITE VICTORY

How could peasants armed with agricultural implements hope to contend with well-armoured and supremely confident knights wielding modern weapons? Whether it was lateral thinking, divine inspiration or previous experience, Jan Zizka found the answer in the use of pitchforks.

KEY FACTS

WHO A Hussite force numbering approximately 9000 under Jan Zizka (1360–1424), opposed an army of the Holy Roman Empire numbering 80,000, led by the Emperor Sigismund (reigned 1410–37).

WHAT Roman Empire troops suffered a devastating flank attack whilst assaulting an outpost of besieged Prague.

WHERE The hill of Vitkov, now known as Ziscaberg, to the east of Prague in the Czech Republic.

WHEN 14 July 1420

WHY The population had risen against the Catholic Church's attempt to suppress the Hussite heresy and held Prague.

OUTCOME The rout carried away the greater part of the main Imperial army. They lifted the siege and the mostly mercenary army partially dispersed.

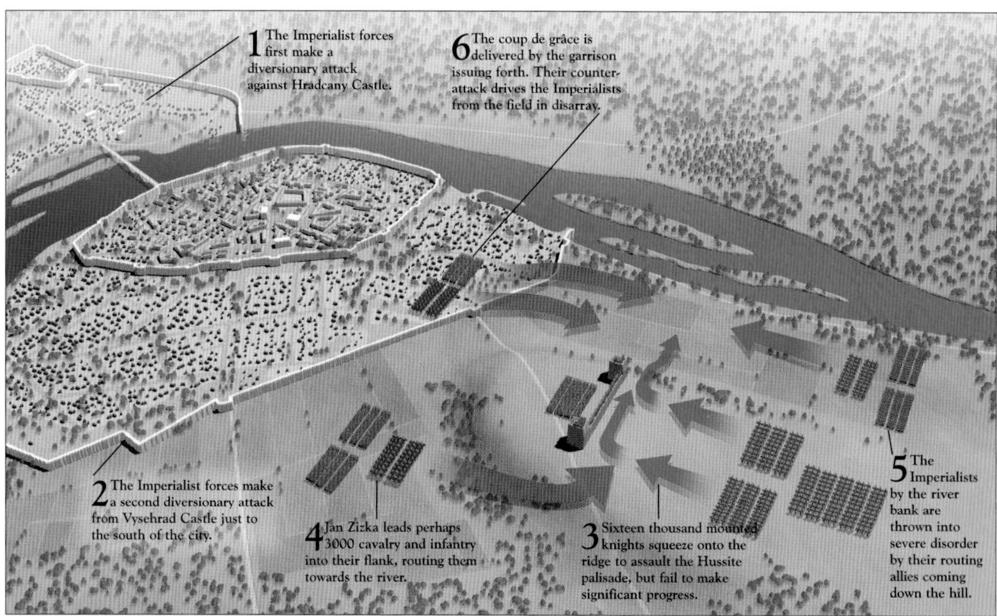
1 The Imperialist forces first make a diversionary attack against Hradcany Castle.
6 The coup de grâce is delivered by the garrison issuing forth. Their counter-attack drives the Imperialists from the field in disarray.
2 The Imperialist forces make a second diversionary attack from Vysehrad Castle just to the south of the city.
4 Jan Zizka leads perhaps 3000 cavalry and infantry into their flank, routing them towards the river.
3 Sixteen thousand mounted knights squeeze onto the ridge to assault the Hussite palisade, but fail to make significant progress.
5 The Imperialists by the river bank are thrown into severe disorder by their routing allies coming down the hill.

Jan Zizka may have been half-blind, but he certainly knew how to read the terrain for the advantages it held for his simple peasant army in its task of overcoming the might of the Holy Roman Empire.

Jan Zizka was a half-blind but sharp-minded former royal gamekeeper. When the Holy Roman Emperor Sigismund arrived at the head of an 80,000-strong army to stamp out the Hussite heresy in Bohemia, Zizka had a chance to put his shrewd tactical brain to work, improvising with whatever weapons were to hand. His was an army of the people, the great majority being foot soldiers equipped with agricultural tools such as flails, billhooks and axes used as weapons with little modification.

Sigismund's army moved to lay siege to Prague, but Zizka had foreseen that they would first attack the nearby palisade on Vitkov Hill, to secure supply lines. Zizka stationed a force of soldiers on one side of the ridge, and these surprised the Imperialist army, whose massed ranks of cavalry were forced to dismount as they tried to exit via the cliffs on the northern side. Thrown into confusion, many riderless horses broke free, and as they came careering down the slope, those of Sigismund's army at the foot of the hill took stock of the view of routing friends and terrified horses and also turned and fled. A pitchfork army, equipped mainly with the tools of their agricultural trade, had won a notable victory.

LOCATION

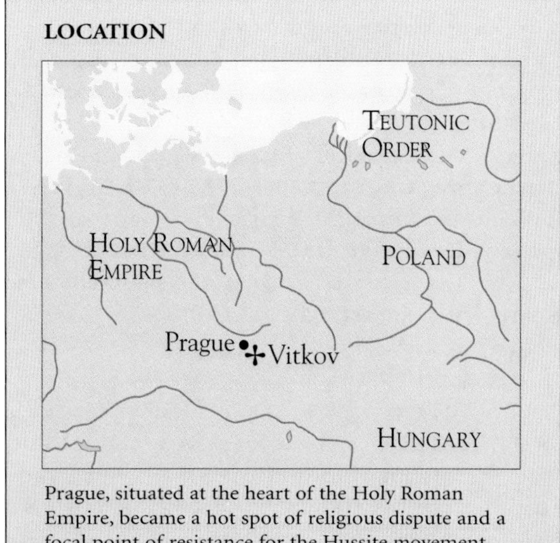
Teutonic Order
Holy Roman Empire
Poland
Prague
Vitkov
Hungary

Prague, situated at the heart of the Holy Roman Empire, became a hot spot of religious dispute and a focal point of resistance for the Hussite movement.

TIMELINE

1500–1000BC	1000–500BC	500BC–0AD	0–500AD	500–1000AD	1000–1500AD	1500–2000AD

Verneuil 1424

HUNDRED YEARS WAR

ENGLISH VICTORY

By 1424, having been on the back foot in the Hundred Years War for so long, the French badly needed victory to lift morale. But at Verneuil, even with the spirited support of their less jaded Scottish allies, they were unable to secure it.

KEY FACTS

WHO John, Duke of Bedford leads the English army against the Dauphin's French army, under Viscount Aumale, backed by their Scottish allies, who were led by John Stewart, Earl of Buchan, and Archibald Douglas, Earl of Douglas.

WHAT Once again the accuracy and skill of the English longbowmen proved decisive. Both Scottish earls were killed, and Aumale drowned in the town moat during the cavalry retreat.

WHERE Verneuil, Normandy, France.

WHEN 16 August 1424

WHY The French had been trying to regain the initiative in the Hundred Years War by attacking English-held towns in Normandy.

OUTCOME This was another crushing defeat for the French, with most of the north down to the Loire in English control.

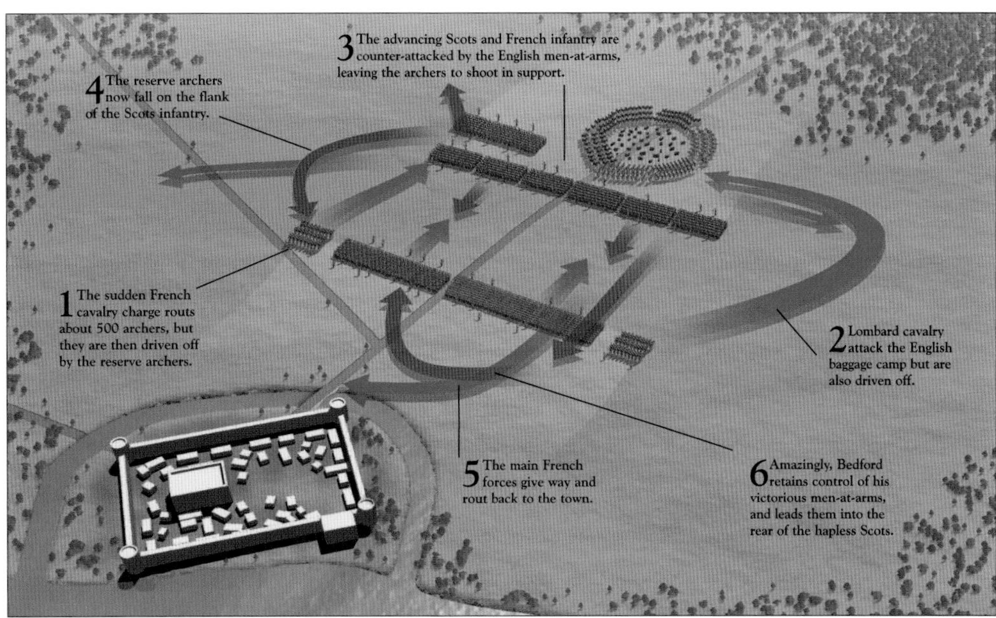

3 The advancing Scots and French infantry are counter-attacked by the English men-at-arms, leaving the archers to shoot in support.
4 The reserve archers now fall on the flank of the Scots infantry.
1 The sudden French cavalry charge routs about 500 archers, but they are then driven off by the reserve archers.
2 Lombard cavalry attack the English baggage camp but are also driven off.
5 The main French forces give way and rout back to the town.
6 Amazingly, Bedford retains control of his victorious men-at-arms, and leads them into the rear of the hapless Scots.

The English would once again owe much of their success at Verneuil to the skills of their bowmen. But on this occasion, they would also incur almost as heavy casualties as those suffered by their enemy.

LOCATION

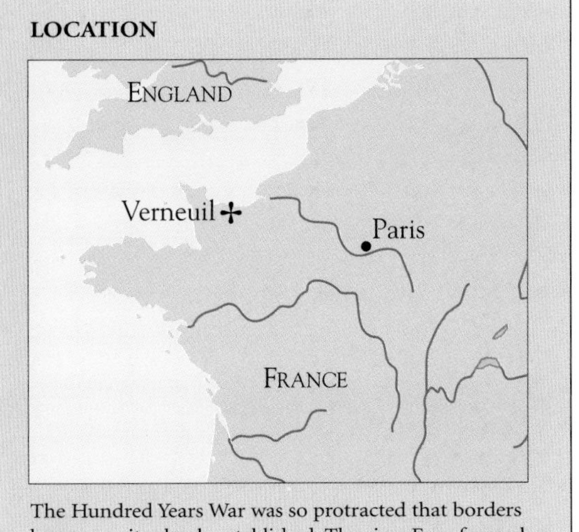

England
Verneuil
Paris
France

The Hundred Years War was so protracted that borders became quite clearly established. The river Eure formed one such boundary and saw considerable skirmishing.

By 1424, with memories of Agincourt still poignant, French commanders were reluctant to engage the English in another major battle. French memories of the hail of arrows at that battle were still fresh, but France's Scottish allies, led by John Stewart, Earl of Buchan, were eager to provoke a fight against their old adversaries. When Verneuil, which had been in English hands, was occupied, they got their wish.

Drawing their lines up in front of the moated and walled town, a French cavalry charge caught the English archers before they got their stakes in place and routed many of them. But English men-at-arms counter-charged the French, who were then forced to fight within range of the awesome English bowmen. The French fled back towards the town moat, pursued by the English.

ENGLISH TRIUMPH

John, Duke of Bedford was able to rally his men and lead them into an attack on the Scottish line. When the English reserve archers joined in, they too broke and fled. Over 7000 men from the allied army died. But the English had also lost 1600 men – far higher than at Agincourt.

TIMELINE

1500–1000BC	1000–500BC	500BC–0AD	0–500AD	500–1000AD	1000–1500AD	1500–2000AD

Siege of Orléans 1428–29

KEY FACTS

Who The French army under the figurehead leadership of Joan of Arc, against the English under the Earl of Shrewsbury.

What The demoralized French lifted a prolonged siege of Orléans and regain the upper hand in a war that seemed lost.

Where Orléans, on the River Loire, north central France.

When 7 May 1429

Why The English, in control of northern France, saw Orléans as a gateway to the south, and France could not withstand its loss.

Outcome After raising the siege, the French went on to drive the English from the Loire region, and the dauphin was crowned King Charles VII at Reims.

In 1429, the fortunes of the French monarchy in the Hundred Years War against England had reached their lowest ebb. But when peasant girl Joan of Arc – the Maid of Orléans – emerged at the Dauphin's gates with her visionary exhortations, a remarkable turnaround was soon underway.

HUNDRED YEARS WAR

FRENCH VICTORY

Joan of Arc arrived at the gates of the Charles VII's castle at Chinon to tell of her visions. The desperate king, running out of options, had little choice but to listen and was personally convinced of her authenticity.

LOCATION

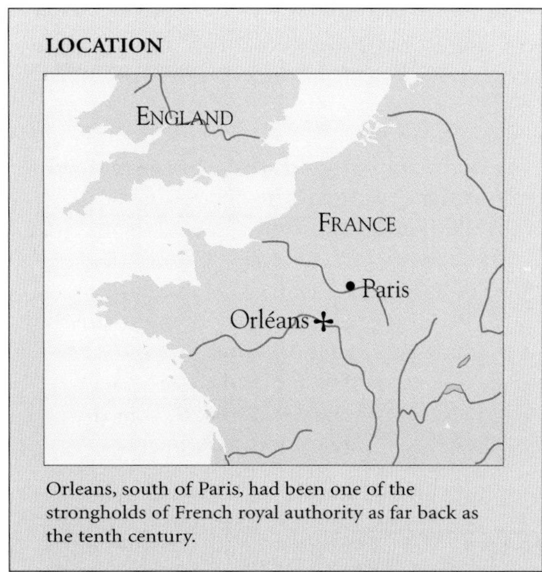
ENGLAND
FRANCE
Paris
Orléans

Orleans, south of Paris, had been one of the strongholds of French royal authority as far back as the tenth century.

When Charles, the Valois heir to the throne of France succeeded his father Charles VI in 1422, he inherited a desperate situation. His authority was recognized only in the south of the country; the English commanded the north, in alliance with Burgundy, and with John, Duke of Bedford effectively acting as regent on behalf of the infant English king Henry VI.

CHANGE OF FORTUNE

It was not until 1429 that Charles's luck began to change, and it could hardly have done so in a stranger, more dramatic way. As the number of French defeats mounted, a peasant girl Joan of Arc claimed to have heard the voices of saints exhorting her to come to the rescue of her country. At first she met with only scorn from military men in her local region of Lorraine. But when she presented herself at the castle of the Dauphin, and was given a personal audience with him, he was struck by her seeming authenticity and he sent her to be assessed by a group of eminent theologians.

The French fightback would eventually push the English out of the Loire region and lead to Charles, the Valois heir to the throne of France, being crowned in Reims Cathedral with Joan of Arc by his side.

Gaining their assurance that she was no heretic, he supplied Joan with a knight's army and horses, and entrusted her with leading the French troops forward to relieve the ongoing English siege of Orléans. As she rode forward, she was dressed in white armour, and carried a banner at her side bearing the symbol of the Holy Trinity and the words 'Jesus, Maria.'

LIFTING THE SIEGE

The English siege of Orléans, a strategically important city if they were to extend their control of French territory into the south, had begun the previous autumn. Because the English lines had not been able to completely block off all routes towards the city, a trickle of supplies and reinforcing troops had managed to sustain the defence, which was led by Jean de Dunois. Even so, time seemed to be fast running out when Joan, accompanied by the Duke of Alençon, arrived to attempt to lift the siege.

The situation was complicated by the fact that while the city lay on the north of the River Loire, a barbican and gatehouse complex, known as Les Tourelles, lay on the south bank. Having taken control of these fortifications, the English had concentrated their forces here. The English had also taken a nearby fort at St Loup and now, as a diversionary tactic, the French launched a successful mission to take it. Further attacks on English posts north of the river forced Shrewsbury to concentrate his men around Les Tourelles, and on the morning of 7 May, Joan, joined by Alençon and Dunois, led a concerted French attack on the complex.

FRENCH FIGHTBACK

Fighting raged throughout the day, and Joan had to retire from the fray when she was wounded in the shoulder. By the end of the day, the French had gained control of the barbican, and Shrewsbury's demoralized troops re-gathered outside the city, ready for a field battle. When it became clear the French would not attack them, they withdrew from the region. The French fightback had begun. It would soon lead to the coronation of the dauphin as Charles VII in Reims Cathedral, with the 'Maid of Orléans' at his side.

TIMELINE

1500–1000BC	1000–500BC	500BC–0AD	0–500AD	500–1000AD	1000–1500AD	1500–2000AD

Siege of Orléans

SIEGE OF ORLÉANS

Has there been a more mystifying episode in European history than how Joan of Arc came to the rescue of the French in the Hundred Years War with England? It's a story by turns sweet, spiritual and, ultimately, tragic. That Joan believed she was divinely inspired there is no doubt, nor that the French king Charles VII – 'le bien servi' – was convinced and energized by her presence. Victory at Orléans proved the turning point in the fighting and she was at his side for his coronation at Reims soon after. That her capture by the English, who burnt her at the stake as a witch, drew no protest from Charles, makes depressing reading – an act of utter betrayal and feebleness from the man she had saved.

Varna 1444

KEY FACTS

WHO A Crusader army largely composed of Hungarians under their king Ulászló I (Vladyslav III of Poland), but also including Germans, Transylvanians, Poles and Wallachians, confronted an Ottoman Turkish army led by Sultan Murad II.

WHAT The Crusader army, outnumbered at least 2:1, fought a day-long battle with the Ottomans.

WHERE Just outside the Bulgarian port of Varna, located on the west coast of the Black Sea, north of Constantinople.

WHEN 10 November 1444

WHY The Crusaders were engaged in an ambitious plan to drive the Turks from the territories they had conquered in the Balkans.

OUTCOME The Crusaders were defeated in a major battle that cost them nearly half of their army.

The Crusade that ended in the Turkish victory at Varna was Western Europe's last serious attempt to save Constantinople from the Ottoman Turks. It was the worst Crusade defeat of the fifteenth century.

OTTOMAN BALKAN WARS

NO CLEAR VICTORY

Janos Hunyadi was a much-celebrated Hungarian military figure, but he was sidelined by the more rash and inexperienced King Laszlo at Varna, a key factor in their defeat.

LOCATION

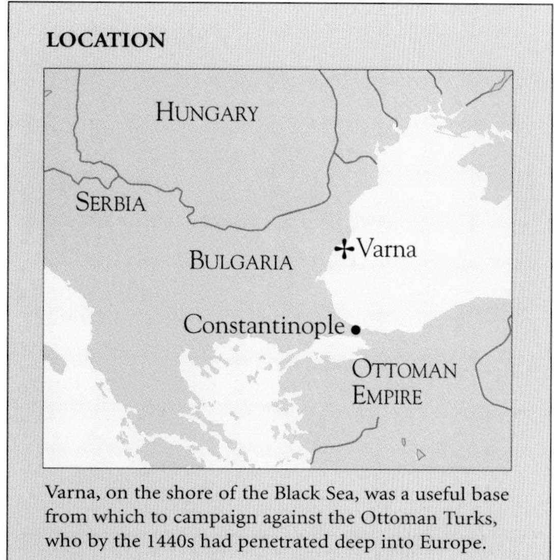
HUNGARY
SERBIA
BULGARIA
Varna
Constantinople
OTTOMAN EMPIRE

Varna, on the shore of the Black Sea, was a useful base from which to campaign against the Ottoman Turks, who by the 1440s had penetrated deep into Europe.

By 1440, the last remnant of the Byzantine Empire was close to defeat at the hands of the expanding Ottoman Turkish sultanate, and in response to the emperor's pleas for help, Pope Eugenius IV agreed to organize a Crusade. When he learnt of the imminent arrival of the Crusaders, the Turkish Sultan Murad II, with a force 40,000–45,000 strong, set out for the threatened Ottoman provinces in Europe, crossing the Bosphorus north of Constantinople late in October 1444. When the Crusaders crossed the Black Sea to Varna, they were dismayed to discover that a large Turkish army was camped nearby.

The Crusade leaders held a council that night. The papal legate Julian proposed a withdrawal, since the Crusaders were heavily outnumbered, and the lie of the land favoured the Turks. Such a move was impractical. There was no clear escape route for the Crusaders, especially in the absence of a fleet of ships. The Black Sea and a lake hemmed them in on two sides, with difficult mountain roads and swampland making a speedy retreat impossible. Instead, the Crusade leaders decided on a rapid attack

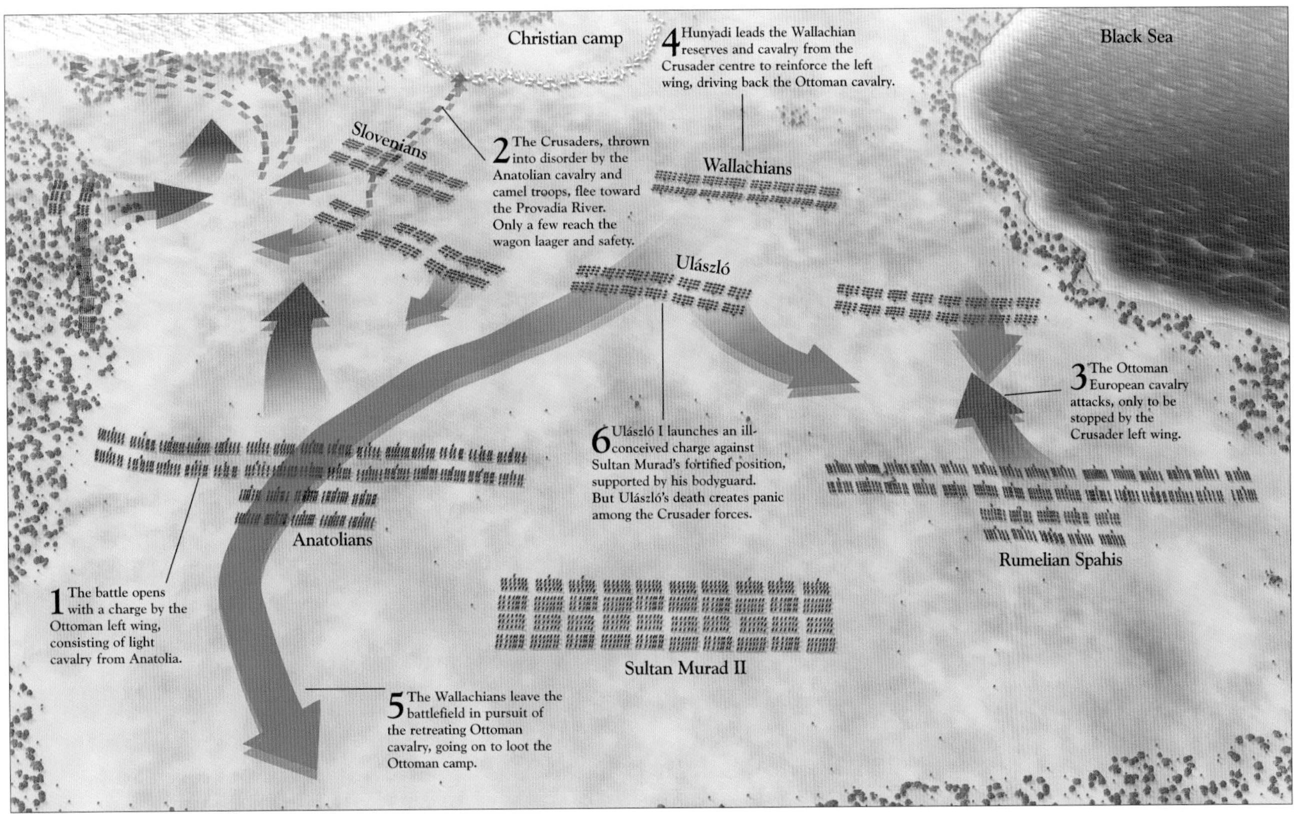

Christian camp
4 Hunyadi leads the Wallachian reserves and cavalry from the Crusader centre to reinforce the left wing, driving back the Ottoman cavalry.
Black Sea
Slovenians
2 The Crusaders, thrown into disorder by the Anatolian cavalry and camel troops, flee toward the Provadia River. Only a few reach the wagon laager and safety.
Wallachians
Ulászló
3 The Ottoman European cavalry attacks, only to be stopped by the Crusader left wing.
6 Ulászló I launches an ill-conceived charge against Sultan Murad's fortified position, supported by his bodyguard. But Ulászló's death creates panic among the Crusader forces.
Anatolians
Rumelian Spahis
1 The battle opens with a charge by the Ottoman left wing, consisting of light cavalry from Anatolia.
Sultan Murad II
5 The Wallachians leave the battlefield in pursuit of the retreating Ottoman cavalry, going on to loot the Ottoman camp.

Varna was characterized by numerous cavalry charges on either side, with heavy losses sustained by both Crusaders and the Turks. The Crusaders retreated with their depleted forces, their aims in tatters, but neither could the Turks claim victory.

against the Turkish army, with Janos Hunyadi, rather than the young and inexperienced Hungarian king Ulászló in overall command.

Murad was wary of the power of the Christians' heavy cavalry against his large numbers of Turkish infantry. He placed his infantry in the centre. The most effective part of this force was the sultan's Janissaries, the elite slave soldiers who had been taken as boys from the Christian parts of the sultanate, converted to Islam, then trained into a highly effective force. Facing him, the Crusader force was poorly balanced, being almost entirely composed of cavalry, and divided into national units.

The battle opened with a charge by the Ottoman left wing. The Christian right wing withstood their attack, but when two further units broke ranks and pursued the retreating Muslims, it exposed the whole Christian right wing to attack.

As the two pursuing Christian units advanced, an Anatolian cavalry force hit them on the flank. Some of the Christians tried to escape to the nearby fortress of Galata. Most were killed or drowned in the Provadia River. The rest of the Christian right wing went quickly to their comrades' aid, but were surrounded. One unit made it safely back to the wagon laager at the rear; few others survived.

While the Christian right wing was being mauled, the cavalry of the Ottoman right wing also attacked. But Janos Hunyadi led a cavalry attack to push them back, while firmly adjuring King Ulászló to stay put, leaving him in nominal command of the Christian centre. This did not suit Ulászló's notions of heroic kingship. Instead, he led his bodyguard against the Janissaries in the Ottoman centre, appearing to seek a personal duel with Murad II. The Ottoman defences and their guns fatally slowed the Christian charge, so much so that Ulászló himself was killed and many of his cavalry slaughtered.

At the end of the day, the two armies disengaged with no clear victory on either side. The Christian losses were so heavy, however, that the Crusader camp disintegrated and the army began to retreat – along narrow, dangerous roads and through swampland, where the Turks could pursue them at leisure. The Ottomans had beaten off the Crusaders, but had also sustained heavy losses.

Tumu 1449

MING–MONGOL WAR

MONGOL VICTORY

When the Mongols invaded China in 1449, Emperor Zhu Qizhen put himself at the head of one of the largest armies in the country's history. It proved a logistical nightmare to move across country, however, especially against foe as mobile as the Mongols.

KEY FACTS

WHO The Mongol cavalry commanded by Esen Tayishi, against the Chinese Ming under emperor Zhu Qizhen and Wang Cheng.

WHAT By withdrawing to a remote steppe region, the Mongols put the marching Chinese army under logistical pressure. Although vastly outnumbered, they were able to prey on the jaded ranks of conscripts when fatigue set in.

WHERE T'umu fortress, Xianfu, China.

WHEN 1 September 1449

WHY The Mongols had invaded China and the emperor massed one of the biggest armies to be gathered during the the Ming Dynasty.

OUTCOME Despite the victory, the Mongols were unable to take the Chinese capital Beijing, and Esen Tayishi would be roundly attacked for his failure to press home the advantage of his victory at Vochan.

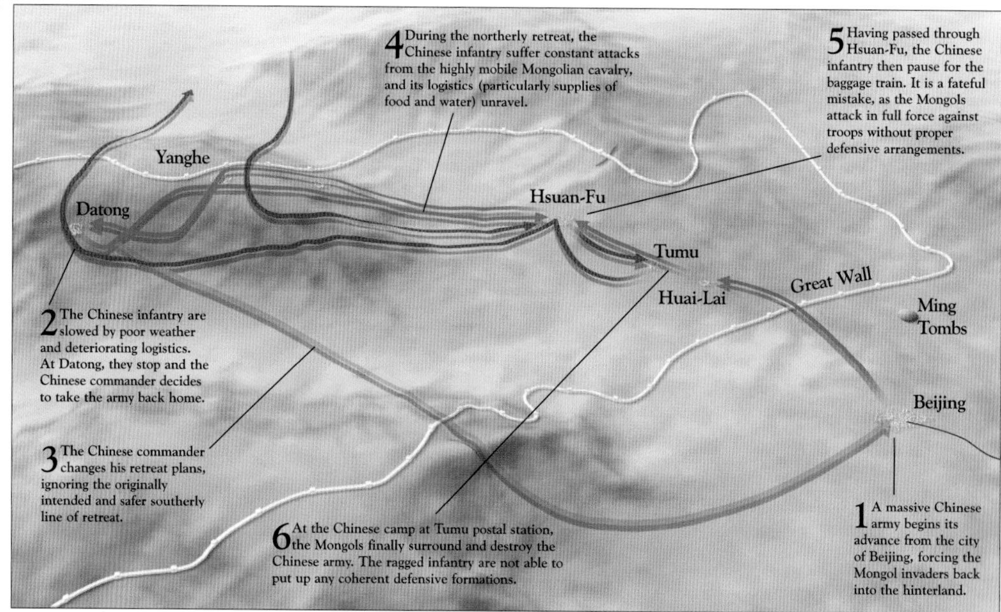

4 During the northerly retreat, the Chinese infantry suffer constant attacks from the highly mobile Mongolian cavalry, and its logistics (particularly supplies of food and water) unravel.
5 Having passed through Hsuan-Fu, the Chinese infantry then pause for the baggage train. It is a fateful mistake, as the Mongols attack in full force against troops without proper defensive arrangements.
Yanghe
Datong
Hsuan-Fu
Tumu
Huai-Lai
Great Wall
Ming Tombs
Beijing
2 The Chinese infantry are slowed by poor weather and deteriorating logistics. At Datong, they stop and the Chinese commander decides to take the army back home.
3 The Chinese commander changes his retreat plans, ignoring the originally intended and safer southerly line of retreat.
6 At the Chinese camp at Tumu postal station, the Mongols finally surround and destroy the Chinese army. The ragged infantry are not able to put up any coherent defensive formations.
1 A massive Chinese army begins its advance from the city of Beijing, forcing the Mongol invaders back into the hinterland.

Tumu was fought by an exhausted Chinese army, proving the logistical folly of attempting to move a huge army across difficult, and often hostile, terrain.

The Chinese Ming assembled a 500,000-strong conscript army in response to a lightning Mongol cavalry invasion. But the Mongol commander Esen Tayishi understood the logistical problems faced by half a million men under forced march. He pulled his forces back into the steppe regions, stretching out the distance for the Chinese troops to travel and maximizing resupply problems.

Torrential rains transformed the ground into a boot-sucking morass for Chinese foot soldiers. As supplies ran down, they camped at Tumu postal station, but the infantry were in an exposed position, and the Mongols closed in.

DISORGANIZATION

Despite a huge Chinese superiority in numbers, they were unable to organize themselves into a coherent response. The marshalled ranks of infantry, so central to defence, crumbled. Up to 250,000 Chinese troops were either killed, wounded or captured. Wang Chen was killed and two days later even the emperor himself fell into Mongol captivity. Mobility had triumphed over infantry mass.

LOCATION

MONGOLIA
Tumu
Beijing
MING CHINA

The battlefield of Tumu was located near the walled town of Huai-Lai. The advance and retreat took the Chinese army through very barren landscapes.

TIMELINE

1500–1000BC	1000–500BC	500BC–0AD	0–500AD	500–1000AD	1000–1500AD	1500–2000AD

Castillon 1453

HUNDRED YEARS WAR

FRENCH VICTORY

KEY FACTS

Who An Anglo-Gascon force under Sir John Talbot, the Earl of Shrewsbury (1390–1453) fought the French forces of Jean Bureau (d. 1463).

What The English cavalry and infantry army attacked the infantry and cannon of the French forces.

Where Castillon, west of the city of Bordeaux, southwest France.

When 17 July 1453

Why After the French capture of Bordeaux in 1451, English King Henry VI (1421–1471) sought to re-establish English control of Bordeaux and Gascony by inflicting a decisive victory on French forces in southwest France.

Outcome Following the outbreak of the Wars of the Roses, the English were no longer able to pursue their claim to the French throne and lost all their land on the continent.

The Battle of Castillon was the last battle fought between the French, the Gascons and the English during the Hundred Years War. With their cannons, the French army demonstrated that victory in battle would in future be determined by gunpowder weapons.

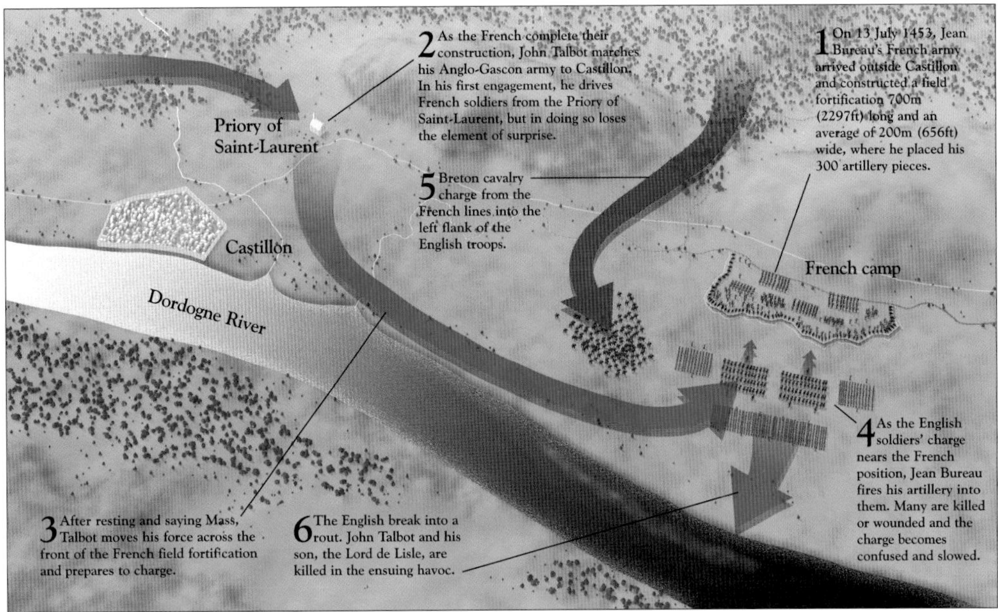

1 On 13 July 1453, Jean Bureau's French army arrived outside Castillon and constructed a field fortification 700m (2297ft) long and an average of 200m (656ft) wide, where he placed his 300 artillery pieces.
2 As the French complete their construction, John Talbot marches his Anglo-Gascon army to Castillon. In his first engagement, he drives French soldiers from the Priory of Saint-Laurent, but in doing so loses the element of surprise.
Priory of Saint-Laurent
5 Breton cavalry charge from the French lines into the left flank of the English troops.
Castillon
French camp
Dordogne River
4 As the English soldiers' charge nears the French position, Jean Bureau fires his artillery into them. Many are killed or wounded and the charge becomes confused and slowed.
3 After resting and saying Mass, Talbot moves his force across the front of the French field fortification and prepares to charge.
6 The English break into a rout. John Talbot and his son, the Lord de Lisle, are killed in the ensuing havoc.

In earlier confrontations in the War, French cavalry had been outdone by the know-how of English bowmen. Now it was the turn of English cavalry and infantry to be outdone by French artillery expertise.

John Talbot, Earl of Shrewsbury and a veteran of the Hundred Years War, was tasked with taking Gascony back from the French. His opposing commander, Jean Bureau, was equally experienced in battle, but while Talbot was a traditional cavalry man-at-arms, Bureau was a gunner, a specialist in fighting with new gunpowder weapons.

When they clashed at Castillon, Bureau had 300 cannons and an even larger number of *couleuvrines à main* and arquebuses at his disposal. Talbot had some gunpowder weapons, but not anywhere near the same number.

Instead of setting up traditional siege lines around the town, spreading out both his gunpowder weapons and soldiers, Bureau built an entrenched camp, where he placed most of his army. When Talbot charged, Bureau turned the full massed force of his cannons and handguns upon them. The English were mowed down by the bombardment, many killed outright by iron and stone gunshots. The battle probably lasted no more than a few minutes. Hardly a Frenchman was injured. Talbot tried fleeing with his troops, but a cannonball killed his horse, pinning him underneath. A French soldier, eschewing a rich ransom, killed the unarmoured general with his axe.

LOCATION

England
Paris
France
Bordeaux
Castillon
Gascony

The castle and walled town of Castillon lay 50km (31 miles) away from Bordeaux, where it defended the access to the city by road and river (the Dordogne).

TIMELINE

1500–1000BC	1000–500BC	500BC–0AD	0–500AD	500–1000AD	1000–1500AD	1500–2000AD

Constantinople 1453

BYZANTINE–OTTOMAN WARS

OTTOMAN TURKISH VICTORY

KEY FACTS

WHO Ottoman Sultan Mehmed II (1432–81, reigned 1444–46 and 1451–81) besieged Constantinople with 120,000 troops, opposed by some 8–10,000 Christian defenders under Emperor Constantine XI Palaeologus (1405–53, reigned 1449–53).

WHAT The Turks used Urban's massive cannon against the finest fortification works in Europe.

WHERE Siege of the Imperial Byzantine capital of Constantinople (Byzantium) on the Bosporus and Sea of Marmara. The city is better known today as Istanbul.

WHEN 5 April–29 May 1453

WHY Mehmed II wished to eliminate this tiny Christian stronghold deep behind the Turkish frontier and make it the new capital of his growing empire.

OUTCOME The fall of Byzantine Constantinople to Mehmed's expanding Ottoman Empire.

The Ottoman Turkish siege of Constantinople in 1453 was one of the greatest sieges of all time. It saw the Turks use – for the very first time – heavy siege artillery to break through the enormous Theodosian Walls that had held off attackers for more than a millennium.

The fall of Constantinople and Byzantium to the Turks sent shockwaves throughout the West. While Byzantium had long been an Eastern-centred empire, a last remaining physical reminder of the days of classical Rome had been smashed.

LOCATION

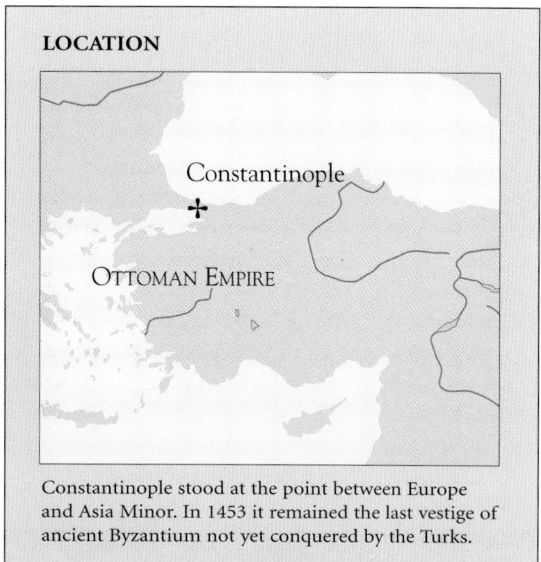

Constantinople
OTTOMAN EMPIRE

Constantinople stood at the point between Europe and Asia Minor. In 1453 it remained the last vestige of ancient Byzantium not yet conquered by the Turks.

Mehmed II, the Ottoman Sultan, had an all-consuming passion to conquer Constantinople and make it the capital of an Ottoman Empire that would straddle the world. In the summer of 1452 he paid a Hungarian gunmaker, Urban, a huge sum to build him a monstrous gun that would be able to breach the city walls. By January 1453, Urban's gun was ready for inspection at Adrianople, the Ottoman capital to the west of Constantinople. The gun barrel measured 8.1m (26ft 8in) in length, had a calibre of 20.3cm (8in) and required a crew of 700, but could lob a cannonball weighing a tonne (1 ton) over 1.6km (1 mile).

Clearly Mehmed II had the hardware for a successful siege of Constantinople which, although a shadow of its former self by 1453, continued to hold great cultural and economic importance for Eastern and Western Europe. Its Theodosian Walls – built in the fifth century in the reign of Emperor Theodosius II (401–450) – remained formidably intact, with 5.7km (3.5 miles) of moats and a triple line of walls and fortified towers stretching from the Sea of Marmara to the Golden Horn.

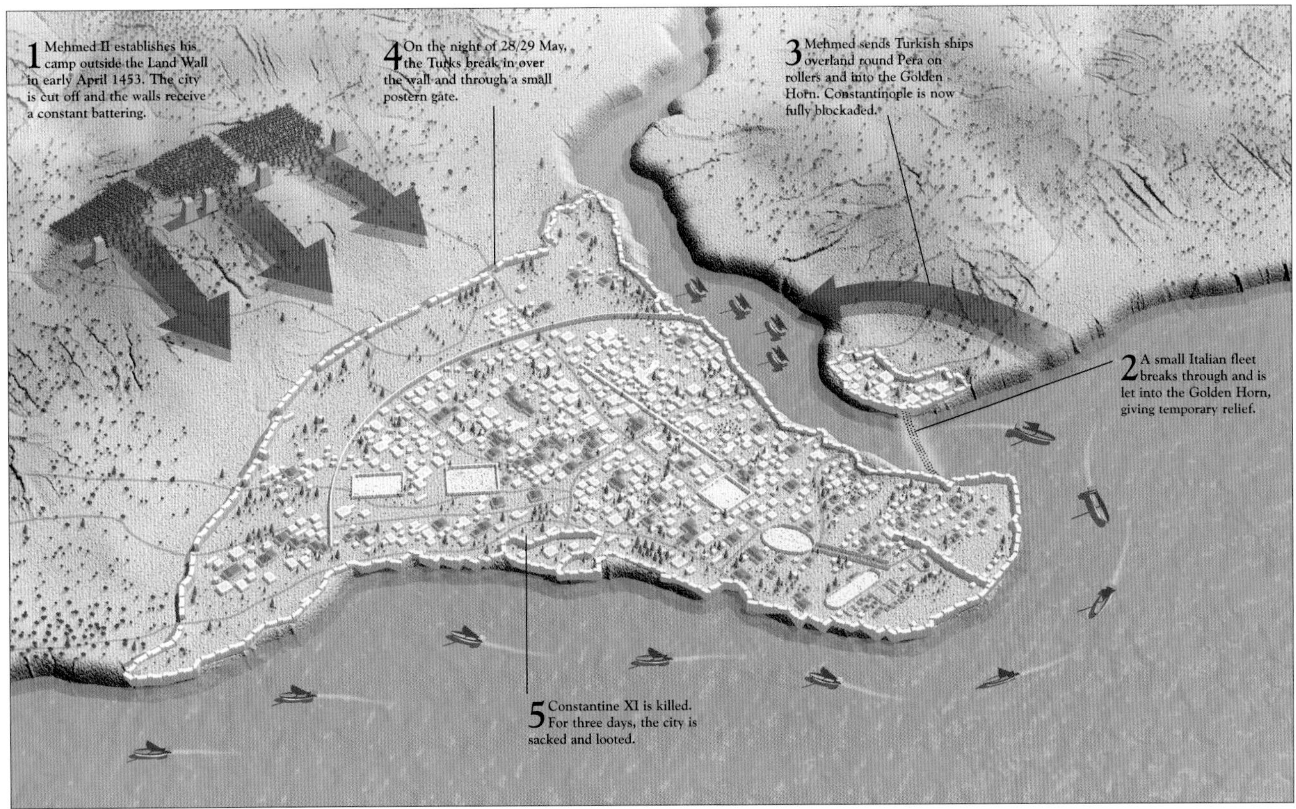
1 Mehmed II establishes his camp outside the Land Wall in early April 1453. The city is cut off and the walls receive a constant battering.
4 On the night of 28/29 May, the Turks break in over the wall and through a small postern gate.
3 Mehmed sends Turkish ships overland round Pera on rollers and into the Golden Horn. Constantinople is now fully blockaded.
2 A small Italian fleet breaks through and is let into the Golden Horn, giving temporary relief.
5 Constantine XI is killed. For three days, the city is sacked and looted.

Constantinople was but a shadow of its former self by 1453, yet the old fortifications remained defiantly intact. They proved a real challenge to the feisty and impatient Ottoman Sultan Mehmed II.

Mehmed amassed a huge army, and the first detachments arrived beneath the walls of Constantinople in the spring of 1453. Since much of the city walls faced the sea, Mehmed concentrated his assault on the massive Land Wall, pitching his red and gold silk tent about 400m (440 yards) from the Land Wall, with his best troops and Urban's monstrous gun around him.

When the Turks took two forts to the west of the Land Wall, Mehmed had the defenders impaled in front of it to show what happened to those who resisted his will. A third fort, on the island of Prinkipo, held out and the garrison chose to burn itself to death rather than fall into the hands of the Turks. Finally the Turks began bombarding the Theodosian Walls, with artillery fire, continuing without interruption for six weeks. The Ottoman guns were heavy and unwieldy, with a tendency to slide off their firing platforms. Urban's giant gun fired only seven times a day, so complex and time-consuming was the process of loading and firing it, but it had a deafening roar and did great damage to the wall and the defenders' nerves.

But Turkish galleys were no match for a fleet of Italian ships that sailed into Constantinople with badly needed supplies of grain. Days later, though, another lone Venetian vessel sailed into the harbour with the devastating news that there would be no Western fleet to save Constantinople. Morale began to slide.

There were problems within the Ottoman camp, too, with many of the Sultan's ministers unimpressed by his arrogance. Mehmed wanted a grand assault during the night of the 28/29 May and agreed to withdraw if that failed. At first things did not go well, with the Christian defenders holding their own. But as the formidable Turkish Janissaries sharpened their scimitars for one last desperate attack, someone discovered that a small gate (Kerkaporta) had been left open between the Blachernae and the Theodosian Walls. The attackers wasted no time in rushing through. The Turks poured in and ran amok in the city, looting, killing and raping, until even Mehmed had had enough and by evening had imposed some order. Some 50,000 Byzantines were enslaved while 4000 were killed in the battle. The greatest siege of all time was over.

CHAPTER 3

The Early Modern Period

Even as increasingly professional armies and the use of artillery became more widespread from the sixteenth century, many forces remained wedded to the fighting principles of an earlier age.

This was the period when bigger wasn't always better. At Breitenfeld (1631), King Gustavus Adolphus of Sweden brought off a brilliant victory over the massive but inflexible Hapsburg Imperial army, using smaller, intermingled battalions of artillery and cavalry. Too slavish an adherence to the massed cavalry charge launched into enfilading artillery fire often resulted in disaster, as at Ramillies (1706), Poltava (1708) and Minden (1757).

Kings still led armies into battle during this period – notably Gustavus Adolphus, and the brilliant Frederick the Great of Prussia at Rossbach (1757) – but increasingly it was the age of the career soldier, such as John Churchill, Duke of Marlborough, whose finest moment came at Blenheim (1704).

◀ **Kahlenburg provided the Hapsburg Empire with a notable victory near Vienna over the Ottomans Turkish army, who were weakened by attempting to fight a battle two fronts.**

Brunkeberg 1471

DANO-SWEDISH WAR

SWEDISH VICTORY

The battle of Brunkeberg not only saved the nascent Swedish nation state from being submerged in a Danish-dominated Scandinavian Union but saw a modern, professional army defeated and routed by a committed and well-organized peasant militia.

KEY FACTS

WHO A royal army of 6000 Danish regulars and German mercenaries led by King Christian I Oldenburg of Denmark, opposed an army of 10,000 Swedish peasant levies led by Sten Sture.

WHAT Professional troops, including heavily armoured knights, were defeated by lightly armed but numerous peasant troops.

WHERE Brunkeberg, west of Stockholm, Sweden.

WHEN 10 October 1471

WHY As part of a long-standing conflict, the Swedes, seeking full independence, clashed with the Danish king, seeking to restore royal (Danish) control over Sweden by seizing Stockholm.

OUTCOME The Danes overconfidently charged the Swedes, who, using superior numbers and knowledge of the local terrain, encircled and defeated their foe.

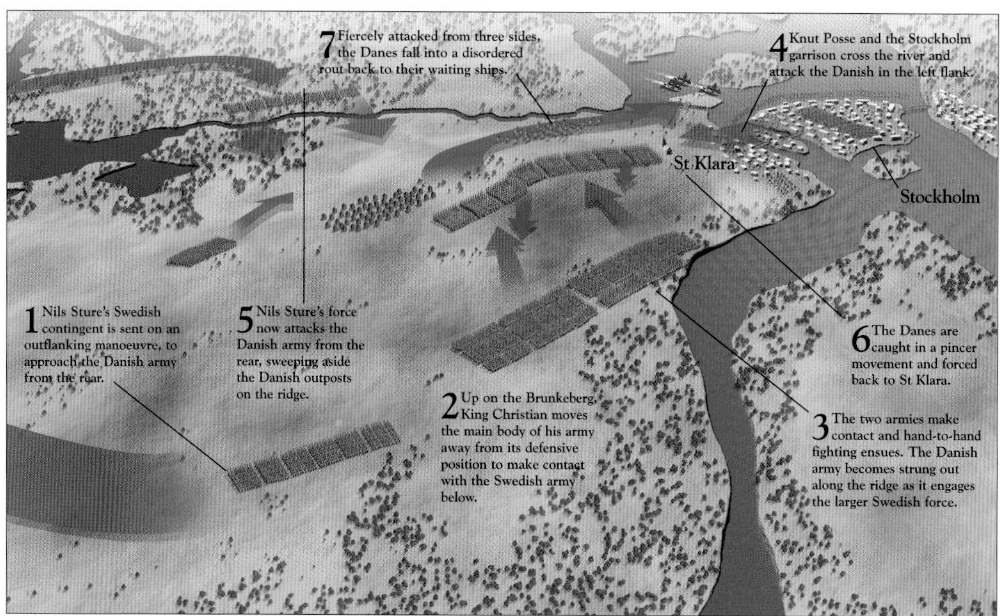
7 Fiercely attacked from three sides, the Danes fall into a disordered rout back to their waiting ships.
4 Knut Posse and the Stockholm garrison cross the river and attack the Danish in the left flank.
St Klara
Stockholm
1 Nils Sture's Swedish contingent is sent on an outflanking manoeuvre, to approach the Danish army from the rear.
5 Nils Sture's force now attacks the Danish army from the rear, sweeping aside the Danish outposts on the ridge.
6 The Danes are caught in a pincer movement and forced back to St Klara.
2 Up on the Brunkeberg, King Christian moves the main body of his army away from its defensive position to make contact with the Swedish army below.
3 The two armies make contact and hand-to-hand fighting ensues. The Danish army becomes strung out along the ridge as it engages the larger Swedish force.

It has never been a foregone conclusion that a powerful modern army will overcome a primitive smaller one. At Brunkeberg, superior local knowledge swung things decisively in favour of Sten Sture.

At Brunkeberg two vastly different armies met. The Danish had mounted knights and hardened professional mercenaries from Germany, who liked to fight regular battles in the open field. The core of the Swedes' army was made up of peasant levies armed with swords, pikes, axes, crossbows and longbows. The favourite tactic among the Swedish peasants was the ambush, and at Brunkeberg, Sten Sture would use that tactic to good effect.

Sture knew that on the high, wooded and boulder-strewn ridge of Brunkeberg, where the Danes had positioned themselves, knights in armour, artillery and regular infantry would not be in their element. While his army attacked the Danes from the front against the slopes leading up to their camp, Nils Sture took his fierce force of Darlecarlians around the ridge to attack the vulnerable rear of the Danish position from the east, overcoming them through a combination of surprise and sheer numbers. Here the training and superior arms of King Christian's king's troops were of little avail as wave after wave of snarling Swedes poured in on them from all sides. Christian lost half his men and Sten Sture had saved Sweden's fledgling statehood and independence.

LOCATION

Brunkeberg
Stockholm
SWEDEN
DENMARK

If Christian I had managed to capture Stockholm, at the centre of the kingdom of Sweden, he would have controlled the whole north-central Baltic.

TIMELINE

1500–1000BC	1000–500BC	500BC–0AD	0–500AD	500–1000AD	1000–1500AD	1500–2000ad

Diu 1509

PORTUGUESE–MAMLUK WAR

PORTUGUESE VICTORY

Dom Francisco de Almeida – 'the Great Dom Francisco' – was a Portuguese adventurer with a great many exploits to his name. When his son was killed in a battle with Egyptian ships, he was determined, as viceroy of Portuguese India, to gain revenge at Diu.

KEY FACTS

WHO Dom Francisco de Almeida leads the Portugese fleet, against the joint fleet and soldiers of the Sultan of Gujarat, the Mamluk Sultanate of Egypt, and the Zamorin of Kozhikode.

WHAT The Egyptians' land-based artillery was little match for the heavy cannon of Dom Francisco's fleet, which simply blocked the harbour and blasted them away.

WHERE Off the Indian coast, near Diu.

WHEN 3 February 1509

WHY The Portuguese Empire was gradually extending its control of the seas, but its ships were subject to frequent attack by the Egyptian fleet.

OUTCOME After victory, the Portuguese were able to consolidate by gaining control of several ports in the region, taking effective control of the Indian Ocean.

Dom Francesco de Almeida arrived at Diu with a high reputation as a military leader, but in reality this was a vengeance mission after the Egyptians had killed his son.

LOCATION

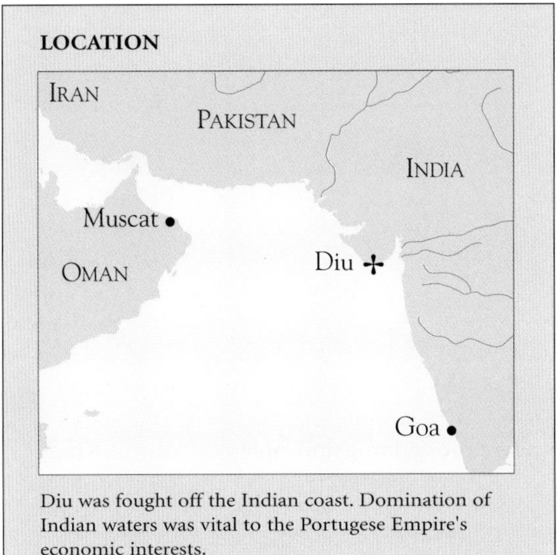
IRAN
PAKISTAN
INDIA
Muscat
OMAN
Diu
Goa

Diu was fought off the Indian coast. Domination of Indian waters was vital to the Portugese Empire's economic interests.

Establishing control of the Indian Ocean was central to Portuguese ambitions to build a naval empire, but it inevitably caused friction with other trading powers in the region. When an attack on Portuguese ships by an allied fleet led by the Mamluk Egyptians resulted in the death of the son of the Indian vicerory Dom Francisco de Almeida, retaliation was inevitable.

A pretext was not hard to find. Diu was a key port in the Indian Ocean, so Dom Francisco launched a gunship bombardment from outside the harbour. The Egyptians attempted to respond by use of artillery encamped within the city, but with little success. The small ships they attempted to launch were no more successful. They were too light to carry cannon, and for those that did manage to get close enough to engage in boarding and hand to hand combat, their sailors were outfought by well-armoured Portuguese equipped with arquebuses and grenades. The result was a rollicking Portuguese victory, to further stamp their emergence as the masters of oceans.

TIMELINE

1500–1000BC	1000–500BC	500BC–0AD	0–500AD	500–1000AD	1000–1500AD	1500–2000AD

Novara 1513

KEY FACTS

Who French general Louis de la Trémoille (1460–1525) against Milanese leader, Maximilian Sforza (1493–1530), and his mercenary Swiss soldiers.

What The French army of 10,000 were besieging Novara, a Milanese city, when attacked by a relief force largely composed of Swiss mercenaries employed by the Duke of Milan.

Where Near Novara, northern Italy.

When 6 June 1513

Why The French had been victorious at Ravenna the previous year. Nevertheless, the French under King Louis XII were driven out of the city of Milan the following month by the Holy League.

Outcome The French defeat by the Swiss pikemen forced Louis XII (1462–1515) to withdraw from Milan and Italy in general.

WAR OF THE LEAGUE OF CAMBRAI

MILANESE/CONFEDERACY VICTORY

By the end of the Middle Ages, the prosperity of Italian city-states led to the employment of large numbers of mercenaries, as these towns constantly fought against each other. Pike-armed mercenaries from Switzerland became especially valued in these conflicts, and the Swiss Way of War was born.

NAVERRA
Meyland
Bauia
Byöffen
CONTE ALEXAND.

Louis II de la Trémoille carefully set up his troop dispositions and then decided to sit back and rest ahead of a battle that he was confident would be on his terms. The Swiss, never conventional fighters, caught him off guard, however.

LOCATION

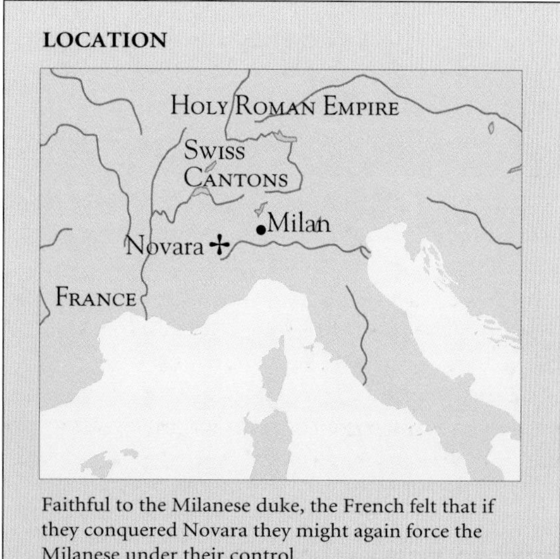
HOLY ROMAN EMPIRE
SWISS CANTONS
Milan
Novara
FRANCE

Faithful to the Milanese duke, the French felt that if they conquered Novara they might again force the Milanese under their control.

The French involvement in Italian affairs stretched back into the previous century when Charles VIII (1483–1498) had been invited by the Milanese to lay claim to the kingdom of Naples. Charles quickly lost whatever Italian prizes he had won, but his successor Louis XII (1498–1515) soon returned to the campaign trail south of the Alps, and enjoyed considerable success. However, despite victory at Ravenna in 1512, the French were chased out of Milan the following month, and in 1513 the French general Louis II de la Trémoille settled for the more modest goal of laying siege to the smaller town of Novara.

At this time Novara was held by mercenaries of the Swiss Confederation, and La Trémoille, keen to engineer battle conditions most favourable to his own army, marched out to a field about a couple of miles away from his siege lines, where he encamped for the night, expecting the Swiss to do battle with him the following morning. The Swiss, however, were unconventional fighters, who prided themselves on not doing the 'expected' thing and decided to surprise the French with a night attack, hoping

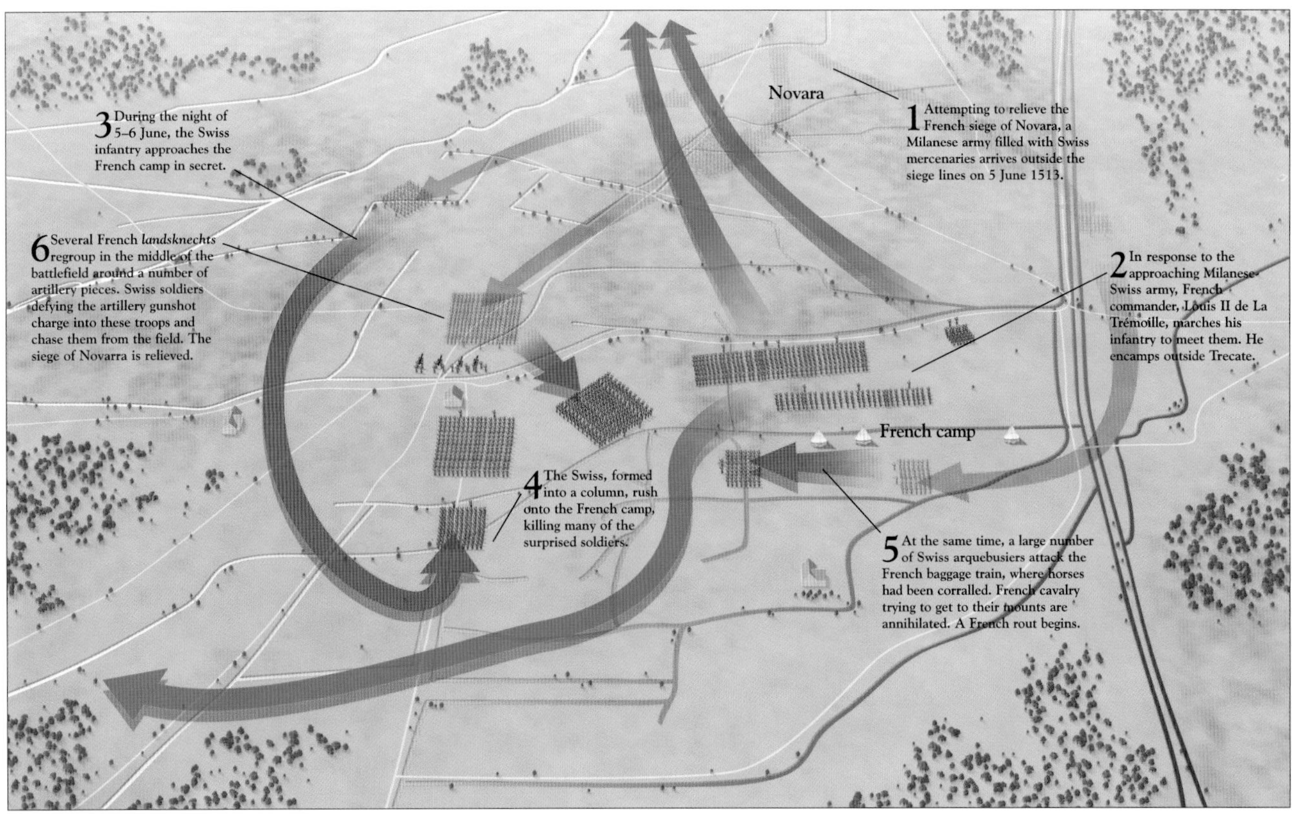
Novara
1 Attempting to relieve the French siege of Novara, a Milanese army filled with Swiss mercenaries arrives outside the siege lines on 5 June 1513.
2 In response to the approaching Milanese-Swiss army, French commander, Louis II de La Trémoille, marches his infantry to meet them. He encamps outside Trecate.
3 During the night of 5–6 June, the Swiss infantry approaches the French camp in secret.
4 The Swiss, formed into a column, rush onto the French camp, killing many of the surprised soldiers.
5 At the same time, a large number of Swiss arquebusiers attack the French baggage train, where horses had been corralled. French cavalry trying to get to their mounts are annihilated. A French rout begins.
6 Several French *landsknechts* regroup in the middle of the battlefield around a number of artillery pieces. Swiss soldiers defying the artillery gunshot charge into these troops and chase them from the field. The siege of Novarra is relieved.
French camp

The French Valois kings dreamt of taking control of large areas of Italy. Milan was one of its richest cities, but gaining control of Novara was crucial before their plans to take it could be further implemented.

to catch many of the French asleep or at least unprepared to fight a battle.

The Swiss Army was almost entirely made up of infantry soldiers, pikemen, polearmers and arquebusiers. Of the 8000–9000 troops, only about 200 were Milanese cavalry. These units marched quietly to the battlefield, trying not to arouse any French scouts or pickets. Arriving outside the camp undetected, the infantry rushed onto the sleeping Frenchmen. La Trémoille's army was entirely surprised. On the left, the Swiss were able to sweep around the camp and the town of Trecate, to fall onto the virtually unprotected French baggage train. The right column came out of the woods and set upon the French cavalry, who were confused and unable to mount any resistance. The arquebusiers in this contingent simply fired round after round of gunshot into the cavalry until they were killed or had fled. The remaining soldiers in this column performed their own flanking attack, joining their middle column in an assault on the French camp.

However, it was the large centre column of the Swiss that did the most damage to the French, whose tents were quickly overrun. Many French soldiers immediately fled in rout. But a large number of *landsknechts* (German mercenaries) regrouped in a defensive line near Trecate, positioning their artillery – which seems largely to have survived the initial attacks – in front of them. The Swiss, too, had regrouped into their columns and, defying the artillery barrage, charged. Contemporary reports, including one written by Florange de la Marck, the commander of the French *landsknechts,* claim that a volley of cannonballs mowed through the Swiss. It did not stop them and, before a second volley could be fired, they were upon the *landsknechts,* killing and wounding with a ruthlessness fitting their reputation. It was over quickly.

As for La Trémoille, it seems he had fled at the initial Swiss attack. Most historians have thus branded him a coward, although some have claimed that he was merely trying to set up a cavalry counter-attack. If so, it never materialized. In fact, most of his cavalry fled with him. Almost all of the French cavalry got away, with only about 40 losing their lives, while more than 5000 infantry lay dead or dying on the battlefield.

Pavia 1525

FRENCH WARS IN ITALY

SPANISH VICTORY

KEY FACTS

WHO The French army led by King Francis I (1515–1547) against the Spanish imperial army under the command of Charles de Lannoy.

WHAT The Imperialist forces caught those of the French in the huge hunting park of Mirabello just outside the city walls, and effectively crushed them.

WHERE Pavia, Lombardy, northern Italy.

WHEN 24 February 1525

WHY The French had lost their territories in Lombardy, and Francis I was determined to regain them, bringing him into conflict with the ascendant power of the Spanish Hapsburg ruler Charles V.

OUTCOME The French king was taken prisoner and forced to sign the Treaty of Madrid, surrendering his claims to Italian territories to Spain.

Francis I was one of the more successful French monarchs on the battlefield, and something of a chivalric throwback to previous centuries. But he met his match at Pavia in 1525, when a heavy defeat by the Imperial army of Spain led to his own capture and the near-wipeout of his army.

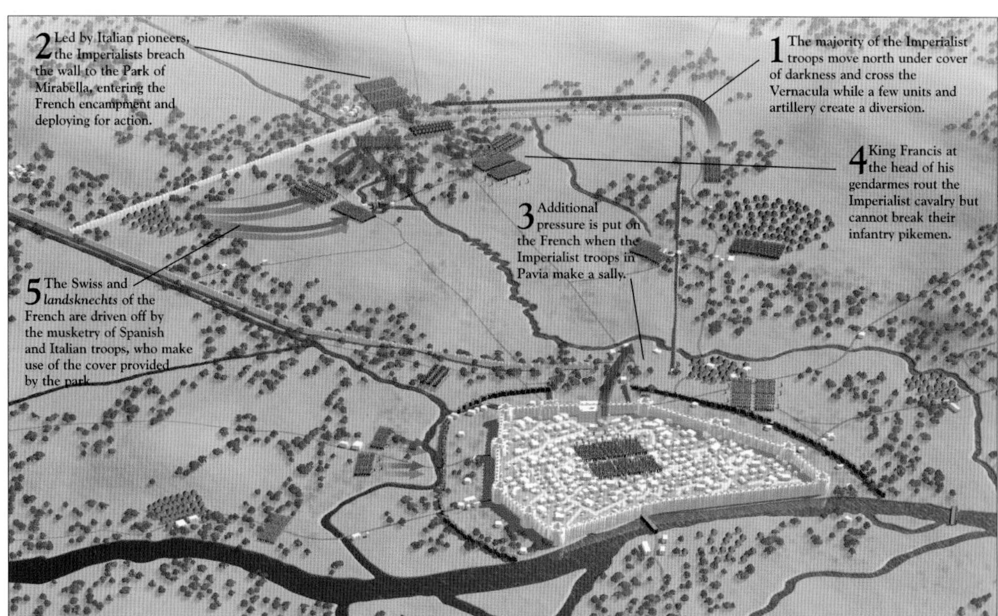

1 The majority of the Imperialist troops move north under cover of darkness and cross the Vernacula while a few units and artillery create a diversion.
2 Led by Italian pioneers, the Imperialists breach the wall to the Park of Mirabella, entering the French encampment and deploying for action.
3 Additional pressure is put on the French when the Imperialist troops in Pavia make a sally.
4 King Francis at the head of his gendarmes rout the Imperialist cavalry but cannot break their infantry pikemen.
5 The Swiss and *landsknechts* of the French are driven off by the musketry of Spanish and Italian troops, who make use of the cover provided by the park.

A ducal hunting park sounds like an unusually idyllic setting for a battle but, surrounded by woods ideal for concealing advancing artillery, it proved to be a trap for Francis I's army.

Francis I had crossed the Alps at the head of a huge army in the autumn of 1524, determined to revive his predecessors' dreams of conquering Milan and the kingdom of Naples. But when he laid siege to the Lombard city of Pavia, a Spanish Imperial army under the command of Charles de Lannoy launched an attack after breaching the wall of the ducal hunting park used by the French as their camp. As the Imperial forces entered the park and deployed into battle order, the garrison within the city also sallied forwards. Caught by surprise, Francis was forced to commit his forces in uncoordinated attacks on several fronts.

Using the concealment provided by nearby woods, the Imperialist forces were able to hide the location of much of their infantry, both pikemen and arquebusiers, which enabled them to be used to maximum effect while securing minimal casualties themselves. Francis I himself fought valiantly on until his horse was killed under him. Surrounded by arquebusiers, he was eventually taken prisoner. The captured king's letter home to his mother – 'All is lost save honour' – summed up the extent of the French debacle.

LOCATION

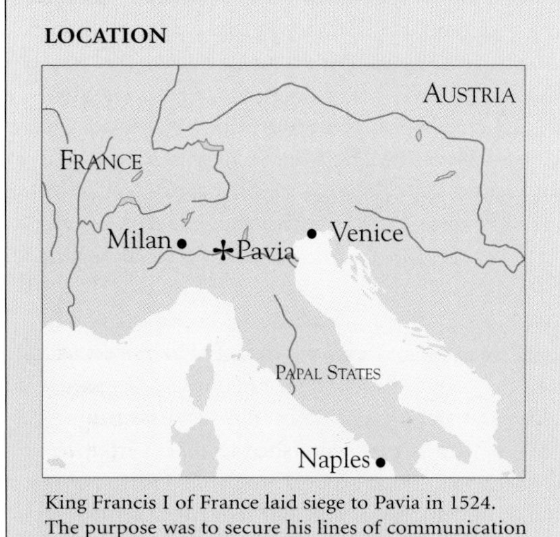

AUSTRIA
FRANCE
Milan
Pavia
Venice
PAPAL STATES
Naples

King Francis I of France laid siege to Pavia in 1524. The purpose was to secure his lines of communication before proceeding to attack Naples.

TIMELINE

1500–1000BC	1000–500BC	500BC–0AD	0–500AD	500–1000AD	1000–1500AD	1500–2000AD

Mohács 1526

KEY FACTS

WHO Ottoman army led by Suleiman the Magnificent, against Hungarian army under King Louis II.

WHAT Rather foolishly, the feeble army of the Hungarians attempted to confront the might of the Ottoman Turks and their formidable artillery, and were predictably blown away in the space of a couple of hours.

WHERE Mohács, near Budapest, Hungary.

WHEN 29 August 1526

WHY Suleiman the Magnificent saw Hungary as a stepping stone for a deeper Turkish advance into Europe.

OUTCOME After their defeat at Mohacs, the days of an independent Hungary were at an end as it was contested and carved up between the Ottomans and Austrians.

King Louis II of Hungary and Bohemia was only 20 at the Battle of Mohács – the same age, in fact, as Alexander the Great when he won his first great battle. Unfortunately, Louis was no Alexander, and his army was blown away by the Turks in a chilling demonstration of the use of artillery.

OTTOMAN CAMPAIGN

OTTOMAN VICTORY

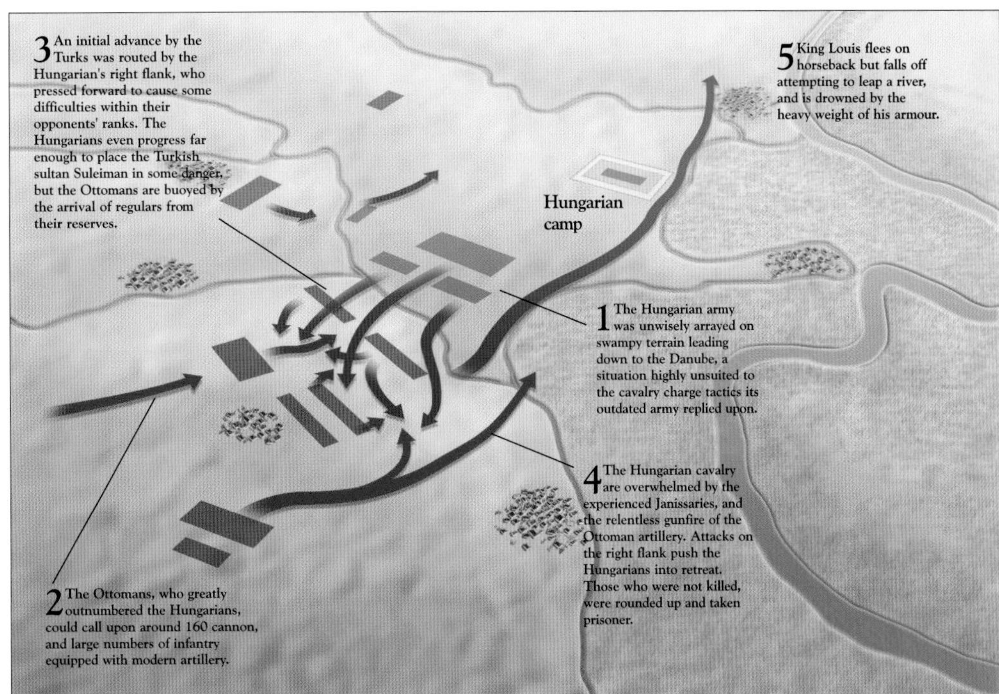
3 An initial advance by the Turks was routed by the Hungarian's right flank, who pressed forward to cause some difficulties within their opponents' ranks. The Hungarians even progress far enough to place the Turkish sultan Suleiman in some danger, but the Ottomans are buoyed by the arrival of regulars from their reserves.
5 King Louis flees on horseback but falls off attempting to leap a river, and is drowned by the heavy weight of his armour.
Hungarian camp
1 The Hungarian army was unwisely arrayed on swampy terrain leading down to the Danube, a situation highly unsuited to the cavalry charge tactics its outdated army replied upon.
4 The Hungarian cavalry are overwhelmed by the experienced Janissaries, and the relentless gunfire of the Ottoman artillery. Attacks on the right flank push the Hungarians into retreat. Those who were not killed, were rounded up and taken prisoner.
2 The Ottomans, who greatly outnumbered the Hungarians, could call upon around 160 cannon, and large numbers of infantry equipped with modern artillery.

The Turkish advance through the battered borders of Eastern Europe was a cause for real concern in the early sixteenth century. The defeat of the Hungarian army at Mohács, predictable as it seems, was a catastrophe.

LOCATION

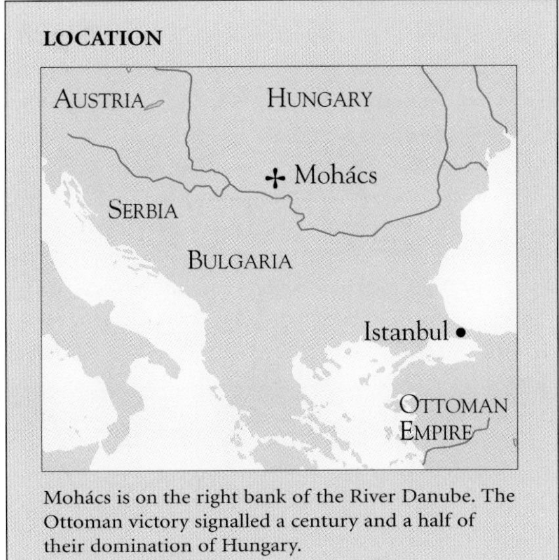
AUSTRIA
HUNGARY
Mohács
SERBIA
BULGARIA
Istanbul
OTTOMAN EMPIRE

Mohács is on the right bank of the River Danube. The Ottoman victory signalled a century and a half of their domination of Hungary.

By the 1520s, the Ottoman advance seemed unstoppable. Only Hungary seemed to stand in its way of moving into Europe. Louis II, king of Hungary and Bohemia, was married to a Hapsburg princess. This was a potentially dangerous alliance, so the sultan Suleiman the Magnificent decided on an invasion. Louis was determined to put up a fight, despite his army being ill-trained and out-dated, and reliant on heavily armoured cavalry, in contrast to the professional Turks, fully equipped with the latest artillery.

CRUSHING LOSS

Louis chose the terrain on which to fight. While an initial attack by his right flank went well, the Ottoman guns soon begun to roll out their fire. Under such a withering onslaught, the Hungarians were shot to pieces in little more than an hour. Louis himself escaped, but his own end was near. When he was thrown from his horse as it tried to leap a river, the weight of his out-moded armour dragged him down and he drowned.

TIMELINE

1500–1000BC	1000–500BC	500BC–0AD	0–500AD	500–1000AD	1000–1500AD	1500–2000AD

Pavia

PAVIA

Francis I of France and Henry VIII of England, in youth at least, had much in common. They were a kind of throwback to the medieval age of chivalry, symbolized by their alliance at the Field of the Cloth of Gold in 1520. Francis I had ambitions to build an empire, but he was old-fashioned in another sense, in that he relied upon cavalry and footsoldiers. At Pavia he was confronted by the future – an imperial army deploying arquebusiers to maximum effect. Francis fought valiantly, but defeat was certain, and his remorseful letter home to his mother – 'All is lost save honour' – has a poetic quality. But poets don't win wars, and Francis would gain more garlands as a patron of the arts.

Kawanakajima 1561

KEY FACTS

Who The *daimyo* army of Takada Shingen of the Kai province, against that of Uesugi Kenshin of the Echigo province.

What A battle in which the Uesugi had seemed to grab the initiative became a test of stamina – including a remarkable scuffle between the two commanders – in which the protagonists fought each other to a standstill.

Where Kawanakajima, in modern-day Nagano, Japan

When 10 September 1561

Why Uesugi Kenshin believed the Kai were planning an attack on his Echigo territories, and amassed a large army to forestall it.

Outcome Although there was no clear winner, with both sides suffering heavy casualties, the Uesugi force withdrew from the region.

This battle was one of five clashes on the plain of Kawanakajima between 1553 and 1564. The participants in these battles remained constant – the armies of Takeda Shingen and Uesugi Kenshin, rivals for power in the Age of the Warring States.

AGE OF THE WARRING STATES

NO CLEAR VICTORY

This battle dissolved into a series of stand-offs between cavalry, bowmen, arquebusiers and footsoldiers, with the two sides fighting each other to a standstill.

LOCATION

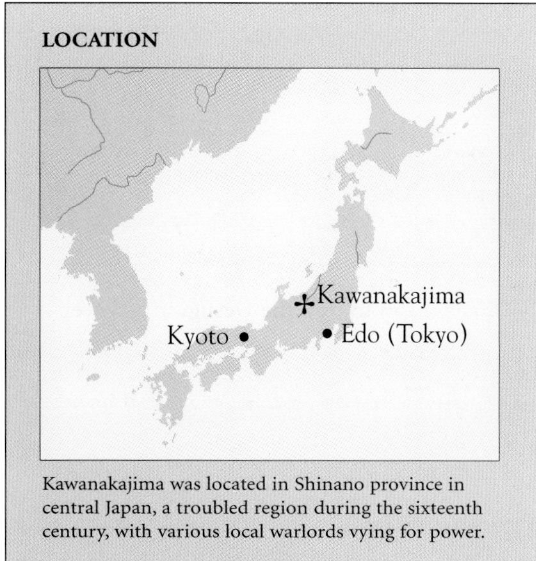
Kawanakajima
Kyoto
Edo (Tokyo)

Kawanakajima was located in Shinano province in central Japan, a troubled region during the sixteenth century, with various local warlords vying for power.

The battleground sits in northern Shinano province, near the city of Nagano. Shinano separated the provinces of the warring parties – Uesugi's Echigo province in the north and Takeda's Kai province in the south-east. In September 1561, Uesugi began a large deployment of forces towards the plain of Kawanakajima, based on the expectation that Takeda was building up to a major invasion of Echigo itself. Takeda had marched out from Kai with an army of around 16,000 warriors on 27 September, reaching Kawanakajima in about six days. At first, he deployed the bulk of his army on the Chausuyama heights to the west of the plain, and effectively blocked the return path for the Uesugi army.

Then, on 8 October, Takeda took his force down from the Chausuyama, crossed the Chikumagawa River that ran along the western portion of the plain, and occupied the fortress in the south-eastern corner, known as Kaizu. This movement was conducted under the noses of the Uesugi, who had their forces deployed on the wooded Saijosan high ground.

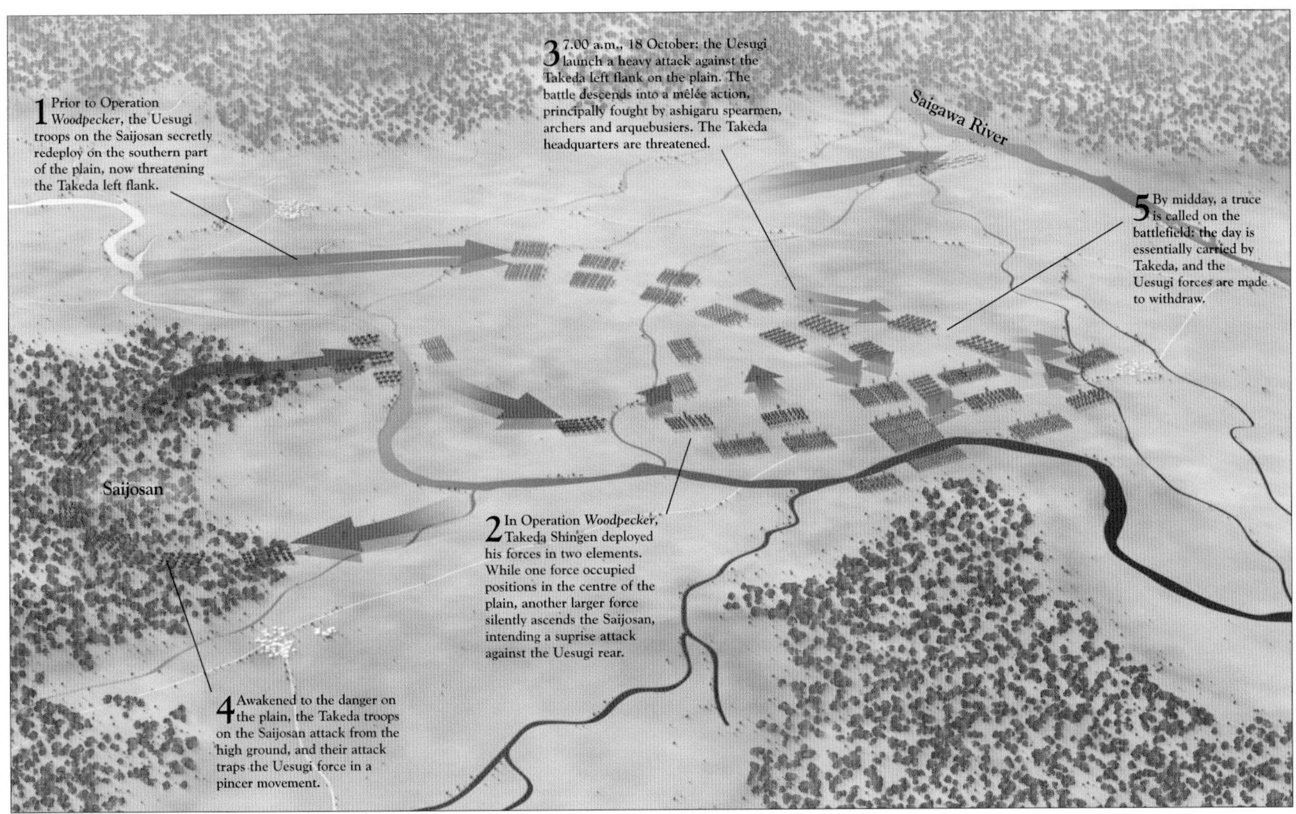
1 Prior to Operation Woodpecker, the Uesugi troops on the Saijosan secretly redeploy on the southern part of the plain, now threatening the Takeda left flank.
3 7.00 a.m., 18 October: the Uesugi launch a heavy attack against the Takeda left flank on the plain. The battle descends into a mêlée action, principally fought by ashigaru spearmen, archers and arquebusiers. The Takeda headquarters are threatened.
Saigawa River
5 By midday, a truce is called on the battlefield: the day is essentially carried by Takeda, and the Uesugi forces are made to withdraw.
Saijosan
2 In Operation Woodpecker, Takeda Shingen deployed his forces in two elements. While one force occupied positions in the centre of the plain, another larger force silently ascends the Saijosan, intending a suprise attack against the Uesugi rear.
4 Awakened to the danger on the plain, the Takeda troops on the Saijosan attack from the high ground, and their attack traps the Uesugi force in a pincer movement.

The Uesgi attempted to take the initiative by moving down onto the plain at night, smothering the noise of their horses' hooves with cloth. It deceived their opponents, but achieved no battle-swinging advantage.

It would surely only be a matter of time before the Uesugi began their assault. In a pre-emptive move, Takeda launched Operation *Woodpecker*. The plan ran as follows. Takeda would take out 8000 men from Kaizu during the night, moving them silently across the Chikumagawa to the centre of the plain. At the same time, a force of 12,000 soldiers was to climb the Saijosan and, when the time was right, attack the Uesugi troops there from the rear. Theoretically, the Saijosan assault would force the Uesugi men down from the mountain on to the plain, where they would be driven onto a crushing flank attack.

Operation *Woodpecker* was launched at midnight on 18 October, although by this time there had already been significant movement in the Uesugi camp. At 10.00pm on 17 October, Uesugi had actually taken his troops down from the Saijosan in secret (even the horses' hooves were wrapped in cloth to dampen the noise), having been alerted by his scouts to the intended movements out from Kaizu. When Takeda rose the following morning, he found the Uesugi forces deployed and waiting for him, ready to do battle.

Takeda's right flank was subjected to a fast and violent assault from the Uesugi mounted samurai at around 7.00am, while arquebusiers blasted out their volleys of gunshot. The Uesugi operated a winding wheel attack system, in which fresh troops were rotated into the attack as battle-tired troops moved out, so maintaining the momentum of the assault. The attack was bearing fruit, and at around 9.00am the Uesugi vanguard even closed on Takeda's headquarters, resulting in an individual combat between the two principal commanders. Uesugi received two injuries in the battle, but his bodyguard force managed to drive away Takeda and his retainers. Yet despite fearful losses, the Takeda defence held out. Furthermore, by this point the Operation *Woodpecker* detachment on the Saijosan had raced down from the mountainside and clashed with the Uesugi rearguard.

Now the Takeda plan to trap the Uesugi in a pincer movement was bearing fruit. Yet such were the level of casualties that at midday a truce was called. The Uesugi force subsequently withdrew from the battlefield, with both sides having suffered 60–70 per cent casualties.

Siege of Malta 1565

KEY FACTS

WHO Knights Hospitallers led by Chevalier Jean de Vallette against a siege army of the Ottoman Empire, led by Mustafa Pasha.

WHAT The Ottomans launched a concerted effort to take the harbour fort of St Elmo, but met with spirited resistance. By the time they had stormed the fortifications, their supplies were running low, and they had lost many soldiers.

WHERE Malta.

WHEN 18 May–11 September 1565

WHY The Ottomans regarded Christian-held Malta as an obstacle to their shipping and lines of communication in the Mediterranean.

OUTCOME The Ottomans remained major players in the Mediterranean, but the failure to take Malta halted efforts to make further inroads into Europe.

How could a little island hope to hold out against the rampant Ottoman Empire? In 1565, the doughty Knights Hospitallers gave an object lesson in resistance that heartened military underdogs for centuries afterwards.

OTTOMAN–HABSBURG WARS

KNIGHTS HOSPITALLERS VICTORY

The Ottomans appeared to hold all the aces at Malta, but Mustafa Pasha was an arrogant commander, not much liked by his generals. His impatience would weaken his army's resolve and the siege would end in failure.

LOCATION

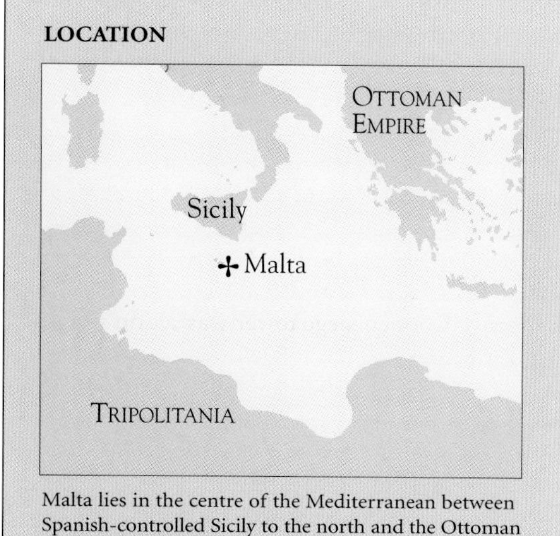
OTTOMAN EMPIRE
Sicily
Malta
TRIPOLITANIA

Malta lies in the centre of the Mediterranean between Spanish-controlled Sicily to the north and the Ottoman province of Tripolitania (Libya) to the south.

As the Ottoman Empire swept through the Balkans and Hungary and menaced the Mediterranean, the Order of the Hospitaller Knights of St John held out on the rocky island of Malta, where they had been based since the fall of Rhodes in 1522 to the Turks. The order had proved a persistent and serious threat to Muslim shipping and lines of communication in the Mediterranean, and Sultan Suleiman 'the Magnificent' was determined to crush it by invading and conquering Malta. As a strategic base in Turkish hands, the island, located south of Sicily and Naples, would be ideally suited for invading Italy and creating trouble for the infidels in the Sultan's Holy War against Christian Europe.

GRAND MASTER

But the Knights and the people of Malta had an indefatigable leader in the Grand Master of the Order, Chevalier Jean Parisot de la Vallette. As a young man, La Vallette had taken part in the siege of Rhodes and was determined to die rather than surrender Malta to an enemy he feared and loathed in equal measure.

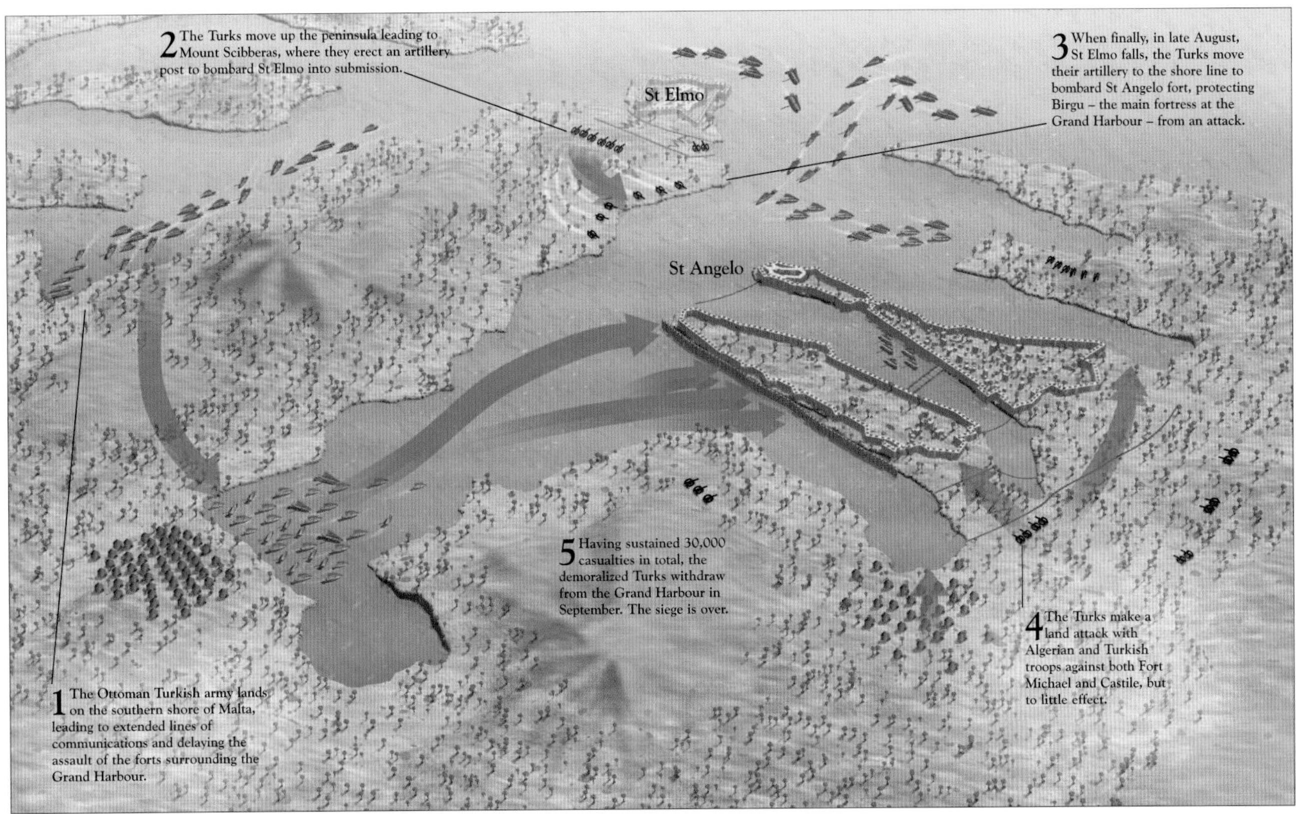
2 The Turks move up the peninsula leading to Mount Scibberas, where they erect an artillery post to bombard St Elmo into submission.
St Elmo
3 When finally, in late August, St Elmo falls, the Turks move their artillery to the shore line to bombard St Angelo fort, protecting Birgu – the main fortress at the Grand Harbour – from an attack.
St Angelo
5 Having sustained 30,000 casualties in total, the demoralized Turks withdraw from the Grand Harbour in September. The siege is over.
4 The Turks make a land attack with Algerian and Turkish troops against both Fort Michael and Castile, but to little effect.
1 The Ottoman Turkish army lands on the southern shore of Malta, leading to extended lines of communications and delaying the assault of the forts surrounding the Grand Harbour.

The fortress of St Elmo was subject to relentless pounding by Ottoman cannon during the siege, but as the weeks passed and Ottoman supplies grew low, their efforts to break in became more frantic.

When the Ottomans, under the leadership of Mustafa Pasha, landed on the island, they began by attacking the fortress of St Elmo, which protected the harbour, expecting to take it in a matter of days. The fortress's perceived weakness was its low position, making it vulnerable to artillery fire. The Turks constructed a parapet on the heights above St Elmo and placed two 60-pounders, ten 80-pounders and a single massive mortar that fired 73kg (160lb) of solid shot inside this battery. They used marble, iron and stone cannon balls to bombard the fort, but their fire made little impression.

Under relentless fire, senior officers urged the Grand Master to evacuate St Elmo, but this only made La Vallette more determined to hold the fortress at all costs. He sacked fainthearted Knights, sent reinforcements and admonished the fort's commandant Luigi Broglia to fight to the death. La Vallette knew that every day that St Elmo held out meant more time for the main forts – and more time for relief to arrive.

Mustafa Pasha, increasingly frantic as the weeks passed, decided to send in waves of *Iayalars*, or volunteers, armed with scimitars. Encouraged by Mullahs shouting verses out of the Koran, and supported by the fire of 4000 musketeers, the *Iayalars* threw themselves at the walls only to be thrown back by the defenders' fire and weapons. The attack left 150 defenders dead, but also more than a thousand *Iayalars*.

By the time the Turks finally broke through a few days later, it had taken nearly one-quarter of their number – 8000 men – to take this, the smallest and weakest of the Maltese forts. When they moved to take the larger fortresses of Birgu and Senglea, they faced similar resistance. A Turkish mine breached the walls of Birgu, and the Turks rushed through, only to face Knights and Maltese defenders led by La Vallette in person. La Vallette was wounded in the leg, but had it dressed only when the city wall was safely back in Christian hands.

Next, a massive wooden siege tower was set on fire by the Knights using their arsenal of inflammables, and after almost three months, the Turks were increasingly demoralized. By the time a small Spanish relief force had arrived, the last Turks had departed, never to return.

Lepanto 1571

KEY FACTS

WHO Don Juan (John) of Austria, at the command of the Holy League fleet, against the Turkish grand admiral Ali Pasha, leading the main Ottoman fleet.

WHAT Against a Turkish fleet still largely committed to fighting sea battles by the old tactic of ramming and boarding, the greater cannon fire that the Christians brought to the fray was decisive.

WHERE Lepanto, Gulf of Patras, off western Greece coast.

WHEN 7 October 1571

WHY The pope had urged a crusade to drive off the advancing Ottoman Turks, who had conquered Cyprus and threatened to take control of the Mediterranean.

OUTCOME Despite their fleet being pounded to destruction, the Ottomans rebuilt fast and remained a major Mediterranean power.

The five-hour battle at Lepanto was the largest sea battle ever fought in the Mediterranean. And in the deployment by the Venetians of the massive galleas, a hybrid ship somewhere between a galley and a galleon, the age of the cannon broadside was born.

OTTOMAN–HABSBURG WARS

HOLY LEAGUE VICTORY

By the time of Lepanto, the Turks were still deploying old-style ramming and boarding tactics, and their vessels proved vulnerable against the guns of the Christian allies.

LOCATION

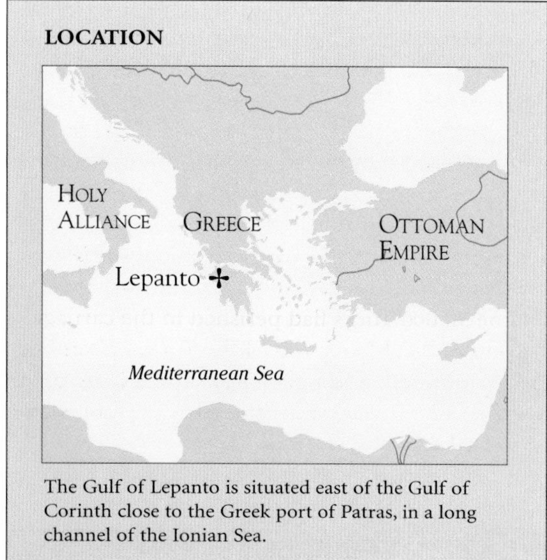
HOLY ALLIANCE
GREECE
OTTOMAN EMPIRE
Lepanto
Mediterranean Sea

The Gulf of Lepanto is situated east of the Gulf of Corinth close to the Greek port of Patras, in a long channel of the Ionian Sea.

By the middle of the sixteenth century, the Ottomans were threatening to take control in the waters of the western Mediterranean. In 1571, the Venetians were in danger of losing the vital port and outpost of Cyprus when Pope Pius V proclaimed a crusade against the Turks. There was not much time to be lost in mobilizing the Christian response – a powerful Turkish fleet was poised to enter the Adriatic Sea.

The fleet the Venetians dispatched to Lepanto would be the largest in the Republic's history, and the best equipped, able to call upon big new ships known as galleasses, specially built to hold the largest cannon available from the Republic's stockpiles. These ships could fire some 147kg (325lb) of shot in every salvo – equivalent to the cannon firepower of five standard galleys of the time. The galleass was, quite literally, a castle on the sea, and it required four smaller vessels to tow them forward. Alongside them was a new and formidable Spanish fleet, under the command of Emperor Philip of Spain's bastard brother, Don Juan of Austria.

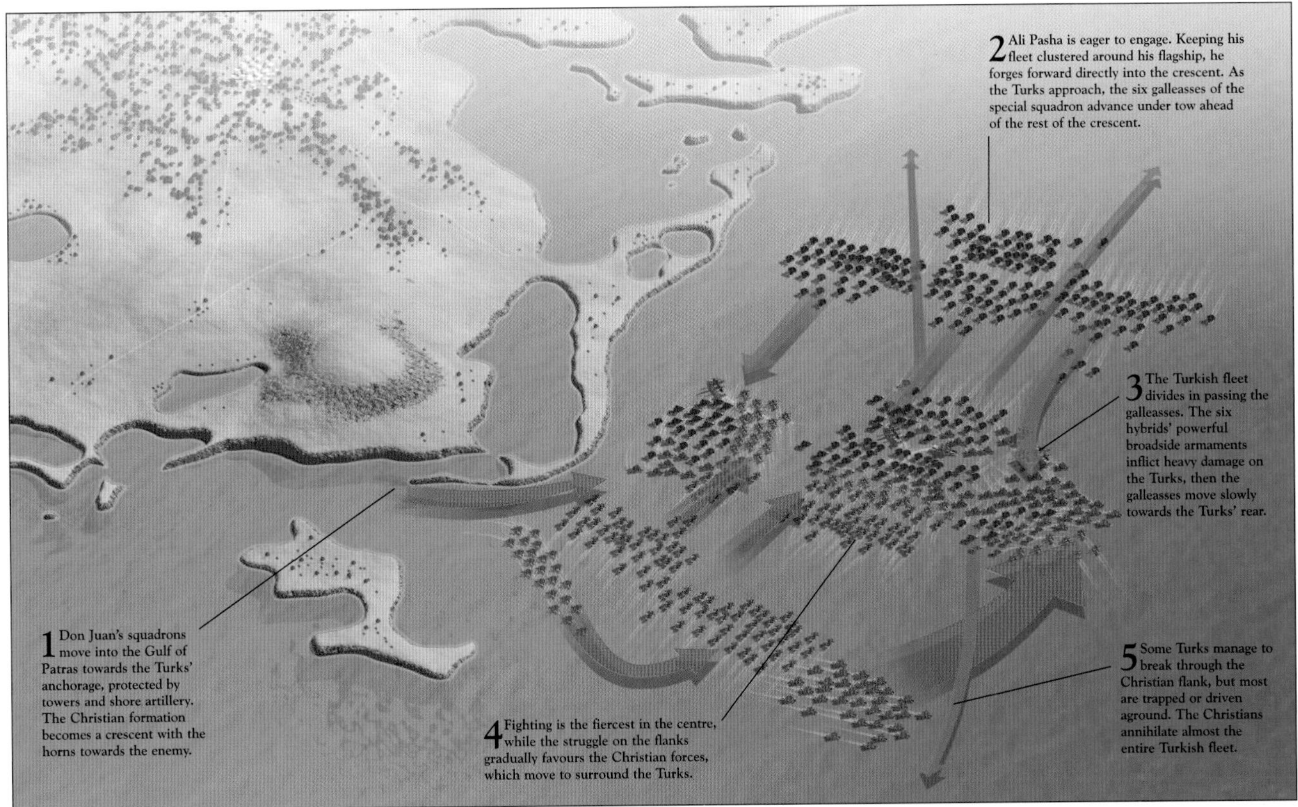
2 Ali Pasha is eager to engage. Keeping his fleet clustered around his flagship, he forges forward directly into the crescent. As the Turks approach, the six galleasses of the special squadron advance under tow ahead of the rest of the crescent.
3 The Turkish fleet divides in passing the galleasses. The six hybrids' powerful broadside armaments inflict heavy damage on the Turks, then the galleasses move slowly towards the Turks' rear.
1 Don Juan's squadrons move into the Gulf of Patras towards the Turks' anchorage, protected by towers and shore artillery. The Christian formation becomes a crescent with the horns towards the enemy.
4 Fighting is the fiercest in the centre, while the struggle on the flanks gradually favours the Christian forces, which move to surround the Turks.
5 Some Turks manage to break through the Christian flank, but most are trapped or driven aground. The Christians annihilate almost the entire Turkish fleet.

Not only did the Christian allies have greater artillery power on their ships, but they were also able to deploy guns on the shores. The Turkish fleet was effectively annihilated by the combined firepower.

As Ali Pasha, the Turkish grand admiral, methodically collected his forces in the Gulf of Patras on the western coast of Greece, the Christian fleet moved slowly eastwards and the two adversaries met off the Greek coast around Lepanto.

Ali Pasha noted the six large vessels – the galleasses – set out as the vanguard of the Christian line and chose to bypass them by ordering his three squadrons to divide and sail around them without engaging. But long-range fire from the broadsides of the galleasses added to the disorder of the Turkish squadrons as they passed. The situation became worse as the Christians moved to engage before the Turkish fleet could reform, and any hope of avoiding the terrible firepower of the galleasses proved vain as the lumbering monsters reversed direction and fell upon the Turkish rear.

The Turkish efforts to reform were not assisted by the clouds of smoke resulting from the cannon of both sides and from the arquebuses with which the crewmen on the Spanish fleet were armed. The Turks were accurate and proficient archers, but matchlocks provided a counter to their arrows. Light artillery pieces on swivels – called *versos*, or murderers – poured fire onto the Turkish decks.

The galleasses' great height of their wooden sides rendered them practically immune to Turkish efforts to board them. The goal of both fleets was to envelop the other, and fierce fighting raged on the flanks of each line. Gunpowder and thick armour began to make a difference in the Christians' favour. As the Turkish marines perished, another calamity befell their ships. The Christian slaves on the benches of the Turkish fleet began availing themselves of weapons dropped in the carnage and attacked their former masters. While the ships were so embroiled, they lost all propulsion and hope of manoeuvre or escape.

When the day ended, 7700 Christians and 12 ships had sunk beneath the reddened waters of the gulf. By contrast, some 30,000 Turks had perished in the carnage and 170 galleys and lighter vessels of the Turkish fleet had been captured. That the galleasses had played a huge part, no one doubted. The West's faith in technology had been amply vindicated at Lepanto.

Nagashino 1575

The Battle of Nagashino was a clash of old and new technologies. The traditional Japanese 'way of the sword' confronted the reality of early firearms, with decisive results that were to change the way battles were fought in Japan.

SENGOKU PERIOD WARS

ODA NOBUNAGA'S VICTORY

KEY FACTS

WHO The daimyo (feudal lord) Takeda Katsuyori (1546–82) fought the combined forces of Oda Nobunaga (1534–82) and Tokugawa Ieyasu (1543–1616).

WHAT Takeda besieged Nagashino Castle, to which Oda and Tokugawa sent a massive relief army that was heavily armed with arquebus gunners.

WHERE The area around Nagashino Castle, in Totomi Province, central Japan.

WHEN 28 June 1575

WHY Takeda had wider territorial ambitions for central Japan and was aiming to defeat the Tokugawa armies and advance against Kyoto.

OUTCOME An eight-hour battle saw the almost complete destruction of Takeda's army, with devastating casualties caused by volley fire from enemy arquebusiers.

Traditional samurai fighting tactics still had a part to play at Nagashino, but by this era artillery and musketry were becoming the decisive factors in warfare.

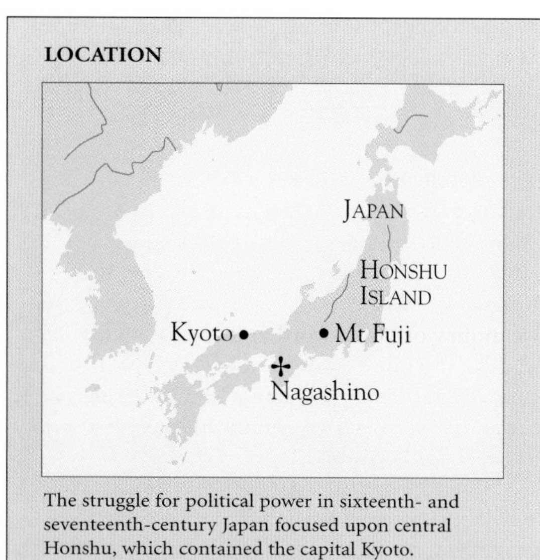
LOCATION
JAPAN
HONSHU ISLAND
Kyoto
Mt Fuji
Nagashino

The struggle for political power in sixteenth- and seventeenth-century Japan focused upon central Honshu, which contained the capital Kyoto.

The Battle of Nagashino took place on a soggy plain some 5km (3.1 miles) from the castle, behind the banks of the Rengogawa River. A three-tiered palisade of wooden stakes just high enough to prevent a horse jumping over was also built a short distance behind the river. Along with the wet ground, this would hamper a cavalry charge, and it also provided cover for Oda Nobunaga's arquebusiers.

Both sides at the Battle of Nagashino used firearms, but it was Oda, drawing on his brutal past experience, who best understood the tactical applications of such weapons. The arquebus, a simple muzzle-lock loaded firearm, had been introduced into Japan from Portugal in 1543. However, while it was light enough to fire from the shoulder, it had nothing in the way of sights, and accuracy was poor: its range was limited to a few hundred metres, misfires were frequent and reloading was laborious. What Oda understood, however, was its great value as a weapon when used in volley. Furthermore, handling an arquebus required a fraction

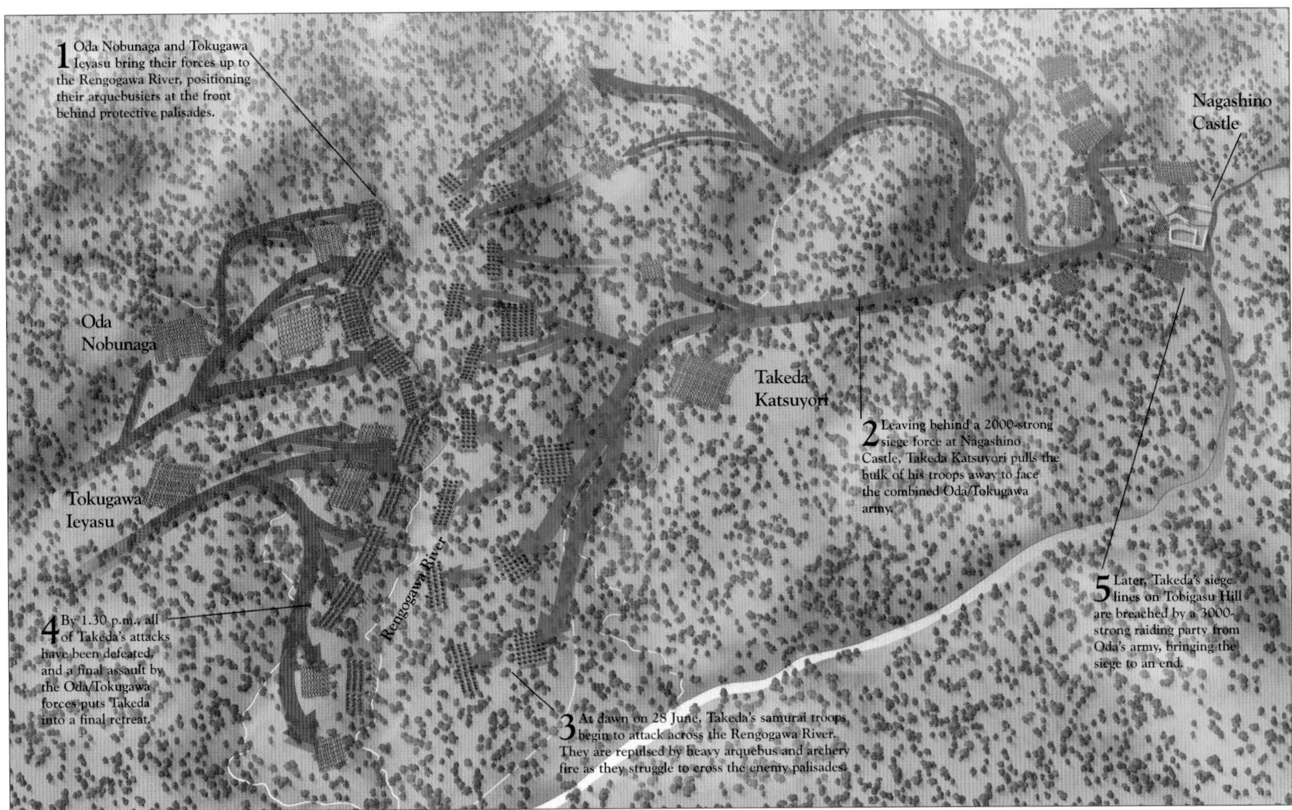
1 Oda Nobunaga and Tokugawa Ieyasu bring their forces up to the Rengogawa River, positioning their arquebusiers at the front behind protective palisades.
Nagashino Castle
Oda Nobunaga
Takeda Katsuyori
2 Leaving behind a 2000-strong siege force at Nagashino Castle, Takeda Katsuyori pulls the bulk of his troops away to face the combined Oda/Tokugawa army.
Tokugawa Ieyasu
Rengogawa River
4 By 1.30 p.m., all of Takeda's attacks have been defeated, and a final assault by the Oda/Tokugawa forces puts Takeda into a final retreat.
5 Later, Takeda's siege lines on Tobigasu Hill are breached by a 3000-strong raiding party from Oda's army, bringing the siege to an end.
3 At dawn on 28 June, Takeda's samurai troops begin to attack across the Rengogawa River. They are repulsed by heavy arquebus and archery fire as they struggle to cross the enemy palisades.

The Battle of Nagashino was fought in wet conditions. Takeda Katsuyori banked on this rendering his opponents' gunpowder ineffective, but in the event it was his old-fashioned cavalry who were disadvantaged by having to charge through mud.

of the skill demanded of a bowman, enabling an army to rapidly increase its firepower.

VOLLEY TACTICS

Oda took 3000 arquebusiers with him to the Nagashino battlefield, and trained them in the application of disciplined volley tactics. During the lulls in reloading, archers would take over to maintain a constant rain of direct fire on the enemy. Takeda also had arquebus-armed troops, but at the time of Nagashino he still relied on cavalry dash. This tactical decision proved to be his ondoing.

When Oda's army arrived on the plain, Takeda, instead of maintaining a defensive position by the castle, opted for military glory by charging across open ground to meet him. Wiser commanders had counselled against this, fearing it would leave them vulnerable to sustaining heavy casualties from ball and arrow. But Takeda opted for a full-frontal attack on Oda's dispositions because he'd surmised that the enemy arquebuses would prove useless because of wet weather. In fact, the arquebusiers' powder had been kept dry, and the principal effect of the rain was to make the terrain even more ill-suited to a fast cavalry charge.

As the horsemen emerged up the far bank, a withering fusillade of fire rippled out from Oda's matchlockmen, arranged behind the palisade in three ranks, each rank firing in turn. Some 9000 rounds were fired in the first three rapid volleys alone, and cavalrymen and horses dropped in horrifying numbers as shot hit their targets from around 50m (55 yards).

CHANGING FACE OF BATTLE

Much bloody hand-to-hand combat, using the traditional samurai sword and spear, did take place, and the fact that the battle raged for eight hours before Takeda finally withdrew his men from the fray suggests that the weaponry of bow, sword and spear still played a major part. Nevertheless, the arquebus had been central to Oda's conclusive victory, causing a high level of casualties and dealing a crushing blow to a force relying on traditional methods of warfare.

Gravelines 1588

KEY FACTS

Who A Spanish fleet of 22 galleons and 108 armed merchant vessels under the Duke of Medina Sidonia, opposed by an English fleet comprised of 35 galleons and 163 other vessels and commanded by the Lord High Admiral, Charles Howard.

What The Spanish intended to invade England in conjunction with a Dutch-based army, who were to be transported by the Armada from the Spanish Netherlands.

Where A series of running engagements in the English Channel, with a decisive battle off Gravelines near the Belgian coast.

When July and August 1588

Why Ongoing conflict between Protestant England and Catholic Spain, largely due to religious differences.

Outcome The Spanish fleet was defeated off Gravelines and was forced to sail north around Britain to return home.

Long-standing tension between Protestant England and Catholic Spain turned into open war in 1585. In July 1588, the Spanish fleet entered the English Channel, intending to invade the British Isles.

ANGLO-SPANISH WAR

ENGLISH VICTORY

The Spanish galleons looked magnificent – with high 'castles' like siege towers at the stern and the grandeur of floating fortresses. But the sleeker English ships were built for carrying cannon, and were more suited to battle on the open sea.

LOCATION

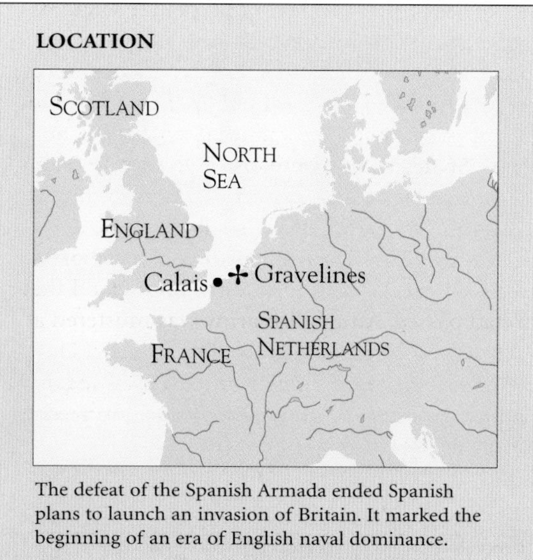
SCOTLAND
NORTH SEA
ENGLAND
Calais
Gravelines
SPANISH NETHERLANDS
FRANCE

The defeat of the Spanish Armada ended Spanish plans to launch an invasion of Britain. It marked the beginning of an era of English naval dominance.

The Spanish Armada sailed on England in May 1588. By July, it was sailing off the Cornish coast, but for some time afterwards nothing more than a series of indecisive engagements occurred. However, when Duke Medina Sidonia was unable to anchor the fleet in the sheltered waters of the Isle of Wight due to harrying by several English ships, he sailed across the Channel to the region of northern France, anchoring off Dunkirk. This meant his ships were unprotected by a harbour, and Admiral Lord Howard, commanding the English, ordered a fireship attack – vessels carrying barrels of gunpowder and loaded with a highly combustible mix of tar and pitch were sent downwind against the Spanish force.

This threw the Spanish fleet into disarray. Although part of Spain's fleet remained in formation, large numbers of vessels were forced to cut their cables, causing great confusion. It also meant the Armada was being driven from its anchorage into open waters, where the lighter, narrower, faster English ships – designed like mobile artillery platforms, in contrast to the old-fashioned

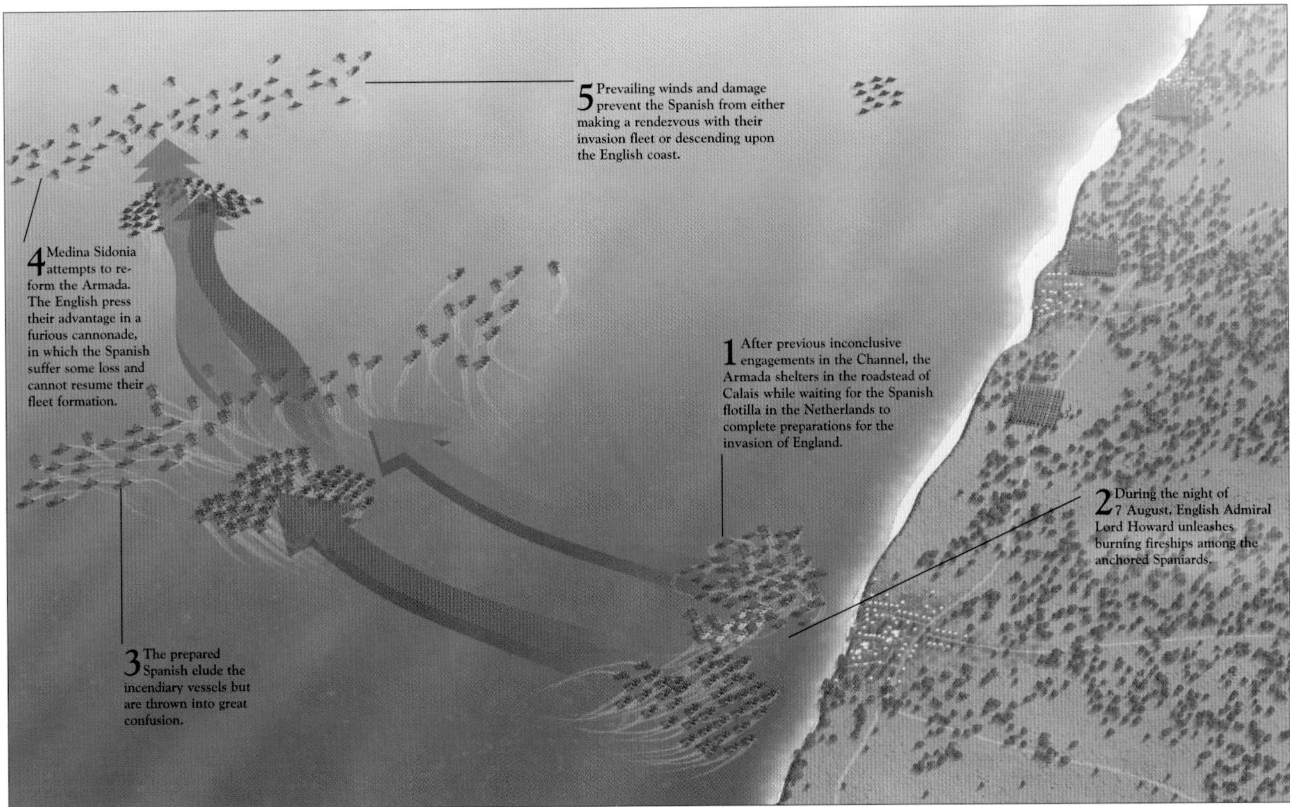
5 Prevailing winds and damage prevent the Spanish from either making a rendezvous with their invasion fleet or descending upon the English coast.
4 Medina Sidonia attempts to re-form the Armada. The English press their advantage in a furious cannonade, in which the Spanish suffer some loss and cannot resume their fleet formation.
1 After previous inconclusive engagements in the Channel, the Armada shelters in the roadstead of Calais while waiting for the Spanish flotilla in the Netherlands to complete preparations for the invasion of England.
2 During the night of 7 August, English Admiral Lord Howard unleashes burning fireships among the anchored Spaniards.
3 The prepared Spanish elude the incendiary vessels but are thrown into great confusion.

The Spanish fleet faced adverse weather conditions, a furious cannonade and the terrifying scenario of incendiary vessels. These factors combined to give victory to the English at Gravelines.

Spanish warships, with their high 'castles' fore and aft like floating siege towers – would have an advantage. As the Armada struggled to regain its formation, it was blown eastwards by the winds. Off Gravelines, it was forced to halt as the Dutch coast became extremely hazardous at this point. Now the English had a chance to fight a decisive action, getting in close to fire where previous long-range bombardment had been ineffective.

To have a chance of penetrating the Spanish ships' thick hulls, the English had to fire from within a range of 100m (109yd), but this was risky since the Spanish wanted to draw their enemies in close in order to grapple and board. However, by maintaining an advantageous windward position, and by means of good seamanship, the English were able to close in, pound the Spanish and then retire to a safe distance.

Spanish gunnery was largely ineffective for several reasons. Their guns were made of bronze and fired more slowly than the English iron guns, and their crews were not well trained. The Spanish were still geared to the old idea of ships primarily being used to carry large contingents of soldiers. Cannonfire would be used sparingly, to force their opponent on the defensive, preparing the way for the anticipated grappling and boarding battle. Against some foes, this was effective, but the English ships were too manoeuvrable to be caught this way. In addition to its tactical disadvantages, the Spaniards' leeward position meant that penetrating hits often occurred below the waterline when the vessel was not heeling over towards the wind, and their guns were pointing at the sky much of the time for the same reason.

Estimates of the losses at Gravelines vary, though no more than 11 Spanish ships were lost in the battle. Many more were damaged, and the Armada was driven into the North Sea, where the English, though almost out of ammunition, pursued them as far as the Firth of Forth in Scotland. At the time, it was not clear in England that the threat had passed. An English army was mustered at Tilbury in case of an invasion up the Thames, and Queen Elizabeth I herself visited this army to deliver an inspiring speech. In the event, the encouragement was not needed. The threat of invasion had been averted.

Gravelines

GRAVELINES

The sight of the Spanish Armada would have been enough to send the fleet of most nations of the sixteenth century scuttling for port. Their ships were built like floating fortresses. They put to sea with the full wind of an empire in their sails. But the English ships were sleeker affairs, gunboats of a later prototype and easier to handle. 'God blew and they were scattered' read the inscriptions on commemorative medals struck to mark the way English ships had blasted their way to victory at Gravelines. The shattered remnants of the Spanish fleet were left to limp back home.

Sacheon 1592

IMJIN WAR

KOREAN VICTORY

By neglecting the development of an effective navy, Japan was courting disaster in its invasion of Korea in 1592. At Sacheon the Korean navy, armed with groundbreaking 'turtle ships', undermined the entire Japanese enterprise.

KEY FACTS

WHO Japanese naval forces, under ultimate command of Toyotomi Hideyoshi (1536–98), were confronted by the smaller but more modern Korean fleet under Admiral Yi Sun-shin (1545–98).

WHAT Admiral Yi attacked a Japanese naval squadron anchored at Sacheon, drawing it out to sea, where he had the advantage of manoeuvrability and superior naval gunnery.

WHERE Sacheon, on the southern coast of the Korean Peninsula.

WHEN 29 May 1592

WHY With Korean land forces being routed by the Japanese, Admiral Yi chose a strategy of interdicting the Japanese maritime supply routes.

OUTCOME Up to 40 Japanese ships lost for no Korean vessels, and the beginning of Korean naval supremacy in the Imjin War (1592–98).

The kobukson, or 'turtle' ship, was an alarming sight when unleashed on the Japanese fleet. The smoky billows from its dragon's head were scary enough, but so too was its enhanced firepower, thanks to extra gunports.

LOCATION

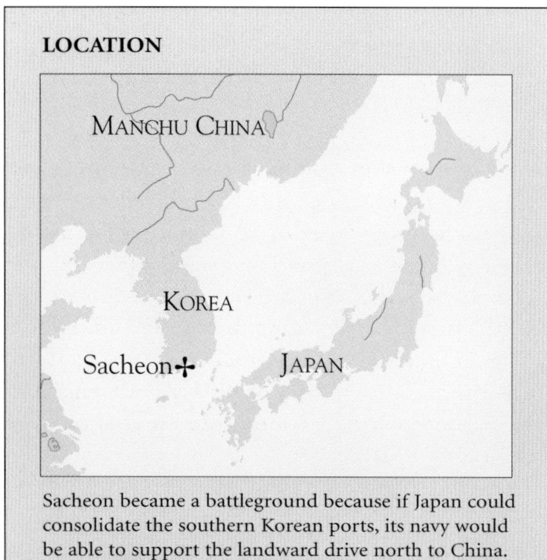
MANCHU CHINA
KOREA
Sacheon
JAPAN

Sacheon became a battleground because if Japan could consolidate the southern Korean ports, its navy would be able to support the landward drive north to China.

Toyotomi Hideyoshi, a Japanese daimyo (feudal lord) with ambitions to conquer China, had launched an invasion of Korea when it refused a request that his army be granted free passage through the kingdom. The Japanese army had readily embraced the relatively new use of firearms by this time, and its military capabilities vastly outstripped those of Korea, who still relied on long-range composite bows as their direct-fire weapons. But as a naval power Korea was less of a pushover, thanks to the efforts of Admiral Yi Sun-shin, and had invested in new naval technology, including long range cannon, sited to give all-round (360°) fire capability.

It is true that the Japanese had more ships, but these were too lightweight for such heavy gunnery, and their crews relied on musketry, and the old marine methods of grappling, boarding and on-deck fighting, for taking control of enemy ships.

As the Japanese land forces were pushing northwards, Admiral Yi saw that they were acutely reliant upon naval logistics to fuel their advance, and began to interdict supply

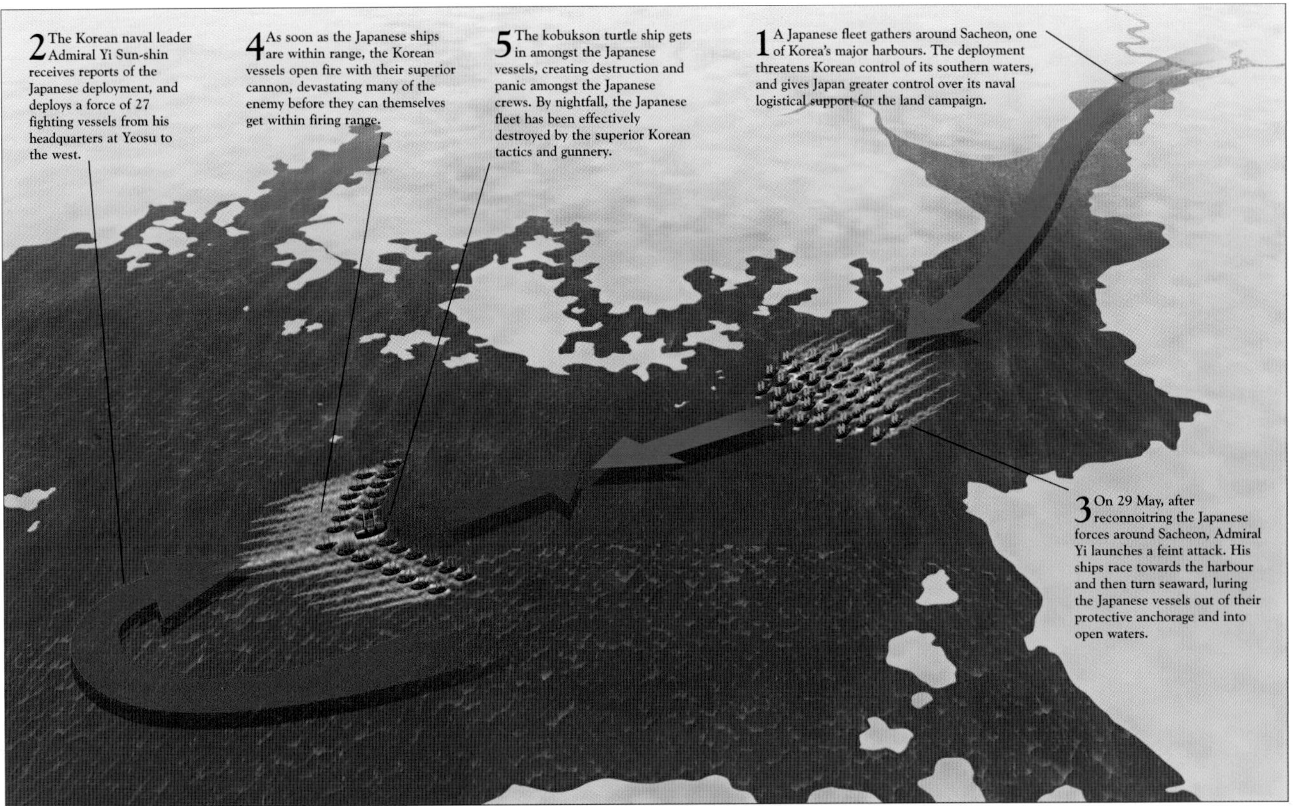
2 The Korean naval leader Admiral Yi Sun-shin receives reports of the Japanese deployment, and deploys a force of 27 fighting vessels from his headquarters at Yeosu to the west.
4 As soon as the Japanese ships are within range, the Korean vessels open fire with their superior cannon, devastating many of the enemy before they can themselves get within firing range.
5 The kobukson turtle ship gets in amongst the Japanese vessels, creating destruction and panic amongst the Japanese crews. By nightfall, the Japanese fleet has been effectively destroyed by the superior Korean tactics and gunnery.
1 A Japanese fleet gathers around Sacheon, one of Korea's major harbours. The deployment threatens Korean control of its southern waters, and gives Japan greater control over its naval logistical support for the land campaign.
3 On 29 May, after reconnoitring the Japanese forces around Sacheon, Admiral Yi launches a feint attack. His ships race towards the harbour and then turn seaward, luring the Japanese vessels out of their protective anchorage and into open waters.

The 'false' retreat wasn't simply deployed in land battles. It worked at sea, too. At Sacheon, the Japanese were lured to their doom by an outnumbered, but shrewdly commanded, Korean navy.

routes. Several naval engagements went as planned by Yi, and the scene was set for the Battle of Sacheon, when he led a force of 26 warships against up to 70 Japanese ships.

Yi needed to draw the Japanese out from the harbour at Sacheon to the open sea, where he would have the advantage in gunnery. To lure them, he had his force sail at speed towards the harbour, then reverse direction, as if suddenly alarmed by the sight of the Japanese warships. The Japanese fell for the ruse, and dispatched up to 40 vessels for a pursuit action. It would be a fatal mistake. The deployment took time, hence the light was fading even as the Japanese put to sea.

Once the Japanese ships were out of the harbour, the Koreans went into action, turning rapidly and using their oars to drive their ships quickly into gunnery range. Korean gunners were taught to begin engaging as soon as they entered cannon range, and soon the Japanese ships were being smashed by shot and arrows. The Japanese could respond only with peppering arquebus shots. One such shot might have changed the course of the entire war when it struck Yi, but the ball did nothing more than deliver a flesh wound to the admiral's left arm.

Now the Koreans played their ace card, launching a kobukson, or 'turtle ship', a new type of warship whose firepower was delivered from around a dozen cannon ports each side of the hull, and from further ports at the stem and stern. The bow also featured a carved dragon's head, from which pumped a sulphurous smoke, serving both to lay down a screen and as a weapon of psychological warfare. The turtle ship sailed into the heart of the Japanese fleet, its cannon delivering crushing broadsides against the lightweight enemy vessels while Japanese musket balls bounced harmlessly off the upper deck and thick hull. The appearance of the kobukson caused panic. Its unusual layout and heavy firepower startled the Japanese sailors and marines, who struggled to see how the ship could be taken and were alarmed at the grinning, smoking dragon's head. By nightfall, every Japanese warship that had sailed out to engage the Koreans was sinking or critically damaged. On the Korean side, casualties amounted to just a handful of sailors injured.

Hansando Island 1592

KEY FACTS

WHO Korean admiral Yi Sun-shin (1545–98) faced the fleet of Toyotomi Hideyoshi (1536–98).

WHAT Admiral Yi destroyed a large fleet of Japanese ships in open waters off the island, resulting in the death of 8000 Japanese sailors.

WHERE East coast of Hansando Island, (in modern South Korea).

WHEN 15 August 1592

WHY Japanese land forces were taking control of Korea's cities, but Admiral Yi recognized they were more vulnerable at sea.

OUTCOME Another win despite the odds for the Korean navy against the larger forces of the Japanese, and one that ended Toyotomi Hideyoshi's over-arching dream of invading China.

At Hansando Island, the seemingly superior Japanese would once again be outwitted by the Korean Admiral Yi Sun-shin, this time in a sea battle that would end Japanese hopes of launching a full-scale invasion of China.

IMJIN WAR

KOREAN VICTORY

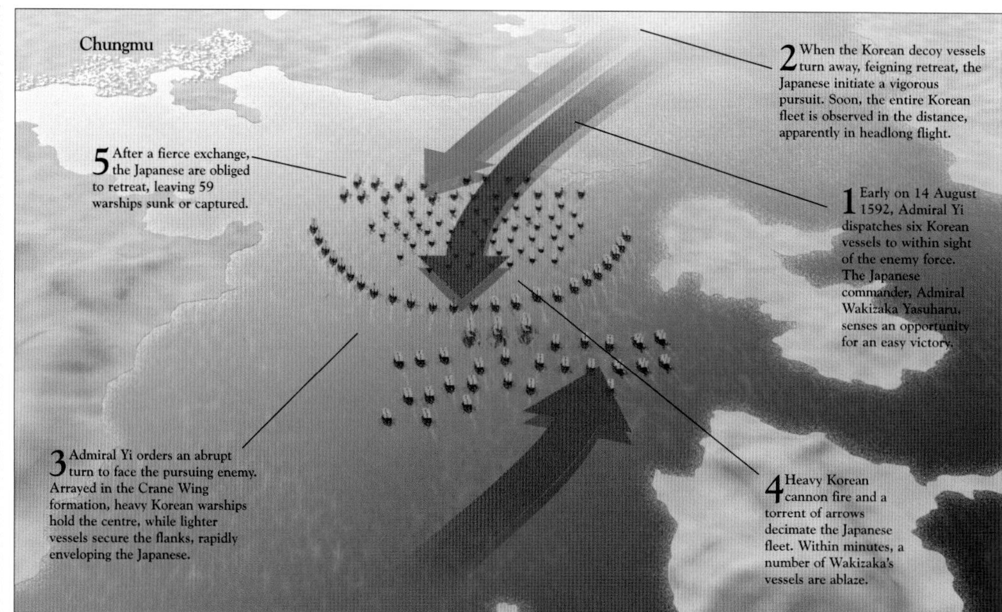

Chungmu
2 When the Korean decoy vessels turn away, feigning retreat, the Japanese initiate a vigorous pursuit. Soon, the entire Korean fleet is observed in the distance, apparently in headlong flight.
5 After a fierce exchange, the Japanese are obliged to retreat, leaving 59 warships sunk or captured.
1 Early on 14 August 1592, Admiral Yi dispatches six Korean vessels to within sight of the enemy force. The Japanese commander, Admiral Wakizaka Yasuharu, senses an opportunity for an easy victory.
3 Admiral Yi orders an abrupt turn to face the pursuing enemy. Arrayed in the Crane Wing formation, heavy Korean warships hold the centre, while lighter vessels secure the flanks, rapidly enveloping the Japanese.
4 Heavy Korean cannon fire and a torrent of arrows decimate the Japanese fleet. Within minutes, a number of Wakizaka's vessels are ablaze.

Japanese territorial ambitions were undermined by inferior naval resources. Once again, at Hansando, the Koreans managed to out-manoeuvre them, by luring them into deep waters where more up-to-date gunships could pick them off.

Warned that a powerful Japanese naval force was approaching, Admiral Yi marshalled the forces of the Korean navy north of the Kyonnaeryang Strait to protect the shipping lanes in the Yellow Sea.

Admiral Yi was aware that the waters where the Japanese had paused were too shallow for his own warships. So he devised a scheme to lure the enemy away from the shoals surrounding Hansando Island and into the open sea, where his heavier panokseon ships and artillery could wreak havoc on the lighter Japanese craft. The Japanese lacked the artillery power of their enemy, whose ships were armed with cannon, and they still had to rely on old marine warfare techniques such as grappling and boarding. While some Japanese ships did get close enough to their opponents to enable this to happen, Yi was largely successful in ensuring that this happened only to Korean ships that were already crippled. Of the 73 Japanese ships deployed, 59 were damaged or sunk, while the Koreans suffered only minor damage to a number of ships. This crushing victory once again proved the superiority of Korean naval weaponry, especially the panokseon ships, as well as Korean tactics.

LOCATION

Beijing

KOREA

Hansando

JAPAN

MING CHINA

If the Koreans were going to repel the Japanese invasion of their country, they would have to destroy the Japanese navy.

TIMELINE

1500–1000BC	1000–500BC	500BC–0AD	0–500AD	500–1000AD	1000–1500AD	1500–2000AD

Siege of Jinju 1593

KEY FACTS

WHO Japanese army against the Korean soldiers and civilians defending the castle of Jinju.

WHAT The Korean defenders were able to resist for 10 days against their assailants, but Japanese sappers used a camouflaged armoured cart to finally make a breach in the walls.

WHERE Jinju in the Jeolla province of Korea (now South Gyeongsang province, South Korea).

WHEN July 1593

WHY Jinju was a key fortress guarding the Jeolla province of Korea.

OUTCOME Once the breach was made, the garrison commander and the entire population defending the fortress, both soldiers and civilians, were put to the sword.

The first siege of Jinju, a year before, had resulted in a Korean victory, but when the Japanese returned, their use of an unusual turtle shell armoured cart helped ensure a more favourable outcome for them.

JAPANESE INVASIONS OF KOREA

JAPANESE VICTORY

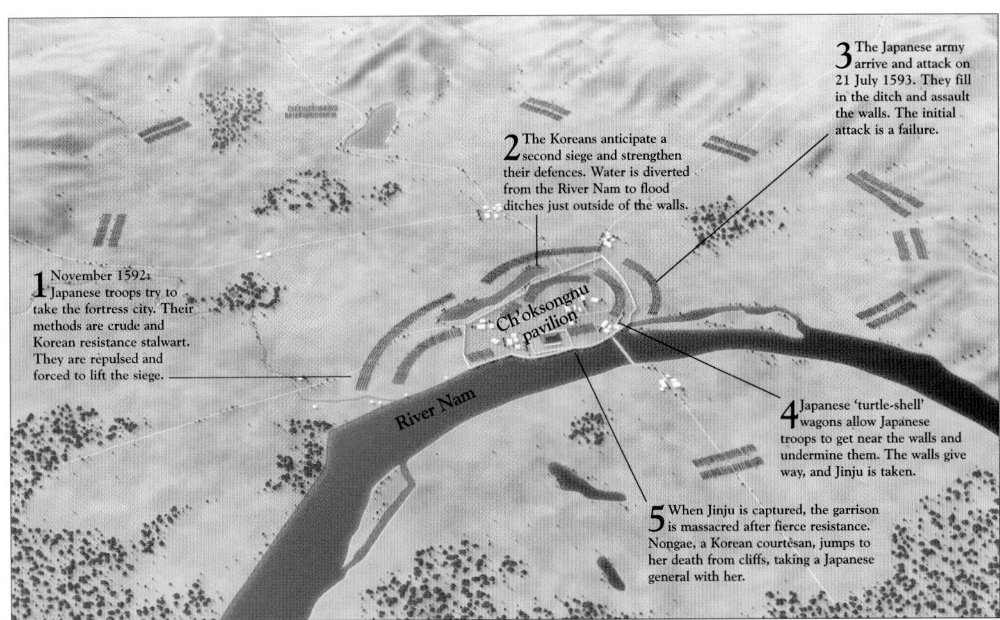

3 The Japanese army arrive and attack on 21 July 1593. They fill in the ditch and assault the walls. The initial attack is a failure.
2 The Koreans anticipate a second siege and strengthen their defences. Water is diverted from the River Nam to flood ditches just outside of the walls.
1 November 1592: Japanese troops try to take the fortress city. Their methods are crude and Korean resistance stalwart. They are repulsed and forced to lift the siege.
Ch'oksongnu pavilion
River Nam
4 Japanese 'turtle-shell' wagons allow Japanese troops to get near the walls and undermine them. The walls give way, and Jinju is taken.
5 When Jinju is captured, the garrison is massacred after fierce resistance. Nongae, a Korean courtesan, jumps to her death from cliffs, taking a Japanese general with her.

Jinju was in the heart of guerrilla fighting territory. Stealth came naturally to fighting men of the area, but the subterfuge involved in the use of a turtle shell wagon to undermine the fortress's defences was ingenious.

By the autumn of 1592, the Japanese invaders had achieved great success on the Korean peninsula. However, Korean partisan fighters were making life increasingly difficult for the invasion force. Jinju was a fortified city that was on the fringe of Korean guerrilla territory in Jeolla Province. By capturing the city, the Japanese would deny the guerrillas a base of support and also open a new road to Jeolla, which could then be conquered.

TURTLE SHELL WAGON

During a first siege of the castle in 1592, the Korean garrison had heroically beaten off all attacks, forcing the Japanese to withdraw. When they returned in 1593, Korean soldiers and civilians once again put up a stout defence, and succeeded in killing many Japanese soldiers. But after 10 days, Japanese sappers used camouflaged, armoured 'turtle shell' wagons to approach and undermine the walls. Eventually, a section of the wall collapsed, allowing the Japanese assault troops to storm in. Fighting was fierce with the Koreans battling to the last, but in the end the whole garrison, including its commander, was put to the sword.

LOCATION

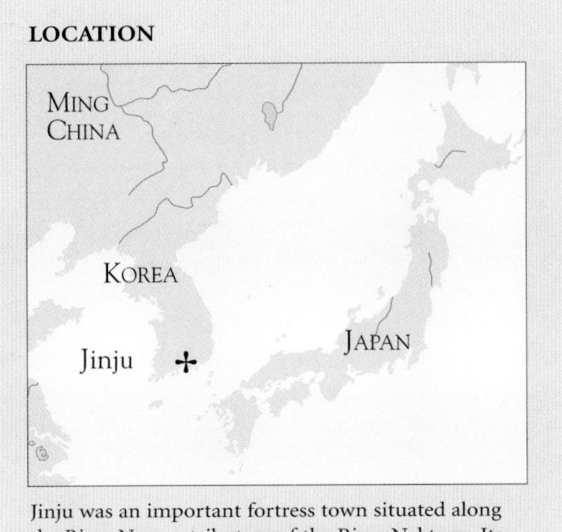

Ming China
Korea
Jinju
Japan

Jinju was an important fortress town situated along the River Nam, a tributary of the River Naktong. Its capture would open another road to the south.

TIMELINE

1500–1000BC	1000–500BC	500BC–0AD	0–500AD	500–1000AD	1000–1500AD	1500–2000AD

Nieuport 1600

When the Dutch general Maurice of Nassau set out to deal with some pirates based at Dunkirk in 1600, in Spanish-controlled territory, he did not expect to have to deal with a full-scale attack at Nieuport. His military expertise turned the situation in his favour, but was ultimately fruitless.

NETHERLANDS WAR OF INDEPENDENCE

DUTCH VICTORY

KEY FACTS

WHO The Dutch general Maurice of Nassau against the Spanish army led by Archduke Albrecht of Austria.

WHAT Maurice found himself engaged, unintentionally, in a full-scale battle with the Spanish army, but was able to overcome the disorganized charges of the Spanish pikemen.

WHERE Nieuport, (in modern Belgium).

WHEN 2 July 1600

WHY Spanish pirates had based themselves in nearby Dunkirk, and preyed on Dutch trading vessels. Maurice of Nassau was ordered to clear them from the area.

OUTCOME Although Maurice managed to defeat the Spanish, inflicting heavy losses upon them, privateers remained at large to prey upon Dutch commerce in the area.

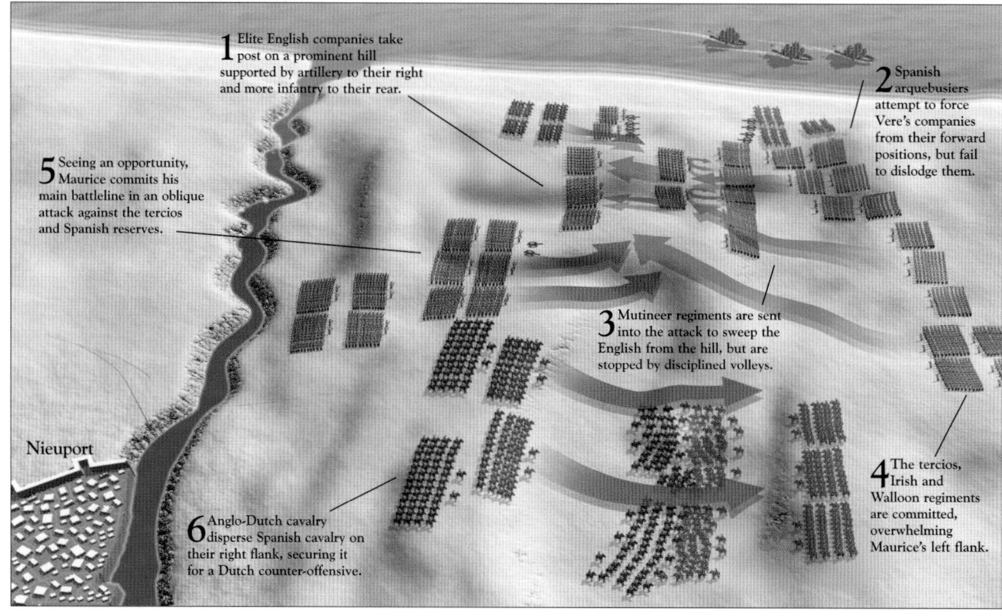
1 Elite English companies take post on a prominent hill supported by artillery to their right and more infantry to their rear.
2 Spanish arquebusiers attempt to force Vere's companies from their forward positions, but fail to dislodge them.
3 Mutineer regiments are sent into the attack to sweep the English from the hill, but are stopped by disciplined volleys.
4 The tercios, Irish and Walloon regiments are committed, overwhelming Maurice's left flank.
5 Seeing an opportunity, Maurice commits his main battleline in an oblique attack against the tercios and Spanish reserves.
6 Anglo-Dutch cavalry disperse Spanish cavalry on their right flank, securing it for a Dutch counter-offensive.
Nieuport

Privateers and pirates were a constant menace in the English Channel in this period, but a clever soldier like Maurice of Nassau would have expected to outwit them easily enough. At Nieuport, however, he had to face the Hapsburg army.

The Dutch general Maurice of Nassau had set out to deal with Spanish privateers in Dunkirk. Mutiny was rife in the Spanish army at this period, and so he could be confident that he would reach his target without opposition. However, Albrecht of Austria moved swiftly to deploy regular Spanish troops, and Maurice soon found himself with his back to the city of Nieuport and a Spanish army across his line of supply and communications.

Archduke Albrecht began his attack with a concerted cavalry charge, soon supported by half his army, to dislodge the English companies in Maurice's employ from a forward defensive position on a hill.

Maurice responded by sending forward his main battle line. The Anglo-Dutch companies met the Spanish veterans head-on, inflicting heavy casualties. When Albrecht dispatched his reserves to the fray, it was enough to break Maurice's left but opened the Spanish oblique advance to Maurice's reserves.

Albrecht had no more troops to commit to the battle, and his cumbersome formations were assailed from both front and flank. Gradually, the Spaniards scattered in all directions, leaving their guns in the field.

LOCATION

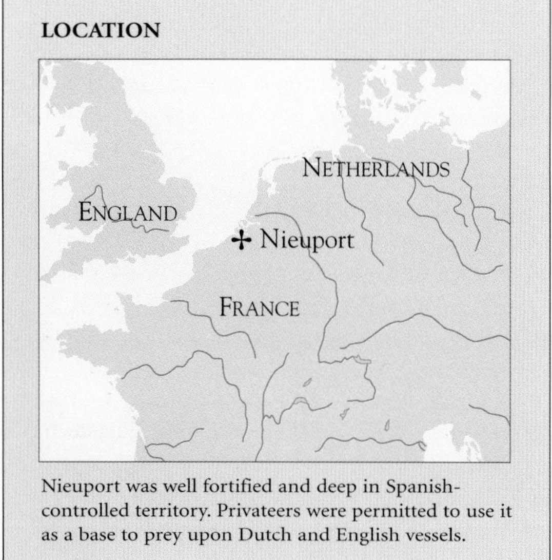
NETHERLANDS
ENGLAND
Nieuport
FRANCE

Nieuport was well fortified and deep in Spanish-controlled territory. Privateers were permitted to use it as a base to prey upon Dutch and English vessels.

TIMELINE

1500–1000BC	1000–500BC	500BC–0AD	0–500AD	500–1000AD	1000–1500AD	1500–2000AD

Sekigahara 1600

KEY FACTS

Who The clans of Tokugawa Ieyasu's Eastern Army against those of the Western Army of Ishida Mitsunari.

What The Western Army entered the battle with a well thought-out tactical plan. Secret negotiations between Tokugawa and several of Ishida's allies meant their defection at key moments in the battle contributed to the Eastern Army's eventual success.

Where Sekigahara, Japan.

When 21 October 1600

Why The death of Toyotomi Hideyoshi, who had acted as unifying figure among the warring Japanese daimyo, had plunged the country into a new battle for power.

Outcome Ieyasu's victory paved the way for him to become shogun, and establish a dynasty that would endure for over two centuries.

Following a century of civil war in Japan, Toyotomi Hideyoshi had succeeded in unifying the island nation. However, his untimely death in 1598 precipitated a bitter struggle for pre-eminence between former subordinates and led to one of the most decisive battles in Japanese history.

SENGOKU PERIOD WARS

EASTERN ARMY VICTORY

The events of the battle of Sekigakara were considered so momentous in Japanese history that they are commemorated by a stone monument on the site of the conflict.

LOCATION

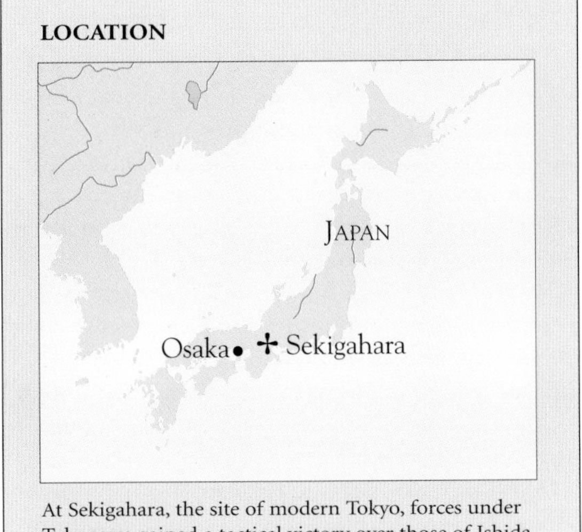
JAPAN
Osaka
Sekigahara

At Sekigahara, the site of modern Tokyo, forces under Tokugawa gained a tactical victory over those of Ishida, giving rise to the powerful Tokugawa shogunate.

The Battle of Sekigahara pitted the forces of Ishida Mitsunari, loyal to the infant son of Toyotomi Hideyoshi, against those of Tokugawa Ieyasu, daimyo (lord) of the Kanto Plain, who was challenging for the succession.

Ishida had carried out a night-time march on Sekigahara, and was already in position by the time the Eastern Army arrived the next morning and had to deploy in a thick fog. Initial clashes went the Western Army's way, and its opponents faced the prospect of being trapped on three sides. But secret negotiations about defecting had taken place between Tokugawa and several of Ishida's lieutenants, including Kobayaka Hideaki, who occupied a critical position in the field.

When Ishida signalled for Kobayaka to attack, he was hesitant and eventually joined the battle on the Eastern side. This moment of treachery was observed by several other generals of the Western Army, and they too now switched sides. Eventually, those who remained loyal to Ishida saw the battle was lost and began to march away.

TIMELINE

1500–1000BC	1000–500BC	500BC–0AD	0–500AD	500–1000AD	1000–1500AD	1500–2000AD

Siege of Osaka 1615

KEY FACTS

WHO Tokugawa shogunate led by Tokugawa Ieyasu against Toyotomi Hideyori and his clan.

WHAT Tokugawa Ieyasu made two attempts to attack Toyotomi Hideyori in his stronghold at Osaka and was finally successful in his summer campaign of 1615.

WHERE Osaka, Japan.

WHEN November 1614–January 1615 and May–September 1615

WHY Tokugawa Ieyasu saw Toyotomi Hideyori as a rival and a threat to Japan's internal stability.

OUTCOME After Tokugawa Ieyasu's victory, he was able to eliminate the Toyotomi clan and re-unite Japan under his leadership.

After his great victory at Sekigahara in 1600, Tokugawa Ieyasu had gone on to became Shogun, before passing on the title to his son. He continued to carry real political and military clout, however, and acted forcefully when the Toyotomi clan seemed about to challenge dynastic stability.

SENGOKU PERIOD WARS

TOKUGAWA VICTORY

While the siege of Osaka Castle would be the key to the success of the Tokugawa campaign, a certain amount of fighting in the field would also have taken place between the rival clans.

LOCATION

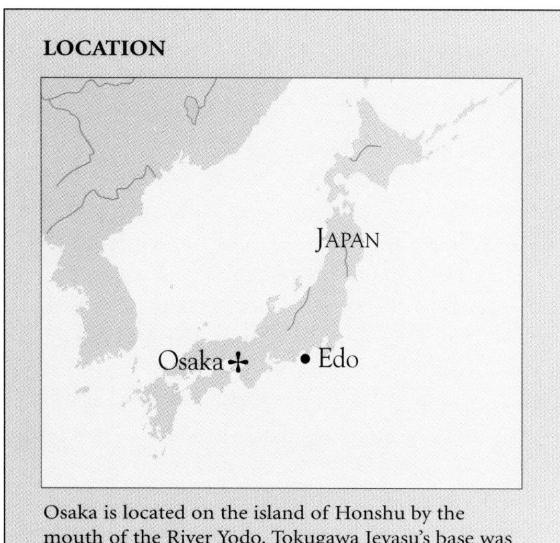
JAPAN
Osaka
Edo

Osaka is located on the island of Honshu by the mouth of the River Yodo. Tokugawa Ieyasu's base was at Edo (Tokyo), 403km (251 miles) away.

Tokugawa Ieyasu had established himself as Shogun in 1603 after defeating all his enemies at the Battle of Sekigahara in 1600. He stepped down in 1605, nominally handing the shogunate to his son Hidetada. It was a transparent move that fooled few people. Ieyasu would control Japan to the end of his life.

But Ieyasu was concerned about the threat from Toyotomi Hideyori, son and heir of former Japanese ruler Toyotomi Hideyoshi. Hideyori's name was a powerful talisman to many who recalled his father. That made him a threat to the continued domination of the Tokugawa family. Ieyasu, who was 68 and determined to secure the kingdom for his dynasty, decided to deal with the problem now, once and for all.

By the summer of 1614, it was clear that war was going to break out between Ieyasu and Hideyori, with the former gathering all the powder and European-style ordnance he could lay his hands on, including five English cannons. But when the fighting finally broke out, Hideyori decided on a purely defensive strategy, remaining in his

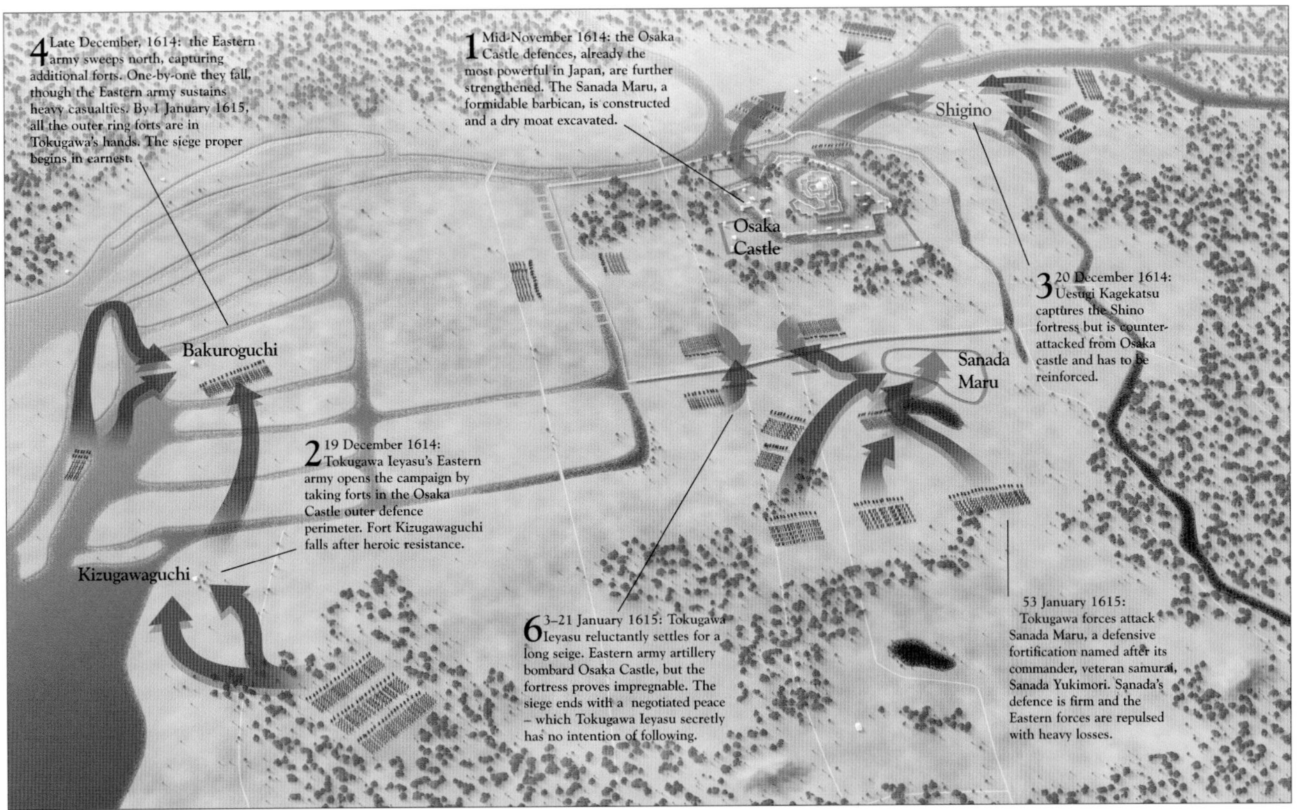
4 Late December, 1614: the Eastern army sweeps north, capturing additional forts. One-by-one they fall, though the Eastern army sustains heavy casualties. By 1 January 1615, all the outer ring forts are in Tokugawa's hands. The siege proper begins in earnest.
1 Mid-November 1614: the Osaka Castle defences, already the most powerful in Japan, are further strengthened. The Sanada Maru, a formidable barbican, is constructed and a dry moat excavated.
Shigino
Osaka Castle
3 20 December 1614: Uesugi Kagekatsu captures the Shino fortress but is counter-attacked from Osaka castle and has to be reinforced.
Bakuroguchi
Sanada Maru
2 19 December 1614: Tokugawa Ieyasu's Eastern army opens the campaign by taking forts in the Osaka Castle outer defence perimeter. Fort Kizugawaguchi falls after heroic resistance.
Kizugawaguchi
6 3–21 January 1615: Tokugawa Ieyasu reluctantly settles for a long siege. Eastern army artillery bombard Osaka Castle, but the fortress proves impregnable. The siege ends with a negotiated peace – which Tokugawa Ieyasu secretly has no intention of following.
5 3 January 1615: Tokugawa forces attack Sanada Maru, a defensive fortification named after its commander, veteran samurai, Sanada Yukimori. Sanada's defence is firm and the Eastern forces are repulsed with heavy losses.

Osaka castle was so well fortified it withstood bombardment by 300 cannons and a painstakingly long and carefully planned siege campaign by the Tokugawa forces. In the event, deceit was required to overcome it.

mighty stronghold of Osaka Castle, passively confident in its powerful defences. It was hoped that Ieyasu would waste time, men and precious resources trying to take an impregnable fortress.

A LONG SIEGE

Ieyasu launched his Winter Campaign against Osaka in November 1614. By this time, Hideyori had had a massive new moat constructed, 73m (240ft) wide and 11m (36ft) deep, and when the waters flowed they rose to a depth of 3.7–10.4m (12–24ft). The castle fortifications were already formidable and Ieyasu settled for a long siege. Three hundred cannons were brought up, and these bombarded the castle on a regular basis. Ieyasu ordered one artillery piece to be trained on a tower where he knew Hideyori stayed. One 6kg (13lb) shot smashed through the tower wall and killed two attendants of his mother, Yodogimi.

The castle took some pounding but had been designed well. In fact, as the new moat made it seemingly impregnable, Ieyasu tried trickery. He managed to persuade Yodogimi, who held a position of much influence over her son, that a truce could be worked out. Foolishly Hideyori agreed, and though most of the Eastern army withdrew, those that remained started to fill in Osaka's moats.

Hideyori protested, but he could make no overt move lest he break the peace agreement. Six months later, Ieyasu resumed the siege, now against defences rather less formidable than they had been.

BREAKTHROUGH

Ieyasu's troops and cannon could get closer than before, and parts of the castle were blasted to rubble. Soon the main keep was aflame and all hope was lost. Hideyori committed suicide and his mother either killed herself or was dispatched by a retainer. Thousands of Toyotomi loyalists were also put to the sword.

The siege of Osaka marked the end of war and great castle-building. Ieyasu had successfully cemented his shogunate. Peace reigned for over 200 years, until the coming of the Western powers in the mid-1800s began a whole new era for Japan.

TIMELINE

1500–1000BC	1000–500BC	500BC–0AD	0–500AD	500–1000AD	1000–1500AD	1500–2000AD

Siege of Osaka

SIEGE OF OSAKA

Castle siege warfare was essentially a medieval form of battle. In Western Europe, its age had largely passed by the seventeenth century. But Osaka Castle remained a massively strong fortification in China in this period, guarding the mouth of the River Yodo. It was a key stronghold of Toyotomi Hideyori and his clan, as it held out against the Tokugawa shogunate of Tokugawa Ieyasu and his son. Ieyasu pounded the castle with 300 western-style artillery and 300 cannons for months, but still the castle held out. When it finally fell, however, it marked the end of the great age of castle-building.

Breitenfeld 1631

KEY FACTS

Who King Gustavus Adolphus of Sweden (reigned 1611–1632), and his Saxon allies, against the Imperial army of the Holy Roman Empire under the command of John Tserclaes von Tilly.

What The Imperial forces launched pistol-firing cavalry attacks against their enemy, but the Swedish tactic of interspersing musket units amongst their cavalry, proved a more concentrated form of artillery attack.

Where Breitenfeld, north of Leipzig, in modern Germany.

When 17 September 1631

Why King Gustavus Adolphus was seeking to rally the Protestant cause and to strike at the Hapsburgs' overweening behaviour in the Baltic.

Outcome After this defeat, Tilly pulled his army back westwards, which was a major boost to the Protestant armies.

During the reign of King Gustavus Adolphus, Sweden soared from being a rather minor Scandinavian power to being a major player on the European stage. Victory at Breitenfeld would be his finest military moment.

THIRTY YEARS WAR

SWEDISH VICTORY

King Gustavus II Adolphus's success at Breitenfeld owed much to the innovative interspersing of artillery units among the conventional ranks.

LOCATION

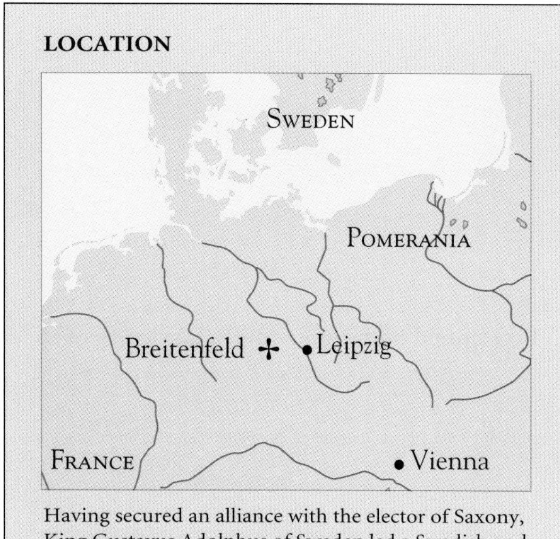
SWEDEN
POMERANIA
Breitenfeld
Leipzig
FRANCE
Vienna

Having secured an alliance with the elector of Saxony, King Gustavus Adolphus of Sweden led a Swedish and Saxon army to liberate Leipzig from the Imperialists.

Gustavus Adolphus had declared war on the Imperial Hapsburgs in 1630, and when he finally launched an invasion of Germany the following year, he gained the support of John George, the elector of Saxony, who had just lost the city of Leipzig to an Imperialist army under John Tserclaes von Tilly.

As Gustavus Adolphus and John George moved their armies towards Leipzig, Tilly moved his forces out to meet them and occupied a ridgeline some 8km (5 miles) north of the city, at Breitenfeld. Tilly placed his infantry on the ridgeline, and planned to launch coordinated cavalry attacks against the enemy's flanks, led by his lieutenant, Gottfried Heinrich Graf von Pappenheim on the left, and Tilly himself on the right.

The initial artillery duel favoured the Swedes. Not only did they have a greater number of cannon, but, because of their cased ammunition, they delivered a greater volume of fire than the Imperialist artillery. The fire of the Swedish artillery clearly had an effect: the pounding inflicted on Pappenheim's cavalry provoked him to move

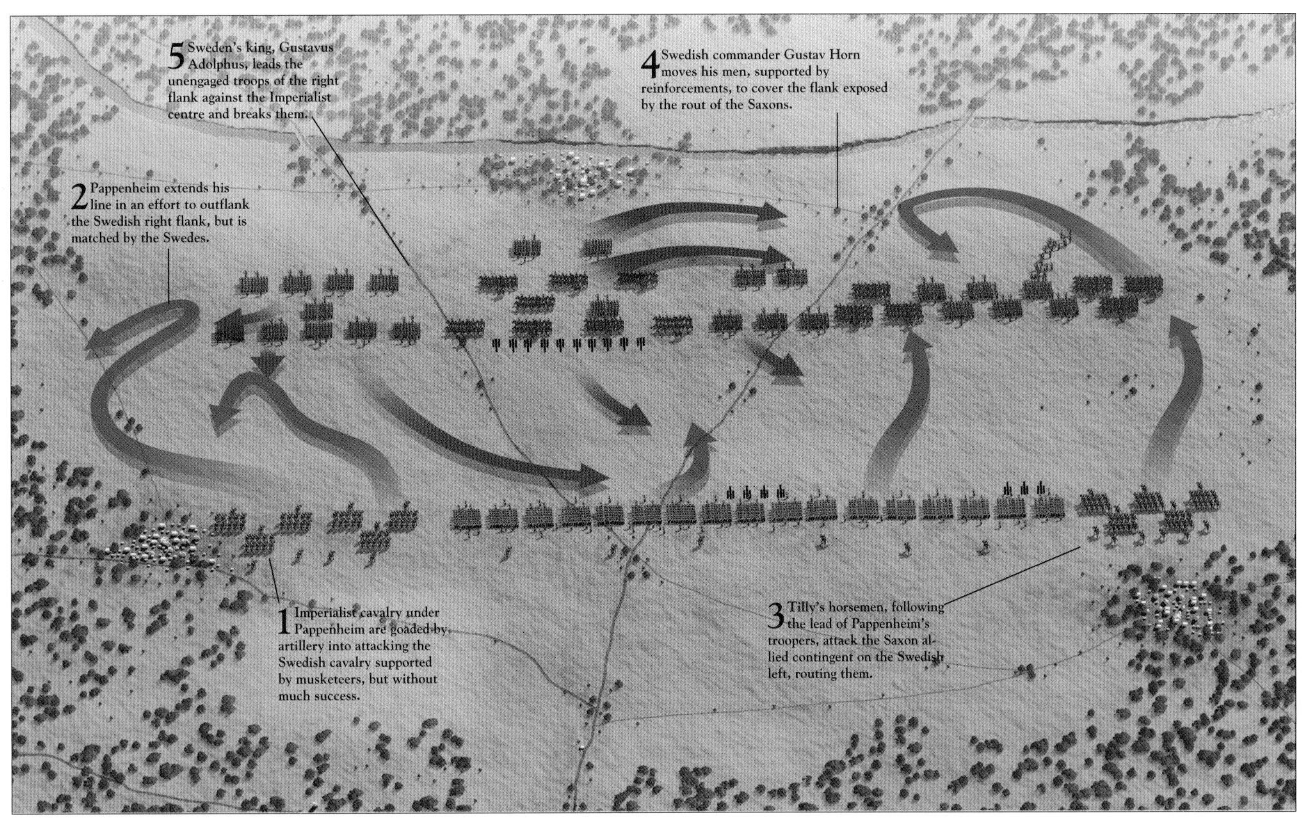
5 Sweden's king, Gustavus Adolphus, leads the unengaged troops of the right flank against the Imperialist centre and breaks them.
4 Swedish commander Gustav Horn moves his men, supported by reinforcements, to cover the flank exposed by the rout of the Saxons.
2 Pappenheim extends his line in an effort to outflank the Swedish right flank, but is matched by the Swedes.
1 Imperialist cavalry under Pappenheim are goaded by artillery into attacking the Swedish cavalry supported by musketeers, but without much success.
3 Tilly's horsemen, following the lead of Pappenheim's troopers, attack the Saxon allied contingent on the Swedish left, routing them.

The imperial army under Von Tilly enjoyed some success with its own cavalry charges at Breitenfeld, but the Swedish formations were more flexible and their artillery firepower was more effectively concentrated in units.

forwards to avoid the Swedish cannon fire. Because this move was unexpected, Tilly did not order his troops to advance at the same time, and Pappenheim's cavalry therefore advanced without support.

Pappenheim's cavalry attacked the Swedish cavalry, not by charging in and engaging in hand-to-hand combat, but by using the caracole formation. This involved riding up to within pistol range, firing and wheeling to reload and repeat the process. This was a similar concept to countermarch fire for infantry. But it was not effective against the Swedish cavalry because they had intermingled detachments of musketeers among the cavalry units. These inflicted significant casualties on the Imperialist horse because their salvo fire was more densely concentrated and their weapons had both greater range and power of penetration.

On the right flank, things went better for the Imperialists. At the sight of Tilly's cavalry charge, the inexperienced Saxon troops turned on their heels and fled. In a single blow, 40 per cent of Gustavus Adolphus' forces had been driven from the field. Fortunately for the king, his deployment and the discipline of his men did not allow the Imperialist cavalry to roll up his left flank. As fresh Swedes from the reserve and other parts of the battle line arrived, they began pushing the Imperialist forces back with their disciplined volleys.

After about five hours, Pappenheim and his cavalry had finally been driven off. Exhibiting the coup d'oeil of a great captain, Gustavus Adolphus recognized that now was the time to attack. At the head of several troops of horsemen, he led an attack on the Imperialist centre, breaking through and capturing Tilly's cannon, which he turned on their former owners. The breaking of their centre and the additional artillery pounding was too much for the Imperialists who finally broke. The Swedish cavalry pursued, leaving some 7600 Imperialist troops dead and another 6000 as prisoners. The Swedes lost 2000 men. Breitenfeld had showed the superiority of the 'Swedish synthesis' combination of firepower and shock coupled with superior discipline and organizational flexibility. Many larger armies in the following years would copy their example.

Lützen 1632

THIRTY YEARS WAR

SWEDISH VICTORY

Gustavus Adolphus, King of Sweden, had declared war on the Hapsburg Empire in 1630 and led the first modern-style professional standing army in Europe to a brilliant victory at Breitenfeld. He would at Lützen, too, but at the cost of his own life and high casualties among his troops.

KEY FACTS

WHO A Swedish army, commanded by King Gustavus Adolphus (1594–1632), opposed by an Imperial army under Prince Albrecht von Wallenstein (1583–1634).

WHAT Despite the death of Gustavus Adolphus, the Swedish army was able to win a hard-fought victory.

WHERE Lützen, near Leipzig in Saxony.

WHEN 6 November 1632

WHY Saxony, a Swedish ally, was threatened with invasion by Imperial forces.

OUTCOME Saxony was preserved, but the war continued for another 16 years.

King Gustavus Adolphus would lead the Swedish troops on a cavalry charge at Lützen, but this talented and innovative military man would also meet his end in the battle.

LOCATION

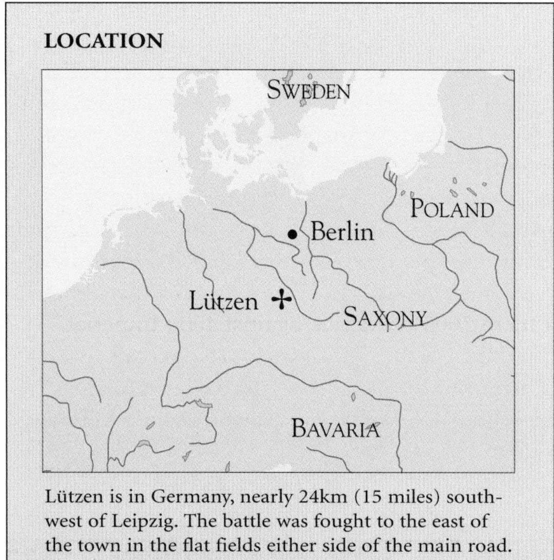

SWEDEN
POLAND
Berlin
Lützen
SAXONY
BAVARIA

Lützen is in Germany, nearly 24km (15 miles) south-west of Leipzig. The battle was fought to the east of the town in the flat fields either side of the main road.

Victory at Breitenfeld allowed the Swedes to overrun much of southern Germany in 1631–32 and the Holy Roman Emperor placed the experienced Prince Albrecht von Wallenstein in command of a fightback. After inflicting an early defeat on the Swedish army, Wallenstein marched into Saxony to go into winter quarters, and detached some of his cavalry. But the Swedes were still in the field and seeking a decisive battle before the ravaged winter countryside ran out of supplies to support their campaign.

Joining forces with the Saxons to create an allied army, they camped overnight near Lützen, on a flat plain that had little shelter, with the Imperial army just 5km (3 miles) away.

Thick fog forced the Allied army to postpone its attack until 1100 the next day, after which their advance was halted by heavy musket and artillery fire. On the right, a primarily Swedish and Finnish force under the personal command of Gustavus Adolphus made more progress, though at a heavy cost in terms of casualties. Fog then descended on the battlefield once more, heavily restricting

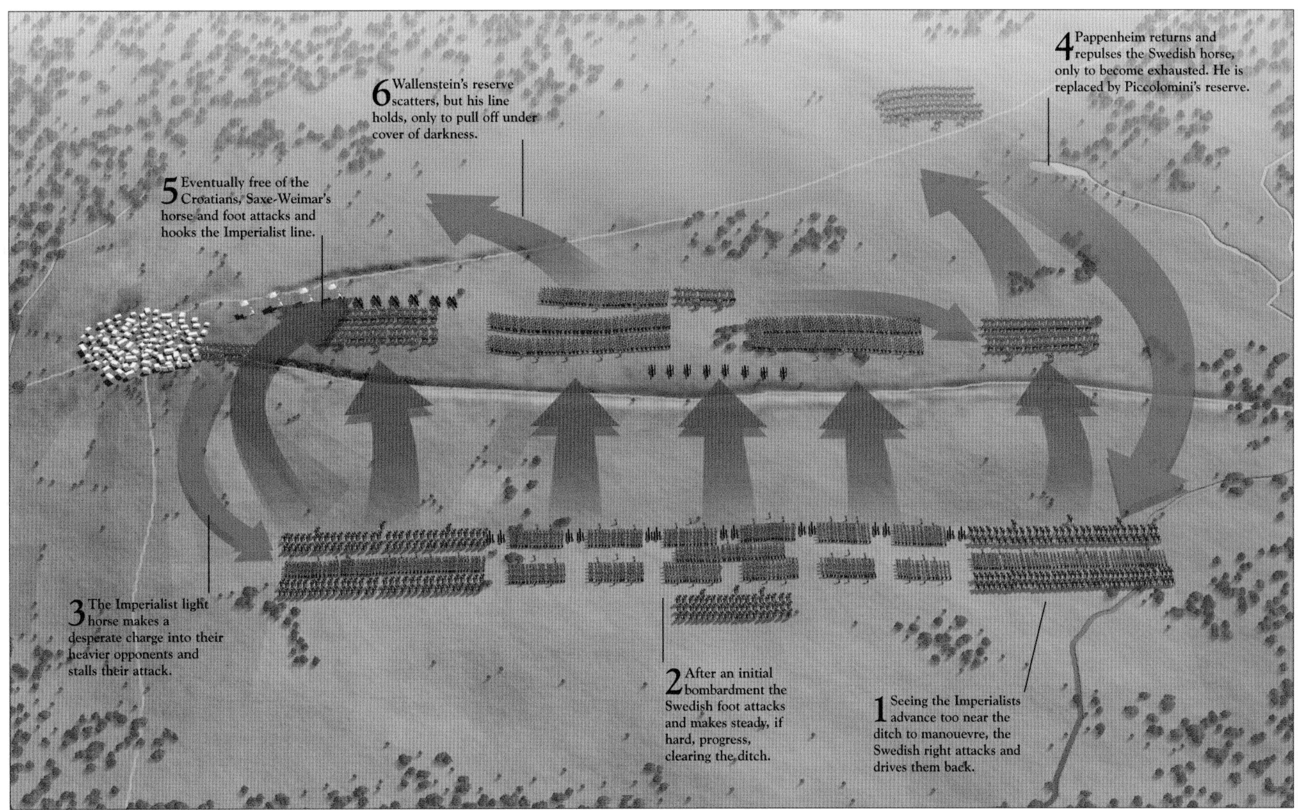
4 Pappenheim returns and repulses the Swedish horse, only to become exhausted. He is replaced by Piccolomini's reserve.
6 Wallenstein's reserve scatters, but his line holds, only to pull off under cover of darkness.
5 Eventually free of the Croatians, Saxe-Weimar's horse and foot attacks and hooks the Imperialist line.
3 The Imperialist light horse makes a desperate charge into their heavier opponents and stalls their attack.
2 After an initial bombardment the Swedish foot attacks and makes steady, if hard, progress, clearing the ditch.
1 Seeing the Imperialists advance too near the ditch to manouevre, the Swedish right attacks and drives them back.

Lützen was fought on a flat plain with little shelter. There was plenty of room for the old favourite of European warfare over the centuries, the cavalry charge, which relied upon speed, manoeuvre and shock force.

visibility. The result was a close-quarters battle of attrition with heavy casualties on both sides.

In the midst of the fighting, Wallenstein's army were buoyed by the arrival of the detached cavalry – 5000 horsemen under Count Pappenheim (1594–1632) – and the Swedish cavalry were almost driven from the field. Meanwhile, Gustavus Adolphus had taken personal command of one of his cavalry units when its commander was wounded. As he led an advance, the fog thickened until it was impossible to see in any direction. This covered the attack of a force of Imperial cuirassiers, who charged into Gustavus' unit.

In the ensuing mêlée, Gustavus Adolphus was shot in the arm and lost his sword as he tried to keep control of his horse. He became separated from his command and was shot again, this time in the back. Despite the efforts of his bodyguard to save him, Gustavus fell from his horse when it was shot, and he was dragged for some distance with his foot caught in a stirrup. He was still alive when the Imperial cavalry found him, and was finished off with a pistol shot. His clothing and weapons were taken as trophies.

Recognizing the wounded horse that fled through their lines, and hearing that the king was dead, the Swedes began to waver. However, the army's second-in-command, Bernhard of Saxe-Weimar (1604–39), was able to rally them and lead an advance. A general attack developed that became a bitter close-range firefight.

In a final effort to break the deadlock, Bernhard of Saxe-Weimar ordered an attack on the Imperial artillery battery located on Windmill Hill. Supported by intense artillery fire, the allies were initially repulsed and a second assault succeeded only after two further hours of close combat. With Windmill Hill in the possession of the allies, the Imperial position was badly compromised.

Wallenstein's army was demoralized and exhausted and, although his opponents were in scarcely better condition, it was the Imperial forces that retreated. The allied victory had cost them 3000 casualties, against 4000 Imperial losses. Despite this battlefield victory, the overall strategic victory sought by Gustavus Adolphus had eluded him, and whatever advantage was gained at Lützen was bought at the price of his own life.

Battle of the Downs 1639

KEY FACTS

WHO The Dutch lieutenant-admiral Maarten Tromp against a Spanish fleet led by Admiral Antonio de Oquendo.

WHAT A belligerent Dutch admiral launched an audacious attack on Spanish ships within neutral English waters.

WHERE The Downs, off the Kent coast, England.

WHEN 31 October 1639

WHY A Spanish fleet was attempting to bring reinforcements to its beleaguered troops in Flanders during the ongoing Eighty Years War.

OUTCOME The Spanish mission to deliver troop reinforcements did to some extent succeed, but the victory was an emphatic statement of growing confidence of the Dutch as a naval power.

By the 1630s, the formidable naval powers of Spain and England were weakening, but the seas they had so recently dominated were witnessing the rise of a belligerently confident new maritime power in the Dutch.

EIGHTY YEARS WAR

DUTCH VICTORY

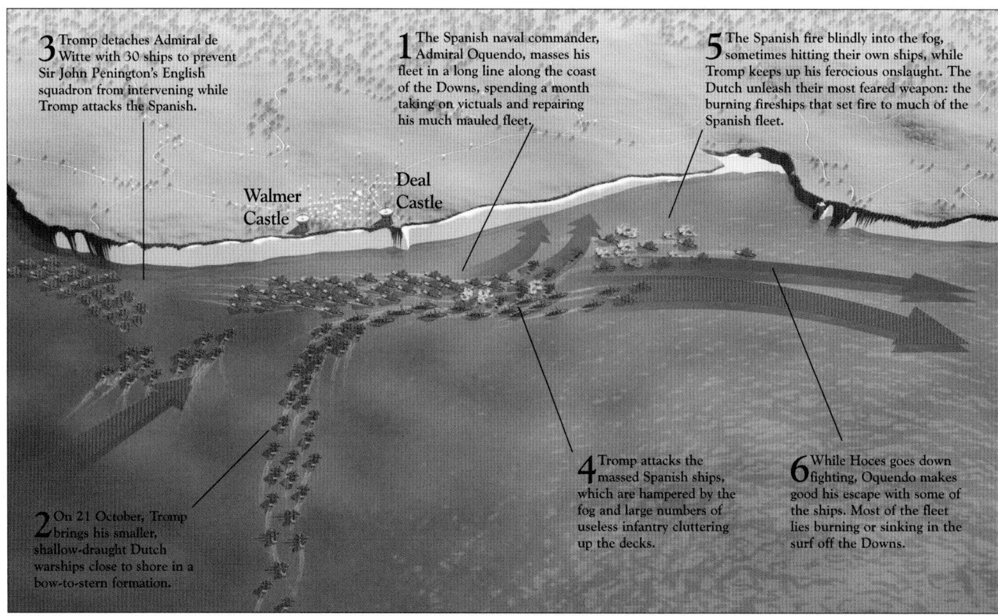
3 Tromp detaches Admiral de Witte with 30 ships to prevent Sir John Penington's English squadron from intervening while Tromp attacks the Spanish.
1 The Spanish naval commander, Admiral Oquendo, masses his fleet in a long line along the coast of the Downs, spending a month taking on victuals and repairing his much mauled fleet.
5 The Spanish fire blindly into the fog, sometimes hitting their own ships, while Tromp keeps up his ferocious onslaught. The Dutch unleash their most feared weapon: the burning fireships that set fire to much of the Spanish fleet.
Walmer Castle
Deal Castle
2 On 21 October, Tromp brings his smaller, shallow-draught Dutch warships close to shore in a bow-to-stern formation.
4 Tromp attacks the massed Spanish ships, which are hampered by the fog and large numbers of useless infantry cluttering up the decks.
6 While Hoces goes down fighting, Oquendo makes good his escape with some of the ships. Most of the fleet lies burning or sinking in the surf off the Downs.

The Battle of the Downs took place in the English Channel, in waters not far from two of Britain's most famous coastal fortresses at Walmer and Deal. But on this occasion, the naval protagonists were the Dutch and Spanish fleets.

A fleet of Spanish ships had been trying to bring reinforcement troops to its army in Flanders when they were sighted by the Dutch Admiral Maarten Tromp, who launched an attack in the English Channel. The Spanish admiral Antonio de Oquendo, more concerned with delivering the soldiers safely than engaging the Dutch in a sea battle, fled with his ships for the dubious safety of Spain's former enemy, England, taking anchorage at the Downs, on the Kent coast.

After waiting for reinforcements, and realizing that the Spanish would not come out to give battle, Tromp attacked, even though he was in technically neutral English water. Firing quick rounds and coming in close for a kill, his crews trusted in their audacity against an inexperienced enemy. The Spanish ships were raked with shot, and Tromp then unleashed his fireships with devastating results.

The *Santa Theresa*, flagship of Admiral de Hoces, exploded, taking both the admiral and his crew to the seabed. Oquendo managed to escape with the remains of his fleet and delivered some of the promised troops to the Cardinal-Infante's army in Flanders.

LOCATION

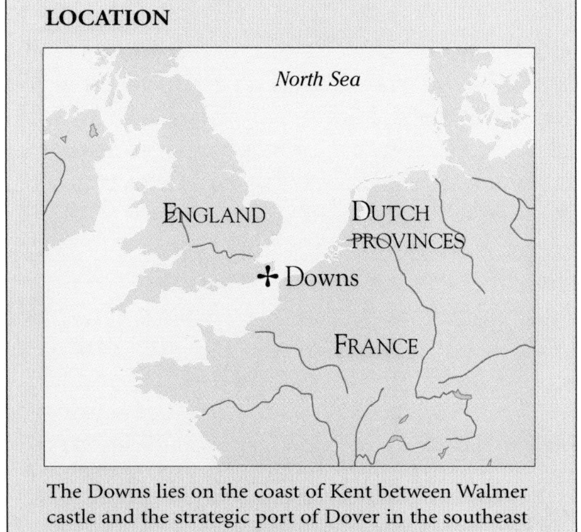
North Sea
ENGLAND
DUTCH PROVINCES
Downs
FRANCE

The Downs lies on the coast of Kent between Walmer castle and the strategic port of Dover in the southeast of England, facing the Channel and France.

TIMELINE

1500–1000BC	1000–500BC	500BC–0AD	0–500AD	500–1000AD	1000–1500AD	1500–2000AD

Edgehill 1642

KEY FACTS

WHO The Royalist army under Charles I against the Parliamentarians under the Earl of Essex.

WHAT The first major battle of the English Civil War involving the king. After inconclusive artillery salvoes, the two sides engaged in fierce hand-to-hand fighting.

WHERE The escarpment of Edgehill, Warwickshire, England.

WHEN 23 October 1642

WHY Charles I's absolutist conceptions of kingship and his arrest of leading parliamentarians when they refused to support his plans for war with Scotland had split the country in two, precipitating civil war.

OUTCOME After a fierce infantry battle, Charles was unable to dislodge Essex's forces, but was eventually able to move on London.

In the autumn of 1642, as England was about to be consumed by full-scale civil war, Charles I attempted to march on London but found his way blocked by the troops of the Earl of Essex.

ENGLISH CIVIL WAR

NO CLEAR VICTORY

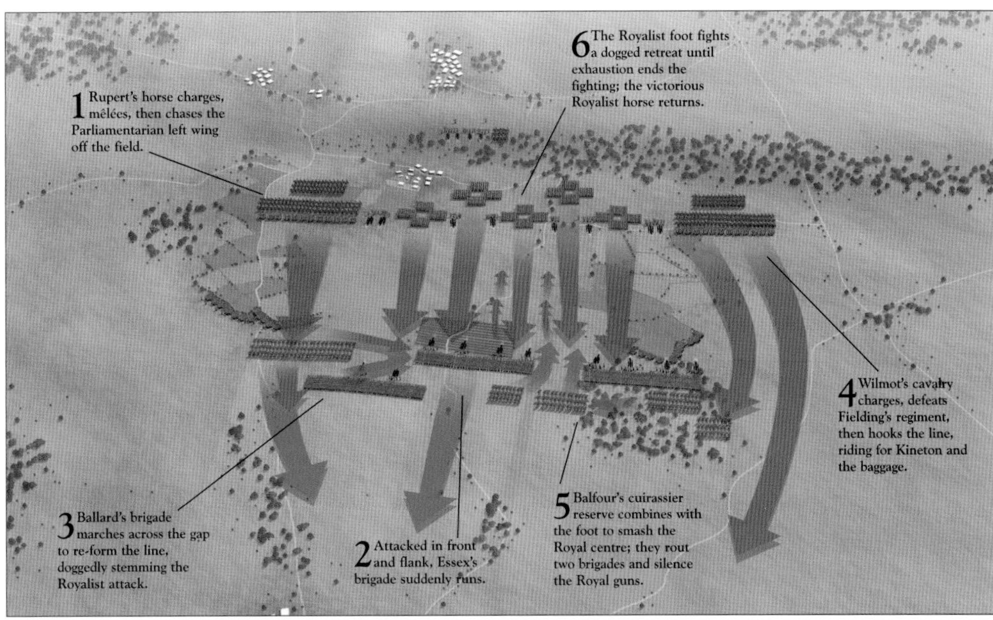
1 Rupert's horse charges, mêlées, then chases the Parliamentarian left wing off the field.
6 The Royalist foot fights a dogged retreat until exhaustion ends the fighting; the victorious Royalist horse returns.
4 Wilmot's cavalry charges, defeats Fielding's regiment, then hooks the line, riding for Kineton and the baggage.
3 Ballard's brigade marches across the gap to re-form the line, doggedly stemming the Royalist attack.
2 Attacked in front and flank, Essex's brigade suddenly runs.
5 Balfour's cuirassier reserve combines with the foot to smash the Royal centre; they rout two brigades and silence the Royal guns.

By the time of Edgehill, artillery was a staple of warfare, but often inexpertly used. The Royalist forces here launched rounds of fusilades which, because of poor positioning, simply lodged harmlessly into the turf of the hill.

King Charles I had manoeuvred his army between the Earl of Essex's Parliamentarians and London, forcing them to offer battle near the foot of Edgehill escarpment, 32km (20 miles) south of Coventry. With both sides deployed, the Royalists chose to attack, first launching their artillery fire. However, they had inexpertly placed their guns up the slope of the hill, so that much of the fire simply plunged uselessly into the turf.

Still, when the royal dragoons on the wings moved forward, they managed to drive back those of their opponents. Following this, Prince Rupert of the Rhine launched a cavalry charge that helped rout the Parliamentarian's central brigade of foot soldiers. However, several other brigades of foot soldiers remained in their ground, and provided enough cover for their cavalry to then break though and punch a hole in the royal lines, breaking up two of their brigades and driving the king's army back to its starting position. Both sides lost around 1500 men, but while Essex's army was still essentially intact when he withdrew from the field, the way was now effectively clear for the king to march on the capital, London.

LOCATION

SCOTLAND
IRELAND
ENGLAND
Edgehill
London

Edgehill is near Kineton in the English Midlands. The battle was fought on open, boggy, moorland. Today much of it is covered by a military depot.

TIMELINE

1500–1000BC	1000–500BC	500BC–0AD	0–500AD	500–1000AD	1000–1500AD	1500–2000AD

The Dunes 1658

FRANCO-SPANISH WAR

FRENCH & ENGLISH VICTORY

The English New Model Army broke with tradition in favour of efficiency in combat. At the time, armies were raised on an ad hoc basis and led by political rather than military figures. The New Model Army promoted professionalism and demonstrated a better way to form a military force.

KEY FACTS

WHO French army led by Vicomte de Turenne, supported by troops from the English Commonwealth, against the Spanish army led by John of Austria the Younger and Louis II de Conde.

WHAT A Spanish army was marching to relive Dunkirk, but found itself caught in the rapid volley fire of the English musketeers.

WHERE Dunkirk, modern France.

WHEN 14 June 1658

WHY France was at the time engaged in war with Spain. Meanwhile, the presence of such a large contingent of Spanish troops across the Channel was seen as a potential invasion force by the English.

OUTCOME Defeat of the Spanish at the Dunes ended the treat of an invasion of England, and the Spanish and French would sign a peace treaty the following year.

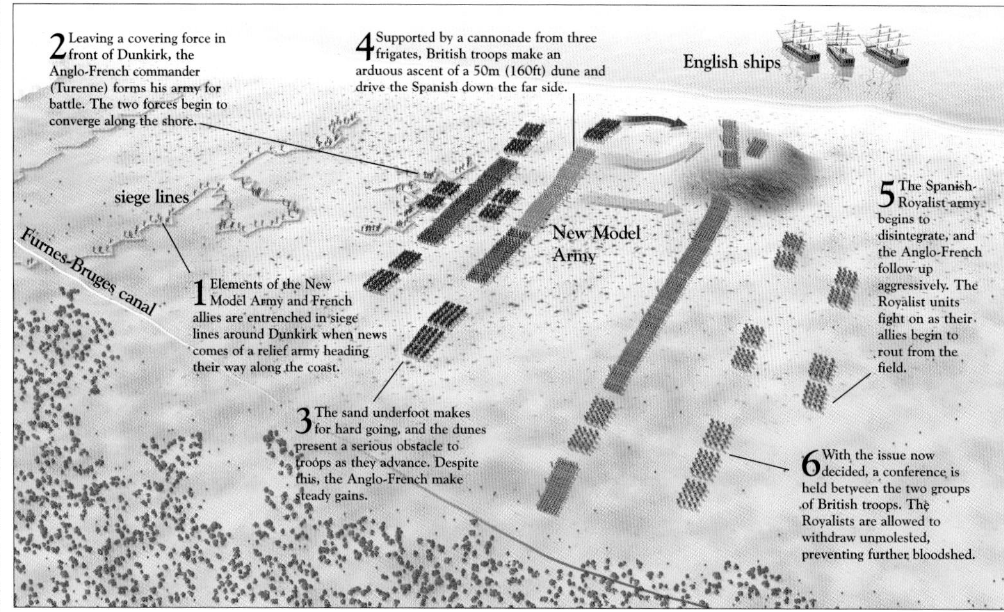

2 Leaving a covering force in front of Dunkirk, the Anglo-French commander (Turenne) forms his army for battle. The two forces begin to converge along the shore.
4 Supported by a cannonade from three frigates, British troops make an arduous ascent of a 50m (160ft) dune and drive the Spanish down the far side.
English ships
siege lines
Furnes-Bruges canal
New Model Army
5 The Spanish-Royalist army begins to disintegrate, and the Anglo-French follow up aggressively. The Royalist units fight on as their allies begin to rout from the field.
1 Elements of the New Model Army and French allies are entrenched in siege lines around Dunkirk when news comes of a relief army heading their way along the coast.
3 The sand underfoot makes for hard going, and the dunes present a serious obstacle to troops as they advance. Despite this, the Anglo-French make steady gains.
6 With the issue now decided, a conference is held between the two groups of British troops. The Royalists are allowed to withdraw unmolested, preventing further bloodshed.

The discipline of the much vaunted New Model Army would be thoroughly tested in the sandy, unstable terrain at The Dunes, when it had to negotiate a steep climb of around 50m (160ft) before it could force its opponents into a retreat.

In 1654, the New Model Army, which had performed so well in the English Civil War, found itself fighting alongside French troops against the Spanish, led by John of Austria the Younger and Louis II de Conde. Dunkirk had been occupied by Spanish troops and when a Spanish relief force marched on the town, the Anglo-French army offered battle on a coastal terrain characterized by many sand dunes.

The musketeers of the English units proved especially effective, maintaining a steady fire by the constant rotation of men. After firing, the front rank retired to the rear to reload while men with weapons ready replaced them and, using forked stands to support their heavy firearms, took aim and fired at the enemy before pulling back in turn. Thus a constant, rolling fire was maintained without exposing the unit to countercharge, the covering pikemen ready to repulse anyone who got too close.

When an enemy unit was seen to waver, the pikemen advanced to decide the matter with a 'push of pike.' The Spanish were thrown back on the defensive and sent routing from the field after two hours of hard fighting. Dunkirk itself soon surrendered.

LOCATION

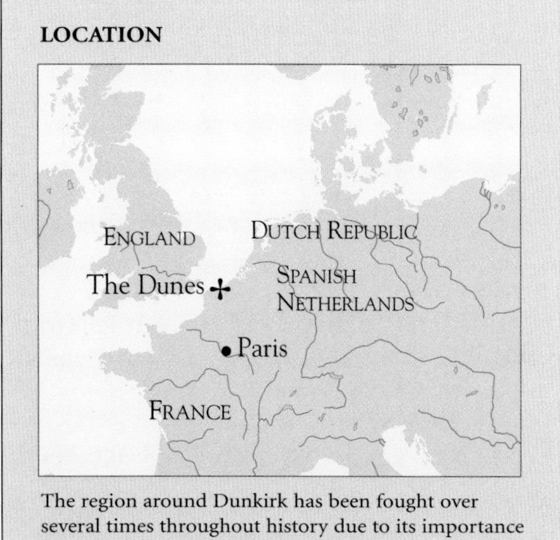

ENGLAND
DUTCH REPUBLIC
The Dunes
SPANISH NETHERLANDS
Paris
FRANCE

The region around Dunkirk has been fought over several times throughout history due to its importance as a Channel port.

TIMELINE

1500–1000BC	1000–500BC	500BC–0AD	0–500AD	500–1000AD	1000–1500AD	1500–2000AD

Medway 1667

KEY FACTS

Who Dutch fleet and marines under the command of Lieutenant Admiral Michiel de Ruyter, against English led by Admiral George Monck, Duke of Albemarle.

What The Dutch were able to sail up the Thames and the Medway rivers and burn 13 English ships and tow away two others.

Where Chatham, England.

When 9–14 June 1667

Why Charles II had procrastinated over signing a peace treaty to end the Anglo-Dutch War.

Outcome The raid forced the English to come to terms more quickly, agreeing to a treaty that was significantly more favourable to the Dutch.

The English were probably being too clever by half when manoeuvring behind the scenes for advantageous terms at the conclusion of the Anglo-Dutch War. But an impudent Dutch raid under their noses meant it would be their opponents who left the negotiating table with the biggest smiles.

SECOND ANGLO-DUTCH WAR

DUTCH VICTORY

The ships that sailed from Chatham and the Medway enabled Britain to command seas around the globe for large periods between the sixteenth and nineteenth centuries. The Dutch raid here was a cause of national embarrassment.

LOCATION

North Sea

England

Dutch Republic

London

Medway

France

The River Medway lies at the outer mouth of the River Thames. The British naval dockyards at Chatham were based a short way up the Medway.

The Dutch fleet under the command of Admiral de Ruyter reached the mouth of the Thames on 7 June with the intention of raiding up the Medway River and forcing England to sue for peace. Three days later, the Dutch attacked Sheerness, clearing the way for the fleet.

The English responded by placing blocking ships, a chain and two gun batteries at the mouth of the river at Gillingham to keep the enemy away from the main English naval base, at Chatham. The Dutch used fireships to smash their way through the English defences on 12 June, burning several ships in the process and capturing HMS *Royal Charles* intact. The following day, the Dutch sailed further up river, but in the face of increasingly heavy English battery fire progress was slow. Another three English vessels were either sunk or captured before the Dutch withdrew to home waters. The raid was a major military and political success for the Dutch, and a serious humiliation for the English navy. A peace agreement was signed on Dutch terms soon afterwards.

TIMELINE

1500–1000BC	1000–500BC	500BC–0AD	0–500AD	500–1000AD	1000–1500AD	1500–2000AD

Kahlenberg 1683

KEY FACTS

WHO An army of the Holy Roman Empire, led by Charles of Lorraine, joined by Jan Sobieski III of Poland, against the Ottoman siege forces of Kara Mustafa.

WHAT The Ottomans laid siege to Vienna, but were weakened by fighting on two fronts – continuing their assault on the city, while trying to beat off the relief army.

WHERE Vienna, Austria.

WHEN 11 September 1683

WHY The Ottomans were intent on taking Vienna as part of ambitions to press further on into central Europe.

OUTCOME The Ottomans sustained heavy and demoralizing losses, and the defeat effectively ended their expansionist ambitions within Europe.

The grand viziers of the Ottoman Empire had nursed ambitions for greater territorial expansion deep into Europe for some time, and the conquest of the strategically vital city of Vienna lay at the heart of their plans.

GREAT TURKISH WAR

HAPSBURG/ROMAN VICTORY

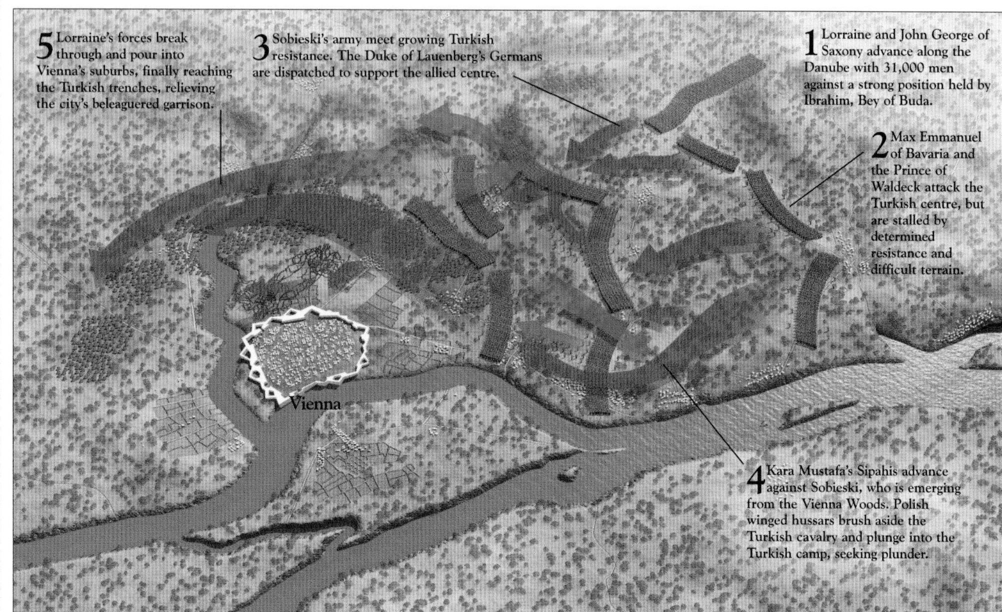
5 Lorraine's forces break through and pour into Vienna's suburbs, finally reaching the Turkish trenches, relieving the city's beleaguered garrison.
3 Sobieski's army meet growing Turkish resistance. The Duke of Lauenberg's Germans are dispatched to support the allied centre.
1 Lorraine and John George of Saxony advance along the Danube with 31,000 men against a strong position held by Ibrahim, Bey of Buda.
2 Max Emmanuel of Bavaria and the Prince of Waldeck attack the Turkish centre, but are stalled by determined resistance and difficult terrain.
Vienna
4 Kara Mustafa's Sipahis advance against Sobieski, who is emerging from the Vienna Woods. Polish winged hussars brush aside the Turkish cavalry and plunge into the Turkish camp, seeking plunder.

The bravery of the Polish cavalry was renowned for centuries. In 1683, the fabulous 'Winged Hussars' swept from the Vienna Woods to lift a prolonged siege by the Turks and end their dreams of conquering Europe.

The Ottoman siege of Vienna had gone on for two months when a relief army of the Holy Roman Emperor, led by Charles of Lorraine, joined by Jan Sobieski III of Poland, arrived on the north bank of the Danube. The Ottoman grand vizier Kara Mustafa was confident Vienna would fall before it could be relieved, and had kept many of his janissaries ready in trenches just outside the walls as sappers continued their attempts to breach them, meaning the attentions of his forces were divided. The combined armies, meanwhile, advanced through the Vienna Woods, sweeping down from the heights of the Kahlenberg mountain.

WINGED HUSSAR ATTACK

Heavy fighting through the Vienna Woods slowed the advance, but Lorraine broke through along the Danube, and the Poles fought their way through on the right. The 'Winged Hussars' of Sobieski's cavalry poured into the Turkish camp in a massive charge. The jannisaries in the trenches were annihilated, and less than three hours after the charge, Vienna had been saved.

LOCATION

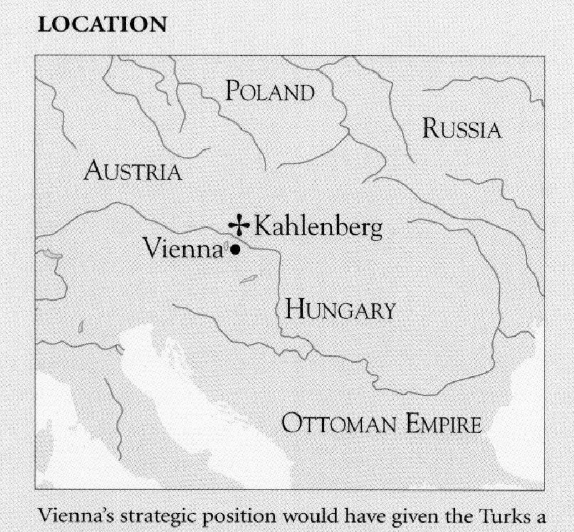
POLAND
RUSSIA
AUSTRIA
Kahlenberg
Vienna
HUNGARY
OTTOMAN EMPIRE

Vienna's strategic position would have given the Turks a foothold in central Europe, threatening future Turkish offensives into Bohemia and southern Germany.

TIMELINE

1500–1000BC	1000–500BC	500BC–0AD	0–500AD	500–1000AD	1000–1500AD	1500–2000AD

Ulan Butung 1690

QING DYNASTY WARS

NO CLEAR VICTORY

KEY FACTS

WHO Zungharians against the Manchu Prince of Yu, leading the Chinese Qing army.

WHAT Galdan Boshughtu and his nomadic Zungharian army, caught by surprise, used their camels as a makeshift defensive wall, enabling them to stave off a heavy defeat.

WHERE Ulan Butung, Outer Mongolia.

WHEN 3 September 1690

WHY The Zungharians had advanced into eastern Mongolia, a buffer zone between them and the Chinese, so the Qing forces were dispatched to eliminate this potential threat to their frontiers.

OUTCOME Although the Chinese claimed a military victory, the Zungharian cavalry were able to ride off to fight another day.

The Chinese Qing army of the seventeenth century was extremely versatile. But when it met the Zungharians at Ulan Butung, having marched across the arid Gobi Desert, its military sophistication was thwarted by a most unconventional 'fortification' – a defensive walls of camels.

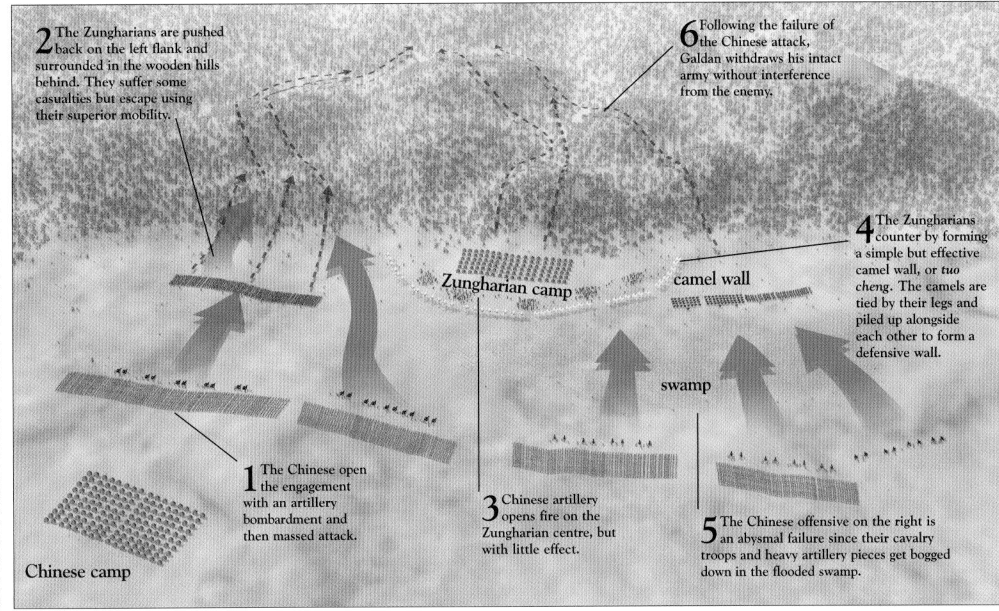

2 The Zungharians are pushed back on the left flank and surrounded in the wooden hills behind. They suffer some casualties but escape using their superior mobility.
6 Following the failure of the Chinese attack, Galdan withdraws his intact army without interference from the enemy.
4 The Zungharians counter by forming a simple but effective camel wall, or *tuo cheng*. The camels are tied by their legs and piled up alongside each other to form a defensive wall.
Zungharian camp
camel wall
swamp
1 The Chinese open the engagement with an artillery bombardment and then massed attack.
3 Chinese artillery opens fire on the Zungharian centre, but with little effect.
5 The Chinese offensive on the right is an abysmal failure since their cavalry troops and heavy artillery pieces get bogged down in the flooded swamp.
Chinese camp

The Chinese army was already on the point of exhaustion after many miles on the march in hot, arid conditions, but encountering an unexpectedly effective 'fortification' made from a wall of camels tested their resilience to breaking point.

The Qing forces found Outer Mongolia a challenging battleground. Their supply lines were stretched to a maximum from early in the campaign, and food and water was difficult to manage. Having finally caught up with the Zungharians amidst the wooden hills of Ulan Butung, the Qing employed a combined force of artillery, infantry and cavalry in a traditional combined-arms attack. Caught by surprise, the Zungharian commander, Galdan, decided to stand and fight.

After suffering an artillery bombardment, the Zungharians protected their camp in a highly unconventional fashion, forming a defensive barrier by trussing up their 10,000 camels into a *tuo cheng*, or camel wall, and firing arrows at the Qing through the gaps. Although the Chinese commander Yu claimed a victory when his troops made a breakthrough on the left flank, the main attack proved a failure, which enabled the bulk of the Zungharian cavalry army to survive and withdraw intact after negotiating a ceasefire.

The camel wall proved decisive, in that the Zungharians were able to hold their positions while at their most vulnerable, allowing them to survive to fight another day.

LOCATION

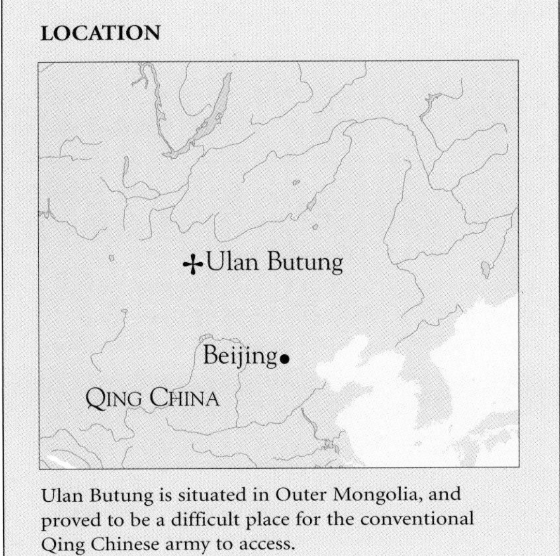

Ulan Butung
Beijing
QING CHINA

Ulan Butung is situated in Outer Mongolia, and proved to be a difficult place for the conventional Qing Chinese army to access.

TIMELINE

1500–1000BC	1000–500BC	500BC–0AD	0–500AD	500–1000AD	1000–1500AD	1500–2000AD

Blenheim 1704

KEY FACTS

Who An Allied force commanded by the Duke of Marlborough (1650–1722) and Prince Eugène of Savoy (1663–1736), opposed by a Franco-Bavarian army under Marshal Count de Tallard (1652–1728).

What The Allies exploited their advantages, notably in infantry and artillery, with bold strategic movement and aggressive tactics on the field of battle.

Where The village of Blenheim in Bavaria.

When 13 August 1704

Why The Grand Alliance sought to limit Franco-Bavarian power by defeating their army in the field.

Outcome A decisive victory for the Allies protected Vienna and forced Bavaria out of the war.

Knowing that the fall of Vienna might spell the end of the Grand Alliance, the Duke of Marlborough embarked upon a daring march from the Low Countries to the Danube, putting his forces in position to defeat a Franco-Bavarian army threatening the Austrian capital.

WAR OF THE SPANISH SUCCESSION

ALLIED VICTORY

The battle was characterized by a day of exhausting attacks and counter-attacks which wore down both sides, before Marlborough's English troops eventually gained the day.

LOCATION

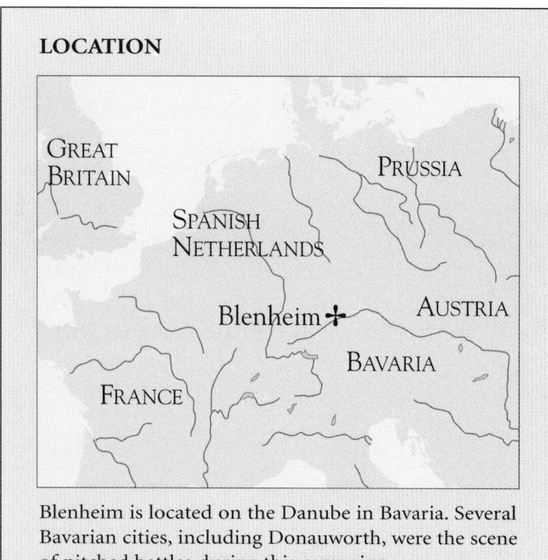
GREAT BRITAIN
PRUSSIA
SPANISH NETHERLANDS
Blenheim
AUSTRIA
BAVARIA
FRANCE

Blenheim is located on the Danube in Bavaria. Several Bavarian cities, including Donauworth, were the scene of pitched battles during this campaign.

France had been generally successful against the Grand Alliance in the War of the Spanish Succession, and with its ally Bavaria now threatening Vienna, there was a danger that Austria, one of the major powers amongst the Allies, could be taken out of the war. John Churchill, later Duke of Marlborough, who was a minister of Queen Anne and an able commander, hit upon a plan to lead an Allied army, currently engaged in the Low Countries, on a daring, rapid march to the Danube to meet the Franco-Bavarian army, commanded by Marshal Count de Tallard.

The Franco-Bavarian army occupied a good defensive position around Blenheim, its right flank secured by the Danube and the left by high, forested, ground. The villages of Blenheim, Oberglau and Lutzingen formed strong points in the line. Low-lying and wet areas formed natural obstacles to any enemy advance. But Marlborough was an aggressive and skilled commander. Wary of Tallard's dispositions, he noted that his personal command on the right flank in front of the village of Blenheim was the strongest part of the Franco-Bavarian line. It seemed likely

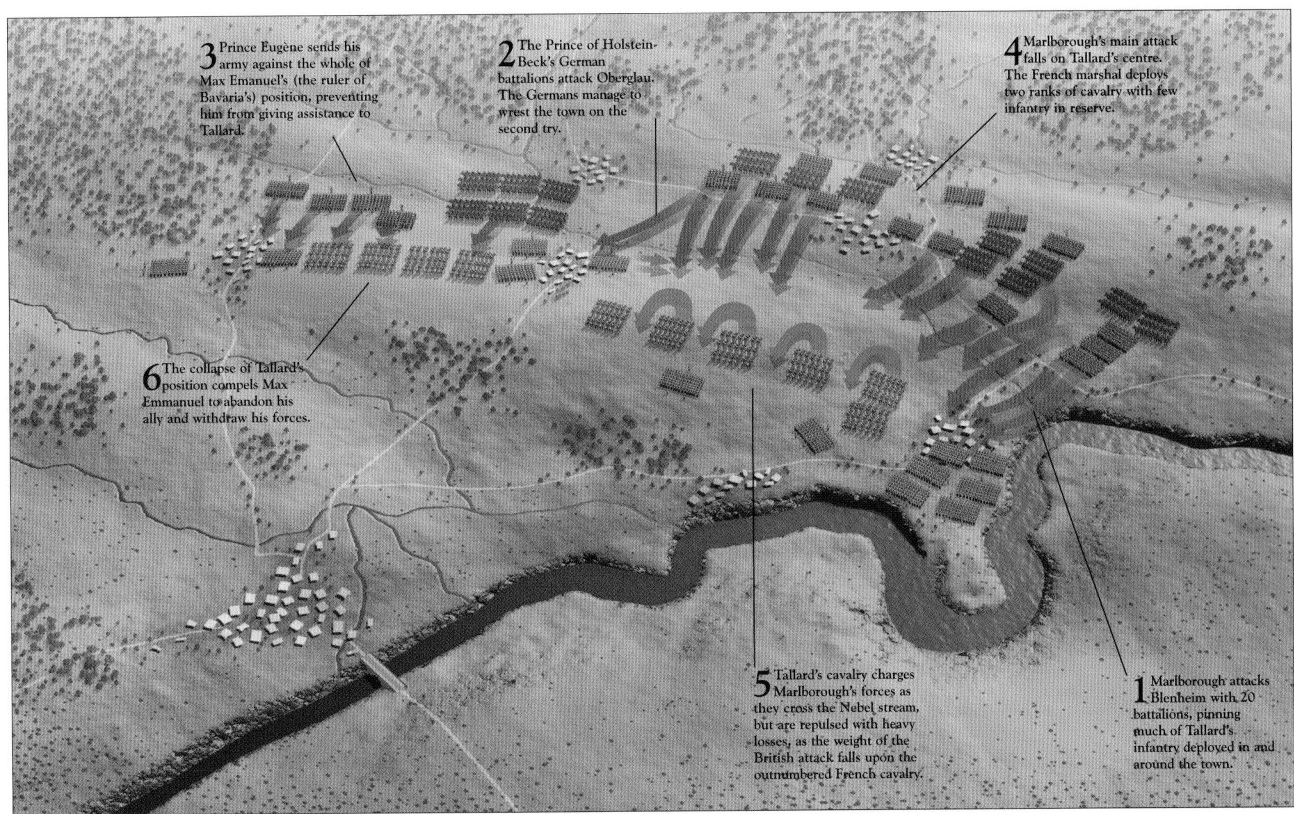
3 Prince Eugène sends his army against the whole of Max Emanuel's (the ruler of Bavaria's) position, preventing him from giving assistance to Tallard.
2 The Prince of Holstein-Beck's German battalions attack Oberglau. The Germans manage to wrest the town on the second try.
4 Marlborough's main attack falls on Tallard's centre. The French marshal deploys two ranks of cavalry with few infantry in reserve.
6 The collapse of Tallard's position compels Max Emmanuel to abandon his ally and withdraw his forces.
5 Tallard's cavalry charges Marlborough's forces as they cross the Nebel stream, but are repulsed with heavy losses, as the weight of the British attack falls upon the outnumbered French cavalry.
1 Marlborough attacks Blenheim with 20 battalions, pinning much of Tallard's infantry deployed in and around the town.

Blenheim was traditionally depicted in later years as a battle in which cavalry played the main role, whereas it actually featured highly intensive use of artillery, weaponry that was becoming increasingly decisive on the battlefield.

to Marlborough that Tallard intended to counter-attack from here if the opportunity presented itself. Marlborough therefore decided to occupy this force while he broke the weaker centre.

Using the army under Prince Eugène of Savoy to occupy the Bavarians holding the enemy left, Marlborough launched the Blenheim pinning attack. The initial attack penetrated Blenheim at a few points, but the Allies were swiftly ejected and were then counter-attacked in the flank by cavalry. Fire from an Allied infantry brigade drove off the counter-attack in turn, allowing a renewed attack to be launched. This drew in French reinforcements, with the result that there were far more men in the village than were necessary to beat off the Allied assault. The attack on Blenheim was an expensive failure, in that it did not drive the French from the village, but it did serve the purpose of pinning large numbers of French troops in a position where they could not influence the critical phase of the battle.

The point of decision was Oberglau, in the centre, held by the French under Ferdinand de Marsin. As the Allied infantry advanced, they were charged by French horsemen, and repulsed by artillery fire. Had Tallard's infantry reserves not been occupied at Blenheim, a French counter-attack at this point might have borne fruit. Instead, additional Allied cavalry, including heavy squadrons sent by Prince Eugène, enabled the French centre to be pushed back into the village of Oberglau, were their infantry were overwhelmed despite a gallant stand.

On the Allied right flank, Prince Eugène personally led another attack, the regimental colour in his hand, just at the moment when some of his troops seemed to be wavering. This finally broke the Bavarian line. Now only the French right flank force still held out in and around Blenheim, but gradually they were pushed into the centre of the village, where they made a stand in a walled churchyard. There, they beat off repeated attacks with heavy casualties on both sides until the Allies offered a parlay. The defenders eventually agreed to surrender, bringing the action to a close. The Grand Alliance remained intact, and Marlborough made a Duke.

Ramillies 1706

KEY FACTS

WHO John, Duke of Marlborough leads an Anglo-Dutch army against the French under the Duc de Villeroi.

WHAT In one of the great cavalry engagements, a well-executed 'secret' redeployment of somve of his cavalry squadrons turned what seemed a fruitless mêlée in Marlborough's favour.

WHERE Ramillies, Belgium.

WHEN 23 May 1706

WHY The French were trying to resist Allied inroads into the Spanish Netherlands.

OUTCOME Marlborough was able to enjoy further military success in the Netherlands and push the French army back beyond the Flemish frontier.

There can seldom have been as great a horse charge as that massed by the French cavalry at Ramillies. Yet the pride of their army, despite immense bravery, were to be cut down by the Anglo-Dutch forces under the Duke of Marlborough, who once again proved his shrewdness on the battlefield.

WAR OF THE SPANISH SUCCESSION

ANGLO-DUTCH VICTORY

At the height of the battle, the fighting descended into a furious melee, with many soldiers crushed to death, and no side seeming to gain an advantage as the combatants swayed back and forth.

LOCATION

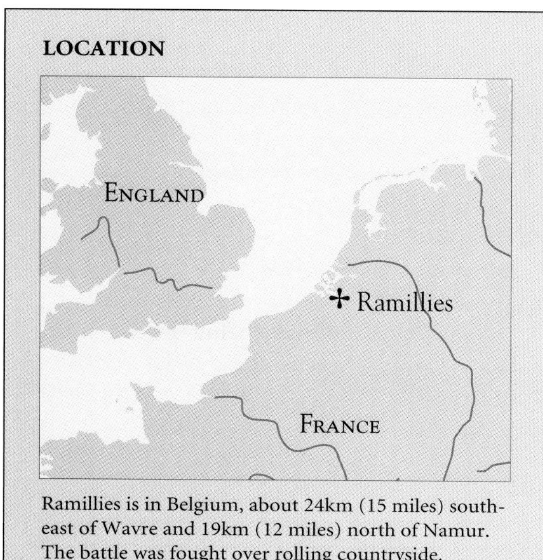
England
Ramillies
France

Ramillies is in Belgium, about 24km (15 miles) south-east of Wavre and 19km (12 miles) north of Namur. The battle was fought over rolling countryside.

Louis XIV had ordered Marshal Villeroi to engage the Duke of Marlborough's Anglo-Dutch army after it had penetrated defensive fortifications in the Spanish Netherlands during the ongoing War of the Spanish Succession.

The two armies engaged near the village of Ramillies on broad, rolling, open country, an almost natural arena unbroken by obstacles and bounded by the village of Ramillies to the north and Taviers to the south. It was Villeroi who had a grand cavalry plan. His massive cavalry arm was to sweep forwards and soften up the numerically inferior Allies. They would then follow on with the sword and drive English cavalry on the left from the field. English cavalry, on the allied right, would not have room nor time to deal with the envelopment. Then the horse would have their day, cutting them down and turning the retreat into a spectacular rout. A fitting revenge for Blenheim, but the plan didn't quite work out.

Marlborough's own cavalry option had a chance if something if something could be done to equalize the

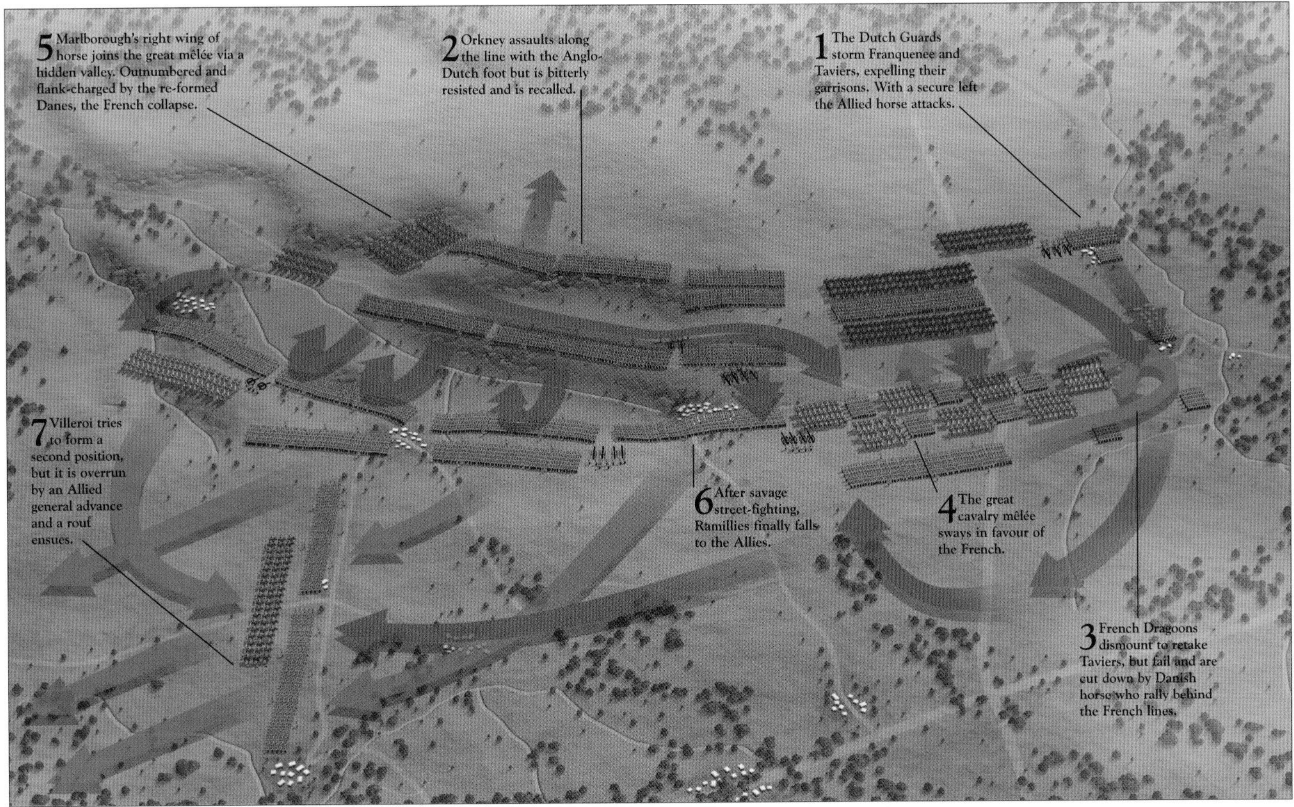
5 Marlborough's right wing of horse joins the great mêlée via a hidden valley. Outnumbered and flank-charged by the re-formed Danes, the French collapse.
2 Orkney assaults along the line with the Anglo-Dutch foot but is bitterly resisted and is recalled.
1 The Dutch Guards storm Franquenee and Taviers, expelling their garrisons. With a secure left the Allied horse attacks.
7 Villeroi tries to form a second position, but it is overrun by an Allied general advance and a rout ensues.
6 After savage street-fighting, Ramillies finally falls to the Allies.
4 The great cavalry mêlée sways in favour of the French.
3 French Dragoons dismount to retake Taviers, but fail and are cut down by Danish horse who rally behind the French lines.

The battle of Ramilles took place in wide open country near the village of Ramillies itself. It was almost a natural arena for warfare – ideal, so it seemed, for the sweeping cavalry charge to be the decisive instrument.

numbers. This meant switching Lumley's cavalry from the right to the left, where their numbers and surprise appearance would make a significant difference. This hinged upon the French not knowing that Lumley was coming. Marlborough sent word to Lumley for the majority of his cavalry to wheel sharply to their left and move off unseen down the shallow Quivelette valley towards the centre. It was a calculated risk and it took some time to effect, but when the first 18 squadrons of Lumley's command arrived, Marlborough had enough horsemen to risk undertaking a mêlée en masse with the best cavalry in Europe.

The battle began with a charge of the much admired French cavalry. With 68 squadrons, a cavalry charge on such a scale had seldom been seen before. Literally thousands of horsemen walked and then slow-trotted forwards, boot to boot. This was no furious charge, but a steady steamroller of an advance. What followed was a furious mêlée, with the two sides crashing into one another at the recommended good round trot, spilling men from the saddle and knocking horses over and sideways in the crush. Both sides' reserves cannoned into the rear of their own formations and sent shockwaves of impetus through the densely packed mass, which swayed back and forth, neither side gaining a clear advantage.

BREAKTHROUGH

The moment of breakthrough came late in the day when Marlborough, placing himself at the head of the 18 newly arrived cavalry squadrons, led them into the battle. It was now a matter of time and attrition. The Allies were winning the cavalry struggle, with a numerical superiority of 87 to 68 squadrons. They drove the French back and then opened up their guns on them. The French Household cavalry had done their best and lived up to their fame, but after nearly two hours of charging and counter-charging, they were finally being overwhelmed. The Allied horse pinned them frontally and surged through the gaps to surround and annihilate them. For the French, it was a final, crushing end to a hard-fought battle; for the Allies, it was a decisive victory.

Ramillies

RAMILLIES

Two hundred years after the defeat of Francis I at Pavia by the Hapsburg guns, the French army, under Francois Villeroi's command at Ramillies, remained wedded to the idea of marching infantry and the 'glorious' cavalry charge. To be fair, the French were still the finest cavalry in Europe, but now they were taking on a shrewd opponent in John Churchill, Duke of Marlborough, who had already secured his reputation with a brilliant victory at Blenheim the year before. Two hours of French charges and counter charges brought only 'the most shameful, disastrous and humiliating of routs'.

Oudenarde 1708

KEY FACTS

Who John Churchill, Duke of Marlborough and Eugène, Prince of Savoy and the Allied army, against the French under Joseph, Duke of Vendome and Louis, Duke of Burgundy.

What The French army was undermined by poor communication, mutual distrust and the different objectives of their commanders, in contrast to Marlborough's swift and efficient deployments and communication networks.

Where Oudenarde, modern Belgium.

When 11 July 1708

Why The French had made another attempt to retake the Spanish Netherlands and seemed poised to cut off the British army's supply lines from the English Channel.

Outcome Defeat was followed by peace negotiations, but Louis XIV would soon return to his attempt to regain the Netherlands.

In contrast to the neat battle formation, and rampaging cavalry charges at Ramillies, the battle between the Allied army and the French at Oudenarde was just a mad, bloody scramble. But it produced the same outcome – a defeat for the French.

WAR OF THE SPANISH SUCCESSION

ANGLO-DUTCH VICTORY

Keeping supply lines open was key for any army on campaign overseas. Oudenarde was a vital fortress if the British were to retain their lines to the English Channel in the War of Spanish Succession.

LOCATION

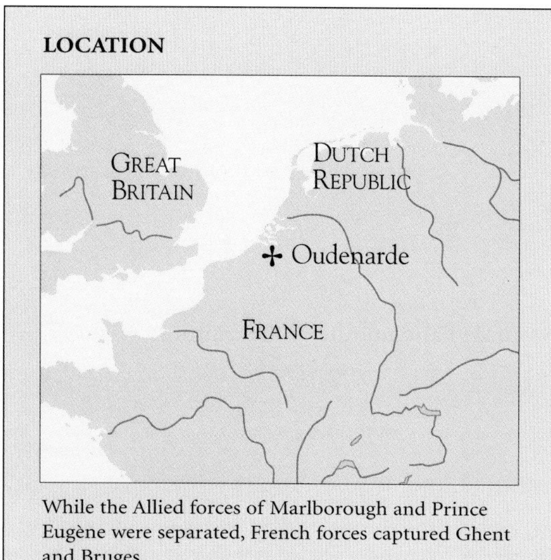
GREAT BRITAIN
DUTCH REPUBLIC
Oudenarde
FRANCE

While the Allied forces of Marlborough and Prince Eugène were separated, French forces captured Ghent and Bruges.

Despite several major battles, such as at Blenheim (1704) and Ramillies (1706), the Spanish War of Succession dragged on. The fighting in the Low Countries had reached stalemate until, in 1708, Louis XIV sent a large army under the joint command of the seasoned old soldier the Duke of Vendôme and his grandson and heir, Louis, the Duke of Burgundy.

As the French army prepared for an invasion of Flanders, the Duke of Marlborough, now seemingly outnumbered, was joined by the Imperial army under Prince Eugène of Savoy. When the French persuaded the citizens of Ghent and Bruges in northern Flanders to turn themselves over, thus cutting Marlborough's lines of supply, the Allies, realizing their fortress at Oudenarde was their only remaining link with the English Channel, decided the best option was to engage the French as swiftly as possible.

An Allied advanced guard under quartermaster general William Cadogan secured Oudenarde before the French under Vendôme could reach it. While the latter was

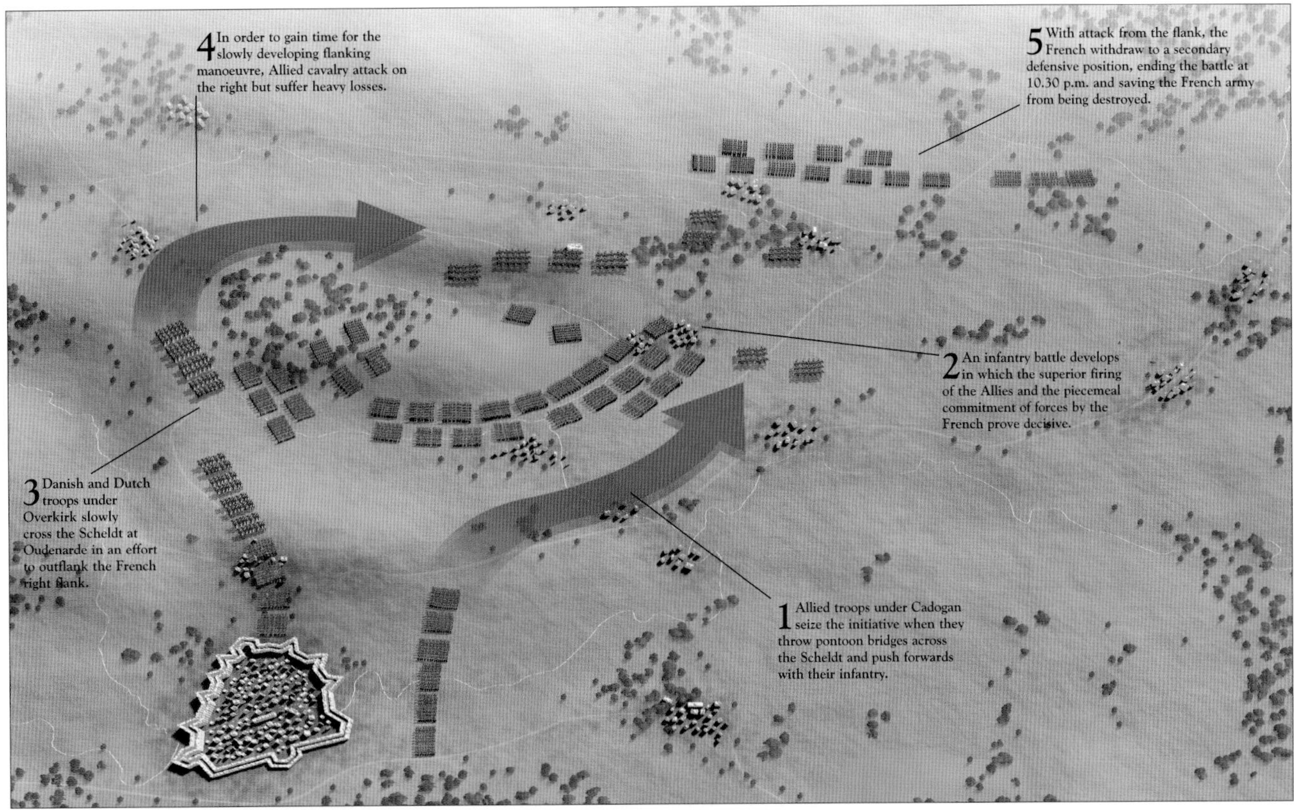
4 In order to gain time for the slowly developing flanking manoeuvre, Allied cavalry attack on the right but suffer heavy losses.
5 With attack from the flank, the French withdraw to a secondary defensive position, ending the battle at 10.30 p.m. and saving the French army from being destroyed.
2 An infantry battle develops in which the superior firing of the Allies and the piecemeal commitment of forces by the French prove decisive.
3 Danish and Dutch troops under Overkirk slowly cross the Scheldt at Oudenarde in an effort to outflank the French right flank.
1 Allied troops under Cadogan seize the initiative when they throw pontoon bridges across the Scheldt and push forwards with their infantry.

Oudenarde was another example of the Duke of Marlborough's effective leadership. By moving his troops across terrain at a rapid pace while the enemy seemed to be dawdling, he enabled the British to assume the advantageous position, despite being outnumbered.

determined to launch an assault on it, he found to his frustration that he was undermined by Burgundy, who argued for adopting a more defensive position along the River Scheldt. Cadogan spotted that Vendôme's forces were moving at only a leisurely pace to redeploy across the river, and sent word back to Marlborough to arrive as quickly as possible, setting up pontoon bridges across the Scheldt to aid him. Marlborough marched at lightning speed, and this audacious crossing by Allied troops had given them the initiative, even though the French had a considerable numerical advantage.

As the battle began, Burgundy ordered six battalions of French infantry towards the village of Groenewald, but the attack got bogged down. Seeing this, Vendôme ordered another six battalions in support and finally led an additional 12 battalions himself. Eventually Vendôme had committed 50 battalions to the attack against the Allies, but was unable to exercise effective command since he was personally engaged in the infantry battle. Unfortunately, Burgundy seemed unaware of what was happening and did little to support the main attack. He sent 16 cavalry squadrons, but their advance was halted by the marshy ground. The battle raged on and the superior platoon fire of the allies took its toll.

On the Allied side of the field, the coordination between Marlborough, who was now commanding the Allied left, and Eugène, Prince of Savoy, was exemplary by contrast. Then critical reinforcements arrived in the form of Count Overkirk and his 24 battalions and 12 squadrons of Dutch and Danish troops. Although the battle raged on for some time longer, the arrival of the Dutch and Danes under Overkirk convinced Burgundy that all was lost and he and his entourage left the field. Vendôme held on a bit longer, but was eventually forced to withdraw, joining Burgundy on the road back to Ghent.

Had Overkirk arrived earlier, the entire French army might have been destroyed. As it was, 5500 French were killed or wounded and another 9000 captured, including some 800 officers. The Allies also took more than 100 standards and colours and 4500 horses and mules, losing just under 3000 killed and wounded from their own strength.

Poltava 1709

KEY FACTS

Who Charles XII of Sweden lead his army against the Russian tsar Peter the Great.

What A Swedish army seriously weakened by a march through the Russian winter, was picked off by a newly efficient Russian artillery power outside Poltava.

Where Poltava, Ukraine.

When 27 June 1709

Why The Swedish had endeavoured to continue their military dominance of the region by invading Russia.

Outcome Swedish military capability had been critically dented, while Russia announced its arrival as a military force.

Sweden was a relatively small European nation that had punched above its weight for years. The Russians, by contrast, had lagged behind. But once Peter the Great finally mobilized his country's potential military capability, the results could be devastating, as demonstrated at Poltava.

GREAT NORTHERN WAR

RUSSIAN VICTORY

The Swedes had to pass through a narrow area of ground flanked by marshes on one side and woods on the other to confront the Russians at Poltava, and their slim front left them an easy target for Peter's the Great's waiting artillery.

LOCATION

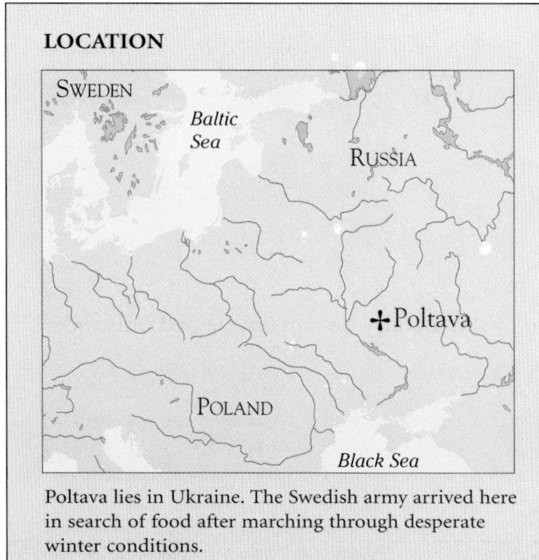
SWEDEN
Baltic Sea
RUSSIA
Poltava
POLAND
Black Sea

Poltava lies in Ukraine. The Swedish army arrived here in search of food after marching through desperate winter conditions.

Poltava marked the arrival of Russia as a military power, but to do so, it first had to defeat the Swedes, who had been in the ascendency for some time. Charles XII, king of Sweden, had continued his nation's domination of the Scandinavian and Baltic region, established by King Gustavus Adolphus earlier in the previous century, but Russia was increasingly impatient to assert its own presence. While the Swedes were absorbed with attacking Denmark and Poland, the Russian army underwent major reform under the tsar, Peter the Great. When Charles invaded Russia in 1708, it was finally able to put out an army that was fully equipped to meet him.

Charles had made the mistake of invading during a Russian winter, meaning that by the time the main armies encountered one another, what had been a 40,000-strong Swedish force was down to around 22,000 men, whittled away by the cold, sickness and failing supplies, and by being picked off in skirmishes with the Russians. En route to Moscow, instead of waiting for troop reinforcements, Charles decided to lay

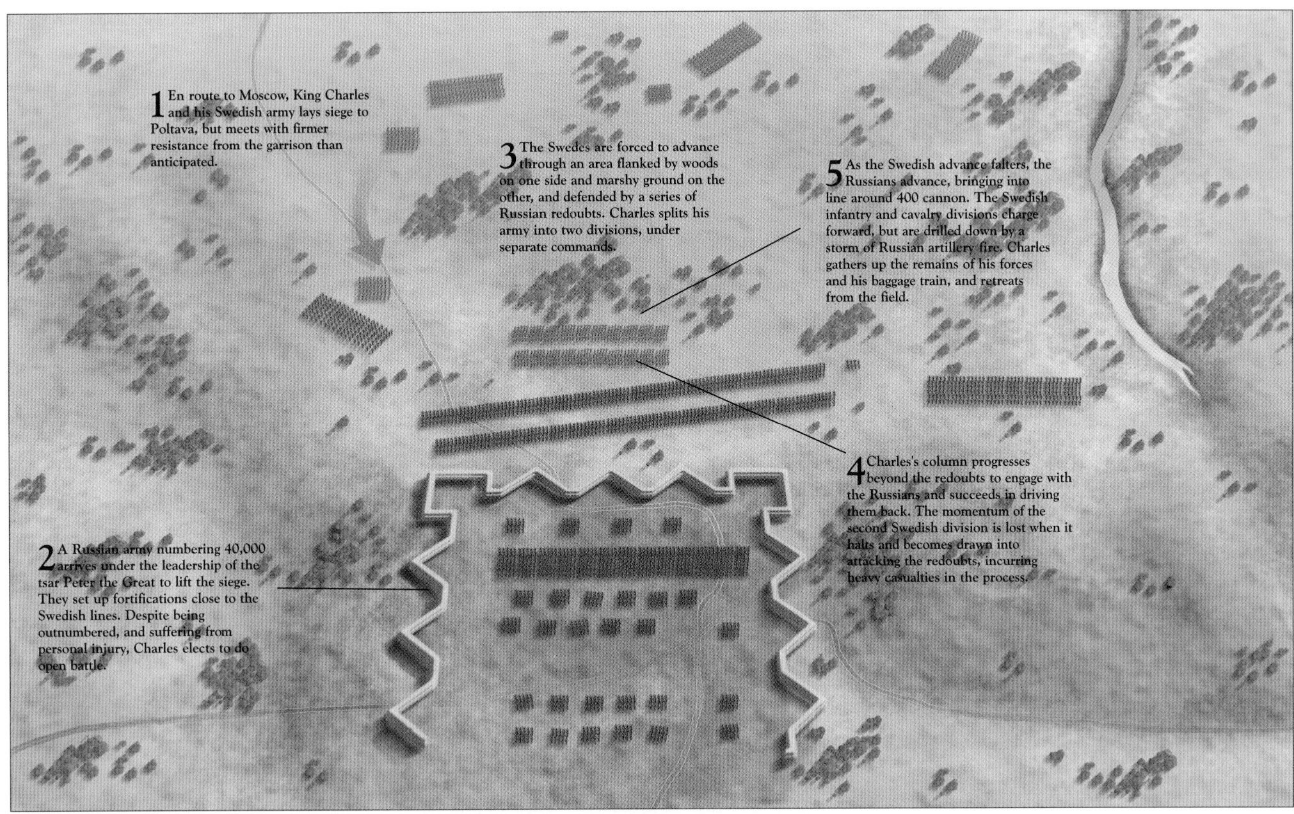
1 En route to Moscow, King Charles and his Swedish army lays siege to Poltava, but meets with firmer resistance from the garrison than anticipated.
2 A Russian army numbering 40,000 arrives under the leadership of the tsar Peter the Great to lift the siege. They set up fortifications close to the Swedish lines. Despite being outnumbered, and suffering from personal injury, Charles elects to do open battle.
3 The Swedes are forced to advance through an area flanked by woods on one side and marshy ground on the other, and defended by a series of Russian redoubts. Charles splits his army into two divisions, under separate commands.
4 Charles's column progresses beyond the redoubts to engage with the Russians and succeeds in driving them back. The momentum of the second Swedish division is lost when it halts and becomes drawn into attacking the redoubts, incurring heavy casualties in the process.
5 As the Swedish advance falters, the Russians advance, bringing into line around 400 cannon. The Swedish infantry and cavalry divisions charge forward, but are drilled down by a storm of Russian artillery fire. Charles gathers up the remains of his forces and his baggage train, and retreats from the field.

Poltava lay on the road to Moscow. Charles of Sweden had invaded during the Russian winter and, with supplies short, was keen to make rapid advances. This would inform his keenness to engage with better-positioned opponents at Poltava.

siege to Poltava, but the garrison within held out longer than anticipated. To add to the problem of dwindling food supplies, gunpowder was also running low.

It was at this moment that a 40,000-strong Russian army arrived under the command of tsar Peter. To make his situation worse, Charles' ability to command was hampered by an infected foot wound, which left him lame.

The sensible move at this point would have been for Charles to draw back as quickly as possible. However, he decided to remain and fight the Russians. The latter had set up fortifications close to the Swedish army, expecting that Charles would aim for a swift resolution of the situation, given his supply issues. They were correct. A Swedish advance meant they had to pass through an area that was flanked by woods on one side and marshy ground on the other. This area was defended by a series of Russian redoubts. Passing the redoubts required splitting the army into two divisions, only one of which could be under Charles's command as he was carried along on a litter.

Unfortunately, Charles was a 'lead from the front' leader who did not find it easy to delegate or communicate ideas to subordinates readily. While Charles's column swept beyond the redoubts to engage and drive back the Russians, the second division, confused about its purpose, paused to attack the redoubts, incurring heavy casualties in the process. With this loss of momentum from the Swedish advance, Peter now bought his own 40,000-strong force forward, together with something in the region of 400 cannon.

TORN TO SHREDS

Once again, wisdom might have dictated a sharp withdrawal, but Charles had, from past military experience, developed contempt for the ability of the Russian soldier to hold his ground. So he launched some 4000 infantry and cavalry on a 600m (660yd) advance into a storm of Russian artillery fire. Inevitably, the Swedes were torn to shreds. The Swedes had met with savage defeat. In a single battle, the baton of Northern European super power had passed from them to Russia.

Poltava

POLTAVA

With all the resources at its disposal, Russia had been punching below its weight for too long on the battlefield, something that Peter the Great was keen to rectify. Fascinated by technology, he invested huge sums in building up his army's artillery firepower. This was unleashed on the Swedes – until then, the mightier fighting force – at Poltava to devastating effect. The battle announced the arrival of Russia as a force to be contended with, and for only one year of Peter's reign the country would not be at war.

Siege of Fredriksten 1718

KEY FACTS

WHO King Charles XII of Sweden against the Norwegian garrison of the town of Fredriksten.

WHAT Frediksten was a key fortress and Charles XII intended to capture it to ensure his army would not be attacked from the rear.

WHERE Fredriksten, near Halden, Norway.

WHEN 12 December 1718

WHY Charles XII was involved in an ongoing battle to capture Denmark-Norway.

OUTCOME Charles XII was killed while making a trench inspection, and the invasion was abandoned.

King Charles XII of Sweden was a fascinating figure, and an able military commander. But leading the army in person at the siege of Fredriksten he was mortally injured by a projectile while inspecting the trenches. His death ended Sweden's hopes of conquering neighbouring Norway.

GREAT NORTHERN WAR

NORWEGIAN VICTORY

5 The death of the king on the evening of 30 November in the forward trench saves the fort from capitulation.
4 Meanwhile the other two forts, Overbjerget and Mellemberget, remain held by the Norwegians. However, due to both a lack of artillery and proximity, they are unable to give fire support for the garrison at Fredriksten.
1 The Swedes erect an artillery position on Studekollen heights to provide fire support for the storming of Gyldenløve fort.
3 Below Gyldenløve, the Swedes now dig a first parallel and begin preparations to dig a second, where they would place heavy siege guns.
2 Not liking formal sieges, the impatient Swedes storm and capture Gyldenløve on 24 November.

Charles XII organized what had seemed likely to be a fruitful siege, but his death while inspecting troops led to its abandonment – and the loss of one of Europe's most accomplished military rulers.

In October 1718, Swedish king Charles XII invaded southern Norway with 35,000 troops, determined to reduce the lynchpin of the enemy's frontier defences at Fredrikshald to rubble through a regular siege, led by a hired professional French artillery officer called Colonel Maigret.

The Swedes, commanded in person by the king, stormed and captured the outer fort of Gyldenløve on 24 November. Three days later, the Swedes, facing only 1400 enemy troops holding the fortress of Fredriksten, dug a parallel trench to the fortress, followed by an approach trench (to a second parallel), and seemed to be on the verge of a great – and relatively easy – victory.

CHARLES XII'S DEMISE

Once the siege artillery had the fortress within range, it could be forced through bombardment to capitulate, as Colonel Maigret had assured the king. But on 30 November Charles XII was killed in the most mysterious of circumstances in the forward trenches, saving the Norwegians from what would have been a humiliating defeat and eventual occupation by their neighbours.

LOCATION

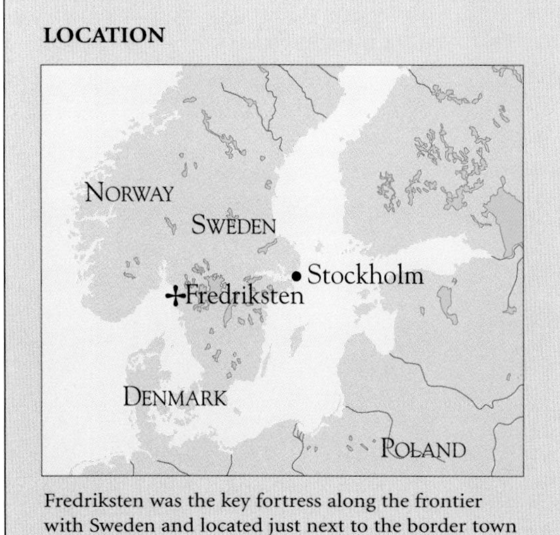

NORWAY
SWEDEN
Stockholm
Fredriksten
DENMARK
POLAND

Fredriksten was the key fortress along the frontier with Sweden and located just next to the border town of Fredrikshald in southeastern Norway.

TIMELINE

1500–1000BC	1000–500BC	500BC–0AD	0–500AD	500–1000AD	1000–1500AD	1500–2000AD

Leuthen 1757

KEY FACTS

WHO Frederick the Great headed a Prussian army against the Austrians under the command of Charles of Lorraine and Field Marshal Leopold.

WHAT Frederick performed a brilliantly executed, rapid redeployment of his men on the battlefield, which threw his opponents into confusion. Despite their superior numbers, they were unable to recover.

WHERE Leuthen, in modern-day Poland.

WHEN 5 December 1757

WHY The Austrians had retaken Silesia during the ongoing Seven Years War and Frederick was determined to win it back.

OUTCOME This was Frederick the Great's finest hour, establishing his reputation as a great general for all time, and ensuring Prussian control of Silesia.

When Frederick the Great led the Prussians at Leuthen in 1757, his reputation as a brilliant general was already secure after his devastating win over the French at Rossbach. After Leuthen, he would earn a place among the greats of legend.

SEVEN YEARS WAR

PRUSSIAN VICTORY

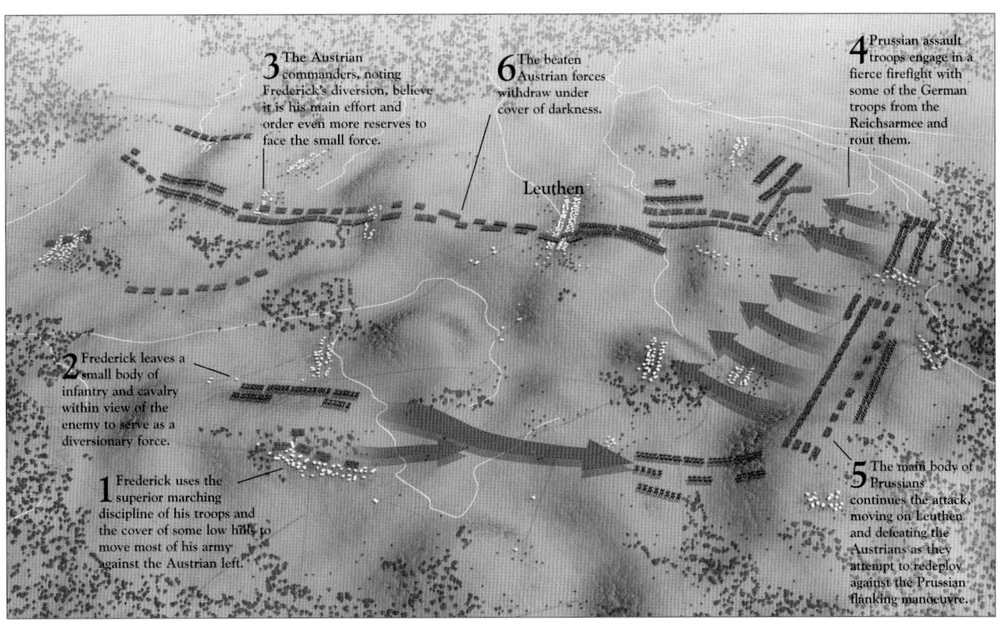

3 The Austrian commanders, noting Frederick's diversion, believe it is his main effort and order even more reserves to face the small force.
6 The beaten Austrian forces withdraw under cover of darkness.
4 Prussian assault troops engage in a fierce firefight with some of the German troops from the Reichsarmee and rout them.
Leuthen
2 Frederick leaves a small body of infantry and cavalry within view of the enemy to serve as a diversionary force.
1 Frederick uses the superior marching discipline of his troops and the cover of some low hills to move most of his army against the Austrian left.
5 The main body of Prussians continues the attack, moving on Leuthen and defeating the Austrians as they attempt to redeploy against the Prussian flanking manoeuvre.

Frederick the Great's manoeuvre at Leuthen was skilfully executed. It required much discipline on the part of his soldiers, and the ability to cover the terrain quickly, having left only a small body of infantry and cavalry to divert the Austrians.

Frederick the Great and his Prussian army met the Austrians at Leuthen under the command of Charles of Lorraine and Field Marshal Leopold Daun while marching on the city of Breslau. Frederick took advantage of the excellent discipline and mobility of his troops, as well as the terrain, to undertake a daring and complex manoeuvre. Using speed and the cover of some low ridges, Frederick marched his army across the front of the Austrian forces and appeared on the Austrian left flank.

EXPOSED FLANK

A small body of infantry and cavalry were left in sight of the Austrians to keep their attention and give the impression he had deployed his army to their front. Frederick quickly attacked the enemy's exposed flank and routed the Reichsarmee units on the far left. The Austrians made an effort to create a new defensive line based on the village of Leuthen, but their slow manoeuvring forced units to attack piecemeal, and so the Austrians were driven out of the town and pushed back. Frederick pursued them, but the arrival of night precluded an utter rout in a battle that had lasted for only three hours.

LOCATION

PRUSSIA
HANOVER
Berlin
Leuthen
FRANCE
AUSTRIA
Vienna

After his victory in Rossbach in Saxony, Frederick the Great quickly moved to Silesia. He then moved on Breslau, encountering the Austrians at Leuthen en route.

TIMELINE

1500–1000BC	1000–500BC	500BC–0AD	0–500AD	500–1000AD	1000–1500AD	1500–2000AD

Rossbach 1757

KEY FACTS

WHO Frederick the Great of Prussia against the combined armies of France and Austria under Charles de Rohan, Prince de Soubise and General Joseph von Saxe-Hilburghausen.

WHAT With skilful planning, adept use of the terrain and an ability to respond decisively to a changing situation, Frederick the Great brought off a stunning victory.

WHERE Near the village of Rossbach, Saxony, Germany.

WHEN 5 November 1757

WHY Frederick the Great was facing invasion on several fronts and determined to deal with the Franco-Austrian threat first.

OUTCOME Frederick's victory re-invigorated him after earlier reverses and he was now able to deal with the further threats to his realm.

Frederick II of Germany was not given the epithet 'the Great' lightly. As a military leader, he was considered a tactical genius, and his brilliance was seldom more evident than at Rossbach.

SEVEN YEARS WAR

PRUSSIAN VICTORY

Frederick the Great was determined to establish Prussia as a European power, which inevitably meant confrontation with two old adversaries, France and Austria.

LOCATION

SWEDEN
PRUSSIA
HANOVER
Berlin
Rossbach
SAXONY
AUSTRIA

Frederick chose Saxony as the place to rest his army after the retreat from Bohemia because it offered him a central position in Germany to react to his enemy.

In 1757 Frederick the Great faced the enmity of Austria, and counted Russia and France among his other enemies. The Prussian kingdom lacked the men and money that his opponents could muster. England sided with the soldier-king, but its commitments were largely focused in Hanover and north Germany. Still, the year had begun well enough. Frederick's occupation of Saxony the previous year allowed him to invade Bohemia in the spring. The first months of the campaign found him before the gates of Prague, yet by summer the tide of war had turned. In May an Austrian relief army under Marshal Browne approached the Bohemian capital. With few troops to spare, Frederick marched to meet Browne and defeated him after a bloody day's combat.

A month later the Battle of Kolin was another desperate affair, in which Frederick himself narrowly escaped capture. After suffering 14,000 casualties, Frederick left the field of battle to his enemy, raised the siege of Prague and limped back to Saxony. The situation worsened. France entered the war in the spring of 1757, soon to be joined by

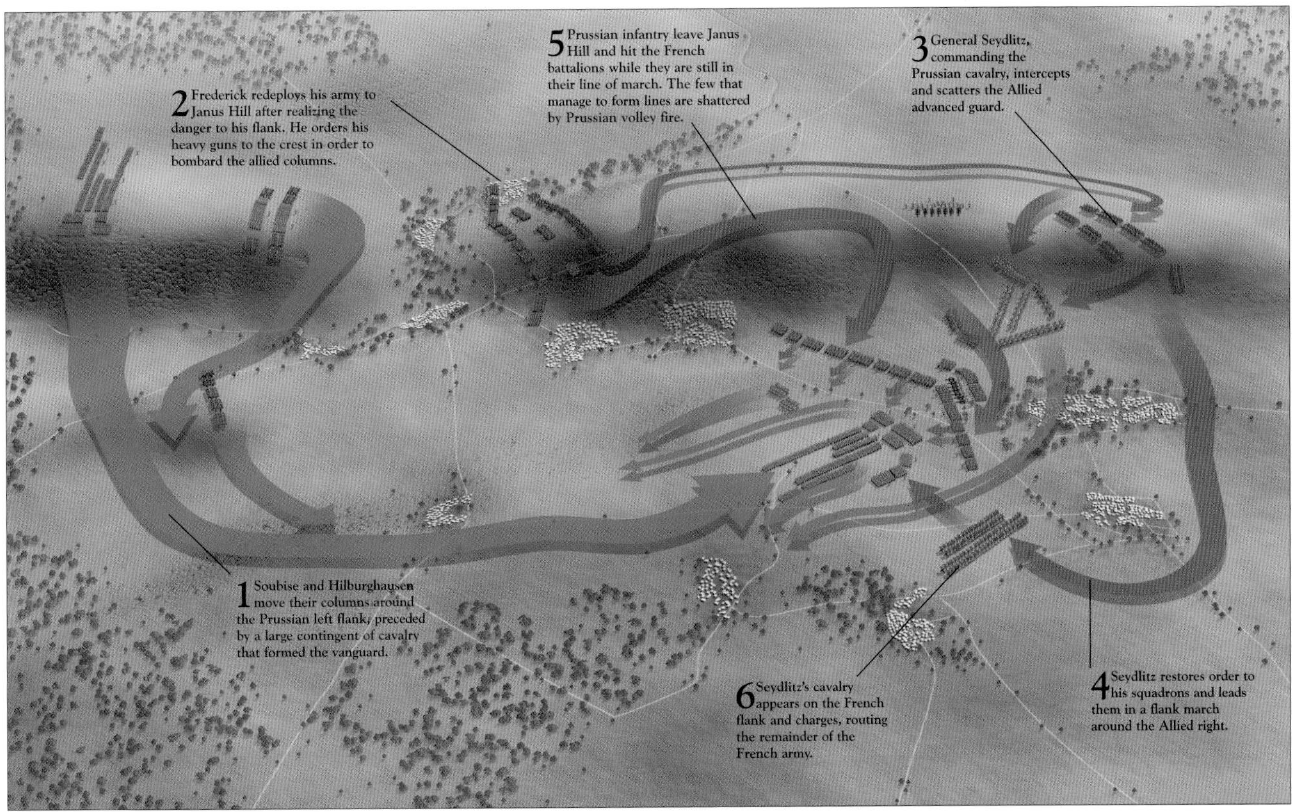

5 Prussian infantry leave Janus Hill and hit the French battalions while they are still in their line of march. The few that manage to form lines are shattered by Prussian volley fire.
3 General Seydlitz, commanding the Prussian cavalry, intercepts and scatters the Allied advanced guard.
2 Frederick redeploys his army to Janus Hill after realizing the danger to his flank. He orders his heavy guns to the crest in order to bombard the allied columns.
1 Soubise and Hilburghausen move their columns around the Prussian left flank, preceded by a large contingent of cavalry that formed the vanguard.
6 Seydlitz's cavalry appears on the French flank and charges, routing the remainder of the French army.
4 Seydlitz restores order to his squadrons and leads them in a flank march around the Allied right.

Success for the Prussians at Rossbach involved an ambitiously redeployment of the entire army, all the more impressive given that the complicated movement was completed within just 90 minutes.

Sweden and Russia, and all were ready to hone in on Berlin.

Frederick determined to deal with the Franco-Austrian threat first, whilst the Russian army was too distant to intervene, even though his army would be outnumbered by two to one. The battle of Rossbach, therefore, where he faced a French army under Charles de Rohan, Prince de Soubise, and General Joseph von Saxe-Hilburghausen commanding the Reicharmee, was a deliberate engagement designed to eliminate a strategic threat.

As preparations were made for battle, Hilburghausen and Soubise, instead of advancing head-on, decided they would screen their camp, and move their columns around the Prussian left flank, catching Frederick unawares. It was a sound plan, but it took most of the morning for the French and Imperialists to organize into three march columns.

Frederick, eventually alert to the situation, ordered General von Seydlitz, his cavalry commander, to take all the cavalry and head off the Allied advance, while the Prussian infantry began to march. Taking advantage of a hill to his rear, he ordered his heavy guns to the crest and proceeded to bombard the French from more than a mile off.

Within 90 minutes, Frederick's entire army had redeployed. When Seydlitz unleashed his 38 cavalry squadrons, the surprised Austrian cavalry were hardly able to respond and were sent into flight. As the Prussian infantry moved down the slope towards the French, the Allies were unable to observe their progress due to a dip between their position and the Prussian army. As they emerged, disciplined volleys poured into the head of the Allied columns.

The French battalions faltered. Now Seydlitz's cavalry re-emerged on the French right. The charge of Prussian heavy squadrons took apart the already shaken army. Whatever control Soubise had, disappeared in moments. Another Seydlitz cavalry charge soon put the Imperialists to flight.

Frederick had not only won the day, but the victory transformed the strategic situation that had depressed the Prussian king through the summer. The battle cost Frederick 500 men. For the French and Imperialists, it was much more expensive: 5000 killed and wounded and another 5000 captured.

Minden 1757

KEY FACTS

WHO An Anglo-German army led by Field Marshal Ferdinand, Duke of Brunswick, against a French army led by the Marquis de Contades.

WHAT Massed cavalry charges by the French proved ineffective against the firepower of vastly outnumbered but disciplined use of musketry.

WHERE Minden, Minden-Ravensburg, now part of North Rhine-Westphalia, Germany.

WHEN 1 August 1757

WHY The French were threatening to take control of Hanover in the Seven Years War.

OUTCOME After the defeat the French army withdrew from Hanover, while the victory was greeted with great jubilation in Britain.

This was the age of the great cavalry charge, and there was no greater advocate of the cavalryman than Frederick the Great of Prussia. Ironically, however, victory for his Allied Army at Minden would be secured by infantry firepower against the glorious, massed French cavalry.

SEVEN YEARS WAR

ANGLO-GERMAN VICTORY

Minden would feature some of the most dramatic examples of massed cavalry charges, as waves of brave French horsemen launched themselves at the Allied guns. The mounted troops were simply blown to shreds.

LOCATION

HANOVER
PRUSSIA
Berlin
Minden
SAXONY
FRANCE
AUSTRIA

Minden is 56km (35 miles) east of Osnabruck. The battlefield is relatively unaltered and is on the open moor on the west bank of the River Weser.

When the French took control of the strategically vital fortress at Minden on the River Weser in Westphalia, Frederick the Great of Prussia was concerned that Hanover might fall into the hands of his enemy. Prince Ferdinand of Brunswick, charged with manoeuvring to deny the French the opportunity of making any further advancement, offered battle to the French under the Marshal, the Marquis de Contades on the plain of Minden.

VAINGLORIOUS CHARGE

The Duke of Marlborough's decisive battles at Blenheim and Ramillies, and the roles played in them by the Allied cavalry, had caught the imagination of public and military men alike. They sent out a signal for the return to shock-mêlée emphasis. Linked to the employment of cavalry 'en masse', Minden was to feature a classic example of the spectacular but utterly vainglorious charge.

The most extraordinary moment came when a misunderstood order – the result of linguistic confusion – set off the advance of an Allied column of attack

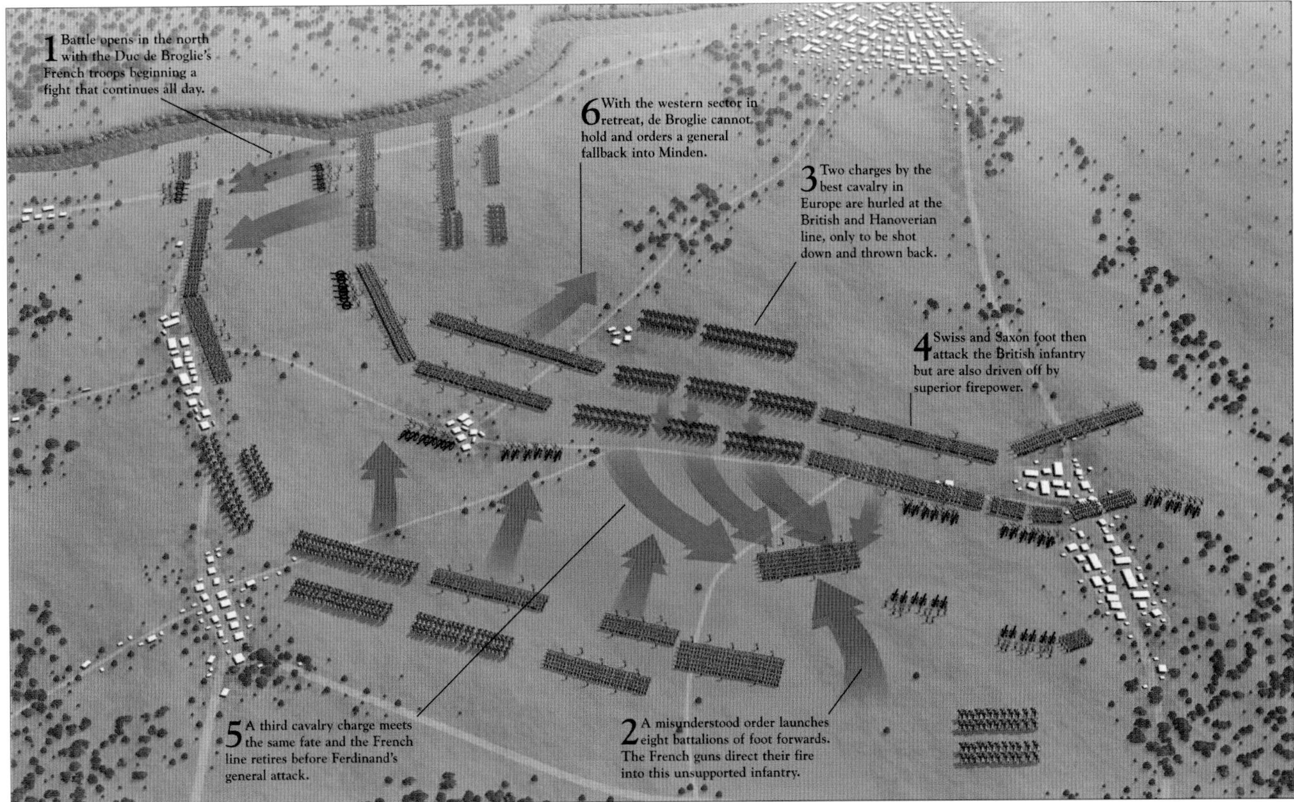
1 Battle opens in the north with the Duc de Broglie's French troops beginning a fight that continues all day.
6 With the western sector in retreat, de Broglie cannot hold and orders a general fallback into Minden.
3 Two charges by the best cavalry in Europe are hurled at the British and Hanoverian line, only to be shot down and thrown back.
4 Swiss and Saxon foot then attack the British infantry but are also driven off by superior firepower.
5 A third cavalry charge meets the same fate and the French line retires before Ferdinand's general attack.
2 A misunderstood order launches eight battalions of foot forwards. The French guns direct their fire into this unsupported infantry.

The French arrived at Minden with the reputation of possessing the finest cavalry in Europe. The battle took place on open moor – suitable terrain for the massed charge of horses – but the cavalry simply crashed into a wall of artillery fire.

commanded by Friedrich von Sporcken and containing six battalions of British infantry, unsupported by cavalry. As they marched, the morning mist lifted to reveal that they were heading directly towards the centre of the French line, where stood the elite French cavalry.

While Ferdinand tried to halt the advance, the redcoat line continued to move forward under heavy fire from two batteries of artillery, with the still fresh French cavalrymen licking their lips behind them. When they launched themselves in a mighty wave at the infantry, their combined squadrons amounted to something like 7500 men. But now the Allied infantry halted and presented muskets. Their first volley crashed into the front rank of the cavalry, bringing down men and horses in a sprawling mass.

Horsemen in the second rank tried to get their mounts to weave between or jump those who had gone down, but they then took a volley from the second rank, which halted most of them. Those that regrouped were dragged from their saddles and impaled on bayonets.

Further waves of cavalry attacks were launched, but Von Sporcken's men closed ranks, redressed and began to advance once more. The finest cavalry in Europe was being ripped to shreds, and there was no hope of rallying them. The technique of the unsupported charge of cavalry en masse was being defeated by the defensive firepower of unsupported infantry in line.

VICTORY FOR MUSKET AND BAYONET

With the French cavalry in ruins and their centre wide open, now was the time for the Allied cavalry to strike and pour through de Contades' line. But their general, Lord George Sackville, did not charge, and his conduct and that of the British and German cavalry was to become a scandal. Their behaviour contrasted with the bravery of the French, who made yet two more cavalry charges, including one straight into the point-blank fire of a large Allied battery in the centre.

Minden was unquestionably a battle won by the musket and the bayonet. The lesson for the cavalry was that if infantry stood and could deliver disciplined firepower at close range they could stop the gallop charge in its tracks.

Siege of Quebec 1759

KEY FACTS

WHO British army and navy under the control of General James Wolfe against Louis-Joseph, Marquis de Montcalm leading the French army.

WHAT The French ineffectively delivered their gunfire from too great a distance, while the English waited until they were within close range and dispensed their front line within two volleys.

WHERE Quebec, Canada.

WHEN 13 September 1759

WHY The British had made an amphibious assault on Quebec, the key possession among France's colonial territories in North America.

OUTCOME Both generals were fatally injured in the battle, but Quebec fell to the British, who would go on to capture the French colonies in North America.

The Battle of Quebec was one of the shortest in history, lasting no longer than 15 minutes. It is ironic, then, that the generals on either side should succumb to mortal gunshot wounds during its brisk interplay of firefighting.

FRENCH AND INDIAN WAR

BRITISH VICTORY

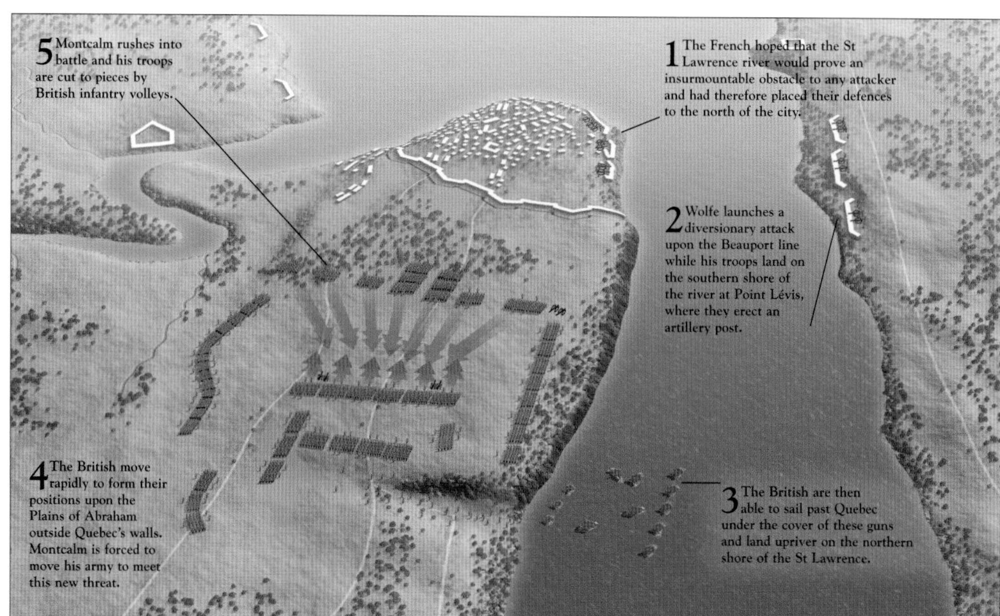

5 Montcalm rushes into battle and his troops are cut to pieces by British infantry volleys.
1 The French hoped that the St Lawrence river would prove an insurmountable obstacle to any attacker and had therefore placed their defences to the north of the city.
2 Wolfe launches a diversionary attack upon the Beauport line while his troops land on the southern shore of the river at Point Lévis, where they erect an artillery post.
4 The British move rapidly to form their positions upon the Plains of Abraham outside Quebec's walls. Montcalm is forced to move his army to meet this new threat.
3 The British are then able to sail past Quebec under the cover of these guns and land upriver on the northern shore of the St Lawrence.

A lot of planning had gone into the defensive siting of Quebec, to make use of the local terrain. In the event, a fierce exchange of artillery fire would be enough swiftly to decide the outcome in favour of the British attacking force.

Quebec was France's much-prized North American colonial capital. When it became plain that General Wolfe, after an amphibious mission along the St Lawrence River, had managed to slip his troops through a gap in the bankside defences to muster above the city, General Montcalm, the French commander, mustered his men as quickly as he could. But Wolfe had caught him off guard, and was effectively able to give battle on the Plains of Abraham on his terms.

Montcalm next made the fatal error of committing his troops too early to battle, instead of taking up a more defensive posture. His men delivered their gunfire from so distant a range that it proved ineffective. By contrast, the English infantry waited until their enemies had advanced well within musket range, then delivered their volleys smartly to maximum effect. The French were swiftly cut to pieces, but both Wolfe and Montcalm died from mortal gunshot wounds received in the short battle. After the bloody battle, the British began erecting siege lines, but the city capitulated once its garrison had been defeated in the field.

LOCATION

CANADA

FRENCH TERRITORY

Quebec

BRITISH COLONIES

Quebec lay in the very centre of the French colony of Canada. It was well fortified, making its capture by Wolfe and his British troops a difficult proposition.

TIMELINE

1500–1000BC	1000–500BC	500BC–0AD	0–500AD	500–1000AD	1000–1500AD	1500–2000AD

Quiberon Bay 1759

SEVEN YEARS WAR

BRITISH VICTORY

The Seven Years War (1756–1763) was not a profitable military venture for France, and at Quiberon Bay, in her own waters, its navy would experience one of its most humiliating defeats.

KEY FACTS

WHO The British navy under Admiral Sir Edward Hawke against Admiral Marquis de Conflans and the French navy.

WHAT An opportunist attack by Admiral Hawke, catching the French in shallow, rocky waters where they believed confrontation was unthinkable, reaped a handsome result for the British.

WHERE Quiberon Bay, near St Nazaire, France.

WHEN 20 November 1759

WHY France planned an invasion of Scotland, but several British warships set out to interrupt the preparation of its fleet near Quiberon Bay.

OUTCOME The defeat shattered the French navy, and put an end to their plans to sail on Scotland.

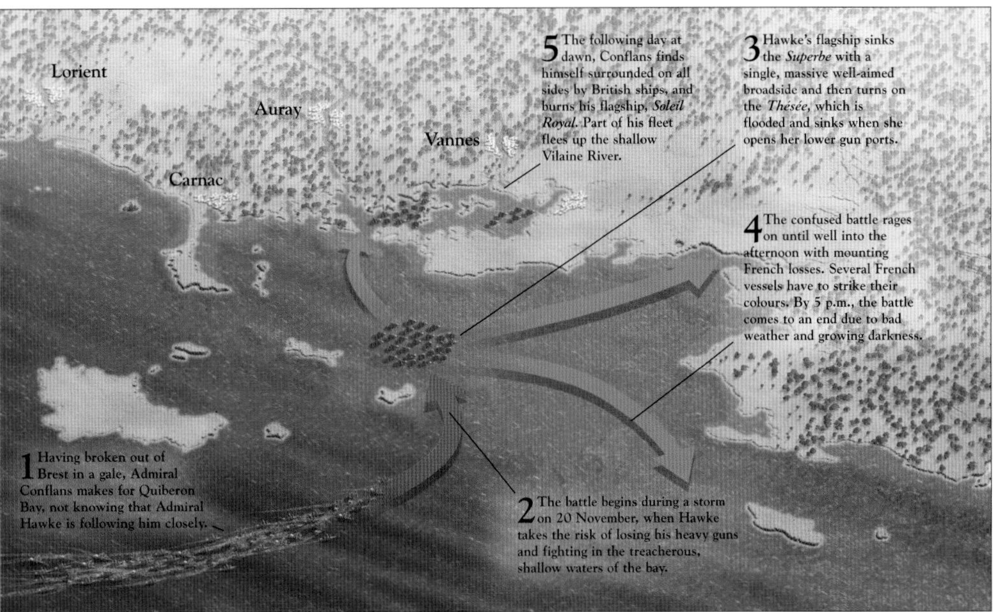

Lorient
Auray
Carnac
Vannes
5 The following day at dawn, Conflans finds himself surrounded on all sides by British ships, and burns his flagship, *Soleil Royal*. Part of his fleet flees up the shallow Vilaine River.
3 Hawke's flagship sinks the *Superbe* with a single, massive well-aimed broadside and then turns on the *Thésée*, which is flooded and sinks when she opens her lower gun ports.
4 The confused battle rages on until well into the afternoon with mounting French losses. Several French vessels have to strike their colours. By 5 p.m., the battle comes to an end due to bad weather and growing darkness.
1 Having broken out of Brest in a gale, Admiral Conflans makes for Quiberon Bay, not knowing that Admiral Hawke is following him closely.
2 The battle begins during a storm on 20 November, when Hawke takes the risk of losing his heavy guns and fighting in the treacherous, shallow waters of the bay.

The treacherous coastline at Quiberon made this an unlikely spot for a set-to between two major naval powers, and Admiral Hawke verged on the reckless in his pursuit of the French into these waters.

Quiberon Bay is a shallow, rocky and dangerous stretch of water and a far from ideal spot for a sea battle. But having shadowed the French to the bay where their commander Admiral Marquis de Conflans hoped to find sanctuary, Admiral Hawke overlooked the obvious dangers, made far worse by a oncoming gale, to signal his captains to 'Go at them!' The French were shocked that their enemy would be so bold as to fight them inside the bay during a gale, and shock turned to panic when Hawke's flagship sunk the *Superbe* with a single broadside. The *Thésée* sunk like a stone in the foaming waves when her captain ordered the lower gun ports opened to fire back at the British with her heaviest guns, allowing water to flood the ship.

VICTORY IN ADVERSITY

The battle raged on with intense ferocity for another three hours, but a critical British naval success had been achieved in potentially treacherous waters. The French plans to sail to attack Scotland were in ruins, and its defeat at Quiberon Bay was described as its 'Trafalgar' of the Seven Years' War – which it would ultimately lose.

LOCATION

ENGLAND

FRANCE

Brest •

✢ Quiberon Bay

Bay of Biscay

Quiberon Bay lies on the Biscay coast near the port of St Nazaire. Passage into the bay can be treacherous in poor weather, with dangerous rocks and shoals.

TIMELINE

1500–1000BC	1000–500BC	500BC–0AD	0–500AD	500–1000AD	1000–1500AD	1500–2000AD

Quiberon Bay

QUIBERON BAY

Admiral Sir Edward Hawke does not have the familiar ring of Admiral Horatio Nelson, perhaps, but he must be chalked up as another in a long line of able British sea commanders. At Quiberon Bay he conducted what to the French seemed an unthinkable, highly risky attack on their navy in shallow, rocky waters off the coast near St Nazaire. Hawke's opportunist success was later recalled as the French 'Trafalgar' of the Seven Years' War. It was undoubtedly a real-life instance of 'He who dares, wins.'

Siege of Havana 1762

KEY FACTS

WHO An amphibious British force led by the Earl of Albermarle, against combined Spanish forces led by Juna de Prado, the commander in chief, and Admiral Gutierre de Hevia.

WHAT The Earl of Albermarle decided that taking the fortress of Morro, at the entrance to Havana harbour, was the key to taking the city itself. But at one point it looked like he had run out of time.

WHERE Havana, Cuba.

WHEN 6 June–14 August, 1762

WHY The British were involved in a colonial war with Spain in the Americas, and Havana was an important Caribbean base for the Spanish fleet.

OUTCOME Havana would actually be returned to Spain as part of the treaty signed at the end of the Seven Years War, but its loss in 1762 was a serious blow to its naval power status.

When the Earl of Albermarle laid painstaking siege to the fortress of Morro, an outpost of Spanish-held Havana, many feared he was wasting precious time, with his men succumbing to yellow fever, and the hurricane season approaching. Could his patient approach pay off?

SEVEN YEARS WAR

BRITISH VICTORY

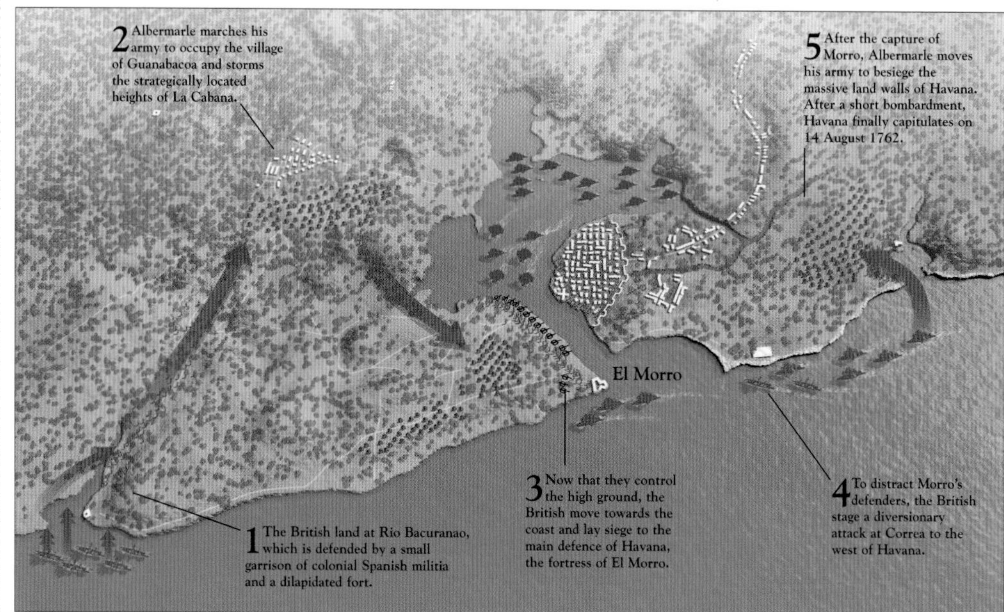
2 Albermarle marches his army to occupy the village of Guanabacoa and storms the strategically located heights of La Cabana.
5 After the capture of Morro, Albermarle moves his army to besiege the massive land walls of Havana. After a short bombardment, Havana finally capitulates on 14 August 1762.
El Morro
1 The British land at Rio Bacuranao, which is defended by a small garrison of colonial Spanish militia and a dilapidated fort.
3 Now that they control the high ground, the British move towards the coast and lay siege to the main defence of Havana, the fortress of El Morro.
4 To distract Morro's defenders, the British stage a diversionary attack at Correa to the west of Havana.

Havana, as an important port, was defended by several fortifications. When the British appeared to spend most time on reducing a single fort guarding the harbour entrance, there were fears they were wasting precious resources.

Moving to wrest the vital port of Havana from Spanish control during the Seven Years War, the British caught their colonial rivals off guard by landing at the mouth of the Bacuranao river and moving swiftly to occupy the strategic heights of La Cabana and the village of Guanabacoa. La Cabana gave the British a commanding position above the Bay of Havana, where they could position artillery before moving to take control of the fortress of Morro, which defended the entrance to Havana's harbour. Albermarle, the British commander, was criticized for his slow but methodical strategy, and it's possible he underestimated the extent of the Morro fortifications. The Morro and its Spanish defenders were able to hold out for many days, costing the British dearly in numbers of men lost to yellow fever in the sticky tropical climate.

However, when it finally fell, it meant that Albermarle could march with his men smartly around the south of the Bay and lay siege to the city itself, which eventually capitulated on 14 August 1762. The siege was over and Britain had won a great victory over her colonial rivals.

LOCATION

Atlantic Ocean
East Florida
Gulf of Mexico
Havana
Bahamas
Cuba
Caribbean Sea

Cuba controlled the shipping lanes into and out of the Mexican Gulf and Florida Straits. Havana was the main port and fortified base on the island.

TIMELINE

1500–1000BC	1000–500BC	500BC–0AD	0–500AD	500–1000AD	1000–1500AD	1500–2000AD

Maymyo 1767

SINO-BURMESE WAR

BURMESE VICTORY

When the might of the Chinese army rolled into Burma at the start of the Sino-Burmese War, victory appeared certain for the larger army. But the Burmese terrain, with its jungles and mountains are ideal for a plucky, and smart, local soldier with the know-how to exploit the situation.

KEY FACTS

WHO Maha Thiha Thura, commander of the Burmese military forces, against the Chinese army led by General Mingrui.

WHAT The Burmese encircled a retreating Chinese army and effectively massacred them, with General Mingrui committing suicide.

WHERE Maymyo, modern-day Pyinoolwin, Burma.

WHEN 1767

WHY The Chinese had invaded Burma and Maha Thiha Thura used his heavily outnumbered infantry in guerrilla warfare tactics.

OUTCOME Sickened by defeat, yet undeterred, the Chinese would launch a further invasion, but once again Maha Thiha Thura would be in the thick of the action to repel them.

2 At least 10,000 Burmese infantry and 2000 cavalry resist the Chinese advance. They cannot stop the onslaught, but delay it significantly.
6 The Ming army attempts to break out of the Burmese trap by attacking through the smaller column to its front. The Burmese infantry make a stand, however, and the Chinese army becomes completely encircled and annihilated.
1 Ming Jui's southern column advances against the Burmese army towards the capital Ava.
3 Burmese troops peel off into the jungle from the main force and loop back to make guerrilla-style attacks on the Chinese flanks.
5 The second Burmese force launches a cutting attack on the Chinese rear. The Chinese are now under threat of encirclement.
4 A second Burmese infantry force under Maha Thiha Thura makes a wide sweep around the rear of the Chinese column.

The massive Ming army must have presented an impressive sight as it rolled forwards, but the outnumbered Burmese were not intimidated. Jungle terrain such as this was custom-ordered for their guerrilla style tactics.

LOCATION

MANCHU CHINA
INDIA
Ava
Maymyo
BURMA
SIAM

Terrain was an important factor in the Chinese defeat at Maymyo. The jungle and mountains of Burma suited Burmese guerrilla-style tactics.

When Miha Thiha Thura caught up with the Chinese army at Maymyo, they were already ailing from tropical diseases, starvation and extreme fatigue as their strategy for taking Burma unravelled. A pincer action against the Burmese capital of Ava failed after one force became isolated and cut off by the Burmese infantry who, naturally enough, had the major advantage of being more familiar with their country's convoluted terrain.

They put up such an impressive defence at Kaughton, a fortified position, that the northern arm of the Chinese pincer was stopped dead in its tracks, and then put into retreat. The Chinese infantry of the southern column, therefore, were left isolated against the increasing Burmese guerrilla-style attacks. Then, as a killer blow, the entire army was encircled by Miha Thiha Thura's men. The Chinese suffered large casualties from Burmese archers and gunners as they moved in for the kill, and General Mingrui, electing not to flee the field, instead committed suicide.

TIMELINE

1500–1000BC	1000–500BC	500BC–0AD	0–500AD	500–1000AD	1000–1500AD	1500–2000AD

CHAPTER 4

The Wars of the Revolution

The battles of the Revolutionary period are dominated by those of the American War of Independence and the wars fought by the various European coalitions against the armies of Napoleonic France. The American battles were small scale – colonial militia pitting their wits and pluck against the British redcoats, exploiting the gaps in their drawn-out chains of command and unfamiliarity with the local terrain.

Napoleon Bonaparte may have been a megalomaniac who roused practically a whole continent to take up arms against him, but he was also a great soldier, respected by his men as one of their own. Some of his finest victories included Austerlitz (1805), but it must be placed against the folly of the ignominious retreat from Moscow (1812). Some of the most pitiless of battles were fought in this period. The French lost 25,000 men and the Prussians 15,000 at Eylau (1807). 'What a massacre!' exclaimed a forlorn Marshal Ney, contemplating the dreadful scene. 'And without a result!'

◀ 1801 Copenhagen – Nelson's grimly-fought battle with the Danes, more intense even than the fighting at Trafalgar, eventually saw an armistice signed and the legend of Nelson firmly established.

Bunker Hill 1775

AMERICAN WAR OF INDEPENDENCE

BRITISH VICTORY

Ever since the Boston Tea Party in 1773, in which the colonials tipped British tea into the harbour as a furious gesture against taxes imposed by the British government, Boston had been at the heart of rising tensions. They were to burst aflame at the Battle of Bunker Hill.

KEY FACTS

WHO British troops under General William Howe against the American militia under overall command of Colonel William Prescott.

WHAT The British launched several determined attempts to break hastily assembled American fortifications on the Charlestown peninsula. They finally succeeded, but at a heavy cost in terms of casualties.

WHERE Charlestown, Massachusetts.

WHEN 17 June 1775

WHY The Americans had laid siege to the port of Boston at an early stage of the War of Independence.

OUTCOME The British would continue to find themselves hemmed in on several fronts, and Howe would eventually have to evacuate Boston.

The American War of Independence seems made for the creation of heroes, as local militia from the colonies confronted the imperial might of the British army.

LOCATION

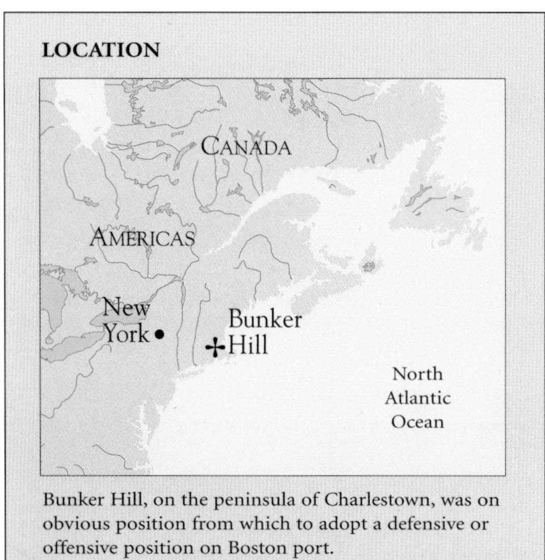
CANADA
AMERICAS
New York
Bunker Hill
North Atlantic Ocean

Bunker Hill, on the peninsula of Charlestown, was on obvious position from which to adopt a defensive or offensive position on Boston port.

At an early stage in the American War of Independence, the British army had found itself under siege at Boston. As the American militia gradually entrenched themselves in the surrounding countryside, a plan had been hatched by the British commander General Gage to gain control of the Charlestown peninsula across the harbour to facilitate a lifting of the blockade. American militia beat him to it, however, rapidly moving in to take control of Bunker Hill and Breed's Hill on the peninsula, and speedily erecting a redoubt upon the latter, from which artillery fire could be more readily directed on Boston.

General William Howe, one of a group of generals sent from London to assist Gage in breaking the siege, was assigned to attack the American positions. He began by landing with his men on the south easternmost shore of the peninsula at Moulton's Point. On arrival, he spotted that the Americans had further troop reinforcements on Bunker Hill, so he sent word back to the mainland to be supplied further soldiers. By then sitting back and waiting for these reinforcements to arrive, Howe lost valuable

The Americans' siege of Boston came at an early stage of the War of Independence. Although the British would manage to lift the siege, they sustained heavy losses, and the rebels at struck an early blow at their morale and future offensive capabilities.

momentum, for at this stage,the American troops had still not been fully deployed around their fortifications.

By mid-afternoon, the British reinforcements had arrived. A force under Brigadier General Robert Pigot began a feinted attack from the left flank on the redoubt, but as it did so it came under heavy sniper fire from the village of Charlestown. Howe now requested that Admiral Samuel Graves, whose boats had been ferrying the British soldiers across the bay, provided support fire. In the process of this, the village was set ablaze, by which time Pigot had pulled back. Howe had also launched an attack on the American left, but as the militia held their ground, he was forced to fall back under an onslaught of heavy artillery fire.

The British regrouped, this time planning for Pigot to launch a full attack on the redoubt while Howe led another assault on the American left. Once again, neither attack was successful, and the British were driven back under heavy fire, some of the companies so badly hit that they were reduced to single figures.

Howe now sent a message back to Boston requesting further soldiers, while persuading a number of those among his wounded to gird themselves for further action. But the Americans commanders were not without their problems either, with several companies beginning to retreat from the fortifications. One such company was brought back into line only when a neighbouring company under Captain John Chester from Connecticut turned and aimed their muskets at them, forcing them to reconsider.

Howe's final attack was made directly on the redoubt, and with the Americans now beginning to run short of ammunitions, they were able to break through. Once inside the redoubt, the battle turned into hand-to-hand fighting in which the British, with their bayonets, were at an advantage.

The Americans were eventually forced off the peninsula, and the British able to fortify Bunker Hill and Breed's Hill. But the cost had been disproportionately high. They had lost twice as many men as the Americans – 40 per cent of their attacking force – and this was not only a blow to morale but would also hinder their capability for future offensives.

Saratoga 1777

KEY FACTS

WHO British troops under General John Burgoyne against the Americans under General Horatio Gates.

WHAT The British general John Burgoyne found his advance on Albany blocked by American troops, and attempted to storm his way through by attacking their fortifications near Saratoga. His outnumbered forces were convincingly repulsed.

WHERE Saratoga County, New York.

WHEN 19 September and 7 October 1777

WHY The British were trying to take New York, which was a stronghold in the American battle for independence.

OUTCOME The American cause was taken increasingly seriously by the French after their victory at Saratoga, and they would soon form an alliance.

The Americans had been lobbying the French for some time for more support in their quest for independence. The resilience and professionalism shown by their army against the British at Saratoga finally induced the French to fully commit to the cause.

AMERICAN WAR OF INDEPENDENCE

AMERICAN VICTORY

For General John Burgoyne, an imaginative but somewhat headstrong commander, surrender to Horatio Gates at Saratoga represented a huge personal blow.

LOCATION

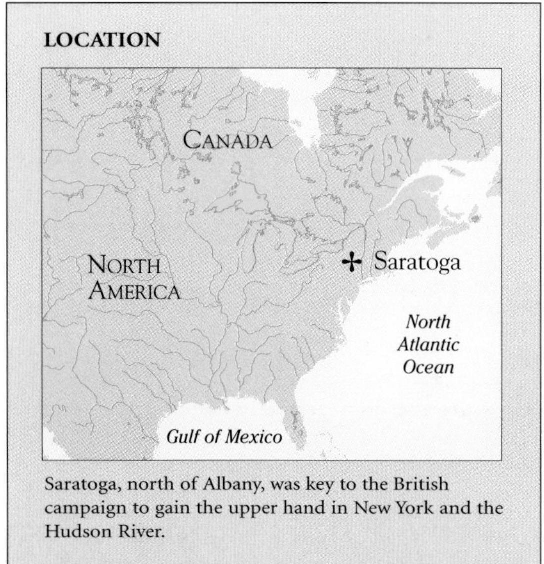
CANADA
NORTH AMERICA
Saratoga
North Atlantic Ocean
Gulf of Mexico

Saratoga, north of Albany, was key to the British campaign to gain the upper hand in New York and the Hudson River.

The British strategy in the US War of Independence placed great importance on subduing New York, an area where it had encountered fiercest resistance. General John Burgoyne understood that gaining control of the valley of the Hudson River and the regional capital Albany was vital, but while he was successful when operating along the waterway, movement over ground proved trickier in an area that had few roads, and which was often blocked by trees felled to slow the progress of British troops. When Burgoyne reached Saratoga, north of Albany, things began to go seriously awry.

Part of the plan involved a force of 1000 men under the command of Barry St Leger joining up with Burgoyne in Albany, having first gained control of central New York. But St Leger's column relied heavily on Indian recruits, and these had a reputation for unreliability. When news reached them of the approach of an American force heading towards them to relieve St Leger's siege of Fort Stanwix, they deserted, and St Leger, finding himself in danger of being trapped by a much larger army, had no

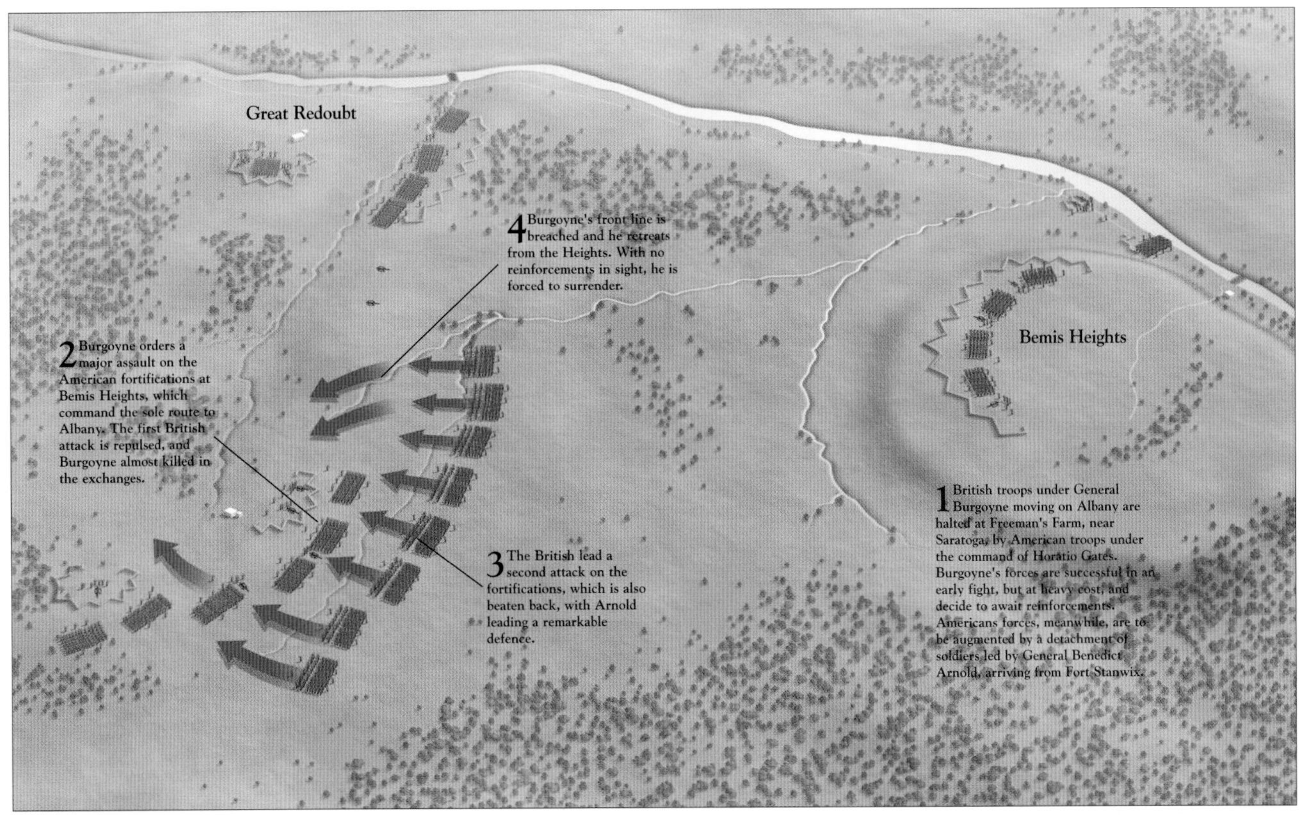

Great Redoubt
4 Burgoyne's front line is breached and he retreats from the Heights. With no reinforcements in sight, he is forced to surrender.
Bemis Heights
2 Burgoyne orders a major assault on the American fortifications at Bemis Heights, which command the sole route to Albany. The first British attack is repulsed, and Burgoyne almost killed in the exchanges.
1 British troops under General Burgoyne moving on Albany are halted at Freeman's Farm, near Saratoga, by American troops under the command of Horatio Gates. Burgoyne's forces are successful in an early fight, but at heavy cost, and decide to await reinforcements. Americans forces, meanwhile, are to be augmented by a detachment of soldiers led by General Benedict Arnold, arriving from Fort Stanwix.
3 The British lead a second attack on the fortifications, which is also beaten back, with Arnold leading a remarkable defence.

The British defeat at the Battle of Saratoga put a major dent in British pride and confidence in North America. In the two battles around Saratoga, the British lost a total of around 1000 men, against 500 casualties on the American side.

choice but to retreat into Canada, effectively taking himself out of the New York campaign.

Next Burgoyne ran into difficulties at Saratoga. German mercenaries in his employ went out scouting for supplies, but their haughty manner prompted many hitherto neutral locals to throw in their lot with the rebels. His Indians soldiers didn't help either by scalping a local girl, Jane McCrae. Even though she was married to a loyalist in Burgoyne's army, the failure to punish those Indians responsible made her a local cause célèbre, and another rallying point for the American rebels.

SEPTEMBER BATTLE

The first Battle of Saratoga took place at Freeman's Farm, after the arrival of American troops led by Horatio Gates, dispatched from Virginia by George Washington to halt Burgoyne's movement on Albany. The clash was won by the British, but as it came with the loss of a considerable number of men, Burgoyne decided to sit tight and await further reinforcements. However, it was the Americans whose numbers were to be augmented, in the shape of the detachment of soldiers led by General Benedict Arnold from Fort Stanwix.

Fearing winter could soon close in, and with sign of relief soldiers on the horizon, Burgoyne ordered a major assault on Bemis Heights, where the Americans had taken up a fortified position, commanding the only route to Albany. Although the rebels had the advantage of position, there were deep divisions within their command structure on the arrival of Arnold, to the extent that Gates had actually removed Arnold from field command.

The first British attack on the American defences was repulsed, with Burgoyne almost losing his life. The second also failed, and was notable for a remarkable appearance by Arnold. Seemingly in a state of considerable agitation, he disobeyed orders and rode into the fray, leading the defence of the American redoubts that the British were attempting to capture. The attack having failed, and with his front line breached, Burgoyne had little option but to retreat. Increasingly surrounded and outnumbered, he would soon surrender to the Americans, for whom victory at Saratoga was seen as a turning point in their cause.

Paulus Hook 1779

KEY FACTS

WHO 'Light Horse Harry' (Major Henry) Lee led the American Continental Army against British and Loyalist forces in charge of the fort at Paulus Hook.

WHAT Lee led a successful raid on an isolated British- and Loyalist-held fort at an important control point on the Hudson River.

WHERE Paulus Hook, New Jersey.

WHEN 19 August 1779

WHY The British had a firm grip on New York, underpinned by naval control of the Hudson and the fortresses alongside it.

OUTCOME The British retained the fort, but many of their soldiers were taken prisoner, and Lee was acclaimed by George Washington and honoured as a hero.

The American War of Independence made heroes of many men, one of whom was the distinguished cavalryman from Virginia, 'Light Horse Harry' Lee. But when he led an impudent night-time raid on the important fort at Paulus Hook in 1759, the British were distinctly unamused.

AMERICAN WAR OF INDEPENDENCE

AMERICAN VICTORY

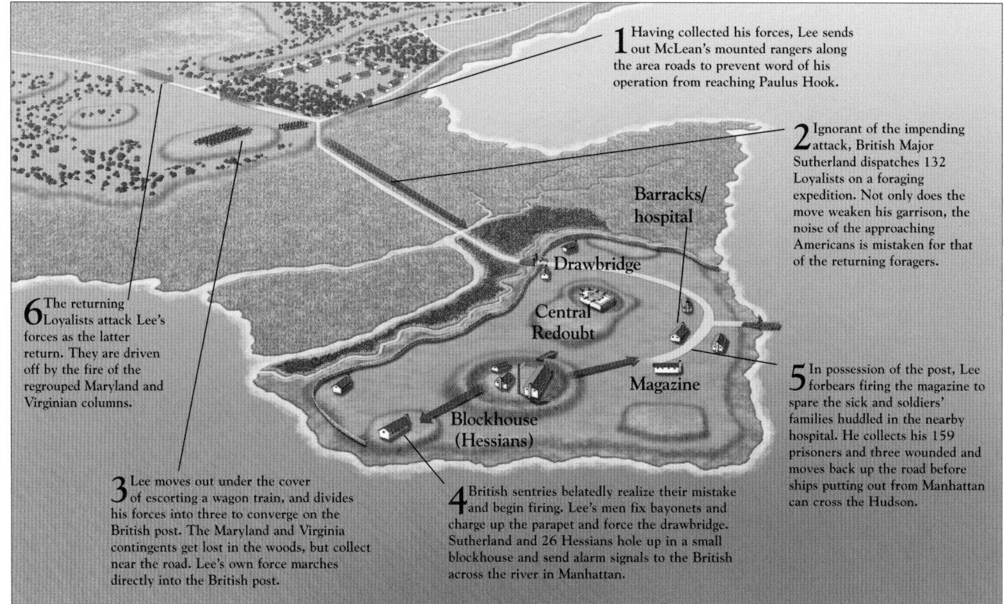
1 Having collected his forces, Lee sends out McLean's mounted rangers along the area roads to prevent word of his operation from reaching Paulus Hook.
2 Ignorant of the impending attack, British Major Sutherland dispatches 132 Loyalists on a foraging expedition. Not only does the move weaken his garrison, the noise of the approaching Americans is mistaken for that of the returning foragers.
Barracks/ hospital
Drawbridge
Central Redoubt
Magazine
Blockhouse (Hessians)
6 The returning Loyalists attack Lee's forces as the latter return. They are driven off by the fire of the regrouped Maryland and Virginian columns.
5 In possession of the post, Lee forbears firing the magazine to spare the sick and soldiers' families huddled in the nearby hospital. He collects his 159 prisoners and three wounded and moves back up the road before ships putting out from Manhattan can cross the Hudson.
3 Lee moves out under the cover of escorting a wagon train, and divides his forces into three to converge on the British post. The Maryland and Virginia contingents get lost in the woods, but collect near the road. Lee's own force marches directly into the British post.
4 British sentries belatedly realize their mistake and begin firing. Lee's men fix bayonets and charge up the parapet and force the drawbridge. Sutherland and 26 Hessians hole up in a small blockhouse and send alarm signals to the British across the river in Manhattan.

The British seemingly did not hear 'Lighthorse Harry' Lee's approaching army. Despite a few of his men getting lost in the woods, Lee was able to bring off one of the most daring escapades of the American War of Independence.

LOCATION

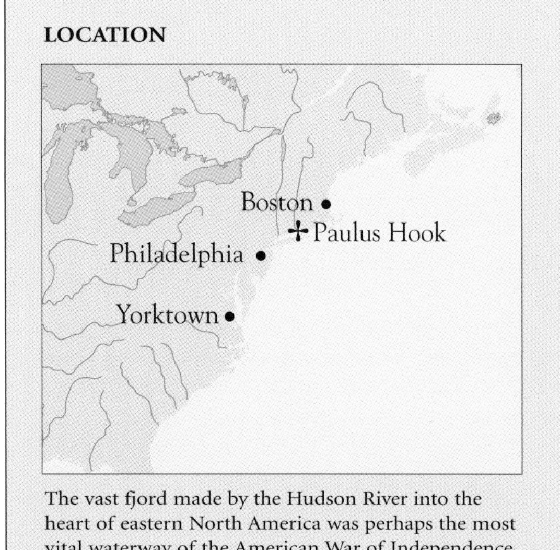
Boston
Paulus Hook
Philadelphia
Yorktown

The vast fjord made by the Hudson River into the heart of eastern North America was perhaps the most vital waterway of the American War of Independence.

The British grip on New York, won at a staggering cost to the Americans in a series of battles in late 1776, remained a hindrance and a threat to the American Continental cause until the final British withdrawal in November of 1783. British vessels of war prowled up the Hudson as far as the great American bastion of West Point, while soldiers and supplies took advantage of Manhattan's superb harbour and transportation system. Neither Washington nor his subordinate commanders were willing to leave matters as they stood. The isolated British and Loyalist bastion across the Hudson at Paulus Hook allowed the British to control access to the river, but it also offered an inviting target.

A 'BRILLIANT' ATTACK

'Light Horse Harry' Lee launched a nocturnal raid on the outpost, leading his men stealthily through approach woods, intending to set fire to the fort's barracks. Finding it occupied by sick soldiers and civilians, he instead carried off 159 rebel prisoners. George Washington described Lee's attack as a 'brilliant' success. The British were considerably unnerved by this audacious escapade into the very heart of their defences.

TIMELINE

1500–1000BC	1000–500BC	500BC–0AD	0–500AD	500–1000AD	1000–1500AD	1500–2000AD

Guilford Courthouse 1781

AMERICAN WAR OF INDEPENDENCE

BRITISH VICTORY

In 1781, Lord Cornwallis's British army was sick and weary and suffering from desertions. Despite this, when he learnt of the presence of the enemy near Guilford Courthouse, he could not resist the urge to engage in battle. Technically, he won, but at considerable cost to his troops and British strategy.

KEY FACTS

WHO General Lord Cornwallis leads the British forces against Americans under General Nathanael Greene.

WHAT Cornwallis had made camp to rest his tired troops, when reports came that Greene's men were also encamped nearby. He seized upon the moment to attack.

WHERE Modern-day Greensboro, Guilford County, North Carolina.

WHEN 15 March 1781

WHY The British were engaged in a bitter war in the southern colonies. The appointment of Greene buoyed the Americans, yet the British looked like they were in a position to nail their advantage in the south.

OUTCOME Cornwallis was able to drive the Americans off, but lost a quarter of his men, forcing him to withdraw.

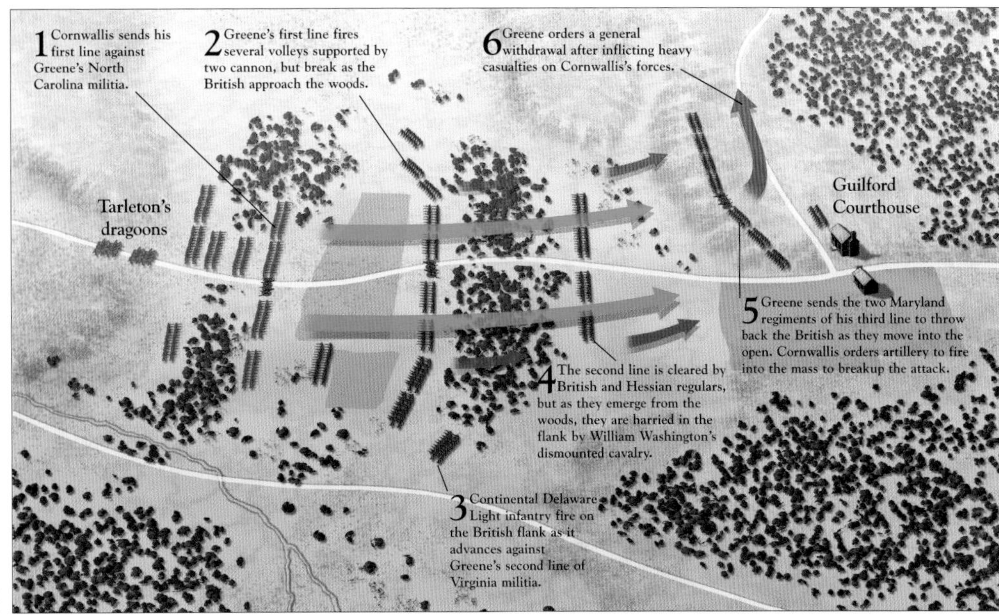
1 Cornwallis sends his first line against Greene's North Carolina militia.
2 Greene's first line fires several volleys supported by two cannon, but break as the British approach the woods.
6 Greene orders a general withdrawal after inflicting heavy casualties on Cornwallis's forces.
Tarleton's dragoons
Guilford Courthouse
5 Greene sends the two Maryland regiments of his third line to throw back the British as they move into the open. Cornwallis orders artillery to fire into the mass to breakup the attack.
4 The second line is cleared by British and Hessian regulars, but as they emerge from the woods, they are harried in the flank by William Washington's dismounted cavalry.
3 Continental Delaware Light infantry fire on the British flank as it advances against Greene's second line of Virginia militia.

Guilford Courthouse was really a battle Cornwallis and the British could have done without. They won through in the end, but the tricky terrain, with plenty of woodland cover, provided plenty of opportunities to ensnare them with artillery fire.

The British hoped that fighting in the south would draw the southern colonies firmly behind them, and ultimately help break the stalemate in the north. But when General Nathaniel Greene was appointed the new commander of the American forces, he was able to assemble an army twice the size of that under Lord Cornwallis, and waged a war of attrition.

HOLLOW VICTORY

The gradual erosion of British forces took its toll, and Cornwallis had withdrawn to make camp at Hillsbororough, North Carolina, when he received news that Greene's men were themselves camped not far away. Cornwallis decided to give battle and, despite coming under heavy fire from American guns whose range was longer than those of his own, managed to drive the Americans from the field. But in doing so he lost half of the 1900 men he had at his disposal during the engagement. He now had to abandon his campaign in Carolina, withdrawing to Wilmington to rest and re-supply, before marching north into Virginia, where he was later besieged at Yorktown.

LOCATION

Boston
New York
Rhode Island
Yorktown
Guilford Courthouse

The British campaign in the southern colonies was designed to break the stalemate that had developed in the north.

TIMELINE

1500–1000BC	1000–500BC	500BC–0AD	0–500AD	500–1000AD	1000–1500AD	1500–2000AD

Yorktown 1781

AMERICAN WAR OF INDEPENDENCE

FRANCO-AMERICAN VICTORY

KEY FACTS

Who A British army of 8000 men under Major-General Charles Cornwallis (1738–1805), opposed by a 17,000-strong Franco-American army under Lieutenant-General George Washington (1732–99) and Lieutenant-General Jean-Baptiste de Rochambeau (1725–1807).

What Cornwallis advanced into Virginia without orders, placing his force in a compromising position. He then retreated to Yorktown, where he was besieged.

Where Yorktown, on the York River in Virginia.

When 28 September–19 October 1781

Why Cornwallis believed that an advance into Virginia would improve the British hold on the southern states.

Outcome The British army was forced to surrender, convincing Parliament that the war in the colonies could not be won.

After realizing that advancing into Virginia was a mistake, the British had withdrawn to the coast – the right decision had the Royal Navy enjoyed its usual supremacy at sea. But French naval forces were able to blockade Yorktown, cutting off supplies and troop reinforcements.

The British forces surrender at Yorktown came after an attempt by Major-General Charles Cornwallis to break out across the river was thwarted by bad weather.

LOCATION

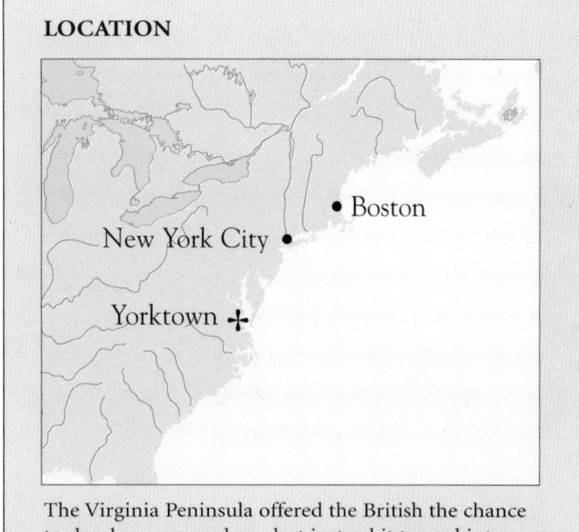
Boston
New York City
Yorktown

The Virginia Peninsula offered the British the chance to develop a secure base, but instead it turned into a trap when control of the sea lanes was lost.

Despite winning battles, the British had failed to achieve victory in the north, and so transferred troops southwards to seek a decisive action there. Clearing the Carolinas of regular enemy forces, Cornwallis made the fateful decision to advance into Virginia, eventually marching to Yorktown, on Chesapeake Bay.

The British war effort in America depended upon sea links for communication, resupply and the movement of reinforcements, so a position on the coast made strategic sense. Dominance of the seas around North America was taken almost for granted. Certainly there was nothing that the American colonists could do to challenge the Royal Navy. However, the same was not true of the French navy, and a failure to intercept their ships aided the Franco-American strategic position. The French were also able to bring in reinforcements and artillery to be used in the siege of Yorktown, which began on 28 September, in a combined effort of the Franco-American army under George Washington and the French commander General de Rochambeau.

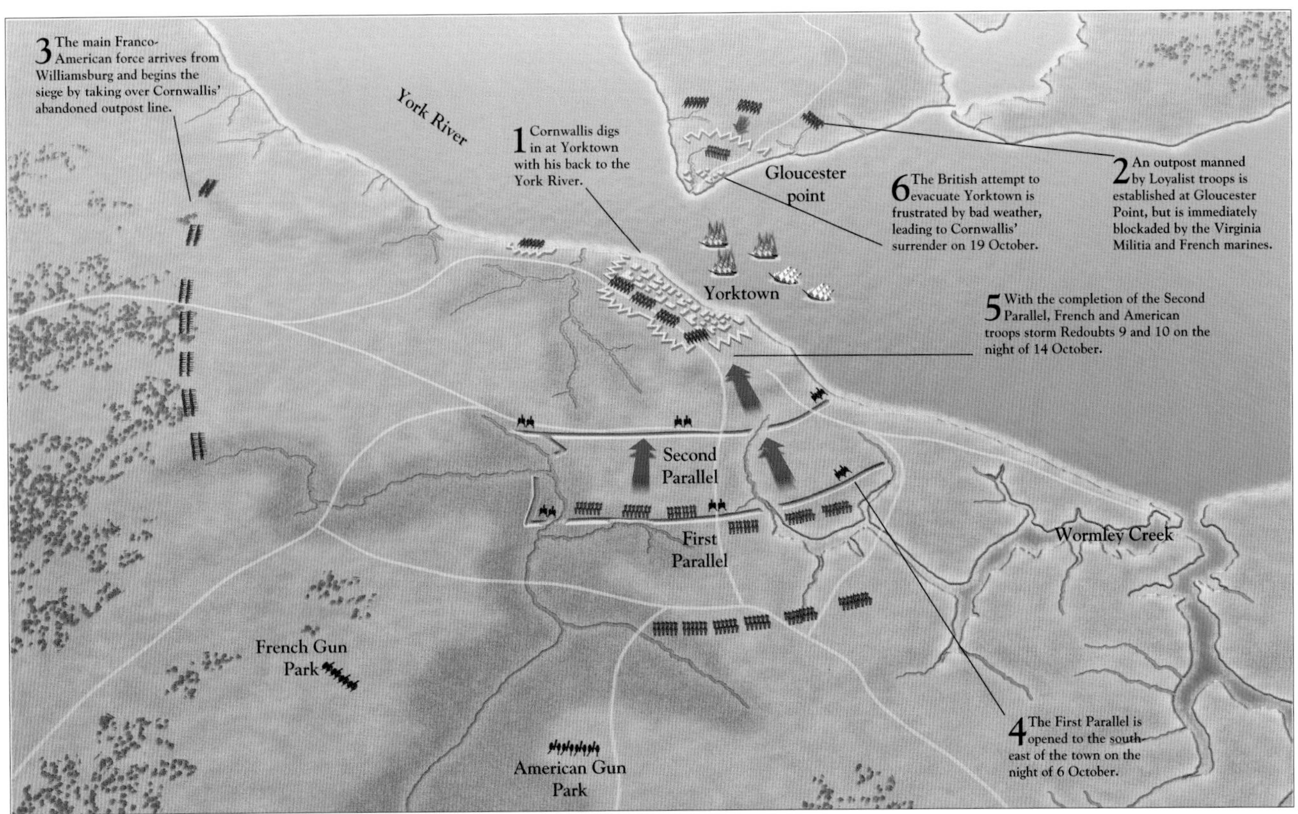
3 The main Franco-American force arrives from Williamsburg and begins the siege by taking over Cornwallis' abandoned outpost line.
York River
1 Cornwallis digs in at Yorktown with his back to the York River.
Gloucester point
6 The British attempt to evacuate Yorktown is frustrated by bad weather, leading to Cornwallis' surrender on 19 October.
2 An outpost manned by Loyalist troops is established at Gloucester Point, but is immediately blockaded by the Virginia Militia and French marines.
Yorktown
5 With the completion of the Second Parallel, French and American troops storm Redoubts 9 and 10 on the night of 14 October.
Second Parallel
First Parallel
Wormley Creek
French Gun Park
American Gun Park
4 The First Parallel is opened to the south-east of the town on the night of 6 October.

The British forces attempted to dig in at Yorktown, while they also attempted to retain control of the sea. Despite doughty resistance, the combined forces of the Americans and French would force their eventual surrender.

Cornwallis was dismayed at his predicament, but ensured a system of defences and outworks were put in position and manned. Yorktown was defended by seven main redoubts, with artillery batteries covering the river narrows as well. An inner line of earthworks protected the town itself.

The British were already short of food, and now slaughtered a large proportion of their horses to avoid having to feed them. Enough were retained to allow a foraging party of cavalry to be sent out on 3 October, but this force was chased back into the siege lines, which continued to tighten as the besiegers began work on a trench parallel to the defences.

The defenders' artillery positions came under fire from heavier and more numerous guns in the Franco-American siege train. The barrage covered the digging of a second parallel (a system of trenches), much closer to the defence lines. This was ready by 12 October, though it was not a complete encirclement because two British-held redoubts blocked the path to the river. These were named Redoubts 9 and 10 by the British.

As work continued to construct trenches ever closer to the British lines, Washington planned an assault on the outlying redoubts. These were blasted with artillery for an extended period, but were still formidable when the assault went in. The French attack on Redoubt 9 was held up by abatis, large obstructions constructed of wood with spikes or blades sticking out. The French were challenged and then fired on as they began their assault, but were able to break through. The American force took Redoubt 10 after a ferocious bayonet fight that finally overwhelmed the defenders.

With the redoubts lost, Yorktown came under artillery fire from three directions. It was clear that the defenders could not hold out much longer unless the artillery bombardment was slackened. A few British soldiers did manage to get across the York River in a desperate escape plan by Cornwallis, but bad weather prevented a mass break-out. With more artillery being moved into position by the besiegers, the military situation in Yorktown was completely hopeless. On 19 October, the British force finally surrendered.

Yorktown

van Blarenberghe 1784

YORKTOWN

When General Cornwallis's cornered British army surrendered at Yorktown to the Americans in 1781, news filtered back to England. Lord North, the prime minster, cried out, 'Oh God! It is all over.' He knew that the attempt to the thwart the American fight for independence was finally lost. Victory had been achieved thanks to a massive artillery bombardment and the successful storming of the redoubts from which the British had attempted to defend their positions. It was the biggest humiliation yet suffered by the British army.

Karansebes 1788

KEY FACTS

WHO Hussars of the Austrian army and their fellow infantry inadvertently fire on each other.

WHAT Panic had broken out in an Austrian camp. Thinking they were about to be attacked by Turks, and in fading light, the Austrians began defending themselves against what, as it turned out, were their own comrades.

WHERE Karansebes, now Caransebes, in modern Romania.

WHEN 1788

WHY The Hapsburgs had made an alliance with Russia against the Ottoman Turks.

OUTCOME The Turks arrived on the scene some time later to discover 10,000 dead or maimed Austrian soldiers.

Joseph II was a ruler with 'advanced' ideas on the role of the monarch, in sharp contrast to his reactionary mother, the Empress Marie Theresa. He wasn't a great fighting man, though, and the farce of Karansebes, assuming it really occurred, would have added no feathers to his cap.

AUSTRO-TURKISH WAR

TURKISH VICTORY

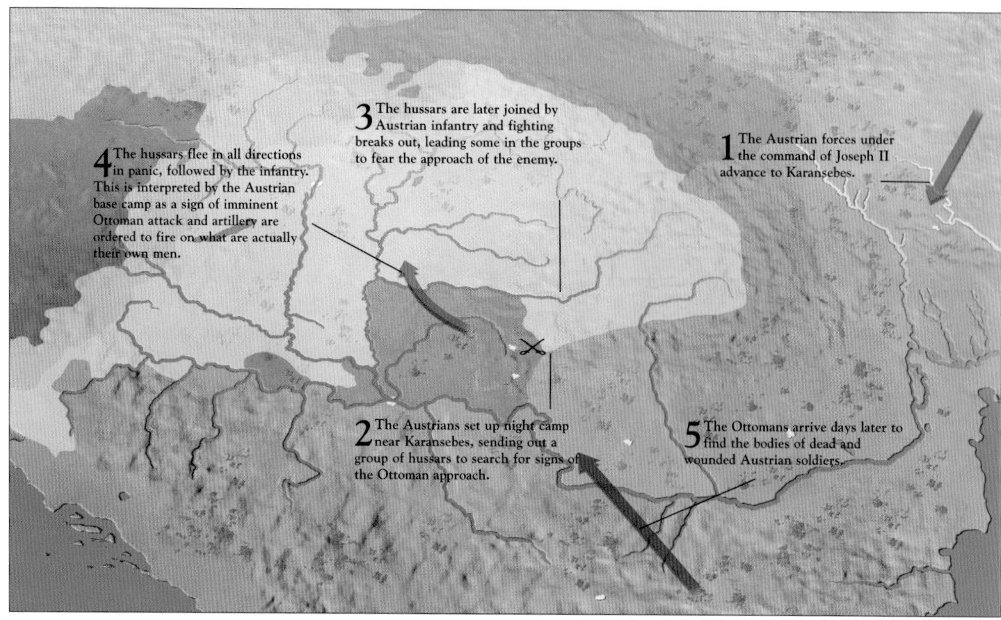
1 The Austrian forces under the command of Joseph II advance to Karansebes.
2 The Austrians set up night camp near Karansebes, sending out a group of hussars to search for signs of the Ottoman approach.
3 The hussars are later joined by Austrian infantry and fighting breaks out, leading some in the groups to fear the approach of the enemy.
4 The hussars flee in all directions in panic, followed by the infantry. This is interpreted by the Austrian base camp as a sign of imminent Ottoman attack and artillery are ordered to fire on what are actually their own men.
5 The Ottomans arrive days later to find the bodies of dead and wounded Austrian soldiers.

The Battle of Karansebes is one of the most excessive examples of 'friendly fire' in history. The battle was fought and 'lost' by the Austrians without the enemy even making an appearance.

Of all the unlikely episodes in military history, the farce of Karansebes takes the gold star. So incredible were the events, in fact, that many doubt that it ever happened – and with good reason, as the first account of the 'battle' was not written up until half a century after it allegedly occurred.

Austria had declared war on the Ottoman Turks. Emperor Joseph II, no great shakes as a general, led the troops on the front line. His army had set up a night camp near Karansebes, when, so the story goes, hussars were sent out to check for any sign of the enemy. They were later joined by some infantry and a scuffle seems to have broken out over alcohol, leading one infantryman to cry out in jest, 'Turks! Turks!'. His fellow soldiers – many of different nationalities, a fact that underscores the potential for misunderstanding – failed to see the joke. The hussars panicked and fled in all directions, followed by many of the infantry. Back at base camp, an officer interpreted it as a sign of imminent Ottoman attack and ordered his artillery to fire. When the Ottomans did arrive, a couple of days later, all they found were thousands of dead and wounded Austrian soldiers.

LOCATION

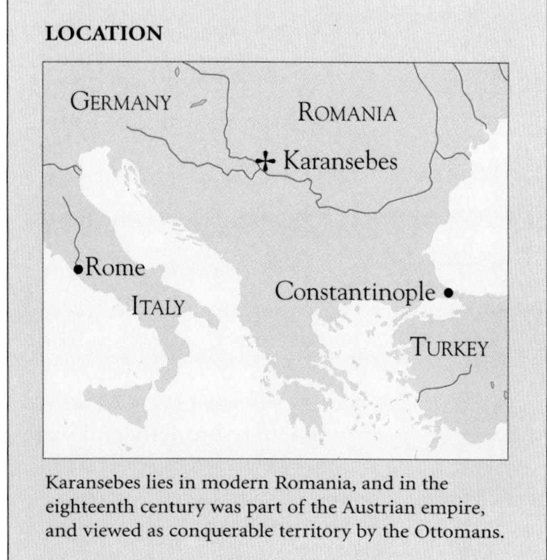
GERMANY
ROMANIA
Karansebes
Rome
ITALY
Constantinople
TURKEY

Karansebes lies in modern Romania, and in the eighteenth century was part of the Austrian empire, and viewed as conquerable territory by the Ottomans.

TIMELINE

1500–1000BC	1000–500BC	500BC–0AD	0–500AD	500–1000AD	1000–1500AD	1500–2000AD

Svensksund 1790

KEY FACTS

WHO A Swedish flotilla under the personal command of King Gustavus III of Sweden against a Russian fleet led by its commander Prince Charles von Nassau-Siegen.

WHAT The Russians underestimated the strength of the fleet they were attacking, and lost almost 10,000 men and nearly 90 vessels when they fell into a Swedish trap.

WHERE Svensksund, southern Finland.

WHEN 8–10 July 1790

WHY The Swedes had declared war on Russia to try to regain territories lost in Finland earlier in the century.

OUTCOME The Swedish were successful at Svensksund, but when the treaty to end the Russo-Swedish war was signed the following month it brought them no territorial gains.

Svensksund was the greatest naval defeat Russia had ever experienced by the time the battle took place and, even though it ended the Russo-Swedish War, it remains curiously uncelebrated in Sweden.

RUSSO-SWEDISH WAR

SWEDISH VICTORY

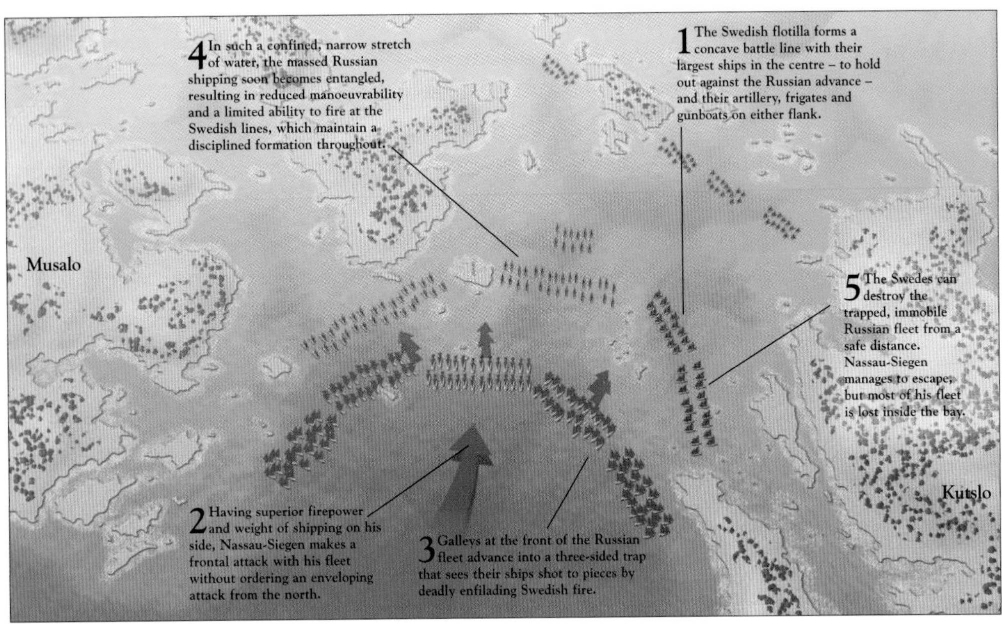

4 In such a confined, narrow stretch of water, the massed Russian shipping soon becomes entangled, resulting in reduced manoeuvrability and a limited ability to fire at the Swedish lines, which maintain a disciplined formation throughout.
1 The Swedish flotilla forms a concave battle line with their largest ships in the centre – to hold out against the Russian advance – and their artillery, frigates and gunboats on either flank.
Musalo
5 The Swedes can destroy the trapped, immobile Russian fleet from a safe distance. Nassau-Siegen manages to escape, but most of his fleet is lost inside the bay.
Kutslo
2 Having superior firepower and weight of shipping on his side, Nassau-Siegen makes a frontal attack with his fleet without ordering an enveloping attack from the north.
3 Galleys at the front of the Russian fleet advance into a three-sided trap that sees their ships shot to pieces by deadly enfilading Swedish fire.

The Russians deployed a larger fleet at Svenskund, but made a huge mistake by opting for a purely frontal offensive. They sailed right into a Swedish trap, leaving them open to flanking fire on both sides, and negating their numerical advantage.

King Gustavus III of Sweden had been keen to provoke a fight with Russia, partly to regain land lost in Finland to the Russians 50 years earlier. But earlier battles hadn't gone well, and the first battle of Svensksund, in 1789, had been lost. The following year, however, King Gustavus, in personal command of a 250-strong flotilla, waited with his ships in a strong defensive position along the northern edge of the bay in anticipation of another Russian attack.

SWEDISH TRAP

Underestimating his enemy's strength and leadership, the Russian commander Charles von Nassau-Siegen signalled his 150 vessels to make a frontal assault. As his ships advanced, they sailed into the trap the Swedes had laid for them, coming under heavy enfilading fire from their flanks. In the confusion, the Russian vessels drifted ever deeper into the Swedish trap until they could no longer move or manoeuvre properly and were shot to pieces. Nassau-Siegen finally admitted defeat, but the signalled retreat could not be executed. The Russians lost 7400–9500 men and almost 90 vessels were either sunk or captured.

LOCATION

SWEDEN

Svensksund

St Petersburg

Stockholm

RUSSIA

Baltic Sea

Svensksund, or 'Swedish Sound', is situated in the eastern part of the Finnish archipelago, south of the towns of Kotka and Fredrikshamn (Hamina).

TIMELINE

1500–1000BC	1000–500BC	500BC–0AD	0–500AD	500–1000AD	1000–1500AD	1500–2000AD

Glorious First of June 1794

KEY FACTS

Who Admiral Lord Howe leads the British fleet against the French fleet led by Vice-Admiral Louis Thomas Villaret de Joyeuse, protecting a French grain convey.

What Admiral Lord Howe tried to divide the French line so the ships could be picked off individually, but his plan was misunderstood by his captains, and while the French ships sustained significant damage, the convoy got through.

Where Atlantic Ocean.

When 1 June 1794

Why With famine looming in France, a convoy had been sent to secure supplies from its American colonies.

Outcome Britain's naval superiority saw the French lose seven ships, yet the ultimately successful arrival of the convoy was treated as a victory by the French.

In 1794, the French, in the midst of a series of wars with its neighbours and with its ports under blockade, was facing serious food shortages. It had to turn to its colonies across the Atlantic for aid.

FRENCH REVOLUTIONARY WARS

NO CLEAR VICTORY

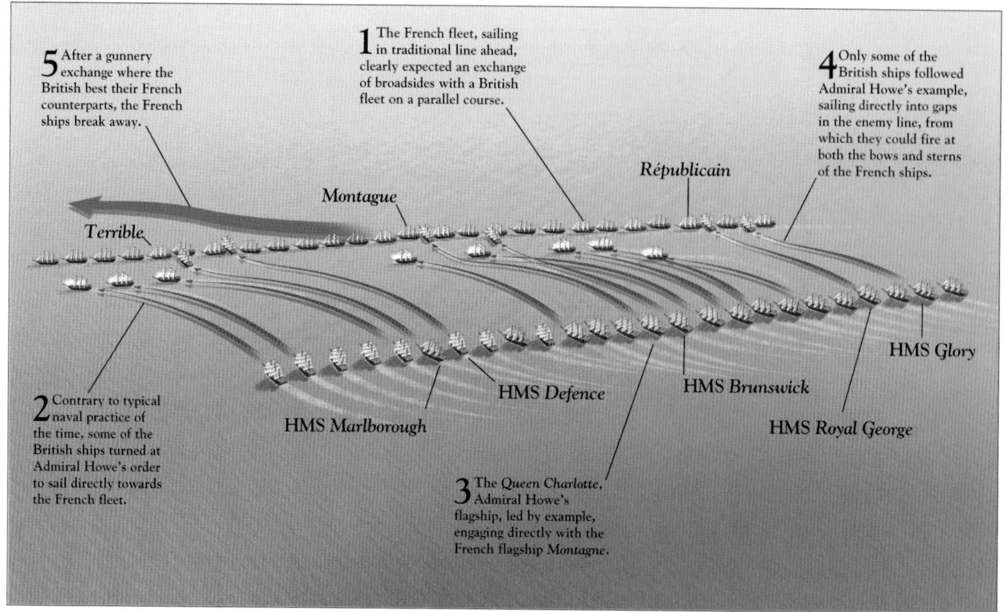

1 The French fleet, sailing in traditional line ahead, clearly expected an exchange of broadsides with a British fleet on a parallel course.
2 Contrary to typical naval practice of the time, some of the British ships turned at Admiral Howe's order to sail directly towards the French fleet.
3 The Queen Charlotte, Admiral Howe's flagship, led by example, engaging directly with the French flagship Montagne.
4 Only some of the British ships followed Admiral Howe's example, sailing directly into gaps in the enemy line, from which they could fire at both the bows and sterns of the French ships.
5 After a gunnery exchange where the British best their French counterparts, the French ships break away.
Montague
Républicain
Terrible
HMS Glory
HMS Defence
HMS Brunswick
HMS Marlborough
HMS Royal George

Admiral Lord Howe broke with the conventional pattern of a naval exchange of the time, which usually involved parallel lines of boats firing broadsides at each other, by sailing directly into the lines of his opponents.

As a French convoy, loaded with grain, made its return journey across the Atlantic, Admiral Lord Howe at the head of the British fleet made ready to intercept it, finally catching up with the French fleet that was escorting it home on 1 June, a month after it had departed the shores of Virginia.

Howe boldly planned to send his ships to pierce the French line individually and break through to their leeward, cutting off the French line of retreat. This would allow him either to scatter or destroy the ships in a piecemeal fashion. However, he only partially succeeded – most of his captains misunderstood or ignored his signals.

Howe's flagship, *Queen Charlotte*, and five other British vessels pierced the French line in a ragged attack, saved from serious damage by poor French gunnery. The battle became a confused mêlée, as ships engaged in individual duels. After some fierce exchanges, the French finally broke away, leaving seven captured and sunk ships behind. However, the British fleet was too badly damaged to pursue. Only one of the actual cargo ships had been lost when the convoy finally reached Brest.

LOCATION

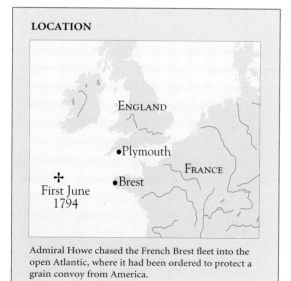

England
Plymouth
France
Brest
First June 1794

Admiral Howe chased the French Brest fleet into the open Atlantic, where it had been ordered to protect a grain convoy from America.

TIMELINE

1500–1000BC	1000–500BC	500BC–0AD	0–500AD	500–1000AD	1000–1500AD	1500–2000AD

Fleurus 1794

KEY FACTS

WHO General Jean-Baptiste Jourdan, general-in-chief of the French army, faced a large Austrian and Dutch relief force led by the Prince of Sachsen-Coburg.

WHAT Jourdan had laid siege to Charleroi, and managed to beat off an attempted relief force at nearby Fleurus.

WHERE Fleurus, Belgium.

WHEN 26 June 1794

WHY The French had occupied Belgium and Holland, but the Coalition armies had succeeded in driving them back to the French frontier.

OUTCOME Victory enabled the French to push on with their conquest of Belgium and, eventually, the Netherlands.

The Battle of Fleurus, which featured the first use of 'airpower' in warfare – in the shape of an air balloon used by the French for reconnaissance – was a key battle in the French Revolutionary Wars. By winning it, the French paved the way for the ultimate break-up of the Dutch Republic.

FRENCH REVOLUTIONARY WARS

FRENCH VICTORY

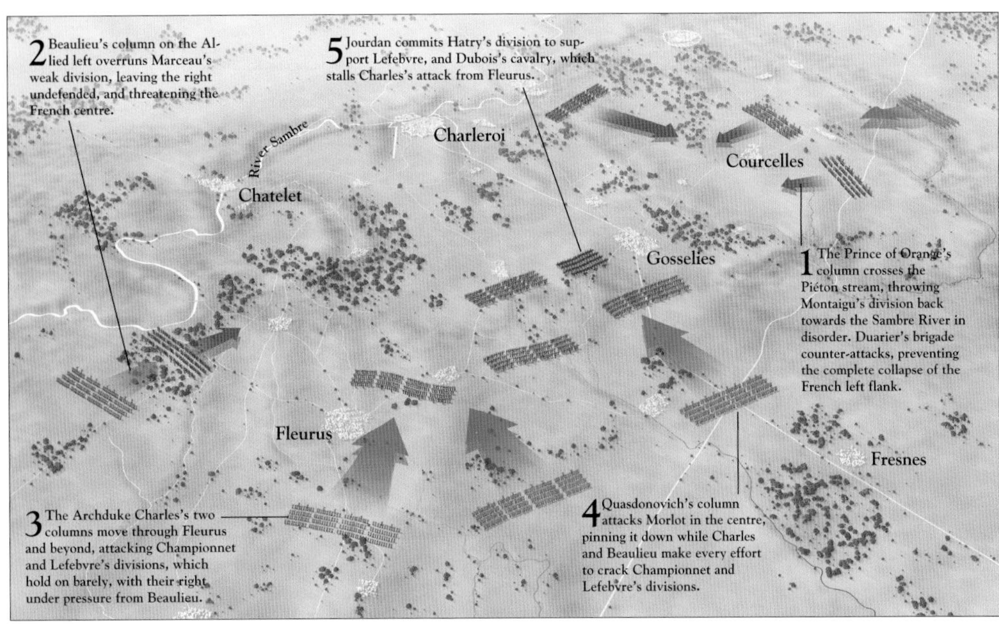
2 Beaulieu's column on the Allied left overruns Marceau's weak division, leaving the right undefended, and threatening the French centre.
5 Jourdan commits Hatry's division to support Lefebvre, and Dubois's cavalry, which stalls Charles's attack from Fleurus.
River Sambre
Charleroi
Chatelet
Courcelles
Gosselies
1 The Prince of Orange's column crosses the Piéton stream, throwing Montaigu's division back towards the Sambre River in disorder. Duarier's brigade counter-attacks, preventing the complete collapse of the French left flank.
Fleurus
Fresnes
3 The Archduke Charles's two columns move through Fleurus and beyond, attacking Championnet and Lefebvre's divisions, which hold on barely, with their right under pressure from Beaulieu.
4 Quasdonovich's column attacks Morlot in the centre, pinning it down while Charles and Beaulieu make every effort to crack Championnet and Lefebvre's divisions.

The occupation of the Low Countries by the French Revolutionary Army inevitably caused alarm in neighbouring countries, and a coalition of various interests was formed, converging on the French near Fleurus.

The Austrian and Anglo–Allied armies successfully threatened the French occupation of Belgium and Holland in the spring of 1794, with a counteroffensive forcing them to withdraw their armies to the French frontiers. The Committee of Public Safety set up during the French Revolution dispatched the bloodthirsty deputy Louis de St-Just to ensure the armies and their commanders understood the severity of the situation.

SIEGE OF CHARLEROI

General Jean-Baptiste Jourdan, temporarily removed from command in 1793, was appointed general-in-chief of a new invasion force and crossed the Sambre river to besiege Charleroi. The Prince of Sachsen-Coburg headed an Austrian-Dutch attempt to relieve the city, but Jourdan deployed his army in a semicircle to prevent it reaching its destination, at Fleurus.

After a desperate battle in which Jourdan's flanks broke, his ability to deploy his reserves rapidly, combined with the steadfastness of his centre, forced the allies to withdraw from the field with heavy casualties. The French were able to push on with their conquest.

LOCATION

Great Britain
Sachsen-Coburg
Brussels
Fleurus
Paris
Austria
France

After several failed attempts to capture Charleroi, the French finally succeeded in June 1794, defeating the relief army under the Prince of Sachsen-Coburg.

TIMELINE

1500–1000BC	1000–500BC	500BC–0AD	0–500AD	500–1000AD	1000–1500AD	1500–2000AD

Rivoli 1797

KEY FACTS

WHO Napoleon Bonaparte at the head of the French Army of Italy against Baron General Jozsef Alvinczy's Austrians.

WHAT The Austrians, despite outnumbering the French, found themselves caught on unfavourable high ground above Rivoli, where their columns became disordered, and the greater experience of the French proved decisive on rough terrain.

WHERE Rivoli, Italy.

WHEN 14–15 January 1797

WHY Napoleon Bonaparte had laid siege to the city of Mantua, a key location for the Austrians as they attempted to fight back against the French onslaught in Italy.

OUTCOME After one of his greatest military victories, Bonaparte was able to further assert his hold on northern Italy.

Napoleon Bonaparte had invaded northern Italy in 1796, keen to sweep away the Austrians and set up a Republic. It was never going to be that easy, but at Rivoli he scored one of his most emphatic military victories.

FRENCH REVOLUTIONARY WARS

FRENCH VICTORY

Louis Albert Guislain Bacler d'Albe, French artist, cartographer and advisor to Napoleon from 1796-1814, depicts here Napoleon and Masséna. Napoleon made Bacler d'Albe a Baron of the Empire and Masséna a Marshal of the Empire.

LOCATION

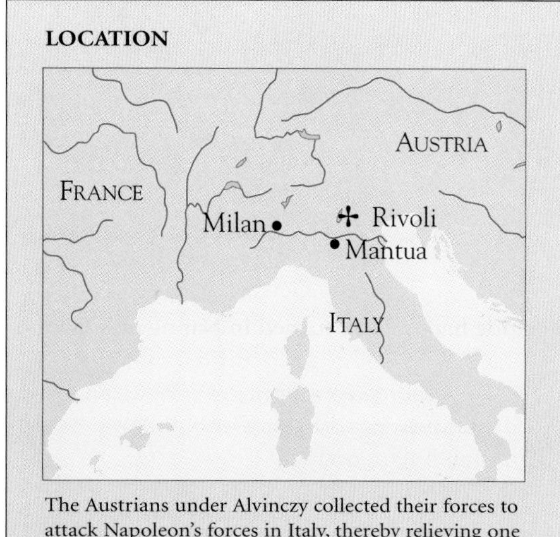
AUSTRIA
FRANCE
Milan
Rivoli
Mantua
ITALY

The Austrians under Alvinczy collected their forces to attack Napoleon's forces in Italy, thereby relieving one of their armies trapped in the fortress of Mantua.

Mantua was the last major town controlled by the Austrians, and its fortress had been besieged by Napoleon. Determined to lift the siege, the Austrians reinforced their army in northern Italy under Baron General Jozsef Alvinczy.

The plan was for Alvinczy's 28,000-strong force to come down the Adige valley from the north, forcing the narrow bottleneck in the mountains near Rivoli. When news reached Napoleon that the French under General Joubert had retreated to high ground at Rivoli, he ordered a division under General André Masséna at Verona to proceed there with all haste. When Napoleon himself arrived, he prepared for an immediate attack.

Alvinczy had divided his force into six separate assault columns. Three columns would attack the heights to which the French had retreated. Two other columns were to march along both banks of the Adige and attempt to scale the gorge on to the heights. A sixth column, under General Lusignon, was to undertake a flanking manoeuvre along the French right, coming in on the rear of Napoleon's army and cutting off their escape.

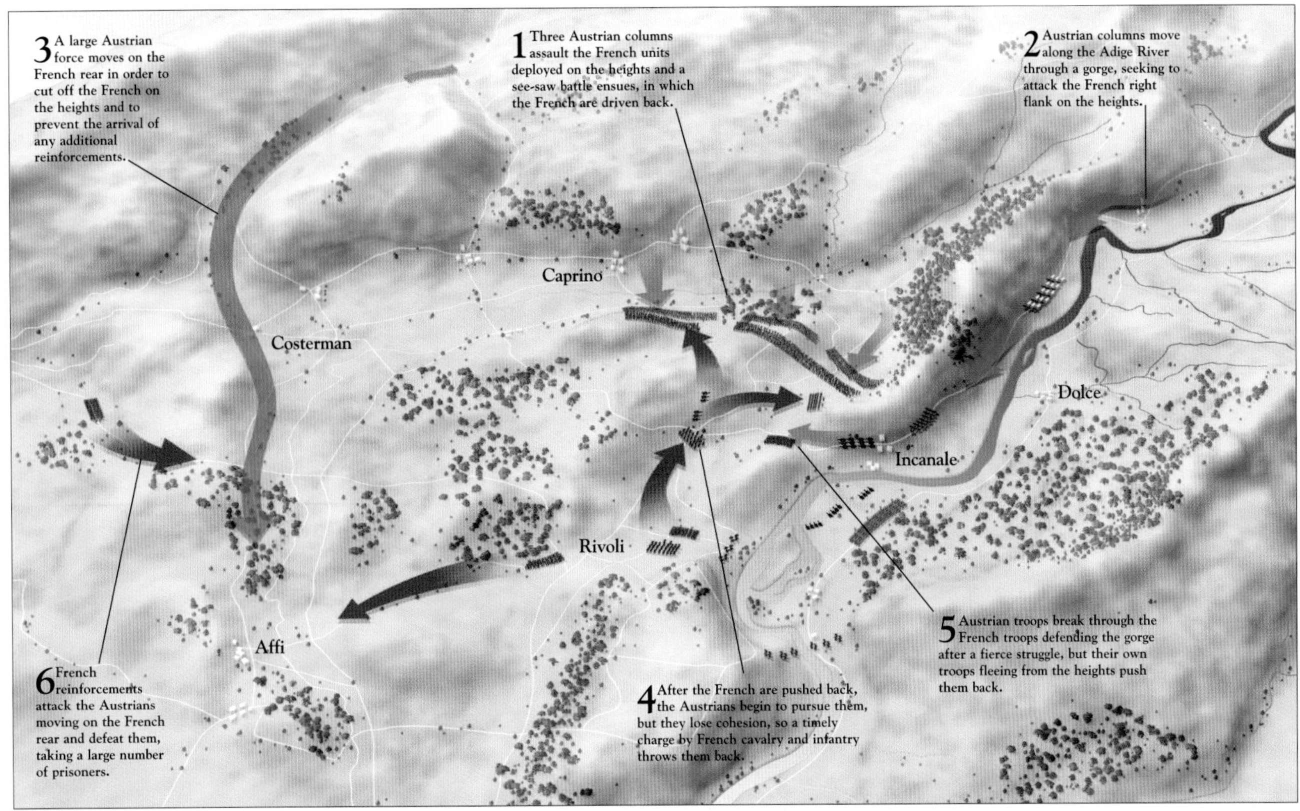
3 A large Austrian force moves on the French rear in order to cut off the French on the heights and to prevent the arrival of any additional reinforcements.
1 Three Austrian columns assault the French units deployed on the heights and a see-saw battle ensues, in which the French are driven back.
2 Austrian columns move along the Adige River through a gorge, seeking to attack the French right flank on the heights.
Caprino
Costerman
Dolce
Incanale
Rivoli
Affi
5 Austrian troops break through the French troops defending the gorge after a fierce struggle, but their own troops fleeing from the heights push them back.
6 French reinforcements attack the Austrians moving on the French rear and defeat them, taking a large number of prisoners.
4 After the French are pushed back, the Austrians begin to pursue them, but they lose cohesion, so a timely charge by French cavalry and infantry throws them back.

The Battle of Rivoli took place on tricky North Italian upland terrain. The deep, narrow gorges were especially perilous for the Austrians, many lacking the campaign experience of Napoleon's men.

The majority of Joubert's troops, including 18 artillery pieces, were on the heights, and they attacked the Austrians at first light. Despite being outnumbered by a factor of 4:3, the French attack went well at first, with the French capturing a key village from the Austrians.

But as the attack slowed, the Austrians were able to attack the exposed left on the French line, causing the unit of the 85th Demi-Brigade to flee. Only reinforcements brought by General Masséna were able to stabilize the now vulnerable left flank. Meanwhile, in the French centre, a battalion of Austrian grenadiers overran a French battery in front of the 14th Demi-Brigade. Only a last-ditch bayonet charge enabled the French to recapture it.

The French right flank was also opened up when the 39th were forced from their defensive works. However, the difficult nature of the terrain slowed the advance of the Austrian forces, and a house provided with a large enclosure served as a rallying point for the units, soon to be augmented by reinforcements rrived from Lake Garda.

Things looked bleak for the French, and got worse. Volleys were heard from their rear – Lusignon's column had competed its flanking move, blocking not only the line of retreat but also the route the reinforcements would take. Responding to the dismay of some of his officers, Napoleon is reported to have said simply: 'They are ours.'

On the plateau, the French were able to sway the situation in their favour, as a small body of 200 cavalry attacked the Austrians troops. The Austrians were tired, and had lost much of their cohesion now that they were in pursuit. As a result, they were easily overthrown by this small body of cavalry. The panic that ensued, spread from one column to another, some even fleeing into the gorge, thereby pushing back the troops trying to ascend the heights. This allowed Joubert to lead a regiment to the edge of the gorge and fire on to the troops below, driving them back. Shortly thereafter, fresh French reinforcements arrived, trapping Lusignon's column between two enemy bodies. The tide had quickly turned in Napoleon's favour.

The battle had been won by the late afternoon, leaving Joubert merely to conduct a mopping up operation. Mantua fell the following month, and Napoleon continued his march through Italy.

Rivoli

RIVOLI

The Austrian baron General Jozsef Alvinczy was, apparently, a keen admirer of the Prussian military mastermind Frederick the Great. He was keen to put his hero's ideas into operation with his own army. But Alvinczy was no Frederick, and his soldiers lacked experience. When he attempted to deploy a complicated formation at Rivoli, he came unstuck against one of the fighting greats of own time, Napoleon Bonaparte. Napoleon was a practical man as much as a thinker, able to react to fast-changing situations. He was at his peak in the mountain passes at Rivoli – as the more theoretical Alvinczy found to his cost.

Nile 1798

FRENCH REVOLUTIONARY WARS

BRITISH VICTORY

At the Battle of the Nile, Horatio Nelson dealt a body blow to the French fleet, caught napping in the Aboukir Bay. While the British fleet destroyed many of France's finest ships, it also left a certain Napoleon Bonaparte stranded in a foreign land.

KEY FACTS

Who British forces led by Rear-Admiral Horatio Nelson, against the French Navy led by Vice-Admiral François Breuys.

What Nelson caught the French fleet in the bay at Aboukir unprepared for battle and partially unmanned. Most of the French ships were either sunk or taken by the British.

Where Aboukir Bay, Egypt.

When 1 August 1798

Why Napoleon had invaded Egypt, intending to continue on to British India, opening up new fronts in the war between the two nations. The ships that had delivered his army remained in Aboukir Bay.

Outcome The destruction of the French fleet undid the successful campaign waged on land in Egypt by Napoleon – and left him stranded. It also put the British Navy in control of the Mediterranean.

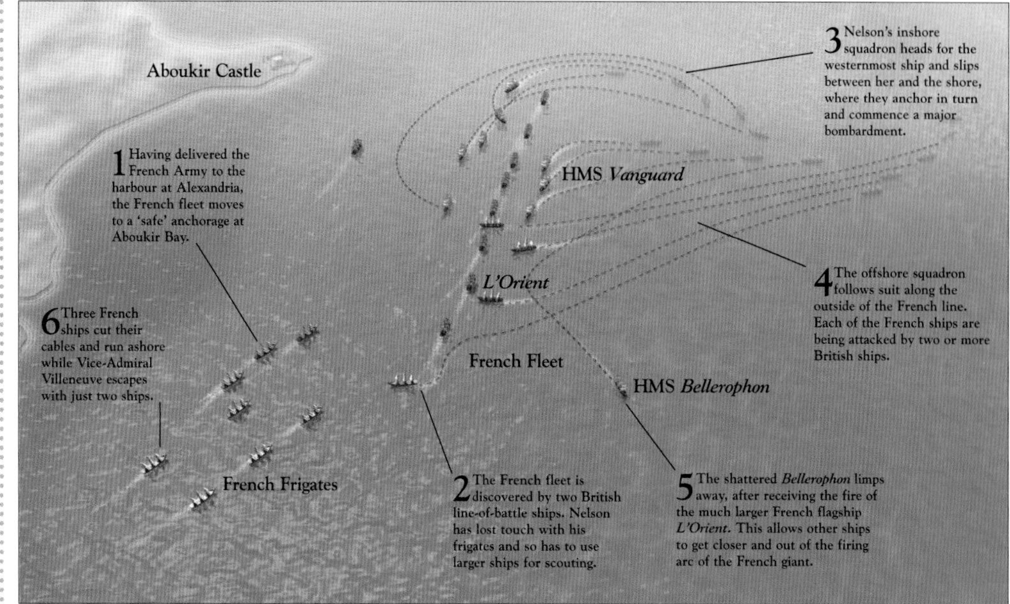
Aboukir Castle
1 Having delivered the French Army to the harbour at Alexandria, the French fleet moves to a 'safe' anchorage at Aboukir Bay.
3 Nelson's inshore squadron heads for the westernmost ship and slips between her and the shore, where they anchor in turn and commence a major bombardment.
HMS Vanguard
L'Orient
4 The offshore squadron follows suit along the outside of the French line. Each of the French ships are being attacked by two or more British ships.
6 Three French ships cut their cables and run ashore while Vice-Admiral Villeneuve escapes with just two ships.
French Fleet
HMS Bellerophon
French Frigates
2 The French fleet is discovered by two British line-of-battle ships. Nelson has lost touch with his frigates and so has to use larger ships for scouting.
5 The shattered Bellerophon limps away, after receiving the fire of the much larger French flagship L'Orient. This allows other ships to get closer and out of the firing arc of the French giant.

Nelson's deployment of his fleet at the Battle of the Nile meant that, although his force was technically outnumbered, there would be two of his ships to each one of the French.

After a French army, led by Napoleon, had disembarked on its Egyptian land campaign, the escorting fleet then anchored at Aboukir Bay. When Vice-Admiral Brueys learnt of the sudden approach of the British fleet, he chose to fight with his ships at anchor.

Admiral Nelson's battle plan involved splitting his ships into divisions, one to attack on the seaward side of the French, the other to cut in between where the fleet was anchored and the shoreline. It meant that the French would be caught in crossfire, and that even though, overall, Brueys had more ships and superiority in firepower, there would effectively be two British ships to every French one.

While the French centre held for a time, gradually this told. When the flagship Orient suddenly exploded, Brueys was killed. His flag captain was also fatally wounded shortly afterwards.

With several French ships badly damaged, two others slipped out of line, then beached themselves, before surrendering. Just four French ships made good their escape. Nelson's victory also left the French army – and Napoleon – trapped in the Middle East.

LOCATION

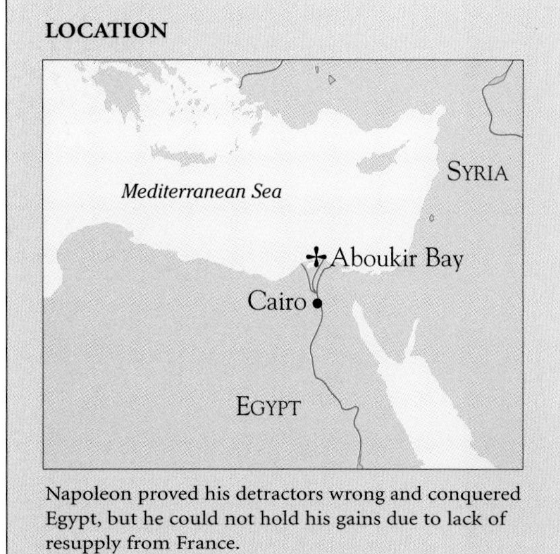
Mediterranean Sea
SYRIA
Aboukir Bay
Cairo
EGYPT

Napoleon proved his detractors wrong and conquered Egypt, but he could not hold his gains due to lack of resupply from France.

TIMELINE

1500–1000BC	1000–500BC	500BC–0AD	0–500AD	500–1000AD	1000–1500AD	1500–2000AD

Copenhagen 1801

The Battle of Copenhagen has gone down in history as the occasion when Lord Nelson, under orders to retreat, put his telescope to his blind eye and pretended not to see the signal. The result was one of his most hard-earned victories.

FRENCH REVOLUTIONARY WARS

BRITISH VICTORY

KEY FACTS

WHO Admiral Sir Hyde Parker and Vice-Admiral Lord Nelson led the British Navy against the fleet of Denmark-Norway

WHAT In a grimly fought battle, the exchanges grew so intense that Admiral Sir Hyde Parker actually directed a retreat signal at Nelson, who nonetheless persisted, enabling the superior gunnery of his ships eventually to come out on top.

WHERE Off-shore of Copenhagen, Denmark.

WHEN 2 April 1801

WHY British trade in the Baltic had been threatened by the formation of a League of Armed Neutrality, which the Scandinavian countries had joined.

OUTCOME An armistice was signed and Copenhagen re-opened to British trading ships.

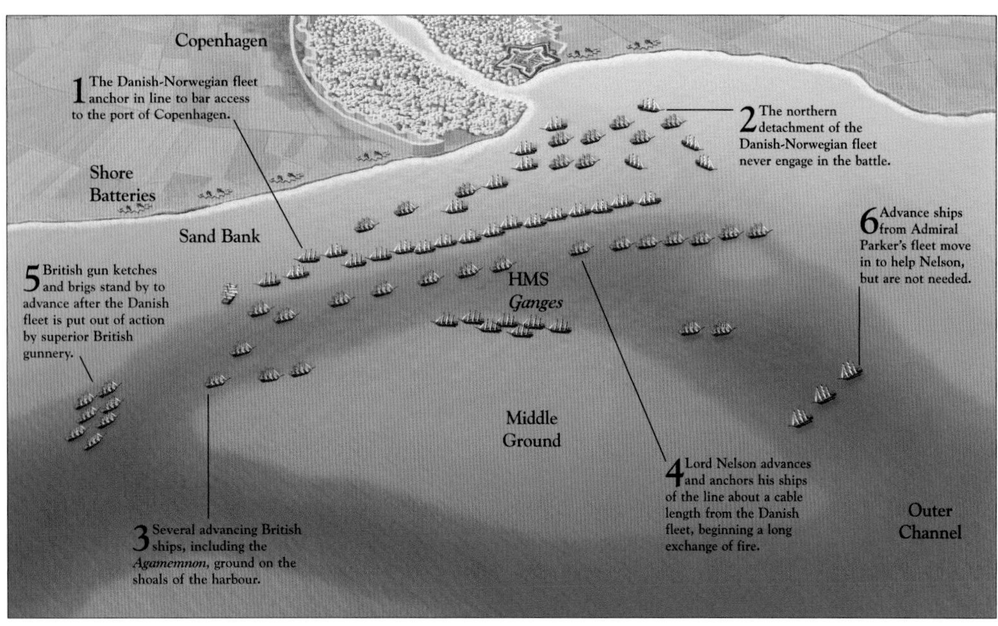
Copenhagen
1 The Danish-Norwegian fleet anchor in line to bar access to the port of Copenhagen.
2 The northern detachment of the Danish-Norwegian fleet never engage in the battle.
Shore Batteries
Sand Bank
6 Advance ships from Admiral Parker's fleet move in to help Nelson, but are not needed.
5 British gun ketches and brigs stand by to advance after the Danish fleet is put out of action by superior British gunnery.
HMS Ganges
Middle Ground
4 Lord Nelson advances and anchors his ships of the line about a cable length from the Danish fleet, beginning a long exchange of fire.
Outer Channel
3 Several advancing British ships, including the Agamemnon, ground on the shoals of the harbour.

Copenhagen was a long, hard slog, with the two adversaries lining their ships alongside each other and pounding away with their guns. It was a battle that added to the legend of Nelson.

Admiral Sir Hyde Parker sent his second-in-command, Horatio Nelson, into Copenhagen harbour with 12 ships of the line that had relatively shallow draughts, along with the smaller vessels in the fleet. Consequently, three British ships grounded while entering the harbour, but the remaining vessels anchored about 180m (200yd) from the Danish ships and batteries. From this position the two sides proceeded to fire broadsides at each other until each ship was disabled.

BREACH OF ORDERS

In light of the heavy Danish resistance, Parker signalled a retreat, which Nelson disregarded, famously putting his telescope to his blind eye and remarking to his captain: 'I have only one eye. I have a right to be blind sometimes.' Nelson was justified as superior gunnery disabled the Danish ships and British bomb vessels were able to approach the city. The battle ended when the Danes accepted an offer of truce.

Copenhagen is often considered to be Nelson's hardest fought battle, surpassing even the intensive fighting that took place at Trafalgar.

LOCATION

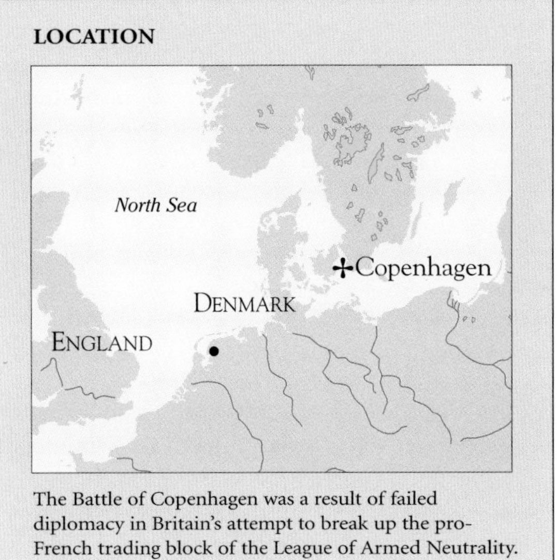
North Sea
Copenhagen
DENMARK
ENGLAND

The Battle of Copenhagen was a result of failed diplomacy in Britain's attempt to break up the pro-French trading block of the League of Armed Neutrality.

TIMELINE

1500–1000BC	1000–500BC	500BC–0AD	0–500AD	500–1000AD	1000–1500AD	1500–2000AD

Trafalgar 1805

NAPOLEONIC WARS

BRITISH VICTORY

KEY FACTS

WHO A Franco-Spanish fleet of 33 ships under Admiral Pierre Villeneuve (1763–1806), opposed by an English fleet of 27 ships under Vice-Admiral Horatio Nelson (1758–1805).

WHAT Rather than a conventional engagement between lines of battle, the English made a risky attack that allowed them to gain local superiority over the enemy.

WHERE Off Cape Trafalgar near the Straits of Gibraltar.

WHEN 2 December 1805

WHY The English needed to cripple the Franco-Spanish fleet to protect England from invasion.

OUTCOME The Franco-Spanish fleet was decisively defeated.

The war between England and France was a clash between a great naval power versus a great land power. In the same year that Emperor Napoleon of France won his major land victory at Austerlitz, his chance to invade the British Isles was forever lost off the coast of Spain.

Trafalgar saw many ships crammed together and fighting at point-blank range. Whoever could keep up the highest rate of fire and cause the most significant damage would come off best.

LOCATION

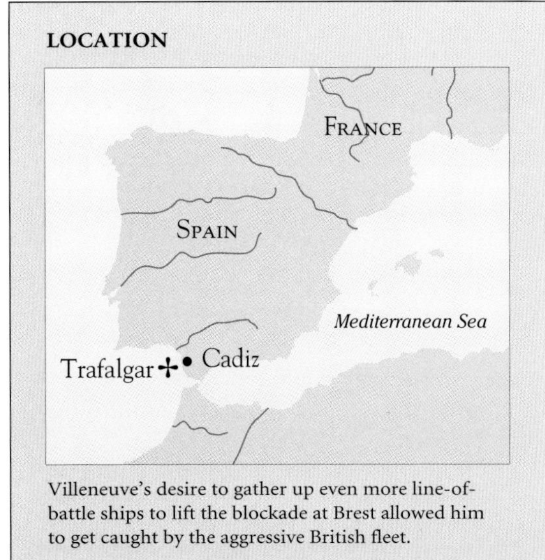
France
Spain
Mediterranean Sea
Trafalgar
Cadiz

Villeneuve's desire to gather up even more line-of-battle ships to lift the blockade at Brest allowed him to get caught by the aggressive British fleet.

If Napoleon's dream of invading and defeating Britain was ever to reach fruition, he knew he would also have to defeat its navy. Appointing Pierre Villeneuve to command his fleet, Napoleon planned for it to link up with Allied naval forces from Spain and clear the English Channel of British warships. This would enable a fleet of small boats to land Napoleon's 'Army of England' in Britain.

When word arrived that the Combined Fleet was in Cadiz, preparations began to send a British fleet to engage it, led by Nelson, on HMS *Victory*. Nelson eventually caught up with Villeneuve's fleet off Cape Trafalgar, in the Straits of Gibraltar. The Combined Fleet seemed in some disorder as the British formed up into two columns with the intent of punching through the enemy line and achieving local superiority by 'doubling up' on enemy ships. This manoeuvre was risky because it exposed the lead ships – including HMS *Victory* – to broadside fire. However, Nelson felt that the poorly trained enemy gunners could not inflict much damage, especially since a rising sea made gunnery difficult.

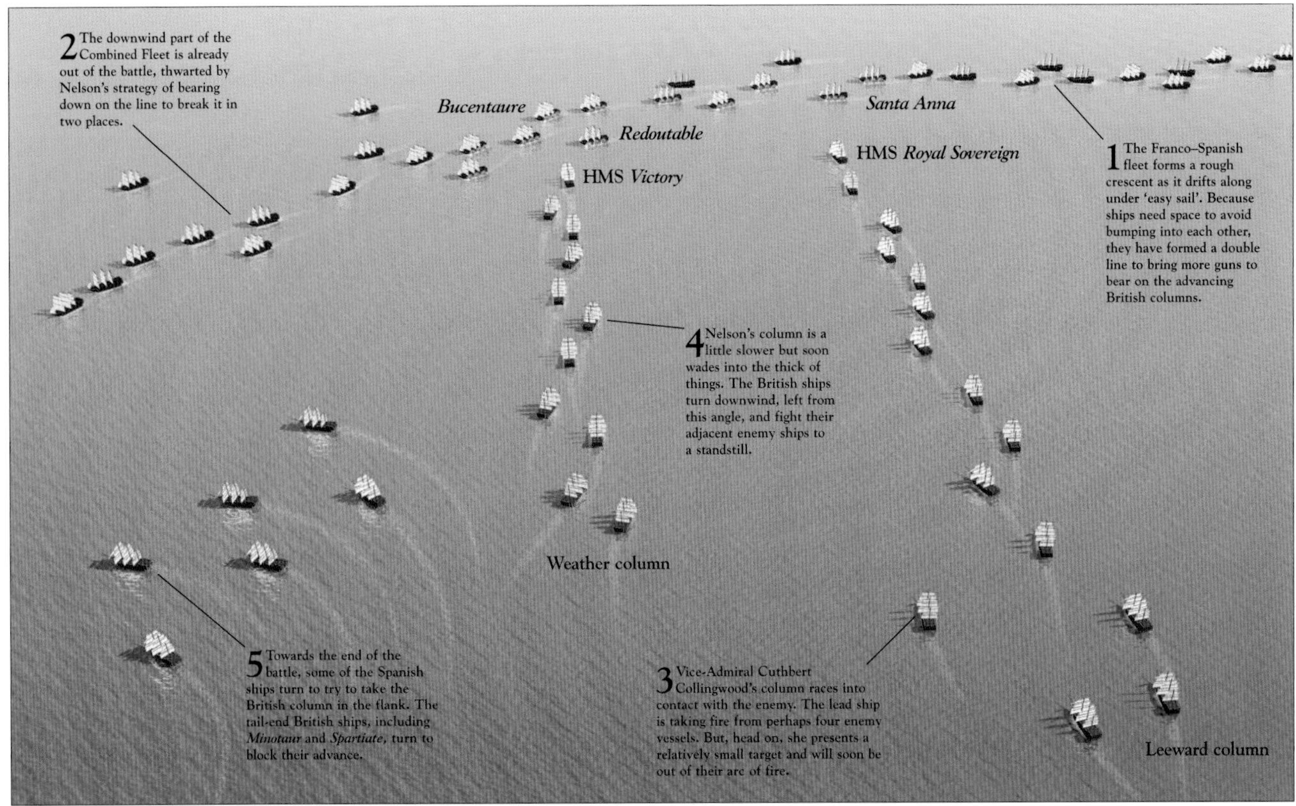

2 The downwind part of the Combined Fleet is already out of the battle, thwarted by Nelson's strategy of bearing down on the line to break it in two places.
Bucentaure
Redoutable
HMS Victory
Santa Anna
HMS Royal Sovereign
1 The Franco–Spanish fleet forms a rough crescent as it drifts along under 'easy sail'. Because ships need space to avoid bumping into each other, they have formed a double line to bring more guns to bear on the advancing British columns.
4 Nelson's column is a little slower but soon wades into the thick of things. The British ships turn downwind, left from this angle, and fight their adjacent enemy ships to a standstill.
Weather column
5 Towards the end of the battle, some of the Spanish ships turn to try to take the British column in the flank. The tail-end British ships, including Minotaur and Spartiate, turn to block their advance.
3 Vice-Admiral Cuthbert Collingwood's column races into contact with the enemy. The lead ship is taking fire from perhaps four enemy vessels. But, head on, she presents a relatively small target and will soon be out of their arc of fire.
Leeward column

Breaking the enemy line, as Nelson did, was a risky approach, but had a high payoff if the ships in column managed to cut the line in two. As the British ships passed into the French line, they were able to deliver full broadside fire.

Within minutes of the first shots of the battle being fired, *Victory* was engaged with four enemy vessels. These included the most powerful warship in the world, the Spanish 136-gun first-rate *Santissima Trinidad* along with *Heros*, *Redoubtable* and the French flagship *Bucentaure*. Despite serious damage, *Victory* was able to pass under the stern of *Bucentaure*, allowing her entire broadside to fire down the length of the French flagship. With damage to her masts and steering, *Victory* was difficult to control and it was almost impossible to tell what was going on as a confused mêlée of ships began to develop. Nelson had refrained from making detailed plans with his captains, instead making them aware that they could do little wrong if they put their ship alongside one of the enemy and pounded it with guns.

Victory next engaged the *Redoubtable* and became entangled with her. Captain Jean-Jacques Lucas of the *Redoubtable* was aware of the limitations of his crew. Since gunnery and sailing training were problematic while under blockade, Lucas had drilled his crew in boarding actions and sharpshooting from the rigging.

Morale was high aboard *Redoubtable*, which carried a large force of marines. One of her sharpshooters hit Nelson, the bullet lodging in his spine. Nelson was taken below, where he died three hours later. In the meantime, Lucas and his crew were preparing to board *Victory*. Their attempt was disrupted when the second British ship in the line, the 98-gun *Temeraire*, fired into the crew assembled on *Redoubtable*'s deck.

Under fire from *Victory* and *Temeraire*, *Redoubtable* fought on until her crew had sustained almost 90 per cent casualties, most of them fatal. Then she finally struck her colours (indicating surrender), permitting *Victory* and *Temeraire* to double up on *Bucentaure*. Other ships fired into the French flagship as they passed, or joined the cannonade. *Santissima Trinidad* suffered the same treatment, refusing to surrender for hours despite not having any guns left to fight with.

By the time that a shattered *Bucentaure* surrendered to HMS *Conqueror*, the battle was ending. The French and Spanish had lost some 22 ships, the British none, though many vessels were severely damaged.

Austerlitz 1805

NAPOLEONIC WARS

FRENCH VICTORY

KEY FACTS

WHO 73,000 French troops under Emperor Napoleon Bonaparte (1769–1821), opposed by an 85,000-strong Austro-Russian army commanded by Emperor Francis II (1768–1835) and Czar Alexander I (1777–1825).

WHAT The Allies were drawn into an attack on the French left. Once committed on the flank, their centre was broken by a French attack.

WHERE Near Austerlitz in Bohemia, 113km (60 miles) north of Vienna.

WHEN 2 December 1805

WHY The Allies feared that Napoleon intended to dominate Europe and moved to oppose him. The French responded with a brilliant campaign culminating in the victory at Austerlitz.

OUTCOME The Allies were totally defeated, greatly weakening the Third Coalition that had formed to oppose Napoleon.

The war between England and France was a clash between a great naval power and a great land power. In the same year that Emperor Napoleon of France won his greatest land victory at Austerlitz, his chance to invade the British Isles was forever lost off the coast of Spain.

Austerlitz resulted in another victory for Napoleon Bonaparte, but with desperately high numbers of casualties suffered by both sides.

LOCATION

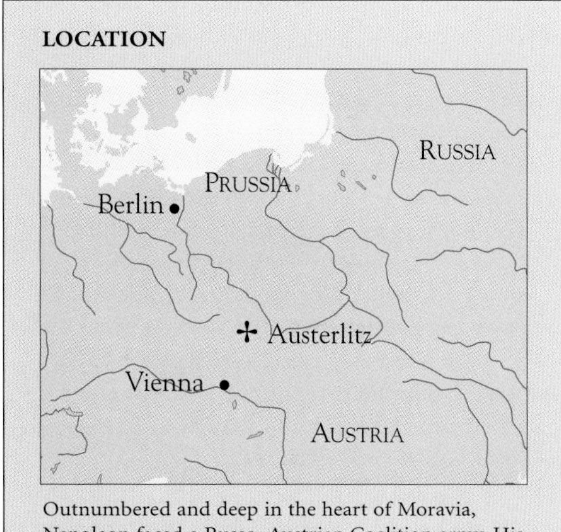
RUSSIA
PRUSSIA
Berlin
Austerlitz
Vienna
AUSTRIA

Outnumbered and deep in the heart of Moravia, Napoleon faced a Russo–Austrian Coalition army. His victory at Austerlitz was his greatest achievement.

When Napoleon, having decided that an invasion of Britain was impracticable, turned his full concentration on his mainland continental foes at the end of 1805 and occupied Vienna, the Austrian army chose not to fight and lose in a vain attempt to protect the capital. Instead, it moved off to prepare for a better opportunity for eventual victory. Napoleon, however, aware of the threat as long as his enemy's army remained in the field, determined to push on and seek a decisive action.

Reaching Brunn (Brno, now in the Czech Republic), he decided that he wanted to fight the Allies at a nearby location, next to the Pratzen Heights and the village of Austerlitz. To draw out the opposition, Napoleon posted forces on the Pratzen Heights and in Austerlitz, then hurriedly withdrew them as the enemy approached. To further consolidate the impression that he was in a bad position and wanted to avoid a battle, he entered into negotiations, and these were carried out with less of the arrogant self-confidence that characterized his usual manner.

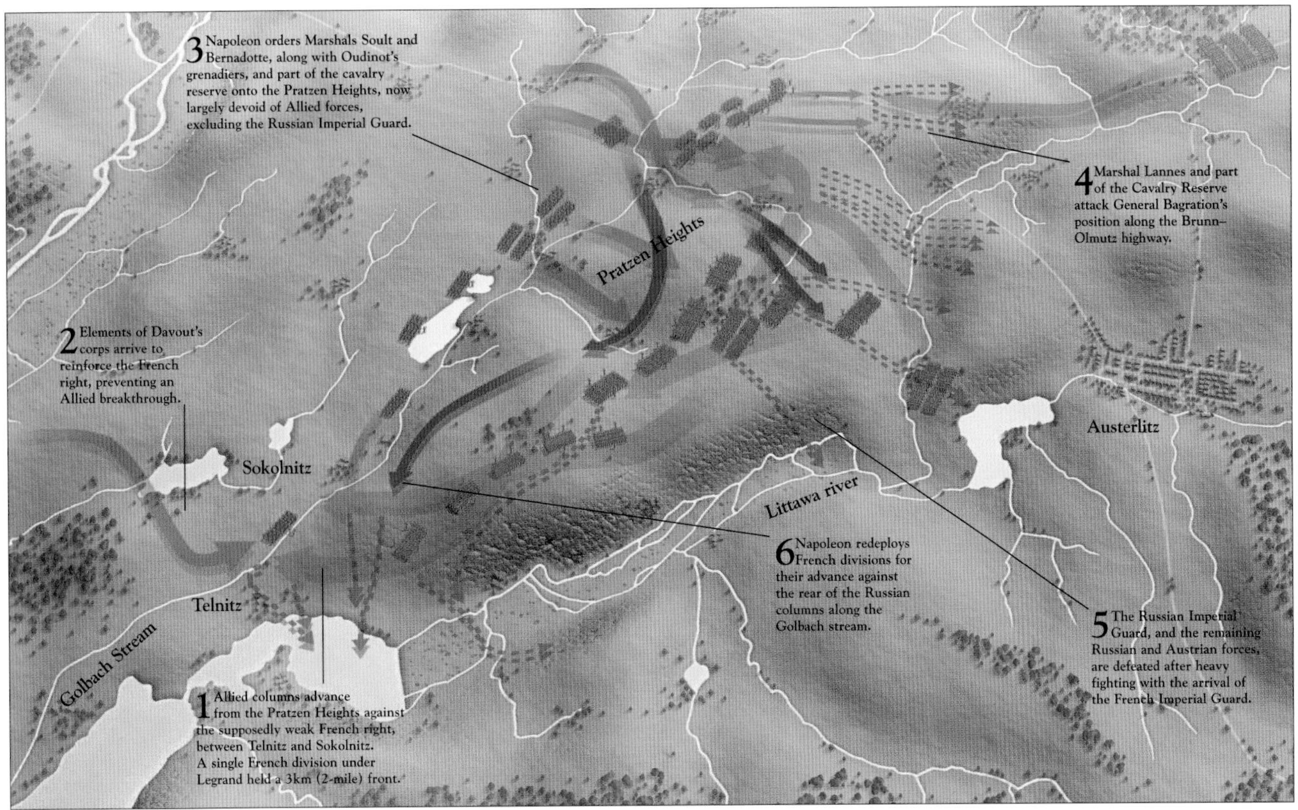
3 Napoleon orders Marshals Soult and Bernadotte, along with Oudinot's grenadiers, and part of the cavalry reserve onto the Pratzen Heights, now largely devoid of Allied forces, excluding the Russian Imperial Guard.
4 Marshal Lannes and part of the Cavalry Reserve attack General Bagration's position along the Brunn–Olmutz highway.
Pratzen Heights
2 Elements of Davout's corps arrive to reinforce the French right, preventing an Allied breakthrough.
Austerlitz
Sokolnitz
Littawa river
6 Napoleon redeploys French divisions for their advance against the rear of the Russian columns along the Golbach stream.
Telnitz
Golbach Stream
5 The Russian Imperial Guard, and the remaining Russian and Austrian forces, are defeated after heavy fighting with the arrival of the French Imperial Guard.
1 Allied columns advance from the Pratzen Heights against the supposedly weak French right, between Telnitz and Sokolnitz. A single French division under Legrand held a 3km (2-mile) front.

The raised ground of Pratzen Heights was the scene of most of the fighting during the Battle of Austerlitz. The battle showed the talents of Napoleon as a commander and tactician at their best, and his victory essentially destroyed the Third Coalition.

As most of their commanders were convinced that the French forces were weak and hesitant, the Allies decided to strike at the French right flank, which was understrength and in exposed positions. The intent was to break this flank while making a subsidiary attack on the opposite flank, opening the way for a final blow to rout the French army. This was exactly what Napoleon wanted them to try. They proceeded with their plan on the morning of 2 December 1805. The attack opened with an advance against the village of Tellnitz on the French right flank, but although there was a real danger for the French at this point that a determined Allied attack could drive in the flank as planned, the Allied advantage was not pressed home.

Napoleon waited until the Allies were fully committed to the attack on his right flank and had largely vacated the Pratzen Heights and then gave the order to attack. At the same time, he ordered a French corps to ascend the Heights, concealed in mist for at least some of the way, and take possession of them. A series of Russian counter-attacks failed to dislodge the French, who consolidated their position until they were in firm control of the centre of the battlefield.

Czar Alexander also ordered his Imperial Guard to retake the Heights. Despite heavy resistance, they broke through the first French line and caused thousands of French soldiers to flee. As the French clung to the Heights, the Horse Grenadiers of the French Imperial Guard charged into action, beginning a mêlée that drew in large numbers of horsemen from both sides. This engagement was very closely fought, but the French, supported by horse artillery and steady infantry, gained the upper hand.

Now the Allies were weakening. Their flank attacks had failed and the surviving units were heavily engaged in close fighting, while the centre was shattered. On the French right, the Allies finally broke and began to flee across the frozen lakes. The French artillery caused additional casualties by firing into the lakes to break the ice. However, there was little pursuit; the French, too, were exhausted by the heavy fighting. In addition to reducing Austria to military impotence, the legend of Napoleonic invincibility was greatly enhanced.

Austerlitz

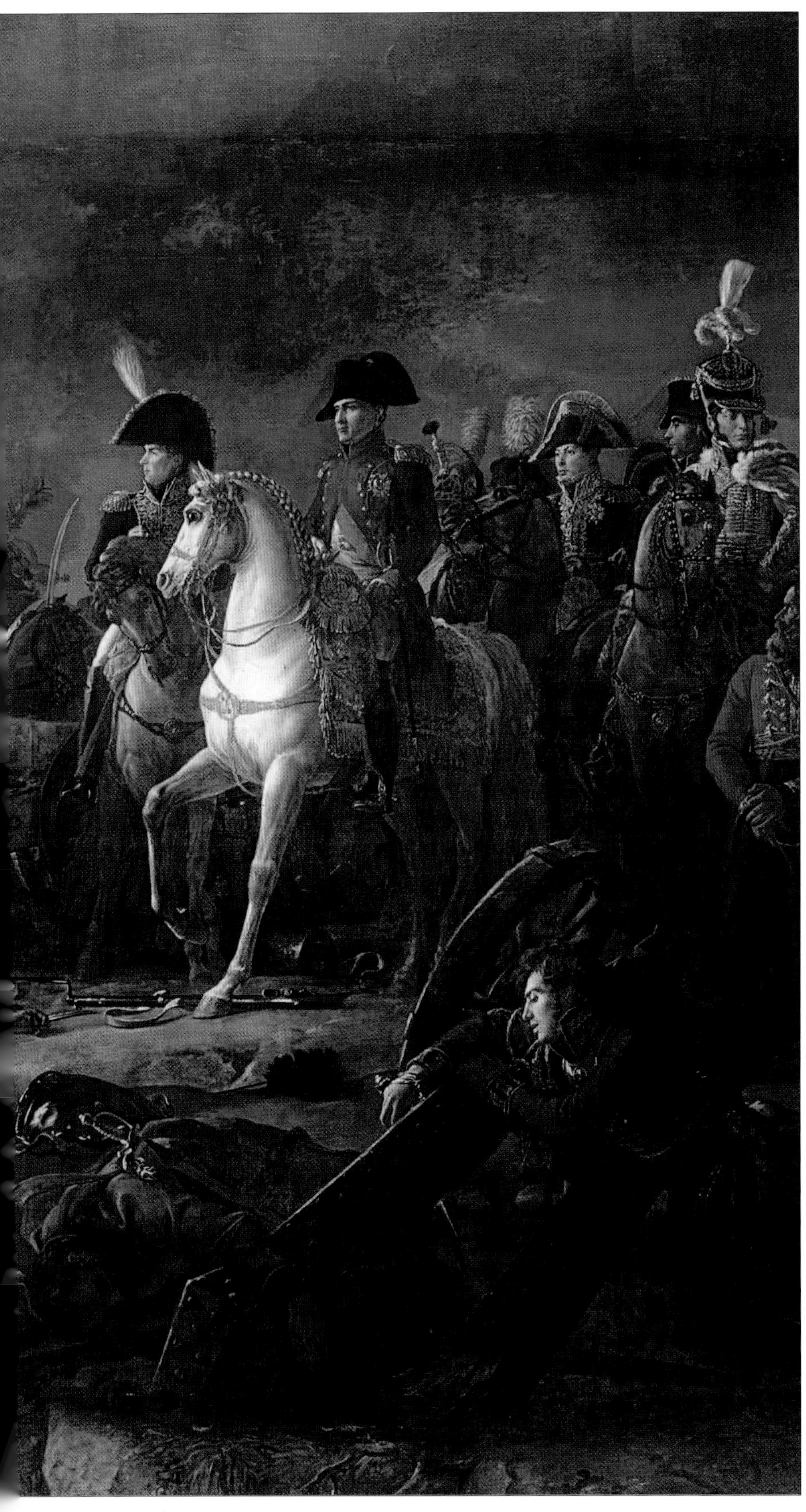

AUSTERLITZ

The Battle of Austerlitz took place on the high ground of Pratzen Heights, and was an example of Napoleon Bonaparte's brilliance in engineering a situation to ensure that a stand-off took place on terrain of his own choosing. His Austrian and Russian opponents were desperate to prevent him from marching on Vienna, and came up with a complicated plan to stop him, but Napoleon outmanoeuvred them, including a feint to convey the impression that he considered himself to be in an unfavourable position, and catching them with a surprise attack as a concealing mist lay over the battlefield. This was one of the victories that made Napoleon's reputation.

Auerstädt 1806

KEY FACTS

Who A corps of the French army under Marshal Louis Davout against Prussians led by the Duke of Brunswick.

What Napoleon had sent corps to attack the rear of the Prussian army, but they found themselves under attack from a greater concentration of enemy forces at Auerstädt.

Where Auerstädt, Germany.

When 14 October 1806

Why Napoleon had launched an attack into Saxony in response to the signing of a new alliance between Prussia and Russia.

Outcome Napoleon was able to march on to further victories in Prussia, paving the way for an all-out assault on Russia.

The French army by the early 1800s was a highly efficient fighting machine. But as events at Auerstädt proved, scouting methods of the period still left much room for improvement.

NAPOLEONIC WARS

FRENCH VICTORY

Napoleon's army was never more ruthless than at Auerstädt. After defeating the Prussians, they pursued their beaten remnants for four hours after they'd fled the field.

LOCATION

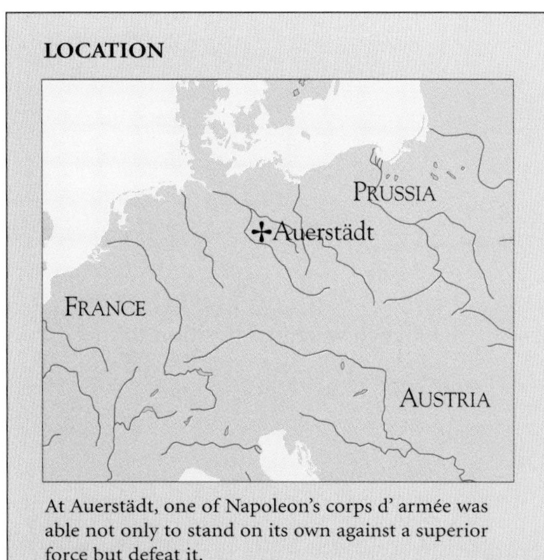
PRUSSIA
Auerstädt
FRANCE
AUSTRIA

At Auerstädt, one of Napoleon's corps d' armée was able not only to stand on its own against a superior force but defeat it.

In the summer of 1806, after the Prussians had formed an alliance with Russia, Napoleon crossed the borders of Saxony at the head of the French army. He had every reason to be confident in the manpower at his disposal. La Grande Armée used a flexible organizational structure, within which units could be transferred between formations at need. The basic unit was the corps, into which the French army had been divided since 1800. Each corps was a self-contained all-arms force of infantry, artillery and cavalry, capable of dealing with many opponents unsupported and defending itself until assistance arrived if it encountered a superior force.

By contrast, the Prussian army was 'a walking museum piece', scarcely changed since the days of Frederick the Great. Its poor command structure meant many positions were held by more than one officer.

Napoleon reached Jena, where he prepared to meet the Prussian army. To crush his enemies more completely, he ordered the III corps under Marshal Louis Davout and the I corps under Jean Bernadotte to move to the east of the

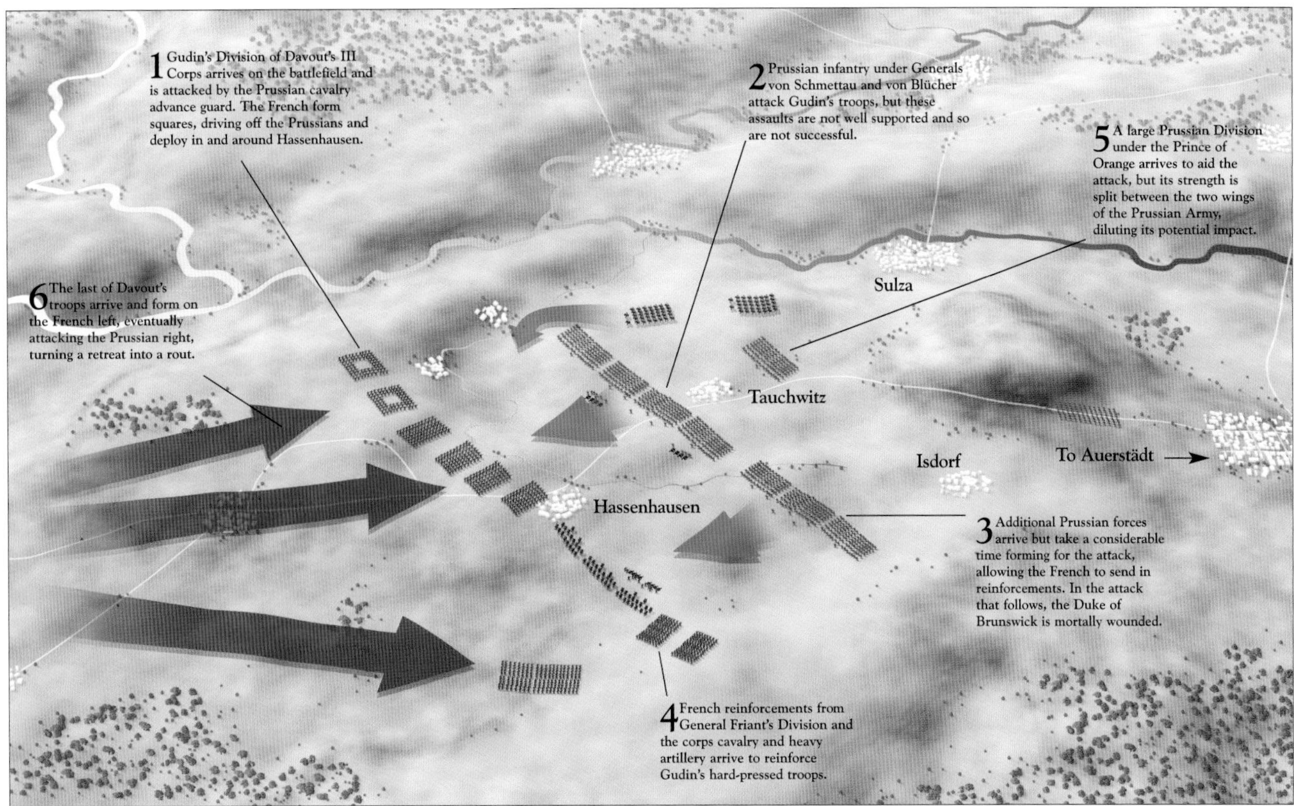
1 Gudin's Division of Davout's III Corps arrives on the battlefield and is attacked by the Prussian cavalry advance guard. The French form squares, driving off the Prussians and deploy in and around Hassenhausen.
2 Prussian infantry under Generals von Schmettau and von Blücher attack Gudin's troops, but these assaults are not well supported and so are not successful.
5 A large Prussian Division under the Prince of Orange arrives to aid the attack, but its strength is split between the two wings of the Prussian Army, diluting its potential impact.
6 The last of Davout's troops arrive and form on the French left, eventually attacking the Prussian right, turning a retreat into a rout.
Sulza
Tauchwitz
Isdorf
To Auerstädt
Hassenhausen
3 Additional Prussian forces arrive but take a considerable time forming for the attack, allowing the French to send in reinforcements. In the attack that follows, the Duke of Brunswick is mortally wounded.
4 French reinforcements from General Friant's Division and the corps cavalry and heavy artillery arrive to reinforce Gudin's hard-pressed troops.

The Prussian army was a shadow of its former days under Frederick the Great when it took to the field at Auerstädt. Worse still, it was facing a highly efficient French army at the peak of its power and confidence.

town and make for the rear of the Prince of Hohenlohe's forces, cutting off their line of retreat.

FACE TO FACE

Davout's progress was slow since there was heavy fog and the terrain was a difficult climb. Worse still, and unknown to Napoleon, just about to do battle with what he had mistakenly been informed was the entire Prussian army on the heights above Jena, Davout's march was to bring him face to face with the main army, under the Duke of Brunswick, based at Auerstädt.

Almost immediately, Davout found himself under attack from an impetuous charge of two squadrons of Prussian dragoons. Ordering one brigade to form square, this was easily repulsed and, as the fog lifted, a horse battery under the command of General Etienne Gudin knocked out a Prussian battery and drove back some of their horse and foot. Davout then ordered Gudin to occupy the village of Hassenhausen, supported by the divisional artillery, where they drove back several uncoordinated attacks by Prussian infantry and cavalry.

Among these included one led by Gebhard Von Blücher who, impetuous as ever, had his horse shot out from under him, though he was able to return to his lines unharmed. At this critical moment French reinforcements arrived, just as William, the Prince of Orange, arrived with his division. Unfortunately, rather than keeping the division together and bringing its mass to bear on one of the flanks of the French Army, he was ordered to divide his command between the two flanks of the Prussian Army, thereby denying the opportunity to apply mass at a decisive point.

RELENTLESS PURSUIT

Further repeated Prussian charges were driven back. This, combined with the advance of fresh enemy troops, took the fight out of the Prussian infantry, which began to retire. By noon, the French were in a position to make a general advance, turning the retreat into a rout. The French were relentless and kept up the pressure on the retreating Prussians for nearly four hours, covering several miles before they halted, utterly exhausted.

Maida 1806

NAPOLEONIC WARS

BRITISH VICTORY

In 1806, the southern peninsula of Italy was in turmoil, after the French invasion of Naples had forced its king to flee. Was there anything that stood in the way of them taking Sicily?

KEY FACTS

WHO General Sir John Stuart in charge of the British army against French troops commanded by General Jean Reynier.

WHAT General Sir John Stuart was able to position his troops advantageously, so that they were able to inflict heavy losses on the advancing French lines while sustaining few himself.

WHERE Maida, Calabria, Italy.

WHEN 4 July 1806

WHY The French were intending to invade Sicily, always a crucial island for its strategic position for trade, and the British were waging a campaign against them on the southern Italian peninsula.

OUTCOME The British, by stoking up local opposition to the French, were able to stave off an invasion of Sicily.

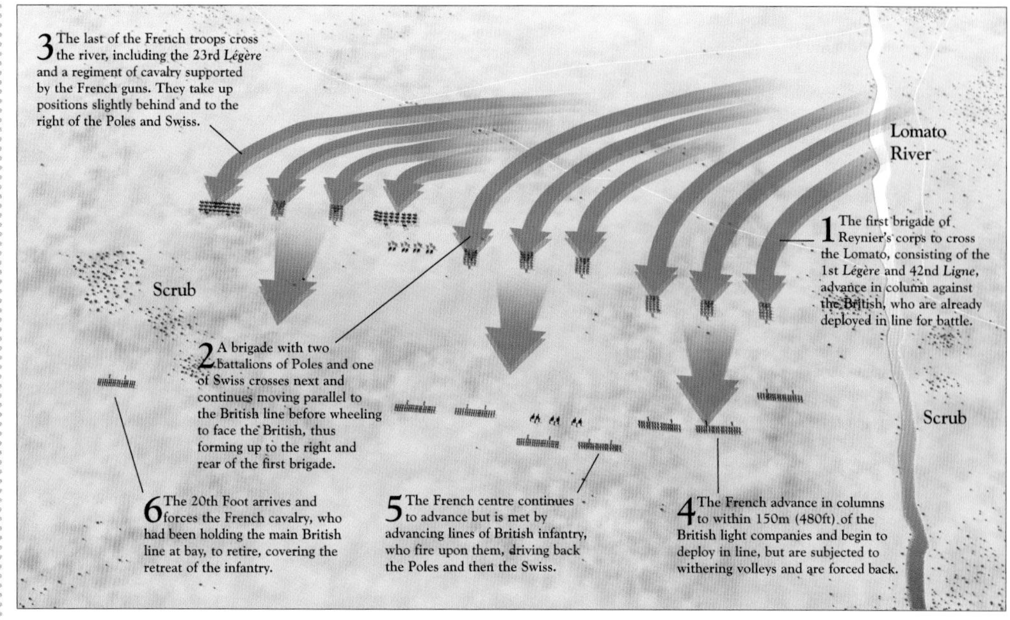
3 The last of the French troops cross the river, including the 23rd Légère and a regiment of cavalry supported by the French guns. They take up positions slightly behind and to the right of the Poles and Swiss.
Lomato River
1 The first brigade of Reynier's corps to cross the Lomato, consisting of the 1st Légère and 42nd Ligne, advance in column against the British, who are already deployed in line for battle.
Scrub
2 A brigade with two battalions of Poles and one of Swiss crosses next and continues moving parallel to the British line before wheeling to face the British, thus forming up to the right and rear of the first brigade.
Scrub
6 The 20th Foot arrives and forces the French cavalry, who had been holding the main British line at bay, to retire, covering the retreat of the infantry.
5 The French centre continues to advance but is met by advancing lines of British infantry, who fire upon them, driving back the Poles and then the Swiss.
4 The French advance in columns to within 150m (480ft) of the British light companies and begin to deploy in line, but are subjected to withering volleys and are forced back.

Maida lay on the tip of Naples and near the island of Sicily, for centuries an island whose considerable strategic significance, by virtue of its location, far outweighed its actual size.

General Sir John Stuart had landed a force of some 5000 infantry, supported by a battery of foot artillery, in Calabria in southern Italy with the dual intention of stirring local unrest against French occupation, and engaging the French in battle.

A French force under General Reynier met Stuart's army on a plain north of the Lomato River near the village of Maida. Since the French were south of the river, they had to march perpendicular to the British line of advance. While Stuart's troops formed for battle, the French crossed the Lomato and then wheeled to advance on the British. This forced Reynier's units to advance in an oblique battle order and did not allow them to deploy from column into line.

DEVASTATING VOLLEYS

The British units waited until the leading French columns were in range and unleashed devastating volleys. Most of the French infantry were forced to fall back, covered by cavalry who managed to prevent the British from fully exploiting what was already a sizeable tactical victory.

LOCATION

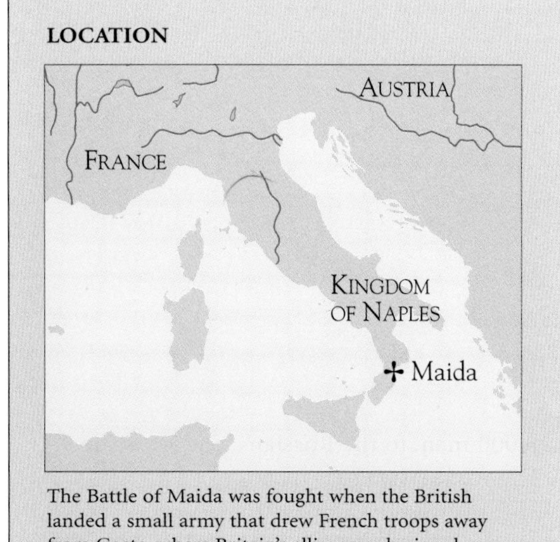
AUSTRIA
FRANCE
KINGDOM OF NAPLES
Maida

The Battle of Maida was fought when the British landed a small army that drew French troops away from Gaeta, where Britain's allies were besieged.

TIMELINE

1500–1000BC	1000–500BC	500BC–0AD	0–500AD	500–1000AD	1000–1500AD	1500–2000AD

Eylau 1807

NAPOLEONIC WARS

STALEMATE

KEY FACTS

WHO General Levin von Bennigsen leading a Russian army against the French led by Napoleon Bonaparte.

WHAT A gruelling battle in the snow, in which the French sustained heavy losses from Russian cannon, while the French retorted with a bloody cavalry charge. The Russians eventually retreated, but the French were too exhausted to pursue.

WHERE Preussische-Eylau, near Kalingrad.

WHEN 7–8 February 1807

WHY After routing the Prussians, Napoleon was now ready to carry his campaign into Russia.

OUTCOME The two sides slogged away for 14 hours and, with heavy casualties on both sides, no clear winner emerged. Napoleon would have to wait until the summer for the victory that would force the Russians to seek peace terms.

Fighting a battle in winter is generally inadvisable, and never was there a better illustration than at Eylau. Many who weren't killed suffered a perhaps worse fate by freezing to death whilst lying injured.

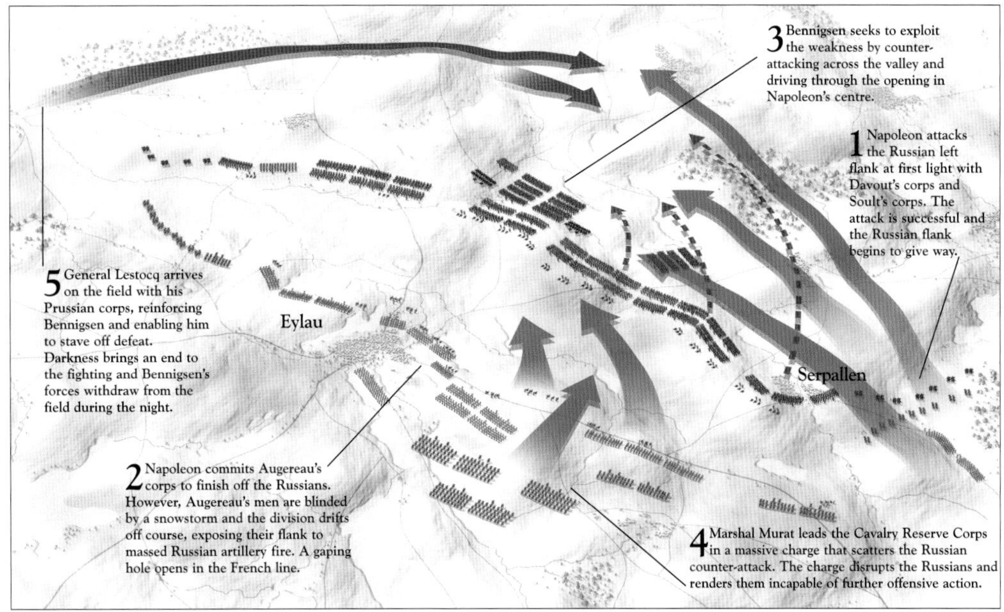

3 Bennigsen seeks to exploit the weakness by counter-attacking across the valley and driving through the opening in Napoleon's centre.
1 Napoleon attacks the Russian left flank at first light with Davout's corps and Soult's corps. The attack is successful and the Russian flank begins to give way.
5 General Lestocq arrives on the field with his Prussian corps, reinforcing Bennigsen and enabling him to stave off defeat. Darkness brings an end to the fighting and Bennigsen's forces withdraw from the field during the night.
Eylau
Serpallen
2 Napoleon commits Augereau's corps to finish off the Russians. However, Augereau's men are blinded by a snowstorm and the division drifts off course, exposing their flank to massed Russian artillery fire. A gaping hole opens in the French line.
4 Marshal Murat leads the Cavalry Reserve Corps in a massive charge that scatters the Russian counter-attack. The charge disrupts the Russians and renders them incapable of further offensive action.

Some of the most punishing battles in history have been fought on Russian soil. Eylau took place in a snowstorm, and many combatants wounded in the exchanges simply froze to death.

Snow was falling when Napoleon launched a full-scale attack on General Levin von Bennigsen's lines at Eylau. Marshal Louis Davout conducted a brilliant attack that threatened to envelop the left flank of the Russian Army, but a supporting corps stumbled blindly through a snowstorm, lost its way and wandered directly into the path of the Russian main gun line. Torn to pieces by grapeshot, the corps fled from the field, leaving a gaping hole in Napoleon's line.

The Russians would have prevailed had not Marshal Joachim Murat launched a massive attack with the French Cavalry Reserve, which checked the Russian advance and saved the day. Bennigsen was reinforced by General Lestocq's Prussian corps late in the battle, and with these fresh troops he was able to stabilize his position, before staging a full retreat. The French were so exhausted they could not pursue them, having lost perhaps 25,000 men, to the Russians' and Prussians' 15,000. Many of the wounded froze to death. Marshal Ney, who had arrived late in the battle, tellingly surveyed the scene and commented: 'What a massacre! And without a result!'

LOCATION

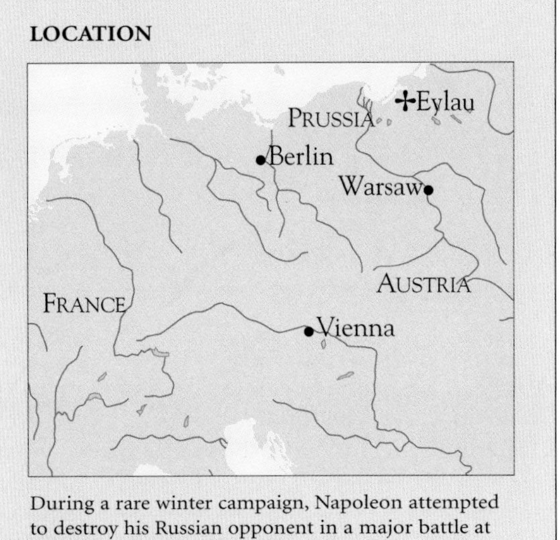

Eylau
PRUSSIA
Berlin
Warsaw
FRANCE
AUSTRIA
Vienna

During a rare winter campaign, Napoleon attempted to destroy his Russian opponent in a major battle at the village of Eylau, in Russian Poland.

TIMELINE

1500–1000BC	1000–500BC	500BC–0AD	0–500AD	500–1000AD	1000–1500AD	1500–2000AD

Maida

MAIDA

Italy, in the years before its unification in the mid-nineteenth century, was perpetually caught up in the machinations of the colonial powers of Europe, with the Austrians and the Spanish Bourbons among those who took a hand in controlling its affairs. By the beginning of the nineteenth century, it was the French under Napoleon who seemed set to take control of the entire peninsula. This was a disaster for a trading nation like Britain, which needed access to the Mediterranean. Maida was fought in a plain near the Lomato River by a British army under General Stuart and thwarted French plans to invade strategically vital Sicily.

Friedland 1807

NAPOLEONIC WARS

FRENCH VICTORY

KEY FACTS

Who The Russian army under General Levin von Bennigsen against la Grande Armée of Napoleon.

What The French deployed close-range, rapid artillery fire to open the way for a decisive victory.

Where Friedland, modern day Pravdinsk, Russia.

When 14 June 1807

Why Napoleon had launched a major invasion of Russia, having previously defeated their Prussian allies.

Outcome Russia quickly sought terms with Napoleon, but peace would be short-lived.

The battle of Friedland was notable as the moment when artillery truly came of age as a combat arm that was the equal of the cavalry and the infantry, a truly independent element of manoeuvre on the battlefield. It was a major moment on the road to modern warfare.

Light cavalry, usually used for pre-battle reconnaissance and pursuit after enemy lines had been broken, played a full part in the mounted charges at Freidland.

LOCATION

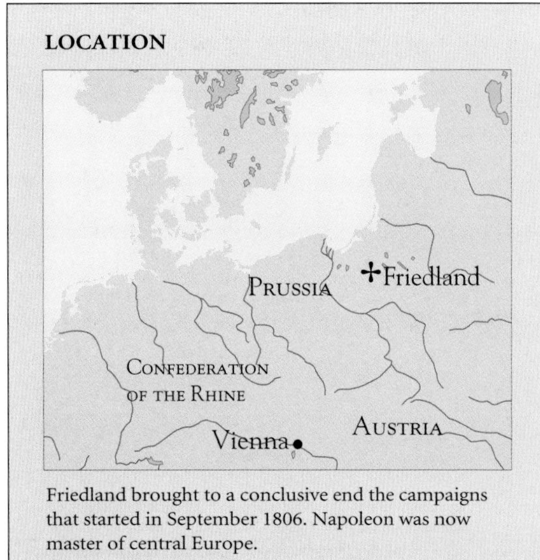
Friedland
Prussia
Confederation of the Rhine
Austria
Vienna

Friedland brought to a conclusive end the campaigns that started in September 1806. Napoleon was now master of central Europe.

The Russian army under General Bennigsen was crossing the River Alle at Friedland when a French army marching under the command of Marshal Jean Lannes was sighted on the western bank of the river overlooking the town. Lannes apparently being unsupported, Bennigsen decided to cross the river and destroy his force. By deciding on this course of action, Bennigsen committed himself to fight with a river at his back.

Further, he had his pontonniers construct three bridges leading into Friedland and nowhere else, though he also had the civilian bridge over the river at his disposal. This plan of action limited Bennigsen's ability to withdraw quickly if necessary. Lannes immediately sent couriers galloping off to find Napoleon and the main French Army and proceeded to fight an expert delaying action against the Russians.

The French general never had more than 26,000 men at his disposal to face 60,000 Russians. Not only did Bennigsen fail to destroy Lannes' corps, he deployed almost his entire force against it, so when Napoleon

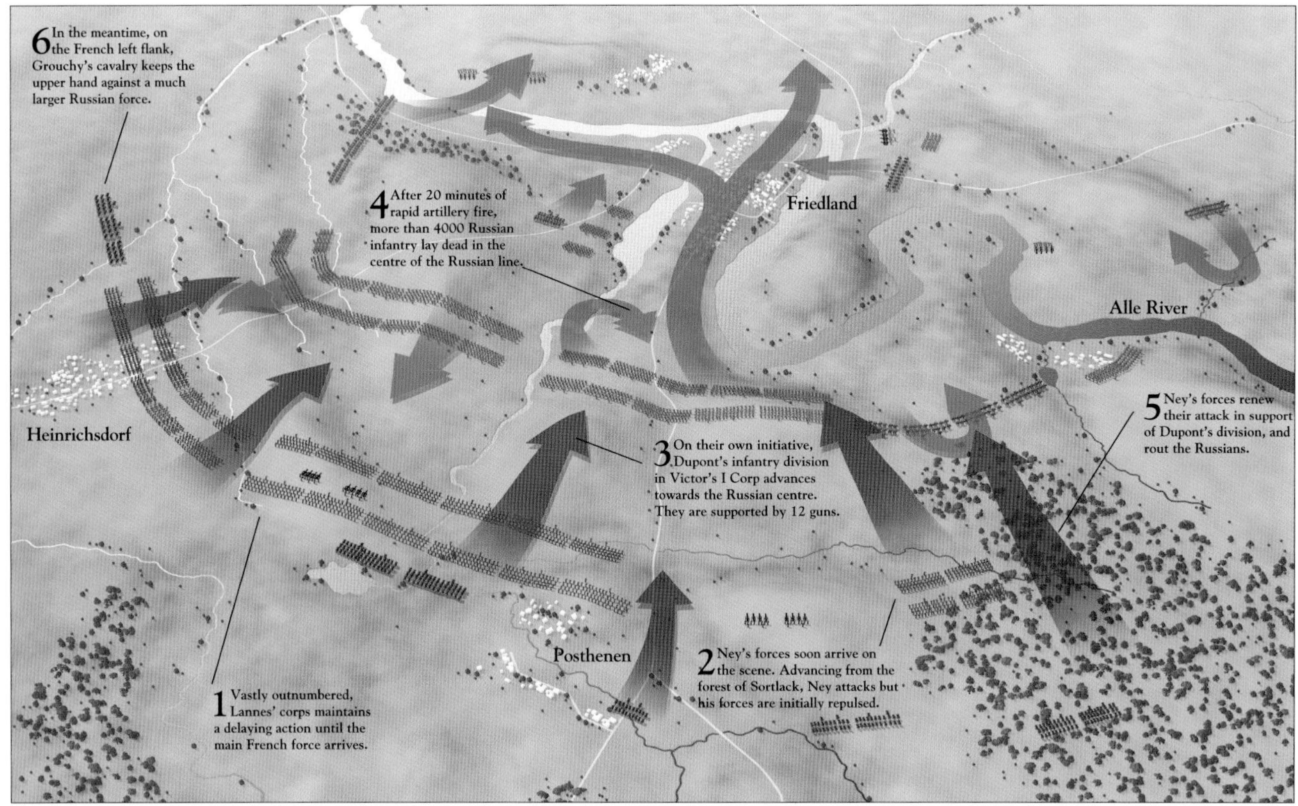
6 In the meantime, on the French left flank, Grouchy's cavalry keeps the upper hand against a much larger Russian force.
4 After 20 minutes of rapid artillery fire, more than 4000 Russian infantry lay dead in the centre of the Russian line.
Friedland
Alle River
Heinrichsdorf
3 On their own initiative, Dupont's infantry division in Victor's I Corp advances towards the Russian centre. They are supported by 12 guns.
5 Ney's forces renew their attack in support of Dupont's division, and rout the Russians.
Posthenen
2 Ney's forces soon arrive on the scene. Advancing from the forest of Sortlack, Ney attacks but his forces are initially repulsed.
1 Vastly outnumbered, Lannes' corps maintains a delaying action until the main French force arrives.

While the cavalry charge played a big role at Friedland, this was the first time artillery was used as an independent element of attack on the battlefield. Horse-drawn mobile artillery enabled commanders to concentrate fire at key moments and points in a battle.

finally arrived, he was presented with a golden opportunity to capitalize.

In the French centre, General Sénarmont, the corps chief of artillery in I Corps, successfully requested the use of the entire corps artillery contingent, 36 guns, to join in an advance by General Pierre Dupont. Sénarmont initially formed the artillery into two 15-gun batteries on the flanks of Dupont's division. The other six guns were kept in reserve along with the ammunition caissons. The artillery batteries soon outpaced Dupont, and Sénarmont took the responsibility of ordering them forward against the Russian centre. They advanced by bounds, opening fire on the Russians at approximately 410m (450 yards) from the centre of the enemy line. The Russian infantry stood firm. After firing five or six salvoes, Sénarmont ordered his companies forward, stopping at a range of 230m (250 yards) to open fire once again.

Ordering his guns to cease firing, Sénarmont again ordered the companies forward, stopping once again to open fire, this time at 135m (150 yards) from the Russian positions. Just over 20 minutes later, more than 4000 Russians littered the field and the Russian centre was destroyed. This was the decisive action of the battle.

An attack by Marshal Ney followed up Sénarmont's manoeuvre. Dupont had also brought his division forward in support and defeated the Russian Guard infantry in close combat. Sénarmont was counter-attacked by the cavalry of the Russian Guard, and his artillery companies changed front and gave the Russian horsemen two canister volleys, shattering their charge.

ARTILLERY MANOEUVRE

The remainder of the battle was almost anticlimactic. The Russian left was crushed and there was a rush for the bridges. Ney and Dupont continued to advance and now Sénarmont supported the French advance on Friedland, their combined efforts nearly destroying the Russian Army. Friedland was one of the outstanding victories of the French Empire and its artillery tactics, repeated on other battlefields, marked the first time artillery had been used as an independent manoeuvre element on the battlefield in an offensive role.

Somosierra 1808

NAPOLEONIC WARS

FRENCH VICTORY

Spain had assisted Napoleon in his conquest of Portugal, but then found itself the object of his imperial attentions. The capital Madrid had risen up against him earlier in 1808, however, and now he found himself having to march on the city to stamp his control.

KEY FACTS

WHO Napoleon Bonaparte and the French Army, with the assistance of the Polish cavalry, against Benito San Juan leading a makeshift Spanish army, including conscripts and reservists.

WHAT Napoleon's advance on Madrid occurred when a mountain pass was blocked by Benito San Juan's army. A charge by the Polish cavalry was crucial to the French bursting through and continuing on to the capital.

WHERE The mountain pass near Somosierra, north of Madrid.

WHEN 30 November 1808

WHY Napoleon Bonaparte had launched an invasion of Spain, but despite the efficiency of the French army, there was much local resistance.

OUTCOME Napoleon was able to march on to Madrid, which fell to him a week later.

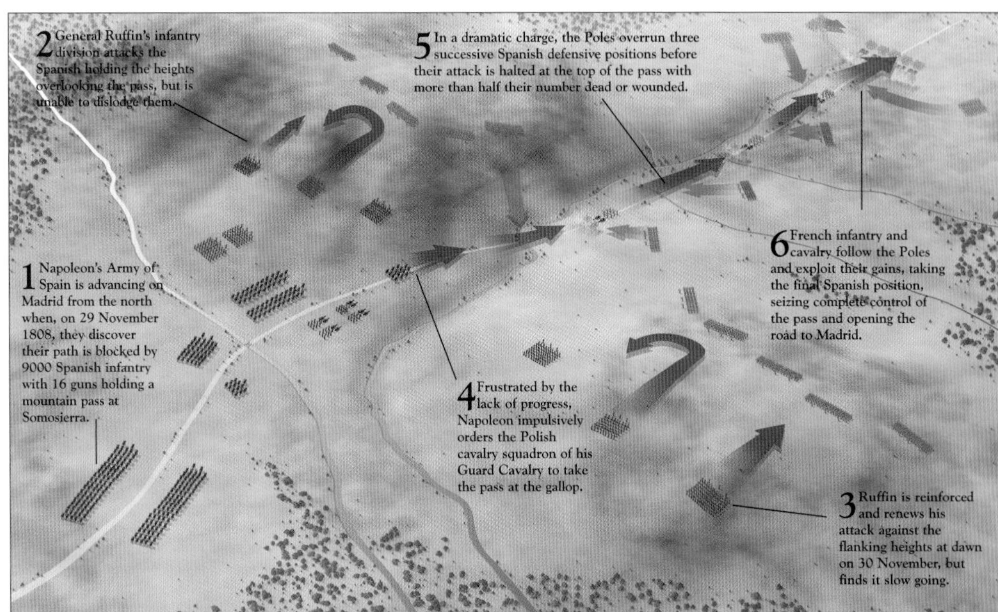
2 General Ruffin's infantry division attacks the Spanish holding the heights overlooking the pass, but is unable to dislodge them.
5 In a dramatic charge, the Poles overrun three successive Spanish defensive positions before their attack is halted at the top of the pass with more than half their number dead or wounded.
1 Napoleon's Army of Spain is advancing on Madrid from the north when, on 29 November 1808, they discover their path is blocked by 9000 Spanish infantry with 16 guns holding a mountain pass at Somosierra.
6 French infantry and cavalry follow the Poles and exploit their gains, taking the final Spanish position, seizing complete control of the pass and opening the road to Madrid.
4 Frustrated by the lack of progress, Napoleon impulsively orders the Polish cavalry squadron of his Guard Cavalry to take the pass at the gallop.
3 Ruffin is reinforced and renews his attack against the flanking heights at dawn on 30 November, but finds it slow going.

Even if the golden age of the cavalry was passing, mounted troops could still play a key part in warfare. At Somosierra, much was owed to the exploits of the Polish cavalrymen who took the mountain pass at a gallop.

Napoleon's 40,000-strong Army of Spain was driving towards the capital Madrid. But Benito San Juan had managed to put together a respectably sized force, based around local militia, reservists and conscripts. And with 16 guns ensconced in fortified positions astride a mountain pass winding past the town of Somosierra, he had blocked the route.

CLEARING THE WAY

General Francois Ruffin's infantry division attempted but failed to clear the Spanish from the heights overlooking the pass, but progress was slow. As Napoleon fumed at the delay, one of the advance Spanish batteries fired on his headquarters. At his order, his Polish escort squadron of 125 troopers charged forward and overran the first gun battery, then pressed on, capturing two more gun positions and practically clearing the road all the way to the summit before heavy casualties brought them to a halt. French infantry and cavalry then rushed forward and captured the final Spanish position at Somosierra, thus opening up the road to Madrid, which Napoleon captured shortly afterwards.

LOCATION

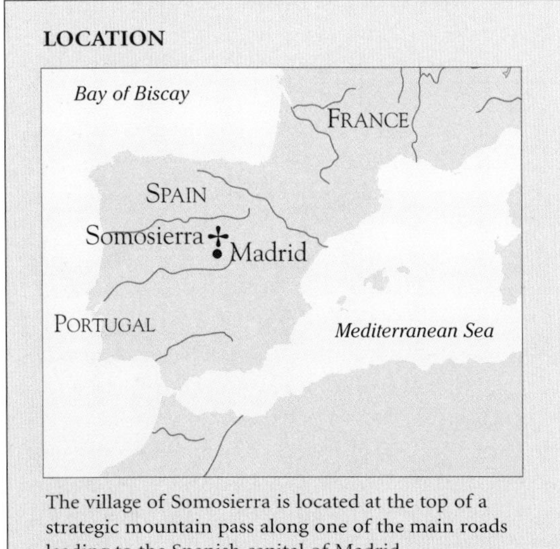
Bay of Biscay
FRANCE
SPAIN
Somosierra
Madrid
PORTUGAL
Mediterranean Sea

The village of Somosierra is located at the top of a strategic mountain pass along one of the main roads leading to the Spanish capital of Madrid.

TIMELINE

1500–1000BC	1000–500BC	500BC–0AD	0–500AD	500–1000AD	1000–1500AD	1500–2000AD

Wagram 1809

NAPOLEONIC WARS

FRENCH VICTORY

Napoleon Bonaparte had just suffered his first major defeat on the battlefield when he leapt back into action a few weeks later. Victory at Wagram somewhat restored his tarnished lustre, but at a huge cost in human life. For the second time, his army suffered immense caualties.

KEY FACTS

WHO Napoleon Bonaparte and the French Army, against the Austrians, led by Archduke Charles of Austria.

WHAT In a punishing battle, marked by extensive use of artillery, Napoleon was able to gain a morale-boosting win after recent setbacks.

WHERE Deutsch-Wagram, near Vienna, Austria.

WHEN 5–6 July 1809

WHY The Austrians, believing Napoleon would be preoccupied by the Peninsular War, had launched a fightback.

OUTCOME The French actually suffered huge losses in the battle, as did the Austrians, leading to the signing of a peace treaty framed much in Napoleon's favour.

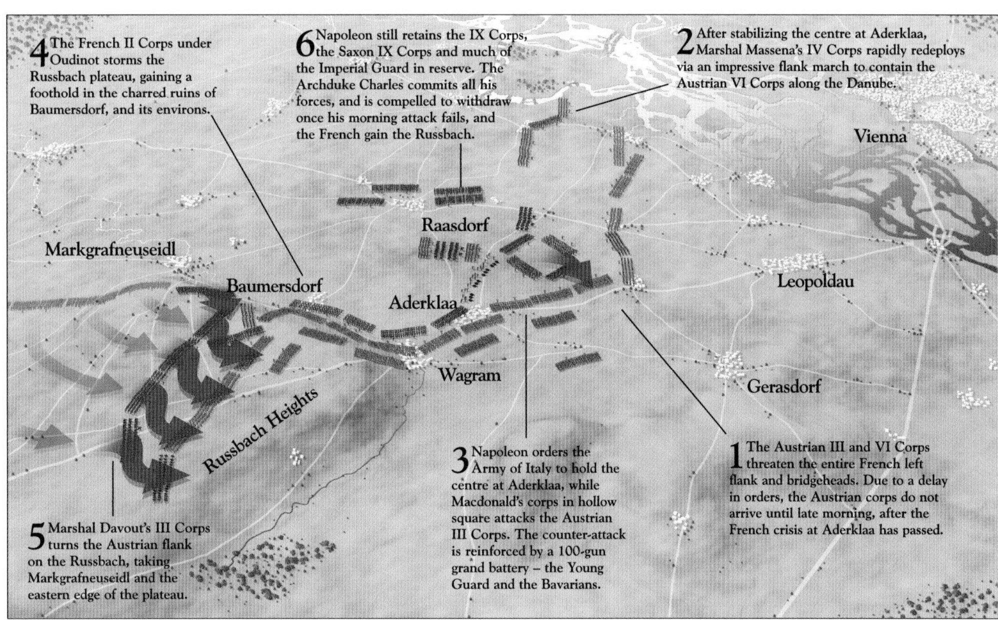
4 The French II Corps under Oudinot storms the Russbach plateau, gaining a foothold in the charred ruins of Baumersdorf, and its environs.
6 Napoleon still retains the IX Corps, the Saxon IX Corps and much of the Imperial Guard in reserve. The Archduke Charles commits all his forces, and is compelled to withdraw once his morning attack fails, and the French gain the Russbach.
2 After stabilizing the centre at Aderklaa, Marshal Massena's IV Corps rapidly redeploys via an impressive flank march to contain the Austrian VI Corps along the Danube.
Vienna
Raasdorf
Markgrafneuseidl
Baumersdorf
Aderklaa
Leopoldau
Wagram
Gerasdorf
Russbach Heights
3 Napoleon orders the Army of Italy to hold the centre at Aderklaa, while Macdonald's corps in hollow square attacks the Austrian III Corps. The counter-attack is reinforced by a 100-gun grand battery – the Young Guard and the Bavarians.
1 The Austrian III and VI Corps threaten the entire French left flank and bridgeheads. Due to a delay in orders, the Austrian corps do not arrive until late morning, after the French crisis at Aderklaa has passed.
5 Marshal Davout's III Corps turns the Austrian flank on the Russbach, taking Markgrafneuseidl and the eastern edge of the plateau.

The French success at Wagram owed much to a nighttime river manoeuvre that bore more similarities to a modern special forces operation than a conventional battle.

Little more than month after a heavy defeat by the Austrians at Aspern-Essling, on the Danube near Vienna, Napoleon decided to return to the battlefield, determined not to repeat the mistakes that had led to that defeat. This time, the French Army constructed gun emplacements, deployed heavy batteries and built numerous pontoon bridges for a second crossing of the Danube. They then managed a remarkably swift and efficient night-time crossing, which resembled an early nineteenth-century special forces operation rather than a conventional battle. The Austrian divisions guarding the bank were overwhelmed, and within four hours Napoleon had three full corps across the river. A violent battle characterized by extensive artillery bombardment ensued, during which the French would lose 30,000 men (it had lost as many at Aspern-Essling). The Austrians, however, fared even worse.

After Wagram, Austria was unable to summon the will to continue the hostilities, and agreed to an armistice. The terms of the peace treaty were shaped more to Napoleon's liking than to his opponent's.

LOCATION

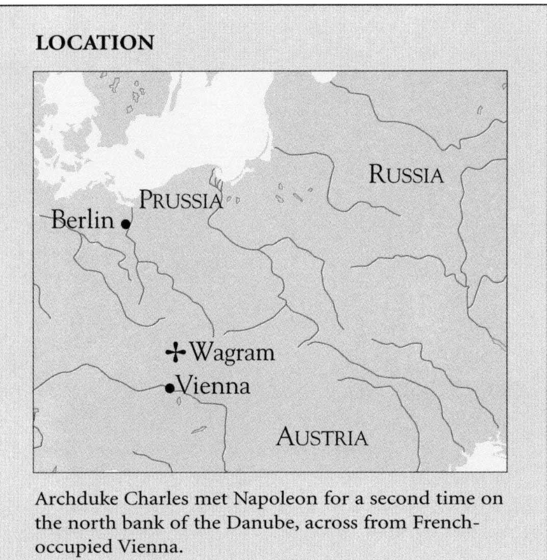
Russia
Prussia
Berlin
Wagram
Vienna
Austria

Archduke Charles met Napoleon for a second time on the north bank of the Danube, across from French-occupied Vienna.

TIMELINE

1500–1000BC	1000–500BC	500BC–0AD	0–500AD	500–1000AD	1000–1500AD	1500–2000AD

WAGRAM

Napoleon Bonaparte was nothing if not the nineteenth-century comeback kid of both the political and military arenas. He fought Wagram just weeks after a bad shaking at the hands of the Austrians at Aspern-Essling, but this time he was triumphant. However, victory at Wagram, achieved with much use of artillery bombardment ensued, came at a heavy price. The French would lose 30,000 men, following on from similarly heavy casualties in the earlier battle. That said, the Austrians lost even more soldiers, and it was Napoleonic France that emerged distinctly the stronger from the resultant armistice.

Grand Port 1810

KEY FACTS

WHO Captain James Willoughby of the HMS *Nereide*, against a small squadron of the French navy under Captain Guy-Victor Duperre.

WHAT Captain Willoughby attempted to lure French ships into a trap at Grand Port, Ile de France, but the plan backfired and ultimately led to much loss of life.

WHERE Off Grand Port, Ile de France, Mauritius.

WHEN August 1810

WHY The British and French navies were battling to attain supremacy in the Indian Ocean, with French corsairs attacking British trade ships.

OUTCOME After this embarrassing British naval defeat, Willoughby was blamed for giving misleading information about the extent of the threat posed by the French force.

During the Napoleonic period, the British and French fleets battled furiously for control of the Indian Ocean. Generally, the British had the stronger presence, but they endured a substantial setback in 1810.

NAPOLEONIC WARS

FRENCH VICTORY

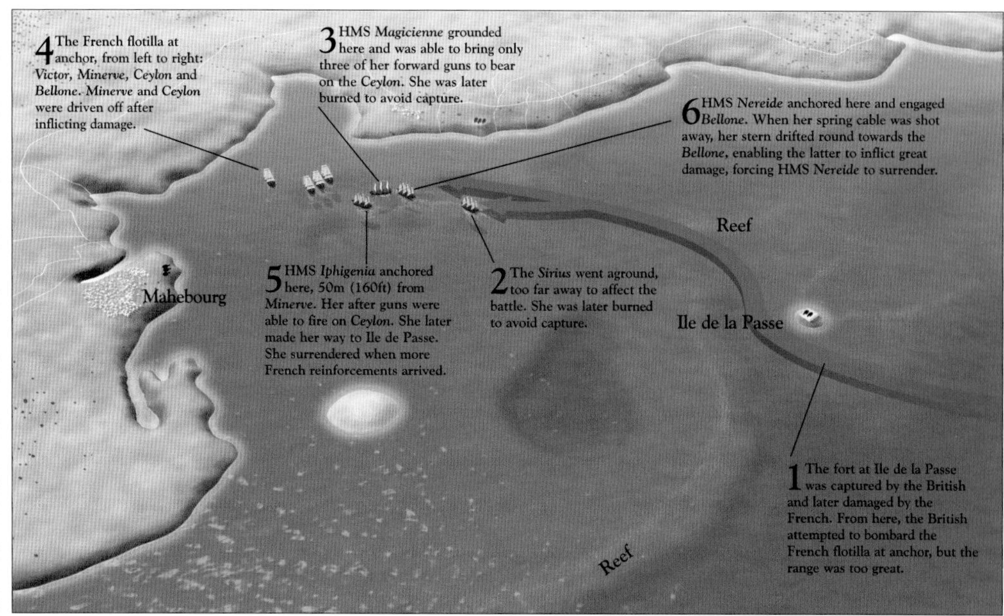

4 The French flotilla at anchor, from left to right: Victor, Minerve, Ceylon and Bellone. Minerve and Ceylon were driven off after inflicting damage.
3 HMS Magicienne grounded here and was able to bring only three of her forward guns to bear on the Ceylon. She was later burned to avoid capture.
6 HMS Nereide anchored here and engaged Bellone. When her spring cable was shot away, her stern drifted round towards the Bellone, enabling the latter to inflict great damage, forcing HMS Nereide to surrender.
Reef
Mahebourg
5 HMS Iphigenia anchored here, 50m (160ft) from Minerve. Her after guns were able to fire on Ceylon. She later made her way to Ile de Passe. She surrendered when more French reinforcements arrived.
2 The Sirius went aground, too far away to affect the battle. She was later burned to avoid capture.
Ile de la Passe
1 The fort at Ile de la Passe was captured by the British and later damaged by the French. From here, the British attempted to bombard the French flotilla at anchor, but the range was too great.
Reef

The defeat of the British fleet in this confrontation in the Indian Ocean would be one of the biggest setbacks the Royal Navy suffered during the Napoleonic Wars.

The British sought to respond to French harassment of its ships sailing to and from its Indian colonies by blockading Grand Port on the French held Ile de France. Captain James Willoughby of the HMS *Nereide*, the senior British officer and an old India hand, had been dispatched to capture a battery on the island, but spotted the approach of five French frigates.

CUNNING TACTICS

Realizing the French were unaware of his presence, he sought to lure them into the harbour by raising the French tricolour. As the first ship, a small corvette, came close, Willoughby opened fire and sent small boats to capture the ship. They could not reach it, however, and the other French ships, by now wise to Willoughby's ruse, returned fire – one caused an explosion on the island, killing several of Willoughby's men. With many others of his crew in small boats offshore, the opportunity to cause significant damage to the French ships had been lost.

Subsequently the French were able to inflict great damage on the remainder of the British squadron, leading to its worst naval defeat in the Napoleonic Wars.

LOCATION

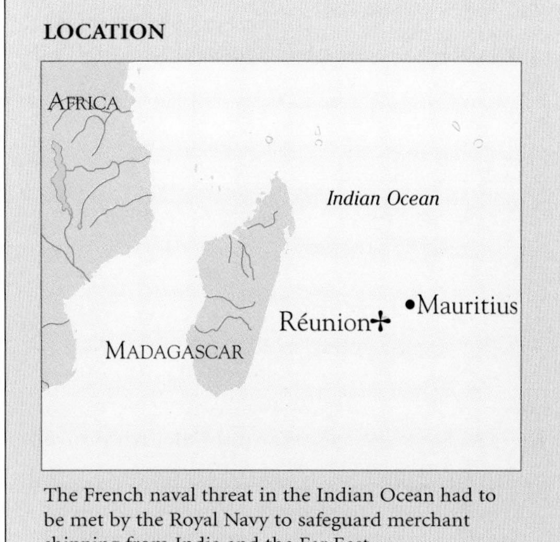

AFRICA
Indian Ocean
Mauritius
Réunion
MADAGASCAR

The French naval threat in the Indian Ocean had to be met by the Royal Navy to safeguard merchant shipping from India and the Far East.

TIMELINE

1500–1000BC	1000–500BC	500BC–0AD	0–500AD	500–1000AD	1000–1500AD	1500–2000AD

Siege of Badajoz 1812

The Duke of Wellington was a great general, but the sieges he led were not well handled. Badajoz was an example where, though he finally prevailed, it actually cost the lives of nearly 5000 soldiers in his command.

PENINSULAR WAR

ANGLO-PORTUGUESE VICTORY

KEY FACTS

WHO General Armand Philippon heads a French garrison against the British army under the command of the Duke of Wellington.

WHAT At the third attempt the British were able to take the castle, after great valour on the part of both sides.

WHERE Badajoz, Spain.

WHEN 6 April 1812

WHY Badajoz was one of the keys to Spain. The Allied army had to take it if they were to penetrate inland and on into southern France.

OUTCOME Although the siege finally succeeded, the British infantry marred the achievement by indulging in a three-day orgy of rape, drunkenness and plunder against the local population.

The effort of the British 88th Foot in scaling the walls at Badajoz would be decisive to securing victory, after attempts to breach the fortifications with gunfire had failed.

LOCATION

Bay of Biscay

FRANCE

PORTUGAL

Madrid

Badajoz

SPAIN

Mediterranean Sea

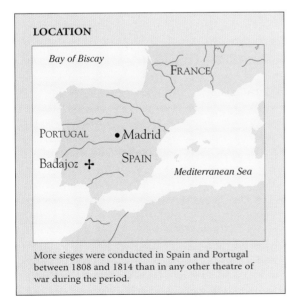

More sieges were conducted in Spain and Portugal between 1808 and 1814 than in any other theatre of war during the period.

The British twice had tried and failed to take Badajoz in the Peninsular War before a third attempt was made in the spring of 1812. The garrison of about 5000 men was ably commanded by the redoubtable General Armand Philippon, who had rendered it as difficult as possible to assail. Obstacles had been built in the ditch to render it unusable as a customary rallying place. Although the walls were breached, the defenders erected more obstacles within them and shored up the defences.

SUCCESSFUL SIEGE

Major-General Thomas Picton's attack on the castle at first failed, and Picton himself was wounded. He rallied his men, however, and they gained a foothold on the lower walls. Scaling ladders were raised and the British poured over the parapet. Resistance was savage, but the British fought through adversity, taking the castle but with heavy casualties. General Philippon and the garrison withdrew into San Cristobal, where they surrendered the next day.

TIMELINE

1500–1000BC	1000–500BC	500BC–0AD	0–500AD	500–1000AD	1000–1500AD	1500–2000AD

Salamanca 1812

KEY FACTS

WHO Arthur Wellesley (Duke of Wellington) leads the British army against Auguste Marmont in charge of the French and Anglo-Portuguese army.

WHAT The British army, seemingly in retreat, were able to turn a cautious defensive position into an offensive and tear into a larger French army that had become overstretched.

WHERE Arapiles, Salamanca, Spain.

WHEN 22 July 1812

WHY Wellington and the British army were attempting to thwart French efforts to cement their control of Portugal and Spain.

OUTCOME Wellington was able to move on Madrid and take it back from the French.

The Duke of Wellington was known as a sound commander, and a master of the defensive situation. At Salamanca, he was able to demonstrate that he could also orchestrate a brilliantly executed attack.

PENINSULAR WAR

BRITISH VICTORY

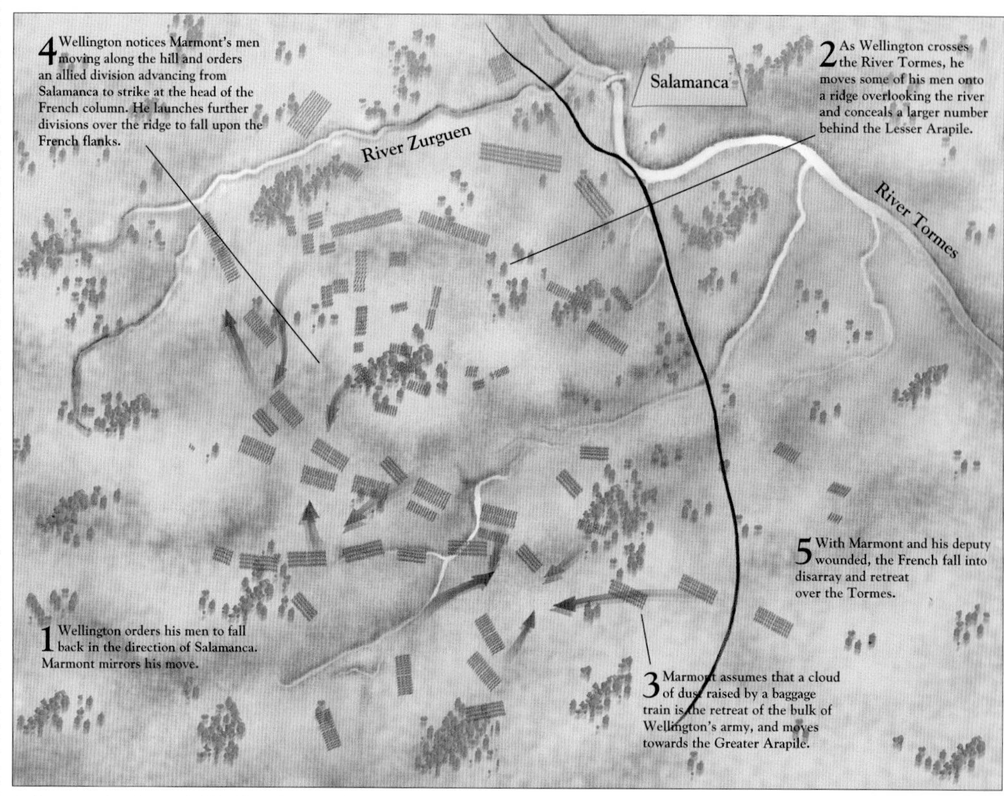
4 Wellington notices Marmont's men moving along the hill and orders an allied division advancing from Salamanca to strike at the head of the French column. He launches further divisions over the ridge to fall upon the French flanks.
Salamanca
2 As Wellington crosses the River Tormes, he moves some of his men onto a ridge overlooking the river and conceals a larger number behind the Lesser Arapile.
River Zurguen
River Tormes
5 With Marmont and his deputy wounded, the French fall into disarray and retreat over the Tormes.
1 Wellington orders his men to fall back in the direction of Salamanca. Marmont mirrors his move.
3 Marmont assumes that a cloud of dust raised by a baggage train is the retreat of the bulk of Wellington's army, and moves towards the Greater Arapile.

Salamanca has been dubbed 'Wellington's masterpiece'. Two years before his triumph at Waterloo, he was already revealing himself to be a tactical genius.

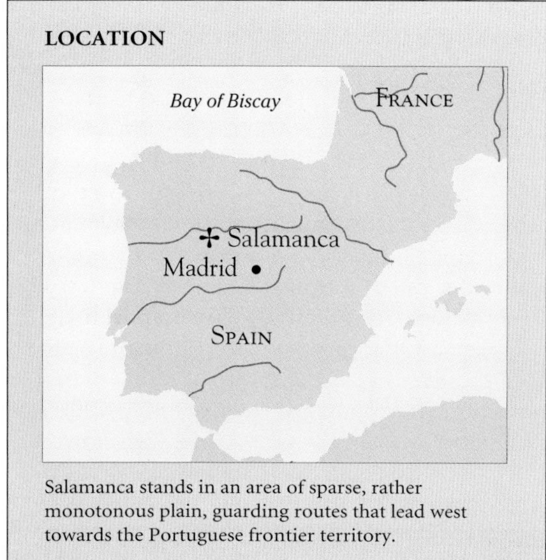
LOCATION
Bay of Biscay
FRANCE
Salamanca
Madrid
SPAIN

Salamanca stands in an area of sparse, rather monotonous plain, guarding routes that lead west towards the Portuguese frontier territory.

France, under Napoleon Bonaparte, had occupied Spain, overthrown the ruling Bourbon family and placed Napoleon's brother Joseph on the throne. The high-handed nature of the French occupation quickly stirred up local resentment, however, and a rebellious spirit spread across the entire Iberian peninsula. A British force under Sir John Moore was despatched to exploit the situation and save Portugal from being completely overrun. While Moore was successful in this objective, he lost his life and his army suffered heavy losses when it was pursued by the French and cornered at Coruna on the northern tip of Spain in 1809.

A new force under Arthur Wellesley, soon to be elevated to the peerage as the Duke of Wellington, was sent out to consolidate the hold on Portugal. A series of minor battles took place at fortresses along the Portuguese and Spanish frontier between the British and the French and these culminated in the Battle of Salamanca, often dubbed 'Wellington's masterpiece.'

Wellington had noted, with some concern, that the

Neither side especially desired a confrontation in the lead-up to the Battle of Salamanca, with the preceding days involving an element of 'shadowing', as the two forces moved in close proximity through the plains near the city.

number of soldiers at the disposal of the French army under the command of Marshal Auguste Marmont appeared to be increasing, and so he had ordered his men to fall back in the direction of Salamanca. His move was mirrored by Marmont. The French commander was under pressure from Joseph Bonaparte to attack the British, but he was wary of getting engaged in a major battle. Wellington, too, was in a cautious mood, believing his army to be outnumbered, but he was prepared to wait for the circumstances to turn in his favour. As he crossed the River Tormes, nearing Salamanca, he moved some of his men onto a ridge overlooking the river, while moving a larger number behind a hill, the Lesser Arapile, effectively concealed from the view of the enemy.

Marmont, meanwhile, observing the British movements from a distance, saw a cloud of dust that was raised by a baggage train moving off towards Ciudad Rodrigo, but which he interpreted as a sign that the bulk of Wellington's army was in retreat, with merely the rearguard left to face him on the ridge. He determined on executing a south and then westwards manouevre along the side of the hill, the Greater Arapile, which ran parallel to the Lesser Arapile across the valley. His plan was to pin Wellington's army to its position, effectively cutting its communication lines with Portugal. However, as his men moved along the hill, Wellington noticed that the French divisions had become too strung out and that they had become exposed on the flanks.

QUICK THINKING

Spotting an opportunity, he rushed to meet a division under the control of his brother-in-law Edward Pakenham, which was advancing from Salamanca with the Portuguese cavalry, and ordered it to meet and strike at the head of the French advance column. He then launched further divisions over the ridge to fall upon the French flanks. Early on in the attack, Marmont himself and his deputy General Bonet were wounded by shrapnel fire, and in the absence of their command the French fell into disarray. While a measure of control was regained, overall recovery was impossible and those French who were not slaughtered left to beat a hasty retreat over the Tormes.

Borodino 1812

NAPOLEONIC WARS

NO CLEAR VICTORY

KEY FACTS

WHO The French Emperor Napoleon, leading some 130,000 men, opposed by a Russian army totalling around 120,000 men (including militia), commanded by Prince Mikhail Illarionovich Golenishchev-Kutuzov (1745–1813).

WHAT The main French force was advancing on Moscow. After a series of attempts at resistance, the Russians established a defensive position at the village of Borodino.

WHERE The village of Borodino on the Moskowa River.

WHEN 7 September 1812

WHY The breakdown of the Treaty of Tilsit resulted in renewed war between Imperial Russia and Republican France. Napoleon hoped to force a new treaty on Russia.

OUTCOME A bloody and indecisive action. The French retained the battlefield and thus claimed victory. The advance on Moscow continued.

Napoleon had not intended to march so deep into Russia, but he was unable to force a decisive engagement, and was drawn onwards. Taking Moscow seemed to offer a way to end the campaign in victory. As the over-extended Grande Armée advanced, the defenders made a stand at Borodino.

The Russian success at Borodino – though not technically a win at all – was considered so significant it is celebrated as Russian Military Glory Day on its anniversary.

LOCATION

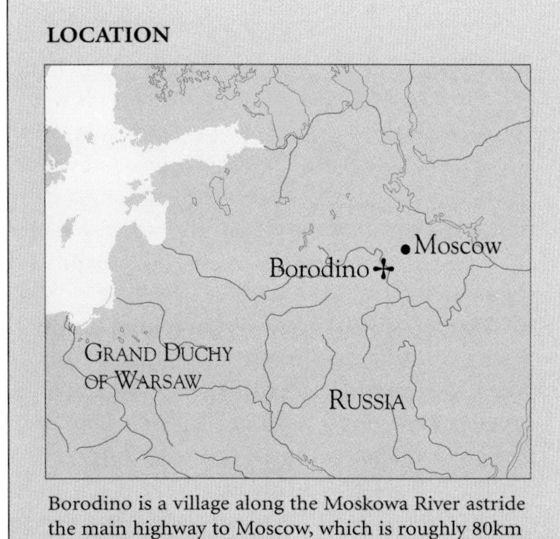
Moscow
Borodino
Grand Duchy of Warsaw
Russia

Borodino is a village along the Moskowa River astride the main highway to Moscow, which is roughly 80km (50 miles) east of the village.

After the short-lived Treaty of Tilsit, Napoleon was soon at war again with Russia. But when his Grande Armée crossed the border, it was with supplies that were barely sufficient to maintain a short campaign – a state of affairs that was acceptable to the Emperor, who intended to win a decisive battle early on.

SUPPLY PROBLEMS

The ability of the French army to move rapidly was mostly due to its skill in foraging on the march and thus travelling light. This worked in the fertile countryside of central Europe, but in Russia there was little forage to be had. Its supply line was also subject to Russian attacks from the very beginning of the campaign, mostly by bands of fast-moving Cossacks who favoured ambush attacks, using their lances and sabres. As the French supply line lengthened, the army gradually weakened to disease, accidents, harassment by irregular forces and straggling. The reduced capability of the French to fight played into the hands of the retreating commander of

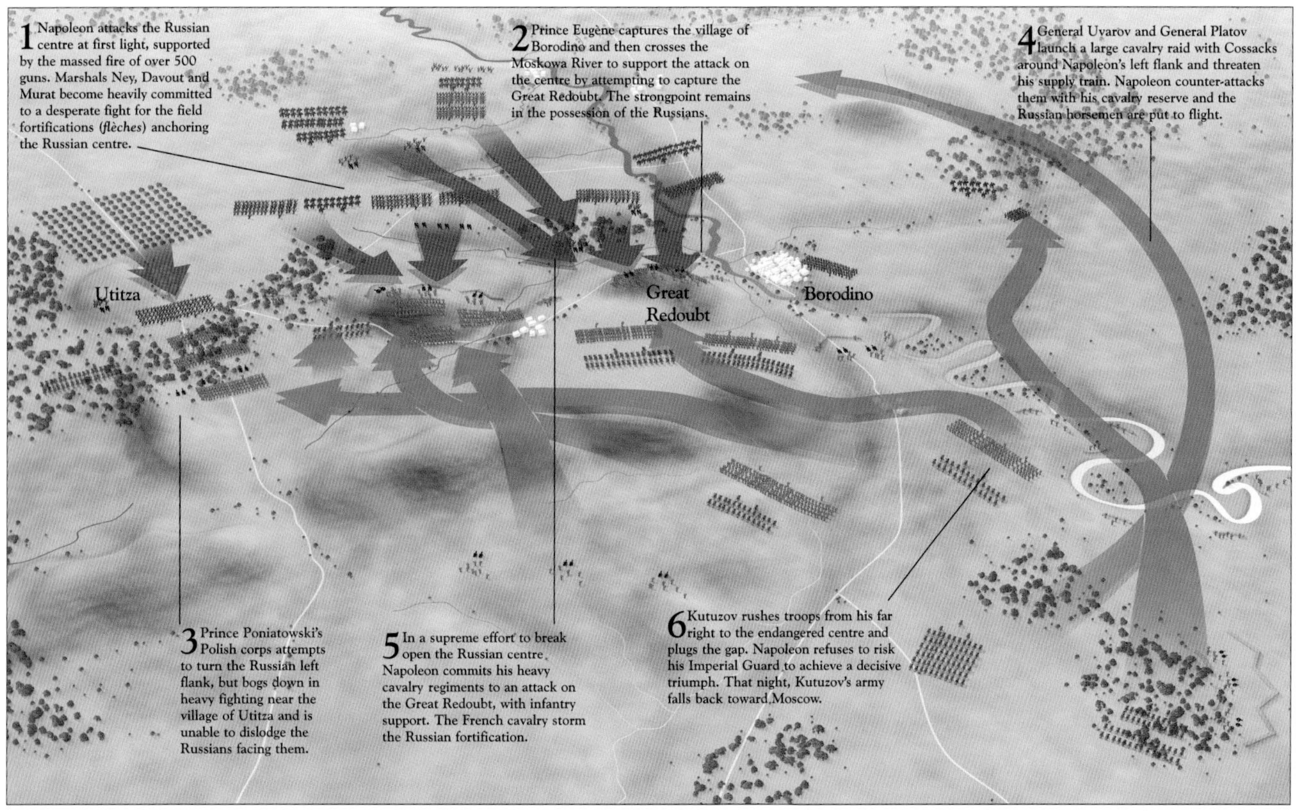
1 Napoleon attacks the Russian centre at first light, supported by the massed fire of over 500 guns. Marshals Ney, Davout and Murat become heavily committed to a desperate fight for the field fortifications (flèches) anchoring the Russian centre.
2 Prince Eugène captures the village of Borodino and then crosses the Moskowa River to support the attack on the centre by attempting to capture the Great Redoubt. The strongpoint remains in the possession of the Russians.
4 General Uvarov and General Platov launch a large cavalry raid with Cossacks around Napoleon's left flank and threaten his supply train. Napoleon counter-attacks them with his cavalry reserve and the Russian horsemen are put to flight.
Utitza
Great Redoubt
Borodino
3 Prince Poniatowski's Polish corps attempts to turn the Russian left flank, but bogs down in heavy fighting near the village of Utitza and is unable to dislodge the Russians facing them.
5 In a supreme effort to break open the Russian centre, Napoleon commits his heavy cavalry regiments to an attack on the Great Redoubt, with infantry support. The French cavalry storm the Russian fortification.
6 Kutuzov rushes troops from his far right to the endangered centre and plugs the gap. Napoleon refuses to risk his Imperial Guard to achieve a decisive triumph. That night, Kutuzov's army falls back toward Moscow.

The Russian approach at Borodino was predicated on the assumption that Napoleon, after a long time in the field and on the march, with supplies under great strain, would want to come to battle as quickly as possible.

the Russian army Prince Mikhail Kutuzov, who set up a defensive position near Borodino, spanning the approach to Moscow.

Napoleon decided on a straightforward frontal attack, hoping to use the superior fighting power of his army to punch his way through the heavily defended Russian positions. To support this, he deployed a Grand Battery of 102 guns to face the main Russian positions at a series of earthworks known as *flèches* (after their arrowhead shape). Many of these guns were heavy 12-pounders capable of inflicting serious damage on the defenders, despite the protection of their earthworks. As the guns opened fire, the infantry advanced and were able to take control of the *flèches*, but then came under fire themselves from the Russian Imperial Guard and supporting elite Grenadier formations, with artillery support.

The greatest of the fortifications that strengthened the Russian line was the Great Redoubt, which the French, again using artillery fire, were able to force their way into and ultimately hold. However, it was only after a titanic effort that the French did so. A pause to reorganize and rest drew out into a gradual wind-down of the action, though the artillery of both sides continued to fire, and skirmishing took place all across the battlefield for some time.

INCONCLUSIVE OUTCOME

Although the defensive line had been broken and the Russians had been pushed back, they were not defeated in any real sense. Napoleon refused to commit the French Imperial Guard for one last push, perhaps because it was his only remaining reserve, so the Russians were able to retreat without pursuit. This left the French in possession of the battlefield, the traditional measure of victory. However, they had not in practice achieved any of their strategic aims. Both sides had lost 30,000–40,000 men, but, unlike the Russians on home soil, the French could not replace theirs. Strung out at the end of a long supply line, the French needed a decisive victory while the Russians only had to avoid total defeat. The Russians, although bloodied, had hurt the invaders badly, denying Napoleon the short campaign he had envisaged.

Borodino

BORODINO

Many of Napoleon's battles involved severe numbers of casualties, but Borodino and its bloody aftermath could be described as a holocaust. Technically, since it was the Russians who withdrew from the Borodino battlefield, the day belonged to Napoleon's army, but his opponents' army, despite heavy casualties, was essentially intact, while his was adrift in a foreign land, weary and short of supplies. It has been estimated that Borodino, combined with the subsequent ignominious French retreat from Moscow in the thick of winter, resulted in around one million casualties, a horrid foretaste of the losses during World War I a century later.

Retreat from Moscow 1812

NAPOLEONIC WARS

RUSSIAN VICTORY

After what was a disputed victory at Borodino, Napoleon arrived in Moscow – the pinnacle of his Russian objective – to find a deserted city. Combined with the earlier slaughter on both sides, the losses sustained on the long march home meant this campaign had seen about a million lives lost.

KEY FACTS

WHO The French Emperor Napoleon, and a Russian army commanded by Prince Mikhail Illarionovich Golenishchev-Kutuzov.

WHAT Napoleon had to beat a retreat through a perishing Russian countryside in winter, his men starving, wracked by disease and assailed by fast moving Cossack light cavalrymen.

WHERE Moscow, Russia.

WHEN October–December 1812

WHY Napoleon had invaded Russia, but entered Moscow to find merely a deserted, burnt-out city.

OUTCOME Napoleon's magnificent Grande Armée had been virtually wiped out, and now France faced a group of enemies salivating for revenge.

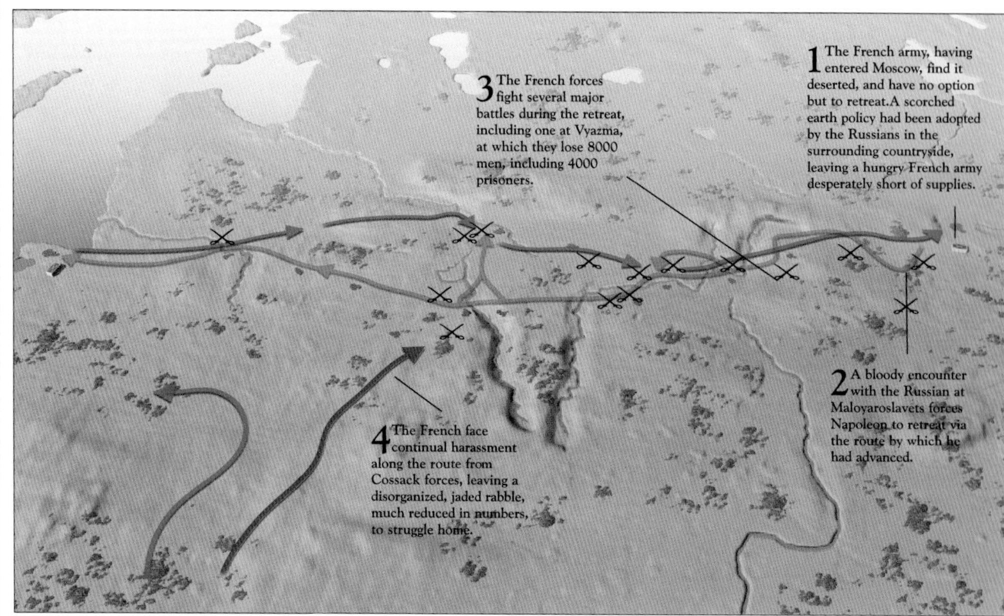
1 The French army, having entered Moscow, find it deserted, and have no option but to retreat. A scorched earth policy had been adopted by the Russians in the surrounding countryside, leaving a hungry French army desperately short of supplies.
2 A bloody encounter with the Russian at Maloyaroslavets forces Napoleon to retreat via the route by which he had advanced.
3 The French forces fight several major battles during the retreat, including one at Vyazma, at which they lose 8000 men, including 4000 prisoners.
4 The French face continual harassment along the route from Cossack forces, leaving a disorganized, jaded rabble, much reduced in numbers, to struggle home.

When the French arrived in Moscow they effectively found an empty city, denuded of the supplies and comforts they desperately craved after a long campaign and the draining encounter at Borodino.

After the ordeal at Borodino, Prince Mikhail Kutuzov realized that his army was in no condition to fight another battle. For his part, Napoleon took Moscow, but was effectively left in control of an empty city, with little to eat and no prospect of resupply. The only option was a retreat.

Returning via the same route as used for the advance seemed impractical, as this had been denuded of supplies by foraging, and a deliberate scorched earth policy by the Russians. But another bloody clash at Maloyaroslavets forced a rethink, and Napoleon had to retire along his original route of advance.

MAJOR CASUALTIES

Casualties during the Moscow Retreat were immense, from hunger, cold and on-going attacks by Russian forces, including continual harassment by the Cossack cavalry. In the end, only about 30,000–40,000 troops of the 630,000 that had entered Russia re-emerged in formed units. About the same number eventually straggled to safety, having endured unimaginable suffering.

LOCATION

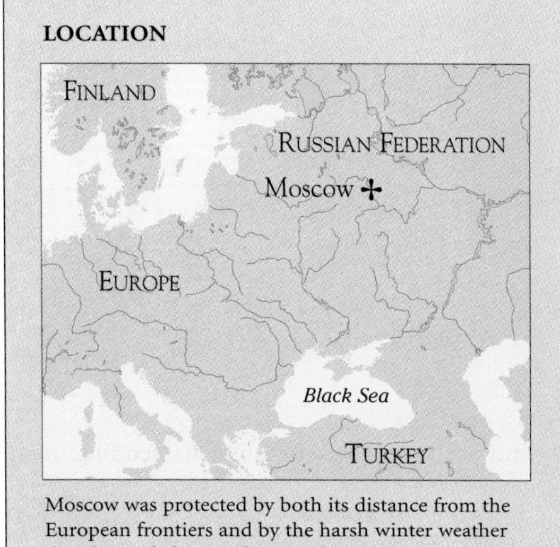
FINLAND
RUSSIAN FEDERATION
Moscow
EUROPE
Black Sea
TURKEY

Moscow was protected by both its distance from the European frontiers and by the harsh winter weather that descended upon the French troops.

TIMELINE

1500–1000BC	1000–500BC	500BC–0AD	0–500AD	500–1000AD	1000–1500AD	1500–2000AD

Hamburg 1813

NAPOLEONIC WARS

RUSSIAN-PRUSSIAN VICTORY

Marshal Davout was a soldier with a distinguished record. At Auerstädt in 1806 and Eylau in 1807, he had played a distinguished part in two of the great French victories of the Napoleonic era. Now, as the curtain came down on Bonaparte's greatest years, there was time for one last stand.

KEY FACTS

WHO A French force under Marshal Davout's XIII Corps, against a Russian army under General Bennigsen.

WHAT Marshal Davout, under strict orders not to let the fortified city of Hamburg fall, put up a spirited defence, despite limiting provision before the final command came to submit.

WHERE Hamburg, Germany.

WHEN December 1813–May 1814

WHY After defeat in Russia, France's enemies were attempting to regain ground. Hamburg was an important city that the French desperately wanted to retain.

OUTCOME Having been the most successful defence of a fortified position during the Revolutionary and Napoleonic periods, Davout's valiant stand would be studied by professional soldiers for years to come.

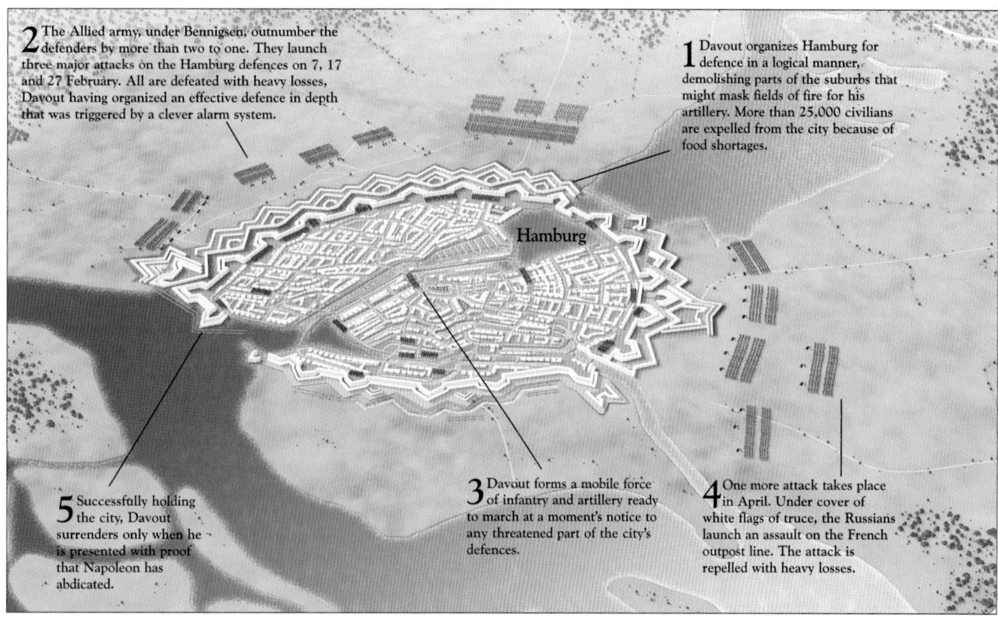
1 Davout organizes Hamburg for defence in a logical manner, demolishing parts of the suburbs that might mask fields of fire for his artillery. More than 25,000 civilians are expelled from the city because of food shortages.
2 The Allied army, under Bennigsen, outnumber the defenders by more than two to one. They launch three major attacks on the Hamburg defences on 7, 17 and 27 February. All are defeated with heavy losses, Davout having organized an effective defence in depth that was triggered by a clever alarm system.
Hamburg
3 Davout forms a mobile force of infantry and artillery ready to march at a moment's notice to any threatened part of the city's defences.
4 One more attack takes place in April. Under cover of white flags of truce, the Russians launch an assault on the French outpost line. The attack is repelled with heavy losses.
5 Successfully holding the city, Davout surrenders only when he is presented with proof that Napoleon has abdicated.

Marshal Davout was an experienced and loyal general, much respected in the French army. His defiant stand at Hamburg came in the dying years of the Napoleonic era.

LOCATION

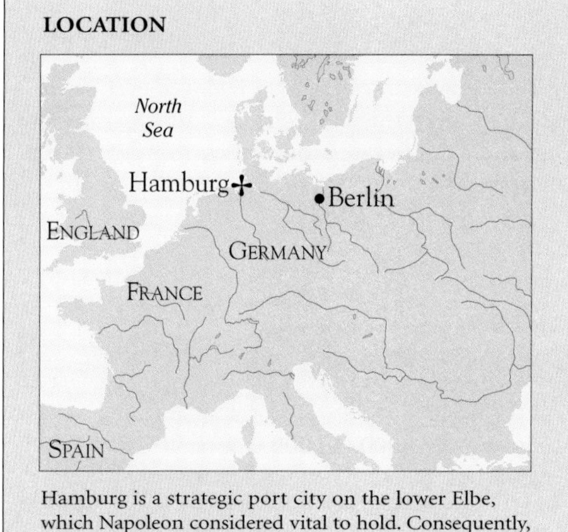
North Sea
Hamburg
Berlin
ENGLAND
GERMANY
FRANCE
SPAIN

Hamburg is a strategic port city on the lower Elbe, which Napoleon considered vital to hold. Consequently, Marshal Davout was tasked with its defence.

Marshal Davout was tasked with holding Hamburg as the Russian-Prussian alliance fought back after Napoleon's Moscow debacle. By the time a siege began, Davout was increasingly isolated. With no news from the main army, he could only assume he was on his own.

Davout had taken every precaution to defend the city to the last. Neglected defences had been improved, and civilians were warned to start storing food for a siege. Russian General Bennigsen's forces outnumbered Davout's by more than two to one, yet three major attacks on the Hamburg defences were all defeated.

DEFIANT STAND

Bennigsen settled down to starve his opponent into submission. One more attack took place when, under cover of white flags of truce, the Russians launched an assault on the French outpost line. The French, however, were ready and neatly repelled the Russians, sending them back to their lines with heavy losses. At last, word came that Napoleon had abdicated in April. Davout, defiant to the end, refused to surrender until he was ordered to by competent French authority.

TIMELINE

1500–1000BC	1000–500BC	500BC–0AD	0–500AD	500–1000AD	1000–1500AD	1500–2000AD

Lake Erie 1813

WAR OF 1812

US VICTORY

KEY FACTS

WHO British naval squadron under Commander Robert Heriot Barclay against American soldiers and sailors led by Lieutenant Jesse Elliot and Master Commandant Oliver Hazard Perry.

WHAT An increasingly confident American navy cornered and destroyed a small squadron of British ships, thanks in part to the resourceful leadership of its commander.

WHERE Lake Erie, near Put-in-Bay, Ohio.

WHEN 10 September 1813

WHY The US had declared war on Britain after the latter had blockaded her trade ships from Continental Europe.

OUTCOME The British lost control of Lake Erie, and the American victory was a massive boost to the morale of its increasingly confident navy.

While the big beasts of France, Prussia, Russia and Austria thundered around on the European stage, slowly a fledgling nation across the Atlantic was starting to flap its wings. In 1813, the United States was still a minor player, but it was being taken increasingly seriously.

Oliver Hazzard Perry, the master commandant who led the American fleet to victory at Lake Erie, was forced to abandon his flagship at one stage of the fighting.

LOCATION

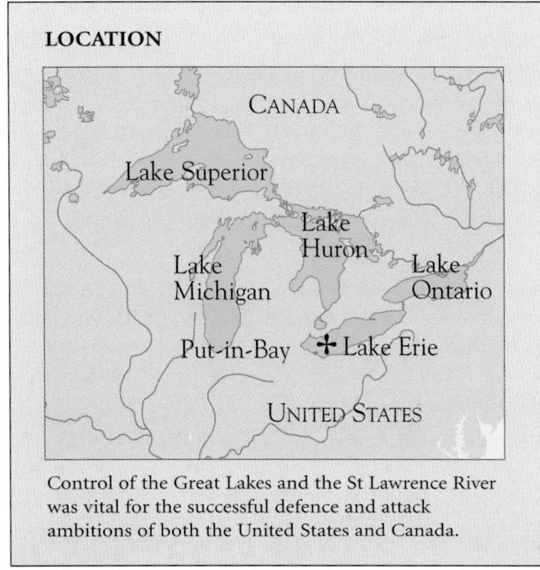
CANADA
Lake Superior
Lake Huron
Lake Michigan
Lake Ontario
Put-in-Bay
Lake Erie
UNITED STATES

Control of the Great Lakes and the St Lawrence River was vital for the successful defence and attack ambitions of both the United States and Canada.

Just 30 years old, the group of Great Britain's tiny former colonies now known as the United States of America had set itself on a course of expansion with minimum pretext. The United States attacked and conquered additional territory from the southern Native Americans and amongst the Spanish colonies of Florida and Miami. It negotiated the purchase of New Orleans from France and turned its avaricious gaze northwards to Canada. True, here there was some provocation. Britain had been mounting an effective blockade of Continental Europe, with whom the United States wanted to trade. Also, US merchantmen had been stopped and searched by the Royal Navy, looking for seamen deserters.

Frustrated by the British blockade, President James Madison (1751–1836) declared war and ordered the US Navy to build squadrons to wrest naval superiority from the British. Super-strong frigates would be built to a standard normally reserved for line of battle ships. These would challenge such ships as could be isolated from the British fleet.

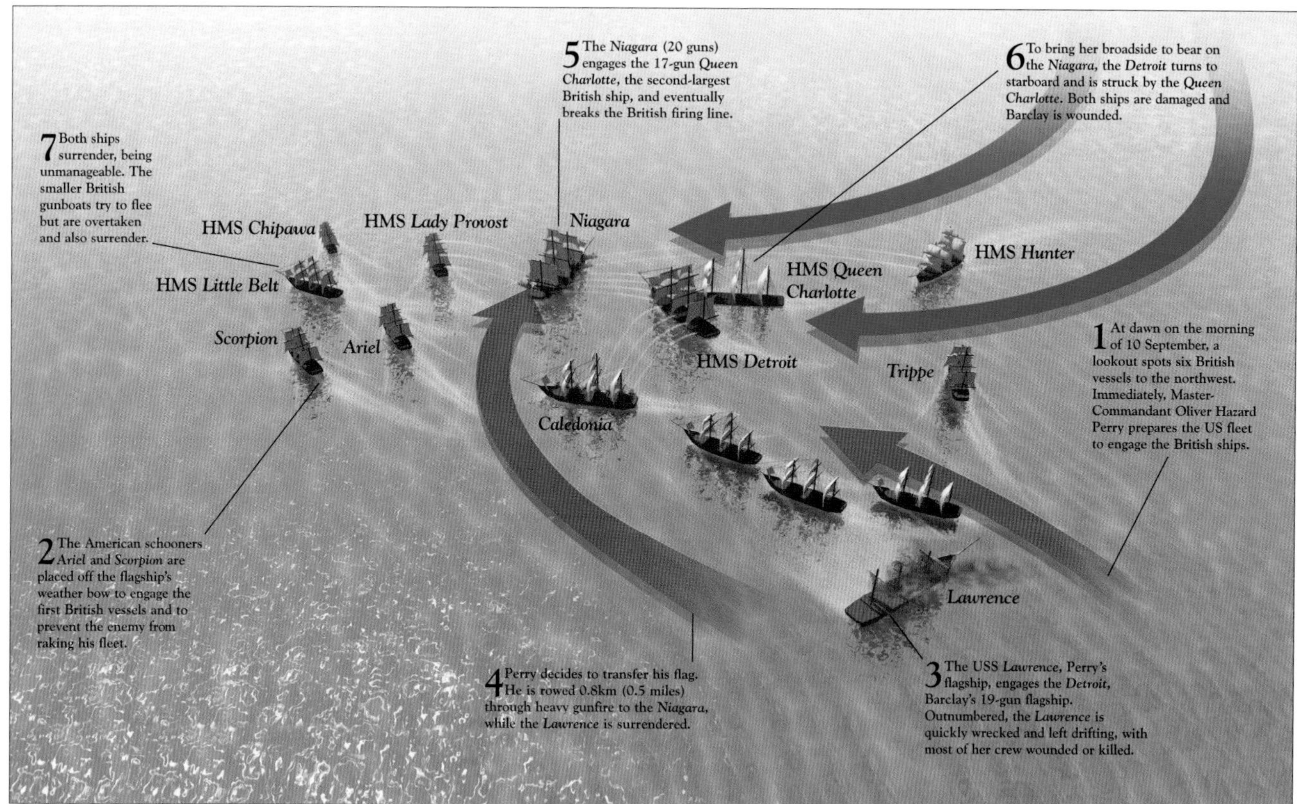

5 The *Niagara* (20 guns) engages the 17-gun *Queen Charlotte*, the second-largest British ship, and eventually breaks the British firing line.

6 To bring her broadside to bear on the *Niagara*, the *Detroit* turns to starboard and is struck by the *Queen Charlotte*. Both ships are damaged and Barclay is wounded.

7 Both ships surrender, being unmanageable. The smaller British gunboats try to flee but are overtaken and also surrender.

HMS *Chipawa*

HMS *Lady Provost*

Niagara

HMS *Queen Charlotte*

HMS *Hunter*

HMS *Little Belt*

Scorpion

Ariel

HMS *Detroit*

Trippe

1 At dawn on the morning of 10 September, a lookout spots six British vessels to the northwest. Immediately, Master-Commandant Oliver Hazard Perry prepares the US fleet to engage the British ships.

Caledonia

2 The American schooners *Ariel* and *Scorpion* are placed off the flagship's weather bow to engage the first British vessels and to prevent the enemy from raking his fleet.

4 Perry decides to transfer his flag. He is rowed 0.8km (0.5 miles) through heavy gunfire to the *Niagara*, while the *Lawrence* is surrendered.

Lawrence

3 The USS *Lawrence*, Perry's flagship, engages the *Detroit*, Barclay's 19-gun flagship. Outnumbered, the *Lawrence* is quickly wrecked and left drifting, with most of her crew wounded or killed.

The fighting on Lake Erie began with the Americans cruising off the Detroit River, in what proved to be a successful attempt to provoke a response from the British flotilla. The American vessels had the advantage of superior numbers and, eventually, favourable winds.

A small new force, comprising the *Oneida* and six adapted lake ships, was ready on 8 November 1812. The force chased but did not catch two British ships. As winter closed in, both sides directed their energies to their shipyards and built more vessels. The British responded by constructing a 30-gun frigate and two corvettes and transferring 450 experienced sailors from the Royal Navy.

The Americans pressed ahead with building a new corvette, the 24-gun Madison, modifying the *Lady of the Lake* and starting work on their own frigate of 26 guns. Both sides also equipped several sail- and oar-powered launches with a single gun in the bows. By August 1813 both sides were ready to begin operations. Large parts of the US–Canadian border passed through the Great Lakes area, and here some of the major action took place. The forces again involved consisted of small ships carrying small guns.

The Americans and the British now had squadrons of warships on both Lake Ontario and Lake Erie. The American commander, Master-Commandant Oliver Hazard Perry (1785–1819) began by cruising off the Detroit River, trying to provoke a response from the British flotilla. It eventually had the desired effect. The British emerged on 10 September with a favourable breeze, and their two lead ships concentrated on the *Lawrence*, Perry's flagship. The next in the American line, the *Caledonia*, was lagging behind. Within just a few minutes, the American *Lawrence* was a wreck, with two-thirds of her crew casualties.

Perry got himself rowed over to the *Niagara* to continue the battle. However, the British officer corps was suffering badly from the American gunnery. *Detroit*, *Queen Charlotte*, *Hunter* and *Prevost* all lost their first lieutenants, and the British commander-in-chief was also mortally wounded. As the British attempted to sort themselves out, Perry charged his ship into their line, firing broadsides in both directions. The *Detroit* attempted to turn downwind to bring her broadside to bear but was run into by the *Queen Charlotte*, which had not responded similarly. This was clearly a mess, and with eight US ships in the immediate vicinity compared with four serviceable vessels in the British flotilla, the latter surrendered.

TIMELINE

1500–1000BC	1000–500BC	500BC–0AD	0–500AD	500–1000AD	1000–1500AD	1500–2000AD

Leipzig 1813

KEY FACTS

Who French army of Napoleon and his allies, against the Sixth Coalition, including Russia, Prussia, Austria, Sweden and Saxony.

What After three days of close fighting, with heavy casualties on both sides, Napoleon was forced to stage a planned retreat.

Where Leipzig, Germany.

When 16–19 October 1813

Why A grand Coalition of European nations had formed against the empire of Napoleon Bonaparte.

Outcome Napoleon had lost a major part of his army, and all of his German territories.

The Battle of Leipzig was a catastrophic defeat for the once ascendant Napoleon. His defeat in Germany against a large coalition army led to the Allied invasion of France itself, and to Napoleon's abdication and temporary exile to the island of Elba in the Mediterranean.

NAPOLEONIC WARS

SIXTH COALITION VICTORY

The Battle of Leipzig took place within view of the Baroque towers of the historic German city, and cost the combatants more than 100,000 casualties.

LOCATION

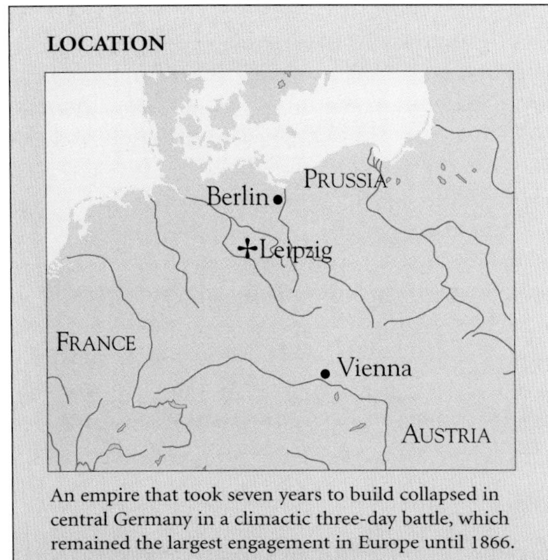
Prussia
Berlin
Leipzig
France
Vienna
Austria

An empire that took seven years to build collapsed in central Germany in a climactic three-day battle, which remained the largest engagement in Europe until 1866.

By October 1813, Napoleon was under attack from Allied armies closing in from the north and south, so he withdrew his army to Leipzig, closer to his Rhenish allies, to prepare for battle.

Leipzig differed from previous Napoleonic battles in that the emperor's enemies coordinated their operations and cooperated effectively. Also known as the 'Battle of the Nations', it was the largest battle fought in Europe until the wars of German unification of 1866 and 1870–71. Almost half a million soldiers from more than a dozen European states were engaged during the three days of fighting. In the end, Napoleon lost a large part of his army, and all of Germany.

Napoleon intended to attack Schwarzenberg's Austrian army while keeping Blücher's Prussians at bay, but neither man intended to pass the initiative to the Frenchman. The Austrian field marshal was well aware that he faced the bulk of Napoleon's army. Confident that he could bring greater numbers to bear, Schwarzenberg ordered a general advance, hoping to turn Napoleon's flank to the east while

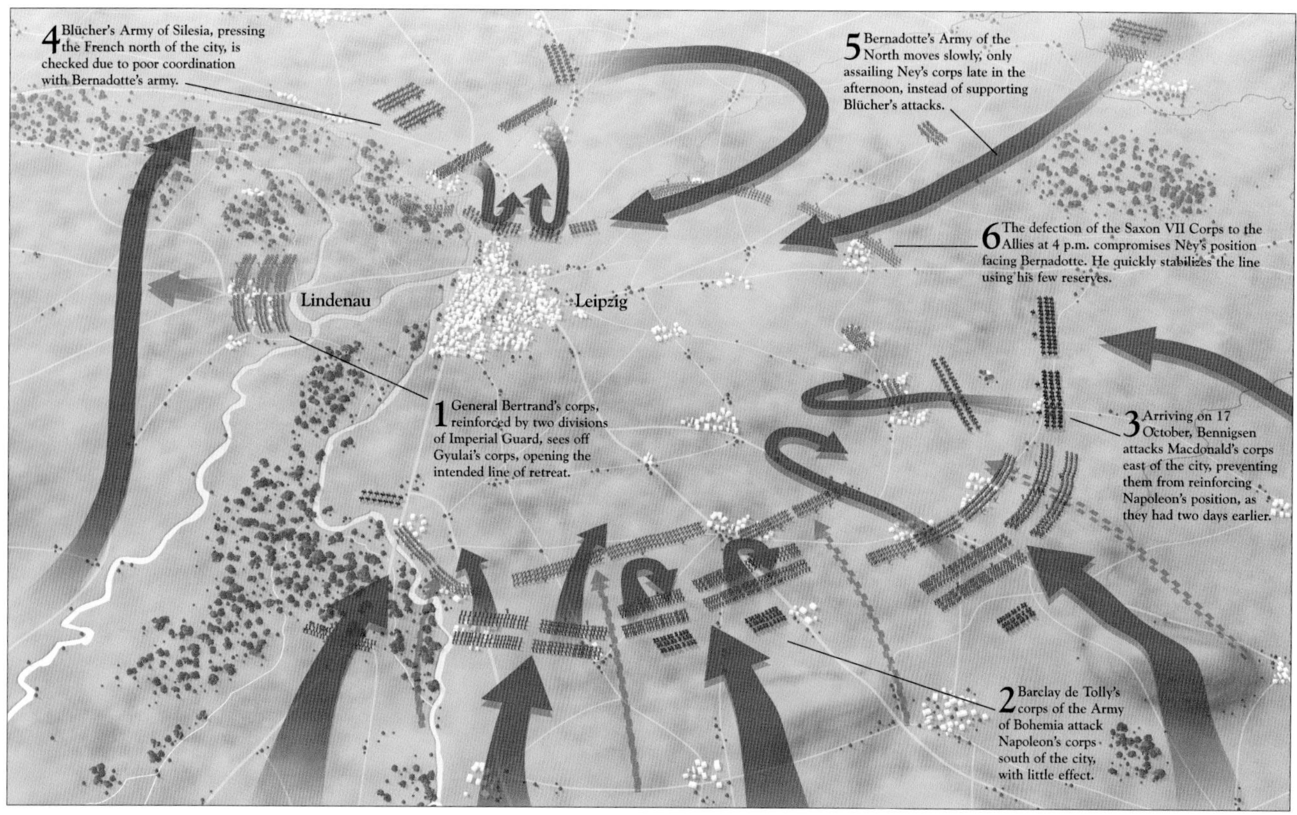
4 Blücher's Army of Silesia, pressing the French north of the city, is checked due to poor coordination with Bernadotte's army.
5 Bernadotte's Army of the North moves slowly, only assailing Ney's corps late in the afternoon, instead of supporting Blücher's attacks.
6 The defection of the Saxon VII Corps to the Allies at 4 p.m. compromises Ney's position facing Bernadotte. He quickly stabilizes the line using his few reserves.
Lindenau
Leipzig
1 General Bertrand's corps, reinforced by two divisions of Imperial Guard, sees off Gyulai's corps, opening the intended line of retreat.
3 Arriving on 17 October, Bennigsen attacks Macdonald's corps east of the city, preventing them from reinforcing Napoleon's position, as they had two days earlier.
2 Barclay de Tolly's corps of the Army of Bohemia attack Napoleon's corps south of the city, with little effect.

At Leipzig, Napoleon knew that defeat in the battle would mean the collapse of his ambitions in central Europe. His attempt to stage a managed withdrawal to stave off the worst of the consequences proved unsuccessful.

he pinned the larger part of the French Army south of the city. Blücher was to vigorously attack Leipzig from the north, preventing the French corps in that vicinity from moving to support Napoleon. To complete the destruction of the French imperial army, Schwarzenberg dispatched Count Ignaz Gyulai's Austrian corps west of the Elster, with Lindenau and Napoleon's line of retreat as its objective.

The fighting began with an advance of Russian and Prussians under General Ludwig Wittgenstein, but the fire from Napoleon's massed heavy batteries was so intense that no advantage was gained, and after two hours of fighting the French launched a counter-attack. Although Napoleon's attack on the enemy centre met with some success, nightfall and exhaustion meant decisive victory eluded his men.

After a day of recuperation, Napoleon's position grew more precarious with the arrival of Bernadotte's Swedish troops to bolster Allied ranks, and Blücher pushed the French back towards the city. While Napoleon understood that wholesale withdrawal would provide the Allies with a tremendous victory and no doubt lead to the collapse of his empire in Germany, he began to prepare for a general retreat, hoping his army would wound the Allies before escaping towards the Rhine.

After a day of combat, night fell without the Allies having reached the city. Napoleon's luck had held, but he knew it would not do so for much longer. He ordered a phased withdrawal of corps through the city and across the Elster river. Engineers were given orders to blow charges on the bridge once the army was across. On 18 October, they began to move to the west bank of the Elster. The Allies launched attacks into the city's suburbs, reaching the walls by late morning. Hard fighting around the city gates continued until 1 p.m., prematurely destroying the bridge. More than 30,000 French and imperial troops were trapped in Leipzig. With Napoleon leading his army away to the west, the defenders surrendered.

Leipzig was a tremendous coalition victory at a heavy price. Napoleon suffered 70,000 killed, wounded or taken prisoner. The Allies lost 54,000 men. Despite this, the Allies had succeeded in bringing their armies together in overwhelming numbers, producing a strategic victory.

Leipzig

LEIPZIG

By 1813, Napoleon was running out of time, no longer the 'lucky general' of yesteryear. Other European powers, of course, had long since sickened of his deeds, but now they bound themselves together to form a massive coalition of a dozen states, including Russia, Prussia, Austria, Sweden and Saxony. Altogether, around half a million men would be involved in three days of fighting at Leipzig, the greatest battle of the era when horses took their place alongside muskets on the battlefield. Both sides lost large numbers of men, but it was the ageing Napoleon who suffered the severest dent to his standing.

Lützen 1813

KEY FACTS

WHO Napoleon Bonaparte and the French Army against the Allied Forces of Prussia and Russia under Count von Blücher.

WHAT A spectacular artillery attack blew a hole in the Allied forces' centre, paving the way for Napoleon himself to lead a decisive infantry assault.

WHERE Near Lützen, Germany.

WHEN 2 May 1813.

WHY Napoleon had rebuilt his Grande Armée after it was crushed at Borodino and was desperate to repel the newly confident alliance of Prussia and Russia.

OUTCOME Napoleon had shown he still had teeth, but further challenges lay ahead.

After Napoleon's disastrous Russian campaign, the momentum seemed now to lie with his enemies. Their foe, however, was desperate not to concede much further ground. An unexpected encounter at Lützen showed there was life in the French lion yet.

NAPOLEONIC WARS

FRENCH VICTORY

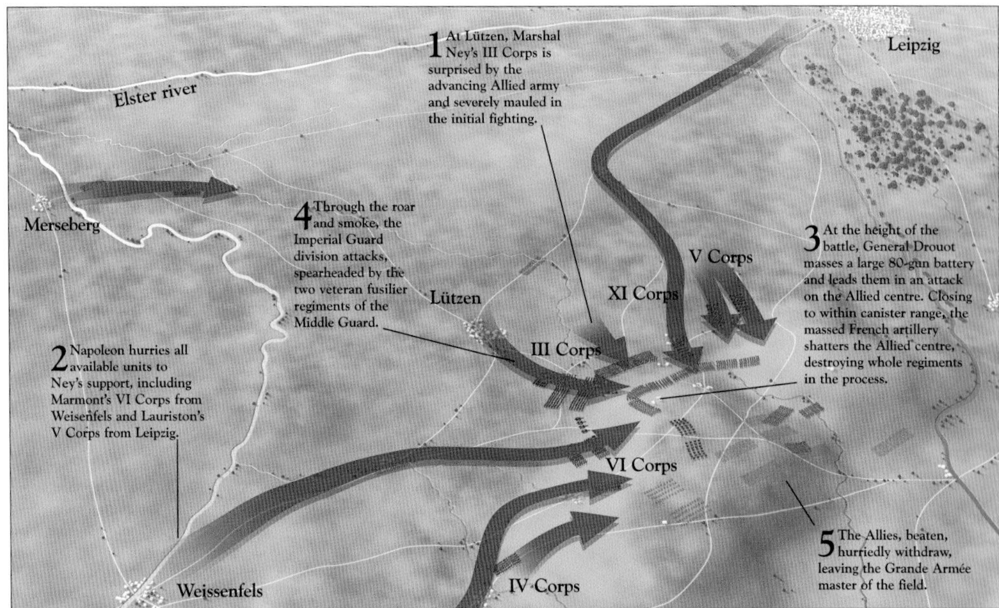

1 At Lützen, Marshal Ney's III Corps is surprised by the advancing Allied army and severely mauled in the initial fighting.
Leipzig
Elster river
Merseberg
4 Through the roar and smoke, the Imperial Guard division attacks, spearheaded by the two veteran fusilier regiments of the Middle Guard.
Lützen
V Corps
XI Corps
III Corps
3 At the height of the battle, General Drouot masses a large 80-gun battery and leads them in an attack on the Allied centre. Closing to within canister range, the massed French artillery shatters the Allied centre, destroying whole regiments in the process.
2 Napoleon hurries all available units to Ney's support, including Marmont's VI Corps from Weisenfels and Lauriston's V Corps from Leipzig.
VI Corps
5 The Allies, beaten, hurriedly withdraw, leaving the Grande Armée master of the field.
Weissenfels
IV Corps

The fighting at Lutzen included some spectacular artillery fire from both sides. While this was one of Napoleon's last victories, his troops were so exhausted they were unable to finish off their opponents.

After his disastrous Russian campaign, Napoleon rebuilt the shattered Grande Armée and by April 1813 was advancing into Germany to link up with Prince Eugène's Army of the Elbe. The new Grande Armée was numerically superior to its Allied antagonists, but except for the Imperial Guard, the army was in large part made up of new conscripts with less than a year's service and therefore experience.

ARTILLERY STRIKE

Count von Blücher's army caught Napoleon by surprise near Lützen, but spectacular artillery action led by General Drouot turned the action in the French favour. Drouot organized and led forward 80 artillery pieces from the Imperial Guard and line artillery. Massed within canister range of the Allied centre, these literally blew a hole in the Allied line and paved the way for the decisive infantry assault by the Guard infantry, led by Napoleon. Whole Allied infantry regiments were destroyed, covering the ground with dead and wounded. However, because the French were shattered from their earlier march, the Allies were able to withdraw from the battlefield in good order.

LOCATION

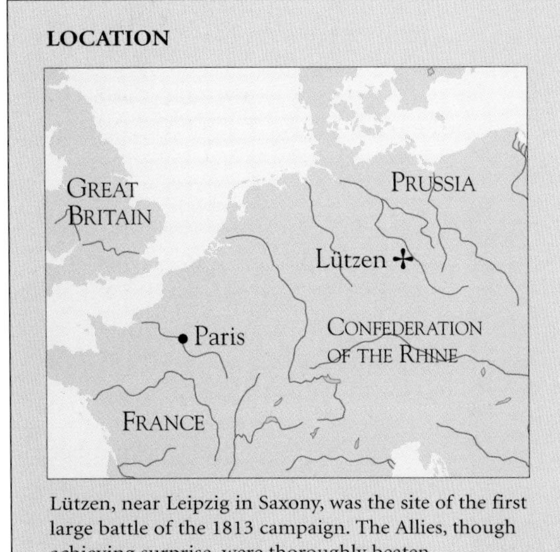

GREAT BRITAIN
PRUSSIA
Lützen
Paris
CONFEDERATION OF THE RHINE
FRANCE

Lützen, near Leipzig in Saxony, was the site of the first large battle of the 1813 campaign. The Allies, though achieving surprise, were thoroughly beaten.

Quatre Bras 1815

NAPOLEONIC WARS

NO CLEAR VICTORY

In the Hundred Days War, Napoleon faced an offensive on two fronts, so he divided his Armée du Nord in two. While he dealt with the Prussians, it fell to Marshal Michel Ney to deal with Wellington and his allies.

KEY FACTS

Who A contingent of the French led by Marshal Ney against the British led by the Duke of Wellington.

What A critical delay by Marshal Ney, concerned not to encounter the full might of the Anglo-Dutch army, allowed a rushed Wellington more time to deploy and avoid defeat.

Where Crossroads of Quartre Bras, modern Belgium.

When 16 June 1815

Why The French needed to obstruct the Anglo-Dutch and Prussian forces linking up, and Quatre Bras was a strategically vital crossroads.

Outcome Wellington withdrew towards Waterloo, for his showdown with Napoleon.

Quatre Bras was a bitterly contested battle which ended in a draw. The French cavalry attacks led by Marshal Ney were undermined by poor coordination.

LOCATION

England

Belgium

Quatre Bras

France

Quatre Bras was a tiny hamlet in southern Belgium located at a vital crossroads of the main highway to Brussels some 40km (25 miles) to the north.

Napoleon had ordered Marshal Ney to take possession of the key crossroads of Quatre Bras. Ney moved cautiously forward, fearful of encountering the Duke of Wellington's main Anglo–Allied Army. However, this meant Wellington was able to rush to the scene of action, and deploy his forces to give stubborn resistance. Ney's position was further weakened when Comte d'Erlon's corps were called by Napoleon to support the main French army, engaged in a concurrent battle with the Prussians at Ligny.

Napoleon also ordered Ney to speed his capture of Quatre Bras in order to fall upon the Prussian rear. A furious Ney hurled his cavalry forward in a desperate attempt to smash the Anglo–Allied forces. With reinforcements arriving steadily, Wellington repulsed Ney's attack and, by early evening, the French were outnumbered. Wellington counter-attacked, driving Ney's forces back to their original starting positions, though the battle ended in a draw. Wellington withdrew from the field the next day, retreating to fight the decisive Battle of Waterloo.

TIMELINE

1500–1000BC	1000–500BC	500BC–0AD	0–500AD	500–1000AD	1000–1500AD	1500–2000AD

Waterloo 1815

NAPOLEONIC WARS

BRITISH AND ALLIED VICTORY

A series of defeats for Napoleon Bonaparte (1769–1821) led to his exile on the island of Elba. However, he escaped back to France, reassembled his army and crossed the French border, intending to prevent an Allied invasion. Allied forces retaliated, bringing about his decisive defeat at Waterloo.

KEY FACTS

Who British, German, Belgian and Dutch allies, led by the Duke of Wellington, plus 50,000 Prussian troops under Marshal Blücher, against Napoleon's reformed French army.

What Napoleon resolved to attack the Allied forces before other powers could come to their aid.

Where Approximately 5km (3 miles) south of the village of Waterloo, 13km (8 miles) south of Brussels.

When 18 June 1815

Why In 1814, 25 years of European war ended and the major European powers started restoring their countries to normality. Napoleon's return from Elba threatened to jeopardize this.

Outcome The Quadruple Alliance, signed by those who fought at Waterloo, was designed to protect the balance of power.

The chateau of Hougoumont was focal point of French attacks at Waterloo, a miscalculation by Napoleon, since it drew his troops away from the British centre.

LOCATION

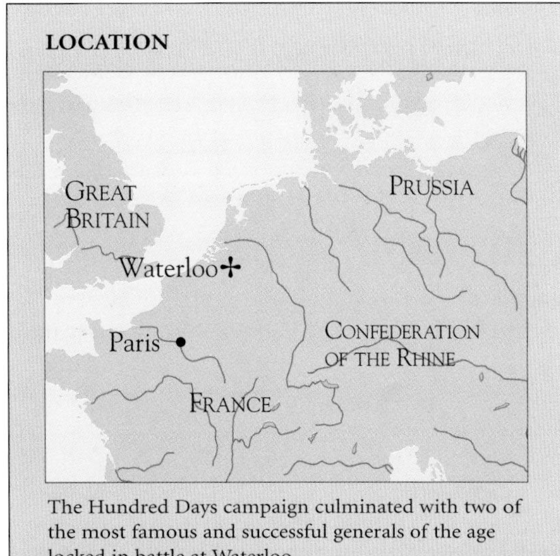
GREAT BRITAIN
PRUSSIA
Waterloo
Paris
CONFEDERATION OF THE RHINE
FRANCE

The Hundred Days campaign culminated with two of the most famous and successful generals of the age locked in battle at Waterloo.

When Napoleon escaped exile on Elba in 1815, he returned to France to remobilize the army, and move on Brussels. Wellington, at the head of the Allies, and the Prussian army under Marshal Gebherd von Blücher, were mobilized to meet him.

At Ligny, Napoleon was able to defeat Blücher's army, but it was not a killer blow, and the Prussians were able to retreat and, critically, join up with Wellington's army at Waterloo, some 13km (8 miles) south of Brussels.

The Waterloo battle was to be fought over terrain comprising a network of small roads, orchards and farms. The centre of action chosen by Wellington lay in the valley situated in front of the right wing of his front line. This was the château of Hougoumont Farm. Two other farms in the valley played a crucial role – Germans troops occupied La Haye Sainte and the French appropriated the nearby La Belle Alliance as their headquarters.

The battle began with a French attack on the chateau at Hougoument Farm, with Napoleon calling on howitzers to shell the château, which caught fire. Then Marshal

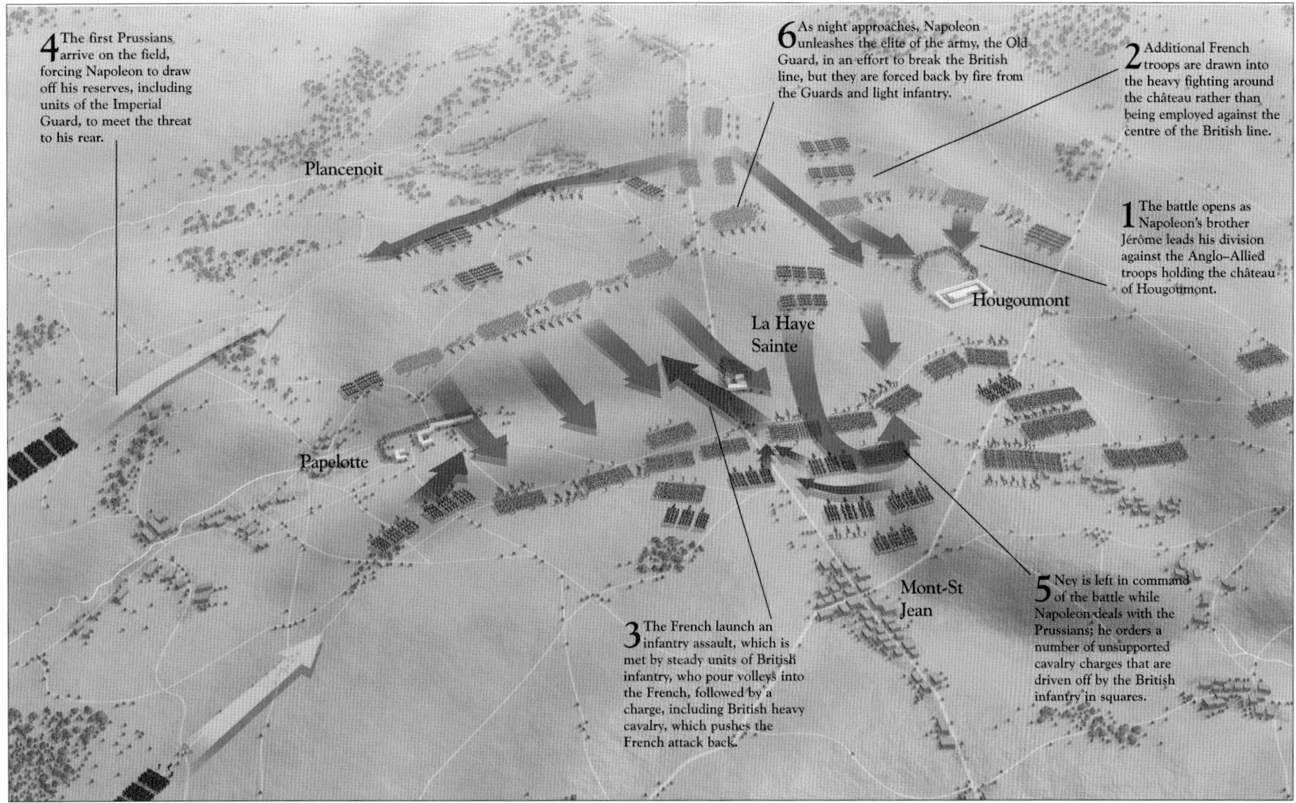
4 The first Prussians arrive on the field, forcing Napoleon to draw off his reserves, including units of the Imperial Guard, to meet the threat to his rear.
6 As night approaches, Napoleon unleashes the elite of the army, the Old Guard, in an effort to break the British line, but they are forced back by fire from the Guards and light infantry.
2 Additional French troops are drawn into the heavy fighting around the château rather than being employed against the centre of the British line.
1 The battle opens as Napoleon's brother Jérôme leads his division against the Anglo-Allied troops holding the château of Hougoumont.
Plancenoit
La Haye Sainte
Hougoumont
Papelotte
Mont-St Jean
3 The French launch an infantry assault, which is met by steady units of British infantry, who pour volleys into the French, followed by a charge, including British heavy cavalry, which pushes the French attack back.
5 Ney is left in command of the battle while Napoleon deals with the Prussians; he orders a number of unsupported cavalry charges that are driven off by the British infantry in squares.

Waterloo was fought in difficult terrain for combat: a sleepy countryside of hedgerows, narrow lanes, small farms and orchards. These features, however, would play important roles in defining the course of the battle.

Michel Ney, one of Napoleon's most trusted aides, brought forward 74 French guns over the ridge opposite La Haye Sainte, followed by 17,000 infantry, to start the attack on Wellington's centre and left.

The effect of the French cannonade was partly lessened by an order from Wellington that his infantry battalions should move behind the ridge and lie down for protection, shielding them from the worst of enemy fire. As the French troops under Ney approached the top of the ridge, they were greeted with a fierce volley and a bayonet charge from the infantry division lead by General Sir Thomas Picton.

The French suffered a major setback when Ney thought he saw signs of Allied withdrawals, and led his attacking force of Cuirassiers cavalry – men equipped with helmets and breast plates – in a series of charges. But the Allied army, far from having withdrawn, had formed into squares interlaced with artillery barriers, which created a solid defensive position that the exhausted French troops could not overcome, leaving the slope littered with Ney's troopers.

Things got worse with the delayed arrival of Blücher's army, slowed by heavy rain in the approaching network of boggy, narrow lanes. While Ney pleaded for more troops to attack the enemy centre, Napoleon concentrated on keeping Wellington's and Blücher's troops apart. By deploying his Young Guard on the Prussians, he gave Wellington time to regroup, and Ney's chance of pressing home a decisive attack had gone.

Late in the day, Napoleon led out the Old and Middle Guards, but it soon collided with the men of the British Brigade of Foot Guards, urged on by Wellington, who commanded, 'Up Guards, ready'. The Foot Guards fired a volley and charged with their bayonets, forcing the French Guard back. It took 15 minutes for Wellington to appear on the skyline and wave his hat, giving the signal for the all-out pursuit of the retreating French, and a mêlée of Allied forces quickly attacked. The French retreat became a rout. Three battalions of the Old Guard hung on to enable the Emperor to escape. He made no attempt to stay and rally his soldiers or conduct their retreat, but rode for his life. The Battle of Waterloo was over.

Index

Picture Credits

AKG Images: 7 bottom (Peter Connolly), 16 (Erich Lessing), 30–31 (Maximilianeum Collection), 36 (Peter Connolly), 64–65, 72 (Coll. Archiv F. Kunst & Geschichte), 74 (Cameraphoto), 81 (Coll. Archiv F. Kunst & Geschichte), 86–87, 89 (Westfaelisches Schulmuseum), 90–91 (Bibliotheque Nationale), 108 (World History Archive), 111 (Bibliotheque Nationale), 126 (Cameraphoto), 128–129 (Cameraphoto), 140 (Coll. Archiv F. Kunst & Geschichte), 156 (British Library), 168 (Coll. Archiv F. Kunst & Geschichte), 172–173 (Erich Lessing), 179 (Visioars), 180–181 (Jerome da Cunha), 196–197 (Erich Lessing), 198 (IAM), 244 (Coll. Archiv F. Kunst & Geschichte), 270

Alamy: 48–49 (North Wind Picture Archives), 52 (Art Directors & TRIP), 104 (North Wind Picture Archives), 118 (Art Archive), 132 (Classic Images), 154 (Timewatch Images), 164–165 (Art Archive), 178 (Classic Image), 222 (Art Gallery Collection), 272–273 (Art Archive), 278–279 (Art Archive), 300–301 (Art Archive)

Amber Books: 6, 7 top

Art Archive: 120–121 (National Museum Damascus/Gianni Dagli Orti), 146–147 (Pharonic Village, Cairo/Gianni Dagli Orti), 264–265 (Musée du Château de Versailles/Gianni Dagli Orti)

Art-Tech/MARS: 276, 288, 295, 312

Bibliotheque Nationale de France: 102

Bridgeman Art Library: 18–19 (Look & Learn), 26, 38–39 (Giraudon), 40 (Alinari), 56 (Anne van Biema Collection), 117 (Giraudon), 170 (Agra Art), 182 (Archives Charmet), 202 (Giraudon), 208–209 (Society of Apothecaries), 227 (Maidstone Museum & Art Gallery), 234–235 (National Army Museum), 238 (Pushkin Museum), 240–241, 250–251, 254–255 (Stapleton Collection), 282 (Galleria d'Arte Moderna), 286–287 (Mansell Collection), 292–293 (Stapleton Collection), 296 & 297 (National Army Museum), 306, 308–309 (State Central Artillery Museum), 311 (National Army Museum)

Corbis: 8–9 (Historical Picture Archive), 10 (Richard T. Nowitz), 13 (Jose Fuste Raga), 14 (Sandro Vannini), 44 (Bettmann), 50 (Araldo de Luca), 76 (Richard T. Nowitz), 96–97 (Stefano Bianchetti), 142 (Bettmann), 188–189 (Art Archive/Alfredo Dagli Orti), 200 (Araldo de Luca), 204 (Asian Art Archaeology), 210 (Reuters/Kim Kyung-Hoon), 216 (Werner Forman)

De Agostini: 42

Mary Evans Picture Library: 28 (Edwin Mullan Collection), 34, 63, 68, 82, 122, 138, 163, 174, 220, 232, 236

Getty Images: 20 (Superstock), 54 (Hulton Archive), 98 (Hulton Archive)

Library of Congress: 256, 257, 258, 304

Malta Tourist Authority: 152

Photos.com: 92, 100, 160, 206, 230, 262, 278

Photo12.com: 41 (Oronoz), 136–137 (Anne Ronan Picture Library), 158–159 (Bibliotheque Nationale), 162 (Hachette), 186 (EUK-Opid), 215 (JTB Photo)

Leven Smits Creative Commons Licence: 114–115

TopFoto: 58 (Granger Collection), 246 (Ullsteinbild), 298 (RIA Novosti)

Werner Forman Archive: 218–219 (Kuroada Collection)